Raising Scores & Hands

- Develop concepts with solid time on task
- Practice with plentiful, meaningful activities
- Meet the needs of every child
- Teach real-life solutions with real-life problems
- Integrate technology for practical application

Math in my World

McGraw-Hill School Division

Problem Solvers for Life.

Motivate with Content

Students apply math skills developed through real-life themes that match their interests, problems that challenge and engage, situations they can share and investigations they can carry out.

Explore with Focus

Hands-on activities in Explore Lessons provide time on task — to assure understanding of key concepts and skills.

Practice with Purpose

Abundant practice in all different standardized and state test formats helps raise scores through skill mastery and critical thinking.

Assess with Assurance

Mixed Reviews, Mixed Applications, Midchapter Reviews, Chapter Reviews, and Cumulative Reviews maintain mastery and ensure achievement over time. Chapters are designed with built-in-the-Pupil's Edition assessment that starts with "What Do You Know?" for pre-assessment, includes Chapter Tests, and finishes with "What Did You Learn?" and "What Do You Think?" features.

Prepare for the Future with Technology

Math in my World is the first math program to come with technology that was developed side-by-side with the print program. Math Van delights students while teaching the same content, chapter by chapter, as the print program. Integrated software for teachers simplifies lesson planning and assessment. And Resource Village, our website for teachers, provides rich alternative instruction for every pupil edition chapter, too.

Problem Solving: Learn it! Use it! Keep it!

Solve Problems with Strategies

Problem solving through mixed applications and other strategies in "Problem Solvers at Work," "Problem-Solving Strategies," and "Real-life Investigations" builds the foundation for continued success in math.

Meet Diverse Needs with Teaching Choices

Teachers can meet the needs of every child with Alternative Teaching Strategies in every lesson, extensive ESL support, comprehensive Spanish language instruction, Reteaching and Remediation tools for all objectives, lesson resources and components for every special requirement.

The Difference Means Results – for all Children!

Discover Simplicity – with Point-of-Use Features

Algebra

Teaching support and features for meeting individual needs, are found chapter by chapter and lesson by lesson at point of use — right where teachers need them. Important topics that appear throughout the program — like algebra preparation — are clearly indicated with bold icons.

Math in my World

Raising Scores & Hands

Program Components

	K	1	2	3	4	5	6
Teacher's Edition Volume 1	•	•	•	•	•	•	•
Teacher's Edition Volume 2		•	•	•	•	•	•
Pupil Edition, Consumable	•	•	•				
Pupil Edition, Non-Consumable				•	•	•	•
Testing Program Blackline Masters	•	•	•	•	•	•	•
Teacher's Assessment Resources	•	•	•	•	•	•	•
Practice Workbook	•	•	•	•	•	•	•
Reteach Workbook		•	•	•	•	•	•
Extend Workbook	•	•	•	•	•	•	•
Quick Review Blackline Masters		•	•	•	•	•	•
Daily Review Transparencies		•	•	•	•	•	•
Home/School Connection				•	•	•	•
Read-Aloud Anthology	•	•	•	•	•	•	•
Math Vocabulary Cards	•	•	•	•	•	•	•
Math Center Activity Pad	•	•	•	•	•	•	•
Problem of the Day Flip Chart	•	•	•	•	•	•	•
Teacher's Lesson Planner	•	•	•	•	•	•	•
Interactive Lesson Planner	•	•	•	•	•	•	•
Teacher Aids Blackline Masters	•	•	•	•	•	•	•
Calculator Blackline Masters		•	•	•	•	•	•
Puppet (Panda, Rhino, Toucan)	•	•	•				
Rubber Self-inking Stamps (Panda, Rhino, Toucan)	•	•	•				
Manipulative Counters (Panda, Rhino)	•	•					
Professional Handbook (one for K–6)	•	•	•	•	•	•	•
Jumbo Activity Book and Stickers	•	•	•				
Literature Big Books (six titles per grade)	•	•	•				
Floor Mats	•	•	•				
Student Workmats	•	•	•				
Problem Solving Audio Cassettes		•	•	•	•	•	•
Math Songs Audio Cassette (one for K–2)	•	•	•				
Customized Grade Level Manipulative Kits (K–2, 3–6)	•	•	•	•	•	•	•
Overhead Manipulative Kit (K–2, 3–6)	•	•	•	•	•	•	•
Essential Manipulative Kit	•	•	•	•	•	•	•
Supplementary Manipulative Kit	•	•	•	•	•	•	•
Teaching Aids Transparencies		•	•	•	•	•	•
Testing: Preparation and Strategies Video	•	•	•	•	•	•	•
Math Van Software	•	•	•	•	•	•	•
Computer Test Generator Software				•	•	•	•
Internet Project Handbook				•	•	•	•
Math for You and Me! Comprehensive Kit		•	•				

Program Authors

Math in My World was developed by an experienced team of authors and consulting experts. The authors who collaborated to create the program represent McGraw-Hill's commitment to the most current thinking in mathematics education, and our deep sensitivity to the real-life challenges of today's classrooms.

DR. DOUGLAS H. CLEMENTS
Professor of Mathematics Education
State University of New York at Buffalo

Douglas H. Clements conducts research on computer applications in education, early development of mathematical ideas, and the learning and teaching of geometry. Dr. Clements taught kindergarten for five years and contributed to NCTM's Addenda series.

LOIS GORDON MOSELEY
Independent Mathematics Consultant Houston, Texas

While she fulfilled her pivotal responsibilities as Coordinator of the Region IV Education Service Center in Houston, Lois Gordon Moseley served as the chairperson for the statewide Mathematics Texas Essential Knowledge and Skills writing team for grades PK - 12. She also served on the board of directors for the Association of African-American Mathematics Educators. Now she consults with Texas school districts and dedicates herself to the improvement of math education.

KENNETH W. JONES
Director OVEC - University of Louisville, Kentucky
Partnership for Professional Development

Ken Jones works closely with school districts in the Louisville region to develop ongoing professional development opportunities for teachers and administrators and to facilitate school improvement. He has been a middle school teacher and the director of several nationally-funded grant programs in mathematics. His special interest is performance assessment and portfolios.

DR. LINDA SCHULMAN
Professor of Mathematics and Mathematics Education
Lesley College
Cambridge, Massachusetts

Linda Schulman began her career as an elementary school teacher and is a leading author of innovative supplementary materials for the teaching of mathematics. Currently, her work focuses on the use of investigations and alternative assessment strategies in the elementary classroom.

Math in my World

Raising Scores & Hands

Contributing Authors

DR. KATHY KELLY-BENJAMIN
Former Associate Professor -
Mathematics Education
Florida Institute of
Technology, Melbourne, Florida
Dr. Kelly-Benjamin is an instructional design manager and educational consultant with expertise in instructional technology and assessment. Dr. Kelly-Benjamin has also been a middle school mathematics teacher, consultant and writer.

CHRISTINE A. FERNSLER
First Grade Teacher
Sidwell Friends School
Washington, D.C.
Christine Fernsler is a recognized authority on classroom practice in elementary math education. She has served as a school mathematics coordinator, presented workshops for NCTM, Virginia Council for Teachers of Mathematics (VCTM) and V-Quest. Ms. Fernsler has also taught courses at George Mason University and Catholic University.

DR. LIANA FOREST
Executive Director
National Association for
the Study of Cooperation
in Education
Felton, California
Dr. Forest has taught at levels from preschool to graduate school. For twenty years she has conducted research and written on learning and teaching in cooperative settings. She also facilitates professional development for teachers, professors and administrators with a focus on cooperative student groups, collaborative school teams and creating cooperative communities. Dr. Forest writes for and is Executive Editor of Cooperative Learning Publications for the International Association for the Study of Cooperatives in Education (IASCE), where she also serves on the Executive Board.

MARIA R. MAROLDA
Mathematics Specialist
Behavioral Neurology/Learning
Disabilities Program
Children's Hospital
Boston, Massachusetts
Maria R. Marolda has extensive expertise and practical experience in mathematics learning profiles, alternative assessment techniques, and differentiated teaching approaches designed to address learning differences in mathematics.

DR. RICHARD H. MOYER
Professor of Science Education
University of Michigan - Dearborn
Dearborn, Michigan
Dr. Richard H. Moyer is a senior author of Macmillan/ McGraw-Hill Science as well as numerous other books and publications. Dr. Moyer, who has taught at all levels, is the recipient of many teaching awards and consults on the use of inquiry teaching methods both nationally and abroad.

DR. WALTER G. SECADA
Professor of Curriculum
and Instruction
University of Wisconsin -
Madison
Madison, Wisconsin
Dr. Walter Secada has written extensively about equity, the education of bilingual learners of mathematics, and the reform of school mathematics. In addition, he has conducted workshops involving authentic assessment, how children reason when they do mathematics, and multiculturalism in the mathematics curriculum. Dr. Secada is editor of an NCTM series of professional books, *Changing the Faces of Mathematics*, which helps teachers address the diversity of today's classrooms.

Text and Technology

Integrated Technology for Management and Instruction

Math in my World management technology helps teachers develop and manage lesson plans, assess student performance, and interact with other teachers using the program. Instructional technology aids students in mastering key math concepts with multimedia and Internet-based lessons that are fully integrated with every chapter in their textbook.

PLANNERPLUS INTERACTIVE LESSON PLANNER

A good instructional plan is the heart of effective instruction. Teachers need easy access to the range of options available to them in each lesson. PlannerPlus shows every element of the program electronically, including:

- objectives
- resources and materials
- lesson content
- all blackline masters

It's easy for teachers to tailor their plans to meet individual needs.

Because teachers have little time to master complex software programs, PlannerPlus is designed to be intuitive and easy to use.

Based on the structure of the Teacher's Edition, teachers can create lesson plans on a daily, weekly, or chapter basis, using suggested outlines or creating custom lessons with their own materials.

In addition to identifying the components and references used in the lesson plan, PlannerPlus can display and print any *Math in my World* blackline master. Every curricular resource is available when needed, for group or individual lessons.

MATH IN MY WORLD TEST GENERATOR

The integrated Test Generator for Grades 3–6 comes with a computer databank of test items for each chapter correlated to:

- state standards
- national standardized testing objectives
- chapter content

Teachers can create tests customized to evaluate student progress from any perspective they need.

The Test Generator gives teachers the choice to:

- use existing questions or create their own
- print tests or give tests online
- customize based on any criteria the teacher selects

Each test item references the math program textbooks and/or technology.

MATHTALK FORUM

Always seeking ways to assist teachers in staff development, McGraw-Hill has established the MathTalk Forum, an online community of classroom teachers.

Hosted by math experts, MathTalk Forum is available for teachers to pose questions about teaching math, share classroom ideas, and gain new insights about their profession. MathTalk expands the professional community and provides the opportunity to participate in "teacher talk" about math with teachers from classrooms everywhere.

MATH VAN MULTIMEDIA SOFTWARE

Math Van is a feature-rich multimedia package developed to go hand-in-hand with the pupil editions of *Math in my World*.

Both the primary K-2 and the intermediate 3-6 programs include:
- grade-appropriate software
- teacher's guide
- user's guide

Special activity cards at intermediate grades support independent exploration and practice of key mathematical concepts.

Every chapter in every grade level of the Teacher's Edition includes a fully integrated, alternative lesson using Math Van, for flexible integration of multimedia technology into instruction. These alternative Teaching with Technology lessons explore the same objective identified in the introduction of each text chapter.

Math Van primary and intermediate activities challenge students to apply the knowledge they've gained in the classroom, and incorporate:
- colorful graphics
- engaging mathematical problems
- flexible tools

Math Van meets individual needs with:
- review and reinforcement of concepts and skills
- exploration and extension of content
- instructional support at every proficiency level

Other Math Van options provide:
- on-screen manipulatives for problem solving, skills practice and decision-making
- Tech Links that highlight opportunities for students to use manipulatives, tables and graphs
- online notes for more practice, reteaching, and extension
- an on-screen calculator
- a built-in notebook that allows students to save and print work, and to keep track of progress for assessment and sharing

INTERNET LESSONS AND CYBERSCOUT

Teachers with Internet access often struggle to find appropriate web sites for instruction. *Math in my World's* Internet resources offer easy access to web-based lesson plans that support guided explorations. Teachers simply select the chapter to teach, review the lesson plan, print the project sheet and answer keys, and they're ready.

For help in designing their own web-linked lessons, teachers can turn to Cyberscout, a classroom-specific search utility. Key-in basic information about the lesson being planned, and a reply e-mail will come back with a list of appropriate websites — so it's simple to develop unique online lessons without spending hours net-searching alone.

MATH IN MY WORLD INTEGRATES TECHNOLOGY

Students today deserve the preparation that both text and technology give them. But technology integration must be natural, closely connected to the expectations for achievement.

Math in my World is the most technologically rich program available. Full integration with the text, flexible application of the tools, and a focus on the needs of students and teachers together bring the power of technology to the service of instruction.

TEACHER'S EDITION
McGRAW-HILL MATHEMATICS

PART 1

Math in my World

DOUGLAS H. CLEMENTS

KENNETH W. JONES

LOIS GORDON MOSELEY

LINDA SCHULMAN

McGraw-Hill
School Division

New York   Farmington

Contributors

Author Team

Program Authors

Dr. Douglas H. Clements

Kenneth W. Jones

Lois Gordon Moseley

Dr. Linda Schulman

Contributing Authors

Christine A. Fernsler

Dr. Liana Forest

Dr. Kathleen Kelly-Benjamin

Maria R. Marolda

Dr. Richard H. Moyer

Dr. Walter G. Secada

Multicultural and Educational Consultants

Rim An
Teacher
UN International School
New York, New York

Sue Cantrell
Superintendent of Schools
Madison County Schools
Marshall, North Carolina

Mordessa Corbin
Instructional Specialist
Mathematics Pre K - 12
Gilbert, Louisiana

Dr. Carlos Diaz
Project Director
Cultural Foundations in Education
Florida Atlantic University
Boca Raton, Florida

Carl Downing
Director of Native American
Language Development Institute
Oklahoma City, Oklahoma

Linda Ferreira
Teacher
Pinellas Park, Florida

Judythe M. Hazel
Elementary School Principal
Tempe, Arizona

Roger Larson
Mathematics Coordinator
Ramsey, Minnesota

Josie Robles
Mathematics Coordinator
Silver Springs, Maryland

Veronica Rogers
Director, Secondary Education
Mobile, Alabama

Telkia Rutherford
Mathematics Facilitator
Chicago, Illinois

Sharon Searcy
Teacher
Mandarin, Florida

Elizabeth Sinor
Teacher/Trainer
Mathematics and Assessment
Waddy, Kentucky

Michael Wallpe
Curriculum Development
Indianapolis, Indiana

Claudia Zaslavsky
Author, Africa Counts
New York, New York

Career Professionals

Jim Anderson
Stained Glass Artist

Robert Beard
Leather Carver

Bill Becoat
Inventor

Jack Bertagnolli
Rancher

Alex Bhattacharji
Reporter, Sports Illustrated

Dr. Sherrilyn Brannon
Veterinarian

Yvonne Campos
Marketing Executive

Theresa Cebuhar
Highway Maintenance Worker

Dave Chin
School Adjustment Counselor

Steve Crockett
Engineer

Susannah Druck
Program Coordinator,
Ecosphere Magazine

Larry Felix
Communications Officer

La Tondra Finley
Veterinarian's Receptionist

Charlotte Garcia
School Superintendent

Rich Garcia
American League Umpire

Alyssa Goodman
Astrophysicist

Marla Grossberg
Market Researcher

Clair Hain, Jr.
President of Great Coasters
International

Ruth Handler
Designer of Barbie and Ken Dolls

Kevin Hanson
Track Official

Kim Harrison
Marine Biologist

Beverly Harvard
Chief of Police

Maria Hayashida
Musher, Winner of 1996
Alaskan Iditarod Race

Colleen Heminger-Cordell
Business Owner

Patrick Hong
Automobile Road-Tester

David Juarez
Olympic Mountain Biker

Pat Kambesis
Speleologist

Frank Mazzotti
Wildlife Biologist

Mishelle Michaels
Meteorologist

Sterling Monroe
Statistician

Rusty Moore
Cordwainer

Sharon O'Connell
Founder of the Sadako/Paper
Crane Project

Sandy Pandiscio
Treasury Analyst

**Martha Puente &
Beatrice Gonzalez**
Interior Decorators

Tom Rittenberry
Sales Representative,
Sun Microsystems

Raymond Rye
Museum Director

Susan Solomon
Ozone Researcher

Monty & Ann Stambler
Game Inventors

Donald Stull
Architect

Priscilla Warren
Rug Weaver

Tina Yao
Graphic Designer

Suzanne Yin
Marine Biologist

McGraw-Hill School Division

A Division of The McGraw-Hill Companies

Copyright © 1999 McGraw-Hill School Division, a Division of the Educational and Professional Publishing Group of The McGraw-Hill Companies, Inc.

McGraw-Hill School Division
1221 Avenue of the Americas
New York, New York 10020

Printed in the United States of America
ISBN 0-02-110332-1 / 4, Pt. 1
2 3 4 5 6 7 8 9 073 04 03 02 01 00 99 98

Contributors

Thanks to all of the teachers, students, and schools who contributed to this project.

Educators and Schools

Phyllis Adcock
West Lake Elementary School
Apex, North Carolina

Leigh Anne Akey
Pauline O'Rourke Elementary School
Mobile, Alabama

Linda Allen
Goshen Elementary School
Goshen, Kentucky

Harriet Anagnostopoulos
John J. Shaughnessy
Humanities School
Lowell, Massachusetts

Susan Ardissono
Shoreline, Washington

Catherine Battle
Snowden Elementary School
Memphis, Tennessee

Sylvia Bednarski
Centerfield Elementary School
Crestwood, Kentucky

Lorraine Bege
Luis Munoz Marin School
Bridgeport, Connecticut

Tricia Bender
Pauline O'Rourke Elementary School
Mobile, Alabama

G. Renee Black
Pauline O'Rourke Elementary School
Mobile, Alabama

Sandy Blagborne
McPherson Middle School
Howell, Michigan

Denise Blume
Slidell, Louisiana

Kaye Bybee
Southland Elementary School
Riverton, Utah

Betty Byrne
Snowden Elementary School
Memphis, Tennessee

Brent Caldwell
Madison Middle School
Marshall, North Carolina

Ellen Carlson
Northwest Elementary School
Howell, Michigan

Walter Carr
Mandarin Middle School
Jacksonville, Florida

Hope Carter
Pauline O'Rourke Elementary School
Mobile, Alabama

Cynthia Carter
Mandarin Oaks Elementary School
Jacksonville, Florida

Denise Clark
Crestwood Elementary School
Crestwood, Kentucky

Patsy Cohen
Louisville Collegiate School
Louisville, Kentucky

Linda Colburn
E.N. Rogers School
Lowell, Massachusetts

Tammy Cooper
Latson Road Elementary School
Howell, Michigan

Lynne Copeland
John Yeates Middle School
Suffolk, Virginia

Naomi Damron
Southland Elementary School
Riverton, Utah

Peg Darcy
Kammerer Middle School
Louisville, Kentucky

Talmdage Darden
John Yeates Middle School
Suffolk, Virginia

Mary Davis
Snowden Elementary School
Memphis, Tennessee

Winifred Deavens
St. Louis Public Schools
St. Louis, Missouri

Terri Dickson
Snowden Elementary School
Memphis, Tennessee

Kris Dillon
Elephant's Fork Elementary School
Suffolk, Virginia

Karen Doidge
West Lake Elementary School
Apex, North Carolina

Hope Donato
Piney Grove Elementary School
Charlotte, North Carolina

Jo Doty
Mandarin Oaks Elementary School
Jacksonville, Florida

Marna Draper
Hawthorne Elementary School
Indianapolis, Indiana

Renee Duckenfield
West Lake Elementary School
Apex, North Carolina

Susan Farrar
Hawthorne Elementary School
Indianapolis, Indiana

Mary Jo Farrell
John J. Shaughnessy
Humanities School
Lowell, Massachusetts

Katrina Fives
Pauline O'Rourke Elementary School
Mobile, Alabama

Katie Flaherty
East Cobb Middle School
Marietta, Georgia

Ellen Flamer
Piney Grove Elementary School
Charlotte, North Carolina

Winston Fouche
Webster Middle School
St. Louis, Missouri

Gil French
Baltimore, Maryland

Melissa Garrone
Snowden Elementary School
Memphis, Tennessee

Dana Geils
P.S. 144/District 28 Queens
Forest Hills, New York

Vera Greer
Snowden Elementary School
Memphis, Tennessee

Paul Groth
Highlander Way Middle School
Howell, Michigan

Marguerite Guthrie
Anchorage Public School
Anchorage, Kentucky

Terri Haarala
Pauline O'Rourke Elementary School
Mobile, Alabama

Carol Harris
Elephant's Fork Elementary School
Suffolk, Virginia

Beverly Hartz
Elephant's Fork Elementary School
Suffolk, Virginia

Lori Harvey
Snowden Elementary School
Memphis, Tennessee

Judy Haskell
Northwest Elementary School
Howell, Michigan

Mary Lynne Havey
McPherson Middle School
Howell, Michigan

Diane Hayes
Pauline O'Rourke Elementary School
Mobile, Alabama

Gayle Hendershot
Garland, Texas

Hector Hirigoyen
Miami, Florida

Janice Holland
Elephant's Fork Elementary School
Suffolk, Virginia

Daisy Irvin
Luis Munoz Marin School
Bridgeport, Connecticut

Barbara Jacobs
H.B. Slaughter School
Louisville, Kentucky

Lisa James
Carroll Middle School
Carrollton, Kentucky

Roberta Johnson
Anchorage Public School
Anchorage, Kentucky

Barbara Jones
Mandarin Oaks Elementary School
Jacksonville, Florida

Faye Jones
West Lake Elementary School
Apex, North Carolina

Lori Jones
Mandarin Middle School
Jacksonville, Florida

Steve June
West Lake Elementary School
Apex, North Carolina

Sydell Kane
P.S. 144/District 28 Queens
Forest Hills, New York

Alisha Kelly
Southwest Elementary School
Howell, Michigan

Kathy Kelly
Hawthorne Elementary School
Indianapolis, Indiana

Mona Kennedy
Southland Elementary School
Riverton, Utah

Larry Kiernan
Raymond Park Middle School
Indianapolis, Indiana

Dina Kruckenberg
Ira Ogden Elementary School
San Antonio, Texas

Cathy Kuhns
Coral Springs, Florida

Judy Lane
Hawthorne Elementary School
Indianapolis, Indiana

Carol Lehrman
P.S. 144/District 28 Queens
Forest Hills, New York

Eleanor Levinson
West Lake Elementary School
Apex, North Carolina

Contributors

Clarice Loggins
Snowden Elementary School
Memphis, Tennessee

Jim Long
Snowden Elementary School
Memphis, Tennessee

Melanee Lucado
Snowden Elementary School
Memphis, Tennessee

Diane Lucas
Pauline O'Rourke Elementary School
Mobile, Alabama

Debra Luke
Pauline O'Rourke Elementary School
Mobile, Alabama

Debbie Lytle
Piney Grove Elementary School
Charlotte, North Carolina

Jim Madsen
Southland Elementary School
Riverton, Utah

Maria Marquez
Ira Ogden Elementary School
San Antonio, Texas

Ofelia Martinez
Ira Ogden Elementary School
San Antonio, Texas

Lisa Martire
Luis Munoz Marin School
Bridgeport, Connecticut

Rae Ann Maurer
P.S. 144/District 28 Queens
Forest Hills, New York

Ellen McClain
Hawthorne Elementary School
Indianapolis, Indiana

Kelley McDaniel
South Oldham County Middle School
Crestwood, Kentucky

Debra McElreath
Mandarin Oaks Elementary School
Jacksonville, Florida

Nancy McLaughlin
DeSoto, Texas

Jim McMann
Lowell Public Schools
Lowell, Massachusetts

Debbie Miller
Hawthorne Elementary School
Indianapolis, Indiana

Milvern Miller
South Bend, Indiana

Melinda Monserrate
Gateway Middle School
St. Louis, Missouri

Phyllis Moore
Madison Middle School
Marshall, North Carolina

Joan Murphy
E.N. Rogers School
Lowell, Massachusetts

Vickey Myrick
West Lake Elementary School
Apex, North Carolina

Dennis Nelson
Tempe, Arizona

Martha O'Donnell
St. Francis School
Goshen, Kentucky

Tom O'Hare
E.N. Rogers School
Lowell, Massachusetts

Wanda Peele
Emma Elementary School
Asheville, North Carolina

Linda Perry-Clarke
Elephant's Fork Elementary School
Suffolk, Virginia

Taylor Phelps
John Yeates Middle School
Suffolk, Virginia

Alda Pill
Mandarin Oaks Elementary School
Jacksonville, Florida

Kay Pitts
Snowden Elementary School
Memphis, Tennessee

Barbara Rea
North Oldham County Middle School
Goshen, Kentucky

Susan Rhyne
Piney Grove Elementary School
Charlotte, North Carolina

Mary Riley
Madison, Wisconsin

Carolyn Rooks
Snowden Elementary School
Memphis, Tennessee

Nancy Rose
Luis Munoz Marin School
Bridgeport, Connecticut

Jeffrey Rosen
East Cobb Middle School
Marietta, Georgia

Charlene Ruble
Centerfield Elementary School
Crestwood, Kentucky

Patricia Sanford
Mandarin Oaks Elementary School
Jacksonville, Florida

Jim Santo
Luis Munoz Marin School
Bridgeport, Connecticut

Lee Sawyer
West Lake Elementary School
Apex, North Carolina

Virginia Schurke
Mandarin Oaks Elementary School
Jacksonville, Florida

Shadonica Scruggs
Snowden Elementary School
Memphis, Tennessee

Ellen Sears
Anchorage Public School
Anchorage, Kentucky

Tim Sears
Anchorage Public School
Anchorage, Kentucky

Mary Sevigney
John J. Shaughnessy
Humanities School
Lowell, Massachusetts

Ann Sievert
Highlander Way Middle School
Howell, Michigan

Laura Silverman
P.S. 144/District 28 Queens
Forest Hills, New York

Ada Simmons
East Cobb Middle School
Marietta, Georgia

Dot Singleton
Winston Salem, North Carolina

Jo Ann Sipkin
West Lake Elementary School
Apex, North Carolina

Hilda Skiles
South Oldham County Middle School
Crestwood, Kentucky

Sue Slesnick
Louisville Collegiate School
Louisville, Kentucky

Venus Smith
Snowden Elementary School
Memphis, Tennessee

Judy Smizik
Pittsburgh, Pennsylvania

Doug Soards
Mt. Washington Middle School
Mt. Washington, Kentucky

Kristen Sousa
Pauline O'Rourke Elementary School
Mobile, Alabama

Nancy Souza
North Oldham County Middle School
Goshen, Kentucky

Laura Stander
John J. Shaughnessy Humanities School
Lowell, Massachusetts

Trish Strain
Mandarin Oaks Elementary School
Jacksonville, Florida

Mary Sullivan
Pauline O'Rourke Elementary School
Mobile, Alabama

Jeff Swensson
Raymond Park Middle School
Indianapolis, Indiana

Rebecca True
Raymond Park Middle School
Indianapolis, Indiana

Charlie Waller
Pauline O'Rourke Elementary School
Mobile, Alabama

Judy Wayne
E.N. Rogers School
Lowell, Massachusetts

Vickie Wheatley
LaGrange Elementary School
LaGrange, Kentucky

Carol Wietholter
Hawthorne Elementary School
Indianapolis, Indiana

Christine Wilcox
Centerfield Elementary School
Crestwood, Kentucky

Kathryn Williams
Pauline O'Rourke Elementary School
Mobile, Alabama

Ronna Young
Hawthorne Elementary School
Indianapolis, Indiana

Karen Zinman
Rye Brook, New York

Field Test Schools

Alexander Middle School
Huntersville, North Carolina

**Benjamin Franklin
Elementary School**
Yorktown Heights, New York

Bow Elementary School
Detroit, Michigan

Burrville Elementary School
Washington, DC

Candler Elementary School
Candler, North Carolina

Cattell Elementary School
Des Moines, Iowa

Crestwood Elementary School
Crestwood, Kentucky

David Cox Elementary School
Henderson, Nevada

Emma Elementary School
Asheville, North Carolina

JHS 263K
Brooklyn, New York

Longfellow Elementary School
Des Moines, Iowa

Onalaska Middle School
Onalaska, Wisconsin

Studebaker Elementary School
Des Moines, Iowa

W.C. Pryor Middle School
Fort Walton Beach, Florida

Contents

a These lessons develop, practice or apply algebraic thinking through the study of patterns, relationships and functions, properties, equations, formulas, and inequalities.

iii

3 Time, Data, and Graphs

4 **Multiplication and Division Facts**

 These lessons develop, practice or apply algebraic thinking through the study of patterns, relationships and functions, properties, equations, formulas, and inequalities.

v

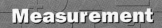

7 Measurement

 These lessons develop, practice or apply algebraic thinking through the study of patterns, relationships and functions, properties, equations, formulas, and inequalities.

10 Fractions and Probability

 These lessons develop, practice or apply algebraic thinking through the
study of patterns, relationships and functions, properties, equations,
formulas, and inequalities.

ix

11 Using Fractions

x

12 Decimals

 These lessons develop, practice or apply algebraic thinking through the study of patterns, relationships and functions, properties, equations, formulas, and inequalities.

Chapter 1 AT A GLANCE: Theme: Amazing Facts Suggested Pacing: 10–13 days

Place Value and Number Sense

WEEK ONE

DAY 1 — PREASSESSMENT

Introduction p. xii

What Do You Know? p. 1
CHAPTER OBJECTIVES: 1A, 1B, 1C, 1D
RESOURCES Read-Aloud Anthology pp. 1–2
Pretest: Test Master Form A, B, or C
Diagnostic Inventory

Portfolio Journal **NCTM STANDARDS:** 1, 2, 3, 4, 6

DAY 2 — LESSON 1.1

EXPLORE ACTIVITY
Numbers in Your World pp. 2–3

CHAPTER OBJECTIVES: 1A
MATERIALS newspaper, tape, scissors
RESOURCES Reteach/Practice/Extend: 1
Math Center Cards: 1
Extra Practice: 484

Daily Review TE p. 1B
Technology Link **NCTM STANDARDS:** 4, 6

DAY 3 — LESSON 1.2

EXPLORE ACTIVITY
Build to Thousands pp. 4–7

CHAPTER OBJECTIVES: 1B
MATERIALS place–value models (TA 22)
RESOURCES Reteach/Practice/Extend: 2
Math Center Cards: 2
Extra Practice: 484

Daily Review TE p. 3B
Technology Link **NCTM STANDARDS:** 4, 6

WEEK TWO

LESSON 1.5

PROBLEM-SOLVING STRATEGY
Make a Table pp. 14–15

CHAPTER OBJECTIVES: 1D
MATERIALS calculators (opt.)
RESOURCES Reteach/Practice/Extend: 5
Math Center Cards: 5
Extra Practice: 486

Daily Review TE p. 13B
Technology Link **NCTM STANDARDS:** 1, 2, 3, 4

MIDCHAPTER ASSESSMENT

Midchapter Review p. 16
CHAPTER OBJECTIVES: 1A, 1B, 1C, 1D

Developing Number Sense p. 17

REAL-LIFE INVESTIGATION:
Applying Place Value and Number Sense pp. 18–19

Portfolio Journal **NCTM STANDARDS:** 1, 2, 3, 4, 6

LESSON 1.6

Round Numbers pp. 20–23

CHAPTER OBJECTIVES: 1C
RESOURCES Reteach/Practice/Extend: 6
Math Center Cards: 6
Extra Practice: 486

Daily Review TE p. 19B

Algebraic Thinking
Journal
Technology Link **NCTM STANDARDS:** 6

WEEK THREE

CHAPTER ASSESSMENT

Chapter Review pp. 32–33
MATERIALS calculators (opt.)

Chapter Test p. 34
RESOURCES Posttest: Test Master Form A, B, or C

Performance Assessment p. 35
RESOURCES Performance Task: Test Master

Math · Science · Technology Connection pp. 36–37

Portfolio **NCTM STANDARDS:** 1, 4, 6

DAY 4

LESSON 1.3

Thousands pp. 8–11

CHAPTER OBJECTIVES: 1B

RESOURCES Reteach/Practice/Extend: 3
Math Center Cards: 3
Extra Practice: 485

TEACHING WITH TECHNOLOGY
Alternate Lesson for
Thousands, TE pp. 11A–11B

Daily Review TE p. 7B

a Algebraic Thinking

Technology Link

NCTM STANDARDS: 4, 6

LESSON 1.7

EXPLORE ACTIVITY

Millions pp. 24–27

CHAPTER OBJECTIVES: 1B

MATERIALS calculators (opt.)

RESOURCES Reteach/Practice/Extend: 7
Math Center Cards: 7
Extra Practice: 487

Daily Review TE p. 23B

a Algebraic Thinking

Technology Link

NCTM STANDARDS: 4, 6

DAY 5

LESSON 1.4

Compare and Order Numbers pp. 12–13

CHAPTER OBJECTIVES: 1C

RESOURCES Reteach/Practice/Extend: 4
Math Center Cards: 4
Extra Practice: 485

Daily Review TE p. 11D

Journal

Technology Link

NCTM STANDARDS: 6

LESSON 1.8

PROBLEM SOLVERS AT WORK

Interpret Data pp. 28–31

CHAPTER OBJECTIVES: 1D

MATERIALS self-stick notes, calculators (opt.)

RESOURCES Reteach/Practice/Extend: 8
Math Center Cards: 8
Extra Practice: 487

Daily Review TE p. 27B

Technology Link

NCTM STANDARDS: 1, 2, 3, 4, 11

Assessment Options

FORMAL

Chapter Tests

STUDENT BOOK
- Midchapter Review, p. 16
- Chapter Review, pp. 32–33
- Chapter Test, p. 34

BLACKLINE MASTERS
- Free-Response Test: Form C
- Multiple-Choice Test: Forms A and B

COMPUTER TEST GENERATOR
- Available on disk

Performance Assessment
- What Do You Know? p. 1
- Performance Assessment, p. 35
- Holistic Scoring Guide, Teacher's Assessment Resources, pp. 27–32
- Follow-Up Interviews, p. 35
- Performance Task, Test Masters

Teacher's Assessment Resources
- Portfolio Guidelines and Forms, pp. 6–9, 33–35
- Holistic Scoring Guide, pp. 27–32
- Samples of Student Work, pp. 37–72

INFORMAL

Ongoing Assessment
- Observation Checklist, pp. 4, 24
- Interview, pp. 2, 20, 28
- Anecdotal Report, pp. 8, 12, 14

Portfolio Opportunities
- Chapter Project, p. xiF
- What Do You Know? p. 1
- Investigation, pp. 18–19
- Journal Writing, pp. 1, 12, 16, 21
- Performance Assessment, p. 35
- Self-Assessment: What Do You Think? p. 35

Chapter Objectives	Standardized Test Correlations
1A Identify how numbers are used	MAT, CAT, SAT, ITBS, CTBS,TN*
1B Read and write whole numbers to millions	MAT, CAT, SAT, ITBS, CTBS,TN*
1C Compare, order, and round whole numbers	MAT, CAT, SAT, ITBS, CTBS
1D Solve problems, including those that involve place value and making a table	MAT, CAT, SAT, ITBS, CTBS,TN*

*Terra Nova

NCTM Standards Grades K-4

1 Problem Solving	8 Whole Number Computation
2 Communication	9 Geometry and Spatial Sense
3 Reasoning	10 Measurement
4 Connections	11 Statistics and Probability
5 Estimation	12 Fractions and Decimals
6 Number Sense and Numeration	13 Patterns and Relationships
7 Concepts of Whole Number Operations	

Meeting Individual Needs

LEARNING STYLES

- AUDITORY/LINGUISTIC
- LOGICAL/ANALYTICAL
- VISUAL/SPATIAL
- MUSICAL
- KINESTHETIC
- SOCIAL
- INDIVIDUAL

Students who are talented in art, language, and physical activity may better understand mathematical concepts when these concepts are connected to their areas of interest. Use the following activity to stimulate the different learning styles of some of your students.

Visual/Spatial Learners

Students may use models to make numbers. Assign values to different pattern blocks. The green triangles can be ones, the orange squares can be tens, the tan parallelograms can be hundreds, the blue parallelograms can be thousands, the red trapezoids can be ten thousands, and the yellow hexagons can be hundred thousands. Using no more than 9 of each block, students can make a picture and find the number value of their design. If pattern blocks are not available, use another abstract model, such as different kinds of beans or macaroni.

See Lesson Resources, pp. 1A, 3A, 7A, 11C, 13A, 19A, 23A, 27A.

GIFTED AND TALENTED

Students who are ready can work with larger numbers by playing a game called "Get Closer To." This game reinforces place-value skills, rounding, and number sense. Prepare a chart like the one below with a given number in the center.

GET CLOSER TO:

_ _ _	100	_ _ _
_ _ _	200	_ _ _
_ _ _	500	_ _ _
_ _ _ _	1,000	_ _ _ _
_ _ _ _	1,500	_ _ _ _
_ _ _ _	2,000	_ _ _ _
_ _ _ _	3,000	_ _ _ _
_ _ _ _	5,000	_ _ _ _
_ _ _ _ _	10,000	_ _ _ _ _
_ _ _ _ _ _	100,000	_ _ _ _ _ _

Make a spinner with the digits 0, 1, 2, 3, 4, 5, 6, 7, 8, 9. One student spins and writes a digit on one of the blank spaces. Students take turns with the spinner until all of the blanks are filled in. The side that is closest to the number given scores a point, and the team with the most points wins.

See also Meeting Individual Needs, pp. 9, 24.

EXTRA SUPPORT

Some students may need to use number lines and place-value models throughout the chapter. As they become more familiar with place value, they will rely less on these concrete aids.

Specific suggestions for ways to provide extra support to students appear in every lesson in this chapter.

See Meeting Individual Needs, pp. 2, 4, 8, 12, 14, 20, 24, 28.

EARLY FINISHERS

Students who finish their class work early may interview other students to get their impressions of what a million is—what the word *million* makes them think of, how long it might take to collect a million of something, what a million dollars might buy. If possible, tape the interviews and later have students write an article about them for the school newspaper. (See *Chapter Project*, p. xiF.)

See also Meeting Individual Needs, pp. 2, 6, 8, 10, 12, 14, 22, 26, 30.

LANGUAGE SUPPORT

You may wish to display place-value names (ones, tens, hundreds, etc.) so that students acquiring English may refer to them when saying numbers. Encourage students to name the place value of specific digits. When referring to digits use the names of the place values as often as possible.

See also Meeting Individual Needs, pp. 5, 9, 21, 26, 30.

ESL APPROPRIATE

INCLUSION

- For **inclusion** ideas, information, and suggestions, see pp. 4, 22, 26, 28, T15.
- For **gender fairness** tips, see pp. 30, T15.

USING MANIPULATIVES

Building Understanding To model larger numbers make a set of lay-over cards. The ones cards will overlap the tens cards, which will overlap the hundreds.

Lay the cards on the floor in order. As students say or write numbers, one student can pick up the numbers and overlap them to show the given number. To model expanded notation, spread cards out with plus signs in between.

Easy-to-Make Manipulatives Use different sized pieces of oaktag to make the cards. You may wish to laminate them.

Write on the ones cards: 0; 1; 2; 3; 4; 5; 6; 7; 8; 9. Write on the tens cards: 00; 10; 20; 30; 40; 50; 60; 70; 80; 90.

Continue as needed for the hundreds, thousands, ten thousands, hundred thousands, and millions.

| Thousands | hundreds | tens | ones |

ESL APPROPRIATE

USING COOPERATIVE LEARNING

Concentric Circles This strategy helps build a sense of community by sharing ideas or answers.

- **Form a circle and count off by twos.**
- **The "Ones" take a step in towards the center and face outward, forming two concentric circles.**
- **Facing pairs share something specified by the teacher.**
- **Then the inner circle stays in place and the outer circle moves to the left, and participants share with a new partner.**

USING LITERATURE

Use the article *Record Breakers of the Land* to introduce the chapter theme, Amazing Facts. This article is reprinted on pages 1–2 of the Read-Aloud Anthology.

Also available in the Read-Aloud Anthology is the article *Setting a Limit*, page 3.

PLACE VALUE AND NUMBER SENSE

Linking Technology

This integrated package of programs and services allows students to explore, develop, and practice concepts; solve problems; build portfolios; and assess their own progress. Teachers can enhance instruction, provide remediation, and share ideas with other educational professionals.

 ## CD-ROM ACTIVITY

In *Amazing Places!,* students use place-value models to keep track of the highest, longest, and biggest places on Earth. Students can use the online notebook to write about the process they develop. To extend the activity, students use the Math Van tools to write down the same number in several different ways. **Available on CD-ROM.**

 ## CD-ROM TOOLS

Students can use Math Van's place-value models to explore the concepts of place value and number sense. The Tech Links on the Lesson Resources pages highlight opportunities for students to use this and other tools such as drawing, tables, graphs, online notes, and calculator to provide additional practice, reteaching, or extension. **Available on CD-ROM.**

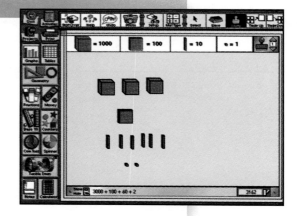

 ## WEB SITE   http://www.mhschool.com

Teachers can access the McGraw-Hill School Division World Wide Web site for additional curriculum support at http://www.mhschool.com. Click on our Resource Village for specially designed activities linking Web sites to place value. Motivate children by inviting them to explore Web sites that develop the chapter theme of "Amazing Facts." Exchange ideas on classroom management, cultural diversity, and other areas in the Math Forum.

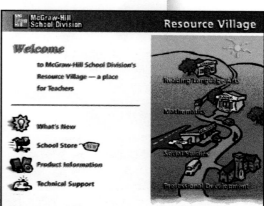

Chapter Project COUNTING COLLECTIONS

1 Starting the Project

Read the story *If You Made a Million* in the Grade 4 Math Read-Aloud Anthology to the students. Brainstorm ways they might collect or otherwise achieve a million of something. Consider ways parents or community members may participate.

Have students select a book of fiction, choose a page full of text, and count the number of *es* (the most frequently used letter in our language) on that page. Then have students predict how many pages they would have to check to find 100, 1000, 10,000, 100,000 and 1,000,000 *es*. Have students share methods they used to make their predictions. Ask if they could use their prediction for 100 to help predict the other figures.

Assist them by writing a place-value chart on the chalkboard. Conclude that each column in the chart is made up of 10 of the previous column numbers.

2 Continuing the Project

- Students work in small groups selecting an item and beginning to collect 1,000,000. Daily, they count the items or data and record it on group charts and graphs. They construct a new graph for every new place-value category reached. (i.e. 1000, 10,000, etc.)
- Each project should consist of a poster board displaying the item or type of data, charts and graphs recording daily/weekly collections; a prediction of the time required to reach 1,000,000 if the group did not reach their goal.

3 Finishing the Project

Students present their projects to the class. They share their understanding of large numbers, explaining the place value of the numbers representing the items.

Have students predict changes that would occur in the data if the whole class or the whole fourth grade had selected a single project.

Community Involvement

Display students collection graphs for Parent's Night.

Parents who have stamp, shell, or button collections can visit the class and show the class part of their collection.

Highlighting the Math

- collect, organize, display, and analyze data
- use data to predict changes over time
- identify and use place-value patterns to predict changes in data over time

BUILDING A PORTFOLIO

Each student's portfolio should include a description of the item or data selected, charts and graphs showing the progress of the collected data, student work showing how the data was used to make projections for larger numbers, and a statement of individual effort for completing the group project.

To assess students' work, refer to the Holistic Scoring Guide on page 27 in the Teacher's Assessment Resources.

PURPOSE Introduce the theme of the chapter.

Resource Read-Aloud Anthology, pages 1–2

Using Literature

Read "Record Breakers of the Land" from the Read-Aloud Anthology to introduce the chapter theme "Amazing Facts."

Developing the Theme

Encourage students to talk about amazing facts they have heard, read about, or seen. They may recall some amazing world records or amazing facts about animals.

Organize students into cooperative groups. Have each group create a poster illustrating one amazing fact. For more ideas, students may want to look through a book of world records. Encourage students to choose a fact that involves numbers in some way.

Display the posters around the classroom. Students may refer to the posters while working on this chapter.

Amazing facts about the following topics are discussed in this chapter:

feats	pp. 2–3	world records	pp. 14–15, 24–27
paper cranes	pp. 8–9	Earth	pp. 20–23
altitudes	p. 12		

CHAPTER 1

PLACE VALUE AND NUMBER SENSE

THEME   Amazing Facts

People are always looking for ways to break world records. In this chapter, you will learn about some world records and other amazing facts. You may even create your own record!

Chapter Bibliography

Counting on Frank by Rod Clement. Milwaukee: Gareth Stevens Inc., 1991. ISBN 0–8368–0358–2.

"High Divers of Mexico" from *The Hayes Book of Daring Deeds* by Teri Kelly with Stef Donev, Mary Kaizer Donev and Dan Mackie. Milwaukee: Penworthy Publishing Company, 1986. ISBN 0–8761–025–4.

On Top of the World: The Conquest of Mount Everest by Mary Ann Fraser. New York: Henry Holt and Company, 1991. ISBN 0–8050–1578–7.

Community Involvement

Have students plan an Amazing Facts about the Community panel discussion featuring three or four senior members of the community. Students can brainstorm a wide-ranging list of seniors or other adults to invite, including men and women retired from local factories, from public office, members of the Chamber of Commerce, or guides at a local tourist attraction. In their letter inviting panelists, students can politely challenge them to bring with them the most amazing fact about the community.

What Do You Know

Estimate the number of stars you think you can draw in 1 minute.

1 Work with a partner to test your estimate. Time each other to see how many stars each of you can really draw in 1 minute. Copy and complete the table.

Minute Draw		
Item	Estimate	Exact Number

2. Possible answers: The estimate was more/less than the exact number, close to the exact number, or 50 stars more/less than the exact number.

2 Write a statement that compares your estimate to the exact number of stars you drew.

3 Josh's group drew 134 stars in 1 minute. Show how you can group 134 things so that they are easy to count. Draw a picture of the grouped stars or of place-value models. Possible answer: Group by tens first, then group the tens into hundreds.

●●

Use Illustrations Tess drew 25 shapes in one minute. What shapes do you think she drew? Illustrate them.

2. 2 groups of 10 shapes and 5 single shapes

When you are reading, the illustrations can give you a better idea of what the author means. Sometimes a picture gives additional information.

1 What information does your illustration give that is not in the paragraph? Possible answers: what the shapes are, their color(s), their size(s)

2 How could you illustrate the paragraph to show tens and ones? See above.

Vocabulary

place value, p.4	period, p.8	round, p.20
digit, p.8	is less than (<), p.12	line plot, p.28
standard form, p.8	is greater than (>),	data, p.28
expanded form, p.8	p.12	

Place Value and Number Sense 1

Reading, Writing, Arithmetic

Use Illustrations Discuss with students the various kinds of illustrations that they might come across in reading or math. Some possibilities include: graphs, charts, diagrams, time lines, photographs, and pictures. Review how each kind of illustration can help a reader get a better idea of what an author is describing or what a math problem is asking.

Vocabulary

 Students may record new words in their journals. Encourage them to show examples and draw diagrams to help tell what the words mean.

PURPOSE Assess students' ability to apply prior knowledge of place value of whole numbers.

Materials have available: place-value models

Assessing Prior Knowledge

Ask students to suggest different ways that the number of students in the classroom can be represented. Make a web on the board like the one below, using the ideas given by students.

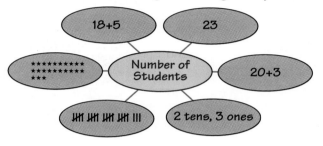

Have students work in pairs for item 1. Encourage students to use whatever methods they wish to answer items 1–3. Observe them as they work. Notice the ways that students show how to group 134 things for item 3.

BUILDING A PORTFOLIO

 Item 3 can be used as a benchmark to show where students are in their understanding of place value.

A Portfolio Checklist for Students and a Checklist for Teachers are provided in Teacher's Assessment Resources, pp. 33–34.

Prerequisite Skills

- *Can students represent whole numbers to hundreds in different ways?*
- *Can students compare whole numbers to hundreds?*
- *Can students compare whole numbers to hundreds?*

Assessment Resources

DIAGNOSTIC INVENTORY
Use this blackline master to assess prerequisite skills that students will need in order to be successful in this chapter.

TEST MASTERS
Use the multiple choice format (form A or B) or the free response format (form C) as a pretest of the skills in this chapter.

1

LESSON 1.1

EXPLORE ACTIVITY

Numbers in Your World

OBJECTIVE Identify types and uses of numbers that exist in the world.

RESOURCE REMINDER
Math Center Cards 1
Practice 1, Reteach 1, Extend 1

SKILLS TRACE

GRADE 3	• Explore the types and uses of numbers in the world. *(Chapter 2)*
GRADE 4	• Explore the types and uses of numbers in the world.
GRADE 5	• Read/write whole numbers through hundred millions and understand the meaning of their digits. *(Chapter 1)*

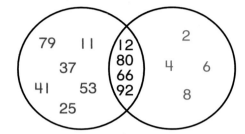

MANIPULATIVE WARM-UP

Cooperative Groups   **Logical/Analytical**

OBJECTIVE Use number sense to analyze and sort groups of numbers.

Materials per group: hundred chart (TA 1), scissors

▶ Draw the diagram below on the chalkboard.

79   11   12   2
37   80   4   6
41   53   66
25   92   8

▶ Ask how the numbers are sorted. For example, students may label the circles "two-digit numbers" and "even numbers," and the overlapping section, "even two-digit numbers." Discuss other ways numbers can be sorted.

▶ Have groups cut apart numbers in the hundred chart, mix the numbers, choose 15 to sort, and show their work on the chalkboard. Encourage the class to decide how the numbers are sorted.

SOCIAL STUDIES CONNECTION

Cooperative Pairs   **Auditory/Linguistic**

OBJECTIVE Connect number sense and history.

▶ As a class, brainstorm ways in which numbers might have appeared in newspaper headlines from earlier times in history. For example:

102 Pilgrims Land at Plymouth Rock
55 Delegates Meet to Write New Constitution
Louisiana Purchase Adds 827,987 Square Miles to U.S.

▶ Then have pairs of students create a similar headline. Encourage students to use their Social Studies books for reference or ideas.

▶ The headline should include numbers in some way and may refer to a time before newspapers were available. Students may draw pictures to go with their headlines. Allow time for pairs to share their headlines.

Daily Review

PREVIOUS DAY QUICK REVIEW

Find how many groups of 4 can be made from the following:

1. 16 *[4]*
2. 32 *[8]*
3. 28 *[7]*
4. 20 *[5]*

FAST FACTS

1. 1 + 1 *[2]*
2. 2 + 2 *[4]*
3. 3 + 3 *[6]*
4. 4 + 4 *[8]*

Problem of the Day • 1

Maria ran a lap around the school in 3 minutes and 27 seconds. It took Keith 220 seconds to run the same distance. Who completed the lap in the least amount of time? How do you know? *[Maria; 3 minutes, 27 seconds is the same as 207 seconds, and 207 is less than 220]*

TECH LINK

ONLINE EXPLORATION

Use our Web-linked activities and lesson plans to connect your students to the world of amazing facts.

MATH FORUM

Management Tip I begin each day with the Fast Facts, Previous Day Quick Review, or Problem of the Day. I use a different activity each day to keep my students interested.

Visit our Resource Village at http://www.mhschool.com to access the Online Exploration and the Math Forum.

MATH CENTER

Practice

OBJECTIVE Identify ways of using numbers.

Materials per student: Math Center Recording Sheet (TA 31 optional)

Students identify ways of describing themselves using numbers, such as their address, age, and height. They organize this information in a chart that categorizes the numbers by use, and compare their personal description with other students.

PRACTICE ACTIVITY 1

MATH CENTER
Partners

Number Sense • You've Got My Number

There are many numbers that help describe you. How many days did you go to school this month? Who wakes up first in your family? second? What is your height?

- On your own, make a chart like the one below. Complete the chart with numbers that describe you. Write as many numbers as you can in each category.
- Compare your chart to your partner's. Were the ways you used numbers to describe yourselves the same? different?

Category	Numbers That Describe Me
To count	_____ years old
To show order	
To name	
To measure	

Chapter 1, Lesson 1, pages 2–3

Place Value

NCTM Standards

- Problem Solving
- ✓ Communication
- ✓ Reasoning
- ✓ Connections

Problem Solving

OBJECTIVE Use a drawing to identify different ways in which numbers are used.

Materials per student: Math Center Recording Sheet (TA 31 optional)

Students identify the different ways numbers are used in a drawing of a room. They write a plan and make a similar drawing of a room in their home using numbers in as many different ways as possible.

PROBLEM-SOLVING ACTIVITY 1

MATH CENTER
On Your Own

Logical Reasoning • Drawing Rooms

- Record the different ways numbers are used in the drawing.
- Write a plan for how you would make a similar drawing of a room in your home.
- Make a drawing of the room and use numbers in as many different ways as you can.

Chapter 1, Lesson 1, pages 2–3

Place Value

NCTM Standards

- ✓ Problem Solving
- ✓ Communication
- ✓ Reasoning
- ✓ Connections

Lesson 1.1 continued

EXPLORE ACTIVITY
Numbers in Your World

OBJECTIVE Identify types and uses of numbers that exist in the world.

Materials per group: newspapers

 **Introduce**

Have students describe ways in which numbers are used in the Olympics. Have them consider:
- **How are numbers used to record distances and time?**
- **How are numbers used to identify players?**

 **Teach**

▶ **LEARN Work Together** Explain to students that "phrases" include numbers and the words that modify those numbers. The words will help them organize the numbers into categories.

Review with the class how to make a tally table.
- **What does each tally represent?** *[1]*
- **How are the tallies grouped?** *[in sets of 5]*
- **Why are the tallies grouped?** *[to make them easier to count]*

MAKE CONNECTIONS
After students have created their own categories, ask them how they use numbers every day. Have students assign those numbers to one of the categories they created. If their categories are different from Mike's, have students also classify their numbers using Mike's categories.

3 Close

▶ **Check for Understanding** using items 1–5, page 3.

CRITICAL THINKING
Discuss instances when an estimate would not be used (giving an address) and instances when it might (describing a size or a total).

▶ **PRACTICE**
Assign ex. 1–8 as independent work.
- For ex. 1–6, have students write a sentence in which the number is used in another way.

Numbers in Your World

In the newspaper you can find many ways that numbers are used in our world.

Work Together
Work in a group to read two or three pages in a newspaper. Record as many phrases with numbers in them as you can find.

Decide on different ways or categories you will use to organize your numbers.

Create a table like the one below. List your categories. Tally, then count the number of examples in each category. Include an example from the newspaper for each category.

▶ How did you choose the categories that you used? **Possible answer: There can be a category for each way numbers are used.**

Make Connections
Mike's group organized their numbers this way.

> **Cultural Note**
> The first printed newspaper was a Chinese circular, *The Peking Gazette*, that was printed around A.D. 700.

How We Organized the Numbers We Found			
Category	Tally	Number of Examples	Example in Newspaper
To count	⳾⳾ ⳾⳾ ||	12	343,000 bees
To show order	|||	3	The 23rd Olympic Games
To name	⳾⳾ ⳾⳾ ⳾⳾	15	WR 67 Derbyshire Fire & Rescue Service
To measure	⳾⳾ ⳾⳾ ⳾⳾ ⳾⳾		21	80 pounds

2   Lesson 1.1

Meeting Individual Needs

Early Finishers
Have students make a list of all the numbers they can find in the classroom. Ask them to sort the numbers into the categories *to count, to measure, to name,* and *to show order.*

Extra Support
Students having difficulty categorizing should make a list of numbers they use every day, then describe each number's importance to them.

Ongoing Assessment
Interview Determine if students understand uses of numbers. Ask:
- **Is the number in the headline, "100 Days Without Rain" used to count, show order, name, or measure?** *[to count or to measure]*

Follow Up If students have difficulty understanding the categories of numbers, let groups discuss and write examples for each or assign **Reteach 1.**

Students who understand categories of numbers may try **Extend 1.**

▶ What categories did your group use? How are they different from those shown on page 2? **Check students' work.**

▶ Find examples from your data that can be placed in the categories Mike's group chose. **Check students' work.**

Check for Understanding
Tell if the number is used to count, show order, name, or measure.

1 The World Trade Center in New York City has about 50,000 people working in it and about 90,000 visitors daily. **to count**

2 Bernard Lavery grew a cabbage that weighed 124 pounds. **to measure**

3 The first American woman in space was Sally Ride. **to show order**

Critical Thinking: Summarize   Explain your reasoning.

4 Give examples of how numbers can answer questions such as *What? When? Where? How big?* and *How many?* **See below.**

5 What other types of questions can be answered using numbers? **Possible answer: How high? How long? Why?**

4. Answers may vary. Possible answers: What is the address?—1600 Maple Street; When is the game?—at 2:00 P.M.; Where is David?—in the third room; How big is the table?—about 4 feet wide; How many people do you expect?—200 people.

Practice

Tell if the number is used to count, show order, name, or measure.

1 The largest single windows are 164 feet high. **to measure**

2 About 350 million people in the world visit zoos each year. **to count**

3 The first woman to climb Mount Everest was Junko Tabei. **to show order**

4 The survey shows that people prefer the Jaguar XJ7. **to name**

5 George Adrian picked 15,830 pounds of apples in 8 hours. **to measure**

6 The New York City subway system has 469 stations. **to count**

7 Write four newspaper headlines. Use numbers to count, show order, name, and measure. Have other students categorize each number. **Students may use different categories of numbers in their headlines.**

8 **Data Point** Predict the number that you read, say, or hear most often in a day. Use a tally table to record all the numbers you find in a day. Was your prediction correct? **Students' predictions should be based on their tables.**

Extra Practice, page 484

Place Value and Number Sense   **3**

Alternate Teaching Strategy

Materials per pair: 20 two-color counters

In cooperative pairs, have students use two-color counters to demonstrate how numbers can be used:

- to measure
- to show order
- to count
- to name

Ask students to write a statement describing what their counters show.

For example, to show order, students can make a line of 10 counters all the same color except the fifth counter. This model shows order by highlighting the fifth counter. The students might write, "The fifth counter is different from the rest."

ESL APPROPRIATE

PRACTICE • 1

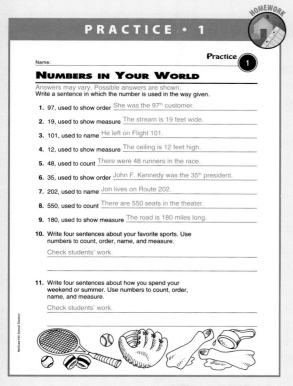

Name: _____   Practice 1

NUMBERS IN YOUR WORLD

Answers may vary. Possible answers are shown.
Write a sentence in which the number is used in the way given.

1. 97, used to show order   She was the 97th customer.
2. 19, used to show measure   The stream is 19 feet wide.
3. 101, used to name   He left on Flight 101.
4. 12, used to show measure   The ceiling is 12 feet high.
5. 48, used to count   There were 48 runners in the race.
6. 35, used to show order   John F. Kennedy was the 35th president.
7. 202, used to name   Jon lives on Route 202.
8. 550, used to count   There are 550 seats in the theater.
9. 180, used to show measure   The road is 180 miles long.
10. Write four sentences about your favorite sports. Use numbers to count, order, name, and measure.
   Check students' work.
11. Write four sentences about how you spend your weekend or summer. Use numbers to count, order, name, and measure.
   Check students' work.

RETEACH • 1

Name: _____   Reteach 1

NUMBERS IN YOUR WORLD

Each of these magazine stories uses numbers in a different way.

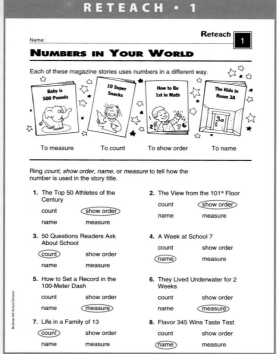

To measure   To count   To show order   To name

Ring *count, show order, name,* or *measure* to tell how the number is used in the story title.

1. The Top 50 Athletes of the Century
   count   (show order)
   name   measure

2. The View from the 101st Floor
   count   (show order)
   name   measure

3. 50 Questions Readers Ask About School
   (count)   show order
   name   measure

4. A Week at School 7
   count   show order
   (name)   measure

5. How to Set a Record in the 100-Meter Dash
   count   show order
   name   (measure)

6. They Lived Underwater for 2 Weeks
   count   show order
   name   (measure)

7. Life in a Family of 13
   (count)   show order
   name   measure

8. Flavor 345 Wins Taste Test
   count   show order
   (name)   measure

EXTEND • 1

Name: _____   Extend 1

NUMBERS IN YOUR WORLD

Numbers in Writing
You need: red, blue, green, yellow crayons

Write a paragraph about your day. Use a number in each sentence. You might answer questions such as: How long did it take you to get to school? Where were you in the line to get on the bus or to go to lunch? How many students attend your school? What room number is your classroom?

Check students' work for use of numbers.

_____

_____

_____

Look back at each of the numbers included in your paragraph. How is it used? Find its category in the chart below and circle the number using the color given. Check students' work.

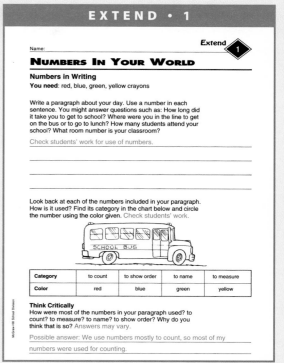

Category	to count	to show order	to name	to measure
Color	red	blue	green	yellow

Think Critically
How were most of the numbers in your paragraph used? to count? to measure? to name? to show order? Why do you think that is so? Answers may vary.

Possible answer: We use numbers mostly to count, so most of my numbers were used for counting.

LESSON 1.2

EXPLORE ACTIVITY
Build to Thousands

OBJECTIVE Represent numbers up to 1,000 in different ways.

RESOURCE REMINDER
Math Center Cards 2
Practice 2, Reteach 2, Extend 2

SKILLS TRACE

GRADE 3
• Explore the concept of place value and regrouping to name numbers through hundreds in different ways. *(Chapter 2)*

GRADE 4
• Explore the concept of place value and regrouping to name numbers through thousands in different ways.

GRADE 5
• Read/write whole numbers through hundred millions and understand the meaning of their digits. *(Chapter 1)*

MANIPULATIVE WARM-UP

Cooperative Pairs   **Logical/Analytical**

OBJECTIVE Review place values to hundreds.

Materials per pair: 2 blank number cubes; markers

▶ Have each pair label one number cube with the numbers 0, 20, 30, 40, 50, and 60 and the other number cube with the numbers 4 through 9.

▶ Tell students they are going to play Haywire Weather. For each of the 12 monthly temperatures on the chart below, pairs roll two number cubes and record the numbers that appear. To create their Haywire Weather, they add these two numbers to the month's temperature.

▶ Each triple-digit temperature wins a newspaper headline to be composed by the team, such as "Triple-Digit Temperatures Trounce All Records!" Each pair reports its results and headlines to the class.
   • **What was the highest double-digit temperature for your team?**
   • **What was the lowest triple-digit temperature?** *[Answers may vary.]*

Jan.	Feb.	Mar.	Apr.	May	June	July	Aug.	Sept.	Oct.	Nov.	Dec.
12	18	31	46	59	68	74	71	61	49	33	18

CULTURAL CONNECTION

Cooperative Pairs   **Auditory/Linguistic**

OBJECTIVE Connect place value with how ancient Arabic numbers were written.

▶ Tell students that ancient Arabic numbers were written in the reverse order of how numbers are written today. Explain that the number *three hundred sixty-two* was written as *two and sixty and three hundred,* or *2 and 60 and 300.*

▶ In cooperative pairs, have each student write five numbers using the ancient Arabic form. Partners exchange papers and rewrite the numbers as they are written today. They should write the numbers both numerically and in word form.

▶ Have partners check each other's work.

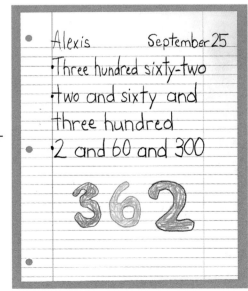

Daily Review

PREVIOUS DAY QUICK REVIEW

Use the number 8 in the way given.
[Sample answers are shown.]

1. to show order [row 8]
2. to measure [8 yards]
3. to name [room 8]
4. to count [8 books]

FAST FACTS

1. 1 + 2 [3]
2. 6 + 3 [9]
3. 4 + 1 [5]
4. 5 + 3 [8]

Problem of the Day • 2

In Georgia's class, 5 students have red hair, 15 students have brown hair, 2 students have black hair, and 7 students have blond hair. How many students do not have brown hair? [14]

TECH LINK

MATH VAN

Tool You may wish to use the Place-Value Model tool with this lesson.

MATH FORUM

Cultural Diversity My students enjoy learning the names for numbers in different languages. I encourage students to make a poster showing number names in a language of their choice.

Visit our Resource Village at http://www.mhschool.com to see more of the Math Forum.

MATH CENTER

Practice

OBJECTIVE Show numbers in different ways.

Materials per pair: place-value models; per student: Math Center Recording Sheet (TA 31 optional)

Students take turns showing numbers through thousands using place-value models and identifying the numbers being shown.

PRACTICE ACTIVITY 2

MATH CENTER
Partners

Manipulatives • What's My Number?

YOU NEED
■ place-value models

1,296

Take turns.
- Use place-value models to show a number from 9 to 2,000.
- Your partner writes the number shown. Check your partner's work.
- Your partner uses place-value models to show the same number in a different way.

Continue until each of you has had five turns.

Chapter 1, Lesson 2, pages 4–7   Place Value

NCTM Standards
  Problem Solving
✓ Communication
✓ Reasoning
  Connections

ESL APPROPRIATE

Problem Solving

OBJECTIVE Use spatial reasoning to solve problems.

Materials per student: Math Center Recording Sheet (TA 31 optional)

Students use a key to make a drawing to show a number. Then they make up their own key and drawing and have their partner figure out the number.

PROBLEM-SOLVING ACTIVITY 2

MATH CENTER
Partners

Spatial Reasoning • Do You See It?

This design shows 448.
- Show your partner where all the lines that stand for 1 are found in the design. Find all the 10 and 100 shapes as well. Have your partner explain how the design shows the number.
- Take turns picking a 3-digit number. Each person uses the key to draw a design to show their number. Check each other's work.
- Make up your own symbols to stand for ones, tens, and hundreds. Use your symbols to show a different 3-digit number. Make a key for your symbols.
- Challenge your partner to read the drawing of your number.

Key:
| = 1   [] = 10   ■ = 100

Chapter 1, Lesson 2, pages 4–7   Place Value

NCTM Standards
✓ Problem Solving
✓ Communication
✓ Reasoning
  Connections

EXPLORE ACTIVITY
Build to Thousands

OBJECTIVE Represent numbers up to 1,000 in different ways.

Materials per pair: place-value models—ones, tens, hundreds, and thousands (if available)

Vocabulary place value

 **1 Introduce**

Ask students to think of all the different ways to represent the number 26. *[Possible answers: 26, twenty-six, one quarter and one penny]*

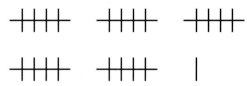

Discuss the representations and their uses. *[Possible answers: 26—page number, counting number; twenty-six—on a check, in the text of a book; one quarter and one penny—in a store advertisement; 26 tally marks—score for a game]*

 **2 Teach**   *Cooperative Pairs*

▶ **LEARN Work Together** Review with students what each of the place-value models represents. Have volunteers show the class how the models can be used to represent the number 367.

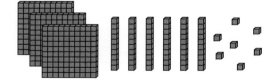

To help students as they work, ask them to consider the following:
- **Are there ways of showing 43, 121, and 1,310 other than the ones you've already used?** *[Possible answers: showing 43 and 121 with only ones models and 1,310 with only tens models]*
- **Which representation was the easiest to make? Why?** *[Accept all reasonable answers.]*

Talk It Over Ask the students:
- **Describe all the ways you can show 1,001, 1,010, and 1,100.** *[Possible answers: using only ones models, using only tens models, using tens and hundreds models, using tens, hundreds, and thousands models]*
- **Which method uses the fewest number of models?** *[representing numbers using place value]*
- **Which method uses the greatest number of models?** *[representing numbers with ones models]*

Building to Thousands

L E A R N

You can use **place-value models** to show numbers in different ways.

You will need
- ones, tens, hundreds, and thousands place-value models

Work Together
Work with a partner. Use a table to record your results.

Number	Thousands	Hundreds	Tens	Ones
43 (ones only)				
43 (tens and ones)				

Show 43 using:
▶ only ones models.
▶ tens and ones models.

Show 121 using:
▶ only tens and ones models.
▶ hundreds, tens, and ones models.

Show 1,310 using:
▶ only hundreds and tens models.
▶ thousands, hundreds, and tens models.

place value The value of a digit depending on its place in a number.

Talk It Over
▶ How would you show each of these numbers using the least number of models? the greatest number of models? **See below.**

  A 1,001

  B 1,010

  C 1,100

A. 1 thousand and 1 one; 1,001 ones

B. 1 thousand and 1 ten; 1,010 ones

C. 1 thousand and 1 hundred; 1,100 ones

4   Lesson 1.2

Meeting Individual Needs

Extra Support

In their math journals, have students draw groups of place-value models that show 1,000 in three different ways.

 ESL **APPROPRIATE**

Inclusion

Spend time helping visually-challenged students become familiar with the place-value models. Let them describe the models they touch. Ask them to describe the relative dimensions.

Ongoing Assessment

Observation Checklist Determine students' understanding of place value by observing how they show 231, 312, and 123 with place-value models.

Follow Up For more practice with place value, have students use place-value charts. Then assign **Reteach 2**.

To challenge students, assign **Extend 2**.

Make Connections

A place-value chart can help you understand numbers greater than 1,000.

thousands	hundreds	tens	ones
1	2	5	7

You can think of 1,257 as:
1 thousand 2 hundreds 5 tens 7 ones,
or 12 hundreds 5 tens 7 ones,
or 1,257 ones.

• How can you find 1 hundred more than 1,257? 1 hundred less? What are the new numbers? Explain your reasoning. **Increase the digit in the hundreds place by 1; decrease the digit in the hundreds place by 1; 1,357 and 1,157.**

Check for Understanding

Write the number.

1  216

2 59

3  507

4  1,142

5  2,301

6 9 hundreds 5 tens 8 ones **958**

7 1 thousand 7 hundreds 9 tens **1,790**

Complete.

8 1,082 = 1 thousand ■ tens 2 ones **8**

9 ■ = 1 thousand 5 tens **1,050**

10 958 = 9 ■ 5 tens 8 ones **hundreds**

11 131 = 1 hundred 3 tens ■ ones **1**

12 1,900 = 1 ■ 9 ■ **thousand, hundreds**

13 460 = 4 hundreds 6 ■ **tens**

Critical Thinking: Generalize **Explain your reasoning.**

14 Write steps that explain to another student how you would find the following: **See page T17.**

a. 10 more than 765 **b.** 100 less than 765 **c.** 1,100 more than 765

Turn the page for Practice.
Place Value and Number Sense   **5**

MAKE CONNECTIONS

Discuss how students can use a place-value chart to find different ways of representing a number. For example, to represent 1,257 using only tens and ones models, students look at the 3-digit number that ends in the tens column (125), and show that number of tens. They then look in the ones column, and show that number of ones (7).

Ask students:
• **How would you show 1,692 if you didn't have any tens models?** [1 thousands, 6 hundreds, 92 ones]
• **What kinds of numbers can you show when you have no ones models? No tens and ones models?** [Possible answers: multiples of ten, or numbers that have a 0 in the ones place; multiples of one hundred, or numbers that have zeros in the tens and ones places]

3 Close

Check for Understanding using items 1–14, page 5.

CRITICAL THINKING
Students may want to use place-value models to help explain their reasoning in clear and simple language. Encourage students to write a numerical representation of what they do.
• **What operation are you using when you increase a number by 100?** [addition]
• **What operation are you using when you decrease a number by 100?** [subtraction]

Practice See pages 6–7.

Language Support

Some students may have difficulties with the numbers *eleven*, *twelve*, and *thirteen*, which are named in some languages as *ten and one, ten and two,* and *ten and three,* respectively. Suggest that students make a two-column chart as a reference. In the first column show the numbers 1–20 in their native language and in the second column, show the numbers in English.

Read Albert Shanker's article in *The New York Times,* Sunday, July 9, 1995, "Where We Stand: Eleven, Twelve, Thirteen" for more information.

ESL APPROPRIATE

▶ **PRACTICE**

Materials have available: place-value models—ones, tens, and hundreds

Options for assigning exercises:
A—Odd ex. 1–29; all ex. 31–35; **Cultural Connection**
B—Even ex. 2–30; all ex. 31–35; **Cultural Connection**

- Remind students that "and" is never used when naming a whole number; "and" is only used when naming a decimal.
- Ex. 8, 9, 10, 11, 12, 13, 15, and 16 involve numbers in which zero is used as a placeholder. Remind students that after writing the digit in the greatest place, they must write a digit in each of the lesser places.
- Some students may need to use place-value models and charts to solve ex. 23–30. Encourage students to draw pictures of the models as well.
- For **Make It Right** (ex. 31), see Common Error below.

Cultural Connection Explain to students that in addition to record keeping, the Incas used *quipus* to relay statistical messages over long distances. Invite students to do further research on the Inca *quipus*. Ask them to find out how *quipus* were used to articulate mathematical messages and how these messages traveled from one place to another.

Encourage students to draw or make a device similar to *quipus* showing 2-digit and 3-digit numbers.

Practice

Write the number.

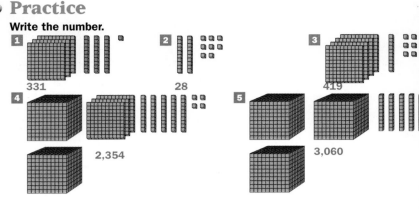

1 331 **2** 28 **3** 419

4 2,354 **5** 3,060

6 1 thousand 4 hundreds 1 ten 2 ones **1,412**
7 8 hundreds 9 tens 2 ones **892**
8 1 hundred 9 tens **190**
9 3 hundreds 4 tens **340**
10 6 hundreds 5 ones **605**
11 1 thousand 3 hundreds **1,300**
12 1 thousand 9 tens **1,090**
13 1 thousand 5 ones **1,005**
14 87 tens 5 ones **875**
15 14 hundreds **1,400**
16 100 tens **1,000**

Complete.

17 385 = ■ hundreds 8 tens 5 ones **3**
18 1,090 = 1 thousand ■ tens **9**
19 990 = 9 hundreds 9 ■ tens
20 1,504 = 1 thousand 5 ■ 4 ones hundreds
21 ■ = 7 hundreds 3 ones **703**
22 ■ = 1 thousand 7 ones **1,007**
23 Find 10 more than 1,719. **1,729**
24 Find 10 less than 821. **811**
25 Find 100 more than 652. **752**
26 Find 100 less than 1,050. **950**
27 Find 1 more than 800. **801**
28 Find 1 less than 1,000. **999**
29 Find 1,000 more than 604. **1,604**
30 Find 1,000 less than 1,229. **229**

··················· **Make It Right** ···················
31 Luis wrote the number in standard form. Explain what the mistake is. *7 hundreds 8 ones = 78*

Possible answer: Luis used the wrong place value; since the 7 is in the hundreds place and there are no tens, he should write 708.

6 Lesson 1.2

Meeting Individual Needs

Early Finishers

Have students write number sentences for ex. 23–30. For example, ex. 23 could be written as 1,719 + 10 = 1,729.

COMMON ERROR

Some students may not notice the place value of digits in a number. As in **Make It Right** on page 6, students may forget to use a zero to hold the tens place. Those who regularly make this error may draw place-value charts to assist them. Students will notice a missing space in the chart more easily and will know to write a zero.

MIXED APPLICATIONS
Problem Solving

32 Una tiled her bathroom floor. She used square mats of 100 tiles, strips of 10 tiles, and some single tiles. If she used 9 mats, 8 strips, and 7 single tiles, how many tiles did she use in all? **987 tiles**

33 Logical reasoning I am a four-digit number. My hundreds digit is less than 1. You write my tens and ones digits as 67 ones. If you add my digits you get 14. What number am I? **1,067**

34 Each story of the World Trade Center is about 10 feet (ft) high. About how many stories high was Philippe Petit? **SEE INFOBIT. 135 stories**

35 Data Point Survey your classmates to find which season they like the most. Show your results in a tally. How many students like spring most? **Students use their survey results to determine how many students chose spring.**

INFOBIT
In 1974, Philippe Petit walked across a high wire between the towers of the World Trade Center. At 1,350 feet, this was the highest high-wire feat ever done.

Cultural Connection Inca Quipu

About 500 years ago, the Inca lived along the western coast of South America. They kept records using *quipus* (KEE-pooz) like the one shown.

Knots were tied in different positions on each cord to show hundreds, tens, and ones.

hundreds
tens
ones

SOUTH AMERICA
Inca Empire

26   143

Give the number that is shown on the cords.

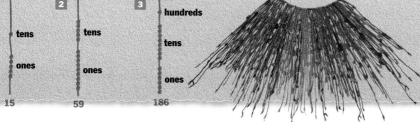

1 tens ones **15**

2 tens ones **59**

3 hundreds tens ones **186**

Extra Practice, page 484

Place Value and Number Sense **7**

Alternate Teaching Strategy

Materials per group: 0–9 spinner (TA 2), place-value charts (TA 4), place-value models—30 ones, 30 tens, 30 hundreds

Have students in each group take turns generating numbers through 999 using the spinner. They record each number randomly in the ones, tens, or hundreds column of the place-value chart.

When they have a digit in each of those three columns, have students:
• show the number with place-value models
• say the number
• record the number in words

Then ask each group to show 1,000 using place-value models. Have them write and say the number in the place-value chart, and record the number in words.

Extend the activity by having students generate numbers through 9,999 using the spinner. Then have them repeat the steps of the activity.

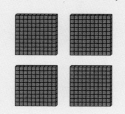
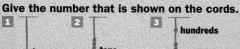
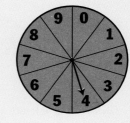

7

LESSON 1.3

Thousands

OBJECTIVE Represent numbers up to 999,999 in different forms and identify the place and value of digits.

Teaching with Technology
See alternate computer lesson, pp. 11A–11B.

RESOURCE REMINDER
Math Center Cards 3
Practice 3, Reteach 3, Extend 3

SKILLS TRACE

GRADE 3	• Read/write numbers through hundred thousands. *(Chapter 2)*
GRADE 4	• Represent numbers up to 999,999 in different forms and identify the value and place of digits.
GRADE 5	• Read/write whole numbers through hundred millions and understand the meaning of their digits. *(Chapter 1)*

MANIPULATIVE WARM-UP

Cooperative Groups — **Visual/Spatial**

OBJECTIVE Explore place value and representations of numbers.

Materials per group: number cube, blank spinner marked 1, 2, and 3 (TA 3); per student: place-value chart (TA 4)

▶ Each student in a group tosses the number cube four times and records the four numbers in the thousands, hundreds, tens, or ones column on the place-value chart. Students take turns reading the numbers and telling how many thousands, hundreds, tens, and ones are in the number.

▶ Next, students take turns spinning the spinner, writing the number spun in the hundreds column on the chart, and adding. Students read the sum and tell how many thousands, hundreds, tens, and ones are now in the number.

▶ Have groups repeat the activity several times.

ESL **APPROPRIATE**

SOCIAL STUDIES CONNECTION

Cooperative Pairs — **Logical/Analytical**

OBJECTIVE Connect place value in greater numbers with facts about the United States.

Resources almanacs, encyclopedias, maps

▶ Have pairs of students research amazing facts about the United States. You may suggest finding the length of the longest river, the height of the tallest building, the size of the largest state, and the highest average rainfall.

▶ Students can make a chart that compares these facts with their state's facts.

Daily Review

PREVIOUS DAY QUICK REVIEW

Write the number.

1. 4 hundreds 2 tens [420]
2. 68 tens 9 ones [689]
3. 1 thousand 6 ones [1,006]
4. 343 tens 2 ones [3,432]

FAST FACTS

1. 8 − 1 [7]
2. 7 − 2 [5]
3. 6 − 3 [3]
4. 9 − 4 [5]

Problem of the Day • 3

Karen makes and sells hair bows to her friends. Yesterday, Karen sold two hair bows for $2 each. She sold a number of larger hair bows for $3. Karen collected a total of $13. How many large hair bows did she sell? [3]

TECH LINK

MATH VAN

Activity You may wish to use *Amazing Places!* to teach this lesson.

MATH FORUM

Management Tip I allow students who struggle with place value to use place-value models as well as place-value charts until they are comfortable with the pencil-and-paper process.

Visit our Resource Village at http://www.mhschool.com to see more of the Math Forum.

MATH CENTER

Practice

OBJECTIVE Write numbers in different forms.

Materials per student: 0–9 spinner (TA 2); Math Center Recording Sheet (TA 31 optional)

Students use a spinner to randomly generate 6-digit numbers. They write the numbers in standard form, as a word name, and in expanded form. [*Answers may vary. Check students' work.*]

PRACTICE ACTIVITY 3   MATH CENTER On Your Own

Number Sense • Numbers, Numbers

Copy the boxes shown below.

☐ ☐ ☐ , ☐ ☐ ☐

YOU NEED
: spinner (0–9)

• Spin the spinner. Write the number in one box. Repeat until all the boxes are filled.
• Write the word name for the number you made. Then write the number in expanded form.
• Now use the same digits to write another 6-digit number. Make it greater than the first number.
• Write the number in standard form, as a word name, and in expanded form.

five hundred thousand, fifty

500,050

500,000 + 50

NCTM Standards
  Problem Solving
✓ Communication
✓ Reasoning
  Connections

Chapter 1, Lesson 3, pages 8–11   Place Value

Grade Level 4   McGraw-Hill School Division

Problem Solving

OBJECTIVE Use place value to solve riddles.

Materials per student: Math Center Recording Sheet (TA 31 optional)

Students solve riddles using what they learned about place value. Then students create their own riddles. [**1.** 75,580; **2.** 252,640. Check students' work.]

PROBLEM-SOLVING ACTIVITY 3   MATH CENTER Partners

Logical Reasoning • What Number Am I?

• Solve the riddles.

  1. I am a 5-digit number. My ones period can be written as five hundred eighty. The value of one of my digits is 5,000. The digit in my ten thousands place is 10 minus 3. What number am I?

  2. I am a 6-digit number. My first three digits can be written as two hundred fifty-two thousand. The value of one of my digits is 600 and the value of another is 40. My only remaining digit is a zero. What number am I?

• Compare your answers with your partner.
• Make up your own riddles and share them with each other.

I am a 4-digit number.

NCTM Standards
✓ Problem Solving
✓ Communication
✓ Reasoning
  Connections

Chapter 1, Lesson 3, pages 8–11   Place Value

Grade Level 4   McGraw-Hill School Division

Thousands

OBJECTIVE Represent numbers up to 999,999 in different forms and identify the place and value of digits.

Materials 14 index cards, counters

Vocabulary digit, expanded form, period, standard form

❶ Introduce

Introduce the Egyptian number system shown below. Write the number 435,500 in Egyptian symbols on the chalkboard.

Explain how the Egyptian number system works and then have students write a few numbers using the system.

Hindu-Arabic	100,000	10,000	1,000	100	10	1
Egyptian						

Then ask:

- **How is the Egyptian system different from the Hindu-Arabic system we use?** *[Possible answers: Place value is not used; pictures are used to represent numbers.]*
- **In which system is it easier to write numbers, the Egyptian system or the Hindu-Arabic system? Why?** *[Possible answer: Hindu-Arabic, because place value makes it possible to use fewer symbols to write numbers.]*

❷ Teach · *Whole Class*

Cultural Connection Read the **Cultural Note.** You may wish to discuss Peace Park, Hiroshima. The first atomic bomb was dropped on Hiroshima during World War II. Deaths numbered nearly 130,000 and 90 percent of the city was destroyed. Most of Hiroshima has been rebuilt. Peace Park is a memorial.

▶ **LEARN** Discuss with students the three different ways to write a number. Ask students for examples.

Talk It Over Discuss place value by showing 835 written in the Hindu-Arabic system and in the ancient Egyptian system. Ask:

- **If you changed the order of the Egyptian symbols, would they show the same number? Why or why not?** *[Possible answer: Yes; the digit's value doesn't change—there are still 8 hundreds, 3 tens, and 5 ones showing.]*
- **What happens when you change the order of the digits in 835 to 385?** *[Possible answer: The number changes because there are now 3 hundreds and 8 tens.]*

PLACE VALUE

Thousands

Do you know that over 435,500 origami paper cranes are hanging from a memorial at Peace Park in Hiroshima, Japan? In the United States, the Sadako/Paper Crane Project collects origami cranes to donate to the Peace Park.

A place-value chart shows the value of the **digits** in a number.

Each group of three digits is called a **period.**

IN THE WORKPLACE
Sharon O'Connell is the founder of the Sadako/Paper Crane Project.

Thousands Period			Ones Period		
Hundreds	Tens	Ones	Hundreds	Tens	Ones
4	3	5	5	0	0

You can read or write numbers in different ways.

Standard Form: 435,500   Note: Commas are used to separate periods.

Word Name: four hundred thirty-five thousand, five hundred

Expanded Form: 400,000 + 30,000 + 5,000 + 500

Check Out the Glossary
digit
period
standard form
expanded form
See page 544.

Talk It Over
▶ How do the places in the thousands period relate to each other? How are they similar to the places in the ones period? How do the places help you read the number?

▶ What is the value of each digit in 435,500? How are the values used in the expanded form?
400,000; 30,000; 5,000; 500; 0; 0; possible answer: you add the values of the digits to get the expanded form.

Cultural Note
In Japan, it is customary to make a garland of origami paper cranes for a friend who is ill.

8   Lesson 1.3

place or of it; e has hundr
and ones places; read each set of hundreds, tens, and ones the sam
read the word *thousand* after the numbers in the thousan

Meeting Individual Needs

Early Finishers

Have students look through newspapers, magazines, and other materials to find numbers with four to six digits. Students should then write the numbers as word names and in expanded form.

Extra Support

Have students put place-value models beside the numbers on a place-value chart. Tell them to show 10 more or 100 more of the number by removing one tens model or one hundreds model from the mat.

ESL APPROPRIATE

Ongoing Assessment

Anecdotal Report Make notes on students' ability to write numbers in standard form, as word names, and in expanded form. Also note if students are able to increase and decrease the value of a number by recognizing the effect this has on only one or two place values.

Follow Up Let students who need help use a place-value chart and complete **Reteach 3.**

For students who need a challenge, assign **Extend 3.**

What if you have 629,509 folded-paper cranes. How many cranes will you have if you make 10 more? 100 more?

A place-value chart can help you see changes in the places of a number.

Thousands Period			Ones Period		
Hundreds	Tens	Ones	Hundreds	Tens	Ones
6	2	9	5	0	9
6	2	9	5	1	9
6	2	9	6	0	9

← 10 more cranes
← 100 more cranes

▶ How would you show 200 fewer cranes? 2,000 more cranes? **Decrease the hundreds digit by 2; increase the thousands digit by 2.**

More Examples

A 240,000 can be written as two hundred forty thousand.

B 57,480 can be written as 50,000 + 7,000 + 400 + 80.

C 800,975 can be written as 800 thousand, 975.

D 2,000 less than 690,000 is 688,000.

E 10 more than 79,995 is 80,005.

1. eight thousand, four hundred twenty-five; 8,000 + 400 + 20 + 5

2. nineteen thousand, eight hundred forty-one; 10,000 + 9,000 + 800 + 40 + 1

3. seventy-five thousand, three; 70,000 + 5,000 + 3

4. six hundred five thousand, nine hundred eleven; 600,000 + 5,000 + 900 + 10 + 1

Check for Understanding

Write the word name for the number. Then write the number in expanded form. See above.

1 8,425   **2** 19,841   **3** 75,003   **4** 605,911

5 Find 300 less than 8,769. **8,469**

6 Find 4,000 more than 21,695. **25,695**

Critical Thinking: Analyze   Explain your reasoning.

7 Aida says you can rename 35,725 as 3 + 5 + 7 + 2 + 5. Do you agree or disagree? **Disagree; 35,725 = 30,000 + 5,000 + 700 + 20 + 5.**

8 When you increase a number by 1,000, do you need to change only the thousands place? Show an example to support your reasoning. See below.

8. When the thousands place has the digit 9, it is necessary to also change one or more other places because of regrouping; 1,000 more than 99,020 is 100,020.

Turn the page for Practice.

Place Value and Number Sense   **9**

CHECK

Ask students to look carefully at the numbers in the place-value chart. After discussing the questions at the top of the page, ask:

• **If you increased the number of cranes by 50, how would the original number change? What is the new number?** *[The digit in the tens place would increase by 5; 629,559]*

• **If you increased the number of cranes by 3,000, which digits would change? What is the new number?** *[thousands and ten thousands; 632,509]*

• **If you decreased the number of cranes by 60, which digits would change? What is the new number?** *[tens and hundreds; 629,449]*

More Examples For each example, ask students to name another way the number can be written. For Example A, students could give the expanded form: 200,000 + 40,000.

3 Close

▶ **Check for Understanding** using items 1–8, page 9.

CRITICAL THINKING
To help students understand item 7, ask:

• **Find 3 + 5 + 7 + 2 + 5.** *[22]*

• **What is the value of each of the digits in the number 35,725?** *[30,000; 5,000; 700; 20; and 5]*

• **Why is Aida incorrect?** *[She did not consider place value.]*

Practice See pages 10–11.

Gifted And Talented

Have students create their own numbering system, using colors or symbols to represent place value. For example, they could decide that a green dot represents a ten, and a red dot represents a one. Three green dots and two red dots would represent 32.

After creating their number system, have students write addition and subtraction problems in their system. They then exchange problems and solve them.

Language Support

Encourage students to compare the construction of word names for numbers in their primary language with the equivalent constructions in English. For example, in the German language, numbers greater than one digit are often read in an expanded format. The numeral 26 is read *six and twenty*. Compare and contrast the forms used.

ESL APPROPRIATE

▶ **PRACTICE**

Options for assigning exercises:

A—Odd ex. 1–17; all ex. 19–27; **Number Tic-Tac-Toe Game; Mixed Review**

B—Even ex. 2–26; **Number Tic-Tac-Toe Game; Mixed Review**

- In ex. 5–10, remind students to use zero as a place holder when needed.
- For ex. 11–18, students are asked to write the word names for numbers. Remind students that 2-digit numbers such as seventy-eight and twenty-five are always hyphenated.

Algebra Being able to analyze data and determine how data is related is a skill necessary for writing algebraic equations. In ex. 19, students analyze data in a table and find a rule to complete the table. In ex. 20–23, students use algebraic thinking to determine the missing numbers.

Number Tic-Tac-Toe Game Give students time to play the game. After playing one round, encourage students to think about the numbers to use on their game sheet. What if they used a number with the same digits? How would that affect their chances of winning? Why? *[Possible answer: Using a number with the same digits would decrease your chances because you would have to draw that number.]*

Mixed Review/Test Preparation Students review writing numbers in standard form. You may wish to have them write the numbers in expanded form as well.

---

11. four hundred seventy-eight; 400 + 70 + 8   12. six thousand, one hundred twenty-five; 6,000 + 100 + 20 + 5
13. nine thousand, five hundred one; 9,000 + 500 + 1   14. seventy-four thousand, seventy-six; 70,000 + 4,000 + 70 + 6

Practice

Write the number in standard form and in expanded form.

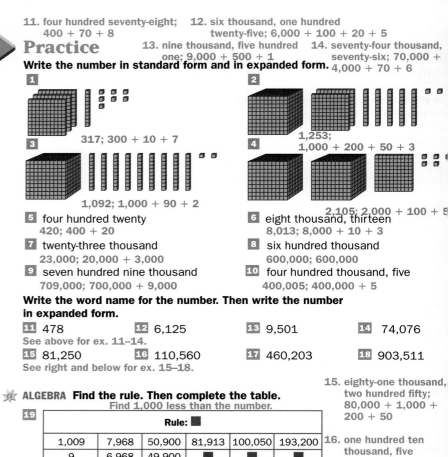

1 317; 300 + 10 + 7

2 1,253; 1,000 + 200 + 50 + 3

3 1,092; 1,000 + 90 + 2

4 2,105; 2,000 + 100 + 5

5 four hundred twenty
420; 400 + 20

6 eight thousand, thirteen
8,013; 8,000 + 10 + 3

7 twenty-three thousand
23,000; 20,000 + 3,000

8 six hundred thousand
600,000; 600,000

9 seven hundred nine thousand
709,000; 700,000 + 9,000

10 four hundred thousand, five
400,005; 400,000 + 5

Write the word name for the number. Then write the number in expanded form.

11 478   **12** 6,125   **13** 9,501   **14** 74,076
See above for ex. 11–14.

15 81,250   **16** 110,560   **17** 460,203   **18** 903,511
See right and below for ex. 15–18.

ALGEBRA Find the rule. Then complete the table.

19 Find 1,000 less than the number.

Rule: ■					
1,009	7,968	50,900	81,913	100,050	193,200
9	6,968	49,900	■	■	■

80,913 99,050 192,200

Fill in the missing numbers.

20 3,039 = 3,000 + ■ + 9   30

21 80,720 = 80,000 + ■ + 20   700

22 73,296 = 70,000 + ■ + 200 + 90 + ■   3,000; 6

23 456,750 = 400,000 + ■ + 6,000 + 700 + ■   50,000; 50

24 Find 100 more than 6,985. 7,085

25 Find 3,000 less than 81,290.
78,290

26 Find 2,000 less than 8,903. 6,903

27 Find 300,000 more than 265,900.
565,900

15. eighty-one thousand, two hundred fifty; 80,000 + 1,000 + 200 + 50

16. one hundred ten thousand, five hundred sixty; 100,000 + 10,000 + 500 + 60

17. four hundred sixty thousand, two hundred three; 400,000 + 60,000 + 200 + 3

18. nine hundred three thousand, five hundred eleven; 900,000 + 3,000 + 500 + 10 + 1

Meeting Individual Needs

Early Finishers

Ask students to write the numbers in exercises 1–10 using the ancient Egyptian system of numbers.

COMMON ERROR

Some students may forget to regroup when adding to or subtracting from a number. When students complete exercises that require regrouping, such as exercise 21 or 23, have them describe the computation place by place, and help them to record any regrouping.

Possible answer: Write 4-digit numbers that do not have the same digit in any given place—this strategy gives a better chance of having the place value chosen.

Number Tic-Tac-Toe Game!

First, make one set of cards for each of the numbers 0 through 9. Make another set with the words *ones, tens, hundreds,* and *thousands.* Put each set of cards in a separate pile.

You will need
- *counters*
- *index cards*

| thousands | hundreds | tens | ones |

7,128	4,309	9,000
2,093	5,100	1,631
3298	6214	8,123

Next, make a game sheet like the one shown. You may choose any 4-digit numbers to fill in the grid.

Play the Game

▶ Mix up each pile of cards. Decide the order in which you will play.

▶ When it is your turn, pick a card from each pile. Then place counters on any number on your game sheet that has the digit in the place shown.

▶ The first player to get three counters in a row, column, or diagonal wins the round. The winner gets a point.

▶ Create new game sheets. Continue playing until a player has 5 points.

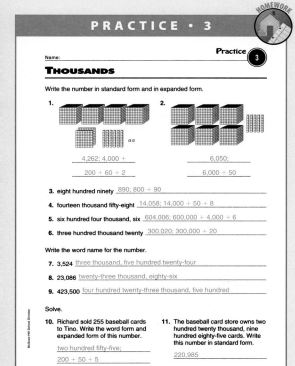

How did you decide what numbers to place on your game sheet?
See above.

mixed review · test preparation

Write the number in standard form.

1 8 hundreds 2 tens
820

2 6 hundred thousands 7 thousands 8 tens
607,080

3 two thousand-seven
2,007

4 4 thousands 6 hundreds 3 tens 8 ones
4,638

Extra Practice, page 485

Place Value and Number Sense **11**

Alternate Teaching Strategy

Materials per student: place-value chart (TA 4)

Display a place-value chart with the number 526,471 and have students write that number on their own place-value charts. Then have them determine the value of each digit. Point to each place and ask questions such as the following:

- **How many hundred thousands are there?** [5]
- **How many ten thousands are there?** [2]
- **How many thousands are there?** [6]

As students identify the value shown in each place, write each part of the expanded form of the number. [500,000 + 20,000 + 6,000 + 400 + 70 + 1]

Then have pairs of students work together to repeat this activity for numbers such as 604,579 and 85,003. Encourage them to find the value of the digit in each place and to write the expanded form step by step.

PRACTICE · 3

Name: _____

Practice **3**

THOUSANDS

Write the number in standard form and in expanded form.

1.
4,262; 4,000 +
200 + 60 + 2

2.
6,050;
6,000 + 50

3. eight hundred ninety   890; 800 + 90

4. fourteen thousand fifty-eight   14,058; 14,000 + 50 + 8

5. six hundred four thousand, six   604,006; 600,000 + 4,000 + 6

6. three hundred thousand twenty   300,020; 300,000 + 20

Write the word name for the number.

7. 3,524   three thousand, five hundred twenty-four

8. 23,086   twenty-three thousand, eighty-six

9. 423,500   four hundred twenty-three thousand, five hundred

Solve.

10. Richard sold 255 baseball cards to Tino. Write the word form and expanded form of this number.
two hundred fifty-five;
200 + 50 + 5

11. The baseball card store owns two hundred twenty thousand, nine hundred eighty-five cards. Write this number in standard form.
220,985

RETEACH · 3

Name: _____

Reteach **3**

THOUSANDS

You can read or write numbers in different ways.
Each group of three digits is called a **period** and is separated by a comma.

	Thousands Period			Ones Period		
	Hundreds	Tens	Ones	Hundreds	Tens	Ones
	6	4	1	3	2	5
Expanded Form	600,000 +	40,000 +	1,000 +	300 +	20 +	5
Word Name	six hundred forty-one thousand, three hundred twenty-five					
Standard Form	641,325					

Fill in the missing numbers.

1. 8,923 = ___8,000___ + 900 + 20 + ___3___

2. 14,247 = 10,000 + ___4,000___ + 200 + ___40___ + ___7___

3. 422,978 = ___400,000___ + 20,000 + 2,000 + ___900___ + 70 + 8

Complete.

	Standard Form	Expanded Form	Word Name
4.	532	500 + 30 + 2	five hundred thirty-two
5.	4,532	4,000 + 500 + 30 + 2	four thousand, five hundred thirty-two
6.	74,532	70,000 + 4,000 + 500 + 30 + 2	seventy-four thousand, five hundred thirty-two
7.	674,532	600,000 + 70,000 + 4,000 + 500 + 30 + 2	six hundred seventy-four thousand, five hundred thirty-two

---

EXTEND · 3

Name: _____

Extend **3**

THOUSANDS

Crossnumber Puzzle

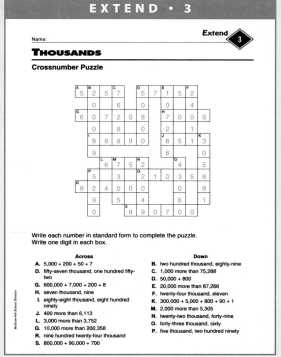

Write each number in standard form to complete the puzzle.
Write one digit in each box.

Across
A. 5,000 + 200 + 50 + 7
D. fifty-seven thousand, one hundred fifty-two
G. 600,000 + 7,000 + 200 + 8
H. seven thousand, nine
I. eighty-eight thousand, eight hundred ninety
J. 400 more than 6,113
L. 3,000 more than 3,752
Q. 10,000 more than 200,358
R. nine hundred twenty-four thousand
S. 800,000 + 90,000 + 700

Down
B. two hundred thousand, eighty-nine
C. 1,000 more than 75,288
D. 50,000 + 800
E. 20,000 more than 87,266
F. twenty-four thousand, eleven
K. 300,000 + 5,000 + 800 + 90 + 1
M. 2,000 more than 5,305
N. twenty-two thousand, forty-nine
O. forty-three thousand, sixty
P. five thousand, two hundred ninety

11

Teaching With Technology

Build to Thousands

OBJECTIVES Students use Place-Value Models to represent numbers to thousands. Students represent large numbers in different forms.

 Resource Math Van Activity: *Amazing Places!*

SET UP
Provide students with the activity card for *Amazing Places!* Start **Math Van** and click the *Activities* button. Click the *Amazing Places!* activity on the Fax Machine.

USING THE MATH VAN ACTIVITY

1 Getting Started Students use Place-Value Models to show the height of the Sears Tower in Chicago, IL and the Empire State Building in New York, NY. Students fill in place-value chart with the heights of the two buildings.

2 Practice and Apply Students are presented with amazing facts that were misprinted. Students use Place-Value Models to show the correct numbers. Students then enter the correct information in the place-value chart.

3 Close Discuss how the Place-Value Models can help students identify the value and place of digits.

Extend Students use an Almanac to find facts about other interesting places. They challenge a friend to use the Place-Value Models to show the number. They write numbers in different forms.

TIPS FOR TOOLS

Remind students that they can use the *Undo* button to erase the last action that they performed.

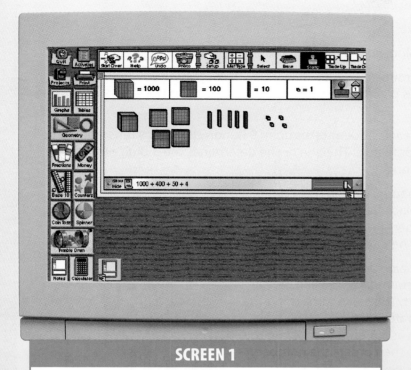

SCREEN 1

Students use Place-Value Models to show the height of the Sears Tower in Chicago, IL.

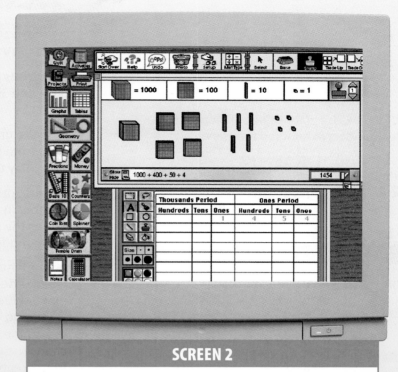

SCREEN 2

Students look at the Place-Value Models and enter the number 1,454 into the place-value chart.

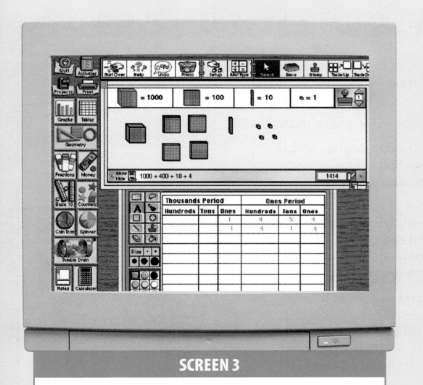

SCREEN 3

Students use Place-Value Models to show the height of the Empire State Building and enter the numbers into the place-value chart.

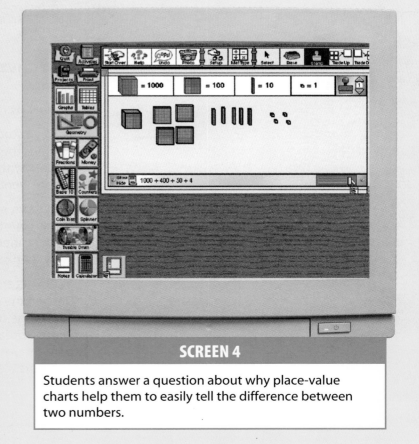

SCREEN 4

Students answer a question about why place-value charts help them to easily tell the difference between two numbers.

LESSON 1.4

Compare and Order Numbers

OBJECTIVE Use place value to compare and order numbers to hundred thousands.

RESOURCE REMINDER
Math Center Cards 4
Practice 4, Reteach 4, Extend 4

SKILLS TRACE

GRADE 3
• Compare and order numbers up to hundred thousands. *(Chapter 2)*

GRADE 4
• Compare and order numbers up to 999,999.

GRADE 5
• Compare and order numbers through hundred millions. *(Chapter 1)*

MANIPULATIVE WARM-UP

Cooperative Groups   **Kinesthetic**

OBJECTIVE Explore comparing and ordering numbers.

Materials per group: 3 large containers, each containing 20 hundreds, 30 tens, and 30 ones place-value models; place-value chart (TA 4); 0–9 spinner (TA 2)

▶ In the group, each student takes up to 9 hundreds, up to 9 tens, and up to 9 ones from the containers. Then he or she determines the 3-digit number shown by their models.

▶ Students take turns writing the 3-digit number in the place-value chart. The group orders the numbers from greatest to least, using models to help them compare.

▶ Students in their groups discuss how they could order greater numbers using only a place-value chart. They take turns using the spinner to generate 5 digits, and then they record the digits as a 5-digit number on the chart. The group then orders the numbers from greatest to least.

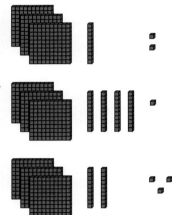

ESL APPROPRIATE

STATISTICS CONNECTION

Cooperative Pairs   **Kinesthetic**

OBJECTIVE Compare and order 2-digit numbers generated by a classroom activity.

Materials clock or watch with a second hand

▶ Have students estimate the number of times they can hop in one minute. Discuss with the class a range of possible answers.

▶ In pairs, one student hops and keeps count of the hops while the other student times one minute. They then switch roles.

▶ Collect the data and write the numbers on the board. Work with the class to arrange the list of numbers from the least to greatest. Have students compare this list to the list of estimated numbers.

Daily Review

PREVIOUS DAY QUICK REVIEW

Write in expanded form.

1. 8,256 *[8,000 + 200 + 50 + 6]*
2. 46,921 *[40,000 + 6,000 + 900 + 20 + 1]*
3. 130,840 *[100,000 + 30,000 + 800 + 40]*

FAST FACTS

1. 2 + 3 *[5]*
2. 1 + 5 *[6]*
3. 3 + 4 *[7]*
4. 6 + 2 *[8]*

Problem of the Day • 4

Ken has one shirt and one pair of shorts in each of these colors: red, yellow, blue. What different combinations of clothes does he have? *[red shirt, red shorts; red shirt, yellow shorts; red shirt, blue shorts; blue shirt, red shorts; blue shirt, yellow shorts; blue shirt, blue shorts; yellow shirt, red shorts; yellow shirt, yellow shorts; yellow shirt, blue shorts]*

TECH LINK

MATH VAN

Tool You may wish to use the Place-Value Model tool with this lesson.

MATH FORUM

Combination Classes When I teach place value to my combination class, the only change I make is the number of digits in the numbers I use in my questions.

Visit our Resource Village at http://www.mhschool.com to see more of the Math Forum.

MATH CENTER

Practice

OBJECTIVE Order numbers.

Materials per group: 4 sets of number cards for 0–9 (TA 29); Math Center Recording Sheet (TA 31 optional)

Students randomly generate numbers to make 4-, 5-, or 6-digit numbers. As a group they order them from least to greatest. The player with the greatest number wins. *[Answers may vary. Check students' work.]*

PRACTICE ACTIVITY 4

MATH CENTER
Small Group

Game • Who Has the Greatest?

- One person mixes up the number cards and passes them out so each group member receives four cards.
- Each person uses his or her cards to make the greatest 4-digit number possible.
- Record the numbers. As a group, order them from least to greatest. Discuss your reasoning.
- The player with the greatest number wins.

Play again with each person receiving five or six cards and making 5- or 6-digit numbers.

YOU NEED
4 sets of number cards (0–9)

NCTM Standards
- Problem Solving
- ✓ Communication
- ✓ Reasoning
- Connections

Chapter 1, Lesson 4, pages 12–13

Place Value

ESL APPROPRIATE

Problem Solving

OBJECTIVE Use logical reasoning to create greatest and least numbers.

Materials per group: number cube, number cards for 0–9 (TA 29); Math Center Recording Sheet (TA 31 optional)

Students use a number cube and number cards to generate numbers. They use logical reasoning to position digits so as to create the greatest number they can using the numbers on their cards. Students repeat the activity to try to create the least number they can.

PROBLEM-SOLVING ACTIVITY 4

MATH CENTER
Small Group

Logical Reasoning • Greatest, Least

Take turns making numbers.

- Toss the number cube. The number you toss is how many digits there are in the number you make.
- Choose that number of cards. Make the greatest possible number using the digits on the cards. Record your number.
- When everyone has had a turn, order all the numbers. The student with the greatest number earns a point.
- Keep playing. The winner is the first person to earn five points.

Play again, but this time make the least possible number.

YOU NEED
- number cube
- number cards (0–9)

98,520

2 5 8 9 0

NCTM Standards
- ✓ Problem Solving
- ✓ Communication
- ✓ Reasoning
- Connections

Chapter 1, Lesson 4, pages 12–13

Place Value

ESL APPROPRIATE

Lesson 1.4 continued

Compare and Order Numbers

OBJECTIVE Compare and order numbers.

Vocabulary is greater than, is less than

 **Introduce**

Write on the chalkboard the following records from the Guinness Book of World Records:

Lou Scripa, Jr. did 70,715 sit-ups in 24 hours.
Charles Sirvizio did 46,001 push-ups in 24 hours.
Lou Scripa, Jr. did 41,788 leg lifts in 12 hours.

Then ask students the following questions:

- **Which is the greater number, the record for sit-ups or the record for push-ups?** *[the record for sit-ups]*
- **If Lou Scripa, Jr. did twice as many leg lifts in 24 hours, would that number be more or less than the number of sit-ups? Explain.** *[More; twice the number of leg lifts is over 80,000, and 80,000 > 70,715.]*

 **Teach**   *Whole Class*

LEARN Write three numbers between 40,000 and 70,000 on the board so that the ones digits line up. Show students how to compare the numbers, starting with the digits in the ten thousands place. Ask these questions about the numbers you write:

- **Where on the number line would you put this number?**
- **Would this number go to the right or left of that number?**

Encourage students to create ways to remember the *greater than* and *less than* symbols. Some see that the symbols point to the smaller number. Others make symbols with thumb and forefinger of each hand. The left-hand symbol looks like the capital letter *L* and is the less than symbol.

 **Close**

▶ **Check for Understanding** using items 1–4, page 12.

CRITICAL THINKING

 Students have an opportunity to relate the process of alphabetizing to place value. Accept a wide variety of explanations.

▶ **PRACTICE**

Options for assigning exercises:

A—All ex. 1–18; **Mixed Review**

B—Odd ex. 1–15; all ex. 16–18; **Mixed Review**

- Students may find it helpful to use a number line to compare numbers.

Mixed Review/Test Preparation Students review writing the word name for numbers, a skill learned in Lesson 3.

Compare and Order Numbers

L E A R N

Here are some amazing heights reached by helicopters and balloons! Compare them.

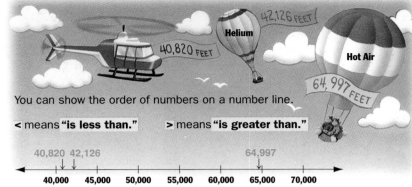

You can show the order of numbers on a number line.

< means **"is less than."**   > means **"is greater than."**

You can also use place value to compare and order numbers.

Line up the ones. Start with the greatest place. Compare the digits.	Compare the digits in the next place.	Write the numbers in order.
40,820 64,997 42,126	40,820 42,126	From greatest to least: 64,997; 42,126; 40,820 From least to greatest: 40,820; 42,126; 64,997
Think: 6 > 4, so 64,997 is the greatest number.	**Think:** 2 > 0, so 42,126 > 40,820.	

The hot-air balloon rose the highest, then the helium balloon, then the helicopter.

> **Check Out the Glossary**
> is less than,
> is greater than
> See page 544.

C H E C K

Check for Understanding

Order the numbers from greatest to least.

1 17,750; 12,000; 17,540   **2** 8,060; 3,594; 6,333   **3** 7,934; 7,958; 3,00
17,750; 17,540; 12,000   8,060; 6,333; 3,594   7,958; 7,934; 3,000

Critical Thinking: Generalize   **Explain your reasoning.**

4 How is writing numbers in order like writing words in alphabetical order?

Possible answer: Comparing the greatest place is like comparing the first letter of words—in both cases if the first place or letter is the same, go to the nex place or letter.

Meeting Individual Needs

Early Finishers

Refer students to the number lines in their book. Point out the intervals for each number line. Students make a number line for the numbers given in one or more of ex. 10–15. They can decide what intervals to use.

Extra Support

When comparing and ordering a set of numbers, students should make sure they always compare two numbers at a time. Remind them to think logically when comparing and ordering more than two numbers.

Ongoing Assessment

Anecdotal Report Make notes on students' ability to use the greater than and less than signs. Ask students to fill in the blank using the appropriate sign:

5,215 ___ 5,500 *[<]*

Follow Up If students need additional help with this skill, assign **Reteach 4**.

For those who are ready for more in-depth activities, assign **Extend 4**.

18. **Answers may vary. Possible answer: Choose AZ because it is less expensive and you leave on March 12.**

Practice

Use the number line to compare. Write >, <, or =.

1. 5,900 ● 4,080 **>**   2. 6,400 ● 6,799 **<**   3. 3,184 ● 3,108 **>**

```
<————|————|————|————|————|————>
    3,000  4,000  5,000  6,000  7,000
```

Compare. Write >, <, or =.

4. 878 ● 794 **>**   5. 8,673 ● 8,654 **>**   6. 1,516 ● 1,112 **>**

7. 8,504 ● 8,515 **<**   8. 10,198 ● 101,980 **<**   9. 254,811 ● 250,811 **>**

Order the numbers from least to greatest.

10. 639; 504; 648 **504; 639; 648**

11. 8,799; 9,411; 9,059 **8,799; 9,059; 9,411**

12. 5,770; 7,707; 5,077 **5,077; 5,770; 7,707**

13. 6,402; 3,499; 3,480 **3,480; 3,499; 6,402**

14. 11,450; 7,760; 8,046 **7,760; 8,046; 11,450**

15. 4,518; 45,108; 4,718 **4,518; 4,718; 45,108**

MIXED APPLICATIONS
Problem Solving

Pencil & Paper · Calculator · Mental Math

16. Order the distances traveled from greatest to least. **SEE INFOBIT.** 24,901 mi, 8,000 mi, 870 mi

17. The first supersonic flight, in a Bell XS-1 rocket plane, reached an altitude of 42,000 ft. The aircraft with the heaviest takeoff load, an Antonov An-225, reached an altitude of 40,715 ft. Which reached the greater altitude? **the Bell XS-1**

18. **Make a decision** You want to fly to Toronto on March 12. You can fly on AZ airline for $175, but you have to change planes and wait 1 hour. You can fly on DRZ airline for $240 nonstop, but you have to leave on March 13. What would you do? **See above.**

INFOBIT
Amazing records: Rick Hansen wheeled his wheelchair 24,901 miles. Plennie Wingo walked 8,000 miles backward. Johann Hurlinger walked on his hands 870 miles.

mixed review · test preparation

1. 548 **five hundred forty-eight**

2. 2,000 + 300 + 10 **two thousand, three hundred ten**

3. 732,907 **seven hundred thirty-two thousand, nine hundred seven**

4. 40,000 + 1,000 + 900 + 20 + 5 **four hundred one thousand, nine hundred twenty-five**

Extra Practice, page 485

Place Value and Number Sense   **13**

Alternate Teaching Strategy

Materials per pair: place-value chart (TA 4)

Write the following on the chalkboard:

Compare

417 ___ 481

Have students write the numbers in a place-value chart.

Thousands			Ones		
hundreds	tens	ones	hundreds	tens	ones
			4	1	7
			4	8	1

417 ≶ 481

Ask questions such as the following to help students compare the two numbers:
- **Which number has more hundreds?** *[Neither; they both have 4 hundreds.]*
- **Which number has more tens?** *[481]*
- **So which number is greater?** *[481]*

Have students write the greater than or less than symbol. *[<]*

After comparing other numbers in the hundreds, have students compare numbers in the thousands, then ten thousands, and then hundred thousands.

Practice 4

Name: _____

COMPARE AND ORDER NUMBERS

Compare. Write >, <, or =.

1. 643 < 943   2. 472 > 427   3. 1,000 < 10,000

4. 5,107 < 5,211   5. 7,316 > 7,309   6. 2,134 > 2,116

7. 30,821 < 31,821   8. 643,927 < 697,625   9. 203,497 > 20,349

10. 10,365 > 8,365   11. 11,091 < 11,901   12. 97,000 > 89,999

13. 65,212 > 56,212   14. 28,545 = 28,545   15. 56,619 < 56,916

Order the numbers from least to greatest.

16. 429; 306; 489 **306; 429; 489**

17. 4,507; 2,698; 2,664 **2,664; 2,698; 4,507**

18. 8,543; 4,876; 4,856 **4,856; 4,876; 8,543**

19. 9,862; 98,438; 98,135 **9,862; 98,135; 98,438**

20. 14,320; 8,940; 13,098 **8,940; 13,098; 14,320**

21. 56,324; 55,873; 55,818 **55,818; 55,873; 56,324**

22. 657,563; 675,843; 657,365 **657,365; 657,563; 675,843**

23. 345,713; 445,713; 234,713 **234,713; 345,713; 445,713**

24. 716,049; 716,490; 716,029 **716,029; 716,049; 716,490**

Solve.

25. There are 325 fourth graders and 340 fifth graders participating in a contest. Which grade has more participants? **fifth grade**

26. The fourth graders scored the following points: 87, 112, 98, 126, 95. Rank these points from least to greatest. **87, 95, 98, 112, 126**

McGraw-Hill School Division

Reteach 4

Name: _____

COMPARE AND ORDER NUMBERS

To compare numbers, compare the digits in each place. You can use a place-value chart.
Compare 4,367 and 4,357.

Thousands	Hundreds	Tens	Ones
4	3	6	7
4	3	5	7

4 = 4   3 = 3   6 > 5

Same number of thousands.   Same number of hundreds.   4,367 has more tens than 4,357.

Think: Start at the left. Look for the first place where the digits are different.

So, 4,367 > 4,357.

Write the numbers in the place-value chart. Then compare. Write >, <, or =.

1. Compare 578 and 589.

Hundreds	Tens	Ones
5	7	8
5	8	9

578 < 589

2. Compare 3,248 and 3,219.

Thousands	Hundreds	Tens	Ones
3	2	4	8
3	2	1	9

3,248 > 3,219

Compare. Write < or >.

3. 4,591 > 1,450   4. 8,329 < 9,230

5. 6,668 < 6,686   6. 2,091 < 2,901

7. 5,113 > 4,555   8. 3,678 < 3,768

9. 23,489 > 21,489   10. 60,281 < 61,002

11. 403,100 < 410,239   12. 932,077 > 912,077

McGraw-Hill School Division

Extend 4

Name: _____

COMPARE AND ORDER NUMBERS

Sunday Papers

The data shows the average number of Sunday newspapers sold for the newspapers listed. Order the newspapers from the least to the greatest circulation. Then write each rank's corresponding code letter in the box below to decode the message. The first one is done for you.

Newspaper	Sunday Circulation	Rank	Code Letter
Atlanta Constitution	287,389	4	T
Boston Globe	509,573	7	N
Chicago Sun Times	554,670	8	E
Columbus Dispatch	257,366	3	L
Denver Post	241,386	2	L
Houston Chronicle	427,844	6	E
Minneapolis Star Tribune	403,300	5	H
Philadelphia Daily News	237,822	1	A
San Francisco Chronicle	556,196	9	W
Washington Post (Washington, D.C.)	812,419	10	S

A	L	L		T	H	E		N	E	W	S
1	2	3		4	5	6		7	8	9	10

Think Critically

The population of Washington, D.C., is about 600,000. Compare this figure with the circulation figure for the *Washington Post*. What conclusion can you draw?

Answers may vary. Sample answer: There are more papers sold than there are people in the city, so people outside of Washington, D.C., read the *Washington Post*.

McGraw-Hill School Division

13

LESSON 1.5

Problem-Solving Strategy: Make a Table

OBJECTIVES Introduce the problem-solving heuristic; make a table to solve a problem.

RESOURCE REMINDER
Math Center Cards 5
Practice 5, Reteach 5, Extend 5

SKILLS TRACE	
GRADE 3	• Solve problems by making a table. *(Chapter 2)*
GRADE 4	• Solve problems by making a table.
GRADE 5	• Solve problems by making a table. *(Chapter 1)*

WARM-UP

Whole Class   Logical/Analytical

OBJECTIVE Use a table to solve problems.

▶ Present this problem:

The stadium shop sells gray team shirts, white team shirts, and blue team shirts. The shop sells white sweat pants and gray sweat pants. How many different combinations of clothes can you make?

▶ Draw this table on the chalkboard. Include at least six blank rows. Ask students how they could use the table to solve the problem.

▶ Have students copy the table and use it to show all of the combinations of clothes.

▶ Extend the problem by adding another choice of clothing, such as socks, in two different colors. Have students discuss how to change the table. Then have them solve the problem.

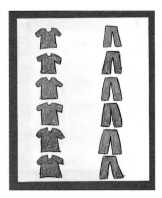

Shirt	Sweat pants
[gray]	*[white]*
[gray]	*[gray]*
[white]	*[white]*
[white]	*[gray]*
[blue]	*[white]*
[blue]	*[gray]*

ALGEBRA CONNECTION

Cooperative Pairs   Logical/Analytical

OBJECTIVE Analyze data in tables to find a pattern.

▶ Display the tables below.

1	2	3	4	5	*[6]*	*[7]*
5	10	15	20	25	*[30]*	*[35]*

1	3	5	7	9	*[11]*	*[13]*
2	4	6	8	10	*[12]*	*[14]*

▶ Ask pairs of students to analyze the data carefully. For each table the pair should determine a rule for the pattern, then use the rule to complete the next two columns.

▶ Discuss the tables. Ask pairs to describe their rules. *[Possible answers: first table, top row— count by 1; bottom row—count by 5; second table, top and bottom rows—add 2.]*

Daily Review

Problem of the Day • 5

Five hundred sixty-seven students at Paro Elementary School are wearing red clothing. Of those students, 316 have red stripes, and 27 have red dots on their clothing. No student has both red dots and red stripes. How many students wearing red are not wearing dots or stripes? [224]

TECH LINK

MATH FORUM

Idea To access real data for student-centered problems, I ask my students to choose their favorite cassette or CD and make a chart showing the names of the songs and their playing time.

Visit our Resource Village at http://www.mhschool.com to see more of the Math Forum.

MATH CENTER

Practice

OBJECTIVE Make tables to solve problems.

Materials per student: Math Center Recording Sheet (TA 31 optional)

Students solve problems by making tables. *[1.Donald will wear the t-shirt and shorts and Tre will wear the suit 2. brown mask, green hair; yellow mask, red hair; purple mask, yellow hair]*

Problem Solving

OBJECTIVE Use logical reasoning to solve problems.

Materials per student: Math Center Recording Sheet (TA 31 optional)

Students are presented with problems that can be solved using tables. Students may choose to solve the problems any way they like. *[1. Maria—red, Anna—green, Sharon—pink, Karen—purple; 2. 6 combinations: Red shorts, red shirt; red shorts, blue shirt; red shorts, white shirt; blue shorts, red shirt; blue shorts, blue shirt; blue shorts, white shirt; 3. Adam—red, Ben—white, Cathy—blue, Dena—black]*

PRACTICE ACTIVITY 5

Logical Reasoning • Cartoon Mix-up

Make a table to solve each problem.

1. Barry was in charge of costumes for the school play. The three main characters are Donald, Margo, and Tre. The costumes will be a suit, T-shirt and shorts, and a dress. Margo's costume is the dress. Tre will not wear the T-shirt and shorts. What will Donald and Tre's costumes be?

2. Jennifer made three masks for the school play. One was yellow, one was brown, and one was purple. One had red hair, one had green hair, and one had yellow hair. The brown mask had green hair. If a mask and its hair cannot be the same color, what color hair did each mask have?

Chapter 1, Lesson 5, pages 14–15   Problem Solving

NCTM Standards

✓ Problem Solving
   Communication
✓ Reasoning
   Connections

PROBLEM-SOLVING ACTIVITY 5

Logical Reasoning • Rainbow Riddles

1. Maria, Anna, Sharon, and Karen each have a different favorite color, either pink, green, purple, or red. Maria's favorite color has 3 letters. Anna's favorite color does not start with *p*. Karen's favorite color is not pink. What is each girl's favorite color?

2. The soccer team is trying to choose new uniforms. They can have red or blue shorts. Their shirts can be either pink, blue, or white. How many possible combinations can the team choose from? List them.

3. Adam, Ben, Cathy, and Dena each like different color cars. One likes blue, one likes red, one likes white, and one likes black. The color Adam likes does not start with *b*. Ben likes white cars. Cathy doesn't like black cars and likes cars that are the same color as her eyes. What color car does each like?

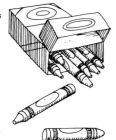

Chapter 1, Lesson 5, pages 14–15   Problem Solving

NCTM Standards

✓ Problem Solving
   Communication
✓ Reasoning
   Connections

Problem-Solving Strategy: Make a Table

OBJECTIVES Introduce the problem-solving heuristic; make a table to solve a problem.

1 Introduce

Ask students to name the world record they find most amazing. Discuss these world records. Then ask:
- **If you wanted to break a world record, which one would you like to attempt?**

2 Teach
Whole Class

▶ **LEARN** Have a volunteer read the introductory problem. Then work through the four-step problem-solving process.
- **What two kinds of information does the problem give you?** *[what was chosen and not chosen by two people]*
- **What part of the answer do you already know?** *[Gene chose the largest drum set.]*
- **What do you still need to find out?** *[the world records that Callie and Claire chose]*

When students consider the Plan step, ask:
- **Can you add or subtract to solve this problem? Explain.** *[No; there are no numbers.]*
- **Why could using a table help you solve this problem?** *[Possible answer: It can help you organize information, keep track of what you know and do not know, and eliminate possibilities in order to find the answer.]*

After students complete the problem-solving process, review the four steps: Read, Plan, Solve, Look Back. Remind students that these steps can help them solve any kind of problem.

3 Close

Check for Understanding using items 1–2, page 14.

CRITICAL THINKING
Discuss the strategies students suggest. Ask students which stategy is easiest to use. Have them explain why.

▶ **PRACTICE**
Materials have available: calculators

Options for assigning exercises:
A—All exercises
B—Choice of six exercises from ex. 1–10

- Ex. 1 and 3 are best suited for the problem-solving strategy Make a Table.
- If students have trouble with ex. 5, suggest that they draw squares and try to make the shapes shown by drawing one line through each square.

Make a Table

L E A R N

Gene, Callie, and Claire read about different world records. Gene reads about the drums. Callie does not read about Scrabble. Which record does each person read about?

Use the questions to help you solve the problem.

Read	What do you know? What do you need to find?	Gene reads about the drums. Callie does not read about Scrabble. Which record does each person read about?
Plan	How can you solve the problem?	Choose a strategy to try: Make a table. Use checks to show what each person read to show what they do not read.
Solve	How can you carry out your plan?	

	Movies	Drums	Scrabble
Gene	X	✔	X
Callie	✔	X	X
Claire	X	X	✔

	Have you answered the question?	Yes. Gene reads about the drums, Callie reads about movies, and Claire reads about Scrabble.
Look Back	Does your answer make sense?	Check. They read about different world records. The answer matches the information given.

Mr. Hughes had seen over 20,000 movies

Jeffery Carlo has 112 pieces in his drum set!

Phil Appleby scored 1,049 in a game of Scrabble!

C H E C K

Check for Understanding

1 **What if** there is a fourth world record. Would you be able to tell which record each person reads about? Why or why not?

Critical Thinking: Analyze **Explain your reasoning.**

2 Solve the problem without using a table. Which method did you use? Which of the two methods do you prefer? Why?

1. Possible answer: No; it would not be possible to tell if Callie reads about the movies or the fourth record, nor which record Claire reads about.

Possible answer: Guess, test, and revise; make a table; it is easier to keep track of the information, and the answer can be found by looking at the table.

14 Lesson 1.5

Meeting Individual Needs

Early Finishers

Present the following clues: 21-23-16 is S-U-N; 5-17-15-7 is C-O-M-E; 8-11-16-6 is F-I-N-D.

Have students decode the following numbers:
21-17-23-16-6 17-8 15-23-21-11-5 *[SOUND OF MUSIC]*

Extra Support

For students who have difficulty following the problem-solving sequence, post a chart of the heuristic and its corresponding questions. Suggest that students start by answering the questions in order.

Ongoing Assessment

Anecdotal Report Make notes on students' ability to use the Make a Table strategy. If students didn't use a table for ex. 1 and 3, ask them to show how to use a table to solve one of those.

Follow Up If students need additional help with this skill, assign **Reteach 5**.

For those who demonstrate mastery, assign **Extend 5**. You may also wish to have them write problems that can be solved by making a table. They can exchange problems and solve.

3. Viv Richards—cricket, Dan Steeles—bowling, Russell Locke—darts

MIXED APPLICATIONS
Problem Solving

1 Patrick has 18 CDs. He has twice as many country CDs as classical CDs. He has 3 more rock CDs than country CDs. How many of each type of CD does he have? **3 classical, 6 country, and 9 rock CDs**

3 Viv Richards, Dan Steeles, and Russell Locke each have one world record. It is in either cricket, darts, or bowling. Viv Richards has the world record in cricket. Dan Steeles does not have the record in darts or cricket. Russell Locke does not have the record in bowling. What record does each person hold? **See above.**

5 **Spatial reasoning** Show which shape you can *not* get by drawing a line through a square. ◯

Use the table for problems 6–10.

6 Which dance had the greatest number of people? the least number of people? **conga line; dancing dragon**

7 Did the dancing dragon or the tap dancers have more people? **tap dancers**

8 Which dance had about 120,000 people? **conga line**

9 Order the dances in the table from greatest to least according to the number of people. Which dance is second? **conga, electric slide, tap, dancing dragon; electric slide**

10 Write newspaper headlines for each dance. Use estimates. Explain how you estimated. **Headlines may vary. Check students' estimates.**

Extra Practice, page 486

2 The world record amount of times that a needle has been threaded is 20,675 in 2 hours (h). Write a newspaper headline that rounds the number to the nearest thousand. **Possible answer: Needle Threaded About 21,000 Times in 2 Hours!**

4 May surveyed students in her class to find out which sport they thought was the most exciting. Her survey showed that 5 named diving, 6 named downhill skiing, 9 named surfing, and 7 named mountain climbing. How many students thought water sports were the most exciting? **14 students**

World Records for Dancing	
Type of Dance	**Number of People Who Joined In**
Electric slide line dance	30,000
Dancing dragon	1,019
Tap dancing	6,196
Conga line dancing	119,986

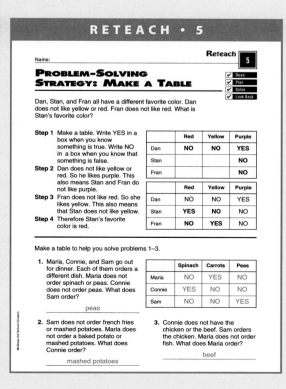

15

Alternate Teaching Strategy

Materials per group: 20 counters

Display the following diagram:

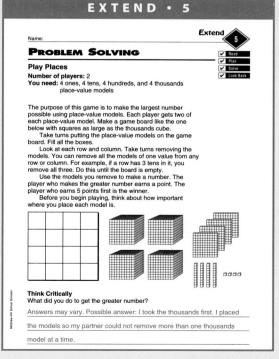

Present this problem:

Place all 20 counters in the colored squares. All red squares must have the same number of counters, and all blue squares must have the same number of counters. Each square cannot have more than 6 counters. How many different combinations can you find?

Discuss methods for solving the problem. Ask students to describe the steps they will follow. Give groups of students 20 counters to try out solutions. Then discuss the problem-solving steps Read, Plan, Solve, and Look Back.

Introduce students to the idea that they could use a table such as the following to solve this problem. Give students a copy of the table and have them fill in the table with counters or numbers to solve.

	1st red square	2nd red square	3rd red square	1st blue square	2nd blue square
Number of Counters	[6]	[6]	[6]	[1]	[1]
	[4]	[4]	[4]	[4]	[4]

PRACTICE • 5

Name: _____

Practice **5**

PROBLEM-SOLVING STRATEGY: MAKE A TABLE

☑ Read ☑ Plan ☑ Solve ☑ Look Back

Solve using the make-a-table strategy.

1. Pam, Tim, and Alex are reporting on one different sports figure each. Tim does not choose Matt Biondi or Larry Bird. Pam does not choose Matt Biondi. Which sports figure does Alex choose?

	Biondi	Bjurstedt	Bird
Pam	✗	✗	✓
Tim	✗	✓	✗
Alex	✓	✗	✗

Biondi

2. Each athlete plays a different sport. Larry Bird does not swim or play tennis. Matt Biondi swims. What sport does Molla Bjurstedt play?

	Bird	Bjurstedt	Biondi
basketball	✓	✗	✗
tennis	✗	✓	✗
swimming	✗	✗	✓

tennis

Solve using any method.

3. Molla Bjurstedt won her first U.S. championship in 1915. Matt Biondi won his in 1984. Whose championship was almost 100 years ago? Molla Bjurstedt

4. Basketball player Larry Bird played in 897 regular season games. He had 8,974 rebounds and 5,695 assists. Did he have more assists or rebounds? rebounds

5. Matt Biondi has won 11 Olympic medals for swimming. He has 4 times as many gold medals as silver medals. He has twice as many silver medals as bronze medals. How many of each type has he won? 8 gold; 2 silver; 1 bronze

6. There were 2,278 fans at a swim meet. There were 2,267 fans at a tennis match. Which had more fans, the swim meet or the tennis match? the swim meet

---

RETEACH • 5

Name: _____

Reteach **5**

PROBLEM-SOLVING STRATEGY: MAKE A TABLE

☑ Read ☑ Plan ☑ Solve ☑ Look Back

Dan, Stan, and Fran all have a different favorite color. Dan does not like yellow or red. Fran does not like red. What is Stan's favorite color?

Step 1 Make a table. Write YES in a box when you know something is true. Write NO in a box when you know that something is false.

	Red	Yellow	Purple
Dan	NO	NO	YES
Stan			NO
Fran			NO

Step 2 Dan does not like yellow or red. So he likes purple. This also means Stan and Fran do not like purple.

Step 3 Fran does not like red. So she likes yellow. This also means that Stan does not like yellow.

	Red	Yellow	Purple
Dan	NO	NO	YES
Stan	YES	NO	NO
Fran	NO	YES	NO

Step 4 Therefore Stan's favorite color is red.

Make a table to help you solve problems 1–3.

1. Maria, Connie, and Sam go out for dinner. Each of them orders a different dish. Maria does not order spinach or peas. Connie does not order peas. What does Sam order?

	Spinach	Carrots	Peas
Maria	NO	YES	NO
Connie	YES	NO	NO
Sam	NO	NO	YES

peas

2. Sam does not order french fries or mashed potatoes. Maria does not order a baked potato or mashed potatoes. What does Connie order? mashed potatoes

3. Connie does not have the chicken or the beef. Sam orders the chicken. Maria does not order fish. What does Maria order? beef

---

EXTEND • 5

Name: _____

Extend **5**

PROBLEM SOLVING

☑ Read ☑ Plan ☑ Solve ☑ Look Back

Play Places
Number of players: 2
You need: 4 ones, 4 tens, 4 hundreds, and 4 thousands place-value models

The purpose of this game is to make the largest number possible using place-value models. Each player gets two of each place-value model. Make a game board like the one below with squares as large as the thousands cube.
  Take turns putting the place-value models on the game board. Fill all the boxes.
  Look at each row and column. Take turns removing the models. You can remove all the models of one value from any row or column. For example, if a row has 3 tens in it, you remove all three. Do this until the board is empty.
  Use the models you remove to make a number. The player who makes the greater number earns a point. The player who earns 5 points first is the winner.
  Before you begin playing, think about how important where you place each model is.

Think Critically
What did you do to get the greater number?

Answers may vary. Possible answer: I took the thousands first. I placed

the models so my partner could not remove more than one thousands

model at a time.

15

PURPOSE Maintain and review concepts, skills, and strategies that students have learned thus far in the chapter.

Using the Midchapter Review

Have students complete the **Midchapter Review** independently or use it with the whole class.

For ex. 1–8, review standard form, word name, and expanded form.

 Responding to this journal question will help students clarify and demonstrate their understanding of place value and ordering numbers.

Possible methods include:
–comparing numbers to find the one with the greatest place value, the second greatest, and so on
–lining up the numbers vertically and ordering the numbers by the number of digits they have
–finding the number whose 7 has the greatest value, second greatest value, and so on.

Vocabulary Review

Write the following words on the chalkboard:

digit	is less than (<)	place value
expanded form	period	standard form
is greater than (>)		

Ask for volunteers to explain, show, or act out the meaning of these words.

Write the number in standard form and in expanded form.

1 seven hundred thirteen 713; 700 + 10 + 3

2 thirty-six thousand, two hundred thirty-nine 36,239; 30,000 + 6,000 + 200 + 30 + 9

3 forty thousand, seventy-five 40,075; 40,000 + 70 + 5

4 two hundred forty thousand, seven hundred twenty-five 240,725; 200,000 + 40,000 + 700 + 20 + 5

Write the number in word form and in expanded form. See right and below.

5 413   **6** 7,075   **7** 42,680   **8** 240,418

Compare. Write >, <, or =.

9 927 ● 772 >

10 2,011 ● 10,031 <

11 8,902 ● 979 >

12 256,723 ● 28,602 >

13 6,400 ● 6,091 >

14 99,804 ● 100,984 <

Order the numbers from least to greatest.

15 73,420; 9,814; 9,836 9,814; 9,836; 73,420

16 4,480; 8,750; 8,040 4,480; 8,040 8,750

Solve.

17 Lin, Rosa, and Lee like either classical music, rock music, or calypso music. None of them like the same type. Lin likes classical music. Lee does not like rock music. Rosa does not like either classical or calypso music. Which types of music do Lee and Rosa like? Lee likes calypso and Rosa likes rock.

18 Ann, Lynda, Paul, and Stephan either swim or play basketball, soccer, or baseball. None are on the same team. Lynda plays basketball. Paul does not swim or play soccer. Stephan does not play soccer or baseball. Which sports do Ann, Paul, and Stephan take part in? Ann plays soccer, Paul plays baseball, and Stephan swims.

19 By May 1994, the musical *The Fantasticks* had been performed 14,095 times; and the play *The Mousetrap*, 17,256 times. Which show had had more performances? *The Mousetrap*

20 Explain how you can use place value to order 7; 7,070; 707; and 70. Answers may vary. Possible answer: The number with more places has more digits, so the numbers can be ordered by the amount of digits.

5. four hundred thirteen; 400 + 10 +
6. seven thousand, seventy five; 7,000 + 70 + 5
7. forty-two thousand, six hundred eighty; 40,000 + 2,000 + 600 + 80
8. two hundred forty thousand, four hundred eighteen; 200,000 + 40,000 + 400 + 10 +

Reinforcement and Remediation

CHAPTER OBJECTIVES	MIDCHAPTER REVIEW ITEMS	STUDENT BOOK PAGES	TEACHER'S EDITION PAGES		TEACHER RESOURCES
			Activities	Alternate Teaching Strategy	Reteach
*1A	1–4	2–3	1A	3	1
*1B	1–8	4–11	3A, 7A	7, 11	2–3
*1C	9–16, 19–20	12–13	11C	13	4
*1D	17–18	14–15	13A	15	5

*1A Identify how numbers are used
*1B Read and write whole numbers to millions
*1C Compare, order, and round whole numbers
*1D Solve problems, including those that involve place value and making a table

developing number sense
MATH CONNECTION

Determine If a Number Is Reasonable

What an amazing claim! Can a baby be 30 feet tall?

To check if 30 feet is reasonable, Rebecca and Ramón used other information they knew.

Rebecca used what she knows about her height.

I think there must be a mistake in the newspaper. I am ten years old, and I am less than 5 feet, which is much less than 30 feet.

Ramón used what he knows about the heights of members of his family.

Even my parents are not 30 feet! I think they must mean 30 inches instead of 30 feet. When my sister was born, she was 20 inches. So 30 inches seems reasonable.

Tell if the claim is reasonable. Explain your thinking. See right.

1. Claim: Simone's mother weighs 5 pounds. **more**
  a. Do you weigh more or less than a 5-pound bag of rice?
  b. Do you think you weigh more or less than an adult? **less**

2. Claim: Hiko's cup holds 300 milliliters (mL) of water. He says that 289 milliliters of water will fill his bathtub.
  a. Compare 300 milliliters with 289 milliliters. **289 < 300**
  b. Is the bathtub smaller or larger than the cup?
  The bathtub should be larger than the cup.

3. Claim: A newspaper article says, "It costs $8 million to clean up one of the beaches in our state!" and "The Governor will sign the state budget for $16 million."
  a. The state pays for services like schools, the police, firefighters, buses, trains, and parks. Do you expect that cleaning up a beach costs more than each of these services? **No, it should be less expensive.**
  b. Compare $8 million and $16 million. Do you think both statements can be correct? Explain your thinking. **No; the state budget should be more than twice the cost of cleaning up a beach.**

1. Not reasonable; since the student weighs more than 5 lb and less than an adult, Simone's mother would be expected to weigh more than 5 lb.

2. Not reasonable; the bathtub should hold more than 300 milliliters of water since it should be larger than the cup.

3. Not reasonable; the budget is too small to pay for all the state services.

Place Value and Number Sense **17**

OBJECTIVE Determine whether numbers are reasonable or unreasonable.

Using Number Sense

Math Connection In Lesson 4, students compared numbers to determine order. In this lesson, students compare numbers given in claims to actual amounts they know to determine whether the numbers are reasonable.

After reading through the opening problem and solutions, ask students:
- **What two measurements did Rebecca compare?** *[5 ft and 30 ft]*
- **Should Rebecca or Ramon compare the height of the baby to the height of an ant? Why?** *[Possible answer: No; the two heights are not related.]*
- **What other comparison could you make to determine if the height of the baby is reasonable?** *[Possible answer: comparing the height of a baby to something they know is 30 ft tall]*

Students may work in small groups or on their own to complete ex. 1–3.

Applying Number Sense

OBJECTIVE Use place value and number sense to compare and predict.

Materials have available: measurement tools such as stop watches, rulers, and scales

1 Engage

Resource Read-Aloud Anthology, pages 1-2

Ask students if they are familiar with any amazing facts or feats. You may wish to have volunteers record examples on the chalkboard.

Then read *Record Breakers of the Land*. Ask students to compare the facts described in the Anthology to their list and to the kind of information recorded in *The Guinness Book of Records*.

- **How are numbers used to record these amazing facts?** *[Possible answers: as a measurement of length, height, or weight, as a count of the number of hits in baseball, to show order]*
- **If you worked for *The Guinness Book of Records*, how would you check the claims made by people wanting to be listed in your book?** *[Possible answers: check with witnesses, ask if they could do it again, send someone to take measurements, look at photographs, or videos]*

2 Investigate

Form groups of four or five students. Ask groups to write a list of activities they enjoy and skills they share that may have record-breaking potential. Students may wish to look over the ideas pictured in the Student Book. Then they can generate a list of 10 to 15 of their own ideas.

Performing Feats After groups have written their lists, suggest that students select four or five feats to perform. If they complete all four steps for each feat before other groups do, they can add one or two extra feats.

3 Reflect and Share

Materials have available: drawing paper, colored markers, scissors, tape, glue, calculators

Report Your Findings Students can illustrate their book in any way they like.

Using the Concentric Circles Strategy, have facing pairs share something they learned in their report.

Use Illustrations Have students display the photographs or drawings of their feat. Ask other students to explain how these illustrations help them understand the feat better.

real-life investigation
APPLYING NUMBER SENSE

Your Own Book of Records

The Guinness Book of Records is a collection of amazing facts and feats performed around the world. In this activity, you will work in teams to create your own feats, make your own record-breaking attempts, and write a book of record-breaking results for your class.

Here are some ideas:

Largest selection of greeting cards

Tallest tower made by stacking number cards

Greatest number of up and down motions with a yo-yo!!

Longest time for hula-hooping

More To Investigate

Predict Possible approaches: If students choose a skill or activity with which they are familiar, then their predictions may be accurate, especially after some practice. Have students record the predictions, then work in pairs to practice and to confirm the results of their performance.

Explore Possible answers: most schools attended, longest time spent jumping rope, largest toothpick building.

Find Answers may vary. Possible answer: According to the *1994 Guinness Book of Records*, the stone-skipping record is 38 skips. The feat was verified on videotape in October 1992.

Bibliography Students who want to learn more about world records and other interesting facts can browse:

The Guinness Book of Sports Records, 1995–1996. New York: Facts on File, 1995. ISBN 0–8160–3263–7.

The World Almanac for Kids, 1996. Mahwah, NJ: World Almanac Books, 1995. ISBN 0–88687–770–9.

Answers may vary.
Check students' work.

See Teacher's Edition
for sample of student work.

DECISION MAKING

Performing Feats

1 Choose feats you wish to measure, and record in your book.

2 Decide on the setup and the measurement tools needed to do each feat.

3 Decide on roles for each member of your team. Roles may include: a timer, a measurer of distances, a counter, and a judge who explains the rules clearly.

4 Compare measurements for each feat to find the best result— fastest, longest, or greatest.

Reporting Your Findings

5 Prepare a book for your team that lists and explains each feat with the best result for that feat. Include the following:

▶ **Use Illustrations** Take photographs or make drawings of the feat.

▶ Choose one feat. Explain how to improve the performance of that feat.

6 Combine your book with the books of other teams to make a class book.

Revise your work.
▶ Are your measurements and comparisons correct?
▶ Is your book clear and organized?
▶ Did you proofread your work?

MORE TO INVESTIGATE
See Teacher's Edition.

PREDICT how well you could perform a feat if you practiced for a while. Choose a feat. Perform the feat. Then compare the results to your prediction.

EXPLORE the different ways to measure feats for going to school, jumping rope, and creating a toothpick building.

FIND the world records for some interesting feats in *The Guinness Book of Records*.

Place Value and Number Sense **19**

Building A Portfolio

This investigation will allow you to evaluate students' ability to organize data, use number sense, and present their findings.

Allow students to revise their work for the portfolio. Each student's portfolio piece should consist of five or more pages explaining and displaying in their own way the feats the team performed. Each page should include a photo or illustration of the feat, a complete description of the feat, the results of the performances by all students in the group, and a mention of the best performance.

The portfolio should also include recommendations for improving the performance of a feat as well as the reasoning behind the recommendation. Place any notes you made about a student's work in his or her portfolio.

You may wish to use the Holistic Scoring Guide to assess this task. See page 27 in Teacher's Assessment Resources.

Students' Work

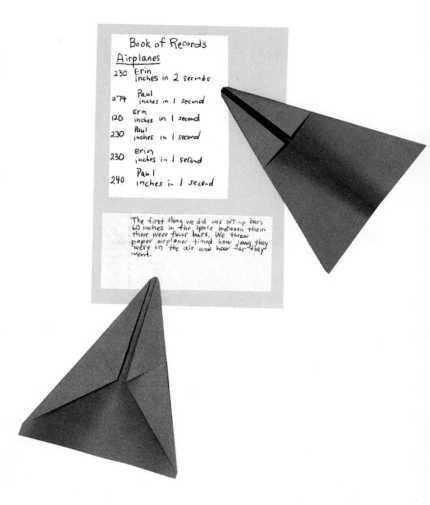

Book of Records
Airplanes
230 Erin inches in 2 seconds
274 Paul inches in 1 second
120 Erin inches in 1 second
230 Paul inches in 1 second
230 Erin inches in 1 second
240 Paul inches in 1 second

The first thing we did was set up bars 60 inches in the space between them there were four bars. We threw paper airplanes timed how long they were in the air and how far they went.

LESSON 1.6

Round Numbers

OBJECTIVE Round numbers to the nearest ten, hundred, and thousand.

RESOURCE REMINDER
Math Center Cards 6
Practice 6, Reteach 6, Extend 6

SKILLS TRACE

GRADE 3
- Explore rounding numbers to the nearest ten or hundred. *(Chapter 2)*

GRADE 4
- Round numbers to the nearest ten, hundred, or thousand.

GRADE 5
- Round whole numbers and decimals, including money amounts. *(Chapter 1)*

MANIPULATIVE WARM-UP

Whole Class   **Logical/Analytical**

OBJECTIVE Make estimates and determine the closest estimate.

Materials four transparent containers; 10 to 100 objects such as play coins, counters, or other small manipulatives

► Count out multiples of 10 objects to fill four containers. Put a multiple of 10 objects in each container.

► Show students the container with the least number of objects. Then show them the size of one of the objects. Ask them to estimate the number of objects in the container. Have a volunteer record the estimates on the board.

► Ask the class to determine which estimate is closest to the actual number of items. Have students whose estimates were closest tell how they chose that number. Continue this process with each container.

SOCIAL STUDIES CONNECTION

Cooperative Groups   **Auditory/Linguistic**

OBJECTIVE Connect rounded numbers with real-life activities.

Materials per student: one section of a newspaper

► Each student in the group scans a section of the newspaper for rounded numbers. Tell students that they may find these numbers in headlines, in articles, or even in advertisements.

► Each group compiles a list of rounded numbers they find. The list includes the phrase or sentence around the rounded number, and the area of the paper where the number was found (headline, article, or advertisement).

► As a class, discuss the numbers that students found.

Daily Review

PREVIOUS DAY *QUICK REVIEW*

Order from least to greatest.

1. 589; 502; 516 *[502; 516; 589]*

2. 7,429; 7,498; 7,470 *[7,429; 7,470; 7,498]*

3. 81,522; 88,940; 85,116 *[81,522; 85,116; 88,940]*

FAST FACTS

1. 7 − 4 *[3]*

2. 5 − 4 *[1]*

3. 8 − 5 *[3]*

4. 6 − 5 *[1]*

Problem of the Day • 6

The school library charges an overdue book 15¢ for the first day, then 10¢ for every additional day. George paid a fine of 95¢ for one overdue book. How many days was his book overdue? *[9]*

TECH LINK

MATH FORUM

Combination Classes I have my more advanced students generate five-, six-, and seven-digit numbers to round. They use a spinner to determine the place to which they should round the number.

Visit our Resource Village at http://www.mhschool.com. to see more of the Math Forum.

MATH CENTER

Practice

OBJECTIVE Round numbers.

Materials per student: newspaper, Math Center Recording Sheet (TA 31 optional)

Students use a newspaper to find 5-digit numbers and use a table to determine whether to round the numbers to the nearest ten, hundred, or thousand. *[Answers may vary. Check students' work. Possible answer: 4,380 rounds to 4,000.]*

PRACTICE ACTIVITY 6

MATH CENTER
On Your Own

Number Sense • Number News

- Check through the newspaper to find as many 5-digit numbers as you can. (Hint: They can be part of a larger number, such as a phone number.)
- Record each number.
- Follow the directions in the table to round each number. Write your answers.

YOU NEED
newspaper

If your number ends in:	Round to the nearest:
3, 7, or 9	ten
2, 5, or 8	hundred
0, 1, 4, or 6	thousand

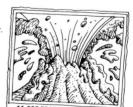

11,035-FOOT VOLCANO ERUPTS

Chapter 1, Lesson 6, pages 20–23   Place Value

NCTM Standards

Problem Solving
Communication
✓ Reasoning
✓ Connections

Problem Solving

OBJECTIVE Round numbers.

Materials per pair: newspaper car advertisements; Math Center Recording Sheet (TA 31 optional)

Students round car prices to the nearest hundred and nearest thousand. They discuss why different methods of rounding are more helpful when making purchasing decisions. *[Answers may vary. Possible answer: Rounding to a higher number helps me to know if I can afford the car. Rounding to the nearest hundred gives a more accurate estimation of the price.]*

PROBLEM-SOLVING ACTIVITY 6

MATH CENTER
Partners

Decision Making • Cars for Sale

Work with your partner.

- Check through the newspaper for ads for new and used cars.
- Record the price of four new cars and four used cars.
- Round the price of the new cars to the nearest thousand.
- Round the price of the used cars to the nearest hundred.

YOU NEED
newspapers

Imagine you are buying one of these cars. Would a car price rounded to a higher or lower number be more helpful? Why? Would rounding to the nearest hundred or to the nearest thousand be more helpful? Why?

Chapter 1, Lesson 6, pages 20–23   Place Value

NCTM Standards

Problem Solving
✓ Communication
✓ Reasoning
✓ Connections

Round Numbers

OBJECTIVE Round numbers to the nearest ten, hundred, and thousand.

Vocabulary round

Introduce

Ask students if they think 759° F is a reasonable sea temperature. Let students brainstorm ways they can check if this number is reasonable. You may wish to tell students that this temperature was recorded in a hot spring 300 miles off the west coast of the United States. The measurement was made in 1985 by a research submarine.

Teach ⁣⁣⁣⁣⁣⁣⁣⁣⁣⁣⁣⁣⁣⁣⁣⁣⁣⁣⁣⁣⁣⁣⁣⁣*Whole Class*

▶ **LEARN** Help students see how the position of the number 759 on the number line helps them determine whether to round to 750 or 760 and to 700 or 800.

- **Which way of rounding the headline is the closest to the actual number?** [Possible answer: rounding to the nearest tenth]
- **Which way of rounding would create the most dramatic headline? Why?** [Possible answer: Rounding to the nearest 100; it would give a greater number for the temperature.]

Talk It Over Ask the students:

- **What place do you look at when you round to the nearest hundred?** [the tens place]
- **Suppose you want to round to a particular place. What rule describes the place that you would look at to help you?** [Possible answers: You look at the place immediately to the right of the one you want to round to; you look at the next smallest place.]

Round Numbers

L E A R N

When you want to give an idea of the size of a number, you can round.

If a newspaper rounded the temperature, what might the headline say?

CITY CHRONICLE

HIGHEST RECORDED SEA TEMPERATURE WAS 759°F

Talk It Over 2. 775–784; the numbers between 775 and 779 are rounded up, and numbers between 780 and 784 are rounded down, to get 780.

759

700 710 720 730 740 750 760 770 780 790 800

Talk It Over 1. Since 737 is nearer to 740 than to 730, round to 740; since 737 is nearer to 700 than to 800, round to 700.

Round to the nearest ten degrees.   Round to the nearest hundred degrees.

Think: 759 is nearer to 760 than to 750. Round 759° to 760°.

Think: 759 is nearer to 800 than to 700. Round 759° to 800°.

DAILY DISPATCH

HIGHEST RECORDED SEA TEMPERATURE WAS ABOUT **760°F!**

MORNING MIRROR

HIGHEST RECORDED SEA TEMPERATURE WAS ABOUT **800°F!**

Talk It Over

▶ How would you round the number 737 to the nearest ten? to the nearest hundred? Explain your reasoning. See above.

▶ What numbers when rounded to the nearest ten are 780? How do you know? See above.

round Finding the nearest ten, hundred, thousand, and so on.

20 Lesson 1.6

Meeting Individual Needs

Extra Support

Remind students that when rounding, all numbers in places to the right of the place being rounded should be changed to zeros. To help students remember when to round up and when to round down, have them write the rules for rounding in their notebooks.

Ongoing Assessment

Interview Determine if students understand rounding by asking:

- **What is 361 rounded to the nearest hundred?** [400]
- **How did you decide how to round?** [Possible answer: When the tens digit is 5 or greater, a number is rounded up to the nearest hundred.]

Follow Up Have students who need additional help with rounding do **Reteach 6**.

Assign **Extend 6** for students who may want a challenge.

Possible answer: When the hundreds digit is 9 and the tens digit is 5 or greater, or when the hundreds digit is 0 and the tens digit is less than 5; 1,968 rounds to 2,000 to the nearest hundred or thousand.

British actor plans to travel around the equator for a television show. If a newspaper rounded the distance around the equator to the nearest thousand, what could the headline say?

24,901 MILES

ound 24,901 to the nearest thousand.

| tep 1 | Look at the place to the right of the thousands place.

24,901 | Step 2 | If the digit is less than 5, round down. If the digit is 5 or greater, round up.

9 > 5, so 24,901 rounds up to 25,000. |

he headline might say, "It's just amazing! British actor to avel about 25,000 miles to get around the equator!"

More Examples

A Round to the nearest hundred.
4,256
↑
5 = 5, so 4,256 rounds up to 4,300.

B Round to the nearest thousand.
89,400
↑
4 < 5, so 89,400 rounds down to 89,000.

Check for Understanding

Round 784 to the nearest ten. **780**

Round 60,750 to the nearest hundred. **60,800**

Round 100,642 to the nearest thousand. **101,000**

ritical Thinking: Generalize **Explain your reasoning.**

When does rounding to the nearest hundred give the same answer as rounding to the nearest thousand? Give an example. **See above.**

Tell why you would or would not round the numbers.
a. John has a fever of 102°F. What should he tell the doctor?
b. The survey showed that 32,563 people watched the game. What will the television news report?

e answer: a. do not round because the doctor has to know how high the fever is; b. only an idea of how many s needed, so round to about 33,000 people.

Turn the page for Practice.

Place Value and Number Sense   **21**

The example on Student Book page 21 involves a number to the ten thousands place. Ask students:
• **What if you rounded the number to the nearest hundred? How much would the number change?** *[Possible answer: The new number is only 1 less than the original number.]*

More Examples Review the procedure for rounding up and rounding down. Some students make the mistake of decreasing a digit by one when rounding down since they increase a digit by one when rounding up.

Clarify that when rounding down, students write a lesser number by writing zeros for all the digits to the right of the place they are rounding to.

③ Close

Check for Understanding using items 1–5, page 21.

CRITICAL THINKING
Ask students to find a number that when rounded to the nearest thousand, hundred, and ten becomes the same answer. Any number that has a nine in both the hundreds and tens place and a five or greater in the ones place, such as 12,997, will work.

Practice See pages 22–23.

Language Support

To round numbers, students need to have a firm understanding of place-value vocabulary. Pair English speakers with students acquiring English to review place-value terms like tens place, hundreds, thousands, and so on.

ESL APPROPRIATE

21

▶ **PRACTICE**
Options for assigning exercises:
A—Odd ex. 1–31; **Mixed Review**
B—Even ex. 2–32; **Mixed Review**

• For Make It Right (ex. 24), see Common Error below.
• Remind students to read all the choices before answering multiple choice questions.

 Algebra Function tables develop algebraic thinking by showing the relationship between a set of numbers.

Mixed Review/Test Preparation Students review writing numbers in standard and expanded forms. Remind them to use zeros as placeholders in ex. 2–5.

Practice

Use the number line. Round to the greatest place.

1. 728 **700**
2. 783 **800**
3. 9,289 **9,000**
4. 9,820 **10,000**

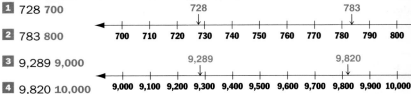

Round to the nearest ten.

5. 451 **450**
6. 23 **20**
7. 9,095 **9,100**
8. 389,995 **390,000**

Round to the nearest hundred.

9. 4,754 **4,800**
10. 1,506 **1,500**
11. 99,984 **100,000**
12. 508,046 **508,000**

Round to the nearest thousand.

13. 8,911 **9,000**
14. 2,099 **2,000**
15. 76,548 **77,000**
16. 109,612 **110,000**

 ALGEBRA Find the rule. Then complete the table.

17. Round to the nearest hundred; 72,100.

Rule: ■	
Input	Output
6,543	6,500
24,063	24,100
72,098	■

18.

Rule: ■	
Input	Output
28,650	27,650
150,987	149,987
59,702	■

Subtract 1,000; 58,702.

19.

Rule: ■	
Input	Output
8,230	18,230
86,500	96,500
293,360	■

Add 10,000; 303,3

Match the number to a rounded number. Tell if the number is rounded to the nearest ten, hundred, or thousand.

20. 6,280 **a; hundred**   a. 6,300

21. 9,800 **d; thousand**   b. 410,000

22. 409,950 **b; thousand or hundred**   c. 98,100

23. 98,096 **c; hundred or ten**   d. 10,000

·························· **Make It Right** ··························
24. Sue Ellen rounded 49,400 to the nearest thousand. Tell what the mistake is, then correct it.   *49,400 rounds up to 50,400.*

Since 400 < 500, she should have rounded down, but she rounded up and kept the hundreds digit in place—the answer is 49,000.

Meeting Individual Needs

Early Finishers

Ask students to create their own tables similar to those shown in ex. 17–19. Have them create their own rules for pairs of numbers. Let students exchange tables and solve each other's problems.

Inclusion

Some students may find it easier to use place-value charts before rounding. This will help them focus on the place to which they are rounding. Circling this number will also help them focus their attention.

ESL ▶ **APPROPRIATE**

COMMON ERROR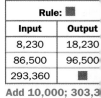

Students may round up or down to a given place, then forget to write zeros in the places to the right of that place. For example, when rounding 875 to the nearest hundred, they may round to 9 hundreds, then write 975 instead of 900.

Use models to reinforce the idea that students are rounding 8 hundreds, 7 tens, and 5 ones to 9 hundreds, and that therefore the tens and ones digits should be changed to zeros.

25. Headline b; possible answer: 22,500 rounded to the nearest thousand is 23,000.
29. Students may write problems about money, approximate distances, and so on.

MIXED APPLICATIONS
Problem Solving
Pencil & Paper   Calculator   Mental Math

25 Steven Newman spent four years walking 22,500 miles for a world record. Which headline would you use? Why? **See above.**
  a. Man walks 200,000 miles
  b. Record broken as man walks 20,000 miles
  c. New 23,000-mile record to beat!

27 For which activity would you *not* use a rounded number? Explain why.
  a. find distance for a bicycle trip
  b. cut lengths to make a frame for a picture
  c. tell how many people attend an event **Possible answer: b; the frame might not fit correctly.**

29 **Write a problem** in which you can find the answer by rounding a number to the nearest ten, hundred, or thousand. Solve it. Have others solve it.
See above.

31 **Data Point** Use the Databank on page 532. Write a headline that uses rounded numbers to compare the average depth of the Indian Ocean with the average depth of another ocean. **See below.**

26 **Spatial reasoning** Show how to make this shape by combining the least number of triangles.

Check students' answers.

28 **Make a decision** The longest paper chain had 400,000 links. The most kites flown in a single line was 11,284. The largest bubble made from dishwashing liquid and water was 50 feet long. Which record would you attempt to beat? Explain why you made your choice. **See below.**

30 What is the greatest number you can make using each of the digits 2, 3, 7, 5, and 1 only once? What is the least number you can make with the digits? **75,321; 12,357**

32 The Arctic Ocean is the smallest ocean on Earth. Its average depth is 3,407 feet. Is this more or less than 1 mile? (Hint: A mile is 5,280 feet.) **less than 1 mi**

mixed review • test preparation

Write the number in standard form and in expanded form.

1 eight hundred fifty-six
  856; 800 + 50 + 6

2 four thousand, eleven
  4,011; 4,000 + 10 + 1

3 sixty-three thousand, twenty-nine
  63,029; 60,000 + 3,000 + 20 + 9

4 seven thousand, two
  7,002; 7,000 + 2

5 eight hundred seven thousand, twenty-three
  807,023; 800,000 + 7,000 + 20 + 3

6 three thousand, nine hundred fourteen
  3,914; 3,000 + 900 + 10 + 4

28. Students' decisions should reflect the choices given.
31. Students may round to the nearest hundred or thousand in writing headlines.

Extra Practice, page 486

Place Value and Number Sense **23**

Alternate Teaching Strategy

Materials place-value models—21 hundreds, 16 tens, 49 ones

Ask a volunteer to use place-value models to show the number 781. To the left of this model, use place-value models to show 800. To the right, show 600. Then ask:
  • **Does the model of 781 look more like the model of 800 or more like the model of 600?** *[800]*
  • **How did you decide?** *[Possible answer: There are almost enough models to make 800, and too many models to look like 600.]*

Repeat with other 3-digit numbers.

ESL APPROPRIATE

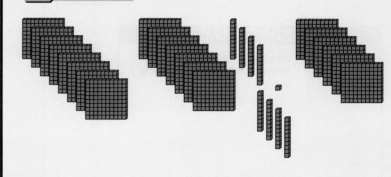

PRACTICE • 6
HOMEWORK

Name: _____   Practice **6**

ROUND NUMBERS

Complete the table.

		Round to the nearest ten.	Round to the nearest hundred.	Round to the nearest thousand.
1.	2,648	2,650	2,600	3,000
2.	7,421	7,420	7,400	7,000
3.	68,725	68,730	68,700	69,000
4.	34,293	34,290	34,300	34,000
5.	387,843	387,840	387,800	388,000
6.	506,027	506,030	506,000	506,000

7. Algebra Find the rule. Then complete the table.

Rule: Add 1,000.		Rule: Subtract 10,000.		Rule: Round to the nearest ten.	
Input	Output	Input	Output	Input	Output
45,897	46,897	17,540	7,540	7,632	7,630
1,324	2,324	85,342	75,342	56,167	56,170
543,918	544,918	791,247	781,247	5,134	5,130
45,715	46,715	54,671	44,671	98,723	98,720
67,159	68,159	178,419	168,419	185,784	185,780
876,532	877,532	732,696	722,696	678,186	678,190

Solve.

8. There were 10,287 people watching the contest. What is this number rounded to the nearest hundred?
  10,300

9. There were 1,876 people in the contest. What is this number rounded to the nearest ten?
  1,880

RETEACH • 6

Name: _____   Reteach **6**

ROUND NUMBERS

A rounded number tells you about how much.
To round to the tens place, check the digit in the ones place.
If the ones digit is less than 5, round down to the nearest ten.
If the ones digit is 5 or more, round up to the nearest ten.

70 71 72 73 74 75 76 77 78 79 80

Round 74 to the nearest ten.   Round 76 to the nearest ten.

Think: 74 is closer to 70 than 80.   **Think:** 76 is closer to 80 than 70.

74 rounds down to 70.   76 rounds up to 80.

Fill in the blanks with tens. Use the number line above to help you.

1. 73 is between __70__ and __80__. It is closer to __70__. 73 rounds to __70__.

2. 77 is between __70__ and __80__. It is closer to __80__. 77 rounds to __80__.

Round to the nearest ten. Use the number line to help you.

50 51 52 53 54 55 56 57 58 59 **60** 61 62 63 64 65 66 67 68 69 **70**

3. 51 __50__   **4.** 66 __70__   **5.** 55 __60__   **6.** 63 __60__

7. 52 __50__   **8.** 67 __70__   **9.** 61 __60__   **10.** 58 __60__

120 121 122 123 124 125 126 127 128 129 **130** 131 132 133 134 135 136 137 138 139 **140**

11. 123 __120__   **12.** 138 __140__   **13.** 129 __130__   **14.** 131 __130__

15. 125 __130__   **16.** 127 __130__   **17.** 135 __140__   **18.** 126 __130__

EXTEND • 6

Name: _____   Extend **6**

ROUND NUMBERS

Rounding Puzzles

1. When rounded to the nearest ten, I'm 770. I have a 7 in the ones place. What number am I?
  __767__

2. When rounded to the nearest ten, I'm 760. I have a 2 in the ones place. What number am I?
  __762__

3. When rounded to the nearest ten, I'm 3,750. I have an 8 in the ones place. What number am I?
  __3,748__

4. When rounded to the nearest ten, I'm 86,300. I have a 7 in the ones place. What number am I?
  __86,297__

5. When rounded to the nearest hundred, I'm 4,600. I have a 3 in the ones place. What numbers could I be?
  4,603; 4,613; 4,623; 4,633; 4,643; 4,593; 4,583; 4,573; 4,563; 4,553

6. When rounded to the nearest hundred, I'm 2,800. I have a 5 in the ones place. What numbers could I be?
  2,805; 2,815; 2,825; 2,835; 2,845

Use the digits 9, 4, 3, 5, 6, 2 to solve exercises 7–10. Answers may vary. Possible responses are given.

7. Make a 6-digit number. When rounded to the nearest ten thousand, it is 690,000.
  693,542

8. Make a 5-digit number. When rounded to the nearest thousand, it is 94,000.
  94,256

9. Make a 6-digit number. When rounded to the nearest ten thousand, it is 460,000.
  459,263

10. Make a 6-digit number. When rounded to the nearest thousand, it is 962,000.
  962,435

23

LESSON 1.7

EXPLORE ACTIVITY
Millions

OBJECTIVE Represent numbers up to 9,999,999 in different forms and identify the value and place of digits.

RESOURCE REMINDER
Math Center Cards 7
Practice 7, Reteach 7, Extend 7

SKILLS TRACE

GRADE 3	Read and write numbers through hundred thousands. (*Chapter 2*)
GRADE 4	Represent numbers to 9,999,999 in different forms and identify the value and place of digits.
GRADE 5	Read/write whole numbers through hundred millions and understand the meaning of their digits. (*Chapter 1*)

LESSON 1.7 RESOURCES

WARM-UP

Cooperative Pairs   **Logical/Analytical**

OBJECTIVE Review place value of numbers up to 1,999.

Materials per pair: place-value chart (TA 4)

▶ Give each pair a place-value chart. Have pairs work together to find the solution for each of the following riddles:

I am a three-digit number. The sum of my digits is 18. The value of my tens digit is the least value possible. What number am I? [909]

I am a four-digit number with four different digits. All of my digits are greater than 5. My thousands digit is 3 more than my ones digit. The value of my tens digit is 80. What number am I? [9,786]

▶ Compare solutions as a class. Then have each pair of students create a riddle.

Thousands			Ones		
hundreds	tens	ones	hundreds	tens	ones
			9	0	9
	9	7	8	6	

SOCIAL STUDIES CONNECTION

Cooperative Groups   **Auditory/Linguistic**

OBJECTIVE Connect greater numbers with the populations of large cities.

Materials per group: world map, almanacs, and encylopedias

▶ Give students a list of large cities, such as Tokyo, Japan; New York City; São Paulo, Brazil; Mexico City, Mexico; Beijing, China; Bombay, India; Buenos Aires, Argentina. Provide students with research materials such as almanacs and encyclopedias and have them find the populations of these cities.

▶ Locate the cities on a world map. Ask students whether or not these populations are estimates. Lead students to see that city populations are always estimates because people move into and out of cities, and people are born and die each day.

Daily Review

PREVIOUS DAY QUICK REVIEW

Round to the nearest thousand.

1. 986 *[1,000]*
2. 4,091 *[4,000]*
3. 72,657 *[73,000]*
4. 107,211 *[107,000]*

FAST FACTS

1. 5 + 1 *[6]*
2. 5 + 0 *[5]*
3. 3 + 2 *[5]*
4. 2 + 4 *[6]*

Problem of the Day • 7

The numbers listed below all have something in common. What is it? Name a 1-digit number that would fit in the group: 16, 34, 511, 124, 610, 412, 700. *[The digits sum to 7; 7.]*

TECH LINK

MATH FORUM

Cultural Diversity My students love to learn words in other languages. I let my students acquiring English teach the class words in their language for million, hundred thousand, and other large numbers.

Visit our Resource Village at http://www.mhschool.com to see more of the Math Forum.

MATH CENTER

Practice

OBJECTIVE Write 7-digit numbers in different forms.

Materials per student: dictionary, picture of telephone key pad, Math Center Recording Sheet (TA 31 optional)

Students use the telephone key pad to change letters of a word into numbers. They write the number in standard and expanded forms. They then give the number form of the word to a classmate to change the numbers into letters and figure out the word. *[Answers may vary. Sample answer: "problem" becomes 7,762,536 and 7,000,000 + 700,000 + 60,000 + 2,000 + 500 + 30 + 6.]*

PRACTICE ACTIVITY 7

MATH CENTER
On Your Own

Number Sense • Information, Please

- Use the dictionary to find a seven-letter word.
- Use the telephone keypad to change the word into a 7-digit number. Use *0* for the letters *Q* and *Z*.
- Write the number in standard and expanded form.
- Give the number in both forms to a friend.
- Challenge the friend to use the telephone keypad to change the numbers into letters and figure out what your word is.

YOU NEED
: dictionary

nations
6,284,667
6,000,000 + 200,000 +
80,000 + 4,000 + 600 +
60 + 7

NCTM Standards
Problem Solving
✓ Communication
✓ Reasoning
Connections

Chapter 1, Lesson 7, pages 24–27

Place Value

Problem Solving

OBJECTIVE Use patterns to predict products.

Materials per student: calculator; Math Center Recording Sheet (TA 31 optional)

Students use a calculator to complete multiplication exercises. They look for patterns to help them predict products. *[**1.** 1,107; 2,214; 3,321; 4,428; 5,535. **2.** 4,444; 5,555; 6,666; 7,777; 8,888; 9,999. **3.** 111,111; 222,222; 333,333; 444,444; 555,555; 666,666; 777,777; 888,888.]*

PROBLEM-SOLVING ACTIVITY 7

MATH CENTER
On Your Own

Patterning • Repeat, Repeat, Repeat

- Use the calculator to do the multiplication. Write each multiplication and product. Stop before you do the last multiplication in each exercise. Look for patterns in the products you have found so far.
- Predict the product of the last multiplication in the exercise.
- Use the calculator to check your prediction.

YOU NEED
: calculator

```
222,222
```

1. 123 × 9 =
123 × 18 =
123 × 27 =
123 × 36 =
Stop and predict.

123 × 45 =

2. 101 × 44 =
101 × 55 =
101 × 66 =
101 × 77 =
101 × 88 =
Stop and predict.

101 × 99 =

3. 37,037 × 3 =
37,037 × 6 =
37,037 × 9 =
37,037 × 12 =
37,037 × 15 =
37,037 × 18 =
37,037 × 21 =
Stop and predict.

37,037 × 24 =

NCTM Standards
✓ Problem Solving
Communication
✓ Reasoning
Connections

Chapter 1, Lesson 7, pages 24–27

Place Value

Lesson 1.7 *continued*

EXPLORE ACTIVITY
Millions

OBJECTIVE Represent numbers up to 9,999,999 in different forms and identify the value and place of digits.

Materials per pair: calculator

1 Introduce

Ask students to name the largest number they have ever seen or heard. Develop a list of all the places they have seen or heard greater numbers, such as references to lottery winnings, world population figures, numbers of insects, and so forth.

2 Teach   *Cooperative Pairs*

▶ **LEARN Work Together** As students fill in their tables, encourage them to look for patterns. Patterns they may suggest include:

– Numbers increase by one place value as you go to the right in the table.

– As the number of push-ups increases, the number needed to reach 10,000 decreases.

Talk It Over Have groups present their methods for computing how long it would take them to do 10,000 push-ups. Encourage them to tell why they used a certain method. Have them compare their choices for ease of use, accuracy, and efficiency.

Millions

L E A R N

The world record for push-ups is held by Paddy Doyle. He did over 1,000,000 in one year!

Work Together
Work with a partner. Use a calculator to solve each problem.

If you did 1,000 push-ups each week, how many weeks would it take to get to:
▶ 10,000 push-ups? **10 wk**
▶ 100,000 push-ups? **100 wk**
▶ 1,000,000 push-ups? **1,000 wk**

If you did 10,000 push-ups each week, how many weeks would it take to get to:
▶ 100,000 push-ups? **10 wk**
▶ 1,000,000 push-ups? **100 wk**

If you did 100,000 push-ups each week, how many weeks would it take to get to:
▶ 1,000,000 push-ups? **10 wk**

Record your answers in a table.

	Number of weeks to get to		
Push-ups each week	10,000 push-ups	100,000 push-ups	1,000,000 push-ups
1,000			

Talk It Over
▶ How many:
   a. thousands are in 10,000? 100,000? 1,000,000? **10; 100; 1,000**
   b. ten thousands are in 100,000? 1,000,000? **10; 100**
   c. hundred thousands are in 1,000,000? **10**

▶ How many push-ups can you do in a week? How many weeks would you take to do 1,000,000 push-ups? **Students may divide the number of push-ups they can do in one week into 1,000,000 to find the answer.**

▶ How did you use the calculator to find your answers? Share your methods with classmates. **Possible answer: Skip-counted by repeatedly adding 1,000; 10,000; or 100,000.**

24 Lesson 1.7

Meeting Individual Needs

Extra Support

For students who have difficulties reading and writing large numbers, have place-value charts available so that they can keep track of the large numbers.

ESL APPROPRIATE

Gifted And Talented

Students use a calculator to find how many push-ups Paddy did a week. They round to the nearest whole number. *[28,851]* Then they use their answer to find how many per day. *[4,122]*

Ongoing Assessment

Observation Checklist Determine if students understand place value of greater numbers by observing them write numbers in word name, standard form, and expanded form.

Follow Up For more practice with place value of greater numbers, assign **Reteach 7.**

For students who need enrichment, assign **Extend 7.**

Make Connections

You can see the relationship of 1,000; 10,000; 100,000; and 1,000,000 in a place-value chart. Each place is ten times greater than the place to its right.

Millions	Thousands			Ones		
Ones	Hundreds	Tens	Ones	Hundreds	Tens	Ones
1	5	0	0	2	3	0

You can read or write the number in different ways.

Standard Form: 1,500,230

Word Name: one million, five hundred thousand, two hundred thirty
  or
1 million, 500 thousand, 230

Paddy Doyle's actual record for push-ups is 1,500,230 in one year!

Expanded Form: 1,000,000 + 500,000 + 200 + 30

Check for Understanding

Write the number in standard form.

1 three million, eighty-two thousand, ten
3,082,010

2 five million, seven hundred sixty-five thousand, one hundred six **5,765,106**

3 seven million, three hundred nine thousand, five hundred thirty **7,309,530**

4 eight million, four hundred forty thousand, two **8,440,002**

Write the number in word form and in expanded form. See above.

5 1,748,235   **6** 1,035,010   **7** 6,526,085

5. one million, seven hundred forty-eight thousand, two hundred thirty-five; 1,000,000 + 700,000 + 40,000 + 8,000 + 200 + 30 + 5

6. one million, thirty-five thousand, ten; 1,000,000 + 30,000 + 5,000 + 10

7. six million, five hundred twenty-six thousand, eighty-five; 6,000,000 + 500,000 + 20,000 + 6,000 + 80 + 5

Critical Thinking: Analyze   Explain your reasoning.

8 What number is 1 greater than 6,999,999? In which places did the digits change?   **7,000,000; the digits changed in each of the 7 places because adding 1 results in regrouping each of the places.**

9 Can 1,500,000 also be written as 15 hundred thousand?

Yes; 10 hundred thousand is 1 million, so 15 hundred thousand is the same as 1 million, 5 hundred thousand.

Turn the page for Practice.
Place Value and Number Sense   **25**

CHECK

MAKE CONNECTIONS

Draw students' attention to the pattern of the place-value names shown in the place-value chart. They should notice that the ones and thousands periods have the same places, namely, hundreds, tens, and ones. Ask students:

- **What do you think the next value to the left in the place-value chart will be?** *[tens]*

Have students compare the examples given for word name and expanded form. Students should recognize the similarities in these two forms. The expanded form uses addition signs to connect the individual values of each digit of a number. The word name uses commas to separate periods of place value.

3 Close

Check for Understanding using items 1–9, page 25.

CRITICAL THINKING
Ask students:

- **What if you rounded 6,999,999 to the nearest ten thousand, hundred thousand, and million? What would the answer be in each case? Why?**
[7,000,000—the same in all cases; because of the nines in each place, rounding up requires the millions digit to be increased by one.]

Practice See pages 26–27.

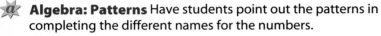

PRACTICE

Options for assigning exercises:
A—Choice of ten from ex. 1–21; all ex. 22–31; **More to Explore**
B—Choice of eight from ex. 1–16; all ex.17–31; **More to Explore**

- Students may want to use a calculator to solve ex. 1 and 2.
- In ex. 25, students can use patterns on a place-value chart to help them find the solution.
- In ex. 29, students can use rounding and mental math (3 × 300,000 or 4 × 250,000) to help them choose the best estimate.
- Have pairs of students work together.

a **Algebra: Patterns** Have students point out the patterns in completing the different names for the numbers.

a **Algebra** Equalities and inequalities are essential algebraic concepts.

More to Explore You may extend the question further by asking students to find answers for hours and days.

---

7. eight hundred seventy-five thousand, six hundred twenty-three **8.** two million, three hundred thousand **9.** nine hundred eight thousand, six hundred seven **10.** six hundred thousand, four **11.** eight million, three hundred ninety-eight thousand, twelve

Practice

a ALGEBRA: PATTERNS **Complete the different names for the number.**

1 2,000,000 = ▨ thousands **2,000**
　　　　　　　▨ ten thousands **200**
　　　　　　　▨ hundred thousands **20**

2 8,000,000 = ▨ thousands **8,000**
　　　　　　　▨ ten thousands **800**
　　　　　　　▨ hundred thousands **80**

Write the number in standard form and in expanded form.

3 one million, four hundred thirty-eight thousand **1,438,000; 1,000,000 + 400,000 + 30,000 + 8,000**

4 four million, eighty-seven thousand, three hundred seven **4,087,307; 4,000,000 + 80,000 + 7,000 + 300 + 7**

5 nine million, two hundred seventy thousand, ninety-one **9,270,091; 9,000,000 + 200,000 + 70,000 + 90 + 1**

6 six million, five hundred three thousand **6,503,000; 6,000,000 + 500,000 + 3,000**

Write the word name for the number.

7 875,623　**8** 2,300,000　**9** 908,607　**10** 600,004　**11** 8,398,012
See above for ex. 7–11.

12 1,004,600　**13** 7,072,234　**14** 5,020,100　**15** 3,205,000　**16** 4,000,050
See below for ex. 12–16.

17 What is 1,000,000 more than 896,000? **1,896,000**

18 What is 1,000,000 less than 4,082,500? **3,082,500**

19 What is 100,000 more than 6,980,400? **7,080,400**

20 What is 10,000 less than 1,067,999? **1,057,999**

21 Tell whether the amount is counted in the millions. Explain your reasoning. **Explanations may vary.**
　a. the number of miles you walk to school **No.**
　b. the number of people living in New York City **Yes.**
　c. the number of dollars needed to run all the schools in your state **Yes.**

a ALGEBRA **Write *true* or *false*.**

22 A > D **False.**

23 B = C **True.**

24 B < A **True.**

25 C > D **False.**

26 B < D **True.**

A = 1,438,095
B = 199,580
C = 1,000 less than 200,580
D = 1,000,000 more than 500,000

12. one million, four thousand, six hundred
13. seven million, seventy-two thousand, two hundred thirty-four
14. five million, twenty thousand, one hundred
15. three million, two hundred five thousand
16. four million, fifty

Meeting Individual Needs

Early Finishers

Have students work with a partner to write a logical reasoning problem similar to ex. 28. The problem should include at least three different numbers. Pairs can exchange their problems with other pairs and solve.

Inclusion

Suggest that students draw place-value charts to help them write numbers in different forms.

Language Support

You might have a Spanish-speaking student demonstrate for the class how they use a decimal point to separate place-value periods in large numbers. They use a comma instead of a decimal point to show numbers less than one. Have students who are used to this system make a chart comparing their method with the method used in the United States.

ESL APPROPRIATE

MIXED APPLICATIONS
Problem Solving

27 If you earned $10,000 a year, how long would it take you to earn $1,000,000? Explain your answer. **100 ten thousands equals 1 million, so it would take 100 y.**

28 Use each digit only once to make the greatest number you can: 0, 2, 5, 7, 8, and 9. **987,520**

29 About how long do you think it would take for 1 million dominoes to topple? Explain your reasoning. **SEE INFOBIT. c**
 a. about 15 minutes
 b. about 5 hours
 c. about 50 minutes
 d. about 5 days

30 **Logical reasoning** A calculator display shows *9586425.* . Later, it shows *9576425.* . Tell how this change could have been made. **Possible answer: 9,586,425 − 10,000 =**

31 **Write a problem** using two or more numbers in the millions. Exchange problems with a classmate. Solve and discuss your answers. **Students should compare their problems and solutions.**

INFOBIT
The greatest number of dominoes set up single-handedly was 320,236 by Klaus Friednich of Germany. He toppled 281,581 of the dominoes within 12 minutes 57.3 seconds.

more to explore

Counting to a Million

How long do you think it would take to count to 1,000,000?

To estimate the time it takes to count to 1,000, you can:
► measure the time it takes to count to 100.
► use your measurement to estimate the time it would take to count to 1,000.

Think: If it takes 2 minutes to count to 100, then it would take ten times as long, or 20 minutes, to count to 1,000.

Measure the time it takes you to count to 100. Then use a calculator to estimate the time it would take to count to:
a. 1,000. **b.** 10,000. **c.** 100,000. **d.** 1,000,000.
Estimates may vary. Check students' work.

Extra Practice, page 487

Place Value and Number Sense **27**

Alternate Teaching Strategy

Materials per group: place-value chart (TA 4), 30–50 counters

Have students place 0 to 9 counters in each column on the place-value chart. Ask students to read the number, write the number in expanded form, in word form, and in standard form.

Write two or three 7-digit numbers on the board. Have pairs work together to show the numbers in the same way.

When they have represented a number correctly, have students first write the number in expanded form, in word form, and then in standard form.

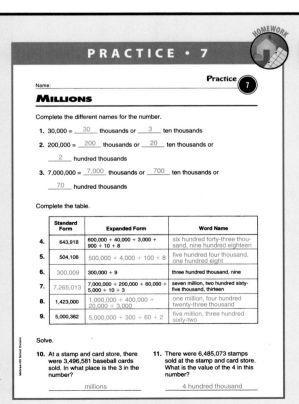

PRACTICE · 7

Name: _____   Practice **7**

MILLIONS

Complete the different names for the number.

1. 30,000 = ___30___ thousands or ___3___ ten thousands

2. 200,000 = ___200___ thousands or ___20___ ten thousands or ___2___ hundred thousands

3. 7,000,000 = ___7,000___ thousands or ___700___ ten thousands or ___70___ hundred thousands

Complete the table.

	Standard Form	Expanded Form	Word Name
4.	643,918	600,000 + 40,000 + 3,000 + 900 + 10 + 8	six hundred forty-three thousand, nine hundred eighteen
5.	504,108	500,000 + 4,000 + 100 + 8	five hundred four thousand, one hundred eight
6.	300,009	300,000 + 9	three hundred thousand, nine
7.	7,265,013	7,000,000 + 200,000 + 60,000 + 5,000 + 10 + 3	seven million, two hundred sixty-five thousand, thirteen
8.	1,423,000	1,000,000 + 400,000 + 20,000 + 3,000	one million, four hundred twenty-three thousand
9.	5,000,362	5,000,000 + 300 + 60 + 2	five million, three hundred sixty-two

Solve.

10. At a stamp and card store, there were 3,496,581 baseball cards sold. In what place is the 3 in the number? _____millions_____

11. There were 6,485,073 stamps sold at the stamp and card store. What is the value of the 4 in this number? _____4 hundred thousand_____

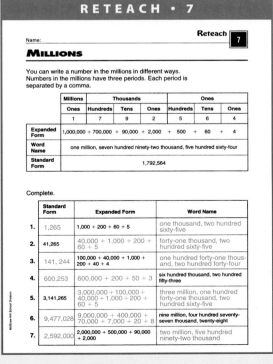

RETEACH · 7

Name: _____   Reteach **7**

MILLIONS

You can write a number in the millions in different ways. Numbers in the millions have three periods. Each period is separated by a comma.

		Millions		Thousands			Ones		
		Ones	Hundreds	Tens	Ones	Hundreds	Tens	Ones	
		1	7	9	2	5	6	4	
Expanded Form	1,000,000 + 700,000 + 90,000 + 2,000 + 500 + 60 + 4								
Word Name	one million, seven hundred ninety-two thousand, five hundred sixty-four								
Standard Form	1,792,564								

Complete.

	Standard Form	Expanded Form	Word Name
1.	1,265	1,000 + 200 + 60 + 5	one thousand, two hundred sixty-five
2.	41,265	40,000 + 1,000 + 200 + 60 + 5	forty-one thousand, two hundred sixty-five
3.	141,244	100,000 + 40,000 + 1,000 + 200 + 40 + 4	one hundred forty-one thousand, two hundred forty-four
4.	600,253	600,000 + 200 + 50 + 3	six hundred thousand, two hundred fifty-three
5.	3,141,265	3,000,000 + 100,000 + 40,000 + 1,000 + 200 + 60 + 5	three million, one hundred forty-one thousand, two hundred sixty-five
6.	9,477,028	9,000,000 + 400,000 + 70,000 + 7,000 + 20 + 8	nine million, four hundred seventy-seven thousand, twenty-eight
7.	2,592,000	2,000,000 + 500,000 + 90,000 + 2,000	two million, five hundred ninety-two thousand

---

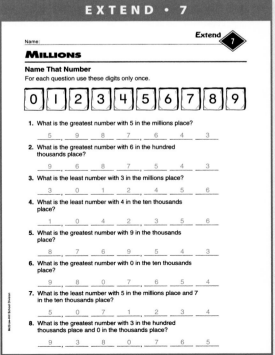

EXTEND · 7

Name: _____   Extend **7**

MILLIONS

Name That Number
For each question use these digits only once.

0	1	2	3	4	5	6	7	8	9

1. What is the greatest number with 5 in the millions place?
 5 , 9 8 7 , 6 4 3

2. What is the greatest number with 6 in the hundred thousands place?
 9 6 8 , 7 5 4 3

3. What is the least number with 3 in the millions place?
 3 0 1 , 2 4 5 6

4. What is the least number with 4 in the ten thousands place?
 1 0 4 2 3 5 6

5. What is the greatest number with 9 in the thousands place?
 8 7 6 9 5 4 3

6. What is the greatest number with 0 in the ten thousands place?
 9 8 0 7 6 5 4

7. What is the least number with 5 in the millions place and 7 in the ten thousands place?
 5 0 7 1 2 3 4

8. What is the greatest number with 3 in the hundred thousands place and 0 in the thousands place?
 9 3 8 0 7 6 5

27

LESSON 1.8

Problem Solvers At Work

OBJECTIVES Solve problems using different strategies. Interpret Data using line plots.

RESOURCE REMINDER
Math Center Cards 8
Practice 8, Reteach 8, Extend 8

SKILLS TRACE

GRADE 3	• Formulate and solve problems involving collecting, displaying, and interpreting data and choosing the best display. *(Chapter 5)*
GRADE 4	• Formulate and solve problems involving interpreting data using a line plot.
GRADE 5	• Formulate and solve problems involving interpreting data using bar graphs. *(Chapter 1)*

WARM-UP

Cooperative Pairs   **Logical/Analytical**

OBJECTIVE Use different strategies to solve problems.

▶ Present the following problem:
Animals drink at a water hole in the morning, at noon, in the afternoon, or in the evening. Lions drink in the afternoon. Giraffes do not drink at noon. Warthogs do not drink in the evening. Hyenas drink before the warthogs. In what order do the animals drink?

▶ Have students work together to solve the problem. Suggest that they try various strategies to solve it. *[hyenas, morning; warthogs, noon; lions, afternoon; giraffes, evening]*

	MORNING	NOON	AFTERNOON	EVENING
Clue 1			lion	
Clue 2	giraffe		lion	giraffe
Clue 3	warthog	warthog	lion	giraffe
Clue 4	hyena	warthog	lion	giraffe

SOCIAL STUDIES CONNECTION

Cooperative Groups   **Visual/Spatial**

OBJECTIVE Find graphic representations of numbers in newspapers.

Materials per group: one section of a newspaper such as *USA Today*, scissors, poster board

▶ Organize students into cooperative groups and give each group a section of a newspaper. Ask groups to look for and cut out graphs and other tools the newspaper uses to graphically represent data.

▶ After collecting as many graphs as possible, the group discusses and analyzes the data given in each one. Have them make a poster for each type of graph.

▶ As a group, have students make a list of the ways in which graphs are used to show information.

Daily Review

PREVIOUS DAY QUICK REVIEW

Complete the different names for 5,000,000.

1. __ thousands *[5,000]*
2. __ ten thousands *[500]*
3. __ hundred thousands *[50]*

FAST FACTS

1. 9 − 5 *[4]*
2. 9 − 6 *[3]*
3. 9 − 7 *[2]*
4. 9 − 8 *[1]*

Problem of the Day • 8

On a recent test, Julio missed one problem because he added 5 when he was supposed to subtract 5. The answer he gave was 17. What was the correct answer? *[7]*

TECH LINK

MATH VAN

Aid You may wish to use the Electronic Teacher Aid with this lesson.

MATH FORUM

Management Tip My students enjoy writing and solving problems and sharing their success with their friends. I give students some time to share their discoveries and methods with the class.

Visit our Resource Village at http://www.mhschool.com to see more of the Math Forum.

MATH CENTER

Practice

OBJECTIVE Interpret data using a line plot.

Materials per student: copy of the same book, Math Center Recording Sheet (TA 31 optional)

Students use a different paragraph of the same book and count the number of times the letters *x, c, t,* and *e* appear in the paragraph. They organize the data into a line plot and compare their data with other members of their group. They then make a group line plot and discuss what they have learned. *[Check students' work.]*

PRACTICE ACTIVITY 8   **MATH CENTER** Small Group 👥👥👥

Using Data • Letters, Letters, Letters

How many times will you see the letters *x, c, t,* and *e* in a paragraph? Look at a book and make a line plot of the data. Everyone uses the same chapter of the book. Each uses a different paragraph from that chapter.

- Count how many times *x, c, t,* and *e* appear in your paragraph.
- Organize the data into a line plot.
- Compare your line plot with other members of your group.
- Then combine your data to make a group line plot.
- Discuss what you learned from making the line plots. What did you discover about these letters?

YOU NEED : book

Chapter 1, Lesson 8, pages 28–31   Problem Solving

NCTM Standards

Problem Solving
✓ Communication
Reasoning
✓ Connections

Problem Solving

OBJECTIVE Use spatial reasoning to solve problems.

Materials mirror; Math Center Recording Sheet (TA 31 optional)

Students observe that some words appear the same in a mirror as they do on the page and write an explanation of why. *[OBOE, CHOICE, HIDE. Answers may vary. Possible answer: The top and bottom of the letters used in these words are the same or almost the same; letters: B C D E H I K O X; HOBO, HEED, DEED, BODE.]*

PROBLEM-SOLVING ACTIVITY 8   **MATH CENTER** On Your Own 👤

Spatial Reasoning • Mirror, Mirror

- Place a mirror on the line.
- Which words can be read the same in the mirror as they can on the page? Write an explanation of why this is so.
- Which letters of the alphabet can you use to write other words like these?
- Write other mirror words.

YOU NEED : mirror

HIDE
PURPLE
CHOICE
SQUARE
OBOE
TABLE

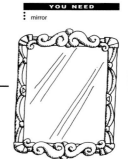

Chapter 1, Lesson 8, pages 28–31   Problem Solving

NCTM Standards

Problem Solving
✓ Communication
✓ Reasoning
Connections

Problem Solvers At Work

OBJECTIVES Solve problems using different strategies. Interpret data using line plots.

Resources drawing program or Math Van Tools

Vocabulary data, line plot

1 Introduce

Materials per student: sticky note

Give each student one sticky note. Draw the following diagram on the chalkboard.

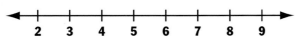

Ask students to draw a large X on their sticky notes. Then have students put their sticky notes above the number on the line that represents the number of letters in their first names.

Compare the line plot your students made to the line plot shown in the text. Discuss how they are similar and different.

2 Teach   *Cooperative Pairs*

PART 1 INTERPRET DATA

LEARN Let students work in pairs to answer the questions. Make sure students are aware that they should answer the questions based on the line plot in their books.

In problem 2, students are asked if there are clusters in the data. You may remind students that clusters are where there are many Xs in one place.

Discuss as a class how a line plot is helpful. Ask students if they think they could have answered the questions by using just the list of numbers.

Use Illustrations For problem 5, ask students what other way the data might be illustrated. Students may suggest a bar graph or tally table. Work with the class to display the data in another form, then invite students to compare the class's illustration with the line plot.

Part 1   Interpret Data

Fourth graders in the River School surveyed their classmates to compare the names to the amazing claim at the right.

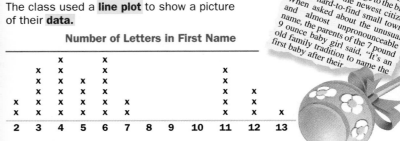

AMAZING CLAIM
LONGEST FIRST NAME GIVEN TO BABY HAS 32 LETTERS

Erehwon, TX — They will have to attach another page to the birth certificate of the newest citizen of this hard-to-find small town. When asked about the unusual name, the parents of the 7 pound 9 ounce baby girl said, "It's an old family tradition to name the first baby after their

Our data:
3, 3, 11, 2, 4, 12, 6, 5, 13, 7, 7, 11, 12, 4, 6, 5, 11,
2, 3, 3, 4, 6, 11, 6, 5, 4, 3, 6, 6, 4, 4, 12, 5, 11

The class used a **line plot** to show a picture of their **data.**

Number of Letters in First Name

```
        x       x
    x   x       x
    x   x   x   x               x
    x   x   x   x               x
x   x   x   x   x   x           x   x
x   x   x   x   x   x           x   x   x
2   3   4   5   6   7   8   9  10  11  12  13
```

Work Together

Use the results of the survey to solve. Explain your methods.

1 How many fourth-grade students are there? How do you know? **34; Possible answers: count the Xs on the line plot; count the amount of numbers in the data.**

2 Are there any clusters in the data? What does this tell you? **Yes, from 2 to 7 letters and from 11 to 13 letters; most of the names are short or very long.**

3 What statement can you make about the number of letters in the first names of the fourth-grade students? **See page T17.**

4 **What if** there are four new students with first names that have 5, 5, 5, and 10 letters. How does the new data affect the statement you made? **See page T17.**

5 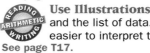 **Use Illustrations** Compare the line plot and the list of data. Which one makes it easier to interpret the data? Why? **See page T17.**

6 Use the survey to explain why having a first name with 32 letters is an amazing claim. If you had to predict the number of letters in a first name, what would your prediction be? Why? **See page T17.**

> **line plot** A graph that shows data using symbols that are lined up.
>
> **data** Information.

Meeting Individual Needs

Extra Support

Present the table to the class:

FAVORITE COLOR

Color	Red	Blue	Yellow
People	213	156	198

Discuss why a line plot would not be used to show the data above.

Ongoing Assessment

Interview Determine if students understand how to read a line plot by asking:

- **How many students in the River School fourth grade class have three letters in their first name?** [5]

Follow Up For students who need more practice interpreting data from a line plot, assign **Reteach 8.**

Students who understand different problem-solving strategies may try **Extend 8.**

Part 2 Write and Share Problems

Erica wrote this problem. Then she chose a paragraph and made a tally table to record the letters she counted.

Letter	Tally	Number of Times the Letter Appears
a	JHT JHT III	13
b	IIII	4
c	JHT	5
d	IIII	4
e	JHT JHT JHT JHT	20

For problems 10–12, see Teacher's Edition.

7 Solve Erica's problem. Explain your reasoning.  See below.

8 Choose a paragraph of your own. Collect data about the five letters. Create a table like Erica's to show your data.
Check students' work.

9 Solve the problem for your own data. Explain how the table helped you to solve the problem.
See below.

10 **Write a problem** of your own where you can use a table to record and organize data to solve the problem.

11 Trade problems. Solve at least three problems written by your classmates.

12 What was the most interesting problem that you solved? Why?

Which letter appears most often: a, b, c, d, or e?

Erica Lester
Snowden Elementary School
Memphis, TN

7. Letter *e*; it appears 20 times, which is greater than any other number.

9. Data and tables may vary. Possible answer: Used the table to record the data and to help find the information easily.

Turn the page for Practice Strategies.

PART 2 WRITE AND SHARE PROBLEMS

Check Ask students to explain how they used the table to solve Erica's problem.

For problem 8, students may choose a paragraph from textbooks or other books in a classroom library.

For problem 9, ask students to write their own problem that requires the use of a table. Many students will simply write another problem about the letters found in a paragraph. Encourage your students to use a different context to write their problems. Remind students to solve the problems on separate pieces of paper so their problems can be shared with classmates.

For problem 10, students may write problems that involve taking a survey and using a table to organize the data. For items 11 and 12, encourage students to discuss the problems they solved and their reasons why a problem was most interesting.

3 Close

Let students discuss the problems they wrote and those of their classmates that they solved. Which problem did they find most challenging? Which problem was the easiest? Were there any problems that they could solve more quickly without the use of a table?

Practice See pages 30–31.

COMMON ERROR

Students may miscount tally marks and Xs in a line plot. Suggest that students double check their counting. They may want to use a straightedge so that they count only the marks above a given number. Students may also find it useful to write the total after counting the first time to keep from making a mistake when going back.

Inclusion

Visually-challenged students may have a difficult time interpreting line plots and tally tables. Let them work with a partner throughout this lesson. Instruct the partner to answer questions the visually-challenged student asks about the graphics, but not to directly answer the problems in the text.

▶ **PART 3 PRACTICE STRATEGIES**

Materials have available: calculators

Students have the option of choosing any five problems from ex. 1–8, and any two problems from ex. 9–12. They may choose to do more problems if they wish. Have students describe how they made their choices.

- For ex. 2, you may want to remind students that drawing a picture can be helpful when solving problems.
- Students can make a table to solve ex. 4.
- Ex. 9–12 will generally take students a little longer to complete. Most require logic and looking for patterns.

At the Computer If computers are not available, students can complete this activity by stacking blocks and counting and recording the number of sides they see. If possible, give students 10 blocks of different colors so that it is easier for them to distinguish each side.

Math Van Students may use the Drawing tool to make the cubes. A project electronic teacher aid has been provided.

Part 3 Practice Strategies

Menu Explanations may vary.
Choose five problems and solve them. Explain your methods.

1 Katy has two books. The first book has 928 pages. The second book is 100 pages longer. How many pages does the second book have?
1,028 pages

2 A tree has 2 limbs. Each limb has 3 branches. Each branch has 3 caterpillars on it. How many caterpillars are there?
18 caterpillars

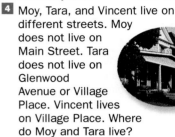

3 **Logical reasoning** I am a number with the digits 0, 3, 4, 5, and 9. If you round me to the nearest thousand or the nearest hundred, you get 44,000. The digit in my tens place is 5. What number am I? **43,950**

4 Moy, Tara, and Vincent live on different streets. Moy does not live on Main Street. Tara does not live on Glenwood Avenue or Village Place. Vincent lives on Village Place. Where do Moy and Tara live?
Moy lives on Glenwood Avenue, Tara lives on Main Street.

5 Which animal do most students have as a pet? fewest students?
a dog; a snake

6 Write a statement that describes the results of this survey. **Possible answer: Very few students have snakes as pets.**

Types of Pets Students Have

Cat	Dog	Fish	Snake	Bird
	x			
x	x			x
x	x	x		x
x	x	x	x	x

7 Order the types of exercise, according to the amount done in an hour, from greatest to least. **See below.**

8 Which type of exercise was done about 3,600 times? Explain your answer. **Squat thrusts; 3,552 rounded to the nearest hundred is 3,600.**

Type of Exercise	World Record Number Done in an Hour
Squats	4,289
Squat thrusts	3,552
Parallel-bar dips	3,726
Burpees	1,840

7. **4,289 squats, 3,726 parallel-bar dips, 3,552 squat thrusts, 1,840 burpees**

30 Lesson 1.8

P R A C T I C E

Meeting Individual Needs

Early Finishers
Ask students to do the **Work Together** problems 1–4 using data from their classroom line plot.

Gender Fairness
Alternate between boys and girls when calling on students. Be sure to call on all students.

Language Support
Let students acquiring English work with English-speaking students to solve problems on pages 30 and 31. Some students may need help with the meanings of some words in the problems.

ESL APPROPRIATE

11a. ▢▢▢ b. ▢▢

Choose two problems and solve them. Explain your methods. Explanations may vary.

9 a. Which of these numbers are Flims?
1,476; 60,000; 412,070; 6,072; 7,307 **1,476; 6,072**

These numbers are Flims.		These numbers are not Flims.	
1,450	2,000	675	750
9,678	4,000	1,735	6,087
7,396	9,996	13,401	700,000
3,044	2,700	82,500	1,975,728

b. Describe a Flim.
an even number in the thousands

10 Use the digits 0, 1, 2, 3, 4, 5, 6, 7, 8, and 9 one time each to replace these circles to make true statements. Compare your statements with other classmates. **Check students' work.**

a. ●●●● < ●●●●

b. ●●●●● < ●●●●●

c. ●●●●● > ●●●●●

d. ●●●●● > ●●●●●

11 Spatial reasoning A design made from toothpicks is shown below.
a. Remove 4 toothpicks and leave only 4 squares that are all the same size.
b. Remove 5 toothpicks and leave only 3 squares that are all the same size. **Answers may vary.**

Possible answers: see above.

12 At the Computer When you stack cubes to form a column, you can see some faces but not others. For example, if you place one cube on a table, you can see five faces but not the face resting on the table.

Use a drawing program to build columns 1 cube high, 2 cubes high, and so on, up to 10 cubes high. Make a table like the one below. Then write about what you notice.

				4	5	6	7	8	9	10
Number of Cubes High	1	2	3	▪	▪	▪	▪	▪	▪	▪
Number of Faces You Can See	5	9	▪	▪	▪	▪	▪	▪	▪	▪
			13	17	21	25	29	33	37	41

Possible answer: Finding 4 times the number of cubes high and adding 1 gives the number of faces that can be seen.

Extra Practice, page 487

Place Value and Number Sense **31**

Alternate Teaching Strategy

Materials: tape or CD player, a tape or CD of a popular song

Draw a chart like the one below on the chalkboard:

Words				
Number of Times Word Is Repeated				

Play a popular song for the class. Ask students to name five words they think are used the most in the song. Then have students copy the chart and write each word on the top of each column. Have students circle the one word they think is used the most.

Play the song and have students listen for the words. Have them draw an X in the column under the word each time they hear it.

As a class, discuss what students' line plots show. Were their guesses about the most-used words correct? What other questions could be answered by using the line plots?

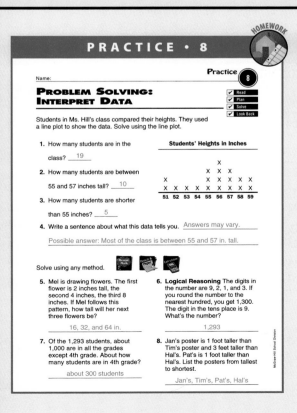

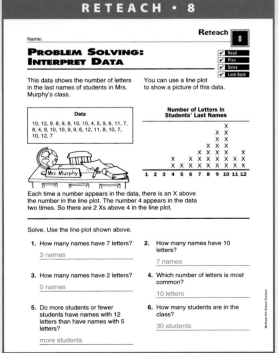

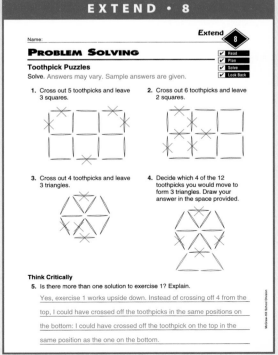

31

PURPOSE Review and assess the concepts, skills, and strategies that students have learned in the chapter.

Materials per student: calculator (optional)

Chapter Objectives
1A Identify how numbers are used
1B Read and write whole numbers to millions
1C Compare, order, and round whole numbers
1D Solve problems, including those that involve place value and making a table

Using the Chapter Review

The **Chapter Review** can be used as a review, practice test, or chapter test.

Think Critically Students' explanations for ex. 26 will show their understanding of place value. In ex. 27, students' explanations will show the depth of understanding they have of rounding and comparing numbers.

Language and Mathematics

Complete the sentence. Use a word in the chart. (pages 2–27)

1 4,000 1 600 1 7 is the ■ of the number 4,607.
expanded form

2 A comma separates the millions and thousands ■ in the number 7,835,082. periods

3 84,600 . 82,900 means 84,600 ■ 82,900.
is greater than

4 To round a number to the nearest thousand, you look at the digit in the ■ place. hundreds

> **Vocabulary**
> periods
> hundreds
> expanded form
> millions
> is greater than
> is less than

Concepts and Skills

Write the number in standard form. (page 8)

5 six hundred forty-three 643

6 seven thousand, nine hundred 7,900

7 three thousand, two hundred seventy-eight 3,278

8 eight hundred sixty-one thousand, four hundred sixteen 861,416

9 six hundred four thousand, thirty-nine 604,039

10 six million, one hundred thousand, nine hundred two 6,100,902

Write the number in word form and in expanded form. (page 8) See below.

11 9,460   12 2,807   13 8,074   14 50,072   15 652,913

Compare. Write >, <, or =. (page 12)

16 983 ● 9,831 <   17 356,700 ● 356,585 >   18 507,120 ● 510,000

Order the numbers from least to greatest. (page 12)

19 1,432; 2,232; 1,475
1,432; 1,475; 2,232

20 67,902; 66,400; 67,050 66,400; 67,050; 67,902

21 443,700; 88,500; 438,600 88,500; 438,600; 443,700

22 Round 9,742 to the nearest hundred. 9,700

23 Round 3,621 to the nearest thousand. 4,000

24 Round 865,398 to the nearest thousand. 865,000

25 Round 999,950 to the nearest thousand. 1,000,000

11. nine thousand, four hundred sixty; 9,000 + 400 + 60
12. two thousand, eight hundred seven; 2,000 + 800 + 7
13. eight thousand, seventy-four; 8,000 + 70 + 4
14. fifty thousand, seventy-two; 50,000 + 70 + 2
15. six hundred fifty-two thousand, nine hundred thirteen; 600,000 + 50,000 + 2,000 + 900 + 10 + 3

Reinforcement and Remediation

CHAPTER OBJECTIVES	CHAPTER REVIEW ITEMS	STUDENT BOOK PAGES		TEACHER'S EDITION PAGES		TEACHER RESOURCES
		Lesson	Midchapter Review	Activities	Alternate Teaching Strategy	Reteach
1A	2-3	2-3	16	1A	3	1
1B	1, 5-15, 26	4-11, 24-27	16	3A, 7A 23A	7, 11, 27	2–3, 7
1C	3-4, 16-25, 27,31-32	12-13, 20-23	16	11C, 19A	13, 23	4, 6
1D	28, 30, 33	14–15, 28–31	16	13A, 27A	15, 31	5, 8

26. The student wrote 3,000 instead of 30,000;
34 thousands = 30,000 + 4,000.

Think critically. (page 8)

26 Analyze. Explain what mistake was made. Then correct it. **See above.**

34 thousand = 3,000 + 4,000

27 Generalize. Write *always, sometimes,* or *never.* Give examples to support your answer.

a. When you round a number to the nearest thousand, you increase the thousands digit by 1. Then, you change the digits that follow to zeros. **Sometimes; possible answer: 43,980 rounds to 44,000; 78,120 rounds to 78,000.**

b. Choose any two whole numbers. The number with more digits is the greater number. **always; possible answer: 789, 650 > 98,400**

. Answers may vary. Possible answers: All are greater than 10,000, all digits are less than 6, all are even numbers, all are multiples of 4.

MIXED APPLICATIONS
Problem Solving Pencil & Paper · Calculator · Mental Math (pages 14, 28)

28 What do all these numbers have in common? **See above.**

1,023,100	45,012	222,400
434,124	131,240	13,232

29 A student surveyed her classmates and made the line plot below. Write a statement that describes the survey. **Students' descriptions should reflect data of line plot given.**

How Many Animals Do You See Each Day?

```
        x   x
        x   x
        x   x
    x   x   x   x
    x   x   x   x   x   x                   x
    1   2   3   4   5   6   7   8   9
```

30 A chain of paper clips was made by 60 students in Singapore in 1992. The chain measured 18,087 feet in length. What was the length of the chain to the nearest thousand feet? **18,000 ft**

Use the information in the table for problems 31–33.

31 Which tunnel or bridge has the greatest length? the least length? **St. Gotthard Tunnel; Howrah Bridge**

32 Which tunnel is longer: the Lincoln or the Mount Royal? **Mount Royal**

33 What is the difference between the length of the Golden Gate Bridge and the Verrazano-Narrows Bridge? **100 ft**

Tunnels or Bridges	Length
Fort McHenry Tunnel, MD	7,200 ft
Golden Gate Bridge, CA	4,200 ft
Lincoln Tunnel, NJ/NY	13,200 ft
Howrah Bridge, India	1,500 ft
Mount Royal Tunnel, Canada	16,900 ft
St. Gotthard Tunnel, Switzerland	53,800 ft
Verrazano-Narrows Bridge, NY	4,300 ft

PURPOSE
Assess the concepts, skills, and strategies that students have learned in this chapter.

Chapter Objectives
1A Identify how numbers are used.
1B Read and write whole numbers to millions.
1C Compare, order, and round whole numbers.
1D Solve problems, including those that involve place value and making a table.

Using the Chapter Test

The **Chapter Test** can be used as a practice test, a chapter test, or as an additional review. The **Performance Assessment** on Student Book page 35 provides an alternate means of assessing students' understanding of place value and number sense.

The table below correlates the test items to the chapter objectives and to the Student Book pages on which the skills are taught.

Assessment Resources

TEST MASTERS

Testing Program Blackline Masters provide three forms of the Chapter Test to assess students' understanding of the chapter concepts, skills, and strategies. Form C uses a free-response format. Forms A and B use a multiple-choice format.

COMPUTER TEST GENERATOR

The Computer Test Generator supplies abundant multiple-choice and free-response test items, which you may use to generate tests and practice worksheets tailored to the needs of your class.

TEACHER'S ASSESSMENT RESOURCES

Teacher's Assessment Resources provides resources for alternate assessment. It includes guidelines for Building a Portfolio, page 6, and the Holistic Scoring Guide, page 27.

Write the word name and expanded form for the number. See below.
1 2,506   **2** 8,067   **3** 30,470   **4** 67,432

Write the number in standard form.
5 5 hundreds 8 ones **508**   **6** 9 hundreds 2 tens 7 ones **927**

7 72 tens **720**   **8** 18 hundreds **1,800**

Tell if the number is used to name, order, count, or measure.
9 Kelly is third in line. **order**   **10** The rope is 9 ft long. **measure**   **11** Fifty people are here **count**
12 The MX6 airplane is in the hangar. **name**   **13** The concert will last seven days. **count**

Compare. Write >, <, or =.
14 375 ● 3,750 **<**   **15** 7,612 ● 7,195 **>**   **16** 4,365 ● 11,628 **<**

Order the numbers from least to greatest.
17 5,826; 6,019; 5,819   **5,819; 5,826; 6,019**
18 68,271; 6,083; 6,826   **6,083; 6,826; 68,271**
19 Round 8,304 to the nearest hundred. **8,300**
20 Round 6,531 to the nearest thousand. **7,000**
21 Round 59,827 to the nearest thousand. **60,000**

1. two thousand, five hundred six; 2,000 + 500 + 6
2. eight thousand, sixty-seven; 8,000 + 60 + 7

Solve.
22 Use the record heights of 6 feet 11 inches, 112 feet, and 90 feet. The largest piggy bank was not 112 feet nor 90 feet high. The figures on Stone Mountain are not 112 feet high. What was the height of the highest recorded sea wave? **112 ft**

23 The actual mountain heights are 7,439 meters, 8,848 meters, and 6,194 meters. Everest is about 9,000 meters. Victory Peak is not about 7,000 meters. How high is McKinley? Order the mountains from greatest to least according to their heights. **7,439 m; Everest, McKinley, Victory Peak**

24 The largest jar of jelly beans had 378,300 beans. The jigsaw puzzle with the most pieces had 204,484 parts. Were there more beans or jigsaw pieces? **beans**

25 Shakespeare's play *Hamlet* has 29,551 words in it. If a newspaper article rounded the number to the nearest thousand, what might a headline say about it? **Possible answer: *Hamlet* has about 30,000 words to say!**

3. thirty thousand, four hundred seventy; 30,000 + 400 + 70
4. sixty-seven thousand, four hundred thirty-two; 60,000 + 7,000 + 400 + 30 + 2

Test Correlation		
CHAPTER OBJECTIVES	**TEST ITEMS**	**TEXT PAGES**
1A	9–13	2–3
1B	1–8	4–11, 24–27
1C	14–21	12–13, 20–23
1D	22–25	14–15, 28–31

See Teacher's Assessment Resources for samples of student work.

What Did You Learn?

Write about the top three immigrant groups in the United States in 1993.

In 1993, there were 65,578 immigrants from China, 18,783 immigrants from Great Britain, 126,561 immigrants from Mexico, 63,457 immigrants from the Philippines, and 17,241 immigrants from Jamaica.

▶ Write a title that includes numbers.

▶ Organize the data in a table. How did you organize the numbers? See page T17.

▶ Write two statements that compare the data about the top three immigrant groups. See page T17.

· · · · · · · · · · · · · · · A Good Answer · · · · · · · · · · · · · · · ·
- organizes the data to allow easy comparisons
- includes a title with numbers that would make people want to read it
- gives accurate comparisons of the data

 You may want to place your work in your portfolio.

What Do You Think ❓
See Teacher's Edition.
1 Can you read and write numbers through hundred thousands? If not, what do you find difficult to do?

2 List all the ways you might use to compare or order numbers.
- Use a place-value chart.
- Use place-value models.
- Use a number line.
- Other. Explain.

Reviewing A Portfolio

Have students review their portfolios. Consider including these items:
- Finished work on the Chapter Project (p. xiF) or **Investigation** (pp. 18–19).
- Selected math journal entries, pp. 1, 12, 16, and 21.
- Finished work on the nonroutine problem in **What Do You Know?** (p. 1) and problems from the Menu (pp. 30–31).
- Each student's self-selected "best piece" from work completed during the chapter. Have each student attach a note explaining why he or she chose that piece.
- Any work you or an individual student wishes to keep for future reference.

You may take this opportunity to conduct conferences with students. The Portfolio Analysis Form can help you report students' progress. See Teacher's Assessment Resources, p. 33.

PURPOSE Review and assess the concepts, skills, and strategies learned in this chapter.

Using the Performance Assessment

Have students read and restate the problems in their own words. Make sure they understand what *immigrants* means in these problems. *[people who come to the United States from other countries]*

Point out the section on the student page headed "A Good Answer." Make sure students understand that you use these points to evaluate their answers.

Evaluating Student Work

As you read students' papers, look for the following:
- *Does the student understand numbers in the thousands?*
- *Can the student compare and order numbers in the thousands?*
- *Can the student organize data into a table?*

The Holistic Scoring Guide and annotated samples of students' work can be used to assess this task. See pages 27–32 and 37–72 in Teacher's Assessment Resources.

Using the Self-Assessment

What Do You Think? Assure students that there are no right or wrong answers. Tell them the emphasis is on what they think and how they justify their answers.

Follow-Up Interviews

These questions can be used to gain insight into students' thinking:
- **Read the numbers of immigrants aloud.**
- **What do you mean by this headline?**
- **What method did you use for comparing the numbers?**
- **What is the basis for your statement? (Ask as you point to one of the students' statements.)**

OBJECTIVE Use place value in a science context.

Resources graphing program, or Math Van Tools

Science

Cultural Connection Read the **Cultural Note** on page 36. Discuss the difference between *extinct* (a species that existed before, but no longer exists anywhere in the world) and *endangered* (a species that is now in danger of becoming extinct).

As you discuss the reasons why species become endangered, ask:

- **How might some of the natural causes listed result in a species becoming endangered?** [*Possible answer: A species of animals could become diseased and then not be able to reproduce.*]
- **What are some ways animals lose their habitats?** [*Possible answers: forest cut for lumber to build homes for people; pollution*]

Math

As students answer the questions on page 37, encourage them to explain how understanding place value helped them.

For item 1 students can explain that since 1,300,000 > 600,000 they know that the number of African elephants has decreased from 1970s to 1990s.

For item 2, have students explain how they identified the animals with populations less than 2,000. Ask:

- **How did you use place value?** [*Possible answer: I looked for those numbers where the thousands digit was less than 2 and did not have digits in any place greater than the thousands.*]

Endangered Species

The snow leopard lives in the mountains of Asia. It is killed for its spotted fur, which is made into fur coats. It is also killed by hunters and by people who think it will kill livestock. The snow leopard is an endangered species.

Reasons why species become endangered include:
a. natural causes such as volcanoes, floods, and disease.
b. loss of habitat (places to live).
c. killings by hunters, by species that are new to the region, or by cars and motorboats.
d. pesticides and poisons.

► What are some ways humans can help endangered species? See above.

Possible answers: protective laws; creating reserves for animals; breeding animals in captivity, then releasing in the wild; recycling; reducing use of chemicals; restoring habitats—for example by planting trees, composting, producing less waste

Extending The Activity

Look for human and natural causes for environmental changes around the school neighborhood. For example, students may find a vacant lot where weeds have taken over a grassy area (natural cause) or where a parking lot was built where a meadow once stood (human cause).

3. Graphs may vary. Check students' work. Possible answer: The bar for the 1990s population is higher than for the 1970s; the bar for the 1990s population is lower than for the 1970s.

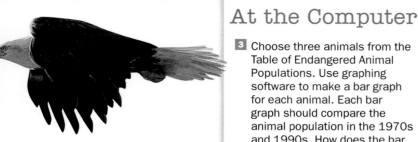

At the Computer

3 Choose three animals from the Table of Endangered Animal Populations. Use graphing software to make a bar graph for each animal. Each bar graph should compare the animal population in the 1970s and 1990s. How does the bar graph show that the population increased? decreased? **See above.**

Change in Population of Florida Cougar

Use the Databank on page 533 for problems 1–5. See page T17.

1 Which species of animals have populations that decreased? increased? How can you tell?

2 Use the populations in the 1990s. Write the animals in order from greatest to least. Which species of animals have populations less than 2,000?

4 Write two statements about the animal populations you chose. **See below.**

5 Use an on-line encyclopedia. Find new information about the population of the animals. Use the information in your graph. What do you notice? Students' observations should be based on their new information.

4. Statements may vary. Possible answer: The population of the African elephant in the 1990s was about half the population in the 1970s, and there was a large increase in the population of the polar bear from the 1970s to the 1990s. Place Value and Number Sense **37**

Technology

Students can work in groups to create their graphs. You may wish to show students how to make a double-bar graph to complete item 3.

In addition to using an online encyclopedia, students may be able to access the internet to find additional information about endangered species. They can also write the U.S. Fish and Wildlife Service.

Math Van Students may use the Graphing tool to make a bar graph for each animal. A project electronic teacher aid has been provided.

Interesting Facts

- **More than 1,000** species were listed by the U.S. Fish and Wildlife Service as endangered or threatened in the early 1990s.

- **Endangered species in the United States** include 32 species of mammals, 61 species of birds, 8 species of reptiles, 5 species of amphibians, 45 species of fish, 3 species of snails, 32 species of clams, 8 species of crustaceans, and 10 species of insects.

Bibliography

The Enormous Egg: You Won't Believe Your Eyes!, by Oliver Butterworth. Boston: Little, Brown & Company, Inc., 1993. ISBN 0–316–11920–2.

Will We Miss Them?: Endangered Species, by Alexandra Wright. Watertown, MA: Charlesbridge Publishing, 1992. ISBN 0–881–06489–0.

Zucchini, by Barbara Dana. New York: HarperCollins Children's Books, 1982. ISBN 0–06–021395–7.

CHAPTER 2 AT A GLANCE: Theme: Smart Shopping   Suggested Pacing: 14–17 days

Money, Addition, and Subtraction

CHAPTER 2 ORGANIZER

WEEK ONE

DAY 1 — PREASSESSMENT

Introduction pp. 38

What Do You Know? p. 39

CHAPTER OBJECTIVES: 2A, 2B, 2C, 2D, 2E

RESOURCES Read-Aloud Anthology pp. 4–6
Pretest: Test Master Form A, B, or C
Diagnostic Inventory

Portfolio   Journal   **NCTM STANDARDS:** 1, 2, 3, 4, 6, 8

DAY 2 — LESSON 2.1

EXPLORE ACTIVITY
Count Money and Make Change
pp. 40–41

CHAPTER OBJECTIVES: 2B
MATERIALS play money (TA 10–11), calculators (opt.)
RESOURCES Reteach/Practice/Extend: 9
Math Center Cards: 9
Extra Practice: 488

Daily Review TE p. 39B
Technology Link   **NCTM STANDARDS:** 4, 6

DAY 3 — LESSON 2.2

Compare, Order, and Round Money
pp. 42–43

CHAPTER OBJECTIVES: 2A
MATERIALS calculators (opt.)
RESOURCES Reteach/Practice/Extend: 10
Math Center Cards: 10
Extra Practice: 488

Daily Review TE p. 41B
Technology Link   **NCTM STANDARDS:** 6

WEEK TWO

LESSON 2.5

Add Whole Numbers pp. 48–51

CHAPTER OBJECTIVES: 2D
MATERIALS calculators (opt.), place-value models (TA 22)
RESOURCES Reteach/Practice/Extend: 13
Math Center Cards: 13
Extra Practice: 489

Daily Review TE p. 47B
Technology Link   **NCTM STANDARDS:** 8

LESSON 2.6

Three or More Addends pp. 52–53

CHAPTER OBJECTIVES: 2D
MATERIALS calculators (opt.)
RESOURCES Reteach/Practice/Extend: 14
Math Center Cards: 14
Extra Practice: 489

Daily Review TE p. 51B
Technology Link   **NCTM STANDARDS:** 8

MIDCHAPTER ASSESSMENT

Midchapter Review p. 54
CHAPTER OBJECTIVES: 2A, 2B, 2C, 2D
MATERIALS play money (bills and coins) (TA 10–11)

Developing Number Sense p. 55

REAL-LIFE INVESTIGATION:
Applying Addition and Subtraction
pp. 56–57

Portfolio   Journal   **NCTM STANDARDS:** 1, 2, 3, 4, 5, 6, 8

WEEK THREE

LESSON 2.9

Subtract Whole Numbers pp. 62–65

CHAPTER OBJECTIVES: 2D
MATERIALS place-value models (TA 22), calculators (opt.)
RESOURCES Reteach/Practice/Extend: 17
Math Center Cards: 17
Extra Practice: 490

Daily Review TE p. 61B

Algebraic Thinking
Journal
Technology Link   **NCTM STANDARDS:** 8

LESSON 2.10

PROBLEM-SOLVING STRATEGY
Choose the Operation pp. 66–67

CHAPTER OBJECTIVES: 2E
MATERIALS calculators, centimeter graph paper (TA 7)
RESOURCES Reteach/Practice/Extend: 18
Math Center Cards: 18
Extra Practice: 491
TEACHING WITH TECHNOLOGY
Alternate Lesson TE pp. 67A–67B

Daily Review TE p. 65B
Technology Link   **NCTM STANDARDS:** 1, 2, 3, 4, 8

LESSON 2.11

Subtract Across Zero pp. 68–69

CHAPTER OBJECTIVES: 2D
MATERIALS calculators (opt.)
RESOURCES Reteach/Practice/Extend: 19
Math Center Cards: 19
Extra Practice: 491

Daily Review TE p. 67D
Technology Link   **NCTM STANDARDS:** 8

DAY 4

LESSON 2.3

MENTAL MATH
Addition Strategies pp. 44–45

CHAPTER OBJECTIVES: 2D
MATERIALS calculators (opt.)
RESOURCES Reteach/Practice/Extend: 11
Math Center Cards: 11
Extra Practice: 488

Daily Review TE p. 43B

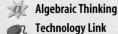 Algebraic Thinking

📓 Journal

🖱 Technology Link

NCTM STANDARDS: 6, 8

LESSON 2.7

MENTAL MATH
Subtraction Strategies pp. 58–59

CHAPTER OBJECTIVES: 2D
MATERIALS calculators (opt.)
RESOURCES Reteach/Practice/Extend: 15
Math Center Cards: 15
Extra Practice: 490

Daily Review TE p. 57B

🖱 Technology Link

NCTM STANDARDS: 6, 8

LESSON 2.12

PROBLEM SOLVERS AT WORK
Find Needed or Extra Information
pp. 70–73

CHAPTER OBJECTIVES: 2E
MATERIALS play money (TA 10–11), calculators (opt.)
RESOURCES Reteach/Practice/Extend: 20
Math Center Cards: 20
Extra Practice: 491

Daily Review TE p. 69B

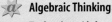 Algebraic Thinking

🖱 Technology Link

NCTM STANDARDS: 1, 2, 3, 4, 8

DAY 5

LESSON 2.4

MENTAL MATH
Estimate Sums pp. 46–47

CHAPTER OBJECTIVES: 2C
MATERIALS calculators (opt.)
RESOURCES Reteach/Practice/Extend: 12
Math Center Cards: 12
Extra Practice: 489

Daily Review TE p. 45B

🖱 Technology Link

NCTM STANDARDS: 5, 6

LESSON 2.8

MENTAL MATH
Estimate Differences pp. 60–61

CHAPTER OBJECTIVES: 2C
MATERIALS calculators (opt.)
RESOURCES Reteach/Practice/Extend: 16
Math Center Cards: 16
Extra Practice: 490

Daily Review TE p. 59B

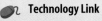 Algebraic Thinking

🖱 Technology Link

NCTM STANDARDS: 5, 6

CHAPTER ASSESSMENT

Chapter Review pp. 74–75
MATERIALS calculators (opt.)

Chapter Test p. 76
RESOURCES Posttest: Test Master Form A, B, or C

Performance Assessment p. 77
RESOURCES Performance Task: Test Master

Math • Science • Technology Connection
pp. 78–79

💾 Portfolio

NCTM STANDARDS: 1, 4, 6

Assessment Options

FORMAL

Chapter Tests

STUDENT BOOK
• Midchapter Review, p. 54
• Chapter Review, pp. 74–75
• Chapter Test, p. 76

BLACKLINE MASTERS
• Test Master Form A, B, or C
• Diagnostic Inventory

COMPUTER TEST GENERATOR
• Available on disk

Performance Assessment
• What Do You Know? p. 39
• Performance Assessment, p. 77
• Holistic Scoring Guide, Teacher's Assessment Resources, pp. 27–32
• Follow-Up Interviews, p. 77
• Performance Task, Test Masters

Teacher's Assessment Resources
• Portfolio Guidelines and Forms, pp. 6–9, 33–35
• Holistic Scoring Guide, pp. 27–32
• Samples of Student Work, pp. 37–72

INFORMAL

Ongoing Assessment
• Observation Checklist, pp. 40, 42, 46, 48
• Interview, pp. 44, 58, 62
• Anecdotal Report, pp. 52, 60, 66, 68, 70

Portfolio Opportunities
• Chapter Project, p. 37F
• What Do You Know? p. 39
• Investigation, pp. 56–57
• Journal Writing, pp. 39, 44, 54, 63
• Performance Assessment, p. 77
• Self-Assessment: What Do You Think? p. 77

Chapter Objectives	Standardized Test Correlations
2A Write, compare, order, and round money amounts	CAT, SAT, ITBS, CTBS,TN*
2B Count money and make change	CAT, SAT, ITBS, CTBS,TN*
2C Estimate the sums and differences of numbers, including money amounts	MAT, CAT, SAT, CTBS,TN*
2D Add and subtract numbers, including money amounts	MAT, CAT, SAT, ITBS, CTBS,TN*
2E Solve problems, including those that involve addition, subtraction, and choosing the operation	MAT, CAT, SAT, ITBS, CTBS,TN*

*Terra Nova

NCTM Standards Grades K–4

1 Problem Solving	8 Whole Number Computation
2 Communication	9 Geometry and Spatial Sense
3 Reasoning	10 Measurement
4 Connections	11 Statistics and Probability
5 Estimation	12 Fractions and Decimals
6 Number Sense and Numeration	13 Patterns and Relationships
7 Concepts of Whole Number Operations	

MONEY, ADDITION, AND SUBTRACTION

Meeting Individual Needs

LEARNING STYLES

- • AUDITORY/LINGUISTIC
- • LOGICAL/ANALYTICAL
- • VISUAL/SPATIAL
- • MUSICAL
- • KINESTHETIC
- • SOCIAL
- • INDIVIDUAL

Students who are talented in art, language, and physical activity may better understand mathematical concepts when these concepts are connected to their areas of interest. Use the following activities to stimulate the different learning styles of some of your students.

Social Learners

Set up a store where students can count money, buy single or multiple items, and make change for their purchases. Students can work with a partner; one child can be the merchant, the other the customer.

Kinesthetic Learners

Some students will need more hands-on practice counting money, adding amounts, and making change than others. Have play coins and bills available for students to use when solving money problems.

See Lesson Resources, pp. 39A, 41A, 43A, 45A, 47A, 51A, 57A, 59A, 61A, 65A, 67C, 69A.

GIFTED AND TALENTED

Give students an ad from a supermarket or department store and a specific amount of play money. Invite students to decide on what to buy and how much change they will get back.

Have students collect register receipts listing items bought from supermarkets. Students could survey and graph items that are purchased most often. Register tapes from different stores could be compared. Students could compare prices of popular items like milk, bread, cereal, and fruit to see which stores have better prices.

See also Meeting Individual Needs, pp. 50, 64.

EXTRA SUPPORT

Some students may wish to use play money throughout the chapter. Students may also use graph paper to help align digits before adding.

Specific suggestions for ways to provide extra support to students appear in every lesson in this chapter.

See Meeting Individual Needs, pp. 40, 42, 44, 46, 48, 52, 58, 60, 62, 66.

EARLY FINISHERS

Students who finish their class work early may research shapes of leaves and then draw, color, and label several leaves—preferably, leaves that are not native to their part of the country. (See *Chapter Project*, p. 37F.)

See also Meeting Individual Needs, pp. 40, 42, 44, 46, 50, 52, 58, 64, 66.

LANGUAGE SUPPORT

Students may be unfamiliar with United States currency. Set up a display showing the types of coins, their names, and their values to help students recognize and count U.S. coins. Encourage students to talk about and bring in currency from their countries. Display the currency and have students compare it to U.S. coins.

See also Meeting Individual Needs, p. 63.

ESL APPROPRIATE

INCLUSION

- • For **inclusion** ideas, information, and suggestions, see pp. 48, 63, T15.
- • For **gender fairness** tips, see p. T15.

USING MANIPULATIVES

Building Understanding Set up a store using cards with pictures of items and cards with prices. Have one group of students match prices with items. Have another group add items that are priced to see if they can buy them with a given amount of money. Have the groups switch roles and continue shopping.

Easy-to-Make Manipulatives Play money or paper money can be stored in plastic bags for groups or pairs of students. This will help with its distribution and collection.

ESL ▶ APPROPRIATE

USING COOPERATIVE LEARNING

Partners Check This strategy develops simple teamwork by allowing students to take turns checking and supporting each other's work.

- **Partners take turns doing a section of the work.**
- **Partners take turns checking each other's work for understanding of a procedure or concept.**
- **Partners correct or appreciate each other's work.**

USING LITERATURE

Use the story from *If You Made A Million* to introduce the chapter theme, Smart Shopping. This story is reprinted on pages 4–6 of the Read-Aloud Anthology.

Also available in the Read-Aloud Anthology is the poem "Ode to Los Raspados," page 7.

MONEY, ADDITION, AND SUBTRACTION

Linking Technology

This integrated package of programs and services allows students to explore, develop, and practice concepts; solve problems; build portfolios; and assess their own progress. Teachers can enhance instruction, provide remediation, and share ideas with other educational professionals.

CD-ROM ACTIVITY

In *Dollars for Collars,* students use money models to buy pet supplies, and in *Coupon Craze,* students use money models, a calculator, and the table tool to figure out how much money is saved using coupons. Students can use the online notebook to write about the process they develop. To extend the activity, students use the Math Van tools to complete an open-ended problem related to the concept of adding and subtracting with money. **Available on CD-ROM.**

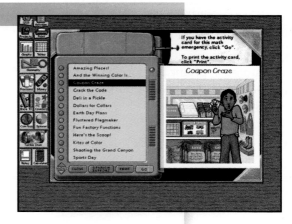

CD-ROM TOOLS

Students can use Math Van's calculator, table, and money models to explore the concepts of adding and subtracting whole numbers using money. The Tech Links on the Lesson Resources pages highlight opportunities for students to use these and other tools such as online notes to provide additional practice, reteaching, or extension. **Available on CD-ROM.**

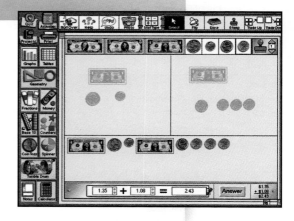

WEB SITE   http://www.mhschool.com

Teachers can access the McGraw-Hill School Division World Wide Web site for additional curriculum support at http://www.mhschool.com. Click on our Resource Village for specially designed activities linking Web sites to addition and subtraction. Motivate children by inviting them to explore Web sites that develop the chapter theme of "Smart Shopping." Exchange ideas on classroom management, cultural diversity, and other areas in the Math Forum.

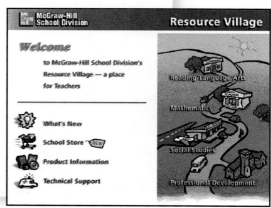

Chapter Project FALL SALE

Highlighting the Math

- collect, organize, and display data
- add and subtract whole numbers, and operate with money
- plan, schedule, and conduct a whole-class event

1 Starting the Project

Introduce the idea of a Fall Sale. Elicit from students items that they can make and sell: leaf placemats, leaf bookmarks, fall postcards, fall recipe cards. Then have them mention the tasks involved in planning and holding the sale:

setting a date and time
creating the items for sale
determining prices
deciding upon and creating the booths

Elicit a list of possible booths, writing each suggestion on the chalkboard. Students will make all displays or items for sale. Consider how family and community members may participate.

2 Continuing the Project

- Each group decides upon a booth. Group members make items for display or sale.
- Group members decide upon prices and attach price-stickers to their items.
- One group makes a poster announcing the Fall Sale and invites another class to attend. The poster may also issue an invitation to parents.

3 Finishing the Project

Hold the sale during a holiday season as part of a larger school arts-and-crafts festival and invite the parents to attend. Have students keep a written list recording the items and amount of each sale.

Community Involvement
Have students donate any profits to a charitable organization—for example, Muscular Dystrophy Association, the March of Dimes, Ronald McDonald House. Have them draft a letter to the organization of their choice, making the donation.

BUILDING A PORTFOLIO

Each student's portfolio should include a photo of their booth, the amount of money earned, and an individual summary of the math used to complete this project.

To assess students' work, refer to the Holistic Scoring Guide on page 27 in the Teacher's Assessment Resources.

CHAPTER 2 ORGANIZER

PURPOSE Introduce the theme of the chapter.

Resources Read-Aloud Anthology, pages 4–6.

Using Literature

Read "If You Made a Million" from the Read-Aloud Anthology to introduce the chapter theme, Smart Shopping.

Developing the Theme

Ask students what *smart shopping* means to them. Encourage discussion of factors, in addition to price, to be considered in deciding where to shop and which products to buy. Factors students mention may include: cost of travel to different stores, personal preferences, quantity of items needed, money available, and so on.

These shopping situations are presented in this chapter:

Flea market	pp. 40–41	Sports store	pp. 55, 60–61
Street fair	pp. 42–43	Catalog	pp. 58–59
Clothing store	pp. 44–45	Fund raiser	pp. 62–63
Toy store	pp. 46–47	Hardware store	pp. 66–67
Trading post	pp. 48–49	Festival	pp. 68–69
Video store	pp. 52–53		

On pages 60–61, students will make decisions about how they would spend $400.

Students may wish to keep track of the different places they shop over a one-week period. They can then create a class list and sort the stores into categories such as food, clothing, music, and so on.

CHAPTER

2

MONEY, ADDITION, AND SUBTRACTION

THEME Smart Shopping

Smart shoppers always save money! In this chapter, you will decide if you will use coupons, buy at a sale, go to a street fair, or buy from a store.

38

Chapter Bibliography

Arthur's Funny Money by Lillian Hoban. New York: HarperCollins Children's Books, 1981. ISBN 0–06–022344–8.

"Big Business" from *Max Malone Makes a Million* by Charlotte Herman. New York: Henry Holt & Company, 1991. ISBN 0–8050–2328–3.

Smart Spending: A Consumer's Guide by Lois Schmitt. New York: Simon & Schuster Books for Young Readers, 1989. ISBN 0–684–19035–4.

Community Involvement

Have students start a Smart Shopper newsletter written for second, third, and fourth graders. Students can work in groups of five to choose a popular game, toy, video, or fad item, then use a telephone directory to research stores in the community that sell it. An editorial team can then organize the data, write one or two opinion columns, and make copies for the class to distribute to local stores, playgrounds, and schools.

3. Check students' answers. Possible answer: Rounded up each price for the plants

What Do You Know ?

and the peat moss to the nearest dollar and added to make sure that the total

Use the information in the price list for problems 1–3. was less than $50.00.

Farmstand Prices

Apples: 69¢ for each pound
Pumpkins: 29¢ for each pound
Large Bag of Peat Moss: $7.99
Small Bag of Peat Moss: $5.75
Large Mum Plant: $5.99
Small Mum Plant: $2.99

1 What is the cost of 2 pounds of apples and a 3-pound pumpkin? **$2.25**

2 **What if** you pay for 1 large mum, 1 small mum, and 1 small bag of peat moss with one $10 bill and two $5 bills. What will be the change? Give three ways to show the change. **$5.27; see page T17.**

3 You have $50.00 to spend at the farm stand. Make a list of the items you can buy with your money. You can buy more than one of each item. Explain how you decided which items to buy. **See above.**

Write a Paragraph A paragraph is a group of sentences about one idea. The first sentence often states the idea. The other sentences tell more about the idea.

Suppose you went to a farm stand. Use the price list above to write a paragraph telling what you bought and how much you spent.

1 What is the topic of your paragraph? **shopping at the farm stand**
Answers may vary. Possible answers: items
2 What details did you include? **bought, prices, total spent**

Vocabulary

estimate, p. 46
sum, p. 46
regroup, p. 48

Associative Property, p. 52
Commutative Property, p. 52

difference, p. 58
subtract, p. 58

Money, Addition, and Subtraction **39**

Reading, Writing, Arithmetic

Write a Paragraph Invite volunteers to read aloud their paragraphs. Ask other students to identify the topic and details in the paragraphs. You might also wish to show students examples of paragraphs in which the main idea is not stated in the first sentence.

Vocabulary

 Students may record new words in their journals. Encourage them to show examples and draw diagrams to help tell what the words mean.

- **Write an addition sentence. Draw a circle around the addends. Draw a box around the sum.**

$$(100) + (45) = \boxed{145}$$

PURPOSE Assess students' ability to apply prior knowledge of adding and subtracting whole numbers and money amounts.

Materials have available: place-value models, play money, calculators (optional)

Assessing Prior Knowledge

Ask volunteers to give examples of problems that can be solved by adding or subtracting. For example:

PROBLEMS THAT CAN BE SOLVED BY

Adding	Subtracting
Joan spent $3 for a book and $2 for notebook paper. How much did she spend altogether?	There were 25 students in our class until 2 students moved away. How many students are in our class now?
Jim has $5.00. He already spent $0.25 for pretzels. How much did he have before	I had 12 cookies. I gave away all but 4. How many did I give away?

Encourage students to use whatever methods they wish to answer items 1–3. Observe them as they work. Notice students' explanations of their method for item 3.

BUILDING A PORTFOLIO

 Item 3 can be used as a benchmark to show where students are in their understanding of adding and subtracting money amounts.

A Portfolio Checklist for Students and a Checklist for Teachers are provided in Teacher's Assessment Resources, pp. 33–34.

Prerequisite Skills

- *Do students know basic addition and subtraction facts?*
- *Do students realize when to add and when to subtract?*
- *Can students show money amounts using coins and bills?*

Assessment Resources

DIAGNOSTIC INVENTORY
Use this blackline master to assess prerequisite skills that students will need in order to be successful in this chapter.

TEST MASTERS
Use the multiple choice format (form A or B) or the free response format (form C) as a pretest of the skills in this chapter.

LESSON

2.1

EXPLORE ACTIVITY

Count Money and Make Change

OBJECTIVE Count on to find amounts of money and make change.

RESOURCE REMINDER
Math Center Cards 9
Practice 9, Reteach 9, Extend 9

SKILLS TRACE	
GRADE 3	• Explore naming the bills and coins needed to equal a given amount. Make change by counting on. *(Chapter 3)*
GRADE 4	• Count on to find amounts of money and make change.
GRADE 5	• Read/write money amounts. *(Chapter 1)* • Subtract money amounts. *(Chapter 2)*

MANIPULATIVE WARM-UP

Cooperative Pairs   **Kinesthetic**

OBJECTIVE Review reading, writing, and representing money amounts.

Materials per pair: 0–9 spinner (TA 2); play money—1 five-dollar bill, 5 one-dollar bills, 5 quarters, 5 dimes, 5 nickels, 10 pennies

▶ One student in each pair spins three numbers and writes them in order as a money amount. For example, if the numbers 2, 3, and 8 are spun, $2.38 is written. The student reads the amount written.

▶ The other student shows the amount using bills and coins.

▶ Students switch roles and repeat the activity.

ESL APPROPRIATE

STATISTICS CONNECTION

Cooperative Groups   **Logical/Analytical**

OBJECTIVE Connect making a line plot with sorting and recording coins.

Materials per group: play coins; centimeter graph paper (TA 7)

▶ Guide students in making a line plot with the labels *1¢, 5¢, 10¢, 25¢,* and *50¢* under five columns on the graph paper.

▶ Students in each group sort their pile of coins by value, arranging them into a column of pennies, a column of nickels, and so on. They count the number of coins in each column. On the graph paper, they place an "X" in a corresponding number of squares.

▶ Ask groups to identify the column on their graph with the greatest number of coins, and the column that represents the greatest value.

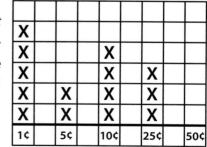

1¢	5¢	10¢	25¢	50¢
X				
X		X		
X		X	X	
X	X	X	X	
X	X	X	X	

ESL APPROPRIATE

Daily Review

Math Van

PREVIOUS DAY QUICK REVIEW

Complete the different names for 3,000,000.
1. thousands *[3,000]*
2. ten thousands *[300]*
3. hundred thousands *[30]*

FAST FACTS

1. 6 + 8 *[14]*
2. 7 + 3 *[10]*
3. 8 + 8 *[16]*
4. 5 + 4 *[9]*

Problem of the Day • 9

Write all the whole numbers that would give a total less than 15.

___ + 6 + 3 *[1, 2, 3, 4, 5]*

TECH LINK

ONLINE EXPLORATION

Use other Web-linked activities and lesson plans to connect your students to the real world of smart shopping.

MATH VAN

Activity You may wish to use *Dollars for Collars* to teach this lesson.

Visit our Resource Village at http://www.mhschool.com to access the Online Exploration and the Math Forum.

MATH CENTER

Practice

OBJECTIVE Count amounts of money.

Materials per pair: play money—coins

Student pairs decide on a coin to leave out of the game. Then they take turns showing amounts of money with all other coins.

PRACTICE ACTIVITY 9

MATH CENTER
Partners

Manipulatives • Change by the Rules

YOU NEED
play money—coins

• Select a type of coin that you will not use, such as a dime. Set all of those coins aside.
• Name an amount of money under $1.00. Be sure you can show that amount with the coins you are using.
• Your partner shows that amount of money using the coins that are left.
• Trade roles. Play until you each have five turns.
• Play again. This time set aside a different kind of coin.

NCTM Standards

    Problem Solving
✓ Communication
✓ Reasoning
✓ Connections

Chapter 2, Lesson 1, pages 40–41

Money

ESL APPROPRIATE

Problem Solving

OBJECTIVE Decide on usefulness of pennies.

Materials per student: Math Center Recording Sheet (TA 31 optional)

Students present an opinion about the use of pennies and explain their reasoning in a paragraph. *[Encourage students to support their opinions with at least three reasons.]*

PROBLEM-SOLVING ACTIVITY 9

MATH CENTER
On Your Own

Decision Making • Pennies or Not?

Some people have suggested that we don't need pennies.
• Think about times when pennies are useful. Think about why having no pennies might make things easier.
• What do you think? Should we keep pennies or should we stop using them? Write a paragraph explaining your opinion. Include at least three reasons to support your idea.

NCTM Standards

✓ Problem Solving
    Communication
✓ Reasoning
✓ Connections

Chapter 2, Lesson 1, pages 40–41

Money

Lesson 2.1 *continued*

EXPLORE ACTIVITY
Count Money and Make Change

OBJECTIVE Count up to find amounts of money and make change.

Materials per pair: play money—1 ten-dollar bill, 1 five-dollar bill, 4 one-dollar bills, 4 quarters, 5 dimes, 5 nickels, 10 pennies

 Introduce

Ask students to describe purchases they make in the cafeteria or school store. Encourage them to discuss their methods of calculating change.

• **How do you know you are getting the correct amount of change?** *[Answers may vary.]*

 Teach　　　　　　*Cooperative Pairs*

▶ **LEARN Work Together** After one student selects an item, pays for it, and his or her partner makes change, have the student verify the amount of change given.

When pairs compare methods, have each try the other's methods. Ask students which method they like best, and why.

MAKE CONNECTIONS

The diagram models *counting up* to find change using the least number of coins. You may want to have students model Martina's solution using play money. Ask students to identify the two steps involved: using coins and bills to count up from the price to the payment given, and counting the coins and bills to find the amount of change.

Have students find other coins to show the change. They should realize that although the coins used to make the change may vary, the total value remains the same.

 Close

▶ **Check for Understanding** using items 1–4, page 41.

CRITICAL THINKING
Before students answer item 4, ask:
• **How do you know when you have found the change with the least number of coins and bills?** *[You can't exchange any of the coins or bills for a greater coin or bill.]*

▶ **PRACTICE**
Materials have available: calculators
Assign exercises 1–10 as independent work.
• You may want to have students draw the money amounts in ex. 4–7.

Count Money and Make Change

Go shopping at the flea market!

Work Together
Work with a partner. Choose an item you would like to buy. Pay for the item with one of the bills shown.

Have your partner use play money to find the change.

You will need
• play money— bills and coins

▶ Discuss your methods with another group. How do they compare? **Methods may include subtraction or counting up in various ways.**

Make Connections
Martina buys a puzzle with $5. She counts up to $5 to find the coins and bills she will get in change.

Think:

Start at
$2.35.　　$2.40　→　$2.50　→　$2.75　→　$3.00　→　$4.00　→　$5.00

40　Lesson 2.1

Meeting Individual Needs

Early Finishers

Using the flea market items, students can write a word problem. Have them illustrate the coins and bills used in their answers.

Extra Support

While making change by counting up from the price to the amount paid, some students may forget the amount paid. You might suggest students keep the amount paid in sight until change has been given.

ESL **APPROPRIATE**

Ongoing Assessment

Observation Checklist Determine if students can make change by observing if they count up from the price and give the change using the least number of coins.

Follow Up Students who are adept at making change can show the change in ex. 8-10 using two different combinations of coins and bills. Also assign **Extend 9.**

For students having difficulty making change, assign **Reteach 9.**

Possible answer: Count up to find the change, then exchange groups of 5 pennies for 1 nickel, groups of 2 nickels for a dime, groups of 2 dimes and 1 nickel for 1 quarter, and groups of 5 dimes for 2 quarters.

To find the amount of change, Martina counts the bills and coins.

Think:

$1.00 → $2.00 → $2.25 → $2.50 → $2.60 → $2.65

The amount of change is $2.65.

- What other coins could you use to count from $2.35 to $3.00? **Answers may vary. Possible answer: 4 dimes and 1 quarter**

- **What if** there are no quarters. How can you find the change to $5? **Possible answer: Use 1 nickel, 6 dimes, and 2 one-dollar bills.**

Check for Understanding

Find the amount of change that will be given.

1. Cost: $2.75
   Amount given: $5.00
   $2.25

2. Cost: $3.98
   Amount given: $5.00
   $1.02

3. Cost: $8.20
   Amount given: $10.00
   $1.80

Critical Thinking: Analyze   Explain your reasoning.

4. What method can you use to give change with the least number of coins and bills? **See above.**

Practice

Write the money amount.

1.  **$3.76**

2.  **$7.81**

3.  **$17.15**   Answers may vary. Possible answers given.

Show the amount of money in two different ways.

4. 67¢ **2 quarters, dime, 7 pennies**
5. 98¢ **9 dimes, 8 pennies**
6. $3.42 **3 one-dollar bills, 4 dimes, 2 pennies**
7. $12.54 **1 ten-dollar bill, 2 one-dollar bills, 2 quarters, 4 pennies**

Find the amount of change.

8. Cost: 47¢
   Amount given: $1.00
   $0.53

9. Cost: $2.15
   Amount given: $5.00
   $2.85

10. Cost: $6.42
    Amount given: $10.00
    $3.58

Extra Practice, page 488   Money, Addition, and Subtraction   **41**

Alternate Teaching Strategy

Materials per pair: play money—1 five-dollar bill, 4 one-dollar bills, 4 quarters, 5 dimes, 5 nickels, 10 pennies; hundred chart (TA 1).

Present this problem:

> Tina bought shampoo for $3.29. She gave the cashier a $5 bill. How much change should she get?

Explain to students that they will use the hundred chart to keep track of the change.

- Locate 29 on the chart.
- Place a penny on 30, a dime on 40, another dime on 50, a quarter on 75, and a quarter on 100. Count out loud, "Three dollars and 30 cents, three dollars and 40 cents, three dollars and 50 cents, three dollars and 75 cents, four dollars."
- Add a dollar bill to this amount and count up to five dollars.
- Count the bill and coins and identify the change as $1.71.

Continue the activity posing other problems with items costing less than $10.

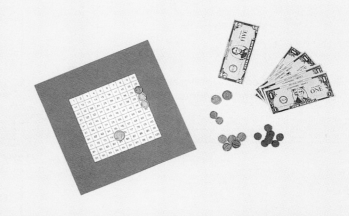

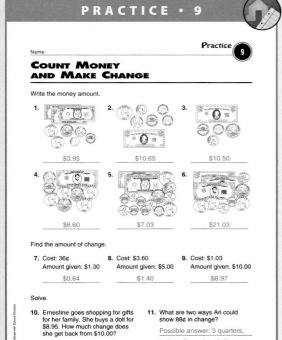

Practice 9

Name:

COUNT MONEY AND MAKE CHANGE

Write the money amount.

1. $3.95
2. $10.65
3. $10.50
4. $6.60
5. $7.03
6. $21.03

Find the amount of change.

7. Cost: 36¢
   Amount given: $1.00
   $0.64

8. Cost: $3.60
   Amount given: $5.00
   $1.40

9. Cost: $1.03
   Amount given: $10.00
   $8.97

Solve.

10. Ernestine goes shopping for gifts for her family. She buys a doll for $8.95. How much change does she get back from $10.00?
    $1.05

11. What are two ways Ari could show 88¢ in change?
    Possible answer: 3 quarters, 1 dime, 3 pennies; 6 dimes, 5 nickels, 3 pennies

---

Reteach 9

Name:

COUNT MONEY AND MAKE CHANGE

To make change, you begin with the cost. Then you count up to the amount given to you. Use the fewest number of bills or coins possible.

You sell a cookie for 20¢. Someone gives you $1.

Think: Change = 80¢

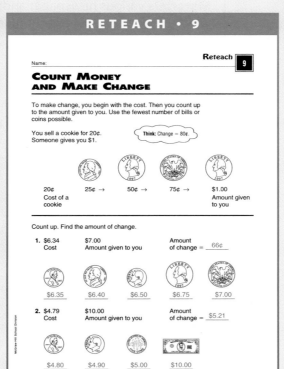

20¢ → 25¢ → 50¢ → 75¢ → $1.00
Cost of a cookie   Amount given to you

Count up. Find the amount of change.

1. $6.34 $7.00   Amount
   Cost   Amount given to you   of change = 66¢

   $6.35 $6.40 $6.50 $6.75 $7.00

2. $4.79 $10.00   Amount
   Cost   Amount given to you   of change = $5.21

   $4.80 $4.90 $5.00 $10.00

Extend 9

Name:

COUNT MONEY AND MAKE CHANGE

Change Exchange

You need: play money—coins and bills

What's in each bucket? Use play money to find at least three ways to make each amount of money. One way has to be the least number of coins and bills possible to make that amount. Record your answers.

Answers may vary. The least number of coins and bills is given.

1. 25¢
   1 quarter

2. 36¢
   1 quarter, 1 dime, 1 penny

3. 74¢
   2 quarters, 2 dimes, 4 pennies

4. 55¢
   1 half dollar, 1 nickel

5. $1.15
   1 dollar bill, 1 dime, 1 nickel

6. $1.75
   1 dollar bill, 1 half dollar, 1 quarter

7. $1.85
   1 dollar bill, 1 half dollar, 1 quarter, 1 dime

8. $2.07
   2 dollar bills, 1 nickel, 2 pennies

9. $2.12
   2 dollar bills, 1 dime, 2 pennies

LESSON 2.2

Compare, Order, and Round Money

OBJECTIVE Compare, order, and round money.

RESOURCE REMINDER
Math Center Cards 10
Practice 10, Reteach 10, Extend 10

SKILLS TRACE

GRADE 3	• Compare, order, and round money amounts. *(Chapter 3)*
GRADE 4	• Compare, order, and round money amounts.
GRADE 5	• Compare, order, and round money amounts. *(Chapter 1)*

WARM-UP

Cooperative Pairs   **Logical/Analytical**

OBJECTIVE Compare and order grocery store coupons.

Materials per pair: 12 grocery store coupons

▶ Give each partner 6 coupons. They arrange their coupons from least to greatest amount. Partners check each other's work.

▶ They select two of their partner's coupons, double the amounts, write the new amount on the coupons, and return them.

▶ Each partner orders the coupons from least to greatest using the new amounts.

▶ Partners then combine coupons and order all from least to greatest.

CONSUMER CONNECTION

Whole Class   **Visual/Spatial**

OBJECTIVE Connect comparing prices and consumer skills.

Materials various newspaper and magazine ads showing the same items, which cost up to $100; tape or glue, markers or crayons, posterboard

▶ Each student chooses and cuts out pictures and descriptions of the same item from various advertisements. Students then arrange the information on posters.

▶ Students can compare prices and benefits and decide from which store they would buy their items. Allow time for students to display and discuss their posters.

Daily Review

PREVIOUS DAY QUICK REVIEW

Find the amount of change from $5.

1. Cost: $1.59 [$3.41]
2. Cost: $4.28 [$0.72]
3. Cost: $3.73 [$1.27]
4. Cost: $2.07 [$2.93]

FAST FACTS

1. 9 + 4 [13]
2. 2 + 7 [9]
3. 8 + 7 [15]
4. 4 + 9 [13]

Problem of the Day • 10

Julio has $1.50 in quarters and nickels. He has the same number of quarters and nickels. How many coins does Julio have? [10 coins— 5 quarters and 5 nickels]

TECH LINK

MATH VAN

Tool You may wish to use the Money tool with this lesson.

MATH FORUM

Combination Classes I pair different-level students and have the higher-level student use play money to show two different money amounts. The lower-level student determines which of the two amounts is greater.

Visit our Resource Village at http://www.mhschool.com to see more of the Math Forum.

MATH CENTER

Practice

OBJECTIVE Round money to the nearest $0.10, $1.00, and $10.00.

Materials per group: 0–9 spinner (TA 2); per student: Math Center Recording Sheet (TA 31 optional)

Students round sums of money and discuss the effects of rounding to different places. *[Sample observation: Rounding to the nearest dime gives the greatest number if the ones and tens places are less than 5. Rounding to the nearest ten dollars gives the greatest number if the ones place is at least 5 and the tens place is less than 5.]*

PRACTICE ACTIVITY 10

MATH CENTER
Small Group

Number Sense • More Money

Copy these blanks onto your paper.

$ _____ _____ . _____ _____

- Each person chooses a different amount to round to: the nearest dime, dollar, and ten dollars.
- One person in your group spins the spinner. Everyone fills in the first blank with the number. Repeat until all the blanks are filled. Everyone in the group should have the same number.
- Each person rounds the number according to his or her amount. Compare each rounded number to see whose is greatest. Did everyone round the same way (up or down)? Why or why not? Change roles and play several times. Discuss which rounded number was most often the greatest. Explain why you think this is so.

Chapter 2, Lesson 2, pages 42–43

YOU NEED
spinner (0–9)

$1790 < $18.00 < $20.00
least ($17.86) greatest

NCTM Standards

✓ Problem Solving
✓ Communication
✓ Reasoning
  Connections

Money

Grade Level 4   McGraw-Hill School Division

Problem Solving

OBJECTIVE Round 5-digit money amounts.

Materials per group: 0–9 spinner (TA 2); per student: Math Center Recording Sheet (TA 31 optional)

Students use the same four digits to write an ordered list of 5-digit money amounts. *[Check students' work.]*

PROBLEM-SOLVING ACTIVITY 10

MATH CENTER
Small Group

Logical Reasoning • Round Up, Round Down

- One player spins to get four digits for the group.
- Each player uses the digits to write five different money amounts. Each money amount must have five digits. You must use all four digits in each amount. Repeat any digit you want.
- Now each player orders their amounts from least to greatest.
- The first player who finishes correctly gets 1 point.
- The first player to earn 5 points wins the game.

Chapter 2, Lesson 2, pages 42–43

YOU NEED
spinner (0–9)

$884.35
$543.84
$445.83
$435.48
$344.85

NCTM Standards

✓ Problem Solving
  Communication
✓ Reasoning
✓ Connections

Money

Grade Level 4   McGraw-Hill School Division

Compare, Order, and Round Money

OBJECTIVE Compare, order, and round money.

Materials have available: play money

 Introduce

Write the following on the chalkboard: $3.25 and $3.62.
Have students discuss the following:

- **How could you compare these two amounts?** *[Possible answer: Compare the numbers in the greatest place, the dollar place, and continue comparing place by place until the two numbers are different.]*
- **At which place would you stop comparing? Explain.** *[The dimes place; the two numbers are different.]*

2 Teach   *Whole Class*

▶ **LEARN** Discuss with students the steps they used to compare whole numbers in the previous chapter. Ask:

- **How is comparing money amounts the same as comparing whole numbers?** *[Each place has to be compared, beginning with the greatest place, until you find a place that has different digits.]*
- **Which do you compare first, dollars or cents? Why?** *[Dollars; dollars are greater than cents.]*

You may wish to review the different notations for cents. For example, point out that 5 cents may be shown as $0.05 or 5¢.

Students may use play money to help them compare and order money amounts.

3 Close

▶ **Check for Understanding** using items 1–8, page 42.

CRITICAL THINKING
After students answer item 8, ask:

- **Name a money amount that would round to $500 whether it was rounded to the nearest dollar, ten dollars, or hundred dollars.** *[Possible answers include all amounts greater than $499.49 and less than $500.50.]*

▶ **PRACTICE**
Materials have available: calculators

Options for assigning exercises:
A—Odd ex. 1–23; **Mixed Review**
B—Even ex. 2–24; **Mixed Review**

- For ex. 1–6, review the *less than* and *greater than* symbols.
- Point out that for ex. 17–20 students should list any item that costs the same as or less than the amount shown.

Mixed Review In ex. 1–3, students review writing numbers in standard form, a skill learned in Chapter 1. In ex. 4–6, students compare greater numbers, a skill learned in Chapter 1.

Compare, Order, and Round Money

Suppose you have saved up for a skateboard. Which of these costs the least? the most?

Compare prices.
Show each amount using play money.

Step 1	Step 2	Step 3
Compare the three amounts	Compare the other two amounts.	Write the amounts in order from least to greatest.
$17.99 **Think:** 5 < 7, so $15.99 $15.99 is the least. $17.25	$17.99 **Think:** 2 < 9, so $17.25 $17.25 < $17.99.	$15.99, $17.25, $17.99

The Thunder costs the least. The Red Flash costs the most.

Which costs about $16.00?
Round each amount to the nearest dollar. $17.99 → $18.00
$15.99 → $16.00
$17.25 → $17.00

The Thunder, at $15.99, costs about $16.00.

Check for Understanding

Show each amount. Then write the amounts in order from least to greatest.

1 $8.43, $10.89, $5.75
$5.75, $8.43, $10.89

2 $37.99, $73.15, $35.50
$35.50, $37.99, $73.15

Round to the nearest dollar and to the nearest 10¢. $232.00, $231.90

3 $4.35   **4** $9.80   **5** $16.55   **6** $99.90   **7** $231.85
$4.00, $4.40 $10.00, $9.80 $17.00, $16.60 $100.00, $99.90

Critical Thinking: Analyze   Explain your reasoning.

8 Beth rounded $463.65 to $500.00. Sam rounded it to $460.00. Alicia rounded it to $463.70. Which one is correct? **See below.**

All are correct—$463.65 to the nearest $100 is $500, to the
42 Lesson 2.2   nearest $10 is $460, and to the nearest 10¢ is $463.70.

Meeting Individual Needs

Early Finishers

Have students practice rounding to the nearest $0.10, $1, $10, and $100 using **Check for Understanding** items 3–7.

Extra Support

Use play money to model $10, $9.19, and $9.25. Order the amounts by comparing the value of the bills and coins. Point out that a money amount with a greater number of digits does not always have the greater value.

ESL> APPROPRIATE

Ongoing Assessment

Observation Checklist Determine if students can compare and order money by observing if they begin comparing the greatest place first then each consecutive place until a different digit is reached.

Follow Up If students have difficulty comparing and rounding money amounts, review rounding and comparing skills using materials from the previous chapter. For students needing additional help, assign **Reteach 10.**

For students who would like a challenge, assign **Extend 10.**

Practice

Compare. Write >, <, or =.

1 $6.58 ● $4.30 **>**   **2** $0.89 ● $1.65 **<**   **3** 88¢ ● 49¢ **>**

4 $37.56 ● $9.98 **>**   **5** $156.18 ● $159.14 **<**   **6** $3,889.99 ● $3,890.99 **<**

Write in order from greatest to least.

7 $8.52, $8.25, $8.79
$8.79, $8.52, $8.25

8 $27.15, $7.98, $14.35, $14.85
$27.15, $14.85, $14.35, $7.98

9 $38.10, $3.81, $38.81, $8.38
$38.81, $38.10, $8.38, $3.81

10 $47.50, $147.50, $4.75, $47.05
$147.50, $47.50, $47.05, $4.75

Round.

11 $7.42 to the nearest dollar **$7.00**

12 $0.98 to the nearest dollar **$1.00**

13 $7.12 to the nearest 10¢ **$7.10**

14 $14.49 to the nearest 10¢ **$14.50**

15 $6.50 to the nearest $10 **$10.00**

16 $27.49 to the nearest $10 **$30.00**

Tell what item or items can be Answers may vary.
bought with the amount. Possible answers are
given.

17 $5.00 markers and
poster board

18 $10.00 poster board
and brushes

19 $15.00

20 $20.00

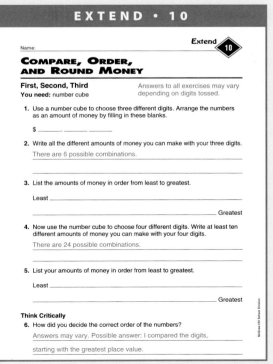

MIXED APPLICATIONS
Problem Solving

21 At the street fair, Loni buys a book for $2.29 and hands the clerk a five-dollar bill. What amount should she receive in change? **$2.71**

22 Sam buys a T-shirt for $6.69 and gives the cashier $20.00. What is the least number of bills and coins he can receive? **See below.**

23 If you have 5 quarters and 11 dimes, do you have enough to buy a ball for $2.00? Why or why not? **See below.**

24 **Write a problem** about buying items shown above. Solve it and have others solve it. **Students should compare problems and solutions.**

mixed review • test preparation

Write the number in standard form.

1 1,000 + 200 + 4
1,204

2 six hundred thousand
600,000

3 80,000 + 4,000 + 900
84,900

Compare. Write >, <, or =.

4 7,510 ● 7,502 **>**

5 11,600 ● 11,690 **<**

6 24,893 ● 106,000 **<**

22. 4 bills and 3 coins: 1 ten-dollar bill, 3 one-dollar bills, 1 quarter, 1 nickel, 1 penny

23. Yes; 5 quarters > $1, 11 dimes > $1, so you have more than $2.

Extra Practice, page 488

Money, Addition, and Subtraction **43**

Alternate Teaching Strategy

Present this problem:

- **One store sells notebooks for $1.50 each. Another store sells the same notebooks for $1.25 each. Which price is less?**

Draw the number line below on the chalkboard.

$0.00 $0.50 $1.00 $1.50 $2.00 $2.50 $3.00 $3.50 $4.00 $4.50 $5.00

Have students mark the prices on the number line to show that $1.25 is less than $1.50.

Continue the activity, having students use the number line to answer additional questions such as:

- **A discount store is having a sale. They are selling the same notebooks for $1.37 each. Is this price greater than or less than $1.25?** [greater than]
- **Which amount is $3.25 closer to on the number line, $3.00 or $4.00?** [$3.00]
- **What would $3.25 rounded to the nearest dollar be? To the nearest ten cents?** [$3.00; $3.30]

PRACTICE • 10

Name: _____

Practice **10**

COMPARE, ORDER, AND ROUND MONEY

Write in order from least to greatest.

1. $9.80, $8.90, $9.98 $8.90, $9.80, $9.98

2. $33.50, $29.50, $602.50 $29.50, $33.50, $602.50

3. $8,203, $5,807, $5,817 $5,807, $5,817, $8,203

4. $23.98, $465.23, $347.76, $238.65 $23.98, $238.65, $347.76, $465.23

5. $3,345.40, $3,256.40, $3,767.40 $3,256.40, $3,345.40, $3,767.40

6. $2,378.42, $2,678.42, $2,234.73 $2,234.73, $2,378.42, $2,678.42

Round.

7. $2.35 to the nearest dollar $2.00

8. $7.95 to the nearest dollar $8.00

9. $23.99 to the nearest dollar $24.00

10. $24.37 to the nearest dollar $24.00

11. $0.18 to the nearest 10¢ $0.20

12. $4.23 to the nearest 10¢ $4.20

13. $16.76 to the nearest 10¢ $16.80

14. $24.32 to the nearest 10¢ $24.30

15. $8.70 to the nearest $10 $10.00

16. $67.34 to the nearest $10 $70.00

17. $13.98 to the nearest $10 $10.00

18. $87.34 to the nearest $10 $90.00

Solve.

19. Sam has $1,045 in his savings account. Lisa has $1,134 in her savings account. Who has more money saved?
Lisa has more.

20. Sam bought a stamp for $12.67. What is this amount rounded to the nearest dollar?
$13.00

RETEACH • 10

Name: _____

Reteach **10**

COMPARE, ORDER, AND ROUND MONEY

To compare amounts of money, you can line up the cents points. Then start comparing at the left.

$28.87
$31.22

2 < 3, so $28.87 < $31.22.

$46.35
$42.79

same
6 > 2, so $46.35 > $42.79.

You can round money amounts to the nearest dollar. When there are 0 to 49 cents, round down to the nearest dollar. When there are 50 to 99 cents, round up.

$38.31 $38.50 $38.74

$38.00 $38.10 $38.20 $38.30 $38.40 $38.50 $38.60 $38.70 $38.80 $38.90 $39.00

$38.31 rounds to $38.00.
$38.50 rounds to $39.00.
$38.74 rounds to $39.00.

Compare. Write >, <, or =.

1. $48.26
$53.26
4 < 5
$48.26 < $53.26

2. $107.15
$105.15
1 = 1
7 > 5
$107.15 > $105.15

3. $53.78 > $34.45

4. $86.45 < $94.65

5. $245.28 < $346.97

6. $19.99 < $119.00

Round to the nearest dollar.

7. $26.90 $27.00

8. $11.48 $11.00

9. $198.44 $198.00

10. $675.19 $675.00

11. $989.85 $990.00

12. $259.56 $260.00

EXTEND • 10

Name: _____

Extend **10**

COMPARE, ORDER, AND ROUND MONEY

First, Second, Third
You need: number cube

Answers to all exercises may vary depending on digits tossed.

1. Use a number cube to choose three different digits. Arrange the numbers as an amount of money by filling in these blanks.

$ _____ . _____

2. Write all the different amounts of money you can make with your three digits.
There are 6 possible combinations.

3. List the amounts of money in order from least to greatest.

Least _____

_____ Greatest

4. Now use the number cube to choose four different digits. Write at least ten different amounts of money you can make with your four digits.
There are 24 possible combinations.

5. List your amounts of money in order from least to greatest.

Least _____

_____ Greatest

Think Critically

6. How did you decide the correct order of the numbers?
Answers may vary. Possible answer: I compared the digits, starting with the greatest place value.

43

LESSON 2.3

MENTAL MATH

Addition Strategies

OBJECTIVE Use strategies to add mentally.

RESOURCE REMINDER
Math Center Cards 11
Practice 11, Reteach 11, Extend 11

SKILLS TRACE

GRADE 3	• Use strategies to add 2-to 3-digit numbers mentally. *(Chapter 3)*
GRADE 4	• Use strategies to add 3-digit numbers mentally.
GRADE 5	• Use strategies to add whole numbers mentally. *(Chapter 2)*

WARM-UP

Cooperative Pairs   **Logical/Analytical**

OBJECTIVE Explore mentally adding 1-digit numbers to 1- and 2-digit numbers.

Materials per pair: 0-9 spinner (TA 2)

► One partner spins a number, mentally adds it to zero, states the addition sentence aloud, and records the sum. The other partner spins a number, mentally adds it to the sum recorded, states the new addition sentence aloud, and records the new sum.

► The game continues with players taking turns spinning a number, adding it to the previous sum, and recording the new sum, until they record a sum of 100 or greater. Players can count the number of turns it took to reach 100, and then play again to see if it takes them more or fewer turns the second time.

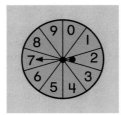

ALGEBRA CONNECTION

Cooperative Groups   **Logical/Analytical**

OBJECTIVE Connect reasoning and addition skills with finding missing numbers.

Materials per group: slips of paper

Write the following incomplete number sentence on the chalkboard:
$14 - \blacksquare = 8$

► Ask groups to find the missing number, allowing time for each group to share the methods they used.

► On slips of paper have students write incomplete number sentences in which a missing number is subtracted from a 2-digit number to give a 1-digit difference. Within groups have students pass the slips of paper around then find the missing numbers. Group members check answers with each other.

Daily Review

PREVIOUS DAY *QUICK REVIEW*

Compare.
1. $7.53__$7.39 *[>]*
2. $18.09__$19.01 *[<]*
3. $237.25__$239.25 *[<]*
4. $554.98__$554.89 *[>]*

FAST FACTS

1. 6 + 3 *[9]*
2. 2 + 9 *[11]*
3. 8 + 7 *[15]*
4. 3 + 4 *[7]*

Problem of the Day • 11

Peter is setting up cones as borders along a race track. The track is 24 yards long. One cone is placed on either side at the start, and then every 8 feet. How many cones will Peter need? *[11 cones]*

TECH LINK

MATH FORUM

Idea When the parents of my students ask how they can help their children in math, I suggest they encourage their children to apply mental-math strategies when shopping.

Visit our Resource Village at http://www.mhschool.com to see more of the Math Forum.

MATH CENTER

Practice

OBJECTIVE Solve addition problems using mental math.

Materials per pair: place-value models, Math Center Recording Sheet (TA 31 optional)

Students experiment with place-value models to find out when it makes sense to use mental math. They decide on which mental math method is best to use. *[Answers may vary. For example, students may decide mental math is best to use if there are not regroupings needed.]*

PRACTICE ACTIVITY 11   **MATH CENTER** Partners

Manipulatives • Even It Out

- Write an addition problem with 2- or 3-digit addends.
- Your partner shows the problem with place-value models. Your partner decides whether to use the mental math method shown or to add left to right mentally instead.
- Circle the problem if your partner uses the method shown here. Now exchange roles and continue.

YOU NEED
place-value models

$$47 + 58$$
$$+3 \downarrow \quad \downarrow -3$$
$$50 + 55$$
$$50 + 55 = 105$$

NCTM Standards
- ✓ Problem Solving
  Communication
  Reasoning
  Connections

Chapter 2, Lesson 3, pages 44–45   Addition

Problem Solving

OBJECTIVE Solve addition and subtraction problems using logical reasoning and mental math.

Materials per student: Math Center Recording Sheet (TA 31 optional)

Students use mental math and logical reasoning to solve a problem involving different numbers of nickels. *[Flora = 163; Suki = 163 + 324 = 487; Alberto = 514 + 163 = 677; Amy = 487 + 211 = 698; Eugene = 698 + 112 = 810. Check students' work.]*

PROBLEM-SOLVING ACTIVITY 11   **MATH CENTER** On Your Own

Logical Reasoning • Begin at the Beginning

- Solve the following problem using addition. Choose mental math strategies to help.

  Five students collect nickels. Suki has 211 fewer nickels than Amy. Flora has 324 fewer nickels than Suki. Alberto has 514 more nickels than Flora. Eugene has the most nickels by 112. If Flora has 163, how many does everyone else have?

- Now make up your own similar problem. Give it to a classmate to solve.

NCTM Standards
- ✓ Problem Solving
- ✓ Communication
  Reasoning
  Connections

Chapter 2, Lesson 3, pages 44–45   Addition

Lesson 2.3 *continued*

MENTAL MATH
Addition Strategies

OBJECTIVE Use strategies to add mentally.

 **Introduce**

Cultural Connection Read the **Cultural Note.** Point out that piña cloth, made from pineapple leaf fibers, is a thin and sheer material, ideal for the humid climate of the Philippines. Ask students to name other natural fibers used for clothing.

 **Teach**   *Whole Class*

▶ **LEARN** Students compare the two problems on page 44 to see why the same strategy was not applied to both: the first problem does not require regrouping, the second problem does.

- **How does the method in the second problem make it easy to add mentally?** *[Possible answer: It makes it possible to add hundreds, tens , and ones separately to a 3-digit number. This is easy to do mentally.]*

Review how to write numbers in expanded form to help students in applying the mental-math strategy for adding.

3 Close

▶ **Check for Understanding** using items 1–5, page 44.

CRITICAL THINKING

 Some students may find it easier to create the examples first, then write the explanation. Encourage them to use clear and simple language in their explanation.

▶ **PRACTICE**
Materials have available: calculators

Options for assigning exercises:
A—Even ex. 2–26; all ex. 27–30; **More to Explore**
B—Odd ex. 1–25; all ex. 27–30; **More to Explore**

- In ex. 30, students can find the sum mentally—first add the dollars, then quarters, dimes, nickels, and pennies.

✹ **Algebra** Students are using the algebraic concept of variables to solve ex. 21–26.

More to Explore Discuss this method by asking:
- **Why does the second addition sentence have the same sum as the first?** *[When one addend is increased, the second addend is decreased by the same number, so there are no changes for the addition sentence.]*
- **When might this method be easiest to use?** *[Possible answer: when one addend is close to a multiple of 100]*

Addition Strategies

Did you know that people make cloth from pineapples? Pineapple cloth is beautiful but expensive. What is the total cost of a $136 pineapple-cloth shirt and a $112 set of mats?

Cultural Note
In the Philippines, pineapple leaves are used to make piña (pihn-YAH) cloth.

Add: $136 + $112
You can add left to right mentally.

$136	$136	$136
+ 112	+ 112	+ 112
2	24	248

Think: $100 + $100 = $200 | **Think:** $30 + $10 = $40 | **Think:** $6 + $2 = $8

The total cost is $248.

What if a tourist buys a shirt for $149 and a curtain for $127. How much does the tourist pay?

Add: $149 + 127
You can also add mentally using this method.

$149
+ 127   **Think:** $149 + $100 = $249
                    $249 + $20 = $269
                    $269 + $7 = $276

The tourist pays $276.

Check for Understanding
Add mentally. Explain your thinking. Explanations may vary.
1 283 + 414 697   **2** 276 + 121 397   **3** 295 + 131 426   **4** $183 + $716
                                                                            $899

Critical Thinking: Summarize

5 Explain why you look for tens or hundreds when you add mentally. Give some examples. See below.

Possible answer: It is possible to use place value to add mentally; think of 30 + 80 as 3 tens + 8 tens = 11 tens = 110, and think of 300 + 800 as 3 hundreds + 8 hundreds = 11 hundreds = 1,100.

Meeting Individual Needs

Early Finishers

Students can make a list of mental-math strategies in their math journals. They can refer to their list when they need help.

Ongoing Assessment

Interview Determine if students understand how to use mental math strategies by asking:
- **How can you add 275 + 143 mentally?** *[Possible answer: Add 275 + 100 = 375, 375 + 40 = 415, 415 + 3 = 418]*

Follow Up Help students identify strategies they can use with exercises with which they are having difficulty. Or assign **Reteach 11.**

For students who would like a challenge, assign **Extend 11.**

Extra Support

When adding two numbers mentally, students should examine the numbers first. If regrouping is not needed, add the numbers from left to right. If regrouping is needed, add the hundreds, tens, and then ones.

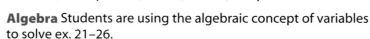

Practice

Add mentally.

1 62 + 37 99 **2** 53 + 24 77 **3** 85 + 11 96 **4** 73 + 22 95

5 85 + 22 107 **6** 75 + 24 99 **7** 86 + 12 98 **8** 129 + 160 289

9 167 + 822 989 **10** 246 + 731 977 **11** $458 + $121 $579 **12** 248 + 550 798

13 120 + 209 329 **14** 498 + 101 599 **15** 232 + 166 398 **16** $749 + $130 $879

17 177 + 221 398 **18** $354 + $215 $569 **19** 201 + 397 598 **20** 586 + 313 899

ALGEBRA Complete. Use mental math.

21 36 + ■ = 59 23 **22** ■ + 246 = 546 300 **23** ■ + $175 = $800 $625

24 391 + ■ = 692 301 **25** 582 + ■ = 797 215 **26** ■ + 672 = 776 104

MIXED APPLICATIONS
Problem Solving

28. No; $48.99 + $28.75 + $28.75 = $106.49, which is more than $103.

27 Tomás counts the number of ties in stock. He finds 287 navy-blue ties and 112 forest-green ties. How many ties are there in all? **399 ties**

28 Mickey has $103 and wants to buy a jacket for $48.99 and 2 hats for $28.75 each. Does she have enough money to buy all the items? Explain. **See above.**

29 Liza bought a skirt for $25.50. She got back a ten-dollar bill and a five-dollar bill in change. How much did she hand to the cashier? **$40.50**

30 In her purse Karen finds 4 one-dollar bills, 6 quarters, 7 dimes, 8 nickels, and 12 pennies. Find the total amount of these coins. **$6.72**

more to explore

Use Hundreds to Add

You can use this method to add mentally.

Add: 298 + 457
+2 ↓   ↓ −2
300 + 455 = 755

Think: Add a number to one addend to make a hundred. Subtract the same number from the other addend.

Add. Use mental math.

1 396 + 175 571 **2** $397 + $156 $553 **3** 295 + 698 993 **4** 427 + 198 625

5 139 + 203 342 **6** 148 + 795 943 **7** $437 + $399 $836 **8** $691 + $259 $950

Extra Practice, page 488

Money, Addition, and Subtraction **45**

Alternate Teaching Strategy

Materials per student: place-value chart (TA 4)

Use the place-value chart to review the value of each digit in 3-, 4-, 5-, and 6-digit numbers. Have students write each number you record in the chart in expanded form.

Present the problem 236 + 197. Elicit that 197 written in expanded form is 100 + 90 + 7. Show how to find the sum using the expanded form of 197 as shown below.

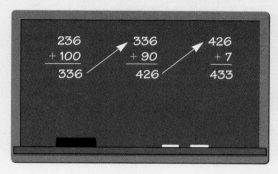

Ask:

• **How is this method different from other ways of adding?** *[Answers may vary. Possible answer: You begin adding in the greatest place instead of the ones place.]*

Continue the activity, giving students other numbers to add. As students become accustomed to this method, encourage them to do more and more of the steps mentally.

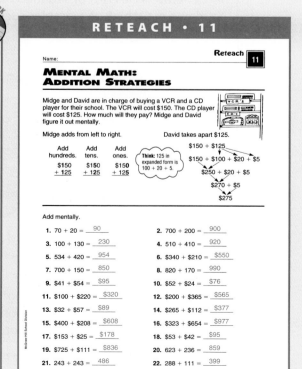

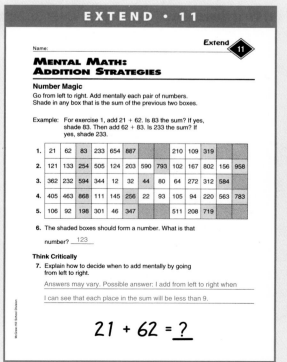

45

MENTAL MATH
Estimate Sums

OBJECTIVE Use rounding to estimate sums, including money amounts.

RESOURCE REMINDER
Math Center Cards 12
Practice 12, Reteach 12, Extend 12

SKILLS TRACE

GRADE 3	• Estimate sums, including money amounts, by rounding. *(Chapter 3)*
GRADE 4	• Estimate sums, including money amounts, by rounding.
GRADE 5	• Estimate sums, including money amounts, by rounding. *(Chapter 2)*

MANIPULATIVE WARM-UP

Cooperative Pairs   **Kinesthetic**

OBJECTIVE Use play money to round dollar amounts and estimate sums.

Materials per pair: 0–9 spinner (TA 2); play money—2 five-dollar bills, 10 one-dollar bills, 6 quarters, 10 dimes, 10 nickels, 10 pennies

► Each student in a pair spins three digits and writes them as a money amount.

► Using play money, each student shows the amount. If the value of the coins is less than 50¢, the student removes the coins. If the value of the coins is equal to or greater than 50¢, the student trades the coins for a one-dollar bill.

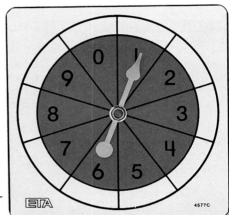

► Each pair writes the rounded amounts in an addition sentence and checks the sum by counting their dollar bills.

► Each pair repeats the activity several times.

LANGUAGE ARTS CONNECTION

Whole Class   **Auditory/Linguistic**

OBJECTIVE Write word problems that involve estimation.

► Generate a class list of situations when an estimation can be used. Students may think of examples such as the following:

> Estimate
> to know whether you have enough money to buy
>   something
> to check answers
> to find out how much or how many
> to write a headline for a newspaper article
> to find an answer when you don't know the exact
>   numbers

► Ask each student to write a word problem involving a situation where an estimate is appropriate. Have students switch papers and solve each other's word problems.

► Review the list created at the beginning of the activity and have students identify the situations that correspond with their word problems. Add to the list any situations suggested by the word problems not already included in the list.

Daily Review

PREVIOUS DAY QUICK REVIEW

Add mentally.
1. 73 + 22 *[95]*
2. 597 + 106 *[703]*
3. $331 + $340 *[$671]*
4. $64 + $18 *[$82]*

FAST FACTS

1. 8 + 3 *[11]*
2. 6 + 4 *[10]*
3. 1 + 7 *[8]*
4. 9 + 1 *[10]*

Problem of the Day • 12

Georgia has two 10¢-stamps, two 5¢-stamps, and ten 1¢-stamps. How many different ways can she make 32¢? *[two ways—two 10¢-stamps, two 5¢-stamps, two 1¢-stamps; two 10¢-stamps, one 5¢-stamp, seven 1¢-stamps]*

TECH LINK

MATH FORUM

Management Tip To practice mentally estimating sums, I have pairs of students work together writing problems for each other to solve. They use calculators to check the reasonableness of their estimates.

Visit our Resource Village at http://www.mhschool.com to see more of the Math Forum.

MATH CENTER

Practice

OBJECTIVE Solve problems using estimation.

Materials per student: Math Center Recording Sheet (TA 31 optional)

Students use estimation to solve addition problems about purchasing party favors and decorations. Then they write their own addition problems. They trade problems with classmates and solve using estimation. *[1. No; 2. Sample answer: chalk and word puzzles or blue streamers and chalk; 3. about $2.50; 4. Check students' problems.]*

PRACTICE ACTIVITY 12

MATH CENTER
On Your Own 👤

Number Sense • Let's Have a Party

Use estimation to solve.

1. Maria is having a party. She has $10 to spend on party favors. Can she buy a bag of jacks and a bag of jump ropes?
2. Greg has $5 to spend. He wants to buy two items. What pairs of items can he buy?
3. About how much money would you need to buy the red streamers and the balloons?
4. Write two more estimation problems about the party items shown. Trade problems with a classmate and solve.

Chapter 2, Lesson 4, pages 46–47   Addition

NCTM Standards
- ✓ Problem Solving
- ✓ Communication
- ✓ Reasoning
- ✓ Connections

Problem Solving

OBJECTIVE Find sums using estimation and mental math.

Materials per student: Math Center Recording Sheet (TA 31 optional)

Students use estimation to decide which addition problem has the greatest sum and which will have the least sum. Then students use mental math to tell if estimates correctly identify the greatest and least sums, and explain why or why not. *[1. 653 + 542; 2. 531 + 111; 3. Estimates may vary. Check students' work.]*

PROBLEM-SOLVING ACTIVITY 12

MATH CENTER
On Your Own 👤

Decision Making • Greatest and Least Sums

Look at these addition problems.

653 + 542 =	529 + 641 =	291 + 655 =	301 + 729 =
211 + 491 =	531 + 111 =	310 + 605 =	729 + 353 =

1. Estimate to decide which has the greatest sum.
2. Estimate to decide which has the least sum.
3. Now use mental math to solve all the problems. Did your estimates correctly identify the greatest and least sums? Explain.

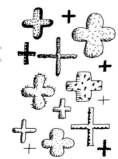

Chapter 2, Lesson 4, pages 46–47   Addition

NCTM Standards
- ✓ Problem Solving
- ✓ Communication
- ✓ Reasoning
- Connections

Lesson 2.4 continued

MENTAL MATH
Estimate Sums

> **OBJECTIVE** Use rounding to estimate sums, including money amounts.
>
> **Vocabulary** estimate, sum

 **Introduce**

Present the following two problems and ask students to identify which number could be an estimate and why:

> **On Friday, the manager of the Tot's Toy Store will give a $100 gift certificate to the 100th customer.**
> **The manager of the Tot's Toy Store wants to know whether more customers are in the store at 9 A.M. or 9 P.M.**

Students should see that estimation would be appropriate in determining how many customers are in the store.

2 Teach *Whole Class*

▶ **LEARN** Read the introductory problem. Have students explain why two numbers are being added and why an estimate is appropriate.

- **How many ways were there for people to learn about the sale? What were they?** *[two ways; newspaper and radio]*
- **How do you know an exact answer isn't needed?** [The question asks "about" how many.]

More Examples In Example C, students should realize that the numbers are rounded to the hundreds place, the greatest place that is common to both numbers.

3 Close

Check for Understanding using items 1–8, page 46.

CRITICAL THINKING
Have students do enough examples of rounding up one addend and rounding down the other addend to discover that the estimated sums may be either greater than or less than the exact sums. Point out that it is important not to generalize from just one or two examples.

▶ **PRACTICE**
Materials have available: calculators

Options for assigning exercises:
A—Odd ex. 1–25; **Mixed Review**
B—Even ex. 2–26; **Mixed Review**

Mixed Review/Test Preparation Standard and expanded forms (ex. 1–2) are taught in Chapter 1. Ordering numbers (ex. 3–5) is taught in Chapter 1.

Estimate Sums

LEARN

Store clerks sometimes survey customers. In this survey, about how many customers knew about the sale?

Estimate: 147 + 162

Round each number to find the **sum** mentally.

Think: Round to the nearest hundred.
147 + 162
↓   ↓
100 + 200 = 300

About 300 customers knew about the sale.

TOT'S TOY STORE
Where did you learn about the sale?

Newspaper	147
Radio	162
Did not know about the sale	117

More Examples

A Estimate: $0.28 + $0.94

   Think: Round to the nearest ten cents.
     $0.30 + $0.90 = $1.20

B Estimate: $3.75 + $5.14

   Think: Round to the nearest dollar.
     $4 + $5 = $9

C Estimate: 3,654 + 225

   Think: Round to the nearest hundred.
     3,700 + 200 = 3,900

D Estimate: 4,954 + 1,425 + 3,567

   Think: Round to the nearest thousand.
     5,000 + 1,000 + 4,000 = 10,000

CHECK

Check for Understanding Estimates may vary. Possible answers are given.
Estimate the sum. Tell how you rounded.

1 $0.68 + $0.72 $1.40; to nearest ten cents

2 $4.78 + $2.32 $7.00; to nearest dollar

3 $41.72 + $57.19 $100; to nearest ten dollars

4 843 + 372 1,200; to nearest hundred

5 6,610 + 385 7,000; to nearest hundred

6 39 + 52 + 46 140; to nearest ten

Critical Thinking: Generalize **Explain your reasoning.**

7 How will an estimated sum compare to an exact sum if you estimate by rounding up both? rounding down both? rounding one up and rounding down the other? Give examples. **See page T17.**

8 Tell how you could round the numbers in ex. 3 and 5 another way to estimate the sums. What would the estimates be? **See below.**

> **estimate** To find an answer that is close to the exact answer.
>
> **sum** The result of addition.

8. Possible answer: 3. round to the nearest dollar, $42 + $57 = $99; 5. round to the nearest thousand, 7,000 + 0 = 7,000.

Meeting Individual Needs

Early Finishers

Students can estimate sums for ex. 17–22 again, this time rounding to the nearest hundred or dollar.

Extra Support

Review the rule for rounding: 1. Decide which place you want to round to. 2. Look at the place to the right. If the digit is less than 5, round down. If the digit is 5 or more, round up.

Ongoing Assessment

Observation Checklist Determine if students understand estimating sums by observing if they round the addends to mentally find the sum of 1,427 + 6,521.

Follow Up Students having difficulty estimating mentally may begin by writing out all the steps, then progress to writing fewer steps as they are able to perform the steps mentally. Or assign **Reteach 12.**

For students who would like a challenge, assign **Extend 12.**

24. Students may estimate or round the prices to find two items that cost less than $50.
26. Students check each other's work by comparing problems and solutions.

Practice

Estimate. Round to the nearest ten or ten cents.

1 22 1 52 **70**   **2** $0.87 1 $0.72 **$1.60**   **3** 78 1 65 **150**   **4** $0.09 1 $0.78 **$0.90**

5 $0.78 1 $0.19 **$1.00**   **6** 499 1 66 **570**   **7** $3.62 1 $0.18 **$3.80**   **8** 43 1 34 1 25 **100**

Estimate. Round to the nearest hundred or dollar.

9 413 1 841 **1,200**   **10** $8.32 1 $2.75 **$11.00**   **11** $3.66 1 $0.88 **$5.00**   **12** 295 1 536 **800**

13 $2.91 1 $7.23 **$10.00**   **14** 7,722 1 198 **7,900**   **15** $3.62 1 $3.76 **$8.00**   **16** 482 1 92 1 29 **600**

Estimate. Round to the nearest thousand or ten dollars.

17 $52.43 1 $36.89 **$90.00**   **18** $20.13 1 $32.45 **$50**   **19** 4,378 1 6,527 **11,000**

20 5,643 1 989 **7,000**   **21** $87.50 1 $7.82 **$100.00**   **22** 6,740 1 271 1 867 **8,000**

MIXED APPLICATIONS
Problem Solving

Use the catalog for problems 23–26.

23 Sean orders one craft kit of each type from the catalog. About how much does his order cost? **about $36.00**

24 Which two items can you buy together for less than $50.00? Explain your answer. **See above.**

25 Tot's Toys had 2,460 customers for its catalog last year. This year it has an additional 1,510 customers. About how many customers does it have this year? **Possible answer: about 4,000 customers**

26 **Write a problem** using the catalog page. Solve it. Have others solve it. **See above.**

Tot's Toys by Mail
- ☆Walkman — $29.75
- ☆Home Planetarium — $29.95
- ☆Craft Kits — $15.19
- ◇Pottery Wheel
- ◇Creature Creator — $12.29
- ◇Sand Art Adventures — $8.99
- ☆Talking Diary — $37.75

mixed review · test preparation

Write the number in standard form and in expanded form.

1 fifty-two thousand, ninety-four **52,094; 50,000 + 2,000 + 90 + 4**   **2** two hundred thousand, one hundred **200,100; 200,000 + 100**

Write in order from least to greatest.

3 467; 678; 464; 644 **464; 467; 644; 678**   **4** 98; 698; 812; 89 **89; 98; 698; 812**   **5** 4,048; 2,480; 8,420; 3,999 **2,480; 3,999; 4,048; 8,420**

Extra Practice, page 489   Money, Addition, and Subtraction   **47**

Alternate Teaching Strategy

Write the following example on the chalkboard. Then explain to students that a quick way to estimate is to add only the front digits.

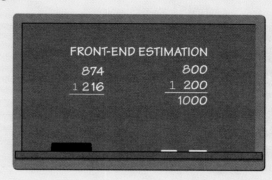

FRONT-END ESTIMATION

874	800
1 216	1 200
	1000

Ask students to explain why they think the estimated sum is greater than or less than the actual sum. Students should recognize that the estimated sum is less than the actual sum because only the front digits were added, and the actual numbers are greater.

Continue estimating sums using other addition examples.

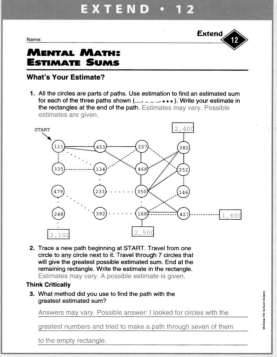

PRACTICE · 12

Name: _____
Practice **12**

MENTAL MATH: ESTIMATE SUMS

Estimate. Round to the nearest

1. ten: 11 1 19 __30__
2. ten cents: $0.67 1 $0.23 __$0.90__
3. ten: 57 1 23 __80__
4. ten cents: $0.94 1 $0.56 __$1.50__
5. ten: 103 1 59 __160__
6. ten: 24 1 67 1 43 __130__
7. hundred: 495 1 313 __800__
8. hundred: 777 1 722 __1,500__
9. dollar: $4.95 1 $2.10 __$7.00__
10. dollar: $9.25 1 $8.95 __$18.00__
11. hundred: 3,765 1 234 __4,000__
12. hundred: 528 1 78 1 142 __700__
13. thousand: 3,965 1 2,100 __6,000__
14. ten dollars: $15.95 1 $4.25 __$20.00__
15. ten dollars: $156.87 1 $36.56 __$200.00__
16. thousand: 5,923 1 569 1 234 __7,000__

Estimate. Tell how you rounded.   Estimates may vary. Possible answers are given.

17. 47 1 32 ____ 80; ten
18. $.07 1 $0.28 ____ $0.40; 10¢
19. $389 1 $67 1 $12 ____ $500; hundred
20. 2,987 1 458 ____ 3,000; thousand

Solve.

21. Ramon wants to buy his mother flowers for $7.50 and a book for $21.95. About how much will he spend? **about $30.00**

22. Ramon's mother plants 37 tulip bulbs and 22 daffodil bulbs. About how many bulbs does she plant in all? **about 60 bulbs**

RETEACH · 12

Name: _____
Reteach **12**

MENTAL MATH: ESTIMATE SUMS

To estimate a sum, you can round each number. Then add the rounded numbers.

Estimate: 128 1 199

Round each number to the nearest hundred. → 100 1 200
Add. → 100 1 200 5 300
So, 128 1 199 is about 300.

Estimate: $3.95 1 $5.25

Round each number to the nearest dollar. → $4 1 $5
Add. → $4 1 $5 5 $9
So, $3.95 1 $5.25 is about $9.

Ring the letter of the correct estimate.

1. Round to the nearest ten dollars: $23 1 $44
   a. $20 1 $40 5 $60
   b. $20 1 $50 5 $70
   c. $30 1 $50 5 $80

2. Round to the nearest hundred dollars: $276 1 $483
   a. $200 1 $400 5 $600
   b. $200 1 $500 5 $700
   c. $300 1 $500 5 $800

3. Round to the nearest dollar: $6.25 1 $2.95
   a. $6 1 $2 5 $8
   b. $6 1 $3 5 $9
   c. $7 1 $3 5 $10

4. Round to the nearest ten: 455 1 110
   a. 400 1 100 5 500
   b. 450 1 100 5 550
   c. 460 1 110 5 570

5. Round to the nearest thousand: 8,999 1 999
   a. 8,000 1 900 5 8,900
   b. 8,000 1 1,000 5 9,000
   c. 9,000 1 1,000 5 10,000

6. Round to the nearest hundred: 653 1 2,901
   a. 600 1 2,900 5 3,500
   b. 700 1 2,900 5 3,600
   c. 700 1 3,000 5 3,700

EXTEND · 12

Name: _____
Extend **12**

MENTAL MATH: ESTIMATE SUMS

What's Your Estimate?

1. All the circles are parts of paths. Use estimation to find an estimated sum for each of the three paths shown (__ __ __ , ● ● ●). Write your estimate in the rectangles at the end of the path. Estimates may vary. Possible estimates are given.

START
(111) (453) (227) (382) → [2,400]
(335) (134) (468) (252)
(479) (233) (350) (146)
(248) (392) (168) (427) → [1,600]
[2,100]   [2,500]

2. Trace a new path beginning at START. Travel from one circle to any circle next to it. Travel through 7 circles that will give the greatest possible estimated sum. End at the remaining rectangle. Write the estimate in the rectangle. Estimates may vary. A possible estimate is given.

Think Critically

3. What method did you use to find the path with the greatest estimated sum?

Answers may vary. Possible answer: I looked for circles with the greatest numbers and tried to make a path through seven of them to the empty rectangle.

47

LESSON 2.5

Add Whole Numbers

OBJECTIVE Add from 2-digit up to 6-digit numbers with regrouping.

RESOURCE REMINDER
Math Center Cards 13
Practice 13, Reteach 13, Extend 13

SKILLS TRACE

GRADE 3	• Add up to 4-digit numbers, including money amounts, with/without regrouping. *(Chapter 3)*
GRADE 4	• Add up to 6-digit numbers, including money amounts, with/without regrouping.
GRADE 5	• Add up to 6-digit numbers, including money amounts, with/without regrouping. *(Chapter 2)*

MANIPULATIVE WARM-UP

Cooperative Pairs   **Kinesthetic**

OBJECTIVE Use place-value models to add 1-, 2-, and 3-digit numbers.

Materials per pair: place-value models—2 hundreds, 9 tens, 9 ones; place-value chart (TA 4)

► Write the following addition exercises on the chalkboard: 8 + 9, 48 + 39, 148 + 139.

► Have pairs of students use place-value models to find each sum. *[17, 87, 287]* Then have them record each addition on a place-value chart.

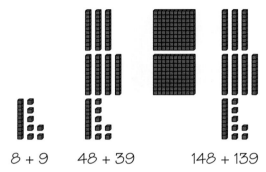

8 + 9   48 + 39   148 + 139

► Discuss the similarities and differences, if any, between adding two 2-digit and two 3-digit numbers. Then discuss whether adding 4- or 5-digit numbers would be any different from adding 2- and 3-digit numbers.

ESL APPROPRIATE

LITERATURE CONNECTION

Whole Class   **Linguistic**

OBJECTIVE Calculate totals for items mentioned in a literature selection.

Resource Read-Aloud Anthology, pp. 7–9

► Read the poem *Ode to Los Raspados*. Ask students to write two categories that can be counted—flavors of snow cones and names of children, for example.

► Read the poem again, and have students count the items in each category. For example, there are 6 flavors and 6 names mentioned in the poems.

► Discuss the items students counted. If totals students found for an item don't agree, reread the corresponding section of the poem and count together.

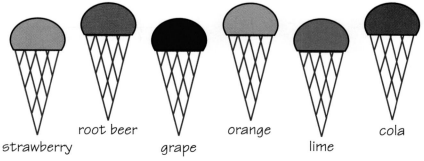

strawberry   root beer   grape   orange   lime   cola

Daily Review

PREVIOUS DAY QUICK REVIEW

Estimate. Round to the nearest hundred or dollar.
1. 709 + 546 *[1,200]*
2. $3.78 + $2.59 *[$7.00]*
3. $9.25 + $7.49 *[$16.00]*
4. 3,475 + 115 *[3,600]*

FAST FACTS

1. 16 − 7 *[9]*
2. 9 − 2 *[7]*
3. 11 − 9 *[2]*
4. 15 − 6 *[9]*

Problem of the Day • 13

Dulcie and Marcus collect marbles. They have the same number of striped marbles. Dulcie has 15 solid marbles. Marcus has 26 solid marbles. Altogether they have 87 marbles. How many striped marbles does each one have?
[23 striped marbles]

TECH LINK

MATH VAN

Tool You may wish to use the Place-Value Model tool and the Calculator with this lesson.

MATH FORUM

Combination Classes While my younger students work with manipulatives to explore and apply addition concepts, my older students use newspapers to write real-world addition problems.

Visit our Resource Village at http://www.mhschool.com to see more of the Math Forum.

MATH CENTER

Practice

OBJECTIVE Solve problems using addition.

Materials per student: Math Center Recording Sheet (TA 31 optional)

Students use addition to determine the value of two of a group of items. Then partners act as game show host and contestant to do problems. *[$924—canoe and bicycle, answers may vary.]*

PRACTICE ACTIVITY 13

MATH CENTER
Partners 👥

Number Sense • Tell That Price!

- Reba is a contestant on "Tell That Price." Before going on the show, she checked prices at local stores. She also made herself a list.

Now she has to tell the exact value of the items in the scene in front of her. Look at her list. What should be her answer?

- With a partner, play game show host and contestant. The host names any two of the items from Reba's list, and the contestant must tell the exact value without using paper and pencil or a calculator. Switch roles and play again.

canoe	$575
mountain bicycle	349
scuba diving classes	250
instant camera	229
table fan	21
sunglasses	79
extra gas can	3
giant beach ball	8
8 oz. sunscreen	7

Chapter 2, Lesson 5, pages 48–51

Addition

NCTM Standards
✓ Problem Solving
   Communication
   Reasoning
✓ Connections

Problem Solving

OBJECTIVE Use logical reasoning to explain mathematical rules.

Materials per student: Math Center Recording Sheet (TA 31 optional)

Students explain the direction in which they work when adding with mental math or paper and pencil.
[Answers may vary. Possible answer: You work right to left when adding with paper and pencil because it makes it easier to regroup. You can use mental math when regrouping isn't required.]

PROBLEM-SOLVING ACTIVITY 13

MATH CENTER
On Your Own 👤

Logical Reasoning • Left to Right or Right to Left?

- Suppose a classmate doesn't understand why you work left to right for mental sums and right to left for paper and pencil sums.

- Try doing mental sums by working from right to left. Try doing paper and pencil sums by working from left to right. What happens?

- Use what you discovered. Write a good explanation for a classmate.

$$54 + 18$$

$$53 + 21$$?

Chapter 2, Lesson 5, pages 48–51

Addition

NCTM Standards
✓ Problem Solving
✓ Communication
✓ Reasoning
   Connections

Add Whole Numbers

OBJECTIVE Add from 2-digit up to 6-digit numbers with regrouping.

Materials calculators (optional)

Introduce

Materials per pair: place-value models—10 hundreds, 19 tens, 19 ones

Have students use place-value models to show the three steps involved in finding the exact sum of 239 and 185 depicted on the page.

Teach   *Whole Class*

Cultural Connection Read the **Cultural Note.** Wampum belts were made by stringing together wampum beads, made from shells. The beads may have originally been white since "wampum" means "string of white beads." The beads were also used to make bracelets and necklaces. The belts, bracelets, and necklaces were used for ornamentation, traded to show good faith, and also used as money. The value of the beads varied depending on the sizes and colors.

▶ **LEARN** Read through the problem at the top of the page. Have students estimate the cost of a wampum bracelet and necklace. Then, ask:
  • **Why do you first make an estimate when an exact answer is needed to solve the problem?** [The estimate will tell you if your answer is reasonable.]

Ask volunteers to describe the steps involved in finding the exact sum. Ask:
  • **When is it necessary to regroup?** [when the sum of the digits in any place is ten or greater]

Encourage students to describe ceremonial ornamentation or dress they may wear for celebrations.

Talk It Over After students answer the first question, ask:
  • **Can an estimate and the exact sum ever be the same number? Give an example.** [Yes; answers may vary. Possible answer: 279 + 221—estimated sum is 300 + 200 = 500, exact sum is also 500.]

Encourage students to include estimating the sum as part of their method in adding 348 and 562.

Add Whole Numbers

Selling Native American crafts shares beauty and keeps traditional arts alive. Each wampum bead takes about two hours to make. How much would a craftsperson earn by selling a wampum bracelet for $239 and a necklace for $185?

Cultural Note
The Iroquois and Chippewa used to trade wampum belts as a promise to keep treaties and to show friendship. Today, the belts are worn during some celebrations.

Add: $239 + $185

Estimate the sum.
Think: $200 + $200 = $400

Find the exact sum.

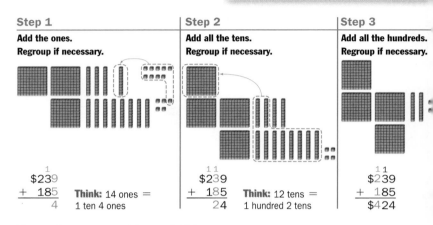

Step 1	Step 2	Step 3
Add the ones. Regroup if necessary.	Add all the tens. Regroup if necessary.	Add all the hundreds. Regroup if necessary.

1 $239 + 185 —— 4	1 1 $239 + 185 —— 24	1 1 $239 + 185 —— $424
Think: 14 ones = 1 ten 4 ones	**Think:** 12 tens = 1 hundred 2 tens	

The craftsperson would earn $424.

Talk It Over
▶ How can you tell that the answer is reasonable? Compare the answer to the estimate—$424 is about $400.
▶ Explain what is regrouped when adding 239 and 185. 9 ones + 5 ones = 14 ones, regrouped as 1 ten 4 ones and 3 tens + 8 tens + 1 ten (from the regrouped
▶ Add 348 and 562. Explain your method.   ones) = 12 tens, regrouped a
   910; explanations may vary.   1 hundred 2 tens.

Meeting Individual Needs

Inclusion

Students may need more practice with manipulatives. Give students play money and addition problems involving dollar amounts. They may find this an easier way to learn to add larger numbers.

ESL APPROPRIATE

Extra Support

Students may forget to align the ones digits when adding numbers with different number of digits. Have them add numbers using a place-value mat and verbalize the numbers they are adding.

Ongoing Assessment

Observation Checklist Note if students can add 2-digit up to 6-digit numbers by observing if they use basic facts and estimation to help them find sums.

Follow Up Students having difficulty can draw place-value models to represent the addends, and identify the places in which they will need to regroup. You may also assign **Reteach 13.**

Assign **Extend 13** for students who would like a challenge.

One design for a wampum belt uses 6,543 beads. The second design uses 5,762 beads. How many beads are needed to make both designs?

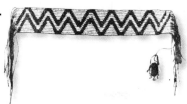

Add: 6,543 + 5,762

Estimate the sum. **Think:** 7,000 + 6,000 = 13,000

You can use paper and pencil to find the exact sum.

Step 1	Step 2	Step 3	Step 4
Add the ones. Regroup if necessary.	**Add all the tens. Regroup if necessary.**	**Add all the hundreds. Regroup if necessary.**	**Add all the thousands.**
6,543 +5,762 5	₁ 6,543 +5,762 05	₁ ₁ 6,543 +5,762 305	₁ ₁ 6,543 +5,762 12,305
	Think: 10 tens = 1 hundred 0 tens	**Think:** 13 hundreds = 1 thousand 3 hundreds	

 You can also use a calculator.   6,543 + 5,762 = *12305.*

To make both designs, 12,305 beads are needed.

More Examples

A
₁ ₁
823
+578
1,401

B
₁
6,456
+ 339
6,795

C  5,743 + 198,400 = *204143.*

Check for Understanding   Estimates may vary depending on the method used. Estimates shown are by rounding.

Add. Estimate to check that your answer is reasonable.

1 468
+593
1,061; 1,100

2 863
+ 42
905; 940

3 $25.80
+ 17.90
$43.70; $50.00

4 6,515
+7,943
14,458; 15,000

5 229,650
+ 94,500
324,150; 290,000

Critical Thinking: Analyze   Show examples.

6 Suppose you add two 4-digit numbers. What is the greatest number of digits that can be in the sum? the least number?
5 digits: 9,999 + 9,999 = 19,998; 4 digits: 1,000 + 1,000 = 2,000

7 When adding two numbers, when would you use mental math? pencil and paper? a calculator?

le answer: Mental math can be used when there is no
ping, pencil and paper when regrouping is needed, and
ılator when the addends are great.

Turn the page for Practice. ➡
Money, Addition, and Subtraction **49**

Read through the problem at the top of page 49. Ask:
- **How are the numbers in this problem different from those in the previous problem?** *[The numbers in this problem have digits in the thousands place.]*

Discuss the four steps shown.
- **How is adding 4-digit numbers different from adding 3-digit numbers? How is it similar?** *[Different: there is an additional column of numbers to add; similar: you still add from right to left, beginning with the ones place, and regroup as necessary.]*

More Examples Example A shows a sum with zero as a digit. Refer students to Step 2 on pages 48 and 49. They can think of 10 tens as 1 hundred and zero tens, write the zero in the sum, and write 1 in the hundreds column to show they regrouped. Example C shows addition of larger addends with a calculator. Remind students that the calculator display does not show a comma.

3 Close

Check for Understanding using items 1–7, page 49.

CRITICAL THINKING
After students answer item 6, ask:
- **If you were to add ten 4-digit numbers, is it possible to get a 6-digit sum? Why or why not?** *[No; the largest 4-digit number is 9,999—adding this number ten times gives 99,990, a five-digit number.]*

Practice See pages 50–51.

▶ **PRACTICE**

Materials have available: calculators

Options for assigning exercises:
A—Ex. 1–14, 19–26, 37–42; **Cultural Connection**
B—Ex. 6–21, 27–42; **Cultural Connection**

• For ex. 19–21, make sure students understand that when money is deposited into an account, the amount is added to the previous balance. You can use the first entry in the checkbook to illustrate this: $376.00 was added to the previous balance of $1,435.00 to get a new balance of $1,811.00.

• For ex. 22–31, point out that estimating saves time in determining which exercises need to be completed.

• For **Make It Right** (ex. 37), see Common Error below.

Cultural Connection Abacuses can be used to add, subtract, multiply, and divide. The words *suan pan* mean "counting tray." The first counting trays contained dust or sand in which people drew numbers.

Abacuses are still used in many parts of the world, such as Japan, Russia, India, and Armenia. Encourage students to describe other adding methods or machines with which they are familiar.

As students use the abacus to complete ex. 11–13, have them demonstrate and explain how to show regrouping on the abacus.

Practice

Add. Remember to estimate.

1	2	3	4	5
67 + 31 **98**	45 + 96 **141**	87 + 37 **124**	246 +923 **1,169**	$2.50 + 7.75 **$10.25**

6	7	8	9	10
9,125 +8,993 **18,118**	2,988 + 699 **3,687**	12,548 + 7,647 **20,195**	$1,560 + 789 **$2,349**	37,118 +89,594 **126,712**

11 257 + 86   **343**   **12** 7,129 + 973   **8,102**   **13** 4,089 + 1,925   **6,014**   **14** 27,517 + 35,650   **63,167**

15 8,918 + 4,546 **13,464**   **16** 29,657 + 3,635 **33,292**

17 $45,851 + $675 **$46,526**   **18** 895,420 + 175,950 **1,071,370**

Complete Mr. Valencia's checkbook balances.

	DATE	DESCRIPTION	AMOUNT	BALANCE
				$1,435.00
	11/7	Deposit: check from sale of computer	$376.00	$1,811.00
19	11/16	Deposit: paycheck	$590.00	▪ $2,401
20	11/18	Deposit: check from Aunt Ina	$135.00	▪ $2,536
21	11/24	Deposit: school loan	$475.83	▪ $3,011.8

Find only those sums greater than 5,000.

22	23	24	25	26
4,890 + 741 **5,631**	965 +998 **less than 5,000**	2,498 + 2,277 **less than 5,000**	5,681 +8,743 **14,424**	4,038 + 975 **5,013**

27	28	29	30	31
9,983 +9,906 **19,889**	3,132 + 1,485 **less than 5,000**	3,602 +1,870 **5,472**	4,610 +1,111 **5,721**	2,163 +2,577 **less than 5,000**

Write two addends for the sum. Each addend must be greater than 500. Answers may vary. Possible answers are given.

32	33	34	35	36
1,460 540 + 920	2,500 999 + 1,501	9,654 9,000 + 654	18,785 17,635 + 1,150	234,112 200,000 + 34,112

· Make It Right ·

37 André lined up the numbers and added. Tell what the mistake is, then correct it. Explain how estimating could help him.

75,896 + 9,420
Sum: 170,096

André represented the number 9,420 as 94,200 before adding—the correct answer is 85,316; estimating, he would know that his answer should be about 80,000 + 10,000, or 90,000.

Meeting Individual Needs

Early Finishers

Students in pairs can take turns tossing a number cube to generate two 5-digit numbers then find the sum. The student with the greater sum rolls the number cube for the next two addends.

ESL APPROPRIATE

Gifted And Talented

Challenge students to determine what the greatest number of digits in the sum can be when two 2-digit numbers are added, when two 3-digit numbers are added, and so on. Have them share answers with the class.

COMMON ERROR

As in the **Make It Right** on page 50, students may make errors related to incorrectly aligning digits. Students may align digits by turning their papers sideways and writing digits between the vertical lines.

MIXED APPLICATIONS
Problem Solving

38 Frederick's Music Store is offering a special sale on a piano: Pay $900 now. Pay $3,400 in one year. What is the total cost of the piano? **$4,300**

40 **Make a decision** A photography store is offering a special. If you have $25.00, which photo or photos would you choose? Explain. **See above.**

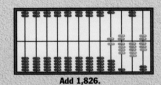

Moment Photography Store

| 8 in. by 11 in. photograph: $7.65 | Sitting fee: $14.85 |
| 5 in. by 7 in. photograph: $3.65 | |

39 Abe sold 465 pieces of pottery on Saturday and 637 pieces on Sunday. About how many pieces did he sell in all? **about 1,100 pieces**

41 **Logical reasoning** The sum of two numbers is 1,000. One addend is 50 more than the other addend. What are the two numbers? **475, 525**

42 **Write a problem** similar to the number puzzle in problem 41. Ask some classmates to solve it. **Students check each other's work by comparing problems and solutions.**

40. Students' decisions should reflect choices given in the ad.

Cultural Connection
The Chinese Abacus

The Chinese abacus, or *suan pan* (swahn pan), can be used to add numbers.

The abacus uses place value. The rod at the right stands for the ones place. The next rod stands for tens, and so on. An upper bead placed next to the crossbar shows 5. A lower bead placed next to the crossbar shows 1.

Here is how you can add 5,637 and 1,826.

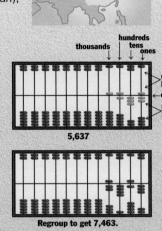

thousands — hundreds, tens, ones
upper beads — crossbar — lower beads

5,637

Add 1,826.

Regroup to get 7,463.

Use the abacus or drawings of the abacus to do ex. 11–13 on page 50.

Check students' work.

China

Extra Practice, page 489

Money, Addition, and Subtraction **51**

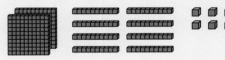

Alternate Teaching Strategy

Materials per group: place-value models—9 hundreds, 19 tens, 19 ones

Present this problem:

> Eric paid $289 for a small blue Navajo rug. He paid $645 for a large red Navajo rug. How much money did he spend on rugs?

Have students show 289 using 2 hundreds, 8 tens, and 9 ones, and below that show 645 using 6 hundreds, 4 tens, and 5 ones. Make sure they align the hundreds, tens, and ones.

- **How many ones are there? Regroup to make tens. How many ones do you have now?** *[14 ones; 4 ones]*
- **How many tens are there? Regroup to make hundreds. How many tens do you have now?** *[13 tens; 3 tens]*
- **How many hundreds are there?** *[9 hundreds]*
- **What number do you have? How much money did Eric spend on rugs?** *[$934]*

Continue the activity with other problems. Include addends with six digits or less.

ESL ▶ **APPROPRIATE**

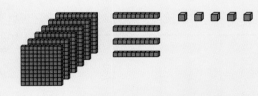

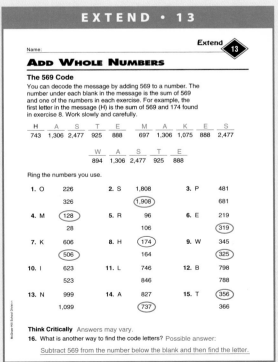

HOMEWORK

Name: _____ Practice **13**

ADD WHOLE NUMBERS

Add. Remember to estimate.

1. 42 $\underline{+\ 21}$ 63	**2.** 48 $\underline{+\ 21}$ 69	**3.** 26 $\underline{+\ 35}$ 61	**4.** $89 $\underline{+\ 12}$ $101	**5.** 32 $\underline{+\ 29}$ 61
6. 287 $\underline{+\ 21}$ 308	**7.** $6.43 $\underline{+\ 2.21}$ $8.64	**8.** 738 $\underline{+\ 65}$ 803	**9.** 579 $\underline{+\ 391}$ 970	**10.** $3.89 $\underline{+\ 0.45}$ $4.34
11. 2,019 $\underline{+\ 1,308}$ 3,327	**12.** 2,908 $\underline{+\ 26}$ 2,934	**13.** 1,256 $\underline{+\ 1,168}$ 2,424	**14.** 2,124 $\underline{+\ 2,999}$ 5,123	**15.** 7,236 $\underline{+\ 999}$ 8,235
16. 36,413 $\underline{+\ 12,236}$ 48,649	**17.** 68,281 $\underline{+\ 12,712}$ 80,993	**18.** 23,786 $\underline{+\ 4,993}$ 28,779	**19.** 12,362 $\underline{+\ 43,748}$ 56,110	**20.** 37,689 $\underline{+\ 7,777}$ 45,466
21. 233,317 $\underline{+\ 142,462}$ 375,779	**22.** 683,924 $\underline{+\ 15,234}$ 699,158	**23.** 562,296 $\underline{+\ 228,421}$ 790,717	**24.** 197,243 $\underline{+\ 35,237}$ 232,480	**25.** 297,152 $\underline{+\ 434,508}$ 731,660

26. $745 + $26 = __$771__

27. 2,165 + 453 = __2,618__

28. 7,621 + 1,296 = __8,917__

29. 8,453 + 3,675 = __12,128__

30. $34,654 + $2,398 = __$37,052__

31. 349,168 + 265,722 = __614,890__

Solve.

32. There were 2,434 people who attended the opening of a new store on Saturday. On Sunday 1,846 people went to the store. How many people went to the store on its first weekend? __4,280 people__

33. The new store took in $110,158 the first week and $98,673 in the second week. How much did it take in during both weeks? __$208,831__

Name: _____ Reteach **13**

ADD WHOLE NUMBERS

Add: 486 + 257

Think: First, estimate the sum. 486 + 257 is about 500 + 300. 500 + 300 = 800.

Step 1 Add the ones. Regroup if you can.

	H	T	O
		1	
	4	8	6
+	2	5	7
			3

Think: 6 ones + 7 ones = 13 ones. 13 ones = 1 ten 3 ones

Step 2 Add the tens. Regroup if you can.

	H	T	O
	1	1	
	4	8	6
+	2	5	7
		4	3

Think: 1 ten + 8 tens + 5 tens = 14 tens 14 tens = 1 hundred 4 tens

Step 3 Add the hundreds. Regroup if you can.

	H	T	O
	1	1	
	4	8	6
+	2	5	7
	7	4	3

Think: 1 hundred + 4 hundreds + 2 hundreds = 7 hundreds

Compare the sum and your estimate. Check that the answer is reasonable.

Add. Show regrouping in exercises 1–8. Remember to estimate.

1. ⬚ 42 $\underline{+\ 19}$ 61	**2.** ⬚ 47 $\underline{+\ 34}$ 81	**3.** ⬚ 95 $\underline{+\ 48}$ 143	**4.** ⬚ 738 $\underline{+\ 215}$ 953
5. ⬚ 178 $\underline{+\ 217}$ 395	**6.** ⬚ 624 $\underline{+\ 192}$ 816	**7.** ⬚ 824 $\underline{+\ 469}$ 1,293	**8.** ⬚⬚ 557 $\underline{+\ 283}$ 840
9. 586 $\underline{+\ 275}$ 861	**10.** 898 $\underline{+\ 129}$ 1,027	**11.** 627 $\underline{+\ 196}$ 823	**12.** 576 $\underline{+\ 637}$ 1,213
13. 6,321 $\underline{+\ 3,497}$ 9,818	**14.** 4,013 $\underline{+\ 5,209}$ 9,222	**15.** 1,365 $\underline{+\ 2,457}$ 3,822	**16.** 8,427 $\underline{+\ 3,796}$ 12,223

Name: _____ Extend **13**

ADD WHOLE NUMBERS

The 569 Code

You can decode the message by adding 569 to a number. The number under each blank in the message is the sum of 569 and one of the numbers in each exercise. For example, the first letter in the message (H) is the sum of 569 and 174 found in exercise 8. Work slowly and carefully.

H	A	S	T	E		M	A	K	E	S
743	1,306	2,477	925	888		697	1,306	1,075	888	2,477

W	A	S	T	E
894	1,306	2,477	925	888

Ring the numbers you use.

1. O	226	**2.** S	1,808	**3.** P	481
	326		(1,908)		681
4. M	(128)	**5.** R	96	**6.** E	219
	28		106		(319)
7. K	606	**8.** H	(174)	**9.** W	345
	(506)		164		(325)
10. I	623	**11.** L	746	**12.** B	798
	523		846		788
13. N	999	**14.** A	827	**15.** T	(356)
	1,099		(737)		366

Think Critically Answers may vary.

16. What is another way to find the code letters? Possible answer: __Subtract 569 from the number below the blank and then find the letter.__

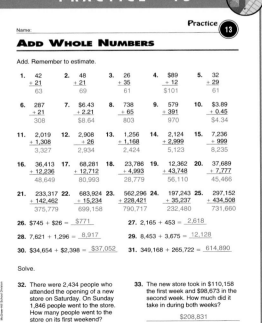

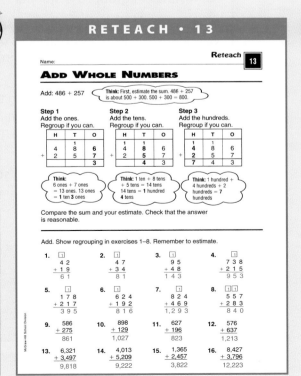

51

LESSON 2.6

Three or More Addends

OBJECTIVE Add three or more addends of 1-, 2-, and 3-digit numbers.

RESOURCE REMINDER
Math Center Cards 14
Practice 14, Reteach 14, Extend 14

SKILLS TRACE

GRADE 3	• Add up to four 4-digit numbers. *(Chapter 3)*
GRADE 4	• Add up to four 4-digit numbers.
GRADE 5	• Add up to four 6-digit numbers. *(Chapter 2)*

WARM-UP

Cooperative Pairs   **Logical/Analytical**

OBJECTIVE Explore palindromes to see when a palindrome added to itself will be another palindrome.

▶ Explain that a palindrome is a word or number that reads the same forward and backward. Pop and dad are word palindromes; 54,745 and 8,338 are number palindromes. Ask:
  • **When is the sum of a palindrome and itself another palindrome?**

▶ Have partners make a three-column table.

▶ In the first column one partner writes five palindromes with three to six digits. In the second column the other partner writes the number in the first column backward. In the third column, partners write the sum of the numbers.

▶ Partners formulate a rule to answer the previous question. Students should find that when adding a palindrome to itself does not involve regrouping, the sum is another palindrome.

Palindrome	Backward Palindrome	Sum
5,005	5,005	10,010
33,133	33,133	66,266
43,234	43,234	86,468

CONSUMER CONNECTION

Cooperative Groups   **Social**

OBJECTIVE Create a spreadsheet.

Materials per group: 0–9 spinner (TA 2), calculator

▶ Show students how to set up a spreadsheet that displays the quarters of a calendar year. Each group decides on a company product and name, and records this on the spreadsheet showing their company's yearly earnings.

▶ One student begins by spinning three numbers. The 3-digit number is recorded as the earnings in the *Jan-Mar* quarter on the spreadsheet. Students take turns spinning and recording numbers until they have earnings recorded for each quarter. They then use a calculator to find the total.

▶ Continue the activity by having students spin one number for each quarter to see how many thousands of dollars they earned above the same quarter last year. Have them record the new earnings and totals.

Jan-Mar	Apr-June	July-Sept	Oct-Dec	Total
$	$	$	$	$

Daily Review

PREVIOUS DAY QUICK REVIEW

Add.
1. 781 + 24 [805]
2. 47,183 + 91,278 [138,461]
3. $45.69 + $10.92 [$56.61]
4. $1,396 + $5,232 [$6,628]

FAST FACTS

1. 10 − 3 [7]
2. 7 − 2 [5]
3. 9 − 6 [3]
4. 10 − 9 [1]

Problem of the Day • 14

The distance from Peg's house to school is 4 miles. The distance from Juanita's house to Peg's house is half the distance from Peg's house to school. How far does Juanita travel to go to school if she stops at Peg's house on her way? [6 mi]

TECH LINK

MATH VAN

Tool You may wish to use the Calculator with this lesson.

MATH FORUM

Idea To check students' understanding of the math skill taught each day, I have them write and solve one problem, and hand it in.

Visit our Resource Village at http://www.mhschool.com to see more of the Math Forum.

MATH CENTER

Practice

OBJECTIVE Add 3 or more addends.

Materials per group: 20 index cards; per student: Math Center Recording Sheet (TA 31 optional)

Prepare Write a different 3-digit number between 100 and 400 on each index card.

Students play a game. They choose and add 3-digit numbers, trying to get a sum that is closest to 1,000.

PRACTICE ACTIVITY 14
MATH CENTER — Small Group

Game • Add 'Em Up to 1,000

- Turn the cards facedown. Choose a card. After you flip over the card, you must call out
  —*Yes* if you plan to add it to make your total 1,000.
  —*No* if you do not plan to add it to your total.
  If you say *yes*, keep the card in front of you. If you say *no*, put the card in a discard pile.
  The next player chooses a card and decides whether to keep or discard it.
- Take turns choosing cards until all cards have been picked up or discarded once. Each player adds all of his or her numbers. The person with the sum that is closest to 1,000 wins. Play again.

YOU NEED 20 index cards—a different 3-digit number between 100 and 400 on each card

455
341
120

NCTM Standards
Problem Solving
✓ Communication
✓ Reasoning
Connections

Chapter 2, Lesson 6, pages 52–53 — Addition

Problem Solving

OBJECTIVE Add three addends.

Materials per pair: inch graph paper (TA 8), 2 counters

Partners each drop a counter on the game board. They each move two times, adding numbers as they move. They must move in a different direction each time.

PROBLEM-SOLVING ACTIVITY 14
MATH CENTER — Partners

Logical Reasoning • Which Way?

- Copy the game board. Each partner drops a counter on the game board to start.
- You can each move two times. You must move in a different direction each time. Add the numbers on your start square and on the two spaces you move to.
- The partner with the greatest sum after two moves wins that round. Play five rounds.

YOU NEED inch graph paper; a counter for each player

243	19	123	147	10
49	854	21	39	542
682	54	797	74	426
88	384	96	984	65

NCTM Standards
✓ Problem Solving
Communication
✓ Reasoning
Connections

Chapter 2, Lesson 6, pages 52–53 — Addition

Lesson 2.6 continued

Three or More Addends

1 Introduce

Ask students to estimate the average length of a movie. Most students will say about 1 1/2 to 2 1/2 hours. Ask students to look at the times for the videos on page 52. Ask:

- **Will watching all three movies take more or less than 5 hours? Explain.** *[More; it would take more than 1 hour to watch Lassie, more than 2 hours to watch Little Women, and more than 2 hours to watch The Sound of Music, which is more than 5 hours total.]*

2 Teach
Whole Class

▶ **LEARN** Read through the problem and discuss how to solve it. Ask:

- **How is solving this problem different from solving problems with two addends? How is it the same?** *[There are more numbers to add in each place; you still add from right to left, regrouping when necessary.]*

Review the Commutative and Associative properties. Ask:

- **Where in the example is the Commutative Property used? the Associative Property?** *[Answers may vary. Possible answers: Commutative Property—where the tens are added, 1 + 9 + 2 + 7 is reordered to 9 + 1 + 7 + 2; Associative Property—where the ones are added, (5 + 2) + 5 is changed to (5 + 5) + 2.]*

3 Close

Check for Understanding using items 1–4, page 52.

CRITICAL THINKING
After answering item 6, ask students to determine how many hours and minutes it will take to watch the three movies. *[6 hours, 32 minutes]*

▶ **PRACTICE**
Materials have available: calculators

Options for assigning exercises:
A—Odd ex. 1–13; **More to Explore**
B—Even ex. 1–12; **More to Explore**

- For ex. 6–11, have students rewrite the problems in a vertical format. Remind students to align digits carefully.

More to Explore Adding zero and adding doubles are two strategies that can be used when adding long columns of numbers. Encourage students to describe other strategies they may use.

Three or More Addends

L E A R N

Does your family rent movies? How long would it take to watch these three movies?

Add: 95 + 122 + 175

Estimate the sum.   **Think:** 100 + 100 + 200 = 400

> **Commutative Property** You can change the order of two addends without changing the sum.
>
> **Associative Property** You can change the grouping of three or more addends without changing the sum.

You can use the **Commutative** and **Associative** properties to help you find the exact sum.

Step 1	Step 2	Step 3
Add the ones. **Regroup if necessary.**	**Add all the tens.** **Regroup if necessary.**	**Add all the hundreds.**
$\begin{array}{r} 1 \\ 95 \\ 122 \\ +175 \\ \hline 2 \end{array}$ **Think:** 5 + 5 = 10 10 + 2 = 12	$\begin{array}{r} 11 \\ 95 \\ 122 \\ +175 \\ \hline 92 \end{array}$ **Think:** 9 + 1 = 10 10 + 7 + 2 = 19	$\begin{array}{r} 11 \\ 95 \\ 122 \\ +175 \\ \hline 392 \end{array}$

 You can also use a calculator.   95 + 122 + 175 = **392.**

It would take them 392 minutes to watch all the movies.

C H E C K

Check for Understanding
Estimates may vary depending on the method used. Estimates shown are by rounding.

Add. Estimate to check that your answer is reasonable.

1 48 + 65 + 72
185; 190

2 4,290 + 740 + 518
5,548; 5,200

3 158 + 74 + 92 + 301
625; 660

Critical Thinking: Analyze   Explain your reasoning.

4 Why is it important to line up the ones digits when adding? Give an example using a 2-, a 3-, and a 4-digit number.

52 Lesson 2.6   Possible answer: to be sure digits having the same place value are added together; examples may vary.

Meeting Individual Needs

Early Finishers

Students can calculate the total number of students in the school or in several classes. Give them the individual class numbers.

Extra Support

To help encourage students to line up the digits before adding, have them complete ex. 1–5 on graph paper.

Ongoing Assessment

Anecdotal Report Make notes on what strategies students use to add columns of numbers. Ask students to describe how to find the sum in a given exercise.

Follow Up To challenge students, have them solve problems with more than three addends or with numbers having more than four digits. Assign **Extend 14**.

If students have difficulty, assign **Reteach 14**.

13. Students' decisions should reflect choices given in the price list.

Practice

Add. Remember to estimate.

1 47	**2** 457	**3** 1,268	**4** $24.69	**5** 1,709
54	35	793	73.45	2,340
+ 36	+ 153	+ 204	+ 86.21	569
137	**645**	**2,265**	**$184.35**	+ 753
				5,371

6 87 + 629 + 4,125 **4,841**

7 54 + 89 + 351 + 822 **1,316**

8 134 + 487 + 5,206 + 978 **6,805**

9 70 + 2,400 + 900 **3,370**

10 $12.52 + $7.45 + $11.89 **$31.86**

11 10,500 + 2,750 + 3,478 **16,728**

 **MIXED APPLICATIONS**
Problem Solving

Use the store ad for problems 12–13.

12 **What if** you can buy a CD player in July if you pay $7 each month until January and then pay $100.95. What would be the total cost? Is this a better price than buying the CD player from JC's Store? **$142.95; yes, the CD player costs $149.95 at JC's.**

13 **Make a decision** If you had $500, what would you buy to get the radio/cassette free? Explain. See above.

JC's Store
—PRICE LIST—
VHS Recorder: $199.95
Each video: $17.99
Rechargeable CD Player: $149.95
AM/FM/CD/Cassette Recorder: $99.95
Each CD: $11.99 Each cassette: $7.99
Zoom Supreme Design Camera: $399.95
Pay $30 now, pay rest next January
NO INTEREST!
Spend $500, get Radio/Cassette FREE!

more to explore

Other Addition Strategies

You can use other addition properties or strategies to help you add.

Add: 396 + 0 + 23

396
+ 23
419

Think: 23 + 0 = 23
If you add zero to a number, you get the number.

Add: 143 + 313 + 242

143
313
+ 242
698

Think:
Look for doubles.

Add. Explain your method. Explanations may vary.

1 582 + 344 + 142
1,068; possible answer: find doubles.

2 2,639 + 0 + 632
3,271; possible answer: add zero.

3 1,056 + 356
1,412; possible answer: find doubles and make tens.

Extra Practice, page 489

Money, Addition, and Subtraction **53**

Alternate Teaching Strategy

Write *898 + 234 + 689* on the chalkboard and show students how to find the sum by marking multiples of 10 and only keeping track of the ones digits.

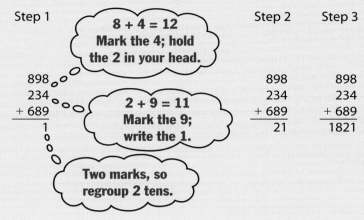

Step 1

8 + 4 = 12
Mark the 4; hold the 2 in your head.

898
234
+ 689
1

2 + 9 = 11
Mark the 9; write the 1.

Two marks, so regroup 2 tens.

Step 2
898
234
+ 689
21

Step 3
898
234
+ 689
1821

Have students use this strategy to solve other problems with three or more addends of 1-, 2-, and 3-digit numbers.

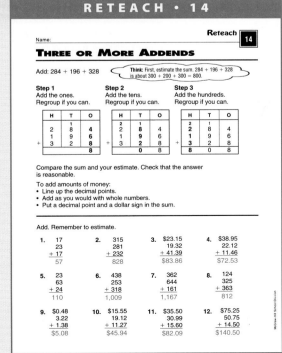

PRACTICE • 14

Name: _____ Practice 14

THREE OR MORE ADDENDS

Add. Remember to estimate.

1. 12	2. $14	3. 12	4. 26
14	82	21	32
+ 22	+ 3	+ 39	+ 65
48	$99	72	123

5. 213	6. 721	7. $895	8. 263
142	20	511	192
+ 324	+ 219	+ 345	+ 859
679	960	$1,751	1,314

9. $32.32	10. 8,239	11. 4,320	12. 3,121
14.53	1,534	1,290	7,383
+ 20.10	+ 121	3,860	2,947
$66.95	9,894	+ 2,199	+ 11,231
		11,669	24,682

13. 61 + 69 + 33 = ___163___

14. 24 + 33 + 73 = ___130___

15. 252 + 514 + 115 = ___881___

16. $13.24 + $6.57 + $18.36 = ___$38.17___

17. 26 + 2,300 + 765 = ___3,091___

18. $263.54 + $54.67 + $582.41 = ___$900.62___

19. 1,599 + 999 + 12,822 = ___15,420___

20. 10,340 + 4,235 + 2,378 = ___16,953___

Solve.

21. Mrs. Endo bought three items at the store. The prices were $1.12, $9.99, and $6.02. How much did she spend altogether?
___$17.13___

22. At the store, 125 people bought a sale item on Monday, 42 on Tuesday, and 37 on Wednesday. How many people bought the sale item on these three days?
___204 people___

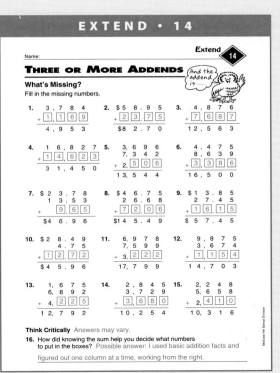

RETEACH • 14

Name: _____ Reteach 14

THREE OR MORE ADDENDS

Add: 284 + 196 + 328

Think: First, estimate the sum. 284 + 196 + 328 is about 300 + 200 + 300 = 800.

Step 1
Add the ones. Regroup if you can.

H	T	O
	1	
2	8	4
1	9	6
+ 3	2	8
		8

Step 2
Add the tens. Regroup if you can.

H	T	O
	1	
2	8	4
1	9	6
+ 3	2	8
	0	8

Step 3
Add the hundreds. Regroup if you can.

H	T	O
	1	
2	8	4
1	9	6
+ 3	2	8
8	0	8

Compare the sum and your estimate. Check that the answer is reasonable.

To add amounts of money:
• Line up the decimal points.
• Add as you would with whole numbers.
• Put a decimal point and a dollar sign in the sum.

Add. Remember to estimate.

1. 17	2. 315	3. $23.15	4. $38.95
23	281	19.32	22.12
+ 17	+ 232	+ 41.39	+ 11.46
57	828	$83.86	$72.53

5. 23	6. 438	7. 362	8. 124
63	253	644	325
+ 24	+ 318	+ 161	+ 363
110	1,009	1,167	812

9. $0.48	10. $15.55	11. $35.50	12. $75.25
3.22	19.12	30.99	50.75
+ 1.38	+ 11.27	+ 15.60	+ 14.50
$5.08	$45.94	$82.09	$140.50

EXTEND • 14

Name: _____ Extend 14

THREE OR MORE ADDENDS

And the addend is ....

What's Missing?
Fill in the missing numbers.

1.   3, 7 8 4
   + 1 1 6 9
     4, 9 5 3

2. $ 5 8 . 9 5
   + 2 3 7 5
    $8 2 . 7 0

3.   4, 8 7 6
   + 7 6 8 7
    1 2, 5 6 3

4.   1 6, 8 2 7
   + 1 4 6 2 3
     3 1, 4 5 0

5.   3, 6 9 6
      7, 3 4 2
   + 2, 5 0 6
     1 3, 5 4 4

6.   4, 4 7 5
      8, 6 3 9
   + 3, 3 8 6
     1 6, 5 0 0

7. $ 2 3 . 7 8
      1 3 . 5 3
   + 9 6 5
    $4 6 . 9 6

8. $4 6 . 7 5
      2 6 . 6 8
   + 7 2 0 6
    $14 5 . 4 9

9. $1 3 . 8 5
      2 7 . 4 5
   + 1 6 1 5
    $5 7 . 4 5

10. $2 8 . 4 9
       4 . 7 5
   + 1 2 7 2
    $4 5 . 9 6

11.   6, 9 7 8
       7, 5 9 9
   + 3, 2 2 2
    1 7, 7 9 9

12.   9, 8 7 5
       3, 6 7 4
   + 1, 1 5 4
    1 4, 7 0 3

13.   1, 6 7 5
       6, 8 9 2
   + 4, 2 2 5
    1 2, 7 9 2

14.   2, 8 4 5
       3, 7 2 9
   + 3, 6 8 0
    1 0, 2 5 4

15.   2, 2 4 8
       5, 6 5 8
   + 2, 4 1 0
    1 0, 3 1 6

Think Critically Answers may vary.

16. How did knowing the sum help you decide what numbers to put in the boxes? Possible answer: I used basic addition facts and figured out one column at a time, working from the right.

53

MIDCHAPTER REVIEW

PURPOSE Maintain and review concepts, skills, and strategies that students have learned thus far in the chapter.

Materials have available: play money—bills and coins

Using the Midchapter Review

Have students complete the **Midchapter Review** independently or use it with the whole class.

Encourage students to solve ex. 13–23 and 30–32 without the use of manipulatives. If they need some assistance, suggest that they draw pictures of place-value models.

 Students may describe the rounding method taught in this chapter, but they may also describe other methods they know. Accept all reasonable answers.

Possible methods include:
–rounding each number to the greatest place
  (200 + 1000 + 3000 = 4200),
–rounding each number to the greatest place common to all
  (200 + 1500 + 2500 = 4200),
–adjusting numbers so that they are easier to add mentally
  (240 + 1,460 = 1,700; 1,700 + 2,500 = 4,200),
–using front-end estimation (200 + 1,000 + 2,000 = 3,200).

Vocabulary Review

Write the following words on the chalkboard:
    Associative Property Commutative Property
    estimate   regroup   sum

Ask for volunteers to explain, show, or act out the meanings of these words and to give examples.

Add mentally.
1 30 + 40 **70**   2 700 + 400 **1,100**   3 4,000 + 8,000 **12,000**   4 12,000 + 5,000 **17,000**

Estimate the sum. Estimates may vary depending on the method used. Estimates shown are by rounding.
5 64 + 19 **80**   6 395 + 654 **1,100**   7 $6.25 + $5.54 **$12**   8 4,186 + 765 **4,800**
9 212 + 689 **900**   10 552 + 74 **670**   11 $33.78 + $65.00 **$100**   12 5,425 + 14,650 **20,000**

Add. Use mental math when you can.

13 75
  + 18
  ‾‾‾
  93

14 6,225
  + 5,859
  ‾‾‾‾‾
  12,084

15 $4.69
  + 8.05
  ‾‾‾‾‾
  $12.74

16 15,308
  + 6,475
  ‾‾‾‾‾
  21,783

17 659
  + 74
  ‾‾‾
  733

18 27 + 43 **70**   19 40 + 30 + 57 **127**   20 500 + 700 + 315 **1,515**

21 586 + 719 **1,305**   22 749 + 89 **838**   23 $712 + $459 + $1,570 + $98 **$2,839**

Write the amount.

24  $9.46   25 $23.31

Find the amount of change.
26 Price of memo pad: $0.89
    Cash given: $5 **$4.11**

27 Price of earrings: $7.35
    Cash given: $10 **$2.65**

Write in order from least to greatest.
28 $62.05, $6.50, $26.50, $62.50
    $6.50, $26.50, $62.05, $62.50

29 $19.62, $119.15, $1.67, $16.92
    $1.67, $16.92, $19.62, $119.15

Solve. Use any method.
30 The Renoir School sponsored an art show. There were 145 ceramic pieces, 274 paintings, and 78 pieces of jewelry. About how many pieces of art were there?
    about 500 pieces

31 On Friday 650 people attended the show. On Saturday 893 people attended the show. On which day did more people attend? **Saturday**

32 Skye bought two pieces of students' work for $8.50 and $12.25. How much did he spend?
    $20.75

33 Explain three different ways you can estimate 239 + 1,468 + 2,529.
    33. Possible answer: Round to the nearest thousand: 0 + 1,000 + 3,000 = 4,000, round to the nearest hundred: 200 + 1,500 + 2,500 = 4,200, round to the greatest place: 200 + 1,000 + 3,000 = 4,200

54 Midchapter Review

Reinforcement and Remediation

CHAPTER OBJECTIVES	MIDCHAPTER REVIEW ITEMS	STUDENT BOOK PAGES	TEACHER'S EDITION PAGES		TEACHER RESOURCES
			Activities	Alternate Teaching Strategy	Reteach
2A	24–25, 31	42–43	41A	43	10
2B	24–29	40–41	39A	41	9
2C	5–12, 30, 33	46–47	45A	47	12
2D	1–4, 13–23, 32	44–45, 48–53	43A, 47A, 51A	45, 51, 53	11, 13–14

*2A Write, compare, order, and round money amounts
*2B Count money and make change
*2C Estimate the sums and differences of numbers, including money amounts
*2D Add and subtract numbers, including money amounts

Use Front Digits to Estimate

Dawn wants to buy a pair of skis that costs $115. She has $95 in her bank account. On her birthday, she gets $38. Does she have enough money?

Use the front digit of each number to estimate the answer.

Estimate: 95 + 38
          ↓   ↓
          90 + 30 = 120   Compare: $120 > $115

Dawn has more than $115. She has enough money to buy the skis.

2. Yes; $2,000 + $3,000 = $5,000, and the total receipts were greater than this amount.

Solve. Use front digits to estimate. Explain your reasoning.

1 Here are the results of a survey on how often customers shopped in Vesta's each month.
- More than 5 times: 247
- 3 to 5 times: 378
- Less than 3 times: 615

Were more or fewer than 1,000 people surveyed? **more than 1,000 people; 200 + 300 + 600 = 1,100 > 1,000**

2 Vesta's will give away a free computer to the Sheerin School if the school can collect $5,000 worth of receipts. In November the school collected $2,650 in receipts. In December the school collected $3,600. Will the school get the free computer? **See above.**

3 Ms. Clark has $200. She wants to buy a bicycle for $99, a fishing rod for $59, and a fishing reel for $75. Does she have enough money? **No; $90 + $50 + $70 = $210 > $200.**

4 Dawn earns $22 dog-sitting and $16 recycling bottles and cans. Does she have enough money to buy a ski jacket for $29.99? **Yes; $20 + $10 = $30 > $29.99.**

5 **Make a decision** Obando's local store sells the book *Long Journey* for $7.95. The book sells at Vesta's for $6.09. Obando can walk to the local store, but he must pay $2.25 for the bus fare to and from Vesta's. What should he do? **Possible answer: It is cheaper to buy the book at the neighborhood store—$6 + $2 = $8 > $7.95.**

6 Freddy is collecting baseball cards. His album holds 200 cards. Last week he bought 64 cards at Vesta's. For his birthday he got 74 cards, and his neighbor gave him 92 cards. Can his album hold all these cards? **No; 60 + 70 + 90 = 220 > 200.**

Money, Addition, and Subtraction **55**

OBJECTIVE Use front-end estimation, without adjustment, to estimate the sum of two or more addends.

Using Number Sense

Math Connection In Lesson 4, students rounded to estimate sums. Here students add only the front-end digits to estimate sums. Faster than rounding, this method always gives an estimate that is less than the exact sum. It is a useful method to apply when the situation calls for a quick estimate, or when an underestimate is needed.

After students read the opening problem and solution, ask:
- **How do you know the exact sum is greater than $120?** *[Since $95 > $90 and $38 > $30, the exact sum is greater than $90 + $30, or $120.]*
- **Will this method always result in an estimate that is less than the exact sum? Explain.** *[Yes; possible answer: you only use the front digits of each number to make the estimate and you think of all the other digits as zero—if any of the other digits are greater than zero, the exact sum will be greater than the estimate.]*

Students may work in pairs or on their own to complete ex. 1–6.

Applying Addition and Subtraction

OBJECTIVE Add and subtract money amounts in the context of budgeting purchases.

❶ Engage

Ask students to recall their last purchase. Have them classify that purchase using the eleven categories shown in the table on page 56 of the Student Book. Then make a class table and compare the results with those in the Student Book table.

• **What might account for the differences?** *[Possible answers: Adults are usually responsible for paying most of the cost for these items, especially #1–5. The households represented by our class are different from the households reflected in the table.]*

❷ Investigate   *Cooperative Groups*

Suggest that students make a three-column table to help organize their answers to the questions on page 56 of the student book. Tell them they should not concern themselves with the total cost. The only limitation is that each item cost less than $400.

Spending Money Students can brainstorm ways of collecting more information about the items they wish to purchase and decide which catalogs each will bring to school for the rest of the group. Students can compare lists for their shopping trip, and team up to find prices. Students can then narrow down their list to ten items that total less than $400.

Students can make a new table to help track spending, like the one shown below. Tell students that "balance" means the amount of money left after making each purchase.

Using the Partners Check Strategy, have partners take turns filling in a section of the table. Partners take turns checking each other's work for understanding of a procedure or concept. Partners correct or appreciate each other's work.

Item	Cost	Balance

❸ Reflect and Share

Materials have available: calculators

Report Your Findings

Write a Paragraph Students can work individually on their reports, then meet again in groups to compare and revise their work. Remind them to check for clearly stated main ideas and details. Suggest they use calculators to check each other's calculations.

real-life investigation
APPLYING ADDITION AND SUBTRACTION

How We Spend Our **Money**

Americans spend their money in many different ways. In this activity, you will work with a group to decide what you would buy if you went on a $400 shopping trip.

What things would you buy?

Where would you buy them?

What prices would you pay?

Ways That Americans Spend Their Money

1 Health
2 Food
3 Rent
4 Items for the home
5 Transportation
6 Personal Expenses
7 Recreation
8 Clothing
9 Charities
10 School fees
11 Personal

56 Real-life Investigation

More To Investigate

Predict Possible approach: Remind students to make predictions without looking at their reports. After working with the sales figures for a while, they should be able to make reasonable predictions.

Explore Possible approach: Students will have more data to work with if they consider not only items they buy but also items their parents purchase for them.

Find Possible answer: This may help the store sell off holiday-related merchandise.

Bibliography Students who want to learn more about comparison shopping and consumer issues of interest to 8-to-14-year olds can read *Zillions* (bi-monthly) published by Consumer's Union of U.S. Inc. 101 Truman Avenue, Yonkers, NY 10703–1057. ISSN 0190–1966.

DECISION MAKING

Spending Money

1 Shop for items your group would like to purchase by:

- ▶ visiting stores, markets, and other places where you can shop.
- ▶ collecting catalogs, newspapers, and store fliers.
- ▶ collecting advertisements, sales brochures, and coupons.

Calculate the prices you would need to pay for the items.

2 Decide on at least ten items you will buy with $400. List them in order of importance.

3 Describe where the items were bought. Include any coupons or advertisements you used.

4 Use a table to keep track of your spending. Record each item you buy, the amount already spent, and the balance or amount that is left.

Reporting Your Findings

5 Prepare a report that describes what you buy. Include the following:

- ▶ Show your record of each item, the total amount spent, and the balance.

Write a Paragraph
Tell what items you bought and how much each one cost. Include the total you spent and how much you have left. Explain how you decided what items to buy and where to buy them.

6 Compare your report with the reports of other groups.

Revise your work.

- ▶ Are your calculations correct?
- ▶ Is your report clear and organized?
- ▶ Did you proofread your work?

MORE TO INVESTIGATE

See Teacher's Edition.

PREDICT the greatest number of items you could buy from your original list with $250. Then check your prediction.

EXPLORE the items you buy in a week and how much money you actually spend.

FIND out why certain items are always on sale each year at the same time.

Money, Addition, and Subtraction **57**

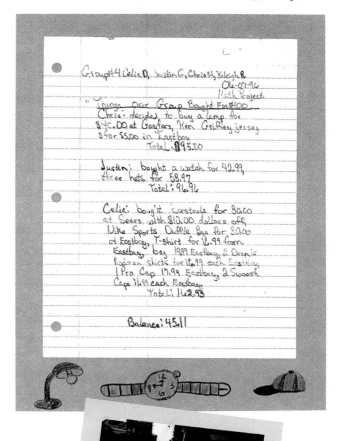

Students' Work

Building A Portfolio

This investigation will allow you to evaluate a student's ability to organize data and to add and subtract money amounts.

Allow students to revise their work for the portfolio. Each student's portfolio piece should consist of two or more pages displaying their record of purchases and written explanations of their choices and their trade-offs. Place any notes you made about a student's work in her or his portfolio.

You may wish to use the Holistic Scoring Guide to assess this task. See page 27 in Teacher's Assessment Resources.

LESSON 2.7

MENTAL MATH

Subtraction Strategies

OBJECTIVE Use properties and strategies to subtract mentally.

RESOURCE REMINDER
Math Center Cards 15
Practice 15, Reteach 15, Extend 15

SKILLS TRACE

GRADE 3
- Use strategies to subtract 2- to 3-digit numbers mentally. *(Chapter 4)*

GRADE 4
- Use strategies to subtract 3-digit numbers mentally.

GRADE 5
- Use strategies to subtract whole numbers mentally. *(Chapter 2)*

MANIPULATIVE WARM-UP

Cooperative Groups   **Social**

OBJECTIVE Subtract 1-digit money amounts from 1- and 2-digit money amounts.

Materials per group: play money—bills

► Player one in each group says, "I have $100 and I am going to spend $___," filling in the blank with a 1-digit number. Player two subtracts the single digit and says, "I have $___ and I am going to spend $___."

► Play continues with players taking turns determining the amount of money they have and how much they will spend, until all the money is gone.

► Have students play the game again, but this time have each group put some limitation on the amount of money that can be spent; for example, they can spend only odd amounts of money.

ALGEBRA CONNECTION

Whole Class   **Logical/Analytical**

OBJECTIVE Use logic to determine the number of counters in a cup.

Materials 2 identical cups, 30 counters, balance

► Ask a volunteer to place up to 30 counters in a cup and a few counters on one side of a balance without the rest of the class seeing.

► Have another volunteer place some counters in an empty cup on the other side of the balance, while students keep count. This continues until the scale is balanced.

► Discuss and choose a method of finding the number of counters the first volunteer put in the cup. Let volunteers test the suggested methods.

Daily Review

Problem of the Day • 15

The postage rate for first class mail is $0.32 for the first ounce and $0.23 for each additional ounce. What is the cost of mailing a letter that weighs 6 ounces? *[$1.47]*

TECH LINK

MATH FORUM

Idea I have my students work on mental-math problems daily. Through continued exposure to these types of problems students often discover their own strategies to make mental math easier.

Visit our Resource Village at http://www.mhschool.com to see more of the Math Forum.

MATH CENTER

Practice

OBJECTIVE Subtract using mental math.

Materials per pair: number cube, Math Center Recording Sheet (TA 31 optional)

Without letting their partner see, students toss a number cube to write a subtraction problem that can be solved mentally using the tossed number. The partner solves the problem and gets a point for correctly identifying the number tossed.

Problem Solving

OBJECTIVE Use a subtraction strategy.

Materials per student: Math Center Recording Sheet (TA 31 optional)

Students use a game board to practice a subtraction strategy. They then create a game board to get a greater score. *[Check students' work.]*

PRACTICE ACTIVITY 15   MATH CENTER · Partners

Number Sense • Toss-Up!

YOU NEED : number cube

- Without letting your partner see, toss a cube to get a number.
- Write a subtraction problem that can be solved mentally using the number you tossed. For example, if you toss a 3, you might write 83–53.
- Your partner solves the problem mentally and tells you what number you tossed. If your partner tells you the number you tossed, your partner gets a point. If not, you get a point.
- Switch roles and keep playing. The first player to get 5 points wins.

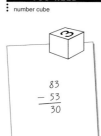

$$\begin{array}{r} 83 \\ -\ 53 \\ \hline 30 \end{array}$$

Chapter 2, Lesson 7, pages 58–59   Subtraction

ESL APPROPRIATE

NCTM Standards
- Problem Solving
- ✓ Communication
- ✓ Reasoning
- Connections

PROBLEM-SOLVING ACTIVITY 15   MATH CENTER · On Your Own

Logical Reasoning • Up, Down, and Sideways

- Pick any two neighboring numbers.
- Subtract the same number from each. The number you subtract by is your score.
  Hint: Subtracting by the largest number possible makes your score higher.
- Repeat three more times. Total your score.
- Play again. This time try for a higher score.
Now make a game board of your own that allows an even greater score!

26	8	31	8
69	46	85	96
29	19	48	29
74	18	76	35
96	39	53	28

Chapter 2, Lesson 7, pages 58–59   Subtraction

NCTM Standards
- ✓ Problem Solving
- Communication
- ✓ Reasoning
- ✓ Connections

Lesson 2.7 *continued*

MENTAL MATH
Subtraction Strategies

OBJECTIVE Use properties and strategies to subtract mentally.

Vocabulary difference, subtract

Write the following subtraction expressions on the chalkboard.

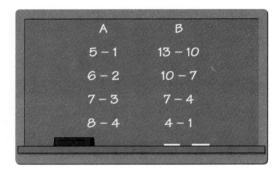

A	B
5 − 1	13 − 10
6 − 2	10 − 7
7 − 3	7 − 4
8 − 4	4 − 1

Have students find the differences and discuss any patterns they see. *[Numbers increase or decrease the same amount from one expression to the next, but the difference remains the same.]*

 **Teach** *Whole Class*

▶ **LEARN** Have students read the introductory problem and study the two solutions. Point out that when the same amount is added to or subtracted from both numbers in the subtraction, the difference does not change.

❸ Close

▶ **Check for Understanding** using items 1–5, page 58.

CRITICAL THINKING
After answering item 5, discuss whether the Associative Property can be used with subtraction.

▶ **PRACTICE**
Materials have available: calculators

Options for assigning exercises:
A—Even ex. 2–16; all ex. 17–22; **Mixed Review**
B—Odd ex. 1–15; all ex. 17–22; **Mixed Review**

Mixed Review/Test Preparation Rounding (ex. 1–5) is taught in Chapter 1. Adding mentally (ex. 6–9) is taught in Lesson 3 of this chapter.

Algebra: Patterns Students explore the Zero Property in ex. 17. Have students point out the pattern when subtracting zero. In ex. 18, students should realize that any number subtracted from itself equals zero.

Subtraction Strategies

LEARN

Kits are popular with 8- to 12-year-olds. An explorer kit is $93 in the catalog. What is the sale price for the kit?

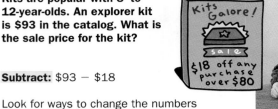

Subtract: $93 − $18

Look for ways to change the numbers so you can find the **difference** mentally.

Think: Add 2 to each number.

$93 − $18
+ 2 ↓   ↓ + 2
$95 − $20 = $75

Think: Subtract 3 from each number.

$93 − $18
− 3 ↓   ↓ − 3
$90 − $15 = $75

The sale price of the kit is $75.

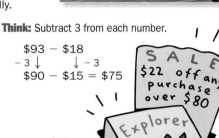

What if the sale is $22 off any purchase over $80. What would be the sale price of the kit?

Subtract: $93 − $22

You can also subtract mentally using this method.

$93
− 22

Think: $93 − $20 = $73
$73 − $2 = $71

The sale price of the kit would be $71.

> **Check Out the Glossary**
> difference
> subtract
> See page 544.

CHECK

Check for Understanding
Subtract mentally. Explain your thinking. Explanations may vary.

1 28 − 18 **10**   **2** 85¢ − 52¢ **33¢**   **3** $276 − $99 **$177**   **4** 485 − 260 **225**

Critical Thinking: Analyze   **Explain your reasoning.**

5 Does subtraction have a Commutative Property like addition? Use place-value models to support your answer.   No; 10 − 7 is not equal to 7 − 10.

58   Lesson 2.7

Meeting Individual Needs

Early Finishers

For ex. 1–16, have students use addition to check their answers. Ask students to analyze the exercises they did wrong and record them in their math journal.

Extra Support

Students can use a number line to help them subtract.

Ongoing Assessment

Interview Determine if students can apply the strategy of subtracting a simpler number by asking:

• **How can you change 435 − 191 so that it is easy to subtract mentally?** *[Possible answer: Add 9 to both numbers, then subtract—444 − 200 = 244.]*

Follow Up Students having difficulty should talk through problems they did incorrectly with another student. For additional help, assign **Reteach 15.**

Have students who are comfortable with subtracting mentally try **Extend 15.**

20. Yes—$15.49 + $9.87 = $25.36, $25.36 − $5 (discount) + $3.95 (delivery) = $24.31.
21. The Birds Around Us kit and two tangram puzzles are cheaper; $15.49 + $17.99 − $5 = $28.48, which is more than $8.99 + $9.87 + $9.87 − $5 = $23.73.

Practice

Subtract mentally.

1 26 − 8 **18**   **2** 31 − 7 **24**   **3** 29 − 19 **10**   **4** 48 − 29 **19**

5 74 − 18 **56**   **6** 96 − 35 **61**   **7** 86¢ − 19¢ **67¢**   **8** 153 − 28 **125**

9 293 − 76 **217**   **10** $7.77 − $1.98 **$5.79**   **11** 645 − 497 **148**   **12** $8.04 − $6.79 **$1.25**

13 592 − 103 **489**   **14** $0.47 − $0.14 **$0.33**   **15** $2.64 − $0.99 **$1.65**   **16** 435 − 197 **238**

ALGEBRA: PATTERNS Find each difference. What pattern do you notice?

17 a. 23 − 0 **23**   b. 59 − 0 **59**   c. 187 − 0 **187**   d. 365 − 0 **365**
When 0 is subtracted from a number, the difference is that number.

18 a. 48 − 48 **0**   b. 546 − 546 **0**   c. 866 − 866 **0**   d. 738 − 738 **0**
When a number is subtracted from itself, the answer is 0.

MIXED APPLICATIONS
Problem Solving

Use the catalog page for problems 19–22.

19 Karen has $9.54. If she buys a Birds Around Us kit, how much money will she have left? **$0.55**

20 Sal has $25. Can he afford the tangram puzzles, electricity kit, and delivery? **See above.**

21 Is it cheaper to buy the Electricity Exploration kit and the Build Your Own Radio kit or the Birds Around Us kit and two tangram puzzles? Explain. **See above.**

22 **Write a problem** using the catalog. Solve it and have others solve it. **Students' decisions should reflect choices given in the catalog.**

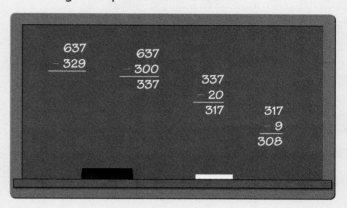

EXPLORATION COMPANY *Sale!*

Elecricity Exploration	$15.49
Build Your Own Radio	$17.99
Make Your Own Camera	$14.85
Plants Around Us	$8.69
Birds Around Us	$8.99
Tangram Puzzles	$9.87
Gift Box	$2.25

Take off an additional $5. for purchases over $25.

DELIVERY
$50.00 and less $3.95
$50.01 - 100.00 .... $6.95
$100.01 and more $9.95

mixed review • test preparation

Round to the nearest hundred and the nearest thousand.

1 721 **700; 1000**   **2** 854 **900; 1,000**   **3** 2,319 **2,300; 2,000**   **4** 3,975 **4,000; 4,000**   **5** 25,542 **25,500; 26,000**

Add mentally.

6 83 + 47 **130**   **7** 48 + 95 **143**   **8** 239 + 403 **642**   **9** 698 + 257 **955**

Extra Practice, page 490   Money, Addition, and Subtraction   **59**

Alternate Teaching Strategy

Materials place-value chart (TA 4)

Use a place-value chart to review the value of each digit in various 3- and 4-digit numbers. Have students record each number in expanded form.

Present this subtraction, 637 − 329. Elicit that 329 written in expanded form is 300 + 20 + 9. Show how to find the difference using the expanded form of 329:

```
  637        637
− 329      − 300       337
           -----      −  20       317
            337      -----      −   9
                      317       -----
                                  308
```

Continue the activity, giving students opportunities to subtract 2- and 3-digit numbers. As students become accustomed to this method, encourage them to do more and more of the steps mentally.

PRACTICE • 15

Practice 15

Name: _____

MENTAL MATH: SUBTRACTION STRATEGIES

Subtract mentally.

1. 36 − 8 = **28**   2. 41 − 9 = **32**   3. 59 − 19 = **40**

4. 82 − 55 = **27**   5. 26¢ − 15¢ = **11¢**   6. 92 − 45 = **47**

7. 73 − 45 = **28**   8. 49 − 17 = **32**   9. 71¢ − 59¢ = **12¢**

10. 68¢ − 15¢ = **53¢**   11. 34 − 12 = **22**   12. 67 − 49 = **18**

13. 45 − 27 = **18**   14. 62 − 56 = **6**   15. 73 − 59 = **14**

16. 974 − 150 = **824**   17. $3.75 − $2.54 = **$1.21**

18. $2.31 − $1.10 = **$1.21**   19. 755 − 245 = **510**

20. $8.45 − $1.55 = **$6.90**   21. 235 − 129 = **106**

22. 743 − 297 = **446**   23. 487 − 126 = **361**

24. 393 − 85 = **308**   25. $5.07 − $0.75 = **$4.32**

26. $6.67 − $5.59 = **$1.08**   27. 452 − 429 = **23**

28. 878 − 534 = **344**   29. $9.85 − 0.63 = **$9.22**

Solve.

30. Kelly has saved all year for bird-watching binoculars. She finally has $126. At the store she discovers that the price has just been raised to $149. How much more will Kelly have to save?
$23

31. Kelly goes to the zoo to see the birds. There are 125 species of birds and 87 are from the area where she lives. How many birds are not from where she lives?
38 birds

RETEACH • 15

Reteach 15

Name: _____

MENTAL MATH: SUBTRACTION STRATEGIES

Subtract mentally: 485 − 249

You can break apart the second number. Then subtract in steps.

Think: 249 = 200 + 40 + 9

Step 1 485 − 200 = 285

Step 2 285 − 40 = 245

Step 3 245 − 9 = 236

485 − 249 = 236

Subtract mentally.

1. 21 − 12 = **9**   2. 55 − 13 = **42**   3. 76 − 25 = **51**

4. 26 − 12 = **14**   5. 89 − 35 = **54**   6. 49 − 17 = **32**

7. 64 − 21 = **43**   8. 85 − 42 = **43**   9. 67 − 22 = **45**

10. 59 − 34 = **25**   11. 57 − 23 = **34**   12. 28 − 19 = **9**

13. 51 − 49 = **2**   14. 73 − 18 = **55**   15. 37 − 15 = **22**

16. 496 − 293 = **203**   17. 547 − 23 = **524**

18. 538 − 125 = **413**   19. 605 − 203 = **402**

20. 685 − 324 = **361**   21. 478 − 352 = **126**

22. 546 − 223 = **323**   23. 878 − 115 = **763**

24. 632 − 410 = **222**   25. 911 − 383 = **528**

EXTEND • 15

Extend 15

Name: _____

MENTAL MATH: SUBTRACTION STRATEGIES

A Puzzling Situation

Use the clues to complete this cross-number puzzle, just the way you would complete a crossword puzzle. Subtract mentally.

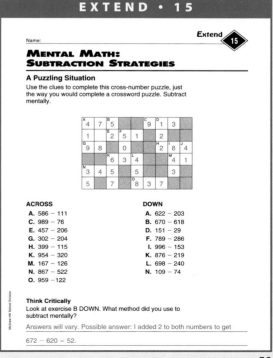

ACROSS
A. 586 − 111
C. 989 − 76
E. 457 − 206
G. 302 − 204
H. 399 − 115
K. 954 − 320
M. 167 − 126
N. 867 − 522
O. 959 − 122

DOWN
A. 622 − 203
B. 670 − 618
D. 151 − 29
F. 789 − 286
I. 996 − 153
K. 876 − 219
L. 698 − 240
N. 109 − 74

Think Critically
Look at exercise B DOWN. What method did you use to subtract mentally?
Answers will vary. Possible answer: I added 2 to both numbers to get
672 − 620 = 52.

59

LESSON 2.8

MENTAL MATH

Estimate Differences

OBJECTIVE Use rounding to estimate differences, including money amounts.

RESOURCE REMINDER
Math Center Cards 16
Practice 16, Reteach 16, Extend 16

SKILLS TRACE

GRADE 3	• Estimate differences, including money amounts, by rounding. *(Chapter 4)*
GRADE 4	• Estimate differences, including money amounts, by rounding.
GRADE 5	• Estimate differences, including money amounts, by rounding. *(Chapter 2)*

MANIPULATIVE WARM-UP

Cooperative Groups   **Visual/Spatial**

OBJECTIVE Explore estimating differences.

Materials per group: 40 two-color counters

▶ Students in each group count out 10 counters for reference.

While the others look away, one student uses some or all of the remaining counters to make two groups of counters of unequal number.

▶ The other students look at the groups of counters and estimate whether the difference between the two groups is greater than or less than 10.

▶ Students count the groups of counters and subtract to check. If the estimate is correct, the first student records a check mark.

▶ The activity continues with students taking turns making the groups and estimating the differences.

ESL APPROPRIATE

LOGICAL REASONING CONNECTION

Cooperative Pairs   **Logical/Analytical**

OBJECTIVE Use rounding to identify subtractions with the same difference.

Materials per pair: 12 index cards

▶ Have pairs write each of the subtractions on an index card: 33 − 22; 28 − 18; 68 − 51; 71 − 48; 89 − 23; 93 − 19; 791 − 402; 831 − 389; 622 − 421; 583 − 392; 389 − 187; 425 − 239; 9,420 − 3,241; 8,801 − 3,022; 5,032 − 2,089; 4,830 − 1,890; 8,210 − 2,900; 7,734 − 3,201

▶ Pairs mix up the cards and place them facedown in 3 rows of 4. Taking turns, each partner turns over two cards. Using rounding to estimate the difference, each partner determines if both subtraction expressions have the same difference.

▶ If the two cards have the same difference, the cards remain faceup. If the two cards do not have the same difference, the cards are placed facedown again. Play continues until all the cards are faceup.

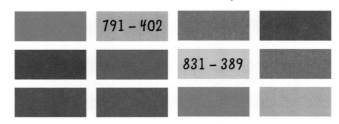

ESL APPROPRIATE

Daily Review

Problem of the Day • 16

Morgan can peel 20 apples in one hour. Ted can peel 15 apples in one hour. How many apples can Morgan and Ted peel in four hours? *[140 apples]*

TECH LINK

MATH FORUM

Idea I ask my students to estimate the number of students at school on any particular day. I give them the total number of students enrolled and the number of absentees.

Visit our Resource Village at http://www.mhschool.com to see more of the Math Forum.

MATH CENTER

Practice

OBJECTIVE Estimate which problem has the greater difference.

Materials per pair: 0-9 spinner (TA 2); per student: Math Center Recording Sheet (TA 31 optional)

Partners write subtraction problems by spinning for 4 digits. They estimate differences and try to identify which problem results in a greater difference.

PRACTICE ACTIVITY 16

MATH CENTER
Partners 👥

Number Sense • Spin Subtraction

YOU NEED
⚬ spinner (0–9)

- Take turns spinning to get four digits.
- Each partner uses the same digits to write two 4-digit numbers and a subtraction problem using the two numbers.
- Players show each other their problems. They estimate to tell which problem has a greater difference. The first to estimate correctly wins the round.
- Play five rounds.

$$6,145 - 5,146$$

$$5,614 - 1,456$$

NCTM Standards

✓ Problem Solving
✓ Communication
✓ Reasoning
✓ Connections

Chapter 2, Lesson 8, pages 60–61   Subtraction

Problem Solving

OBJECTIVE Solve problems involving money.

Materials per student: Math Center Recording Sheet (TA 31 optional)

Students estimate to solve problems. They explain their reasoning. *[Answers may vary. Sample answer: one floppy disk and ten paper clips. To be sure I had enough change from $20, I rounded numbers up to the nearest $0.10.]*

PROBLEM-SOLVING ACTIVITY 16

MATH CENTER
On Your Own 👤

Decision Making • Meter Matter

Helen is shopping for office supplies. She has $20 in bills. Helen needs $0.50 for the parking meter. Choose two or three items that Helen can buy so that she will get at least $0.50 in change. Estimate to solve.

Now find another combination of at least two items Helen can buy to get the change she needs. Write about your strategy.

NCTM Standards

✓ Problem Solving
  Communication
✓ Reasoning
  Connections

Chapter 2, Lesson 8, pages 60–61   Subtraction

Lesson 2.8 *continued*

MENTAL MATH
Estimate Differences

OBJECTIVE Use rounding to estimate differences, including money amounts.

 **Introduce**

Write 827 − 352 on the chalkboard. Ask students what they can tell about the difference from just looking at the numbers, without subtracting. For example, students may point out that the difference will be a 3-digit number and that it will be an odd number.

 **Teach**   *Whole Class*

▶ **LEARN** Read through the example and discuss the method for estimating the difference. Students should recognize that this is similar to the method they were taught in Lesson 4 to estimate sums. Ask:
  • **How do you know an exact answer isn't needed?** *[The question asks "about" how much.]*

More Examples In Example B the numbers are rounded to the greatest place that is common to both numbers—in this case the tens place.

 **Close**

▶ **Check for Understanding** using items 1–9, page 60.

  CRITICAL THINKING
  After discussing item 9, ask:
  • **When would you round to the nearest ten instead of to the nearest hundred?** *[Answers may vary. Possible answer: when you want the estimate to be closer to the exact answer]*

▶ **PRACTICE**
Materials have available: calculators

Options for assigning exercises:
A—Even ex. 2–22; ex. 23–26; **More to Explore**
B—Odd ex. 1–21; ex. 23–26; **More to Explore**

• Remind students that they may need to regroup when subtracting two numbers that do not have the same number of digits.

a **Algebra** In ex. 24, students use algebraic thinking as they explore relationships between pairs of numbers that have the same sum or difference.

More to Explore Remind students that they used front digits to estimate sums in the Developing Number Sense lesson.

Estimate Differences

 LEARN

In-line skates are great, but they are expensive. Suppose you have saved $42 already. About how much more money do you need to save?

Estimate: $98 − $42

Round each number so you can find the difference mentally.

Think: Round to the nearest ten.
$$\begin{array}{c} \$98 \quad - \quad \$42 \\ \downarrow \qquad\quad \downarrow \\ \$100 - \$40 = \$60 \end{array}$$

You need to save about $60 more.

More Examples
A Estimate: 4,378 − 1,542
    Think: Round to the nearest thousand.
    4,000 − 2,000 = 2,000

B Estimate: 564 − 36
    Think: Round to the nearest ten.
    560 − 40 = 520

C Estimate: $19.75 − $6.52
    Think: Round to the nearest dollar.
    $20 − $7 = $13

D Estimate: $2.14 − $0.43
    Think: Round to the nearest ten cents.
    $2.10 − $0.40 = $1.70

CHECK

Estimates may vary. Possible answers are given.
Check for Understanding
Estimate the difference. Tell how you rounded.

1 81 − 66
10; nearest ten

2 $0.89 − $0.26
$0.60; nearest ten cents

3 462 − 239
300; nearest hundred

4 $3.65 − $1.
$3.00; neare dollar

5 7,459 − 3,390
4,000; nearest thousand

6 $38.65 − $11.47
$30.00; nearest ten dollars

7 787 − 69
720; nearest ten

8 $34.78 − $2
$32.00; neare dollar

Critical Thinking: Analyze   Explain your reasoning.

9 Tell how you could round the numbers in ex. 7 and 8 another way to estimate the differences. What would the estimates be? **See below.**

9. Possible answer: 7. round to the nearest hundred, 800 − 100 = 700; 8. round the nearest ten dollars, $30 − $0 = $30.

60   Lesson 2.8

Meeting Individual Needs

Extra Support

Have students tell if the exact answer for each estimation problem is greater than or less than their estimate. A clue they can use is how they rounded the numbers in the problem. Have them use calculators to check their answers.

Ongoing Assessment

Anecdotal Report Make notes on children's ability to round numbers and to use rounding as they estimate with money and whole numbers.

Follow Up Students who can successfully round numbers and estimate differences can do ex. 17–22 again, this time rounding to the nearest hundred or dollar.

For an additional challenge, assign **Extend 16**.

If students need help, assign **Reteach 16**.

Practice

Estimate. Round to the nearest ten or ten cents.

1 85 − 37 **50**   **2** $0.69 − $0.24 **$0.50**   **3** 93 − 45 **40**   **4** 82 − 26 **50**

5 $0.37 − $0.11 **$0.30**   **6** 73 − 33 **40**   **7** 872 − 27 **840**   **8** $2.58 − $0.38 **$2.20**

Estimate. Round to the nearest hundred or dollar.

9 418 − 149 **300**   **10** $7.98 − $6.65 **$1.00**   **11** 645 − 265 **300**   **12** 504 − 294 **200**

13 774 − 286 **500**   **14** 6,803 − 550 **6,200**   **15** $27.62 − $5.28 **$23.00**   **16** 5,295 − 204 **5,100**

Estimate. Round to the nearest thousand or ten dollars.

17 9,683 − 1,078 **9,000**   **18** 2,063 − 1,066 **1,000**   **19** $35.45 − $18.02 **$20.00**

20 6,993 − 6,063 **1,000**   **21** $60.64 − $2.64 **$60.00**   **22** 9,255 − 754 **8,000**

MIXED APPLICATIONS
Problem Solving

24. Possible answer:
   a. 70 − 20, 53 − 3, 200 − 150;
   b. 10 + 60, 35 + 35, 69 + 1

23 This year 357 students registered for the In-line Skating program. Last year 289 registered. About how many more registered this year?
about 100 more students

24 ALGEBRA Find three pairs of numbers that make each a true sentence.
   a. △ − ○ = 50   b. ◇ + □ = 70
   See above.

25 The sale price of a helmet is $35.99. You save $18.97 off the regular price. How much is the regular price for the helmet? **$54.96**

26 Data Point Ask 20 students what type of skating they like most. Record your data in a tally table. How many more students prefer ice skating to in-line skating?
Students' answers should reflect their data.

more to explore

Using Front Digits

You can use the front digits to estimate an answer.

Estimate: 756 − 439   **Think:** 7 hundreds − 4 hundreds = 3 hundreds, or 300
  ↓   ↓
  700 − 400 = 300

Estimate the difference using front digits.

1 35 − 24 **10**   **2** 865 − 565 **300**   **3** 3,712 − 1,630 **2,000**   **4** 7,250 − 3,650 **4,000**

5 $0.92 − $0.54 **$0.40**   **6** $7.89 − $2.25 **$5.00**   **7** $9.43 − $6.25 **$3.00**   **8** $75.98 − $48.89 **$30.00**

Extra Practice, page 490

Money, Addition, and Subtraction   **61**

Alternate Teaching Strategy

Materials per pair: 0–9 spinner (TA 2); play money—2 five-dollar bills, 10 one-dollar bills, 6 quarters, 10 dimes, 10 nickels, 10 pennies

Have each student spin the spinner three times and write the digits as a dollar amount and change. Partners write the two amounts in a subtraction expression, writing the greater amount first.

Then have each student use play money to show his or her amount. If the value of the coins is less than 50¢, the coins are removed. If the value of the coins is equal to or greater than 50¢, the coins are traded for a one-dollar bill.

Each pair writes these rounded amounts in a subtraction expression and finds the difference. They check the difference by comparing the numbers of dollar bills.

ESL APPROPRIATE

PRACTICE · 16

Name: _____   Practice **16**

MENTAL MATH: ESTIMATE DIFFERENCES

Estimate. Round to the nearest

1. ten: 62 − 37 __**20**__
2. ten cents: $0.55 − $0.28 __**$0.30**__
3. ten cents: $0.69 − $0.41 __**$0.30**__
4. ten: 44 − 32 __**10**__
5. ten: 587 − 42 __**550**__
6. ten: 654 − 23 __**630**__
7. hundred: 613 − 385 __**200**__
8. hundred: 895 − 289 __**600**__
9. hundred: 569 − 226 __**400**__
10. dollar: $45.78 − $12.97 __**$33.00**__
11. dollar: $52.35 − $17.04 __**$35.00**__
12. thousand: 8,099 − 3,748 __**4,000**__
13. ten dollars: $23.76 − $13.76 __**$10.00**__
14. ten dollars: $76.98 − $8.54 __**$70.00**__
15. thousand: 6,453 − 1,298 __**5,000**__
16. ten dollars: $62.98 − $4.65 __**$60.00**__
17. thousand: 3,217 − 1,199 __**2,000**__
18. thousand: 3,275 − 1,716 __**1,000**__

Solve.

19. On vacation, Todd's family spent $57.36 on meals on the first day and $46.78 on the second. About how much less did they spend on the second day? ___**about $10 less**___

20. Todd's family drove 334 miles to the beach last year and 425 miles this year. About how much more did they drive this year? ___**about 100 miles**___

RETEACH · 16

Name: _____   Reteach **16**

MENTAL MATH: ESTIMATE DIFFERENCES

Estimate: 4,232 − 368
To estimate differences, you can round each number to its greatest place.

4,232 rounds to 4,000   368 rounds to 400
↑ greatest place is thousands   ↑ greatest place is hundreds

Then subtract to estimate the difference.
4,232 − 368 is about 4,000 − 400.
4,000 − 400 = 3,600

Ring the digit in the greatest place. Then round the number to the greatest place.

1. 6̃53 __**700**__   2. 5̃5 __**60**__   3. 3̃7 __**40**__
4. 2̃,362 __**2,000**__   5. 7̃21 __**700**__   6. 7̃,458 __**7,000**__
7. 1̃,873 __**2,000**__   8. 8̃99 __**900**__   9. 3̃52 __**400**__

Estimate the difference.   *Estimates may vary. Estimates given are by rounding each number to the greatest place.*

10. 72 − 58 __**10**__   11. 42 − 19 __**20**__   12. 87 − 33 __**60**__
13. 59 − 22 __**40**__   14. 536 − 201 __**300**__   15. 781 − 65 __**730**__
16. 186 − 97 __**100**__   17. 312 − 133 __**200**__
18. 389 − 213 __**200**__   19. 1,358 − 500 __**500**__
20. 6,032 − 632 __**5,400**__   21. 8,789 − 352 __**8,600**__
22. 7,025 − 3,809 __**3,000**__   23. 5,778 − 3,201 __**3,000**__

EXTEND · 16

Name: _____   Extend **16**

MENTAL MATH: ESTIMATE DIFFERENCES

Food for Thought

You have $3.00 in your pocket. Choose a lunch from the menu. Pick one main dish, one side dish, and one drink.

SIDE DISHES		MAIN DISHES	
Apple	$0.53	Tuna	$2.93
Orange	$0.76	Peanut butter	$2.48
Banana	$0.64	Turkey	$3.41
Carrot sticks	$0.87	Chicken taco	$2.79
Salad	$0.95	Pork fried rice	$3.84
Pickles	$0.59	Spaghetti	$3.56

DRINKS	
Milk	$0.45
Orange juice	$0.55
Apple juice	$0.66
Grape juice	$0.63
Mineral water	$0.72
Green tea	$0.78

1. Write down your choices.
   Answers may vary. Possible answer: turkey, banana, milk

2. Estimate how much more money you would need in order to buy lunch.
   Answers may vary. Possible answer: $3.41 + $0.64 + $0.45 rounds to $4; $4 − $3 = $1; $1 more is needed.

3. Choose another lunch. Estimate how much more money you would need to buy it. Explain your method.
   Answers may vary. Possible answer: round each amount to the nearest dime or nearest dollar. Add and then subtract the total from $3.00.

4. Choose three items that you can pay for with $3.00. Estimate how much money you would have left. Could you buy a fourth item?
   Answers may vary. Possible answer: salad, orange, and grape juice prices estimate to $2.50. Yes, I could buy milk for $0.45.

Think Critically

5. Suppose you only had dimes to pay for your lunch. How could you best estimate how many you would need? _Possible answer: I would make sure to round up to the nearest ten cents._

LESSON 2.9

Subtract Whole Numbers

OBJECTIVE Subtract 2- to 6-digit numbers, including those with zero.

RESOURCE REMINDER
Math Center Cards 17
Practice 17, Reteach 17, Extend 17

SKILLS TRACE

GRADE 3
• Subtract 4-digit numbers with/without regrouping. *(Chapter 4)*

GRADE 4
• Subtract 6-digit numbers with/without regrouping.

GRADE 5
• Subtract 6-digit numbers with/without regrouping. *(Chapter 2)*

MANIPULATIVE WARM-UP

Cooperative Groups   **Social**

OBJECTIVE Use place-value models to subtract 2- and 3-digit numbers.

Materials per pair: place-value models—2 hundreds, 20 tens, 20 ones; place-value chart (TA 4)

▶ Write the following subtraction exercises vertically on the chalkboard: $212 - 91$, $212 - 95$, $212 - 195$.

▶ Have groups of students use place-value models to find each difference and record each subtraction on a place-value chart. For example, $212 - 91$ is shown below.

▶ Have group members discuss and list how each subtraction is similar to and different from the others, focusing on the regrouping.

▶ Then ask students to describe how subtracting 4- or 5-digit numbers would be similar to and different from subtracting 2- and 3-digit numbers.

ESL **APPROPRIATE**

LANGUAGE ARTS CONNECTION

Cooperative Pairs   **Auditory/Linguistic**

OBJECTIVE Subtract letters from words to make new words.

Materials per pair: drawing paper

▶ Explain to students that a rebus is a riddle that uses pictures and symbols to represent words and phrases. Letters may be subtracted from words to form new words. Present the following rebus of the phrase "out to win":

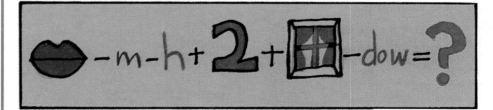

▶ Have students work in pairs to find the phrase the rebus represents. Write the following phrases on the chalkboard: *way to go, time for bed, great work.*

▶ Have each pair choose one phrase to illustrate with a rebus. Allow time for students to display their work. Have other students identify the illustrated phrase.

Daily Review

PREVIOUS DAY QUICK REVIEW

Estimate. Round to the nearest thousand or ten dollars.

1. 6,872 − 3,059 *[4,000]*
2. 2,281 − 899 *[1,000]*
3. $52.45 − $16.86 *[$30]*
4. $75.15 − $5.99 *[$70.00]*

FAST FACTS

1. 14 − 9 *[5]*
2. 8 − 7 *[1]*
3. 10 − 4 *[6]*
4. 6 − 3 *[3]*

Problem of the Day • 17

Karyn and some friends got on the school bus at its first stop. At each of the next two stops 3 students got on the bus. There were then 11 students on the bus. How many friends got on the bus with Karyn? *[4 friends]*

TECH LINK

MATH VAN

Activity You may wish to use *Coupon Craze* to teach this lesson.

MATH FORUM

Idea For a real-world application of subtraction skills, I ask my students to calculate the difference between the morning and afternoon temperatures we record each day.

Visit our Resource Village at http://www.mhschool.com to see more of the Math Forum.

MATH CENTER

Practice

OBJECTIVE Subtract using mental math.

Materials per pair: Math Center Recording Sheet (TA 31 optional)

Students make their partners reach zero in a subtraction game. Then they change the rules of the game and play again. To help with the game, you may wish to give suggestions about numbers to choose. Some examples are numbers between 15 and 19 and numbers less than 7. *[Rules may vary.]*

PRACTICE ACTIVITY 17

MATH CENTER
Partners 👥

Number Sense • Goose Egg

Play a subtraction game. Try to make your partner reach zero first.

- Write 100 at the top of a recording sheet. This will be the game sheet for you and your partner.
- Choose a number less than 20.
- Your partner subtracts that number from the total on the game sheet. The difference is the new total.
- Now your partner chooses a number less than 20. You subtract that number from the total on the game sheet.
- Continue playing until one of you subtracts and gets a difference of zero.
- Play again. Choose different numbers to ask each other to subtract.

```
 100
− 18
  82
 − 5
  77
```

NCTM Standards

   Problem Solving
✓ Communication
✓ Reasoning
   Connections

Chapter 2, Lesson 9, pages 62–65   Subtraction

Problem Solving

OBJECTIVE Solve subtraction problems.

Materials per student: Math Center Recording Sheet (TA 31 optional)

Students solve subtraction problems with missing numbers. Then they rewrite other subtraction problems so that they will not need to regroup. Students exchange problems with their partners and solve.
*[**1.** 480; **2.** 2,770; **3.** 621; **4.** 253; Exercises 5– 8: Students' problems will vary.]*

PROBLEM-SOLVING ACTIVITY 17

MATH CENTER
On Your Own 🧍

Formulating Problems • Don't Regroup

Find the missing numbers.

1.
```
  6,9 5 0
−□,□ □ □
  6,4 7 0
```
2.
```
  3,5 8 2
−□,□ □ □
    8 1 2
```
3.
```
  □ □ □
 − 1 9 0
   4 3 1
```
4.
```
  □ □ □
 −  9 7
   1 5 6
```

On your own, rewrite these exercises so that no regrouping is needed. Trade with a friend and solve.

5.
```
 3,250
− 149
```
6.
```
  658
− 266
```
7.
```
  237
−  49
```
8.
```
 4,231
− 697
```

```
     8
  6.9̸ 5 0
 −   □ 0
  6. 4 7 0
```

NCTM Standards

   Problem Solving
✓ Communication
✓ Reasoning
   Connections

Chapter 2, Lesson 9, pages 62–65   Subtraction

Subtract Whole Numbers

OBJECTIVE Subtract 2- to 6-digit numbers, including those with zero.

Materials have available: place-value models —10 hundreds, 19 tens, 19 ones

1 Introduce

Materials have available: calculators

Present the following situation:
There are 945 concert tickets. The box office sells 367 tickets.
  • **How could you find how many tickets are left?** *[Subtract 945 – 367.]*

Have students estimate the answer then use calculators to find the exact answer.

2 Teach   *Whole Class*

▶ **LEARN** Read through the problem at the top of the page. Ask:
  • **Why do you find an estimate when an exact answer is needed?** *[The estimate will tell you if your answer is reasonable.]*

Ask volunteers to use place-value models to show the three steps involved in finding the exact difference of 725 – 458 as illustrated on the page. Ask:
  • **When is it necessary to regroup?** *[when the number being subtracted is greater than the number subtracted from]*

Talk It Over Encourage students to include estimating the difference as part of their method in subtracting 283 from 564. After they have found the difference, ask:
  • **How can you check that the difference is correct?** *[Add the difference to 283—if the sum is 564, the difference is correct.]*

Subtract Whole Numbers

L E A R N

IN THE WORKPLACE
Larry Felix, Chief of the Office of External Relations, U.S. Dept. of the Treasury

The Department of the Treasury puts together money that has been burned, buried, or torn. Suppose a person brings $725 of burned money to the Treasury and only $458 can be restored. How much is not saved?

Subtract: $725 − $458

Estimate the difference.

Think: $700 − $500 = $200

Find the exact difference.

Step 1	Step 2	Step 3
Regroup if necessary. Subtract the ones.	Regroup if necessary. Subtract the tens.	Regroup if necessary. Subtract the hundreds.

1 15
$ 7 2 5̶
−   4 5 8
—————
           7
	11
	6 1 15
	$ 7̶ 2̶ 5̶
	− 4 5 8
	—————
	       6 7
		11
		6 1 15
		$ 7̶ 2̶ 5̶
		− 4 5 8
		—————
		$ 2 6 7

Think: 2 tens 5 ones = 1 ten 15 ones	**Think:** 7 hundreds 1 ten = 6 hundreds 11 tens	**Check by adding.** $267 + $458 = $725

$267 is not saved.

Talk It Over
▶ How can you tell that the answer is reasonable? **Compare the answer to the estimate: 267 is about 200.**
▶ Subtract 283 from 564. Explain your method. **The difference is 281; explanations may vary.**

62 Lesson 2.9

Meeting Individual Needs

Extra Support

Have pairs of students take turns verbalizing the step by step procedures of subtracting numbers. Students point out the mistake their partners make.

Ongoing Assessment

Interview To determine if children understand how to subtract whole numbers, write 453 – 382 on the chalkboard.
  Do you need to regroup? Explain. *[Yes; there are not enough tens, so you need to regroup 1 hundred as 10 tens.]*

Follow Up Students having difficulty using the algorithm can draw pictures of place-value models. They should identify the places in which they will need to regroup. For additional help, assign **Reteach 17.**

For more challenge, assign **Extend 17.**

Suppose you buried $2,139 in your backyard. If insects destroyed some and only $1,351 was pieced together, how much money was destroyed?

Subtract: $2,139 − $1,351

Estimate the difference.   **Think:** $2,000 − $1,000 = $1,000

You can use paper and pencil to find the exact difference.

Step 1	Step 2	Step 3	Step 4
Regroup if necessary. Subtract the ones.	**Regroup if necessary. Subtract the tens.**	**Regroup if necessary. Subtract the hundreds.**	**Subtract the thousands.**
$ 2,1 3 9 − 1,3 5 1 8	0 13 $ 2,1̸ 3̸ 9 − 1,3 5 1 8 8	10 1 0̸ 13 $ 2,1̸ 3̸ 9 − 1,3 5 1 7 8 8	10 1 0̸ 13 $ 2,1̸ 3̸ 9 − 1,3 5 1 $ 7 8 8

Check: 788 + 1,351 = 2,139

You can also use a calculator.   2,139 − 1,351 = **788.**

The insects destroyed $788.

More Examples

A
```
      11
    3 1̸ 15
    4,2̸ 5̸ 9
  −   7 8 6
    3,4 7 3
```

B
```
       14
     7 4̸ 12
   $ 8 5̸.2̸ 0
   −  5 6.5 0
   $ 2 8.7 0
```

C
```
          15
        6 5̸ 12
    1 8 3,7̸ 6̸ 2̸
  −    7 1,5 7 4
    1 1 2,1 8 8
```

D 256,322 − 89,750 = **166572.**

Check for Understanding

Estimates may vary depending on the method used. Estimates shown are by rounding.

Subtract. Estimate to check that your answer is reasonable.

1
```
   468
 − 399
```
69; 100

2
```
   987
 −  65
```
922; 930

3
```
  $37.25
 − 18.57
```
$18.68; $20.00

4
```
   8,458
 − 6,973
```
1,485; 1,000

5
```
  328,475
 −  90,580
```
237,895; 210,000

Critical Thinking: Analyze   Show examples.

6 To subtract two numbers, when would you use mental math? pencil and paper? a calculator?

Possible answer: Mental math can be used when there is no regrouping, pencil and paper when regrouping is needed, and a calculator when the addends are great.

Turn the page for Practice.

Money, Addition, and Subtraction   **63**

Discuss the steps shown in the problem at the top of the page.

- **How is subtracting 4-digit numbers different from subtracting 3-digit numbers? How is it similar?** [*Different: there is an additional column of numbers to subtract; similar: you still subtract from right to left, beginning with the ones place, and regroup as necessary.*]

Elicit that the difference can be checked by adding it to the number that was subtracted. If the sum is the number you started with, then the difference is correct.

More Examples Example D shows a calculator being used to solve problems with larger numbers. Remind students that calculators don't show commas between periods in a number. Have students read the number in Example D.

3 Close

Check for Understanding using items 1– 6, page 63.

CRITICAL THINKING

JOURNAL Encourage students to give examples of the kinds of problems on which they would likely use each computation method.

Practice See pages 64–65.

Language Support

Some students may have difficulty with the term *regroup*. Encourage them to describe regrouping in their own words. Analyze students' descriptions for accuracy, then use students' terms when working with them.

ESL APPROPRIATE

Inclusion

Subtraction is a concept that may be more difficult than addition for some students. If necessary, allow students to use place-value models while they gain confidence in using the algorithm.

▶ **PRACTICE**

Materials per group: 30 index cards

Options for assigning exercises:
A—Ex. 1–10; all ex. 25–40; **As Close As You Can Game;
Mixed Review**
B—Ex. 11–40; **As Close As You Can Game; Mixed Review**

- Students should try to solve ex. 1–24 mentally.
- For ex. 25–28, encourage students to estimate first in order to eliminate some of the choices.
- For **Make It Right** (ex. 40), see Common Error below.

a **Algebra** Ex. 29–34 give students practice in algebraic thinking. At a later time, variables will be introduced to represent an unknown quantity. Encourage students to use reasoning, number sense, and addition strategies to find the missing numbers.

As Close As You Can Game In playing this game, students try to create a number as close to the target number as possible, without going over the target number.

You may want to place the game in a math center so that students have easy access to it. Repeatedly playing the game will develop number sense and provide practice in subtracting.

Mixed Review/Test Preparation In ex. 1–4, students review addition, a skill learned in Lesson 5 of this chapter. In ex. 5–8, students review writing word names, learned in Chapter 1. Remind students to hyphenate when appropriate.

Practice

Subtract. Remember to estimate.

1	2	3	4	5
66	91	227	768	$5.16
− 23	− 35	− 34	− 544	− 3.08
43	56	193	224	$2.08

6	7	8	9	10
$8.51	6,120	5,475	8,419	$32.65
− 2.72	− 3,600	− 884	− 5,206	− 18.47
$5.79	2,520	4,591	3,213	$14.18

11	12	13	14	15
9,412	3,777	33,454	$2,163	45,223
− 4,063	− 899	− 26,847	− 755	− 6,094
5,349	2,878	6,607	$1,408	39,129

16 $585 − $286 **$299**   17 1,569 − 872 **697**   18 4,113 − 1,099
                                                                        3,014

19 8,291 − 7,408 **883**   20 $75.79 − $16.89   21 8,546 − 7,858 **688**
                                                     $58.90

22 64,245 − 30,757   23 118,491 − 73,508   24 216,843 − 44,579
33,488   **44,983**   **172,264**

Use the sale sign to find the items that have:

25 the greatest difference in price.
    model car/stickers

26 the least difference in price.
    Twister/silk flowers

27 a difference of about $5.
    See below.

28 a difference of $4.04.
    model car/silk flowers

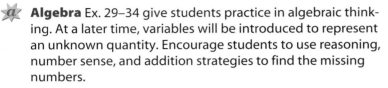

This Week's Sale Items

model car...$16.89   silk flowers....$12.85
stationery.....$5.75   stickers..........$3.39
Twister......$11.69   bath towel......$8.20

a **ALGEBRA** **Find the missing number.**

29 79 + ■ = 90   30 84 − ■ = 54   31 ■ − 65 = 200
     11   **30**   **265**

32 947 − 540 = ■   33 ■ + 183 = 544   34 33 + 79 + ■ = 212
     407   **361**   **Answers may vary. 100**

Write the number as the difference of two numbers. **Possible answers are given.**

35 800   36 575   37 1,600   38 1,845   39 75,211
   900 − 100   **875 − 300**   **3,000 − 1,400**   **2,050 − 205**   **80,000 − 4,7**

> ····················· **Make It Right** ·····················
>
> 40 Here is how Ruth found 3,948 − 1,486.
>   Explain what the mistake is, then correct it.
>
>   ¹⁴   8 1
>   3,9̶4̶8   3,9
>   − 1,486   − 1,4 8
>   2,562   2,4

27. stickers/bath towel or model car/Twister

Meeting Individual Needs

Early Finishers

Have students use addition to check their answers for ex. 1-24. Ask them to analyze the exercises they answered incorrectly and record the notes in their math journal.

Gifted And Talented

Have students play the **As Close As You Can Game** choosing target differences instead of target numbers. Students use the cards to create subtraction expressions closest to the target difference.

COMMON ERROR

As in ex. 40, students may forget to rewrite numbers as they regroup. Suggest that they think of regrouping as a pair of changes: decreasing the number in one place, and increasing the number in another. Every time they regroup, they should check to make sure that they have made two changes.

As Close As You Can Game!

First, make 30 cards—three cards for each of the digits 0 through 9.

Next, choose a 3-digit number, a 4-digit number, and a 5-digit number as target numbers.

You will need
• index cards

Player 1		
Target Number	Number from cards	Score
364	362	2

Play the Game

Play in a group of three or four students.

► Mix up the cards. Give six cards to each player.

► Take turns. Call out one target number. Players then use their cards to make a number as close as possible to the target number.

► To score, find the difference between the target number and the number that was made. Try to get the fewest points that you can.

► Record the information on score sheets. Play two more rounds. Use a different target number for each round. The player with the fewest points at the end of three rounds is the winner.

Target Numbers

364   5,712   10,624

What strategy did you use to make the numbers with your cards? **Possible answer: Found the card that had a digit closest to, but less than, the digit in the greatest place of the target number, then did the same for all the other places.**

mixed review • test preparation

1 28 + 19 **47**   **2** 67 + 39 **106**   **3** 544 + 183 **727**   **4** 947 + 540 **1,487**

Write the number in words.

5 350
three hundred fifty

6 2,306
two thousand, three hundred six

7 38,009
thirty-eight thousand, nine

8 90,014
ninety thousand, fourteen

Extra Practice, page 490

Money, Addition, and Subtraction **65**

Alternate Teaching Strategy

Write the problem 56 + 29 on the chalkboard. Have your students solve the problem. Then ask one or more students to describe how they regrouped. Write the steps for regrouping in addition on the chalkboard.

Write the problem 56 − 29 on the chalkboard. Ask one or more students to describe how to regroup in order to solve this problem. Write the steps for regrouping in subtraction on the chalkboard.

Compare the two lists. Students should see similar things happening.

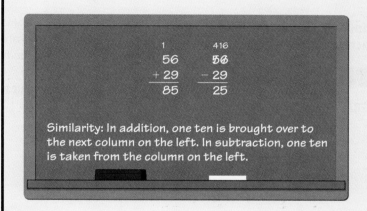

```
    1           4 16
   56          5 6
 + 29        − 2 9
 ────        ─────
   85          2 5
```

Similarity: In addition, one ten is brought over to the next column on the left. In subtraction, one ten is taken from the column on the left.

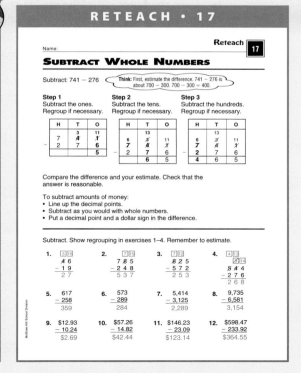

PRACTICE • 17

Practice 17

Name: _____

SUBTRACT WHOLE NUMBERS

Subtract. Remember to estimate.

1. 87 − 31 = **56**	2. 85 − 29 = **56**	3. 578 − 159 = **419**	4. 830 − 799 = **31**
5. 7,987 − 2,174 = **5,813**	6. $3,659 − 1,192 = **$2,467**	7. $7,215 − 2,875 = **$4,340**	8. $15.25 − 3.75 = **$11.50**
9. $15.05 − 9.50 = **$5.55**	10. $29.95 − 16.99 = **$12.96**	11. $17.50 − 8.99 = **$8.51**	12. 25,286 − 11,972 = **13,314**
13. 33,749 − 14,182 = **19,567**	14. 86,219 − 28,103 = **58,116**	15. $198.15 − 109.50 = **$88.65**	16. $7,239 − 5,777 = **$1,462**

17. $20.50 − $11.00 = **$9.50**   18. $42.34 − $10.95 = **$31.39**

19. $18.92 − $9.45 = **$9.47**   20. $56.25 − $18.95 = **$37.30**

Algebra Find the missing number.

21. 68 + **64** = 132   22. **782** − 453 = 329

23. 738 − 256 = **482**   24. 59 + 67 + **23** = 149

25. **469** + 456 = 925   26. 972 − **274** = 698

Solve.

27. Michelle bought 85 tickets for rides at the carnival. If she used 56 tickets, how many did she have left?
29 tickets

28. Lee spent $6.50 on tickets for rides at the carnival. He spent the rest of his money on games. If he had $8.75 at the start of the carnival, how much did he spend on games?
$2.25

RETEACH • 17

Reteach 17

Name: _____

SUBTRACT WHOLE NUMBERS

Subtract: 741 − 276   **Think:** First, estimate the difference. 741 − 276 is about 700 − 300. 700 − 300 = 400.

Step 1 Subtract the ones. Regroup if necessary.

H	T	O
	3	11
7	4̸	1̸
2	7	6
		5

Step 2 Subtract the tens. Regroup if necessary.

H	T	O
	13	
6	3̸	11
7	4̸	1̸
2	7	6
	6	5

Step 3 Subtract the hundreds. Regroup if necessary.

H	T	O
6	3̸	11
7̸	4̸	1̸
2	7	6
4	6	5

Compare the difference and your estimate. Check that the answer is reasonable.

To subtract amounts of money:
• Line up the decimal points.
• Subtract as you would with whole numbers.
• Put a decimal point and a dollar sign in the difference.

Subtract. Show regrouping in exercises 1–4. Remember to estimate.

1. 46 − 19 = **27**	2. 785 − 248 = **537**	3. 825 − 572 = **253**	4. 544 − 276 = **268**
5. 617 − 258 = **359**	6. 573 − 289 = **284**	7. 5,414 − 3,125 = **2,289**	8. 9,735 − 6,581 = **3,154**
9. $12.93 − 10.24 = **$2.69**	10. $57.26 − 14.82 = **$42.44**	11. $146.23 − 23.09 = **$123.14**	12. $598.47 − 233.92 = **$364.55**

EXTEND • 17

Extend 17

Name: _____

SUBTRACT WHOLE NUMBERS

How Much Less?
Use the numbers in the box above each row of exercises to complete the exercises. Use each number only once.

218	428	505	835
348	468	589	964
375	617	776	973

1. 964 − 375 = **589**   2. 973 − 468 = **505**   3. 776 − 348 = **428**   4. 835 − 218 = **617**

136	483	567	925
328	356	597	871
388	739	603	923

5. 925 − 328 = **597**   6. 923 − 356 = **567**   7. 739 − 136 = **603**   8. 871 − 483 = **388**

Think Critically

9. Explain how you solved exercise 5.

Answers will vary. Possible answer: I looked for the number ending in 5 for the top number (925). I looked for a number with a 2 in the tens digit (328 or 923). I subtracted and checked for that number in the box. 925 − 328 = 597

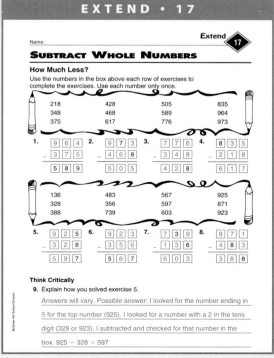

65

LESSON 2.10

Problem-Solving Strategy: Choose the Operation

OBJECTIVE Solve problems by choosing whether to add or subtract.

Teaching With Technology
See alternate computer lesson, pp. 67A–67B.

RESOURCE REMINDER
Math Center Cards 18
Practice 18, Reteach 18, Extend 18

SKILLS TRACE

GRADE 3
• Solve problems involving addition and/or subtraction. *(Chapter 4)*

GRADE 4
• Solve problems involving addition and/or subtraction. *(Chapter 4)*

GRADE 5
• Solve multi-step problems involving addition, subtraction and/or multiplication. *(Chapter 4)*

MANIPULATIVE WARM-UP

Cooperative Groups   **Kinesthetic**

OBJECTIVE Choose an operation to solve a problem.

Materials per group: play money—10 five-dollar bills, 20 one-dollar bills

▶ Present the information on the two fliers.

▶ Then ask the following:
  • How much cheaper is it to buy a pair of sneakers at Big Saver than at Payless? *[$3]* What operation do you use to solve the problem? *[Subtraction]*

▶ Have each group write three word problems using the information from the fliers. Group members play the role of store owners and consumers and act out the problems they wrote.

▶ Allow time for group presentations.

MUSIC CONNECTION

Cooperative Pairs   **Musical**

OBJECTIVE Identify songs and poems that describe addition and subtraction situations.

▶ Have students sing "Bingo." Discuss how in each verse of "Bingo" a clap replaces a letter when *Bingo* is spelled, so you sing fewer and fewer letters each time. Guide students to conclude that this shows subtraction because one letter is subtracted in each verse.

▶ Have pairs of students list other songs or poems they know that show addition or subtraction. Some examples are: "There Was an Old Woman Who Swallowed a Fly" (addition) and "Ten in a Bed" (subtraction).

▶ Allow time for students to share their lists. Have pairs name songs and poems and have other students identify the operation illustrated.

There was a farmer who had a dog
and Bingo was his name-o
B-I-N-G-O!
B-I-N-G-O!
B-I-N-G-O!
And Bingo was his name-o

Daily Review

PREVIOUS DAY QUICK REVIEW

Subtract. Remember to estimate.

1. 82 − 36 *[46]*
2. 5,319 − 702 *[4,617]*
3. $29.55 − $18.38 *[$11.17]*
4. 42,678 − 24,876 *[17,802]*

FAST FACTS

1. 7 − 2 *[5]*
2. 14 − 5 *[9]*
3. 12 − 7 *[5]*
4. 17 − 8 *[9]*

Problem of the Day • 18

George rides his bicycle 30 miles each day. Ned rides his bicycle 25 miles each day. How many more days will it take Ned to bicycle 300 miles than George? *[2 more days]*

TECH LINK

MATH FORUM

Cultural Diversity I encourage students who speak another language to teach other students the words in their language for common items. Students can use these new words in writing word problems.

Visit our Resource Village at http://www.mhschool.com to see more of the Math Forum.

MATH CENTER

Practice

OBJECTIVE Solve problems by choosing the operation.

Materials per student: Math Center Recording Sheet (TA 31 optional)

Students solve a problem using addition and subtraction. *[No; $9; any trip.]*

PRACTICE ACTIVITY 18

MATH CENTER
On Your Own 🧍

Using Data • Cents Sense

Solve.

The Banks family is planning a series of short trips. Each child can plan a trip of not more than 3 days as long as the four children do not plan to spend more than $150.00 altogether. The chart shows what the children planned.

Child	Number of Days	Cost
Laura	2 days	$37.50 total
Rhoda	two 1-day trips	$18.25 each
Elmore	2 days	$37.75 total
Pete	3 days	$49.25 total

Does the family have enough money for all of these trips? How much more money will they need to take all these trips? Which trip or trips could they not take to stay within their budget of $150?

Chapter 2, Lesson 10, pages 66–67

Problem Solving

NCTM Standards

✓ Problem Solving
  Communication
  Reasoning
✓ Connections

Problem Solving

OBJECTIVE Write problems using addition and subtraction.

Materials per student: Math Center Recording Sheet (TA 31 optional)

Students create their own problems about club costs based on numbers that they choose. They exchange and solve each other's problems. *[Students should check that the numbers they supply will make sense. Check students' problems and answers.]*

PROBLEM-SOLVING ACTIVITY 18

MATH CENTER
On Your Own 🧍

Formulating Problems • Club Costs

Fill in each blank with a 1- or 2-digit number. Then use the information to write and solve two or more problems.

- The Explorers Club has a membership fee of $_____.
- The Nature Club has a membership fee of $_____.
- Jack has $_____ saved.
- Angela has $_____ saved.
- The Explorers Club trip will cost $_____.
- The Nature Club luncheon will cost $_____.
- The guest speaker will cost each member $_____.

Chapter 2, Lesson 10, pages 66–67

Problem Solving

NCTM Standards

  Problem Solving
✓ Communication
✓ Reasoning
  Connections

Problem-Solving Strategy: Choose the Operation

OBJECTIVE Solve problems by choosing whether to add or subtract.

 **Introduce**

Write the following on the chalkboard:

Letters—12¢ each   Numbers—8¢ each

Explain that these are prices for letter and number stickers that people use to put their names and addresses on mail-boxes and homes. Ask students to determine the cost of the stickers for their name and address.

 Teach   *Whole Class*

▶ **LEARN** Review the four steps used in the problem-solving process. Then read the problem and work through the solution shown. Ask:

- **What information is needed?** *[the difference in cost between the electronic and travel versions]*
- **What operation should you use? How do you know?** *[Subtraction. Answers will vary. Possible answers include: You use subtraction to find how much greater one quantity is than another.]*
- **About how much more than the travel version does the electronic version cost?** *[about $7.00]*

Make sure students understand the questions that characterize each step of the problem-solving plan.

3 Close

▶ **Check for Understanding** using items 1–4, page 66.

CRITICAL THINKING
If students have difficulty determining the operations needed, suggest that they think of easier numbers to fit the situations described and use models to act out the problem.

▶ **PRACTICE**
Materials have available: calculators, centimeter graph paper (TA 7)
Assign ex. 1–9 as independent work.
- Students may want to use centimeter graph paper to record their answers to ex. 4.
- Before students do ex. 6, they may find it helpful to brainstorm a list of items sold in hardware stores.
- You may want to review how to read a line plot before assigning ex. 7–9.

Problem-Solving Strategy

Read
Plan
Solve
Look Back

Choose the Operation

Read **Bored on a trip? You can buy an electronic version of Wheel of Fortune for $25.50 or a travel version that is not electronic for $18.75. How much more is the electronic version?**

Plan To solve the problem, you need to decide which operation to use.

To find how much more the electronic version costs, find the difference.

Solve Subtract: $25.50 − $18.75 = $6.75

The electronic version costs $6.75 more than the travel version.

Look Back How can you check that your answer is correct? **Answers may vary. Possible answer to check—$6.75 + $18.75 = $25**

Check for Understanding
1 Karen buys two travel games that cost $8.99 and $5.30. What operation would you use to find how much she pays? Why would you use that operation? **Answers may vary. Possible answer: Add to find the total price.**

Critical Thinking: Analyze **Explain your reasoning.**

Which operation would you use to find the answer?

2 You know the number of pieces in a construction set. How many pieces are in five sets? **Possible answer: Add or multiply to find the total.**

3 How much less is the cost of a pint of craft paint than the cost of a quart of craft paint? **Possible answer: Subtract to find the difference between costs.**

4 How much heavier is the electronic Wheel of Fortune than the travel version? **Possible answer: Subtract to find the difference in weights.**

66 Lesson 2.10

Meeting Individual Needs

Early Finishers

Instruct students to use the information in the Databank to write two more word problems. One problem should require addition to solve, the other subtraction.

Extra Support

Encourage students to draw pictures to help them decide which operation to use.

ESL APPROPRIATE

Ongoing Assessment

Anecdotal Report Make notes on students' abilities to determine operations needed to solve word problems. Identify operations or situations with which they have difficulty, if any.

Follow Up Students who are successful at choosing operations can rewrite the situations described in the **Think Critically** section so that the opposite operation is needed. For more challenge, assign **Extend 18**.

For students who are having difficulty, assign **Reteach 18**.

3. Students' answers should reflect their choices.

MIXED APPLICATIONS
Problem Solving

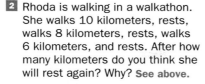

1 Karen estimated that playing Clue would take 35 minutes. The actual time was 26 minutes. Was the actual time longer or shorter than her estimate? How much longer or shorter? **shorter; 9 min shorter**

3 **Make a decision** Suppose you go on a class trip to a Native American museum. You have $7.00 for food and souvenirs. Postcards cost $0.65 each, a small drum costs $4.50, a bracelet costs $2.29, a necklace costs $5.75, fry bread costs $1.59, corn bread costs $1.80, and a fruit juice costs $0.80. How much would you spend?
See above.

5 **Data Point** Use the Databank on page 533. Douglas is hiking up Mount Sunflower, Kansas. He stops for lunch at about 2,000 feet. Abdul is hiking up Mount Rogers, Virginia. He stops for lunch at about 3,000 feet. Who has farther to go to the top? About how much farther does he have to go? **Abdul; about 2,729 ft**

Use the line plot for problems 7–9.

7 How many more students preferred the zoo to City Hall? the Science Museum to City Hall? **5 students; 1 student**

8 How many students voted for the zoo or the Science Museum? **18 students**

9 **What if** the class had also gone to Sea World. How do you think the line plot would change?
Students' answers should reflect the change in the line plot.

2 Rhoda is walking in a walkathon. She walks 10 kilometers, rests, walks 8 kilometers, rests, walks 6 kilometers, and rests. After how many kilometers do you think she will rest again? Why? **See above.**

2. Possible answer: After 4 km; there is a pattern to how far she walks before a rest—10, 8, 6, 4—each distance is 2 km less than the previous distance.

4 **Spatial reasoning** Show four different ways to get from point A to point B by traveling along the lines. **Answers may vary.**

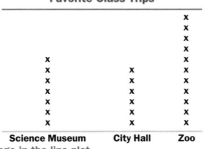

6 **Write a problem** about buying items in a hardware store. The problem needs to be solved by using addition. Then use the same numbers to write a subtraction problem. Ask others to solve your problems and to explain why they chose the operation needed to solve each problem. **Students should compare problems and solutions.**

Favorite Class Trips

	Science Museum	City Hall	Zoo
			X
			X
			X
			X
	X		X
	X	X	X
	X	X	X
	X	X	X
	X	X	X
	X	X	X
	X	X	X

Extra Practice, page 491

Money, Addition, and Subtraction **67**

Alternate Teaching Strategy

Materials per pair: place-value models—5 tens, 19 ones

Present the following problem:

> **Eighteen students were on the school bus. At the fifth stop, 3 students got on. At the sixth and last stop, 5 students got on. How many students rode the bus?**

Using place-value models, students should act out the problem, regrouping as needed. Be sure students realize that since groups are being combined, the problem requires addition to solve. Have a volunteer write the addition sentence on the chalkboard. [18 + 3 + 5 = 26]

Ask students how they could change the problem so that they would use subtraction to solve it. Students will probably suggest that instead of picking up students, the bus drops them off. Have students use models to act out the problem described and record the corresponding subtraction sentence on the chalkboard.

Continue the activity, describing both addition and subtraction problems for students to act out.

ESL **APPROPRIATE**

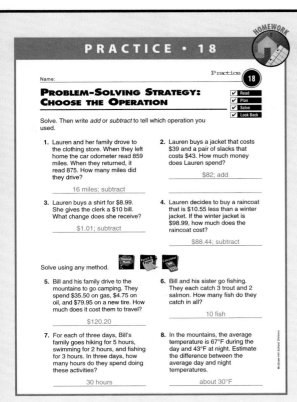

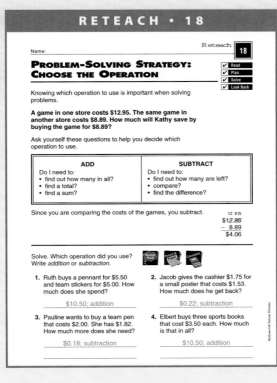

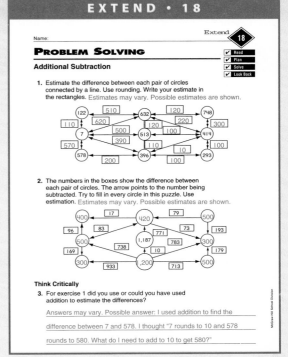

Teaching With Technology

Choose the Operation

OBJECTIVE Students use a table and calculator to solve problems by choosing to use addition or subtraction.

Resource Math Van Activity: *Coupon Craze*

SET UP

Provide students with the activity card for *Coupon Craze*. Start the **Math Van** and click the *Activities* button. Click *Coupon Craze* activity on the Fax Machine.

USING THE MATH VAN ACTIVITY

1 Getting Started Students use a Calculator to add and subtract to find the total cost of art supplies with and without coupons. Students choose the operation they will use.

2 Practice and Apply Students use a Table to find the total cost with and without coupons for other supplies.

3 Close You may wish to have students share the reasons they chose to use addition or subtraction to solve these problems.

Extend Students make up word problems using a flyer from a local grocery store and challenge a partner to solve them.

TIPS FOR TOOLS

When using the Table, students can show the numbers in a different format, such as money, by making that choice in Setup.

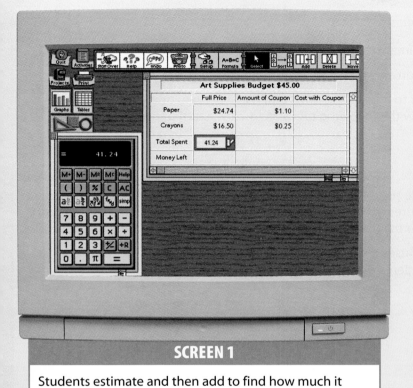

SCREEN 1

Students estimate and then add to find how much it will cost to pay full price for the supplies.

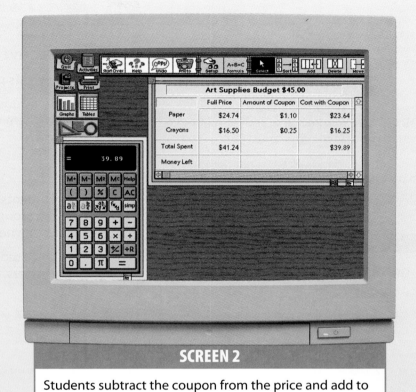

SCREEN 2

Students subtract the coupon from the price and add to find the total cost of the supplies.

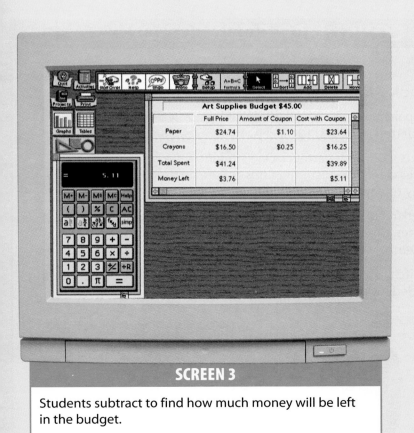

SCREEN 3

Students subtract to find how much money will be left in the budget.

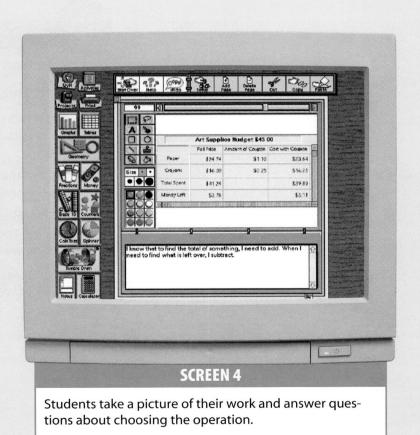

SCREEN 4

Students take a picture of their work and answer questions about choosing the operation.

LESSON 2.11

Subtract Across Zero

OBJECTIVE Subtract 2- to 6-digit numbers with regrouping across zeros.

RESOURCE REMINDER
Math Center Cards 19
Practice 19, Reteach 19, Extend 19

SKILLS TRACE

GRADE 3
• Subtract 4-digit numbers regrouping across zeros. *(Chapter 4)*

GRADE 4
• Subtract 6-digit numbers regrouping across zeros.

GRADE 5
• Subtract 6-digit numbers regrouping across zeros. *(Chapter 2)*

WARM-UP

Cooperative Groups   **Social**

OBJECTIVE Estimate differences.

Materials per group: 4 sets of 1–8 number cards (TA 29), calculator

▶ Tell students to mix up the cards and place them in one pile, facedown. Have them draw the following template on a sheet of paper:

9 0 , 0 0 0
– ☐ ☐ , ☐ ☐ ☐

▶ Students take turns drawing a digit card until 5 cards are chosen. Everyone in the group writes each digit in one box. Students estimate the answers and predict whether the actual answer is greater or less than their estimates.

▶ One student uses the calculator to find the differences of the problems on the papers. Students draw new cards and continue the activity.

ESL APPROPRIATE

CONSUMER CONNECTION

Cooperative Pairs   **Logical/Analytical**

OBJECTIVE Practice making change.

Materials per pair: play money—2 ten-dollar bills, 2 five-dollar bills, 10 one-dollar bills, 5 quarters, 5 dimes, 10 nickels, 10 pennies; catalogs

▶ Have students work with partners. One student is the customer, the other student the sales clerk. The customer finds an item in the catalog and gives the clerk money to pay for the item.

▶ The sales clerk records the price of the item and gives the appropriate change. Together, the sales clerk and customer determine if the correct change was given.

▶ Students switch roles and repeat the activity. Play continues until the sales clerk has recorded more than $300 in sales.

ESL APPROPRIATE

Daily Review

PREVIOUS DAY QUICK REVIEW

Subtract. Remember to estimate.
1. 92 − 14 *[78]*
2. $7.59 − $1.80 *[$5.79]*
3. 5,621 − 3,823 *[1,798]*
4. 48,492 − 6,747 *[41,745]*

FAST FACTS

1. 11 − 7 *[4]*
2. 13 − 9 *[4]*
3. 11 − 9 *[2]*
4. 13 − 8 *[5]*

Problem of the Day • 19

Jane and Ben counted the number of students on two lunch lines. Ben counted 67 more students in his line than Jane counted in her line. They counted 245 students all together. How many students did Jane count? *[89 students]*

TECH LINK

MATH VAN

Tool You may wish to use the Place-Value Model tool and the Calculator with this lesson.

MATH FORUM

Combination Classes I group students and have them work solely with place-value models, place-value models and drawings, or using an algorithm. Each student spends some time in each group.

Visit our Resource Village at http://www.mhschool.com to see more of the Math Forum.

MATH CENTER

Practice

OBJECTIVE Write and solve exercises that require subtracting across zero.

Materials per student: Math Center Recording Sheet (TA 31 optional)

Students write subtraction exercises that require subtracting across zero with three regroupings. They trade exercises with partners and solve. *[Check students' work.]*

PRACTICE ACTIVITY 19 — **MATH CENTER** Partners

Number Sense • Take It Away . . .

• Complete each exercise below so that your partner needs to regroup three times to solve each exercise.
• Exchange papers with your partner. Solve each other's exercises.
• Check that you had to regroup 3 times for every exercise.

11,004	20,090
48,070	
72,600	5,002

1. 11,004 **2.** 20,090 **3.** 48,070 **4.** 72,600
  −□□,□□□   −□□,□□□   −□□,□□□   −□□,□□□

5. 60,387 **6.** 5,002 **7.** 97,309 **8.** 30,051
  −□□,□□□   −□,□□□   −□□,□□□   −□□,□□□

| 30,051 | |
| 97,309 | 60,387 |

Write more exercises of your own to share. Be sure each exercise requires regrouping three times.

Chapter 2, Lesson 11, pages 68–69   Subtraction

NCTM Standards

Problem Solving
✓ Communication
✓ Reasoning
Connections

Problem Solving

OBJECTIVE Identify and continue a pattern.

Materials per student: calculator, Math Center Recording Sheet (TA 31 optional)

Students identify and complete different patterns. Then they choose three subtraction exercises to solve. *[1. 666 555 444 333 222 111; 5,005; 2. 654 543 432 321; 5422; 3. 616 515 414 313 212 111; 5,365; 4. 50 40 30 20 10; 9,550 5. 7,733 6,622 5,511 4,400; 56,935; 6. 5,035 4,024 3,013; 57,678; 7. 5,657 6,768; 76,057; 8. 468 579; 98, 215]*

PROBLEM-SOLVING ACTIVITY 19 — **MATH CENTER** On Your Own

Patterning • Number Shrinking   **YOU NEED**
                                          calculator

• Find the pattern of each subtraction series. Write the missing numbers in each series.
• Subtract to find the final value for three of the exercises.

1. 10,000 − 999 − 888 − 777 − ___ − ___ − ___ = ___
2. 10,000 − 987 − 876 − 765 − ___ − ___ = ___
3. 10,000 − 919 − 818 − 717 − ___ − ___ − ___ = ___
4. 10,000 − 90 − 80 − 70 − 60 − ___ − ___ − ___ = ___
5. 100,000 − 9,955 − 8,844 − ___ − ___ − ___ = ___
6. 100,000 − 9,079 − 8,068 − 7,057 − 6,046 − ___ − ___ = ___
7. 100,000 − 1,213 − 2,324 − 3,435 − 4,546 − ___ − ___ = ___
8. 100,000 − 135 − 246 − 357 − ___ − ___ = ___

NCTM Standards

✓ Problem Solving
Communication
✓ Reasoning
Connections

Chapter 2, Lesson 11, pages 68–69   Subtraction

 ESL APPROPRIATE

Subtract Across Zero

OBJECTIVE Subtract 2- to 6-digit numbers with regrouping across zeros.

1 Introduce

Cultural Connection Read the **Cultural Note.** The Feis was originally a gathering of all the kings, chiefs, and learned men, and lasted for seven days.

Have students talk about or demonstrate steps to dances they may do at festivals or other celebrations.

2 Teach

Whole Class

▶ **LEARN** As students work through the problem shown, discuss how each step pictured with place-value models is represented in the algorithm.

- **When the hundreds were regrouped, how many tens were there? How was the regrouping recorded?** *[10 tens; by rewriting the 3 in the hundreds place as a 2, and the zero in the tens place as a 10]*
- **When the tens were regrouped, how many ones were there? How was the regrouping recorded?** *[10 ones; by rewriting the 10 in the tens place as a 9, and the zero in the ones place as a 10]*

3 Close

▶ **Check for Understanding** using items 1–6, page 68.

CRITICAL THINKING
For item 6, to help students see two different ways to regroup, ask them how they would regroup to subtract ones. Then ask how the regrouping would be different if it were unnecessary to regroup the ones, but necessary to regroup the tens.

▶ **PRACTICE**
Materials have available: calculators

Options for assigning exercises:
A—Even ex. 2–14; ex. 15–19; **Mixed Review**
B—Odd ex. 1–13; ex. 15–19; **Mixed Review**

- Ex. 15–19 require students to use the strategy of Choosing the Operation.

Mixed Review/Test Preparation In ex. 1–4, students review addition, a skill learned in Lesson 5 of this chapter. In ex. 5–9, students review expanded form, learned in Chapter 1.

---

2 SUBTRACTION

Subtract Across Zero

It is fun to go to cultural dance competitions. There were 300 dancers at a feis. Of them, 124 won at least one prize. How many did not win prizes?

Cultural Note
A feis (fesh) is an Irish festival that has Irish dancing competitions.

Subtract: 300 − 124

Estimate the difference.

Think: 300 − 100 = 200

You can use paper and pencil to find the exact difference.

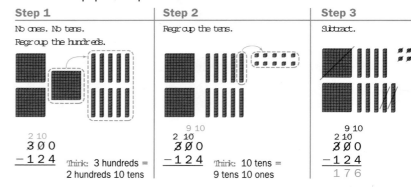

Step 1	Step 2	Step 3
No ones. No tens. Regroup the hundreds.	Regroup the tens.	Subtract.

Step 1:
$$\begin{array}{r} {}^{2\ 10} \\ 3\cancel{0}0 \\ -1\,2\,4 \\ \hline \end{array}$$
Think: 3 hundreds = 2 hundreds 10 tens

Step 2:
$$\begin{array}{r} {}^{9\ 10} \\ {}^{2\ 10} \\ \cancel{3}\cancel{0}0 \\ -1\,2\,4 \\ \hline \end{array}$$
Think: 10 tens = 9 tens 10 ones

Step 3:
$$\begin{array}{r} {}^{9\ 10} \\ {}^{2\ 10} \\ \cancel{3}\cancel{0}0 \\ -1\,2\,4 \\ \hline 1\,7\,6 \end{array}$$

176 dancers did not win prizes.

Check for Understanding
Estimates may vary depending on the method used. Estimates shown are by rounding.
Subtract. Estimate to check that your answer is reasonable.

1 802	**2** 2,502	**3** $70.08	**4** 700	**5** 45,000
− 421	− 726	− 42.90	− 219	− 9,411
381; 400	1,776; 2,000	$27.18; $30.00	481; 500	35,589; 36,000

Critical Thinking: Analyze Explain your reasoning.

6 Give two ways to complete the regrouping: 600 = 5 hundreds ■ tens ■ ones. Possible answer: 5 hundreds 8 tens 20 ones, 5 hundreds 4 tens 60 ones

---

Meeting Individual Needs

Early Finishers

Have students use a calculator to solve List A then try to solve List B without using a calculator. List A:
10,001 − 9 = ■; 10,001 − 99 = ■?
10,001 − 999 = ■? List B:
100,001 − 9 = ■?
100,001 − 99 = ■?
100,001 − 999 = ■?

Extra Support

Review writing numbers in expanded form with students. Emphasize that a zero in a number is a placeholder.

Ongoing Assessment

Anecdotal Report Make notes on whether students understand subtraction across zero. Ask them to describe how they would solve 2,007 − 1,659.
[Regroup 1 thousand as 9 hundreds, 9 tens, and 10 ones. Then subtract.]

Follow Up Students having difficulty can use play money to find change from whole-dollar amounts and record the corresponding subtraction problems. For additional help, assign **Reteach 19.**

For students who demonstrate mastery, assign **Extend 19.**

5. Possible answer: 1,000 − 900 = 100 m—about 100 m higher

Practice

Subtract. Remember to estimate.

1 890 − 457 **433**	**2** 901 − 55 **846**	**3** 400 − 232 **168**	**4** 2,003 − 1,150 **853**	**5** 4,700 − 925 **3,775**
6 $27.00 − 12.60 **$14.40**	**7** $90.70 − 48.05 **$42.65**	**8** 7,024 − 949 **6,075**	**9** 8,000 − 2,450 **5,550**	**10** 9,000 − 6,079 **2,921**

11 105 − 97 **8**   **12** 10,805 − 9,724 **1,081**   **13** $80.60 − $12.85 **$67.75**   **14** $90.00 − $28.48 **$61.52**

MIXED APPLICATIONS
Problem Solving

15 About how much higher is the Carrantuohill than the Wicklow Mountains? SEE INFOBIT. **See above.**

16 Brenda drove 25 miles to the O'Reillys' house. Then she drove another 7 miles to the football game. How far did she drive? **32 mi**

17 **Make a decision** You want to buy potatoes to make Irish stew. A bag of 25 potatoes costs $1.67. You can get a free bag of 15 potatoes if you buy a bag of spinach for $2.38. What would you do? Why? **Students' decisions should reflect their choices.**

18 **What if** you drive 2 miles for gas and then 31 miles to the feis. What is the best estimate of the total distance? **b**
a. 20 miles b. 30 miles c. 40 miles

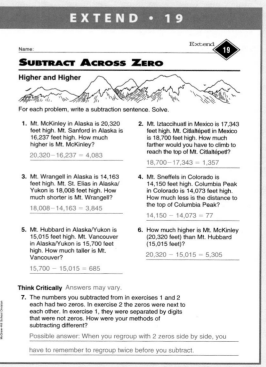

> **INFOBIT**
> The highest point in Ireland is Carrantuohill, which is 1,041 meters high. The Wicklow Mountains, also in Ireland, reach their highest point at 926 meters.

19 Tickets to the feis for Mr. O'Reilly and his 9-year-old daughter, Orla, cost $9.00. Orla's ticket cost $3.25. How much did Mr. O'Reilly's ticket cost? **$5.75**

mixed review · test preparation

1 56 + 12 **68**   **2** 88 + 64 **152**   **3** 349 + 283 **632**   **4** 847 + 671 **1,518**

Write the number in expanded form.   **1,000,000 + 700,000 + 2,000 + 400**

5 803 **800 + 3**   **6** 4,098
4,000 + 90 + 8   **7** 51,800
50,000 + 1,000 + 800   **8** 1,702,400
900,000 + 30,000 + 30 + 2   **9** 930,032

Extra Practice, page 491

Money, Addition, and Subtraction   **69**

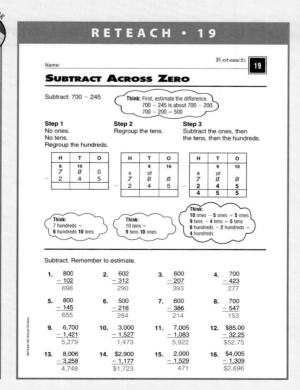

PRACTICE · 19

Name: _____   Practice **19**

SUBTRACT ACROSS ZERO

Subtract. Remember to estimate.

1. 780 − 241 539	2. 702 − 23 679	3. 500 − 236 264	4. 600 − 151 449
5. $60.08 − 13.23 $46.85	6. 7,067 − 3,241 3,826	7. 5,200 − 2,035 3,165	8. 9,000 − 643 8,357
9. $96.00 − 43.34 $52.66	10. 2,030 − 1,304 726	11. $30.20 − 2.49 $27.71	12. 7,000 − 2,415 4,585
13. $60.05 − 14.20 $45.85	14. 5,200 − 1,745 3,455	15. $40.40 − 9.99 $30.41	16. 8,004 − 352 7,652

17. 300 − 183 = __117__   18. 750 − 246 = __504__

19. 1,000 − 527 = __473__   20. 1,600 − 999 = __601__

21. $60.00 − $34.26 = __$25.74__   22. 3,020 − 1,564 = __1,456__

23. 8,000 − 439 = __7,561__   24. 800 − 243 = __557__

Solve.

25. Ricardo had $15.00 when he went to the amusement park. He had $8.35 left at the end of the day. How much did he spend? __$6.65__

26. Ricardo needs 1,000 points to win the dart game at the amusement park. If he scores 720 on his first two shots, how many more points does he need to win? __280 points__

RETEACH · 19

Name: _____   Reteach **19**

SUBTRACT ACROSS ZERO

Subtract: 700 − 245   **Think:** First, estimate the difference. 700 − 245 is about 700 − 200. 700 − 200 = 500

Step 1
No ones.
No tens.
Regroup the hundreds.

H	T	O
6	10	
7̸	0̸	0
2	4	5

Step 2
Regroup the tens.

H	T	O
	9	10
6	1̸0̸	
7̸	0̸	0̸
2	4	5

Step 3
Subtract the ones, then the tens, then the hundreds.

H	T	O
	9	10
6	1̸0̸	
7̸	0̸	0̸
2	4	5
4	5	5

Think:
7 hundreds =
6 hundreds 10 tens

Think:
10 tens =
9 tens 10 ones

Think:
10 ones − 5 ones = 5 ones
9 tens − 4 tens = 5 tens
6 hundreds − 2 hundreds = 4 hundreds

Subtract. Remember to estimate.

1. 800 − 102 698	2. 602 − 312 290	3. 600 − 207 393	4. 700 − 423 277
5. 800 − 145 655	6. 500 − 216 284	7. 600 − 386 214	8. 700 − 547 153
9. 6,700 − 1,421 5,279	10. 3,000 − 1,527 1,473	11. 7,005 − 1,083 5,922	12. $85.00 − 32.25 $52.75
13. 8,006 − 3,258 4,748	14. $2,900 − 1,177 $1,723	15. 2,000 − 1,529 471	16. $4,005 − 1,309 $2,696

EXTEND · 19

Name: _____   Extend **19**

SUBTRACT ACROSS ZERO

Higher and Higher

For each problem, write a subtraction sentence. Solve.

1. Mt. McKinley in Alaska is 20,320 feet high. Mt. Sanford in Alaska is 16,237 feet high. How much higher is Mt. McKinley?

   20,320 − 16,237 = 4,083

2. Mt. Iztaccihuatl in Mexico is 17,343 feet high. Mt. Citlaltépetl in Mexico is 18,700 feet high. How much farther would you have to climb to reach the top of Mt. Citlaltépetl?

   18,700 − 17,343 = 1,357

3. Mt. Wrangell in Alaska is 14,163 feet high. Mt. St. Elias in Alaska/Yukon is 18,008 feet high. How much shorter is Mt. Wrangell?

   18,008 − 14,163 = 3,845

4. Mt. Sneffels in Colorado is 14,150 feet high. Columbia Peak in Colorado is 14,073 feet high. How much less is the distance to the top of Columbia Peak?

   14,150 − 14,073 = 77

5. Mt. Hubbard in Alaska/Yukon is 15,015 feet high. Mt. Vancouver in Alaska/Yukon is 15,700 feet high. How much taller is Mt. Vancouver?

   15,700 − 15,015 = 685

6. How much higher is Mt. McKinley (20,320 feet) than Mt. Hubbard (15,015 feet)?

   20,320 − 15,015 = 5,305

Think Critically Answers may vary.

7. The numbers you subtracted from in exercises 1 and 2 each had two zeros. In exercise 2 the zeros were next to each other. In exercise 1, they were separated by digits that were not zeros. How were your methods of subtracting different?

   Possible answer: When you regroup with 2 zeros side by side, you have to remember to regroup twice before you subtract.

69

LESSON 2.12

Problem Solvers at Work

OBJECTIVE Solve and formulate problems by finding missing or needed information.

RESOURCE REMINDER
Math Center Cards 20
Practice 20, Reteach 20, Extend 20

SKILLS TRACE

GRADE 3
- Formulate and solve problems involving finding missing information. *(Chapter 4)*

GRADE 4
- Formulate and solve problems involving finding missing or needed information.

GRADE 5
- Formulate and solve problems involving extra or needed information. *(Chapter 7)*

WARM-UP

Cooperative Groups   **Social**

OBJECTIVE Describe information found in reference materials.

Materials per group: one reference book, such as dictionary, encyclopedia, almanac, telephone book; or a map; drawing paper and markers

▶ Display each reference book and ask students to describe the kind of information they are usually looking for when they use it. Explain how these materials also contain other information. For example, telephone books often contain maps and area zip codes; dictionaries contain conversion charts for weights and measures; road maps may show mountain elevations.

▶ Have groups look carefully at each section of the books or maps and make a list of the different kinds of information provided.

LANGUAGE ARTS CONNECTION

Whole Class   **Individual**

OBJECTIVE Write word problems involving too much or too little information.

▶ Present the following situation:

> **In 1933, Hack Wilson set the National League record for runs batted in (RBIs). In 1937, Hank Greenberg set the American League record with 183 RBIs.**

▶ Have students discuss what information they need before they can tell who batted in more runs, and how many runs. *[the number of runs Hack Wilson batted in]* Then have them discuss where they could find this information. *[Possible answers: almanac, sports reference book]*

▶ Have students write missing-information problems using the Databank, pages 532–543. Students solve each other's word problems.

> The Grand Fir & Western Hemlock are two trees found in Olympic National Park in Washington State. The Grand Fir is 130 feet high. How much taller is the Grand Fir than the Western Hemlock?

Daily Review

Math Van

PREVIOUS DAY QUICK REVIEW

Subtract. Remember to estimate.

1. 570 − 30 *[540]*
2. 206 − 90 *[116]*
3. 6,000 − 3,098 *[2,902]*
4. $95.60 − $26.85 *[$68.75]*

FAST FACTS

1. 10 − 9 *[1]*
2. 10 − 8 *[2]*
3. 16 − 8 *[8]*
4. 13 − 6 *[7]*

Problem of the Day • 20

Zack got on the elevator on the first floor. The elevator went up three floors where 5 people got on and 2 got off. One person got on at each of the next three floors. After going up 5 more floors, Zach got off. What floor is Zach on? *[12th floor]*

TECH LINK

MATH VAN
Aid You may wish to use the electronic teacher aid with this lesson.

MATH FORUM
Idea After each problem-solving lesson I have my students write and illustrate one problem to be bound in a class book. Students love to flip through the book solving each other's word problems.

Visit our Resource Village at http://www.mhschool.com to see more of the Math Forum.

MATH CENTER

Practice

OBJECTIVE Write problems from given information.

Materials per student: Math Center Recording Sheet (TA 31 optional)

Students use data to write problems that contain extra information. They exchange problems and identify what is extra. Then they solve each other's problems. *[Check students' problems and solutions.]*

PRACTICE ACTIVITY 20
MATH CENTER
Partners

Formulating Problems • Missing or Extra?

- Use the lists below to make up three problems. In each problem include information that is not needed.
- Exchange problems with a partner.
- Look at your partner's problems. Figure out what information is not needed. Circle it.
- Solve the problems.

Zack's spending

Fix Flat Tire on Bike:	$ 9.44
Lunches:	$21.67
Running Shoes:	$71.39
Birthday Card for Mom:	$ 2.36
Computer Magazine:	$ 4.25
Tennis Balls:	$ 3.95

Juha's expenses

Bus:	$10.00
Lunches:	$26.68
Movie with Patti:	$12.00
New Shirt:	$22.58
Phone Bill:	$18.72
New Alarm Clock:	$14.81

NCTM Standards
✓ Problem Solving
✓ Communication
✓ Reasoning
  Connections

Chapter 2, Lesson 12, pages 70–73   Problem Solving

Problem Solving

OBJECTIVE Use logical reasoning to solve a problem.

Materials per group: Math Center Recording Sheet (TA 31 optional)

Students look for extraneous and missing information. They add information needed to solve the problem without giving away the answer. *[Check students work.]*

PROBLEM-SOLVING ACTIVITY 20
MATH CENTER
Small Group

Logical Reasoning • Wayne and Friends

What information do you need to answer the questions? Add any information you wish to help answer the questions, but don't give away the answers. What information is given that you don't need?

Wayne went to the ball game with 5 friends. Juan wore a red hat. Stan wore a black hat. Alex and the person with the white hat ate pizza. Stan and the person with the purple hat didn't eat pizza. They ate cheese sandwiches. Hyun wasn't wearing a purple hat, but he had on purple shorts. Andrej sat near one end. Wayne sat at one end of the group, next to the person with a striped hat.

- What color hat did Andrej wear?
- What was the name of the person Wayne sat beside?

NCTM Standards
✓ Problem Solving
✓ Communication
✓ Reasoning
  Connections

Chapter 2, Lesson 12, pages 70–73   Problem Solving

Problem Solvers at Work

OBJECTIVE Solve and formulate problems by finding missing or needed information.

RESOURCES spreadsheet program, or Math Van Tools

1 Introduce

Ask students to look over the breakfast menu shown in the text. Instruct students to write out what they would order for breakfast. Have them find the total and the amount of change they would receive from $10.

2 Teach   *Cooperative Groups*

PART 1 FINDING NEEDED OR EXTRA INFORMATION

▶ **LEARN** Talk about students' choices for breakfast. Who bought the most expensive and least expensive breakfasts? Ask students:

- **If you only had $3.00 to spend on breakfast, what would you order?** *[Possible answers include homefries and juice or pancakes and water.]*
- **How much money would you need in order to buy pancakes, one egg, and juice?** *[$5.24]*

Work Together For ex. 4, suggest that groups write a description of what they would do to make the prediction. When all groups have completed the exercises, discuss them as a class. Let students talk about the information they needed to solve a problem. Encourage them to share their predicting methods.

Problem Solvers at Work

Read
Plan
Solve
Look Back

Part 1   Find Needed or Extra Information

Ramón eats breakfast at the Morningside Diner.

MENU

Juice	$1.37
Tea	$0.93
Fruit Cup	$1.88
Pancakes	$2.79

1 egg	$1.08
2 eggs	$1.65
Sausage	$2.19
Home Fries	$1.44

TODAY'S SPECIAL
Hearty Meal $6.93
juice or tea, milk
fruit cup, pancakes,
2 eggs

Late Riser $6.28
juice, fruit cup,
sausage,
home fries

Work Together
Tell what information is needed to solve the problem. Tell what information is not needed. Then, solve the problem.

1 Which is less expensive, ordering the Hearty Meal or ordering the items separately? **See page T17.**

2 **What if** you dislike the fruit cup. Should you still order the Late Riser? Tell why. **See page T17.**

3 You want to order eggs Benedict and juice for breakfast. How much does that cost? **See page T17.**

4 **Make a prediction** Predict what item would be chosen most often if your class orders breakfast from the Morningside Diner. How can you check your prediction? **Answers may vary. Possible answer: Take a survey of students in the class and compare the results to the prediction.**

70   Lesson 2.12

Meeting Individual Needs

Extra Support
To help students eliminate extra information, have them write each piece of information on separate index cards. They keep the cards containing information needed to solve the problem and discard the other cards.

Inclusion
Some students may benefit from setting out a clear plan before calculating. Instruct students to write out the steps of their solution. Can they use given information to solve for the information they need? If so, how?

Ongoing Assessment
Anecdotal Report Make notes on students' ability to find the needed information when given too much information. Also note if students can solve a preliminary problem to get the information they need to solve the original problem.

Follow Up If students have difficulty, choose a problem and use questioning to help them identify the information they need. Then assign **Reteach 20**.

For further enrichment, assign **Extend 20**.

5. The costs of a waffle and muffin are needed; the costs of all other food items are extra.

6. Possible answer: The costs of all other food items can be taken out of the problem; $6.94.

Part 2 Write and Share Problems

Sabrina wrote the problem on the right.

5 What information is needed to solve Sabrina's problem? What information is extra? **See above.**

6 Rewrite Sabrina's problem without the extra information. Then, solve it. **See above.**

7 Replace the question in Sabrina's problem with a different question. Find the answer.

For problems 7–10, see Teacher's Edition.

8 Write your own problem that includes extra information.

9 Trade problems. Solve at least three problems written by your classmates.

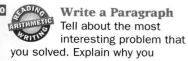

10 **Write a Paragraph** Tell about the most interesting problem that you solved. Explain why you thought it was interesting.

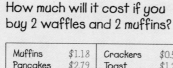

How much will it cost if you buy 2 waffles and 2 muffins?

Muffins	$1.18	Crackers	$0.50
Pancakes	$2.79	Toast	$1.25
Waffles	$2.29	Eggs (2)	$1.65
Juice	$1.37	Bacon	$2.19
Milk	$1.55	Cereal	$1.20

Sabrina Benitez
Shaughnessy School
Lowell, MA

Turn the page for Practice Strategies. ➡

Money, Addition, and Subtraction **71**

PART 2 WRITE AND SHARE PROBLEMS

▶ **Check** Let groups work together to complete exercises 5–9. For exercise 9, instruct students to solve each problem written by members of their group. Tell students to keep track of their answers to each problem and wait to compare answers when all students in the group have completed all the problems.

Discuss ex. 5–9 as a class. Ask students:

• **How is Sabrina's problem different from the problems using the menu?** [Possible answer: Sabrina's problem doesn't have as much unnecessary information.]

• **What technique do you use to deal with unneeded information?** [Possible answers: Write the needed information on paper, highlight needed information, rule out unneeded information.]

Ask students to choose one problem from their group and present it to the class. Give the rest of the students time to solve each problem presented.

 **Write a Paragraph** Have students work with partners as they write and revise their paragraphs. Then invite volunteers to share their finished work. Display the paragraphs on a bulletin board or in a math center.

3 Close

Practice See pages 72–73.

Language Support

Students who speak the same native language may write problems in the native language and trade them. This will give these students more practice solving word problems.

ESL APPROPRIATE

COMMON ERROR

Some students fail to see when a problem requires more than one step. Students may describe the separate steps used to solve the problem and note how problems can be broken down into smaller steps.

▶ **PART 3 PRACTICE STRATEGIES**

Materials have available: play money, calculators

Students have the option of choosing any five problems from ex. 1–8, and any two problems from ex. 9–11. They may choose to do more problems if they wish.

• Have students skim through ex. 1–8 and identify problems they think they can solve by estimating or using mental math.

 Algebra In this lesson, the algebraic concepts of equations and inequalities are represented graphically by balance scales, with values represented by geometric shapes. Use of visual models such as these will help students develop a greater understanding of the essential concepts.

Students may find it helpful to make a table of equivalencies by drawing the equivalencies shown and adding to the table those equivalencies they can determine from the information given.

At the Computer Ex. 11 requires collecting data over a one-week period. If computers are not available, students can write the data in tables and use calculators to find the balances.

Math Van You may wish to have students use the Table tool to create a spreadsheet. A project electronic teacher aid has been provided.

Part 3 Practice Strategies

Menu Explanations may vary.
Choose five problems and solve them. Explain your methods.

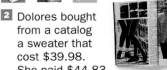

1 The theater sold 357 tickets for the 2 P.M. show and 825 tickets for the 7 P.M. show. About how many tickets were sold for the two shows? **Estimates may vary.**
Possible answer: 1,200 tickets

2 Dolores bought from a catalog a sweater that cost $39.98. She paid $44.83 including delivery and tax. How much was the delivery and tax? **$4.85**

3 Bobby bought a notebook for $2.79 and a binder for $3.65, including tax. How much did he pay for the two items? **$6.44**

4 At a "Buy 2 for the Price of 1" sale, Noah bought 2 boxes of cereal for $4.39 and 2 bottles of fruit punch for $1.59. How much did Noah save? **$5.98**

5 Ellis bought a secondhand bicycle for $27. A similar bicycle sells new for $185. How much money did he save by buying the secondhand bicycle? **$158**

6 Petra and Axel buy food for a part Drinks cost $7.69, cookies, chips and crackers cost $15.54, fruit costs $14.35, and cheese costs $11.89. Will $50 cover their costs? **Yes.**

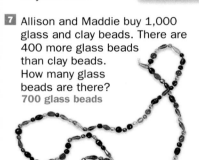

7 Allison and Maddie buy 1,000 glass and clay beads. There are 400 more glass beads than clay beads. How many glass beads are there? **700 glass beads**

8 Write the 1994 populations in order from greatest to least. Alabama: 4,218,792; Arizona: 4,075,052; California: 31,430,697; Delaware: 706,351 Montana: 856,047

31,430,697; 4,218,792; 4,075,052; 856,047; 706,351

Meeting Individual Needs

Early Finishers

Students can work on finishing the displays they created for the carnival advertising the games, rides, and food available. They can also create fliers to distribute to people they wish to invite to the carnival.

Gifted And Talented

Have students write the state names listed in ex. 8 in order from greatest to least population and then greatest to least size (in square miles). Have them compare the two lists and describe what they notice.

Choose two problems and solve them. Explain your methods. *Explanations may vary.*

9 ALGEBRA These two scales are balanced.

Left Side	Right Side	Left Side	Right Side

Suppose these shapes were put on a balance scale. Would the left and right sides balance? If not, tell what you can do to balance them.

a. Left Side Right Side   **b.** Left Side   Right Side

a. Not balanced; possible answer: add 3 cones to the left pan.   b. balanced

c. Left Side Right Side   **d.** Left Side   Right Side

c. Not balanced; possible answer: add a cone to the left pan.   d. balanced

10 Even numbers are numbers like 2, 4, 6, 8, 10, 12, and 14. Odd numbers are numbers like 1, 3, 5, 7, 9, 11, and 13.

a. Tell if the sum will be even or odd. Give examples.
- ▶ sums of two odd numbers even; possible answer: 3 + 5 = 8
- ▶ sums of two even numbers even; possible answer: 6 + 8 = 14
- ▶ sums of one even and one odd number

b. Tell if the sum is correct or incorrect without adding. See below.

12 + 4 = 16 **correct**   27 + 36 = 64 incorrect
154 + 356 = 501   201 + 198 = 399
incorrect   **correct**

11 At the Computer Create a spreadsheet so that you can record your income (any money that you get), your expenses (any money that you spend), and your balance (any money that you have left) for one week. Predict what your balance at the end of the week will be before finding it. Write about what you notice.
Check students' work.

10a. odd; possible answer: 22 + 39 = 61

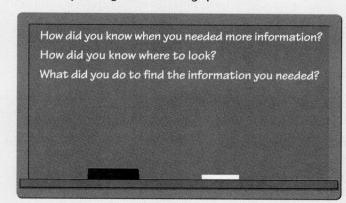

Date	Income	Expense	Balance

Extra Practice, page 491

Money, Addition, and Subtraction   **73**

Alternate Teaching Strategy

Remind students of the Databank, pages 532–543. Instruct students to write word problems that require information from the databank. The data that is provided in the databank should not be repeated in the word problem, but extra information can be given. Also, students should not give clues as to where in the databank the needed information can be found.

Let students trade problems with one or more other students. After students check each other's answers, lead a classroom discussion by asking the following questions:

How did you know when you needed more information?

How did you know where to look?

What did you do to find the information you needed?

PRACTICE • 20

Name: _____   Practice **20**

PROBLEM SOLVING: FIND NEEDED OR EXTRA INFORMATION

☑ Read ☑ Plan ☑ Solve ☑ Look Back

Solve or tell what information is needed to solve the problem. Cross out any extra information.

1. The fourth grade runs a school store. Last week the students had a profit of $137. This week they have a profit of $98. ~~Jeff alone made $59.~~ What was the fourth grade's profit for these weeks?

$235

2. The students sell cameras for $16. ~~Last week one parent bought 7 cameras.~~ Today the students sold 4 cameras. How much did they get for the cameras sold today?

$64

3. If the students sell about 4 cameras each school day for a month, about how much money will they take in at the end of the month?

Needed information—
the price of each camera and
the number of school days in
the month

4. The students sell 23 cameras during Week 1 of September, 28 cameras during Week 2, and 18 cameras during Week 3. ~~The fifth grade bought 16 cameras in September.~~ About how many cameras do the students sell in September?

Needed information—the number of cameras sold by the students in Week 4

Solve using any method.

5. In the school store, a sixth grader buys two gliders at $0.57 each, one camera for $16, and sunglasses for $1.50. What change does she get from $20?

$1.36

6. After closing the store, Tess and Nuru count 6 $10 bills, 2 $5 bills, 13 $1 bills, 20 dimes, 4 nickels, and 30 pennies. How much money do they have?

$85.50

RETEACH • 20

Name: _____   Reteach **20**

PROBLEM SOLVING: FIND NEEDED OR EXTRA INFORMATION

☑ Read ☑ Plan ☑ Solve ☑ Look Back

You do not always need all of the numbers given in a problem.

There are 20 cans of juice in one box and 215 cans in another box. Each can costs 50¢. How many cans of juice are there altogether?

- Read the problem. Think about what you are asked to find.

Think: I am being asked to find how many cans altogether.

- Read the problem again. Look for information you need.

20 cans in one box
215 cans in another box

- Look for information you do not need.

Each can costs 50¢.

- Then solve.

20 + 215 = 235
There are 235 cans altogether.

Solve. Cross out any information you do not need.

1. Julio put 18 cracker boxes and 25 pretzel boxes on a shelf. ~~There is room for 15 more boxes.~~ How many boxes did Julio put on the shelf?

43 boxes

2. Marie and Julio take turns at the cash register. ~~There is about $200 in it.~~ A customer gives Marie $10 and she gives him $6.95 back in change. What was the cost of the item?

$3.05

3. Carrots are $1.99; peas, $2.50; lettuce, $1.98; ~~milk, $1.57.~~ How much do the vegetables cost altogether?

$6.47

4. Julio stacks 75 boxes of cookies ~~on sale for $1.99 a box.~~ At the end of the day, there are 38 boxes left. How many were sold?

37 boxes

EXTEND • 20

Name: _____   Extend **20**

PROBLEM SOLVING

Five in a Row

You need to buy tapes for your school music class. The store sells four different brands.

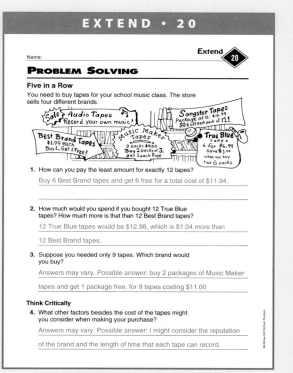

1. How can you pay the least amount for exactly 12 tapes?

Buy 6 Best Brand tapes and get 6 free for a total cost of $11.94.

2. How much would you spend if you bought 12 True Blue tapes? How much more is that than 12 Best Brand tapes?

12 True Blue tapes would be $12.98, which is $1.04 more than
12 Best Brand tapes.

3. Suppose you needed only 9 tapes. Which brand would you buy?

Answers may vary. Possible answer: buy 2 packages of Music Maker
tapes and get 1 package free, for 9 tapes costing $11.00

Think Critically

4. What other factors besides the cost of the tapes might you consider when making your purchase?

Answers may vary. Possible answer: I might consider the reputation
of the brand and the length of time that each tape can record.

CHAPTER REVIEW

PURPOSE Review and assess the concepts, skills, and strategies that students have learned in the chapter.

Materials per student: calculator (optional)

Chapter Objectives

2A Write, compare, order, and round money amounts

2B Count money and make change

2C Estimate the sums and differences of numbers, including money amounts

2D Add and subtract numbers, including money amounts

2E Solve problems including those that involve addition, subtraction and choosing an operation

Using the Chapter Review

The **Chapter Review** can be used as a review, practice test, or chapter test.

Think Critically Students sometimes have difficulty with generalizations using the words *always, sometimes,* and *never.* Suggest that they double-check the accuracy of the statements they answered *always* and *never* by looking at many examples of situations using the numbers described and trying to find an exception.

Language and Mathematics
Complete the sentence. Use a word in the chart. (pages 40–69)

1 The ■ of 100 and 40 is 60. **difference**

2 You can make change by ■. **counting up**

3 An example of the ■ Property is (3 + 2) + 5 = 3 + (2 + 5). **Associative**

4 You ■ to change 45 to 3 tens 15 ones. **regroup**
Commutative

5 The ■ Property lets you change 63 + 78 to 78 + 63.

> **Vocabulary**
> addends
> sum
> difference
> regroup
> Commutative
> Associative
> counting up

Concepts and Skills
Write the money amount. (page 40)

6

7

$16.16 $22.14

Find the amount of change. (page 40)

8 Price: $2.45
Amount given: $5
$2.55

9 Price: $6.73
Amount given: $10
$3.27

10 Price: $12.59
Amount given: $20
$7.41

Compare. Write >, <, or =. (page 42)

11 $14.78 ● $14.53 **>**
12 $25.87 ● $36.14 **<**
13 $6,562 ● $6,852

Add or subtract mentally. (pages 44, 58)

14 40 + 37 **77**
15 12 + 30 + 42 **84**
16 45¢ − 6¢ **39¢**
17 325 − 298

Estimates may vary depending on the method used. Estimates shown are by rounding

Estimate the sum or difference. (pages 46, 60)

18 93 + 85 **180**
19 938 − 654 **200**
20 $8.56 + $7.89 **$17**
21 7,150 − 9?
6,00

22 154
 + 712
 900

23 1,248
 − 879
 100

24 5,625
 − 3,569
 2,000

25 $84.65
 + 39.15
 $120

26 65,12
 − 48,27
 20,00

Reinforcement and Remediation

CHAPTER OBJECTIVES	CHAPTER REVIEW ITEMS	STUDENT BOOK PAGES		TEACHER'S EDITION PAGES		TEACHER RESOURCES
		Lesson	Midchapter Review	Activities	Alternate Teaching Strategy	Reteach
2A	6–7, 11–13	42–43	54	41A	43	10
2B	2, 6–10	40–41	54	39A	41	9
2C	18–26	46–47, 60–61	54	45A, 59A	47, 61	12, 16
2D	1, 3–5, 14–17, 27–45	44–45, 48–53, 58–59, 62–65 68–69	54	43A, 47A, 51A, 57A, 61A, 67C	45, 51, 53, 59, 65, 69	11, 13–15, 17, 19
2E	46–50	66–67, 70–73	54	65A, 69A	67, 73	18, 20

dd or subtract. Use mental math when you can. (pages 44, 58)

7
$$\begin{array}{r} 58 \\ +29 \\ \hline 87 \end{array}$$

28
$$\begin{array}{r} \$7.85 \\ +\ 3.17 \\ \hline \$11.02 \end{array}$$

29
$$\begin{array}{r} 4{,}180 \\ +5{,}932 \\ \hline 10{,}112 \end{array}$$

30
$$\begin{array}{r} 7{,}405 \\ 401 \\ +\ \ 889 \\ \hline 8{,}695 \end{array}$$

31
$$\begin{array}{r} 37{,}956 \\ 9{,}586 \\ +\ \ \ 740 \\ \hline 48{,}282 \end{array}$$

2
$$\begin{array}{r} 63 \\ -19 \\ \hline 44 \end{array}$$

33
$$\begin{array}{r} 504 \\ -\ 78 \\ \hline 426 \end{array}$$

34
$$\begin{array}{r} \$72.35 \\ -\ 18.29 \\ \hline \$54.06 \end{array}$$

35
$$\begin{array}{r} 8{,}047 \\ -3{,}918 \\ \hline 4{,}129 \end{array}$$

36
$$\begin{array}{r} 26{,}045 \\ -\ 8{,}550 \\ \hline 17{,}495 \end{array}$$

7 39 + 51
90

38 6,610 + 2,590
9,200

39 75 + 420
495

40 $843 + $372
$1,215

1 38 − 19
19

42 750 − 297
453

43 $68.37 − $39.55
$28.82

44 6,000 − 4,514
1,486

hink critically. (page 48)

5 Analyze. Tell what the mistake is, then correct it.

$$\begin{array}{r} 4{,}972 \\ +\ 5{,}885 \\ \hline 9{,}757 \end{array}$$

The tens, hundreds, and thousands that were regrouped were not added.

$$\begin{array}{r} {\scriptstyle 1\ 1} \\ 4{,}972 \\ +\ 5{,}885 \\ \hline 10{,}857 \end{array}$$

6 Generalize. Write *always*, *sometimes*, or *never*. Give examples to support your answer. Examples may vary.

a. The sum of two 3-digit numbers is a 3-digit number. sometimes; 34 + 142 = 376, but 952 + 523 = 1,475

b. The difference of two 4-digit numbers is a 5-digit number. never; 9,999 − 1,000 = 8,999

c. The sum of two addends is less than one of the addends. ever, for whole numbers; 23 + 51 = 74

d. The difference of two numbers is greater than one of the numbers. sometimes; 95 − 23 = 72, but 53 − 40 = 13

MIXED APPLICATIONS
Problem Solving

(pages 66, 70)

se the price list for problems 47–50.

7 Carla has $10. Does she have enough to buy 8 hats, 8 plates, 8 napkins, 8 cups, and 8 balloons?
Yes.

8 Jamal hands the cashier a five-dollar bill to pay for party favors and balloons. What is his change?
$1.66

9 Karen buys 8 plates, 8 cups, and 8 napkins. She gets $6.03 back in change. How much did she give the cashier? $10.80

The Party Store

hats (8)..........$1.89   napkins (8)..........$0.79
bugles (8)......$1.59   balloons (8)........$0.59
plates (8)......$2.39   party favors (8)...$2.75
cups (8)..........$1.59   Twister..............$3.47

Party Packages.......$8.99
(consists of 8 plates, 8 cups, 8 napkins, 8 balloons, 8 party favors, Twister game)
(prices include tax)

50 Is the Party Package a good deal? Do you save any money by buying the package instead of buying each item separately? If so, how much?
Yes; $2.59.

Money, Addition, and Subtraction **75**

CHAPTER TEST

Chapter Objectives

2A Write, compare, order, and round money amounts
2B Count money and make change
2C Estimate the sums and differences of numbers including money amounts
2D Add and subtract numbers including money amounts
2E Solve problems, including those that involve addition, subtraction, and choosing an operation

Using the Chapter Test

The **Chapter Test** can be used as a practice test, a chapter test, or as additional review. The **Performance Assessment** on Student Book page 77 provides an alternate means of assessing students' understanding of using money to add and subtract.

Assessment Resources

TEST MASTERS

The Testing Program Blackline Masters provide three forms of the Chapter Test to assess students' understanding of the chapter concepts, skills, and strategies. Forms A and B use a multiple-choice format. Form C uses a free-response format.

COMPUTER TEST GENERATOR

The Computer Test Generator supplies abundant multiple-choice and free-response test items, which you may use to generate tests and practice work sheets tailored to the needs of your class.

TEACHER'S ASSESSMENT RESOURCES

Teacher's Assessment Resources provides resources for alternate assessment. It includes guidelines for Building a Portfolio, page 6 and a Holistic Scoring Guide, page 27.

Write the money amount.

1  $20.39

2  $18.96

Find the amount of change.

3 Price of notebook: $3.29
Amount given: $5 **$1.71**

4 Price of tape: $7.25
Amount given: $10 **$2.75**

5 Price of shirt: $16.58
Amount given: $20
$3.42

6 Price of CD: $14.95
Amount given: $20
$5.05

Compare. Write >, <, or =.

7 $17.27 ● $17.24 **>**   **8** $32.56 ● $29.17 **>**   **9** $4,052 ● $4,115

Estimate the sum or difference. Estimates may vary depending on the method used. Estimates shown are by rounding.

10	**11**	**12**	**13**
258	2,681	$75.60	56,720
+ 316	− 992	+ 47.10	− 43,951
600	**2,000**	**$130**	**20,000**

Add or subtract. Use mental math when you can.

14 73 + 17 **90**   **15** 275 + 125 **400**   **16** $56 − $10 **$46**   **17** 418 − 397

18	**19**	**20**	**21**
$5.28	7,216	$92.14	$26,000
+ 6.19	504	− 68.26	− 18,543
$11.47	+ 372	**$23.88**	**$7,457**
	8,092		

Solve. Use the prices for problems 22–24.

22 Karen bought a T-shirt and shorts. She gave the clerk $30. How much change did she get? **$6.27**

23 Tell if there is needed or extra information. Sue bought 3 sweatshirts and 2 pants. How much did she spend? **Needed information is the price of the pants.**

24 Bob got $20 for his birthday. Does he have enough to get 3 caps? Explain your reasoning. **Yes; 3 caps cost $6.95 + $6.95 + $5 = $18.90,**

Buy two of the same, get the third for $5

Cap	$6.95
T-Shirt	$12.98
Sweatshirt	$15.25
Shorts	$10.75

25 The Petrified Forest contains 93,533 acres. Yosemite has 761,236 acres. Which is larger? **Yosemite**

76   Chapter 2 Test

Test Correlation		
CHAPTER	**TEST ITEMS**	**TEXT PAGES**
2A	1–2, 7–9	42–43
2B	1–6	40–41
2C	10–13	46–47, 60–61
2D	14–21	44–45, 48–53, 58–59, 62–65, 68–69
2E	22–25	66–67, 70–73

Check students' work. See Teacher's Assessment Resources for samples of student work.

What Did You Learn?

Three fourth-grade classes collected money for a children's charity.

Collections for One Week	
Mr. Potter's class	$15.45
Ms. Hale's class	$20.75
Ms. Angelini's class	$12.00

Bob estimates that the total amount collected for the week is about $50.00.

Anita's estimate is $48.00.

▶ Explain how Bob and Anita might have made their estimates. **Possible answer: Bob rounded to the nearest $10.00, and Anita rounded to the nearest $1.00.**

▶ Decide which is a better estimate. Explain your reasoning. **Possible answer: Anita's estimate is better because it includes the ones and tens place while Bob's estimate only includes the tens place—Anita's estimate is closer to the actual answer.**

················ **A Good Answer** ················
• explains how each estimate is made using estimation strategies
• explains logically why one estimate is better by comparing the estimates to the actual total

 You may want to place your work in your portfolio.

What Do You Think
See Teacher's Edition.

1 Can you write, compare, and estimate money amounts? If not, what do you do when you find it difficult to finish a problem?

2 What type of estimation are you comfortable doing?
• Rounding to the greatest place
• Rounding to the nearest ten
• Rounding to the nearest hundred
• Rounding to the nearest thousand
• Other. Explain.

Money, Addition, and Subtraction **77**

Reviewing A Portfolio

Have students review their portfolios. Consider including these items:
• Finished work on the Chapter Project (p. 37F) or **Investigation** (pp. 56–57).
• Selected math journal entries, pp. 39, 44, 54, 63.
• Finished work on the nonroutine problem in **What Do You Know?** (p. 39) and problems from the Menu (pp. 72–73).
• Each student's self-selected "best piece" from work completed during the chapter. Have each student attach a note explaining why he or she chose that piece.
• Any work you or an individual student wishes to keep for future reference.

You may take this opportunity to conduct conferences with students. The Portfolio Analysis Form can help you report students' progress. See Teacher's Assessment Resources, p. 33.

PURPOSE Review and assess the concepts, skills, and strategies learned in this chapter.

Materials have available: calculators (optional)

Using the Performance Assessment

Have students read and restate the problems in their own words.

Point out the section on the student page headed "A Good Answer." Make sure students understand that you use these points to evaluate their answers.

Evaluating Student Work

As you read students' papers, look for the following:
• *Does the student understand that different methods of estimation produce different estimates?*
• *Can the student describe a method of estimation that would have produced each of the estimates?*
• *How well does the student explain why Anita's estimate is better?*

The Holistic Scoring Guide and annotated samples of students' work can be used to assess this task. See pages 27–32 and 37–72 in Teacher's Assessment Resources.

Using the Self-Assessment

What Do You Think? Assure students that there are no right or wrong answers. Tell them the emphasis is on what they think and how they justify their answers.

Follow-Up Interviews

These questions can be used to gain insight into students' thinking:
• **How might Bob have made his estimate?**
• **How might Anita have made her estimate?**
• **What is the actual total?**
• **Which do you think is the better estimate? Why?**
• **What are the advantages of Bob's method of estimation?**

OBJECTIVE Use addition and subtraction of money in a science context.

Materials assorted foreign coins and play money

Resources word-processing program

Science

Cultural Connection Read the **Cultural Note** on page 78. Discuss how before coins were made, people bought things by trading goods and services. Point out that before coins were invented scales were required to weigh metals when used in transactions.

While discussing the questions at the bottom of page 78, if possible, display examples of different metals and coins to help students compare and describe. Then ask:

- **What do you think makes certain metals so valuable?**
  [Possible response: They are rare and beautiful.]

Point out that the U.S. stopped making coins from gold and silver, because the amounts of these metals needed to make a coin were worth more than the coin itself.

Math

If play money is available, allow students to use the coins to help them answer items 1 and 2 on page 79.

Allow students to make up problems similar to item 3 about different coin combinations based on the Databank table on page 534. Have students answer their problems then exchange them with other students.

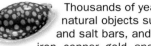

Cultural Note

About 600 B.C. in Lydia, an ancient country that is now part of Turkey, the first "coins" were made. The government of Lydia shaped electrum, a mixture of gold and silver, into bean-shaped lumps of the same weight and stamped them with special symbols. The word *coin* is from a word that means "stamp."

THE MANY FORM$ OF MONEY

Scientists know of about 100 different elements that are found on Earth. Of these, about 80 of them are metals. Metals are easy to form into different shapes and are shiny when polished, so they can easily be used to make coins.

Thousands of years ago, people used natural objects such as feathers, shells, and salt bars, and metals such as iron, copper, gold, and silver as money.

For centuries, coins were made of metals equal to the value of the coin. In the past, coins made of gold, silver, and copper were most common in the United States. Gold was last used for coins in 1933, and silver was removed from most coins in 1965. The five-cent coin (nickel) is still made with some nickel metal in it. All other coins are made from mixtures of copper and zinc.

Feather money was used by the Pacific Islanders of Santa Cruz. Tiny red feathers, glued together, were tied to fiber coils up to 32 ft long.

Today, people use different types of money to buy things. Sometimes, money can be exchanged electronically, using a computer.

Students may name metals used in jewelry, tools, appliances, and so on.

▶ Describe the different types of metals that you have seen. **See above.**

▶ Where do you think we get metals from? **Possible answer: Metals are mined from the earth.**

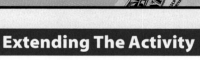

78 Math · Science · Technology Connection

Extending The Activity

Have partners create a checking account register and add and subtract money from an imaginary account to show their balance. Have students start with a balance of $200 and make the following deposits and withdrawals:

Deposit $50. Write checks to pay a $65 electric bill and a $28 water bill. Deposit $15. Write checks to buy a $15 book, $45 video game, and a $12 calculator. Balance is $100. Have partners share and compare methods and results.

At the Computer

Check students' work.

4 What would it be like to have a world without money? What advantages and disadvantages do you think there might be? Use a word processing program to write about your ideas.

Some Notes and Coins

In addition to coins, countries have paper money called notes. The note in the United States is the dollar.

You can make a dollar four ways using only one type of commonly used coin—4 quarters, 10 dimes, 20 nickels, and 100 pennies.

1 Suppose you have 7 coins in your pocket that equal $1.00. What could they be? **Possible answers: 2 quarters, 5 dimes; 3 quarters, 1 dime, 3 nickels**

2 What is the least number of coins you can use to make 87¢? **Possible answer: 8 coins—2 quarters, 3 dimes, 1 nickel, and 2 pennies**

3 Use the Databank on page 534. Look at the money of Botswana. Show three ways to make 47 thebes.

Possible answer: one 25-thebe coin, two 10-thebe coins, and two 1-thebe coins; eight 5-thebe coins, three 2-thebe coins, one 1-thebe coin; four 10-thebe coins, seven 1-thebe coins

Money, Addition, and Subtraction **79**

Technology

Students can work in pairs to write their essays. Have students share and compare ideas by printing out their reports and reading them aloud to the class.

You may wish to have students use a drawing program to design their own coins or bills.

Interesting Facts

- **A stack of pennies 95 miles high** would be worth one million dollars.

- **Coins were made by hand** in medieval times.

- **The United States mints coins** in Philadelphia, Denver, and San Francisco.

- **From 1792 through the early 1900s,** there were gold coins worth $2.50, $5.00, and $10.00.

Bibliography

Coins and Currency, by Brenda Ralph Lewis. New York: Random House, 1993. ISBN 0–679–82662–9.

The Story of Money, by Betsy Maestro. New York: Clarion Books, 1993. ISBN 0–395–56242–2.

Chapter 3

Time, Data, and Graphs

CHAPTER 3 ORGANIZER

WEEK ONE

DAY 1

PREASSESSMENT

Introduction pp. 80

What Do You Know? p. 81
CHAPTER OBJECTIVES: 3A, 3B, 3C, 3D, 3E
RESOURCES Read-Aloud Anthology
pp. 10–13
Pretest: Test Master Form A, B, or C
Diagnostic Inventory

📁 Portfolio   📓 Journal   **NCTM STANDARDS:** 1, 2, 3, 4, 10, 11

DAY 2

LESSON 3.1

Time pp. 82–83
CHAPTER OBJECTIVES: 3A
MATERIALS demonstration clock (if available), calculators (opt.)
RESOURCES Reteach/Practice/Extend: 21
Math Center Cards: 21
Extra Practice: 492

Daily Review TE p. 81B
🖱 Technology Link   **NCTM STANDARDS:** 10

DAY 3

LESSON 3.2

Elapsed Time pp. 84–87
CHAPTER OBJECTIVES: 3B
MATERIALS calculators (opt.)
RESOURCES Reteach/Practice/Extend: 22
Math Center Cards: 22
Extra Practice: 492

Daily Review TE p. 83B
🖱 Technology Link   **NCTM STANDARDS:** 10

WEEK TWO

LESSON 3.5

EXPLORE ACTIVITY
Pictographs pp. 94–95

CHAPTER OBJECTIVES: 3D
RESOURCES Reteach/Practice/Extend: 25
Math Center Cards: 25
Extra Practice: 493

Daily Review TE p. 93B
🖱 Technology Link   **NCTM STANDARDS:** 4, 11

MIDCHAPTER ASSESSMENT

Midchapter Review p. 96
CHAPTER OBJECTIVES: 3A, 3B, 3C, 3D

Developing Technology Sense p. 97

REAL-LIFE INVESTIGATION:
Applying Data and Graphs pp. 98–99

📁 Portfolio   📓 Journal   **NCTM STANDARDS:** 1, 2, 3, 4, 10, 11

LESSON 3.6

EXPLORE ACTIVITY
Bar Graphs pp. 100–103

CHAPTER OBJECTIVES: 3D
MATERIALS calculators (opt.)
RESOURCES Reteach/Practice/Extend: 26
Math Center Cards: 26
Extra Practice: 494

Daily Review TE p. 99B
🖱 Technology Link   **NCTM STANDARDS:** 4, 11

WEEK THREE

LESSON 3.9

PROBLEM SOLVERS AT WORK
Interpret Data pp. 110–113

CHAPTER OBJECTIVES: 3E
MATERIALS calculators (opt.)
RESOURCES Reteach/Practice/Extend: 29
Math Center Cards: 29
Extra Practice: 495

Daily Review TE p. 109D
⭐ Algebraic Thinking
🖱 Technology Link   **NCTM STANDARDS:** 1, 2, 3, 4, 11

CHAPTER ASSESSMENT

Chapter Review pp. 114–115
MATERIALS calculators (opt.)
Chapter Test p. 116
RESOURCES Posttest: Test Master Form A, B, or C
Performance Assessment p. 117
RESOURCES Performance Task: Test Master
Math • Science • Technology Connection
pp. 118–119
Cumulative Review pp. 120–121
MATERIALS calculators (opt.)

🖱 Technology Link
📁 Portfolio   **NCTM STANDARDS:** 1, 4, 10, 11

DAY 4

LESSON 3.3

PROBLEM-SOLVING STRATEGY

Work Backward pp. 88–89

CHAPTER OBJECTIVES: 3E
MATERIALS calculators (opt.)
RESOURCES Reteach/Practice/Extend: 23
Math Center Cards: 23
Extra Practice: 492

Daily Review TE p. 87B

Technology Link

NCTM STANDARDS:
1, 2, 3, 4, 10

LESSON 3.7

Ordered Pairs pp. 104–105

CHAPTER OBJECTIVES: 3D
MATERIALS calculators (opt.)
RESOURCES Reteach/Practice/Extend: 27
Math Center Cards: 27
Extra Practice: 494

Daily Review TE p. 103B

Technology Link

NCTM STANDARDS:
9

DAY 5

LESSON 3.4

EXPLORE ACTIVITY

Range, Median, and Mode pp. 90–93

CHAPTER OBJECTIVES: 3C
MATERIALS inch graph paper (TA 8),
scissors, calculators (opt.)
RESOURCES Reteach/Practice/Extend: 24
Math Center Cards: 24
Extra Practice: 493

Daily Review TE p. 89B

Algebraic Thinking

Journal

Technology Link

NCTM STANDARDS:
4, 11

LESSON 3.8

EXPLORE ACTIVITY

Line Graphs pp. 106–109

CHAPTER OBJECTIVES: 3D
MATERIALS graph paper, calculators
(opt.)
RESOURCES Reteach/Practice/Extend: 28
Math Center Cards: 28
Extra Practice: 495

TEACHING WITH TECHNOLOGY
Alternate Lesson TE pp. 109A–109B

Daily Review TE p. 105B

Journal

Technology Link

NCTM STANDARDS:
4, 11

Assessment Options

FORMAL

Chapter Tests

STUDENT BOOK
- Midchapter Review, p. 96
- Chapter Review, pp. 114–115
- Chapter Test, p. 116
- Cumulative Review, pp. 120–121

BLACKLINE MASTERS
- Test Master Form A, B, or C
- Diagnostic Inventory

COMPUTER TEST GENERATOR
- Available on disk

Performance Assessment
- What Do You Know? p. 81
- Performance Assessment, p. 117
- Holistic Scoring Guide, Teacher's Assessment Resources, pp. 27–32
- Follow-Up Interviews, p. 117
- Performance Task, Test Masters

Teacher's Assessment Resources
- Portfolio Guidelines and Forms, pp. 6–9, 33–35
- Holistic Scoring Guide, pp. 27–32
- Samples of Student Work, pp. 37–72

INFORMAL

Ongoing Assessment
- Observation Checklist, pp. 82, 84, 90, 100
- Interview, p. 88, 110
- Anecdotal Report, pp. 94, 104, 106

Portfolio Opportunities
- Chapter Project, p. 79F
- What Do You Know? p. 81
- Investigation, pp. 98–99
- Journal Writing, pp. 81, 91, 96, 107
- Performance Assessment, p. 117
- Self-Assessment: What Do You Think? p. 117

Chapter Objectives		Standardized Test Correlations
3A	Estimate, tell, and write time	MAT, CAT, SAT, ITBS, CTBS,TN*
3B	Find elapsed time	SAT,TN*
3C	Find the range, median, and mode of a set of data	ITBS,TN*
3D	Read, interpret, organize and display data	MAT, CAT, SAT, ITBS, CTBS,TN*
3E	Solve problems, including those that involve time, data, graphs, and working backward	MAT, CAT, SAT, ITBS, CTBS,TN*

*Terra Nova

NCTM Standards Grades K–4

1 Problem Solving	8 Whole Number Computation
2 Communication	9 Geometry and Spatial Sense
3 Reasoning	10 Measurement
4 Connections	11 Statistics and Probability
5 Estimation	12 Fractions and Decimals
6 Number Sense and Numeration	13 Patterns and Relationships
7 Concepts of Whole Number Operations	

TIME, DATA, AND GRAPHS

Meeting Individual Needs

LEARNING STYLES

- **AUDITORY/LINGUISTIC**
- LOGICAL/ANALYTICAL
- **VISUAL/SPATIAL**
- **MUSICAL**
- **KINESTHETIC**
- **SOCIAL**
- INDIVIDUAL

Students who are talented in art, language, and physical activity may better understand mathematical concepts when these concepts are connected to their areas of interest. Use the following activities to stimulate the different learning styles of some of your students.

Logical/Analytical Learners

Make up logic puzzles for students to solve.

What time is it?
My minute hand is on the four.
My hour hand is between six and seven.

Individual Learners

Make match-up cards showing analog and digital time. Cut cards in half, creating two puzzle pieces. Have students match the analog time with the digital time.

See Lesson Resources, pp. 81A, 83A, 87A, 89A, 93A, 99A, 103A, 105A, 109C.

GIFTED AND TALENTED

Make cards showing analog clocks with different times on the faces. Stack the cards in two piles. Have students work with partners, each turning over one card. Students take turns telling how much time occurs between the two times.

See also Meeting Individual Needs, pp. 85, 91, 102, 111.

EXTRA SUPPORT

Some students may benefit from using demonstration clocks. Specific suggestions for ways to provide extra support to students appear in every lesson in this chapter.

See Meeting Individual Needs, pp. 82, 84, 88, 90, 94, 104, 106.

EARLY FINISHERS

Students who finish their class work early may write a short paragraph about their own much-liked snack, song, movie, or sport. The early-finisher paragraphs may be compiled into a booklet to be shared on the class bookshelf. (See *Chapter Project*, p. 79F.)

See also Meeting Individual Needs, pp. 82, 86, 88, 92, 94, 102, 104, 108, 110, 112.

LANGUAGE SUPPORT

Students acquiring English may not be familiar with telling time using *thirty*. In Spanish, time on the half hour is said ___ and a half. When students are practicing telling time, have them repeat similar times so they can hear a pattern (12:30, 1:30, 2:30, etc.).

See also Meeting Individual Needs, pp. 91, 107, 110.

ESL APPROPRIATE

INCLUSION

- For **inclusion** ideas, information, and suggestions, see pp. 84, 100, 107, 111, T15.
- For **gender fairness** tips, see pp. 112, T15.

USING MANIPULATIVES

Building Understanding To practice telling time and finding elapsed time, students can play a game called "Draw the Time." Give students a recording sheet with three blank clock faces in a row. Write a time on the chalkboard, and have students record the time on the center clock. On the left clock, students write the time two hours earlier. On the clock to the right of the center clock, students write the time three hours later. Have students write the time in digital form underneath all of the clocks.

Easy-to-Make Manipulatives Have students make analog clock faces on paper plates. They can cut out the hands from firm paper or cardboard, punch holes in them, and attach them with paper fasteners.

ESL APPROPRIATE

USING COOPERATIVE LEARNING

People Graphs This strategy helps build a sense of community by grouping students according to several discrete categories, as in a bar graph.

- **Students make several parallel lines according to a shared characteristic (such as the number of books they have read).**
- **Students make and discuss observations about the line-ups.**

USING LITERATURE

Use the story *Hobie Hanson, You're Weird* to introduce the chapter theme, All About Us. This story is reprinted on pages 10–13 of the Read-Aloud Anthology.

Also available in the Read-Aloud Anthology is the selection *The Wonderful Wooden Clock*, page 14.

TIME, DATA, AND GRAPHS

Linking Technology

This integrated package of programs and services allows students to explore, develop, and practice concepts; solve problems; build portfolios; and assess their own progress. Teachers can enhance instruction, provide remediation, and share ideas with other educational professionals.

CD-ROM ACTIVITY

In *Here's the Scoop!,* students use tables and graphs to display and interpret data about an ice cream booth. Students can use the online notebook to write about how they made the graphs from the data. To extend the activity, students use the Math Van tools to make their own graphs. **Available on CD-ROM.**

CD-ROM TOOLS

Students can use Math Van's graph and table tools to explore the concepts of data and graphs. The Tech Links on the Lesson Resources pages highlight opportunities for students to use these and other tools such as online notes and calculator to provide additional practice, reteaching, or extension. **Available on CD-ROM.**

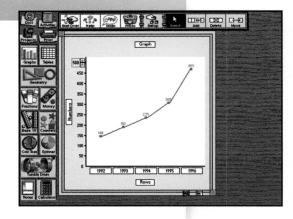

WEB SITE

http://www.mhschool.com

Teachers can access the McGraw-Hill School Division World Wide Web site for additional curriculum support at http://www.mhschool.com. Click on our Resource Village for specially designed activities linking Web sites to displaying and interpreting data. Motivate children by inviting them to explore Web sites that develop the chapter theme of "All About Us." Exchange ideas on classroom management, cultural diversity, and other areas in the Math Forum.

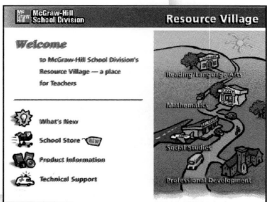

Chapter Project GRAPHICALLY SPEAKING

1 Starting the Project

Introduce the idea of a booklet presenting interesting information about the class in graphs and in written paragraphs. Brainstorm possible types of information to gather, eliciting enough categories so that each group may choose a different one. Examples: favorite snacks, songs, movies, and sports. Students will work in groups of 3 or 4, creating graphs and a brief paragraph analyzing the data the graphs were based upon.

Tell students that the kind of data they collect will determine the kind of graph they use.

Highlighting the Math

- collect, organize, and display data
- construct graphs to represent real-world data
- interpret data by finding the mean, median, and mode
- make generalizations from real-world data

2 Continuing the Project

- Each group selects a topic and begins gathering relevant data from all members of the class. Groups determine methods for gathering and organizing the collection of data.
- Students then select two methods of graphing to best represent the data they've collected. The graphs can be constructed by hand or with a computer.
- Each group writes about the collected data, following an agreed-upon outline:
    1. title
    2. names of students in group
    3. data collected
    4. clumps or gaps in the data

3 Finishing the Project

Each group presents its graph and written analysis to the class, using the outline to organize the presentation if students wish. At two more times during the year the groups might conduct the same survey and make a line graph incorporating the results of their earlier surveys.

Community Involvement
Invite someone from your local newspaper to talk to the class about ways in which graphs are used in journalism. If possible, have parents attend the talk.

BUILDING A PORTFOLIO

Each student's portfolio piece should include a copy of their group's contribution to the booklet, a statement of individual participation in the project, and a summary of the mathematics used in completing the project.

To assess students' work, refer to the Holistic Scoring Guide on page 27 in the Teacher's Assessment Resources.

Favorite Snacks
  crackers
  fruit
  vegetable strips
  raisins

Sports
  soccer
  baseball
  football
  hockey
  surfing

PURPOSE Introduce the theme of this chapter.

Resource Read-Aloud Anthology, pages 10–13

Using Literature

Read "Hobie Hanson, You're Weird" from the Read-Aloud Anthology to introduce the chapter theme "All About Us."

Developing the Theme

Ask students to choose their favorite school subject and about how much time they spend on homework each day. Have a volunteer list all the school subjects on the chalkboard in a column and make a tally mark next to the subject each student names as a favorite.

Ask another student to list the amounts of time—less than 1 hour, 1 hour, 2 hours, or 3 hours—in another column and mark an X next to the amount of time each student spends on homework each day.

After the data have been collected and displayed, ask:
- **What subject is most popular with your class?**
- **What is the longest amount of time spent on homework in your class?**
- **How much time do most students in your class spend on homework?**

CHAPTER

3 TIME, DATA, AND GRAPHS

THEME

All About Us

What do you think fourth graders are like? In this chapter, you will collect information about yourself and others. The information will show interesting facts about you!

80

Chapter Bibliography

City Green by DyAnne DiSalvo-Ryan. New York: Morrow Junior Books, 1994. ISBN 0–688–12786–X.

The Streets Are Free by Kurusa. San Diego: Annick Press, 1995. ISBN 0–55037–370–6.

Community Involvement

Students can work in small groups to survey the collection of a local public library for books written for, or about fourth graders. Each group can count the number of books in a single genre. Groups can graph their results and then design a poster that uses the graph to promote reading. Posters can be given to the library for display.

What Do You Know

2. Possible answer: Swimming is the most popular activity; ballet is the least popular activity; in-line skating is more popular than ice skating.

What are some of the activities you do during summer or winter vacations? On the right are the results of a survey of fourth graders.

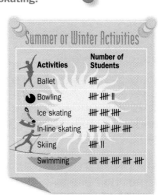

Summer or Winter Activities

Activities	Number of Students
Ballet	ⅢⅡ
Bowling	Ⅲ ⅢⅡ
Ice skating	Ⅲ Ⅲ Ⅲ
In-line skating	Ⅲ Ⅲ Ⅲ Ⅲ
Skiing	Ⅲ Ⅱ
Swimming	Ⅲ Ⅲ Ⅲ Ⅲ Ⅲ

1 What activity is most popular? How do you know? Swimming; it has the most number of tally marks.

2 Make three statements based on the data. See above.

3 Plan an afternoon of activities. Make a schedule that shows how you spend the time. Include activities that take less than a half hour and those that take more than an hour. Check students' work.

 Write: Compare/Contrast When you read, you often find out what something is like by comparing it to something else. Sometimes the writer gives you clues or you have to look for the likenesses and differences.

The table above shows things that fourth grade students like to do during summer or winter vacations. Choose two activities to compare and contrast.

1 How are the two activities alike? How are they different? Students compare and contrast two activities and list their similarities and differences.

Vocabulary

A.M., p. 84	**range,** p. 90	**key,** p. 94
P.M., p. 84	**median,** p. 90	**bar graph,** p. 100
elapsed time, p. 84	**mode,** p. 90	**ordered pair,** p. 104
ordinal numbers, p. 85	**pictograph,** p. 94	**line graph,** p. 106

Reading, Writing, Arithmetic

Write: Compare/Contrast Before students write a compare/contrast paragraph about the two activities, work with them verbally to compare and contrast common classroom objects. Start a topic sentence, for example, "Although textbooks are alike in many ways, they are also different." Then extend the discussion to compare and contrast two graphs.

Vocabulary

 Students may record new words in their journals. Encourage them to show examples and draw diagrams to help tell what the words mean.

PURPOSE Assess students' ability to apply prior knowledge of interpreting tables and making schedules.

Materials have available: graph paper

Assessing Prior Knowledge

Ask students what tallies are. [marks used for keeping a count] Draw this on the board and ask what it means. [5]

ⅢⅠ

Ask for examples of situations where a person might use tallies. [Possible answers: keeping track of how many people give each answer in a survey; given a list of students' heights in inches, figuring out how many students are of each height] Tell students that data is factual information used for drawing conclusions or for calculations.

Encourage students to use whatever methods they wish to answer items 1–3. Observe them as they work. Look at the schedules that students make for item 3.

BUILDING A PORTFOLIO

Item 3 can be used as a benchmark to show where students are in their understanding of elapsed time and making schedules.

A Portfolio Checklist for Students and a Checklist for Teachers are provided in Teacher's Assessment Resources, pp. 33–34.

Prerequisite Skills

- *Can students tell time?*
- *Do students represent and interpret data?*

Assessment Resources

DIAGNOSTIC INVENTORY

Use this blackline master to assess prerequisite skills that students will need in order to be successful in this chapter.

TEST MASTERS

Use the multiple choice format (form A or B) or the free response format (form C) as a pretest of the skills in this chapter.

LESSON 3.1

Time

OBJECTIVE Tell time and choose reasonable time estimates for given activities.

RESOURCE REMINDER
Math Center Cards 21
Practice 21, Reteach 21, Extend 21

SKILLS TRACE

GRADE 3
• Explore choosing reasonable time estimates for given activities. *(Chapter 5)*

GRADE 4
• Tell time and choose reasonable time estimates for given activities.

GRADE 5
• Change between units of time and compute with units of time. *(Chapter 7)*

WARM-UP

Whole Class   **Individual**

OBJECTIVE Record a weekend schedule.

Materials per student: time chart

Prepare Make a copy of the time chart for each student.

▶ Ask students to think about what they do on weekends and share these activities with the class.

▶ Have students list their activities on a schedule or time chart like the one shown on the right.

Time	Activity
7:00 A.M.	
8:00 A.M.	
9:00 A.M.	
10:00 A.M.	
11:00 A.M.	
12:00 A.M.	
1:00 P.M.	
2:00 P.M.	

SCIENCE CONNECTION

Cooperative Groups   **Visual/Spatial**

OBJECTIVE Explore various ways of telling time.

Materials drawing paper, color pencils, markers

▶ Have groups of students brainstorm ideas and names for a new invention for telling time.

▶ From their ideas each group should agree on one invention. Encourage them to add details that enhance the use of their invention.

▶ Groups then write a description of it, including its special features and how it works.

▶ Groups may share their invention with the class.

Daily Review

PREVIOUS DAY QUICK REVIEW

Subtract.
1. 634 − 28 *[606]*
2. 5210 − 4620 *[590]*
3. 9888 − 2626 *[7,262]*
4. $50.25 − $10.21 *[$40.04]*

FAST FACTS

1. 6 + 2 *[8]*
2. 2 + 1 *[3]*
3. 7 + 3 *[10]*
4. 4 + 4 *[8]*

Problem of the Day • 21

Julio scored a total of 25 points in yesterday's basketball game. Julio scored three 1-point free throws and scored two baskets from the 3-point zone. How many 2-point baskets did Julio score? *[8]*

TECH LINK

ONLINE EXPLORATION

Use our Web-linked activities and lesson plans to connect your students to the real world of fourth grade students.

MATH FORUM

Cultural Diversity Students enjoy learning numbers in different languages. I have students give the time in a language that is not their own.

Visit our Resource Village at http://mhschool.com to access the Online Exploration and the Math Forum.

MATH CENTER

Practice

OBJECTIVE Read times on analog clocks.

Materials per student: scissors, drawing paper, Math Center Recording Sheet (TA 31 optional)

Students show the hours on blank clocks. They arrange the clocks so that the 12 is not at the top and ask their partners to identify the time on each clock.

PRACTICE ACTIVITY 21

MATH CENTER
Partners 👥

Spatial Sense • Clock Jumbles

- Work together to draw 12 clocks like the clock shown. Cut out all your clocks. On each clock, show a different time, from 1:00 to 12:00.
- One partner places the clocks face up on the table. Turn them so that the 12 is not at the top.
- Ask your partner to identify each time without moving the clocks. Record all answers, writing them in order as the clocks are placed.
- Switch roles and repeat the activity.

YOU NEED
: scissors
: drawing paper

NCTM Standards

Problem Solving
✓ Communication
✓ Reasoning
Connections

Chapter 3, Lesson 1, pages 82–83   Time

Problem Solving

OBJECTIVE Model time using arms as clock hands.

Materials per pair: 2 Math Center Recording Sheets (TA 31 optional)

Partners use their arms to model a time as it appears on an analog clock. They must identify the time and name events that might occur at that time A.M and P.M.

PROBLEM-SOLVING ACTIVITY 21

MATH CENTER
Partners 👥

Spatial Reasoning • Modeling Clocks

- Write down a time of day. Don't let your partner see your time.
- Use your arms to show your time. Decide which arm will be the minute hand and which will be the hour hand. To show the difference, point the index finger on the minute hand and make a fist on the hour hand.
- Your partner must tell the time you are showing. Then your partner must tell something that might happen if the time were A.M. and something that might happen if the time were P.M. Switch roles with your partner.

NCTM Standards

Problem Solving
✓ Communication
✓ Reasoning
Connections

Chapter 3, Lesson 1, pages 82–83   Time

Lesson 3.1 *continued*

Time

> **OBJECTIVE** Tell time and choose reasonable time estimates for given activities.
>
> **Materials** demonstration clock, if available

Ask students to think of occasions when knowing the time is important to them. For example, students need to get up at a set time in order to get to school on time. Record on the chalkboard the list of occasions generated by the class.

   *Whole Class*

▶ **LEARN** As students read the introductory paragraph, ask a volunteer to show the time on a demonstration clock. If a demonstration clock is not available, draw the face of a clock on the chalkboard and let a volunteer draw the hands in the appropriate positions.

Using a demonstration clock or drawing of a clock face, invite several students to show the time they wake up, go to bed, leave home for soccer practice, or other occasions when knowing the time is important.

When determining the time Lena's brother gets up in the morning, let a student use the demonstration clock to show the answer.

> **Check for Understanding** using items 1–4, page 82.
>
> **CRITICAL THINKING**
> Have students describe the reasoning for their answers to item 4. Ask them to describe ways they could check their answers without doing an activity for an entire day.

▶ **PRACTICE**

Materials have available: calculators

Assign ex. 1–14 as independent work.
- For exercises 1–4, point out examples of different ways to read and write the time as shown on page 82.
- For exercises 5–10, tell students to use their own experiences to determine the most reasonable unit of time.
- In ex. 13, students are given the opportunity to solve a problem that has more than one solution.

Mixed Review/Test Preparation Students review adding and subtracting money amounts, a skill learned in Chapters 1 and 2.

TIME

 Time

1. Possible answers: 8:35, eight thirty-five, thirty-five minutes after eight, twenty-five minutes before nine

Lena, a fourth-grade student, gets up every weekday morning at 7:00 A.M. to get ready for school.

Below are the times for her morning activities.

She gets dressed.	She eats her breakfast.	She leaves for school.
Read: seven-fifteen *or* fifteen minutes after seven *or* a quarter after seven	**Read:** seven-thirty *or* thirty minutes after seven *or* half past seven	**Read:** seven forty-five *or* forty-five minutes after seven *or* a quarter to eight
Write: 7:15	**Write:** 7:30	**Write:** 7:45

▶ Lena's brother gets up 15 minutes (min) earlier than she does. At what time does he get up? How do you know? **6:45; possible answer: count back 15 min from 7:00.**

Check for Understanding
Write the time in two different ways.

2. Possible answers: 11:30, eleven-thirty, thirty minutes after eleven, half past eleven

1 See above.

2

3

Possible answers: 12:17, twelve-seventeen, seventeen minutes after twelve

Critical Thinking: Generalize

4 Name three activities that you enjoy doing that may take this amount of time.
  a. about one minute   **b.** about one hour (h)   **c.** about one day (d)

82   Lesson 3.1
   a. Possible answer: drink milk
   b. Possible answer: play basketball
   c. Possible answer: visit a museum

Meeting Individual Needs

Early Finishers

Have students think of three events that happen in each of the time units:
  a. seconds
  b. minutes
  c. hours
  d. days

Extra Support

Using a schedule of TV programs, read aloud the time of some programs. Ask students to tell the time in at least one different way. You may want to alternate the way you tell the time of the programs as well.

Ongoing Assessment

Observation Checklist Make notes on students' ability to read and write time in more than one form. Students should be successful in reading and understanding both an analog and a digital clock.

Follow Up If students need more practice with time, point out the time throughout the day. Ask students, "About how much time should it take you to get ready for recess?" or assign **Reteach 21.**

As students become more successful with these questions they may try **Extend 21.**

1. Possible answer: 12:07, seven minutes after twelve

2. Possible answers: 4:45, four forty-five, forty-five minutes after four, a quarter to five

3. Possible answer: 9:50, nine-fifty, fifty minutes after nine, ten minutes to ten

Practice

Write the time in two different ways.

1
See above.

2 `4:45`
See above.

3
See above.

4 `10:23`
Possible answers: ten twenty-three, twenty-three minutes after ten

Choose the most reasonable unit of time (seconds, minutes, hours, days, weeks).

5 It takes Lena about 15 ■ to walk her dog. **minutes**

6 A fourth grader goes to school about 180 ■ in a year (y). **days**

Which estimate of time is more reasonable?

7 see a movie
120 seconds (s) or 120 minutes
120 min

8 learn to play a guitar
24 hours or 24 weeks (wk) **24 wk**

9 brush your teeth
2 minutes or 2 days **2 min**

10 drive 600 miles
10 hours or 10 weeks **10 h**

MIXED APPLICATIONS
Problem Solving

11 Sammy buys two notebooks that cost $1.60 each. He gives the cashier a $5 bill. How much change does he get? **$1.80**

12 Kathy goes to a karate class at 4:15 every Tuesday after school. The class lasts an hour. What time does Kathy finish her karate class? **5:15**

13 **Logical reasoning** Karl is putting numbers into three groups: Numbers Greater than 25, Even Numbers, and Numbers with 2 in the Tens Place. Which number fits in all three groups? **c**
a. 29   **b.** 22   **c.** 26

14 **Data Point** Make a class pictograph that shows the time students leave for school. Use clock faces with students' names and place them beside a time. What does the graph tell you about your class? **Students' answers should reflect data shown on the pictograph.**

mixed review · test preparation

1 $52 + $5 **$57**

2 $300 − $200 **$100**

3 $88 − $59 **$29**

4 $127 − $95 **$32**

5 $185 + $705 **$890**

6 $97 − $9 **$88**

Extra Practice, page 492

Time, Data, and Graphs   **83**

Alternate Teaching Strategy

Materials per group: 12 cards showing the numbers 1 through 12, two cardboard clock hands, yarn, paper fasteners

Instruct students in each group to make a clock using the cardboard hands, number cards, and yarn.

Review the difference between the minute hand and the hour hand. Then ask questions such as:

- **How many minutes pass as the hour hand moves from one number to the next?** [60]
- **Where will the hour hand be at 2:30?** [halfway between 2 and 3]
- **How many minutes pass as the minute hand moves from one number to the next?** [5]
- **To what number does the minute hand point when the time is 20 minutes before the hour?** [8]

Let students work together asking each other similar questions.

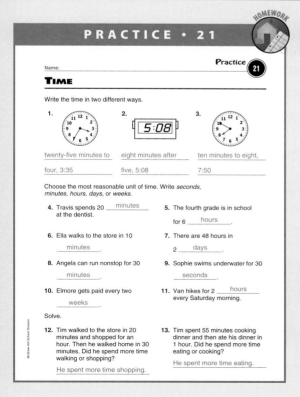

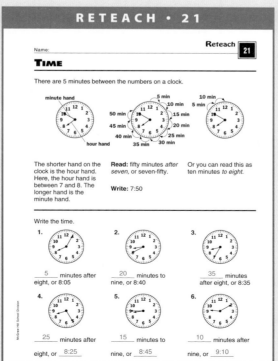

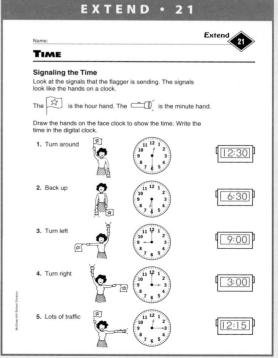

83

LESSON 3.2

Elapsed Time

OBJECTIVES Find and use elapsed times; identify times as A.M. or P.M.; Read and use a calendar.

RESOURCE REMINDER
Math Center Cards 22
Practice 22, Reteach 22, Extend 22

SKILLS TRACE

GRADE 3	• Make and use schedules involving elapsed time. Identify times as A.M. or P.M. *(Chapter 5)*
GRADE 4	• Find and use elapsed times. Identify times as A.M. or P.M.
GRADE 5	• Change between units of time and compute with units of time. *(Chapter 7)*

WARM-UP

Whole Class   **Visual/Spatial**

OBJECTIVE Read, write, and compare times.

► Draw two analog clock faces on the chalkboard.

► On one, draw minute and hour hands to show nine o'clock. Ask a student to tell the time indicated. Write that time beside the clock.

► Have another volunteer come to the chalkboard and draw a minute hand and an hour hand on the second clock face. Ask another student to come to the chalkboard and write the time. As a class, compare the two times.

► Continue this activity until all students have participated.

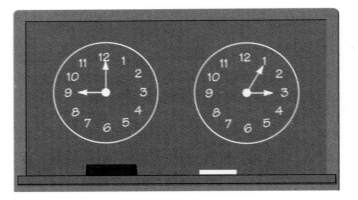

SOCIAL STUDIES CONNECTION

Cooperative Pairs   **Visual/Spatial**

OBJECTIVE Explore the four time zones of the continental United States.

Materials per pair: time zone map of the United States

► Using the time zone map, point out the four time zones in the continental United States: Eastern, Central, Mountain, and Pacific. Explain that for each time zone going east, the time is one hour earlier.

► Have pairs of students play a game similar to "20 Questions."

► One student secretly chooses a state. The second student asks *Yes* or *No* questions about the state chosen. Students should first narrow down the search by asking questions about the time zones: "Is the state in a time zone that is 3 hours ahead of our time?"

► Students should keep track of the number of questions they ask before guessing the state. Have students take turns so each partner has the opportunity to be the questioner at least twice.

Pacific/Mountain/Central/Eastern

Daily Review

Problem of the Day • 22

In the United States, national elections are always held on the first Tuesday following the first Monday in November. Name the possible dates an election could be held. *[Nov. 2nd through Nov. 8th]*

TECH LINK

MATH FORUM

Combination Classes Since my younger students are just learning to tell time, I have them use a play clock to show the times as the older students solve.

Visit our Resource Village at http://www.mhschool.com to see more of the Math Forum.

MATH CENTER

Practice

OBJECTIVE Use elapsed time to write a travel schedule.

Materials per student: Math Center Recording Sheet (TA 31 optional)

Students create a driving itinerary by listing all stops and the amount of travel time. Students determine the total travel time and the time of arrival. *[Answers may vary. Possible answer: Bette buys gasoline each time she stops to eat. Stops: lunch, $\frac{1}{2}$ hour at noon; dinner: 5:30 to 6:30, arrival time, 8:00 P.M.]*

PRACTICE ACTIVITY 22

MATH CENTER
On Your Own

Number Sense • Travel Plans

Bette is planning to drive her family to their cottage on the lake. The total driving time is 10 hours and 30 minutes. She plans to leave at 8:00 A.M. They will have to make several stops along the way.

Write a travel plan for Bette. Include stops for lunch and dinner and one stop for gasoline. You may add another short stop if you like. Write what time she should make each stop and how long each will take. Remember that each stop adds to the time of the trip.

Be sure to include the time they arrive at the cottage. She hopes to get there no later than midnight.

Chapter 3, Lesson 2, pages 84–87

Time

NCTM Standards
- ✓ Problem Solving
- ✓ Communication
- Reasoning
- ✓ Connections

Problem Solving

OBJECTIVE Analyze sequence of events involving elapsed time.

Students read a story and then make a decision based upon elapsed time. They may want to show the sequence of elapsed times on their paper. *[Accept reasonable explanations. Possible answer: If the suspect's story is true, he left the theater at 7:58 P.M. Since the theater is 6 blocks, or 18 minutes, away from the bank, the suspect could not have robbed the bank.]*

PROBLEM-SOLVING ACTIVITY 22

MATH CENTER
On Your Own

Logical Reasoning • The Alibi

A suspect was charged with robbing a bank at 8:04 P.M. the night before. He had an alibi:

- "I left work at 5:04 P.M. Then I walked 8 blocks to the theater. Due to an injury, I can't run. It takes 3 minutes to walk one block. The movie had already started and I had missed 3 minutes. The movie lasted 2 hours and 30 minutes.

- "I left when it was over and walked home 11 blocks. My landlord let me in. I asked her the time, and she said it was 8:28. The bank is 6 blocks from the movie and 9 blocks from my house."

- If the suspect's story is true, could he have robbed the bank? Explain why.

Chapter 3, Lesson 2, pages 84–87

Time

NCTM Standards
- ✓ Problem Solving
- ✓ Communication
- ✓ Reasoning
- Connections

Elapsed Time

OBJECTIVES Find and use elapsed times; identify times as A.M. or P.M.; read and use a calendar.

Vocabulary A.M., elapsed time, ordinal numbers, P.M.

1 Introduce

Ask students to name activities and the duration of those activities. For example, they may know the amount of time set aside for each class, the time it takes for them to walk to school, or the amount of time scheduled for their basketball practice.

Make a list of these activities on the board with their designated times. Ask students to give possible starting and ending times.

2 Teach   *Whole Class*

▶ **LEARN** Read the first example and the solution as a class. Then ask your students to estimate the amount of time it would take to watch a movie. Have them answer the question again using their data. Ask students to describe the methods they used to solve the problem.

Read through the second example and solution. Then ask:
- **How are these two problems similar?** *[They both involve starting and ending times and an elapsed time.]* **different?** *[The first problem asks for a time after a certain amount of time passes, the second asks for time between two times.]*

Talk It Over Ask students what it might be like if morning and afternoon times were not distinguished by A.M. and P.M. Have them give an example of the type of confusion that could result. Be sure students understand the **What If** question by asking them:
- **Can you solve this problem by counting on? Why or why not?** *[No; you must count back because you need a starting time.]*

 TIME

Elapsed Time

L E A R N

You and your friends begin watching a video of last year's Community Dance Expo at 11:30 A.M. The video runs for 2 hours 30 minutes. Will the video be over by the time soccer practice begins at 2:30 P.M.?

You can count on to find the time you will finish the video.

First count on the hours.
Think: 2 hours (2 h)
11:30 A.M.
12:30 P.M. } 1 hour
1:30 P.M. } 1 hour

Then count on the minutes.
Think: 30 minutes (30 min)
1:30 P.M.
2:00 P.M. } 30 minutes

The video will be over at 2:00 P.M., before soccer practice begins at 2:30 P.M.

Your dance partner for this year's Community Dance contest arrives at 4:30 P.M. and leaves at 7:45 P.M. How long do you practice together?

You can count on to find the **elapsed time.**

First count on the hours.
Think: From 4:30 P.M. to 7:30 P.M. is 3 hours (3 h).

Then count on the minutes.
Think: From 7:30 P.M. to 7:45 P.M. is 15 minutes (15 min).

You practice for 3 hours 15 minutes.

Talk It Over
▶ Why do we need A.M. and P.M. when referring to a time? **They tell whether it is between midnight and noon or noon and midnight.**
▶ **What if** the video lasted 1 hour 50 minutes. At what time would you have to begin the video to be finished by 2:00 P.M.? Explain your answer. **12:10 P.M.; start at 2:00 P.M., count back 1 h to 1:00 P.M., then count back 50 min to 12:10 P.M.**

> **Check Out the Glossary**
> A.M.
> P.M.
> elapsed time
> ordinal numbers
> See page 544.

84 Lesson 3.2

Meeting Individual Needs

Extra Support

Some students may have difficulty finding elapsed time when start time is A.M. and end time is P.M. and vice versa. Have them use two play clocks to find elapsed time, one clock for A.M. hours and the other for P.M.

ESL APPROPRIATE

Inclusion

Some students may need to look at a clock when solving problems involving time. Suggest that they draw a clock to help them count back or count on the elapsed time.

ESL APPROPRIATE

Ongoing Assessment

Observation Checklist Determine students' understanding of elapsed time by observing if they can successfully find the starting time, ending time, and elapsed time in a problem.

Follow Up For more practice with elapsed time, students may enjoy a matching game. Ask students to match cards with elapsed times to cards with starting and ending times, or assign **Reteach 22.**

Students who need a greater challenge may make up pairs of cards for the matching game, or try **Extend 22.**

You can also use a calendar to find elapsed time.

Rehearsals for this year's Dance Expo will begin on the Monday after Thanksgiving. They will run every day for 12 days. On what day and date will the last rehearsal be?

Step 1
Use the calendar. Find the Monday after Thanksgiving.

Note: Use **ordinal numbers** when you talk about dates.

The Monday after Thanksgiving is November 30th.

Step 2
Use November 30th as the first day and count on 12 days.

Rehearsals will start on November 30th and end on Friday, December 11th.

The last rehearsal will be on December 11th.

Check for Understanding
Complete the table.

1	Start time: 10:20 P.M.	Elapsed time: 2 h 30 min	End time: ▨	12:50 A.M.
2	Start time: 9:30 A.M.	Elapsed time: ▨	End time: 3:50 P.M.	6 h 20 min
3	Start time: ▨	Elapsed time: 5 h 45 min	End time: 1:00 P.M.	7:15 A.M.
4	Start date: September 1	Elapsed time: 38 days	End date: ▨	October 8
5	Start date: January 12	Elapsed time: ▨	End date: February 2	22 d

Critical Thinking: Analyze   Explain your reasoning.

6 The school art show lasts 3 weeks and ends on December 31st. When does it start? December 11th; count back from the end date to find the start date.

Turn the page for Practice. ➡
Time, Data, and Graphs   **85**

Instruct students to read through the calendar problem. Then ask:
- **Which problem on page 84 is most like the calendar problem on page 85? How are the two problems alike?** *[The calendar problem is similar to the problem shown at the top of page 84; both problems ask for the ending time.]*
- **How are the methods used to solve the two problems similar?** *[Both solutions use counting on.]*

Ask students to write calendar problems similar to the problem given on page 85.

3 Close

Check for Understanding using items 1–6, page 85.

CRITICAL THINKING
After answering item 6, have students further analyze questions about elapsed time by asking:
- **When would you count on to find the elapsed time?** *[when you need to know the ending time]*
- **When would you count back to find the elapsed time?** *[when you want to find the starting time]*

Practice See pages 86–87.

Gifted And Talented

Instruct students to write multi-step problems involving time. Give students the following problem as an example:
On Wednesdays, Ken has both piano and soccer practice. Piano practice starts at 5:30 P.M. and lasts 1 h 20 min. It takes Ken 10 min to get to soccer practice. His Mom picks him up from soccer practice at 9:00 P.M. How long is soccer practice? *[2 h]*

Have students solve the problems they wrote, then exchange their problems with other students and solve them.

▶ **PRACTICE**

Materials have available: calculators (optional)

Options for assigning exercises:
A—Odd ex. 1–17; ex. 18–22; **Cultural Connection**
B—Even ex. 2–16; 18–22; **Cultural Connection**

• Ask students to describe the difference between ex. 1–5 and ex. 6–10. They should notice that for ex. 1–5 they will count up to find the ending time. For ex. 6–10 they will count back to find the beginning time.

• For ex. 18, 20, and 21, suggest that students label the starting time, ending time, and elapsed time.

• Ex. 22 should be completed as a class.

Cultural Connection Discuss the information about Swahili time and locate Kenya and Uganda on a map of Africa. Point out to students that Swahili time is not based on time zones. Swahili time is based on their sunrise, which occurs at 1:00 A.M.

Students may want to determine the current time in Uganda. First have them calculate the time based on standard time. Then have them determine the time in Swahili time.

Ask students if they have friends or relatives who live in another state or country.

• **Why would it be important to know what time zone they live in?** [*Possible answer: to telephone them at a convenient time*]

Practice

Tell what time it will be:

1 in 20 min. **10:55**

2 in 3 h 30 min. **8:45**

3 in 5 h 5 min. **2:00**

4 2 h 50 min after 7:30 A.M. **10:20 A.M.**   **5** 3 h 30 min after 9:15 A.M.
12:45 P.M.

Tell what time it was:

6 a half hour ago. **8:30**   **7** 1 h 10 min ago. **10:50**   **8** 2 h 15 min ago.
11:15

9 2 h 30 min before 10:15 A.M. **7:45** A.M. **10** 5 h 20 min before 4:20 P.M.
11:00 A.M.

Use the calendars for February and March for problems 11–14.

11 What is the date of the third Tuesday in February? **17th**

12 On what day of the week is Groundhog Day? **Monday**

13 If the Presidents' show runs from Presidents' Day through the end of the month, for how many days does the show run? **13 d**

14 If you leave on Valentine's Day and return 16 days later, on what day and date do you return? **Monday, March 2nd**

Complete the table.

15	Start time: 8:15 A.M.	Elapsed time: 3 h 50 min	End time: ■	**12:05 P.M.**
16	Start time: 5:50 A.M.	Elapsed time: ■	End time: 10:40 A.M.	**4 h 50 min**
17	Start date: May 10	Elapsed time: 45 days	End date: ■	**June 24**

Meeting Individual Needs

Early Finishers

Ask students to think of events in their own lives, such as camping or vacationing, where they knew the starting time, ending time, or elapsed time. Ask students to list the event and the starting, ending, and elapsed time.

COMMON ERROR

Students may have difficulties recognizing the difference between starting time and ending time.

Drawing pictures or time lines to represent the duration of an event may help students understand the problems more clearly.

0. Students may use the calendar to count the number of days.
1. Students should compare problems and solutions.

MIXED APPLICATIONS
Problem Solving

3 Joe left on February 20th and returned on March 6th. Wes left on February 18th and returned on March 20th. Whose trip was longer? How much longer? **Wes's; 16 d longer**

0 How many days have passed since the start of the school year? How many days are left? **See above.**

2 **Data Point** Make a line plot for your class like the one shown. Place one check mark above all the ways you have traveled. Can you tell how many students are in your class from the graph? Why or why not? **Line plots may vary. Possible answer: No; some students recorded a check more than once.**

19 **Make a decision** You have $7.20. What would you buy if a fruit salad cost $2.75, a tuna sandwich cost $2.90, a chicken salad cost $3.50, and a cheese melt cost $2.50? **Possible answer: fruit salad and tuna sandwich for $5.65**

21 **Write a problem** about elapsed time. Use a calendar. Have a classmate solve your problem. **See above.**

HOW HAVE YOU TRAVELED?
✓
✓ ✓
✓ ✓ ✓ ✓
by bus | by car | by train or subway | by plane

Cultural Connection Swahili African Time

Many people in the East African countries of Kenya (KEN-yuh) and Uganda (yoo-GAN-duh) start counting the hours of the day at sunrise. Their 1:00 is the same as 7:00 A.M. standard time.

AFRICA
Kenya
Uganda

	Breakfast	**Lunch**	**Dinner**
Standard Time	7:00	12:00	6:00
Swahili Time	1:00	6:00	12:00

Use the chart to answer the question.

1 How can you change Swahili time to standard time? **Add 6 h.**

2 At what time would you get to school in Swahili time? **Answers may vary. Students need to subtract 6 h from the standard time they arrive.**

Extra Practice, page 492

Time, Data, and Graphs **87**

Alternate Teaching Strategy

Materials per pair: demonstration clock

Give each pair a demonstration clock and a copy of the three problems below. Instruct students to make a chart similar to the one shown.

- **Karyn's dance class begins at 7:00 P.M. It takes her 30 minutes to walk to class from home. What is the latest time she can leave her home?** *[6:30 P.M.]*
- **Karyn's mom picks her up from dance class at 9:00 P.M. How long is her class?** *[2 hours]*
- **Karyn's mom can drive home from the dance studio in 10 minutes. When do they arrive home?** *[9:10 P.M.]*

Have students write in the chart the information given in the first problem. Ask students what they need to find. *[the time they have to leave or the starting time]*

Instruct students to show the ending time on the clock and then move the hands backward to show the starting time to indicate the amount of time that has elapsed.

Allow students to use the clocks to complete the last two problems on their own.

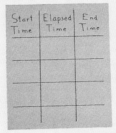

Start Time | Elapsed Time | End Time

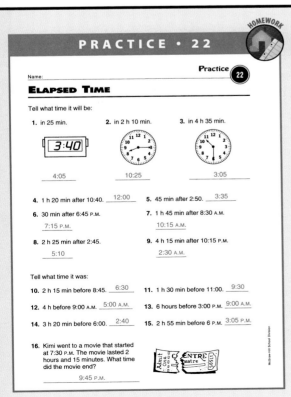

PRACTICE • 22

Practice **22**

Name:

ELAPSED TIME

Tell what time it will be:

1. in 25 min.
3:40 → **4:05**

2. in 2 h 10 min.
10:25

3. in 4 h 35 min.
3:05

4. 1 h 20 min after 10:40. **12:00**

5. 45 min after 2:50. **3:35**

6. 30 min after 6:45 P.M.
7:15 P.M.

7. 1 h 45 min after 8:30 A.M.
10:15 A.M.

8. 2 h 25 min after 2:45.
5:10

9. 4 h 15 min after 10:15 P.M.
2:30 A.M.

Tell what time it was:

10. 2 h 15 min before 8:45. **6:30**

11. 1 h 30 min before 11:00. **9:30**

12. 4 h before 9:00 A.M. **5:00 A.M.**

13. 6 hours before 3:00 P.M. **9:00 A.M.**

14. 3 h 20 min before 6:00. **2:40**

15. 2 h 55 min before 6 P.M. **3:05 P.M.**

16. Kimi went to a movie that started at 7:30 P.M. The movie lasted 2 hours and 15 minutes. What time did the movie end?
9:45 P.M.

CENTRE Theatre

RETEACH • 22

Reteach **22**

Name:

ELAPSED TIME

Tia studied for 35 minutes. She began at 7:45 P.M. What time was it when she stopped?

To find the **elapsed time**, or the time when Tia stopped, you can count on by 5s:

| 5 | 10 | 15 | 20 | 25 | 30 | 35 |
7:45 → 7:50 → 7:55 → 8:00 → 8:05 → 8:10 → 8:15 → 8:20

Tia stopped at 8:20 P.M.

Tell what time it will be:

1. in 15 min.
3:15

2. in 20 min.
8:20

3. in 35 min.
6:05

4. in a half hour.
4:45

5. in a half hour.
7:15

6. in 45 min.
10:55 or five to eleven

7. in 2 h 15 min.
4:15

8. in 4 h 20 min.
9:35

9. in 1 h 25 min.
10:55 or five to eleven

EXTEND • 22

Extend **22**

Name:

ELAPSED TIME

How the Time Flies
Answer each question about airline flights between major U.S. cities. Don't forget the time zones.

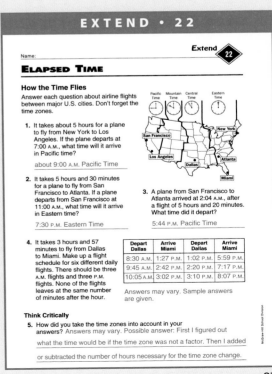

Pacific Time | Mountain Time | Central Time | Eastern Time
San Francisco | New York | Los Angeles | Dallas | Atlanta | Miami

1. It takes about 5 hours for a plane to fly from New York to Los Angeles. If the plane departs at 7:00 A.M., what time will it arrive in Pacific time?
about 9:00 A.M. Pacific Time

2. It takes 5 hours and 30 minutes for a plane to fly from San Francisco to Atlanta. If a plane departs from San Francisco at 11:00 A.M., what time will it arrive in Eastern time?
7:30 P.M. Eastern Time

3. A plane from San Francisco to Atlanta arrived at 2:04 A.M., after a flight of 5 hours and 20 minutes. What time did it depart?
5:44 P.M. Pacific Time

4. It takes 3 hours and 57 minutes to fly from Dallas to Miami. Make up a flight schedule for six different daily flights. There should be three A.M. flights and three P.M. flights. None of the flights leaves at the same number of minutes after the hour.

Depart Dallas	Arrive Miami	Depart Dallas	Arrive Miami
8:30 A.M.	1:27 P.M.	1:02 P.M.	5:59 P.M.
9:45 A.M.	2:42 P.M.	2:20 P.M.	7:17 P.M.
10:05 A.M.	3:02 P.M.	3:10 P.M.	8:07 P.M.

Answers may vary. Sample answers are given.

Think Critically

5. How did you take the time zones into account in your answers? **Answers may vary. Possible answer: First I figured out what the time would be if the time zone was not a factor. Then I added or subtracted the number of hours necessary for the time zone change.**

LESSON 3.3

Problem-Solving Strategy: Work Backward

OBJECTIVE Solve problems by working backward.

RESOURCE REMINDER
Math Center Cards 23
Practice 23, Reteach 23, Extend 23

SKILLS TRACE

GRADE 3	• Solve problems by using the strategy working backward. *(Chapter 8)*
GRADE 4	• Solve problems by using the strategy working backward.
GRADE 5	• Solve problems by using the strategy working backward. *(Chapter 10)*

WARM-UP

Cooperative Pairs   **Visual/Spatial**

OBJECTIVE Solve mazes both forward and backward.

Materials per pair: three or more mazes

► Give each pair two copies of the same maze. Each student will solve the maze by starting from opposite ends at the same time. Give students another maze to complete. This time, students should switch directions so they have solved a maze backward and forward.

► Give students a final maze. Students should choose the method that will allow them to complete the maze more quickly.

► Let students discuss which method—forward or backward—allowed them to complete the maze faster. Which method were they most comfortable with? What did they like and dislike about each method?

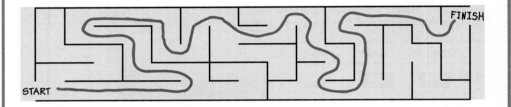

CONSUMER CONNECTION

Cooperative Pairs   **Logical/Analytical**

OBJECTIVE Explore financial planning by using the strategy of working backward.

Materials flyers or newspaper ads on vacation packages, summer camps, games, or shows; calendar, and calculator

► Have each pair of students choose a vacation package, a summer camp, or any games and shows they would want to go to.

► Have students make up a financial plan by making decisions on:
• the starting day of the activity
• the total amount they would have to save
• the amount they plan to save each day
• when they should start saving

► Remind students to use a calendar and then work backward to plan.

► Encourage pairs using a poster to present their work to the class.

Daily Review

PREVIOUS DAY QUICK REVIEW

If it is now 10:00 A.M., tell what time it will be:

1. in 10 min *[10:10 A.M.]*
2. in 2 h 30 min *[12:30 P.M.]*
3. in 8 h 15 min *[6:15 P.M.]*
4. in 9 h 5 min *[7:05 P.M.]*

FAST FACTS

1. 4 + 0 *[4]*
2. 1 + 7 *[8]*
3. 4 + 5 *[9]*
4. 5 + 9 *[14]*

Problem of the Day • 23

A digital clock displays the time as 7:56. What time will it be after 18 digit changes? *[8:14]*

TECH LINK

MATH FORUM

Management Tip My students love to write problems and stories, especially if they can illustrate them. I have my students write, illustrate, and solve the problems in their own mini-books.

Visit our Resource Village at http://www.mhschool.com to see more of the Math Forum.

MATH CENTER

Practice

OBJECTIVE Use a calendar to solve a problem.

Materials per student: Math Center Recording Sheet (TA 31 optional)

Students work backward from the arrival time of 5:00 P.M. to make a schedule of necessary stops and determine the departure time. The schedule allows students to make decisions about how to travel and when to leave. *[Answers may vary. Check students' work.]*

PRACTICE ACTIVITY 23

MATH CENTER
On Your Own

Decision Making • Be Home by 5:00

You and your aunt are going shopping. It's 9:00 A.M. on a Saturday morning. The mall is a 30-minute drive from your house. A bus, which stops at your corner every hour on the hour, takes 45 minutes.

You'd like to leave home as late as possible. You have to be back by 5:00 P.M. You and your aunt need to spend about an hour in each of three stores. Allow 15 minutes to walk between stores. The return bus leaves every hour on the hour. What time should you leave home to get back by 5:00?

Make a schedule to show your answer. If you leave before noon, allow $\frac{1}{2}$ hour for lunch. Your aunt prefers taking the bus. Your schedule will help her decide.

Chapter 3, Lesson 3, pages 88–89

Problem Solving

NCTM Standards

✓ **Problem Solving**
  Communication
✓ **Reasoning**
  Connections

Problem Solving

OBJECTIVE Use logical reasoning to make addition exercises.

Materials per student: 9 index cards; Math Center Recording Sheet (TA 31 optional)

Prepare Write numbers 1–9 on index cards.

Students make addition problems with two 3-digit addends and a 3-digit sum. They use each digit from 1 to 9 once. *[Answers may vary. Possible answers: 157 + 329 = 486, 159 + 327 = 486, 129 + 357 = 486]*

PROBLEM-SOLVING ACTIVITY 23

MATH CENTER
On Your Own

Logical Reasoning • Add It Up

Arrange the cards to make two 3-digit numbers and their sum. Try to make as many different addition examples as you can. Record each example.

YOU NEED
number cards labeled 1 to 9

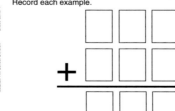

Chapter 3, Lesson 3, pages 88–89

Problem Solving

NCTM Standards

✓ **Problem Solving**
  Communication
✓ **Reasoning**
  Connections

Problem-Solving Strategy: Work Backward

OBJECTIVE Solve problems by working backward.

 **Introduce**

Materials bus schedule

Ask your students if they have ever been on a bus other than a school bus. Ask how they knew when to catch the bus. Help students read the bus schedule. Ask them several questions that can be answered using the bus schedule.

 **Teach**   *Whole Class*

▶ **LEARN** Read the introductory problem as a class and ask students to describe how working backward can help them solve this problem. Have students draw pictures in the order they would occur to represent the problem. For example, pictures could include two people leaving a house, waiting at a bus stop, getting off a bus, and swimming.

Read through the Plan step as a class. Invite students to the board to write information next to the appropriate pictures.

Continue to work through the problem as a class, using the pictures as much as possible. This will help students see more clearly that the problem was solved by working backward.

③ **Close**

Check for Understanding using items 1 and 2, page 88.

CRITICAL THINKING
Ask students if the examples they give can also be solved by working forward. Talk about this example and discuss the fact that there are many ways to solve problems. No one method is more correct than any other.

▶ **PRACTICE**
Materials have available: calculators

Choose eight exercises from ex. 1–10.
- Remind students that not all problems can be solved working backward and that not all problems will be about time. Ask students to read the problems carefully and choose the method they think will work best.
- In ex. 2, students have the opportunity to use the problem-solving strategies Solving Multistep Problems and Choose the Operation.
- For ex. 8, tell students that the three cubes shown are exactly the same. They are simply turned differently so you can see what is on several faces.

Problem-Solving Strategy

Read
Plan
Solve
Look Back

Work Backward

L E A R N

Read Tyler and her mother want to go by bus to a 5:30 P.M. swimming class. This class is at the Midwood Community Center. It takes them about 25 minutes to walk to the Hillsvale bus stop. Which bus should they take? When should they leave home?

Plan You can work backward to solve this problem. Use the bus schedule.

Solve Start by finding the last bus that can arrive at the Midwood Community Center before 5:30 P.M.

> **Think:** A bus arrives at the Community Center at 5:15 P.M. It leaves Hillsvale at 4:45 P.M.

Then find the time Tyler and her mother need to leave home.

> **Think:** End time   4:45 P.M.
> Elapsed time   25 minutes
> Start time   4:20 P.M.

They should take the 4:45 P.M. bus and leave home by 4:20 P.M.

BUS SCHEDULE

LOCATION	P.M.	P.M.	P.M.	P.M.	
Bus Port	2:15	3:00	4:12	4:30	5
Hillsvale	2:25	3:10	4:20	(4:45)	5
Junction North	2:35	3:20	4:35	4:50	5
Maple	2:40	3:25	4:42	4:59	5:4
Ridgewood	2:45	3:30	4:50	5:05	6:0
Tenpal	2:50	3:35	4:55	5:10	6:0
Midwood Community Center	3:02	3:47	5:05	(5:15)	6:2
Corroll	3:12	3:57	5:19	5:30	6:35
Astor	3:17	4:02	5:30	5:41	6:47

Start at 4:20 P.M., take 25 min to walk to the bus stop— 4:45 P.M., take the 4:45 P.M. bus to the Community Center to get there at 5:15 P.M.

Look Back How can you work forward to check your answers? See right.

Check for Understanding

1 **What if** Tyler and her mother want to arrive at the Center about a half hour before the class. Which bus should they take? When should they leave home? Explain your method.

Critical Thinking: Summarize

2 Give examples of problems where you can work backward to find: **Problems may vary.**
   a. the amount of change.   **b.** the time that a concert ends.

They should take the 4:20 P.M. bus from Hillsvale; they should leave home by 3:55 P.M.; explanation may vary.

C H E C K

Meeting Individual Needs

Early Finishers

Have students write more problems that can be solved by working backward using the Midwood Community Center Schedule on page 89.

Extra Support

Have students write a problem that can be solved using a mathematical sentence with an unknown number. For example, ◆ − $12.95 = $7.05. Ask them to explain how working backward can solve the problem.

Ongoing Assessment

Interview Determine if students understand working backward by asking:
- **How does knowing that addition and subtraction are opposite operations help you solve a problem that asks for the number you started with?** *[Possible answer: you can work backward and subtract to find the number you started with.]*

Follow Up If students need more practice working backward, have them share the problems they wrote for ex. 10, or assign **Reteach 23.**

1 Mei wants to finish her exercises by 7:10 P.M. She usually takes 30 minutes to exercise. What is the latest time that she can start? **6:40 P.M.**

3 Kyle likes to create patterns using his calculator. He chooses a number, adds 8, subtracts 4, adds 2, then subtracts 1. His result is 27. What number did he choose? **22**

2 Lee has $5.00 to start. He uses 7 quarters at the arcade. Then he buys a bottle of juice for 89¢. How much money does he have left? **$2.36**

4 Karlene has $57.30 in her savings account at the end of the month. During the month she took out $25 and put in $14.98. How much money did she have at the beginning of the month? **$67.32**

Use the schedule for problems 5–7.

5 How much longer is the swimming class than the dance class? **10 min**

6 Which class is the longest? **swimming**

7 Choose two activities from the schedule that you would like to do. How long is each activity? How much time would you have between the activities? **Students' answers should reflect the times on the schedule.**

Midwood Community Center

Schedule

	Activity	Begin	End
	Gymnastics	10:00 A.M.	11:15 A.M.
	Soccer	11:35 A.M.	12:45 P.M.
	Dance	1:00 P.M.	2:25 P.M.
	Swimming	3:05 P.M.	4:40 P.M.

8 **Spatial reasoning** Three views of the same cube are shown. What shape is on the opposite face from the circle? **the trapezoid**

9 What was the difference between the times Mihir Sen took to swim the Panama Canal and the Palk Strait? SEE INFOBIT. **30 h 15 min**

INFOBIT
In 1966, Mihir Sen of India swam the Panama Canal in 4 hours. He also swam the Palk Strait in 34 hours 15 minutes.

10 **Write a problem** that you can work backward to solve. Use the bus schedule on page 88 or use a bus schedule of your own. **Students may check each other's work by comparing problems and answers.**

Extra Practice, page 492

Time, Data, and Graphs **89**

Alternate Teaching Strategy

Write the following problem on the chalkboard:

Jill walked to the toy store, then to the bakery, and then took a bus home. She spent $5.10 at the toy store, $1.80 at the bakery, and the fare for the bus was $0.75. When she got home Jill had $4.35. How much money did Jill have before she went to the toy store? [$12.00]

Read through the problem with students. Draw a diagram on the chalkboard that shows the events that took place in Jill's day.

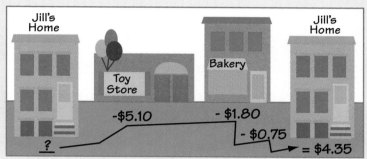

Ask students how the number sentence relates to the problem. They should see that it follows Jill's spending. The missing number is the amount of money Jill had before she went to the toy store.

Tell students that since a piece of information at the beginning of the number sentence is what you are trying to find, it may be easier to work the problem backward. Talk about retracing Jill's steps. Ask students to suggest a number sentence that would allow them to work the problem backward. Sample answer: $4.35 + $0.75 + $1.80 + $5.10 = _____.

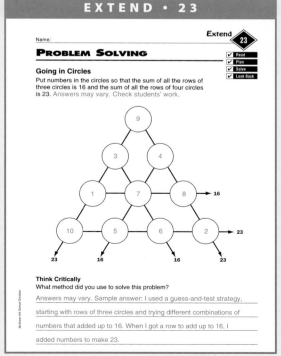
89

LESSON 3.4

EXPLORE ACTIVITY
Range, Median, and Mode

OBJECTIVE Find the range, median, and mode(s) of a set of data and use them to describe the data.

RESOURCE REMINDER
Math Center Cards 24
Practice 24, Reteach 24, Extend 24

SKILLS TRACE

GRADE 3	• *Introduced at grade 4.*
GRADE 4	• Explore finding the range, median, and mode(s) of a set of data and using them to describe the data.
GRADE 5	• Compute the range, median, and mode(s) for a set of data. *(Chapter 3)*

MANIPULATIVE WARM-UP

Cooperative Groups   **Logical/Analytical**

OBJECTIVE Explore analyzing data.

Materials index cards, chart paper, markers

► Students count the number of letters in his or her last name and write each letter on an index card.

A K E M B O
S H I N
G O L D S T E I N

► Pose the following questions to each group:
  • **What is the greatest number of letters in the last names of your group? the least?**
  • **What is the difference between the greatest and the least number of letters in the last names?**
  • **What is the number of letters in a last name that occured most often?**
  [Answers may vary.]

SCIENCE CONNECTION

Cooperative Groups   **Visual/Spatial**

OBJECTIVE Use range, median, and mode to summarize data collected from a science experiment.

► Give students a brief introduction to the two types of memories: *Short-term memory* is used for the temporary storage of information. *Long-term memory* is used for the permanent storage of information.

► Tell students they will be testing their short-term memory. Show the list of words at the right to each group for 5 seconds. Then ask students to write down as many words as they can.

► Have each group calculate the range, median, and mode of the number of words their group members can recall.

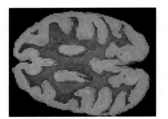

hat   cat   mat

rat   sat   fat   bat

Daily Review

PREVIOUS DAY QUICK REVIEW

Calculate the time.

1. 15 min after 7:25 P.M. *[7:40]*
2. 20 min before 6:15 P.M. *[5:55]*
3. 5 min after 6:00 P.M. *[6:05]*
4. 25 min before 8:00 A.M. *[7:35]*

FAST FACTS

1. 1 + 0 *[1]*
2. 7 + 6 *[13]*
3. 2 + 8 *[10]*
4. 7 + 1 *[8]*

Problem of the Day • 24

Mina started reading a new book. On Monday and Tuesday she read 118 pages each day. On Wednesday she read twice as many pages as she did on Tuesday. On Thursday she read 104 pages and finished the book. How many pages were in the book? *[576 pages]*

TECH LINK

MATH VAN

Tool You may wish to use the Table tool and the Calculator with this lesson.

MATH FORUM

Idea I make number cards and have an odd number of students, each with a card, stand in order in front of the class. The class takes turns asking certain students to step forward to show the median and mode and compute the range.

Visit our Resource Village at http://www.mhschool.com to see more of the Math Forum.

MATH CENTER

Practice

OBJECTIVE Compare and contrast two sets of data by finding the mode, median and range of each set.

Materials per student: calculator, Math Center Recording Sheet (TA 31 optional)

Students create two data sets about different sports balls. They find the range, median, and mode and use these measures to compare and contrast the data sets.

PRACTICE ACTIVITY 24

MATH CENTER
Partners 👥

Number Sense • The Smart Set

The sports storage room at school has 8 kinds of balls: golf balls, bowling balls, tennis balls, footballs, softballs, baseballs, kickballs, and basketballs.

- Working separately, you and your partner list the 8 kinds of balls. Next to each type of ball, write a different number that is less than 15. The number tells how many of each kind of ball the school has.
- Exchange lists with your partner. Each of you works to find the range, median, and mode of the data.
- Then discuss how the two sets of data are alike and different.

YOU NEED
calculator

Chapter 3, Lesson 4, pages 90–93

Statistics

NCTM Standards

- Problem Solving
- ✓ Communication
- ✓ Reasoning
- Connections

Problem Solving

OBJECTIVE Use reasoning to find the sets of numbers that meet various statistical criteria.

Materials per student: calculator, Math Center Recording Sheet (TA 31 optional)

Students are given information including median, mode, and range to identify sets of numbers. They are also asked to add numbers to the set without changing the statistical measures. *[1. 55, 55, 58; or 52, 55, 55; 2. 20, 40, 30; 3. all 1s; 4. Possible answer: 1, 8]*

PROBLEM-SOLVING ACTIVITY 24

MATH CENTER
On Your Own 👤

Logical Reasoning • Above-Average Riddles

Solve each number riddle. There may be more than one answer.

1. A set of 3 mystery numbers has a range of 3. Both its mode and its median are 55. What are the numbers?
2. A set of 3 numbers has a sum of 90. There is no mode, but the median is 30 and the range is 20. What are the numbers?
3. A set of 5 numbers has a median of 1, a mode of 1, and a range of 0. Give the numbers.
4. What numbers can you add to the set below that would not change the mode, the median, or the range?

   0   2   2   4   5   7   10

YOU NEED
calculator

Chapter 3, Lesson 4, pages 90–93

Statistics

NCTM Standards

- ✓ Problem Solving
- ✓ Communication
- ✓ Reasoning
- Connections

Lesson 3.4 *continued*

EXPLORE ACTIVITY
Range, Median, and Mode

OBJECTIVE Find the range, median, and mode(s) of a set of data and use them to describe the data.

Materials per student: inch graph paper (TA 8), scissors

Vocabulary median, mode, range

 Introduce

Discuss with students the books they are currently reading, their favorite books, and their favorite places to read. Let students share their reading experiences and what they enjoy most about a particular book or about reading in general.

Ask students about how many books they read in a week, a month, and a year. Record each student's response on the chalkboard. Ask students:
- **What number of books per year is read most often by our class?**
- **What is the difference between the greatest and least number of books read in a month?**

 Teach   *Cooperative Pairs*

▶ **LEARN** Read through the introductory problem as a class. Ask:
- **Which of the friends reads for the greatest number of hours? least?** *[Katie; Sue]*
- **Is there another way to display the data so that it would be easier to find information?** *[Answers may vary. Students may suggest some kind of graphical representation.]*

Work Together Instruct the group to complete all of the Work Together activities. Tell students to write the names on their strips before they arrange them from least to greatest.

After completing the activity, ask each pair to write its own definitions for the terms *range, median,* and *mode.* Then let the pairs share their definitions with the class.

Talk It Over After discussing the questions given in the text, ask students to compare their data with the data from the table. What do they have in common?

Range, Median, and Mode

Did you know that the more you read, the better you get at it? This table shows the amount of time five friends spend reading. There are many ways to describe the data.

How Much Time Do We Spend Reading	
Friend	**Numbers of Hours**
Alex	2
Sue	1
Roberto	3
Katie	7
Sharella	2

Work Together
Work with a partner. Use inch graph paper to make a strip for the number of hours each friend reads.

Arrange the strips in order from least to greatest.

You will need
- *inch graph paper*
- *scissors*

▶ Compare the shortest strip with the longest strip. The difference between the greatest number and the least number in a set of data is called the **range.**

▶ Look at the strip in the middle. The number in the middle of a set of data that is in order is called the **median.**

▶ Find any strips that are the same length. The number that occurs most often in a set of data is called the **mode.**

Check Out the Glossary
range
median
mode
  See page 544.

Survey seven of your classmates about the time they spend reading books each week. Display your data in a table. Then find the median, mode, and range of your data.

Talk It Over
▶ What are the range, median, and mode of the data above? What do they tell you about time spent reading? **See above.**
▶ What are the range, median, and mode of your data? What do they tell you about how much your friends read? **Answers may vary. Check students' conclusions.**

Question 1. Possible answer h, 2 h; range—largest differe time spent reading is 6 h, m about half of the class spends 1 or 2 h reading, mode— more people read for 2 h.

90   Lesson 3.4

Meeting Individual Needs

Extra Support

Some students may occasionally forget what range, median, and mode mean. Have them write the definitions on 3 index cards and the terms on 3 other cards. Mix and then match the terms and definitions.

Ongoing Assessment

Observation Checklist Determine if students understand range, median, and mode by asking them to find these for a set of data. Have students describe each of these three elements.

Follow Up For more practice with range, median, and mode, have students identify and label their strips of data, or assign **Reteach 24.**

Students who need a greater challenge may combine 3 or 4 strips of data before identifying and labeling them, or try **Extend 24.**

2. No, no, yes; 90 is still between the least and greatest amounts, 90 is still in the middle, the mode changes because both 80 and 90 occur most often.

Make Connections

Tim surveyed 19 students. He showed the data on a line plot and wrote questions he wanted to answer.

You can find the range, median, and mode of the data from the line plot. Each X on the line plot stands for a student's response.

Range Subtract the least number on the scale from the greatest number. $7 - 1 = 6$. The range is 6 books.

Median Cross off an X from each end of the line plot. Repeat this step until only one X is left. Then read the median from the scale below the X. The median is 3 books.

Mode Look at the tallest column of Xs. Then read the mode from the scale. The mode is 2 books.

How many books did you read last month?

Data
6 5 1 2 3 1 2 5 7 2
6 2 5 3 3 1 2 1 3

Number Of Books Read By Students Last Month

```
      x
x  x  x
x  x  x      x
x  x  x      x  x
x  x  x      x  x  x
1  2  3   4  5  6  7
```

1. Did more students read 3 books than any other number of books?

2. What is the greatest difference in the number of books read?

3. Did at least half the students read 3 or more books?

Check for Understanding

1 Find the range, median, and mode from the line plot on the right. **30 pages, 90 pages, 80 pages**

2 **What if** you surveyed one more student who read a book that was 90 pages long. Would the range, median, or mode change? Why or why not? **See above.**

Estimate of the Number of Pages in the Last Book Read

```
x
x   x
x   x   x      x
x   x   x      x
80  90  100   110
```

Critical Thinking: Analyze **Explain your reasoning.**

3 Which of Tim's questions can you answer with the range? the median? the mode? **See page T17.**

4 Which is easiest to read from the line plot, the range, median, or mode? Which is hardest? Why?

Possible answer: Mode; median; the mode is easiest because you can easily see the tallest column, the median is hardest because you have to go through the data to find the middle.

Turn the page for Practice. ➡
Time, Data, and Graphs **91**

CHECK

MAKE CONNECTIONS

Read through the problem. Let students answer the questions below the line plot. Then ask:
- **Which of the three questions refers to the range?** *[question 2]* **the median?** *[question 1]*
- **How did you find the answer for question 3?** *[Answers may vary. Possible answer: by estimating half]*

Read through the information in the first column as a class. Ask students if they used the methods described to answer any of the three questions. Discuss alternative methods students may have used.

Remind students that the median is the middle number only when the set of data is listed in order from least to greatest or greatest to least.

Ask students what the mode would be if 4 students read two books each. Since the greatest amount is shared, there is more than one mode. In this case, the modes would be 1, 2, and 3. If all amounts have the same number of responses, then there is no mode.

3 Close

Check for Understanding using items 1–4, page 91.

CRITICAL THINKING
Have students look again at the line plot for item 3. Ask students to add one response to the data to cause a change in the range and then the median. *[Possible answer: Add 1 more book to the greatest number read to change the range and include 1 more or 1 less student in the survey to change the median.]* Have them explain how they determined where to place the additional responses.

JOURNAL

When is it important to know the range, median, or mode? Have students write one situation for each in their journals.

Practice See pages 92-93.

Language Support

Put students in groups or pairs that include at least one student who is acquiring English. Allow students to find creative ways of remembering the meanings of the words *median, mode,* and *range.*

ESL APPROPRIATE

Gifted And Talented

Tell students that to find the average, or mean, they must first add the numbers in the set of data. Then they divide the sum by the number of numbers in the set of data.

Have students find the mean for each set of data given in this lesson. Tell students to drop any remainders.

▶ **PRACTICE**

Materials have available: calculators

Options for assigning exercises:
A—Odd ex. 1–9; 11–20; **More to Explore**
B—Even ex. 2–10; 11–20; **More to Explore**

- For ex. 1–6, you may want to point out that some sets of data have no mode. Remind students why a set of data may not have a mode.
- For ex. 7–10, tell students their explanation should include median, range, or mode.
- For **Make It Right** (ex. 14), see Common Error below.
- In ex. 16, students are given the opportunity to use the problem-solving strategy, Find a Pattern, to solve the problem.
- In ex. 17, students use the strategy Solving Multistep Problems.
- Students can use the strategy Extra Information to rewrite a problem in ex. 19.

 Algebra: Patterns In ex. 16, students analyze a pattern of scores to determine game-playing abilities.

More to Explore Remind students to list the data from least to greatest before finding the median.

Practice

Find the range, median, and mode for the set of data.

1 Heights of students (in inches):
56 40 36 60 40
24, 40, 40

2 Prices of cassette players:
$60 $80 $80 $38 $72 **$42, $72, $80**

3 Numbers of letters in names:
13 10 5 27 8 16 11
22, 11, none

4 Ages of members of Carla's family:
35 70 2 43 9 7 68
68, 35, none

5 Numbers of students in a class:
21 29 31 28 25 36 25
15, 28, 25

6 Scores of math quiz:
65 90 100 80 75 80 90
35, 80, 80 and 90

Use the data in ex. 1–6 to tell whether the sentence is *true* or *false*. Then explain your answer.

7 More students are 60 inches tall than any other height. **False; mode is 40 in.**

8 At least half the students got 80 or more on the quiz. **True; median is 80.**

9 The longest name is only 2 letters longer than the shortest name. **False; range is 22 letters.**

10 The members of Carla's family have many different ages. **True; there is no mode.**

12 Possible answer: What is the difference between the least and greatest study times? Do at least half of the students study for more than 4 h each week? How long do most students study each week?

Use the data at the right for ex. 11–13.

11 What is the range, median, and mode for the data? **35 min, 30 min, 25 min**

12 Write three questions about the data that can be answered using the range, median, or mode. **See above.**

> *Number of minutes spent studying yesterday by seven students:*
>
> 35 25 60 40 25 30 25

13 Write two statements about the data. Exchange your statements with others. Explain why their statements are true or false. **Check students' statements and explanations. Possible statement: more students study for 5 h than any other time; false, the mode is 4 h.**

·············· **Make It Right** ··············
14 Kara found the median score. Explain what mistake was made, then give the correct answer.

My scores:
80 50 90 40 100
My median score is 90.

Possible answer: Did not put the data in order—the median is 80.

Meeting Individual Needs

Early Finishers

Have students create their own survey. Instruct students to select one question to ask five to ten friends. Have students organize the data in a table, or use strips of inch graph paper to find the range, median, and mode.

COMMON ERROR

As in **Make It Right,** students may forget to order the data before finding the median. Encourage students to think about what the median is in a set of data. Since it is the middle number, or halfway point, the data must be arranged in order from least to greatest or greatest to least before a middle number can be found.

Point out that the mode and range can be found without ordering the data, but it is much easier to find them when the data is arranged in order.

15. Possible answer: The median and mode of Ada's scores is 60, and Jan's median score is 60 also, but her mode is 40.

MIXED APPLICATIONS
Problem Solving

Use the data at the right for problems 15–16.

Game	1	2	3	4	5
Ada	60	60	60	60	60
Jan	40	40	60	80	90

15 How can the score 60 describe Ada's and Jan's scores? Use the words *range*, *median*, or *mode* in your answer. **See above.**

16 ALGEBRA: PATTERNS What patterns do you see in Ada's and Jan's game-playing abilities? **Ada did not improve over time, while Jan improved the more she played.**

17 Seth's game scores are 40, 60, and 80. Sarah's scores are 20, 90, and 90. Which student has the greater total score? By how much? **Sarah; 20 points**

18 The least expensive game in the arcade costs $0.25 to play. The range in the costs of the games is $1.50. How much does the most expensive game cost to play? **$1.75**

19 Rewrite the problem, leaving out any extra information.
Brandon is meeting his friends at the mall at 2:45 P.M. He leaves home at 2:10 P.M. and gets to the mall at 2:59 P.M. Is he early or late? **Students' problems should leave out the time Brandon leaves home.**

20 Data Point Use your data about your classmates' reading time. Write two questions that can be answered and two that cannot. Ask others to answer your questions or explain why they cannot. **Check students' questions and answers.**

more to explore

Where's the Median?

Six students line up according to height. No student has the median height.

To find the median, think about the height halfway between 46 inches and 48 inches. So the median height is 47 inches.

45 in. 45 in. 46 in. 48 in. 49 in. 52 in.

Find the median height, in inches (in.), of the group.

1 40 in., 42 in., 44 in., 45 in. **43 in.**

2 37 in., 44 in., 46 in., 48 in., 49 in. **46 in.**

3 48 in., 48 in., 53 in., 55 in., 56 in., 59 in. **54 in.**

4 39 in., 40 in., 47 in., 53 in., 56 in., 56 in. **50 in.**

Alternate Teaching Strategy

Materials slips of paper

Ask each student in the class to write the name of his or her favorite song on a slip of paper. Have two students collect the papers, organize them by song title, and write the titles across the bottom of the chalkboard. Then have the same students tape the slips of paper above the titles to make a bar graph such as the one below.

Ask students the following questions:

- **What is the greatest number of votes a song received?** *[Answers may vary according to the data collected in your class.]*
- **What is the least number of votes a song received?**
- **What is the range, or difference, between the greatest and the least votes received?**
- **What is the number of votes that occurred most often, or the mode?**
- **List the data from least to greatest. What is the middle number, or median?**

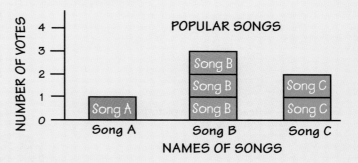

POPULAR SONGS (bar graph; NUMBER OF VOTES on y-axis, NAMES OF SONGS on x-axis: Song A = 1 vote, Song B = 3 votes, Song C = 2 votes)

Name: _____ Practice **24**

RANGE, MEDIAN, AND MODE

Find the range, median, and mode for the set of data.

1. Numbers of items in students' backpacks:
8, 4, 3, 12, 0, 5, 8
_12, 5, 8_

2. Prices of T-shirts:
$9, $13, $23, $15, $14, $13, $13
_$14, $13, $13_

3. Number of hours a week spent helping at home:
7, 5, 11, 5, 1, 5, 4
_10, 5, 5_

4. Number of hours a week spent outside:
24, 9, 8, 21, 7, 8, 11
_17, 9, 8_

Use the data in exercises 1–4 above to tell whether the answer is true or false. Then explain your answer.

5. Most students carry more than 8 items in their backpacks.
False; median is 5.

6. Most students pay $13 for T-shirts. _True; mode is $13._

7. Most students help at home for 5 hours. _True; mode is 5._

8. The greatest amount of time spent outside is 5 hours longer than the least amount. _False; range is 17._

9. The greatest number of items carried in backpacks is 12 more than the least number. _True; range is 12._

Solve.

10. Use the data from exercise 4. Add 14 and 18 as data for 2 more people. How does the range, median, or mode change?
The median changes to 11.

Name: _____ Reteach **24**

RANGE, MEDIAN, AND MODE

Tiko surveys 8 team members to find out how many points each scored in last night's basketball game.

Tiko writes the names and scores in a table.

Points Scored	
Abdul	8
Kesi	9
Steve	7
Palk	19
Laura	12
Tiko	6
Jade	5
Carlos	12
Sean	15

Then she reorders the numbers from greatest to least.

Scores Greatest to Least	
Palk	19
Sean	15
Carlos	12
Laura	12
Kesi	9	← Median
Abdul	8
Steve	7
Tiko	6
Jade	5

The difference between the lowest and highest score is the **range**. The range is 19–5, or 14.

The **median** is the number in the middle of a set of data that is in order from least to greatest. To find the median, cross off a number from each end of the list. Repeat this step until only one number is left. Kesi's score of 9 is the median in this set of data.

The number that occurs most often in a set of data is the **mode**. For this set of data the mode is 12.

Complete the table.

	Data	Reorder Data from Least to Greatest	Range	Median	Mode
1.	6, 8, 8, 5, 4	4, 5, 6, 8, 8	4	6	8
2.	20, 9, 15, 7, 15, 13, 15	7, 9, 13, 15, 15, 15, 20	13	15	15
3.	8, 3, 5, 3, 3, 6, 4	3, 3, 3, 4, 5, 6, 8	5	4	3
4.	68, 75, 90, 90, 85, 92, 78	68, 75, 78, 85, 90, 90, 92	24	85	90
5.	20, 80, 40, 50, 90, 60, 50	20, 40, 50, 50, 60, 80, 90	70	50	50

Name: _____ Extend **24**

RANGE, MEDIAN, AND MODE

A la Mode

1. Ms. Yu is trying to describe the test scores for one of her classes. These are the test scores.

| 73 | 82 | 71 | 95 | 86 | 75 | 73 | 82 | 92 | 68 | 78 | 89 | 96 | 73 | 80 | 78 |

Complete the table by filling in the blanks.

Class 1 Test Scores	
Range	28
Median	79
Mode	73

HINT: When you want to find the median of an even number of items, add the two numbers in the middle of the data set. Then divide the sum by 2.

2. After Ms. Yu scored all the tests for another class, she recorded the range, median, and mode in her book. Later she recorded the students' scores in her grade book. But Ms. Yu could not find Renee's test. Use the data given to find Renee's last test score.

Class 2 Test Scores	
Range	27
Median	85
Mode	92

Student Scores for Class 2	
Sarah - 92	Robert - 71
Mi-ja - 73	Shani - 69
Chester - 80	Victor - 92
Marciano - 90	Renee - 96

Think Critically

3. Explain how you found the answer to exercise 2.

Answers may vary. Sample answer: I knew the range was 27. I added 27 to the lowest score and tested that number against the median and mode. Renee's score was 96.

LESSON 3.5

EXPLORE ACTIVITY
Pictographs

OBJECTIVE Explore reading and making pictographs.

RESOURCE REMINDER
Math Center Cards 25
Practice 25, Reteach 25, Extend 25

SKILLS TRACE

GRADE 3	• Explore reading and making pictographs. *(Chapter 5)*
GRADE 4	• Explore reading and making pictographs.
GRADE 5	• Read and make pictographs. *(Chapter 3)*

WARM-UP

Cooperative Groups   **Logical/Analytical**

OBJECTIVE Determine what numbers are represented by symbols and write numbers using symbols.

► Draw the following symbols and symbol sentences on the chalkboard:

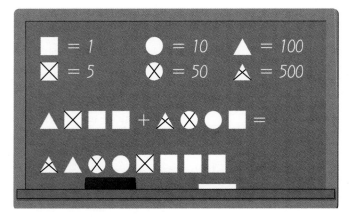

► As a class, translate the symbol sentence into a number sentence.
[107 + 561 = 668]

► In groups, have students write their own symbol sentences and translate each others' sentences.

ESL ► APPROPRIATE

CULTURAL CONNECTION

Cooperative Groups   **Visual/Spatial**

OBJECTIVE Read and write Roman numerals.

Materials per group: 10 index cards

► Roman numerals use letters to represent numbers of different values. Write the following on the chalkboard:

I-1	Addition Positions
V-5	III means 1 + 1 + 1 = 3
X-10	VI means 5 + 1 = 6
L-50	Subtraction Positions
C-100	IV means 5 − 1 = 4
	IX means 10 − 1 = 9

► Discuss how to read Roman numerals, then have each group choose 10 numbers between 10 and 100 and write them on index cards. On the other side they write the Roman numeral.

► They order the new set of cards from least to greatest.

Daily Review

PREVIOUS DAY QUICK REVIEW

Find the range, median, and mode for the set of data.

1. Number of dogs in a pet store: 5, 13, 11, 27, 10, 8, 16 *[22, 11, none]*

FAST FACTS

1. 2 + 0 *[2]*
2. 3 + 7 *[10]*
3. 7 + 9 *[16]*
4. 4 + 2 *[6]*

Problem of the Day • 25

A pictograph in a newsletter shows that 28 students like to read mysteries. The key for the pictograph is ■ = 8 students. How many ■ are shown to represent 28 students? *[3 1/2]*

TECH LINK

MATH VAN

Tool You may wish to use the Table tool and the Graph tool with this lesson.

MATH FORUM

Combination Classes When creating pictographs with my students, I let them use stickers for their symbols. Older students can cut them into fourths or halves.

Visit our Resource Village at http://www.mhschool.com to see more of the Math Forum.

MATH CENTER

Practice

OBJECTIVE Solve and create problems, using a pictograph.

Materials per student: Math Center Recording Sheet (TA 31 optional)

Students use a pictograph to solve a problem. Then they revise the pictograph. *[1. 158; Tomato, 50; mushroom, 12; pepper, 46; spinach, 16; cucumber, 6; cabbage, 2; carrot, 26; 2. tomato, cabbage; 3. Check new graphs. Tomato and carrot fill out the half plates.]*

PRACTICE ACTIVITY 25

MATH CENTER
On Your Own

Number Sense • Salad Bar

Larkin asked all the fourth graders to choose their favorite vegetable to add to a salad. He used the information to make this pictograph.

1. How many fourth graders responded to Larkin's question? How many students voted for each vegetable?

2. What is the most popular vegetable? the least popular?

3. Four students were left out of the survey. When they were asked, 2 of them chose tomato and 2 chose carrot. Draw a new pictograph to include these students.

Favorite Vegetable for Salads

tomato ○○○○○○○○○○○○(
mushroom ○○○
pepper ○○○○○○○○○○○○(
spinach ○○○○
cucumber ○(
cabbage (
carrot ○○○○○○(

Key: ○ • 4 students

Chapter 3, Lesson 5, pages 94–95   Statistics

NCTM Standards
✓ Problem Solving
✓ Communication
✓ Reasoning
  Connections

Problem Solving

OBJECTIVE Create pictographs.

Materials per student: Math Center Recording Sheet (TA 31 optional)

Students represent a data set with 2 pictographs having different keys. They then discuss which key is more appropriate and why. *[Check students' graphs. Possible answer: An appropriate key would be one symbol equals 10 marbles or 1 symbol equals 20 marbles. The latter would result in half symbols, but takes less space.]*

PROBLEM-SOLVING ACTIVITY 25

MATH CENTER
On Your Own

Using Data • Marble Collections

Juan and some of his friends collect marbles.

Use the information about the students' marble collections to make two pictographs with different keys.

Which key works better? Explain why you think so.

Student	Number of Marbles
Dagmar	100
Hasija	70
Juan	50
Kimberly	60
Mengchun	110
Michael	120

Chapter 3, Lesson 5, pages 94–95   Statistics

NCTM Standards
  Problem Solving
✓ Communication
✓ Reasoning
  Connections

EXPLORE ACTIVITY
Pictographs

OBJECTIVE Explore reading and making pictographs.

Vocabulary key, pictograph

 **Introduce**

List on the chalkboard the types of music given on page 94. Ask students to choose their favorite type of music. Have volunteers record on the chalkboard the number of votes each type of music receives.

 **Teach**   *Cooperative Pairs*

▶ **LEARN Work Together** Look at the pictograph on page 94. Ask your students:
- **How many votes does one stick figure represent?** *[8 votes]*
- **What does half a stick figure represent?** *[4 votes]*
- **Describe what you would draw to represent 20 votes.** *[2 stick figures and 1 half stick figure]*
- **Why would you not need to draw two half stick figures in one section of the pictograph?** *[Two halves make a whole stick figure.]*

Organize students in pairs and have them complete the pictograph.

MAKE CONNECTIONS
Have a student read each step for making a pictograph as another student completes each step using the pictograph he or she completed for the data given on page 94. Have students check that the correct number of stick figures has been drawn.

Ask students which step they think is the hardest in making a pictograph? the easiest? *[Possible answers: choosing a key; listing items]*

 **Close**

▶ **Check for Understanding** using items 1 and 2, page 95.

CRITICAL THINKING

Write: Compare/Contrast Have students write a paragraph comparing the table and pictograph on page 94. Then, using students' paragraphs, compile a list of ways the two are alike and different.

▶ **PRACTICE**
Materials have available: calculator

Assign ex. 1–4 as independent work.
- Remind students to complete the table and pictograph for ex. 1–3 before trying to answer the questions.

Pictographs

L E A R N

Does everyone you know like the same kinds of music? The frequency table shows the results of a fourth-grade survey. A **pictograph** of the data has been started.

Work Together
Work with a partner. Copy and complete the pictograph. Then answer the questions.

What is your favorite type of music?

Type of music	Tally	Frequency
Pop	HH HH II	12
Rock	HH HH HH HH IIII	24
Country	HH III	8
R&B	HH HH HH HH	20
Rap	IIII	4
Other	HH III	8

What is your favorite type of music?

Pop	🧍🏃
Rock	🧍 🧍 🧍
Country	🧍
R&B	🧍 🧍🏃
Rap	🏃
Other	🧍

Key: 🧍 stands for 8 votes.
🏃 stands for 4 votes.

▶ How did you decide what symbols to use to show the number of students who chose country music? R&B? **See page T17.**

▶ What type of music is the favorite most of the time? How can you tell by looking only at the pictograph? **Rock music; there are more symbols for rock music.**

▶ **What if** 4 students who chose pop music and 4 students who chose R&B decide they like rock music better. How will the pictograph change?

Symbols shown for rock would be 4 stick figures, R&B would be 2 stick figures, and pop would be 1 stick figure.

Check Out the Glossary
pictograph
key
See page 544.

Meeting Individual Needs

Early Finishers
Instruct students to create alternate pictographs for one or more sets of data in this lesson. Their pictographs should differ only by the number each symbol represents.

Extra Support
Use the pictograph on page 94 as an example. Have one group use one counter for 1 vote and another use one counter for 4 votes. Discuss why choosing an appropriate key is important in making a pictograph.

Ongoing Assessment
Anecdotal Report Note students' abilities to read and make pictographs. Have them answer questions about and create their own graphs.

Follow Up Have students who need more practice find pictographs in the newspaper, write questions or statements about them, and exchange with other students, or complete **Reteach 25**.

Challenge students comfortable with pictographs to recreate them by changing the amount the symbol represents, or assign **Extend 25**.

1. The number of symbols will double; possible answer: the original key because it uses fewer symbols.

Make Connections

To make a pictograph:

- list the items (type of music).
- choose a symbol to represent the responses (number of votes).
- use a key to tell the number each symbol stands for.
- draw symbols to show the responses for each item.
- write a title.

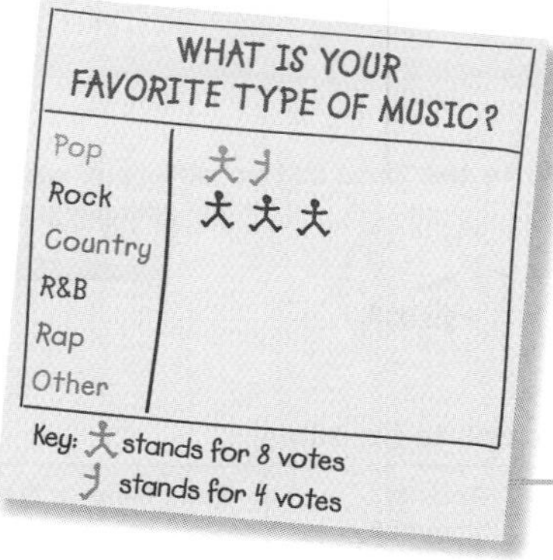

WHAT IS YOUR FAVORITE TYPE OF MUSIC?
Pop
Rock
Country
R&B
Rap
Other
Key: stands for 8 votes
stands for 4 votes

Check for Understanding

1 **What if** you use [symbol] to stand for 4 votes. How will this change the pictograph? Which key do you prefer? Why? **See above.**

Critical Thinking: Compare and Contrast

2 READING ARITHMETIC WRITING **Write: Compare/Contrast** Look at the table and the pictograph on page 94. Which was easier to use to compare the data? **Possible answer: The pictograph was easier to use because you can see more quickly which type of music was most frequently chosen.**

CHECK

Practice

Use the table and the pictograph for problems 1–4.

Favorite sport of students		
Sport	**Tally**	**Total**
Baseball	𝍸 𝍸 𝍸	15
Basketball	𝍸 𝍸 𝍸 𝍸 𝍸 𝍸	■ **30**
Tennis	𝍸 IIII	9
Soccer	𝍸 𝍸 𝍸 𝍸 I	■ **21**

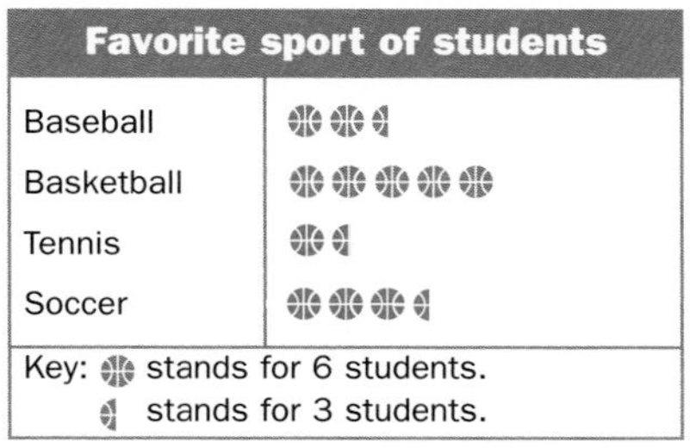

Favorite sport of students
Baseball
Basketball
Tennis
Soccer
Key: stands for 6 students.
stands for 3 students.

PRACTICE

1 Copy and complete the table and the pictograph. Which sport do most students say is their favorite? **basketball**

2 How many more students said baseball, rather than tennis, was their favorite sport? **6 students**

3 How many students were surveyed? Explain how you know. **75 students; it is the total of the responses.**

4 **Data Point** Choose a topic for a "favorite" survey. Survey your classmates or other students in your school. Make a pictograph to show the results. **Students' pictographs should reflect the data from their survey.**

Extra Practice, page 493

Alternate Teaching Strategy

Materials per student: color paper cut to look like tickets; glue

Write the following on the chalkboard.

Karen, Ted, Lily, and Keesha went to an arcade to play Roller Ball. For every 10 points they scored, they received 1 ticket. Karen scored 35 points, Ted scored 50 points, Lily scored 85 points, and Keesha scored 40 points.

Instruct students to make a pictograph showing the number of tickets each person earned. One ticket can represent 10 points, a half-ticket can represent 5 points. They can attach their tickets to the graph using tape or glue.

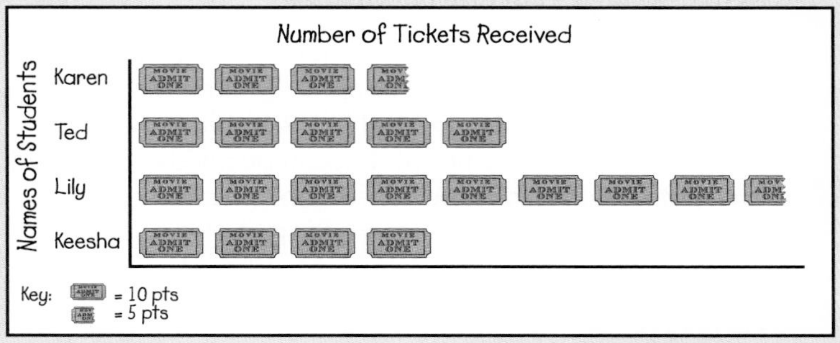

Number of Tickets Received
Names of Students
Karen
Ted
Lily
Keesha
Key: = 10 pts
= 5 pts

When they have finished their pictographs, ask students questions about the pictograph. For example:

- **Who earned the greatest number of points? How many tickets did he or she earn?** *[Lily; she earned $8\frac{1}{2}$ tickets.]*
- **How many tickets did they earn altogether?** *[21 tickets]*

PRACTICE • 25

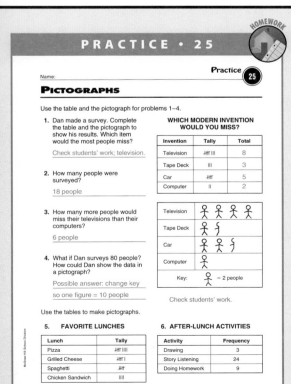

HOMEWORK

Practice 25

Name:

PICTOGRAPHS

Use the table and the pictograph for problems 1–4.

1. Dan made a survey. Complete the table and the pictograph to show his results. Which item would the most people miss?
   Check students' work; television.
2. How many people were surveyed?
   18 people
3. How many more people would miss their televisions than their computers?
   6 people
4. What if Dan surveys 80 people? How could Dan show the data in a pictograph?
   Possible answer: change key so one figure = 10 people

WHICH MODERN INVENTION WOULD YOU MISS?

Invention	Tally	Total
Television	𝍸 III	8
Tape Deck	III	3
Car	𝍸	5
Computer	II	2

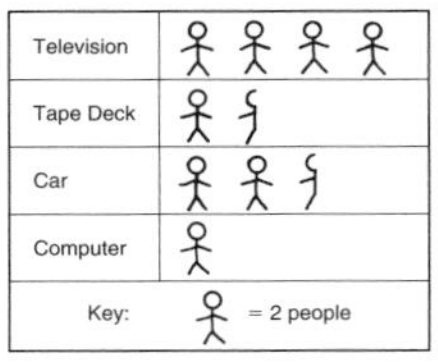

Television
Tape Deck
Car
Computer
Key: = 2 people

Check students' work.

Use the tables to make pictographs.

5. **FAVORITE LUNCHES**

Lunch	Tally
Pizza	𝍸 IIII
Grilled Cheese	𝍸 I
Spaghetti	𝍸
Chicken Sandwich	IIII

6. **AFTER-LUNCH ACTIVITIES**

Activity	Frequency
Drawing	3
Story Listening	24
Doing Homework	9

RETEACH • 25

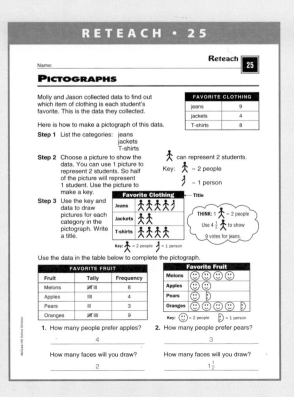

Reteach 25

Name:

PICTOGRAPHS

Molly and Jason collected data to find out which item of clothing is each student's favorite. This is the data they collected.

FAVORITE CLOTHING	
jeans	9
jackets	4
T-shirts	8

Here is how to make a pictograph of this data.

Step 1 List the categories: jeans
jackets
T-shirts

Step 2 Choose a picture to show the data. You can use 1 picture to represent 2 students. So half of the picture will represent 1 student. Use the picture to make a key.

[figure] can represent 2 students.

Key: [figure] = 2 people
[half figure] = 1 person

Step 3 Use the key and data to draw pictures for each category in the pictograph. Write a title.

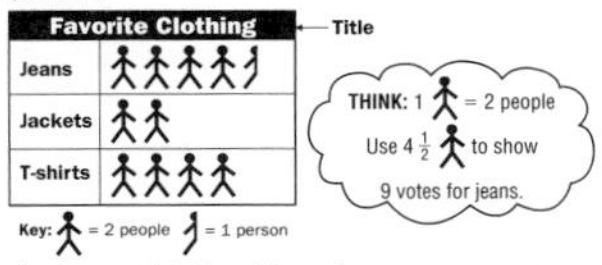

Favorite Clothing
Title
Jeans
Jackets
T-shirts
Key: = 2 people = 1 person
THINK: 1 = 2 people
Use 4 ½ to show
9 votes for jeans.

Use the data in the table below to complete the pictograph.

FAVORITE FRUIT		
Fruit	**Tally**	**Frequency**
Melons	𝍸 III	8
Apples	IIII	4
Pears	III	3
Oranges	𝍸 IIII	9

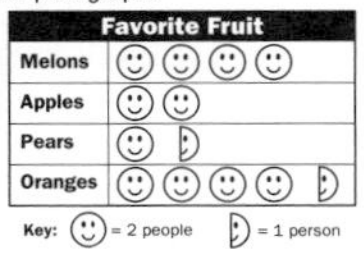

Favorite Fruit
Melons
Apples
Pears
Oranges
Key: = 2 people = 1 person

1. How many people prefer apples?
   4
   How many faces will you draw?
   2
2. How many people prefer pears?
   3
   How many faces will you draw?
   $1\frac{1}{2}$

EXTEND • 25

Extend 25

Name:

PICTOGRAPHS

How Many Children Are There?

Use the clues to complete each pictograph.

1.

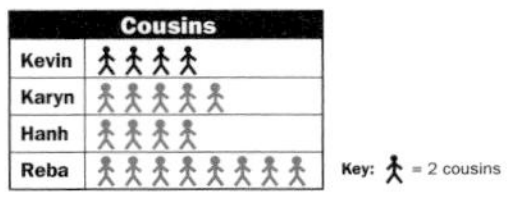

Cousins
Kevin
Karyn
Hanh
Reba
Key: = 2 cousins

Clue 1 Reba has 8 more cousins than Kevin has.
Clue 2 Hanh has 2 fewer cousins than Karyn does.
Clue 3 Kevin and Hanh have the same number of cousins.

2.

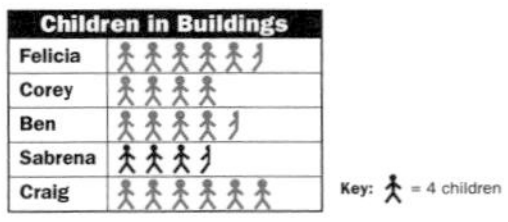

Children in Buildings
Felicia
Corey
Ben
Sabrena
Craig
Key: = 4 children

Clue 1 There are 4 more children in Ben's building than in Sabrena's.
Clue 2 Ben's building has 4 fewer children than Felicia's.
Clue 3 If there were 4 more children in Craig's building, he would have 10 more children than Ben's.
Clue 4 Corey's building has 6 fewer children than Felicia's building.

Think Critically

3. Would it make sense to use 1 stick figure to stand for 8 children in exercise 2? Why or why not? Explain your reasoning.
   Answers may vary. Possible response: No, because you would have to make $\frac{1}{4}$ stick figures, which would be hard to read.

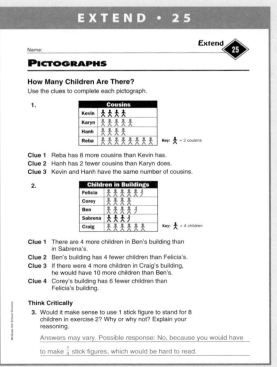

PURPOSE Maintain and review concepts, skills, and strategies that students have learned thus far in the chapter.

Using the Midchapter Review

Have students complete the **Midchapter Review** independently or use it with the whole class.

Encourage students to solve all problems without the use of a demonstration clock or posters displaying the meanings of *median, mode,* and *range.* If they need some assistance, suggest that they draw pictures of clocks and use the memory aides they created. They may also wish to draw pictures or tables to help them organize information.

Students may have their own ideas about how to choose symbols for pictographs. One thing all students should recognize is that the amount the symbol represents should be an amount that can be divided in half. The amount should also allow the student to represent every piece of data using only whole and half symbols.

Vocabulary Review

Write the following words on the chalkboard:

A.M.	elapsed time	key
median	mode	ordinal numbers
pictograph	P.M.	range

Ask for volunteers to explain, show, or act out the meaning of these words.

---

1. Possible answer: 9:47, nine forty-seven
2. Possible answer: ten-fifteen; a quarter past ten
3. Possible answers: 11:19, eleven nineteen, nineteen minutes after eleven

Write the time in two different ways.

1   **2** `10:15`   **3**   **4** `3:35`

Possible answers: 3:35, three thirty-five, thirty-five minutes after three, twenty-five minutes to four

Complete the table.

	Activity	Start Time	Elapsed Time	End Time	
5	Trip to museum	7:30 A.M.	■	12:15 P.M.	4 h 45 min
6	Baseball game	3:45 P.M.	3 hours 20 minutes	■	7:05 P.M.
7	Piano class	■	50 minutes	5:20 P.M.	4:30 P.M.
8	Trip to Peru	■	20 days	May 16	April 27
9	Summer camp	June 18	■	July 2	15 d

Find the range, median, and mode for the set of data.

10 Minidisk player prices:
$89 $101 $95 $95 $101
$12, $95, $95 and $101

11 Number of hours spent studying:
1   3   1   4   4   3   3   3   1
3, 3, 3

12 Number of plays seen:
12   9   3   2   2   7   3
10, 3, 2 and 3

13 Number of languages spoken:
1   1   2   1   2   2   1   3   1
2, 1, 1

14 Number of best friends:
3   4   2   2   5
3, 3, 2

15 Number of states visited:
5   1   3   7   2   8   0
8, 3, none

Use the pictogaph for problems 16–19.

16 Which football team do most people say is their favorite?
Dallas Cowboys

17 How many people say the Buffalo Bills is their favorite team?
27 people

18 How many people were surveyed?
102 people

19 Write a paragraph that compares the data shown in the pictograph.
Check students' work.

20 Describe how you choose a symbol for a pictograph and what the symbol stands for.
Possible answer: Use a symbol that fits the theme of the data and have it stand for an amount that lets you fit the data on the graph.

Favorite Football Team

Miami Dolphins
Dallas Cowboys
San Francisco 49ers
Buffalo Bills

KEY: ▮ stands for 6 people.
▯ stands for 3 people.

Reinforcement and Remediation

CHAPTER OBJECTIVES	MIDCHAPTER REVIEW ITEMS	STUDENT BOOK PAGES	TEACHER'S EDITION PAGES		TEACHER RESOURCES
			Activities	Alternate Teaching Strategy	Reteach
*3A	1–4	82–83	81A	83	21
*3B	5–9	84–87	83A	87	22
*3C	10–15	90–93	89A	93	24
*3D	16–19	94–95	93A	95	25

*3A   Estimate, tell, and write time
*3B   Find elapsed time
*3C   Find the range, median, and mode of a set of data
*3D   Read, interpret, organize, and display data

Graphs and Tables

A computer can help you create tables and graphs that are linked to each other. Create a table, then click on the graph tool to display the data in a bar graph.

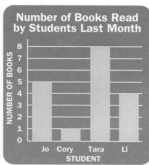

Number of Books Read by Students Last Month

Student	Number of Books Read
Jo	5
Cory	1
Tara	8
Li	4

▶ Change the table so that the number of books Li read is 5. How does this affect the graph? Explain. **The bar above Li rises; the height shows the number of books, so if the number of books increases, the height also increases.**

▶ Lower the bar above Tara to 5. How does this affect the table? Explain. **The number beside Tara in the table is changed to 5; the table shows the same number as the height of the bar.**

1 Show the data below in the table and graph. Include your own data also.

Lena read 2 books last month, Maria read 5 books, and Carl read 3 books. **Check students' work.**

2 Predict how the graph would change if you read 5 more books and Tara read 2 fewer books. **The bar above your name would increase by 5, and the bar above Tara would decrease to show 6.**

Critical Thinking: Generalize
Explain your reasoning.

3 Explain why it is useful to make tables and graphs with a computer. **Possible answer: Changes in one display are automatically shown in the other, so it is not necessary to create new graphs each time a change is made.**

Time, Data, and Graphs **97**

OBJECTIVE Use a spreadsheet program to keep records in tables in linked graphs.

Resources spreadsheet program that links tables and graphs, or Math Van Tools

Using Technology Sense

Math Connection In prior lessons students have used tables and graphs to represent data. Computer tools allow students to create data tables, create graphs linked to the tables, and print the tables and graphs. Here, students create a table and represent the data in the table with a linked bar graph. Then they change a number in the table to see how that affects the graph and they change a bar in the graph to see how that affects the table.

At the Computer Allow students to explore the spreadsheet program before beginning the activities. Suggest that they input data that can be displayed in a graph. Have a volunteer demonstrate how to create a graph that is linked to the data table.

Have students work individually or with a partner to complete the bulleted tasks and items 1–3. Discuss the Critical Thinking question with them.

Extending the Activity Have students add a row to one of the tables for another student. (They can make up the number of books read.) Have them notice how the graph changes after they add the new row.

Math Van Math Van Tools provide easy ways to display data in a variety of ways. Click the *Tables* button in the Math Van toolbar to start a table. To link the Table tool with the Graph tool click the *Link* button below the table. Then click the *Set Up* button and choose the kind of graph you want to make. Click the up or the down arrow next to the vertical axis to change the scale of the graph. A project electronic teacher aid has been provided.

Applying Data and Graphs

OBJECTIVE Use measurement to generate, organize, and graph data, and to find the range, mode, and median.

Materials metric measuring tape (TA 20), centimeter graph paper (TA 7)

 Engage

Have students use a metric measuring tape to measure various objects to the nearest centimeter, such as the length and width of their desks, the thickness of their math textbook, or the length of their pencils. Ask questions to check their understanding of how to use the measuring tape.

- **How do you measure to the nearest centimeter?** *[Possible answer: The nearest centimeter is the number on the tape that is closest to the other end or edge of the object being measured.]*

2 Investigate *Cooperative Groups*

Discuss each measurement listed in the table and decide how each will be measured. Head size, for example, might be the circumference of the head measured across the forehead and above the ears. Arm span could be from outstretched fingertip to outstretched fingertip, or top of shoulder to outstretched fingertip.

Measuring Yourselves Using the People Graphs Strategy, have students make several parallel lines according to the measurements they have taken. Students make and discuss observations about the line-ups.

3 Reflect and Share

Report Your Findings When groups have finished their five tables, ask five volunteers to collect one kind of table from each group. Display tables for height together, tables for head size together, and so on.

Before groups begin work on the class data for one measurement, discuss group findings.

- **What conclusions can you make about the height of the students in this class?** *[Answers may vary. Possible answer: Everyone is within 35 centimeters of each other in height.]*
- **How do the boys' arm spans compare to the girls' arm spans?** *[Possible answer: They are about the same.]*

Suggest that groups use a calculator to check the range of class data before they graph it. When groups choose the measurement they will graph, be sure all measurements are represented by at least one group.

real-life investigation
APPLYING DATA AND GRAPHS

Measure by Measure

How does a doctor know whether you are big or small for your age? Doctors use standard height and size tables. You can create your own tables for fourth graders and report on what you find.

More To Investigate

Predict Possible approach: As they make their predictions, encourage students to picture fifth graders they know.

Explore You may wish to suggest other measurements such as hand span, thumb length, or length of hair.

Find Possible response: In ancient Egypt common units of measure involved fingers, hands, and arms. The digit was one finger width, the hand was five finger widths, and the cubit was the length of the arm from fingertip to elbow.

Bibliography Students interested in the human body can read: *Children's Atlas of the Human Body: Actual Size Bones, Muscles, Organs in Full Color,* by Richard Walker. Vero Beach, FL: Millbrook Publishers, 1994. ISBN 1–56294–503–3.

The Human Body, by Steve Parker. New York: DK Publishing, Inc., 1993; Eyewitness Science Series. ISBN 1–56458–325–2.

Outside and Inside You, by Sandra Markle. New York: Simon & Schuster Children's Books, 1991. ISBN–0–02–762311–4.

See Teacher's Edition
for sample of student work.

DECISION MAKING

Measuring Yourselves

1 Form groups of six or more students. Work in pairs within your group to find the following measurements in centimeters. Copy and complete the table.

How We Measure Up
Height:
Head Size:
Arm Span:
Foot Size:
Length of Giant Step:

2 Decide how you will use each student's measurements to make tables of group measurements. Display all the group tables for everyone to see.

3 Use your group's data for each measurement to predict the range, mode, and median for your entire class. Explain your thinking.

Reporting Your Findings

4 Prepare a group report on one of the measurements you investigated. Include the following:

► A record of that measurement for everyone in your class. Organize the data into a table.

► Make a graph to show the class data for the measurement.

► Write statements about what the graph tells you about your class. Use the words *range*, *median*, and *mode* whenever you can.

5 Explain how your group's predictions compare to the entire class data.

Revise your work.
► Did you measure each person in exactly the same way?
► Do your statements make sense?
► Is your report clear?

MORE TO INVESTIGATE

See Teacher's Edition.

PREDICT what the range, mode, and median measurements might be for a fifth-grade class.

EXPLORE how a measurement other than the one in your report compares with others in your class.

FIND how feet, arms, and hands were used as units of measurement in the past.

Building A Portfolio

This investigation will allow you to evaluate a student's ability to collect and organize data and to use the data to make predictions and conclusions.

Allow students to revise their work for the portfolio. Each student's portfolio piece should consist of a copy of each group's data for the measurement that was chosen, a graph showing the data from all of the group tables for that measurement. The portfolio should also have a summary statement about the graph, including any conclusions that can be made about the range, mode, and median. Place any notes you made about a student's work in his or her portfolio.

You may wish to use the Holistic Scoring to assess this task. See page 27 in Teacher's Assessment Resources.

Students' Work

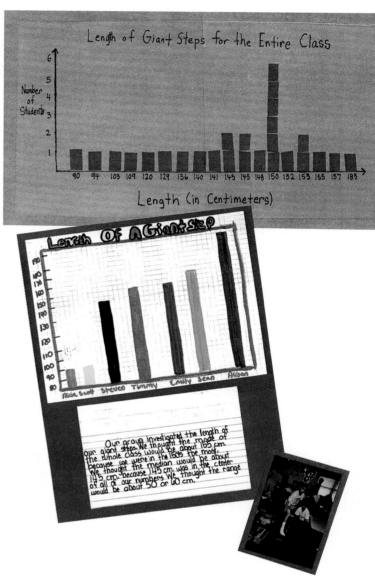

LESSON 3.6

EXPLORE ACTIVITY
Bar Graphs

OBJECTIVE Explore reading and making bar graphs.

RESOURCE REMINDER
Math Center Cards 26
Practice 26, Reteach 26, Extend 26

SKILLS TRACE

GRADE 3	• Explore reading and making bar graphs. *(Chapter 5)*
GRADE 4	• Explore reading and making bar graphs.
GRADE 5	• Read and make single and double bar graphs. *(Chapter 3)*

WARM-UP

Cooperative Groups   **Visual/Spatial**

OBJECTIVE Make a line plot.

Materials chart paper or poster board, markers

▶ Have students in cooperative groups survey the numbers of brothers and sisters each student in the class has. The groups should decide on one or two additional questions that have a numerical answer to ask each student in the class.

▶ After asking the questions and collecting the data, students should make a *line plot* to display each set of data. The finished line plots may be displayed on a large sheet of chart paper or poster board.

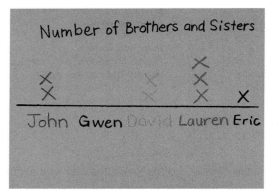

LANGUAGE ARTS CONNECTION

Cooperative Pairs   **Auditory/Linguistic**

OBJECTIVE Connect reading and bar graphs.

Materials large sheet of paper

▶ Have pairs of students select a passage of 20 to 25 words from one of their favorite books. With their partners, have students count the number of letters in each word of the selected passage. While one student counts the letters, the other records the results.

▶ Instruct students to display their results on a bar graph on a large sheet of paper or construction paper. Students then compare their graphs.

▶ Then ask students to rewrite their favorite paragraph, making it shorter. When finished they count and graph the new data and discuss how they shortened their paragraphs.

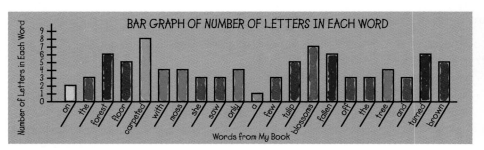

Daily Review

Math Van

PREVIOUS DAY QUICK REVIEW

Find the median height

1. 36 in., 43 in., 45 in., 47 in., 48 in. *[45 in.]*
2. 41 in., 43 in., 45 in., 46 in., 44 in. *[44 in.]*

FAST FACTS

1. $7 - 6$ *[1]*
2. $11 - 4$ *[7]*
3. $12 - 7$ *[5]*
4. $8 - 7$ *[1]*

Problem of the Day • 26

Ted sells four different flavors of ice cream—chocolate, vanilla, chocolate chip, and strawberry—and four different toppings—sprinkles, nuts, strawberries, and chocolate chips. How many different combinations of ice cream and toppings are possible? *[16 combinations]*

TECH LINK

MATH VAN

Tool You may wish to use the Table tool and the Graph tool with this lesson.

MATH FORUM

Idea My students enjoy conducting a school-wide survey on a topic of current interest. The results are published in the school newspaper.

Visit our Resource Village at http://www.mhschool.com to see more of the Math Forum.

MATH CENTER

Practice

OBJECTIVE Create a bar graph.

Materials per student: centimeter graph paper (TA 7), Math Center Recording Sheet (TA 31 optional)

Using the given data about places people want to visit, students create a bar graph. The multiples of 4 allow a scale of zero to 32 with intervals of 4. *[Check students' graphs.]*

PRACTICE ACTIVITY 26

MATH CENTER
On Your Own 👤

Number Sense • Vacation Dreams

Liane asked all the students in her school to name the place they would most like to visit. She used their answers to make a table. Use the information in the table to make a bar graph.

YOU NEED
graph paper

PLACE I'D MOST LIKE TO VISIT	
Grand Canyon	12
London, England	8
Hawaii	32
Japan	20
Zaire	4
Mount Everest	12
New York City	20
Cape Canaveral	12

NCTM Standards

Problem Solving
✓ Communication
✓ Reasoning
Connections

Chapter 3, Lesson 6, pages 100–103

Statistics

Problem Solving

OBJECTIVE Graph the results of a survey.

Materials per pair: graph or drawing paper; per student: Math Center Recording Sheet (TA 31 optional)

Students create a survey form and take a survey. They record the information and use the data to make bar graphs. *[Check students' graphs. Student problems may vary.]*

PROBLEM-SOLVING ACTIVITY 26

MATH CENTER
Partners 👥

Using Data • All About You

Work with a partner. Take a survey. Listed below are some suggestions for questions. You may use them or come up with your own. Ask at least 5 questions. Make bar graphs of the results. Discuss the class favorites.

YOU NEED
graph paper

1. favorite color   red   blue   yellow   green
2. favorite sport   baseball   football   tennis   soccer
3. favorite subject   math   reading   history   science
4. birthday month

NCTM Standards

✓ Problem Solving
✓ Communication
Reasoning
Connections

Chapter 3, Lesson 6, pages 100–103

Statistics

Lesson 3.6 *continued*

EXPLORE ACTIVITY
Bar Graphs

OBJECTIVE Explore reading and making bar graphs.

Vocabulary bar graph

 **1 Introduce**

Talk to students about the number of pets they own. Have students raise their hands as a way to answer the following questions.

- **How many students have 1 pet?**
- **Does anyone have more than 5 pets?**
- **How many students have 3 pets?**
- **How many students have no pets at all?**

If any students have more than 5 pets, let them describe them.

 **2 Teach**   *Cooperative Pairs*

▶ **LEARN Work Together** Ask students to read over the problem and then complete the bar graph with their partner. Point out that the zero on the horizontal bar means a student has no pets at all. Ask them:

- **Which animal is the most popular? the least popular?**
  [panda; elephant]
- **If students only chose one favorite animal, how many students were surveyed?** *[35]*

Talk It Over Tell pairs to answer the questions given. Compare the two graphs as a class.

- **What additional information would you like to know?**
- **What question would you ask?**
- **Which graph would best show the response?**

Bar Graphs

Fourth graders care a lot about people, animals, and the environment. In this survey, students were asked to choose their favorite wild animals.

Use a graph to compare the data quickly and make it easy to read.

Work Together
Work with a partner. Copy and complete the **bar graph**. Then answer the questions.
See graph below.

Cultural Note
Two pandas were given to the National Zoo in Washington, D.C., as gifts from the Chinese government

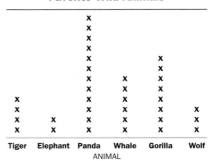

Favorite Wild Animals

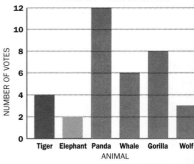

Favorite Wild Animals

Talk It Over

▶ How did you decide what the heights of the bars for the panda, whale, gorilla, and wolf should be? **See page T17.**

▶ Both graphs help you compare the data quickly. Which graph makes it easier to make comparisons? Which makes it easier to read exact numbers? Tell why. **See page T17.**

> **bar graph** A graph that displays data using bars of different lengths.

▶ Your classmate makes the following statements. Do you agree with her? Why or why not?
  a. More students like whales than gorillas. **No; 6 is less than 8.**
  b. Only 2 students chose elephants. **Yes; the bar graph shows 2 students.**
  c. Most students like pandas, gorillas, and whales.
Yes; 26 students like pandas, gorillas, or whales, and only 9 students chose the remaining animals.

100 Lesson 3.6

Meeting Individual Needs

Inclusion

Some students may find it easier to make bar graphs on graph paper. The grid will help them make proportional scales and bars. The lines will help guide the hands of students who have difficulty drawing straight lines.

Ongoing Assessment

Observation Checklist Determine if students understand how to read and make bar graphs by observing them complete ex. 12 on page 103.

Follow Up For more practice with bar graphs, have students make bar graphs from the data given to make pictographs on pages 94 and 95, or try **Reteach 26.**

Students comfortable with bar graphs may create new questions and conduct a survey with another class, or try **Extend 26.**

3. 80 animals; 20 is the least increase and 100 is the greatest; find the difference between the tallest and shortest bars.

Make Connections

To make a bar graph:
► list the items (animals) along the bottom of the graph.
► write a scale with numbers along the left side of the graph, starting with 0.
► draw a bar to match the numbers in the data collected.
► write a title.

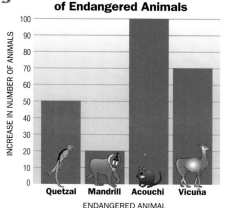

FAVORITE WILD ANIMALS

Number of Students / Animal: Gorilla, Wolf, Tiger

How do the scale numbers in the bar graph increase? What other scale numbers could you have used? **The scale numbers increase by 2; possible answer: could have used scale numbers that increase by 4.**

Check for Understanding

Use the bar graph for problems 1–4.

1 Which animal had the greatest increase in number? How do you know? **Acouchi; it has the tallest bar.**

2 What was the increase in the number of acouchis (a-KOO-cheez)? the number of vicuñas (vī-KOO-nuhz)? **100 acouchis; 70 vicuñas**

3 What is the difference between the largest and smallest increases of endangered animals? How do you know? How can you find this from the bar graph? **See above.**

Critical Thinking: Generalize
Explain your reasoning.

4 When is a bar graph more useful than a line plot? than a pictograph?

Possible answer: when there is a large amount of data or greater numbers are being used; when data that can be read quickly is wanted

Increase in Number of Endangered Animals

INCREASE IN NUMBER OF ANIMALS: 0, 10, 20, 30, 40, 50, 60, 70, 80, 90, 100

ENDANGERED ANIMAL: Quetzal, Mandrill, Acouchi, Vicuña

CHECK

101

MAKE CONNECTIONS

Read through the steps for making a bar graph. Ask students what they would choose as the scale numbers and why. Let several students share their thinking.

Then let students work in pairs to complete the bar graph and to answer the question. If some students complete this part of the lesson before others, have them make another bar graph using the same data but changing the scale numbers.

Cultural Connection Read the **Cultural Note** on page 100. There are 80 pandas in captivity in China, about 20 in captivity in the rest of the world, and about 900 pandas in the wild. The main food source for the giant panda is bamboo. For years bamboo was used in large amounts to build and heat homes. So much of the bamboo was used up that there is not enough for pandas to live on. This is one of the reasons the animals are facing extinction.

3 Close

Check for Understanding using items 1–4, page 101.

CRITICAL THINKING
Ask students to describe the advantages and disadvantages of each of the graphical representations they have learned about so far—bar graph, line plot, and pictograph. Encourage students to explain their reasoning when discussing the advantages and disadvantages.

Practice See pages 102–103.

▶ **PRACTICE**

Materials have available: calculators

Assign ex. 1–15 and **More to Explore** as independent work.

• Ex. 1–3 refer to a line plot. Ask students how knowing how to read a line plot can help them read a bar graph.

• Ex. 4–6 require students to explain how they found their answers. You may require students to give an explanation for other exercises as well.

• In ex. 9, students may use the strategy Interpret Data to solve the problem.

• Ex. 12 can be used to test students on the skills taught in this lesson.

More to Explore Point out the stem-and-leaf plot on page 103. Ask students:

• **How is the stem-and-leaf plot similar to a line plot or a bar graph?** *[Answers may vary. Possible answer: A stem-and-leaf plot uses numbers in the place of Xs or bars.]*

• **How is the stem-and-leaf plot different from line plots and bar graphs?** *[Answers may vary. Possible answer: Individual pieces of data are easier to see in a stem-and-leaf plot.]*

Let students work in pairs to complete the exercises.

---

3. Possible answer: There are more Xs above Thursday and Friday than above Monday and Tuesday.

Practice

Use the line plot for problems 1–3.

1 How many people signed up on Thursday? **5 people**

2 Which day had no sign-ups? **Wednesday**

3 In a school newsletter article, the headline read: "Sign-ups climbed toward the end of the week!" How does the line plot show this? **See above.**

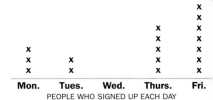

The Comeback of Whales

PEOPLE WHO SIGNED UP EACH DAY

Use the bar graph for problems 4–7. Explain how you found your answer.

4 How long is the dugong? How tall is the panda? **10 ft; 5 ft**

5 How much shorter is the python than the whale? Explain how you know. **See below.**

6 Which animal is between 15 ft and 30 ft in length? **the python**

7 Why do you think the scale numbers increase by 10 rather than by 1? **See below.**

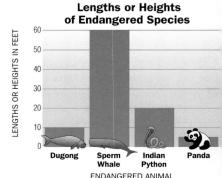

Lengths or Heights of Endangered Species

LENGTHS OR HEIGHTS IN FEET

Dugong   Sperm Whale   Indian Python   Panda

ENDANGERED ANIMAL

Use the bar graph for problems 8–9.

8 Which question can you *not* answer? **b**
  a. How many polar bear videos were borrowed?
  b. Can you borrow an alligator video today?
  c. Are there more than 3 videos on endangered animals?

9 **What if** the library had a video on gorillas and it was borrowed 10 times. Copy the graph and add the new data. **Check students' work.**

Public Library Videos

ENDANGERED ANIMALS VIDEO

Alligator
Bald Eagle
Polar Bear
Snow Leopard
Whooping Crane

NUMBER OF TIMES BORROWED

5. 40 ft; possible answer: find how much higher the bar for the whale is than the bar for the python.

102   Lesson 3.6   7. Possible answer: so that large animals like the whale can fit on the graph

---

Meeting Individual Needs

Early Finishers

Have students predict what would happen to the bar graph on page 100 if the scale numbers increased by 1, 4. Ask students which scale would be easier to work with when dealing with large numbers.

Gifted And Talented

Instruct students to create a set of graphs, one each of the four graphs discussed so far. Have them create booklets to hold this information. You may want to include these in the students' portfolios.

COMMON ERROR

Students may make the mistake of labeling the scale incorrectly. While some forget to use the same increment throughout, others make mistakes when adding the increments. Give students practice in choosing and writing scales for given ranges of data. For example, ask students what scale they would choose and write for data ranging from 65 to 100. *[Possible answer: 0 to 100 in increments of 10—0, 10, 20, 30, 40, 50, 60, 70, 80, 90, 100]*

10. c; possible answer: the bars will be too high if 5 or 10 are chosen, it will be very difficult to read the data if 200 is chosen.

MIXED APPLICATIONS
Problem Solving

Pencil & Paper | Calculator | Mental Math

Use the table for problems 10–13.

10 Make a decision If you wanted to make a bar graph using the data in the table, what scale would you use? Explain. **See above.**
a. 5   b. 10
c. 100   d. 200

Types of Endangered Species	
Species	**Number of Species**
Mammals	338
Birds	243
Fish	113
Reptiles	112
Others	148

11 What is the total number of species that are endangered? **954 species**

12 What if the number of endangered mammals decreased by 50. How would a bar graph of the data change? **Possible answer: The bar for mammals would decrease in height.**

13 Which species has about three times the number of endangered animals as reptiles? about twice the number? **mammals; birds**

14 Write a problem using the data from any of the graphs on pages 100–102. Solve it. Ask others to solve it. **Students should compare problems and answers.**

15 Data Point Survey your classmates to find out what pets they have. Make a bar graph to show the results. **Check students' work.**

more to explore

Stem-and-Leaf Plots
A stem-and-leaf plot is another way to organize data.

1 The stems are the tens digits of the data. What do the leaves stand for? **the ones digits in order from least to greatest**

2 What is the largest class size? the smallest? **42; 27**

3 How many fourth-grade classes are there? **10 classes**

4 Make a stem-and-leaf plot of students in fourth-grade classes in the Union School District: 36 18 32 36 25 28 25 32 20
See page T17.

Data: 40 37 27 37 29
       35 42 42 32 37

Thorndike School District
Students in Fourth-Grade Classes

Stem	Leaf				
2	7	9			
3	2	5	7	7	7
4	0	2	2		

Key: 2 | 7 stands for 27 students.

Extra Practice, page 494

Time, Data, and Graphs **103**

Pages 102–103

Alternate Teaching Strategy

Materials stick-on notes

Have students choose a question whose answer they would like to know. The question should have a limited number of answers.

Create a large bar graph on the chalkboard—answers to the survey questions along the horizontal axis, numbered increments the size of one stick-on note along the vertical axis.

Give each student a stick-on note. Have students place their stick-on notes on the bar graph above their responses to the question.

Discuss the graph as a class. You may want to change the bar graph so that each stick-on note represents a different number of responses. Discuss with students how this would change the graph.

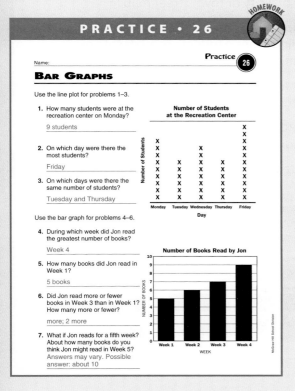

PRACTICE • 26

HOMEWORK

Name:

Practice 26

BAR GRAPHS

Use the line plot for problems 1–3.

1. How many students were at the recreation center on Monday?
9 students

2. On which day were there the most students?
Friday

3. On which days were there the same number of students?
Tuesday and Thursday

Number of Students at the Recreation Center

Use the bar graph for problems 4–6.

4. During which week did Jon read the greatest number of books?
Week 4

5. How many books did Jon read in Week 1?
5 books

6. Did Jon read more or fewer books in Week 3 than in Week 1? How many more or fewer?
more; 2 more

7. What if Jon reads for a fifth week? About how many books do you think Jon might read in Week 5? Answers may vary. Possible answer: about 10

Number of Books Read by Jon

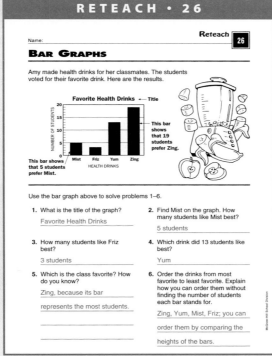

RETEACH • 26

Name:

Reteach 26

BAR GRAPHS

Amy made health drinks for her classmates. The students voted for their favorite drink. Here are the results.

Favorite Health Drinks — Title

This bar shows that 19 students prefer Zing.

This bar shows that 5 students prefer Mist.

HEALTH DRINKS

Use the bar graph above to solve problems 1–6.

1. What is the title of the graph?
Favorite Health Drinks

2. Find Mist on the graph. How many students like Mist best?
5 students

3. How many students like Friz best?
3 students

4. Which drink did 13 students like best?
Yum

5. Which is the class favorite? How do you know?
Zing, because its bar represents the most students.

6. Order the drinks from most favorite to least favorite. Explain how you can order them without finding the number of students each bar stands for.
Zing, Yum, Mist, Friz; you can order them by comparing the heights of the bars.

EXTEND • 26

Name:

Extend 26

BAR GRAPHS

And the Winner Is . . .
Use the Top Sporting Speeds bar graph to make a Winning Speed pictograph.

Top Sporting Speeds

SPORT

1. Put a ring around the faster speed in each group.

Group 1	Group 2	Group 3	Group 4
Bicycling	Luge	Running	Skating
Skiing	Skiing	Bicycling	Luge

Group 5	Group 6	Group 7	Group 8
Bicycling	Skiing	Skating	Luge
Skating	Running	Running	Running

2. Draw a ★ on the Winning Speed pictograph for the faster speed in each group. The sport with the most stars has the winning speed.

Winning Speed	
Bicycling	★ ★ ★
Luge	★ ★
Running	★
Skating	
Skiing	★ ★

Key: ★ = number of wins

3. Write the name of the fastest sport.
bicycling

Think Critically

4. When is a pictograph more useful than a bar graph? Answers may vary. Possible answer: When you want to make data more visually attractive and get people to pay more attention.

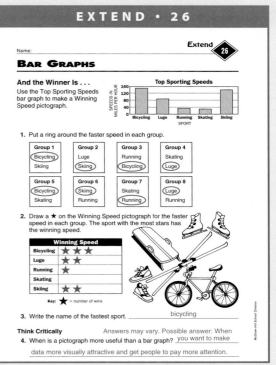

103

LESSON 3.7

Ordered Pairs

OBJECTIVE Use ordered pairs to identify and locate points on a grid.

RESOURCE REMINDER
Math Center Cards 27
Practice 27, Reteach 27, Extend 27

SKILLS TRACE

GRADE 3
• Use ordered pairs to identify and locate points on a grid. *(Chapter 10)*

GRADE 4
• Use ordered pairs to identify and locate points on a grid.

GRADE 5
• Use ordered pairs to identify and locate points on a grid. *(Chapter 8)*

WARM-UP

Cooperative Pairs   **Social**

OBJECTIVE Give and follow directions.

▶ Have students take turns directing their partners from one point in the classroom to another. You may want to set up an obstacle course of desks to challenge the students.

▶ The student must give directions to the blindfolded partner using phrases such as, "Take 2 steps forward and turn left."

▶ After a turn, have each pair discuss their experiences.
  • **What directions were or were not helpful?**
  • **What directions were forgotten by your partner?** *[Answers may vary.]*

> Directions
> 1. Go 3 steps forward.
> 2. Turn left and go 2 steps.
> 3. Turn right and go 4 steps.
> 4. Turn left and go 6 steps.
> 5. Turn right and you are there.

SOCIAL STUDIES CONNECTION

Cooperative Pairs   **Auditory/Linguistic**

OBJECTIVE Use a map to find a location and give directions.

Materials per pair: a small portion of a city or town street map

▶ Instruct each pair to find a location on their map to use as a starting point and another location to be the ending point. Students should write exact directions that lead to the end point, without naming it.

▶ Each pair of students exchanges their directions with another pair. Each pair then follows the directions to the ending point.

▶ Encourage the pairs to discuss problems they had with the directions. Working together, the two pairs should revise their work as needed.

▶ Have pairs share their revised directions with other pairs.

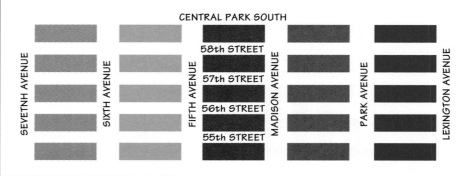

Daily Review

Math Van

PREVIOUS DAY QUICK REVIEW

For the numbers 25, 40, 30, 25, 25, 60 and 35, find:

1. range *[35]*
2. median *[30]*
3. mode *[25]*

FAST FACTS

1. 12 − 8 *[4]*
2. 10 − 7 *[3]*
3. 4 − 4 *[0]*
4. 3 − 2 *[1]*

Problem of the Day • 27

Kelli has her books organized on five shelves, each shelf containing books on only one topic. The books about animals are on the shelf directly below the books about crafts. The books about sports are on a shelf above the books about the planets. The shelf that holds craft books is three shelves below the shelf that holds mystery books. What type of books are on the third shelf? *[books about planets]*

TECH LINK

MATH VAN

Tool You may wish to use the Table tool and the Graph tool with this lesson.

MATH FORUM

Cultural Diversity Some urban areas were designed with roads that look similar to the grid map. Students who live in these areas may enjoy making an accurate map of their neighborhood.

Visit our Resource Village at http://www.mhschool.com to see more of the Math Forum.

MATH CENTER

Practice

OBJECTIVE Solve a riddle using ordered pairs.

Materials per student: Math Center Recording Sheet (TA 31 optional)

Students solve a riddle by locating letters identified by ordered pairs. *[A monkey]*

PRACTICE ACTIVITY 27

MATH CENTER
On Your Own

Spatial Sense • Grid Lock

Follow the directions to answer the riddle.

What kind of key isn't used to start a car?

Use the ordered pair to locate each letter in the answer.

___ ___ ___ ___ ___ ___ ___
(4, 8) (8, 3) (2, 5) (7, 9) (6, 6) (2, 4) (10, 5)

Chapter 3, Lesson 7, pages 104–105

Statistics

NCTM Standards

✓ Problem Solving
  Communication
✓ Reasoning
  Connections

Problem Solving

OBJECTIVE Draw designs using ordered pairs.

Materials per student: graph paper, Math Center Recording Sheet (TA 31 optional)

Students set up a 12 × 12 grid and draw designs going from point to point on the grid. They list the ordered pairs that make up the design on a separate sheet of paper and then exchange lists with their partner. The partners try to duplicate each other's designs.

PROBLEM-SOLVING ACTIVITY 27

MATH CENTER
Partners

Spatial Reasoning • Ordered Designs

YOU NEED
graph paper

- On your graph paper, label horizontal and vertical scales from 0 to 12.
- Create a design on the graph by connecting points with straight line segments.
- On a separate paper, list the coordinates of the points in the order in which you connected them. Then trade lists with your partner. Use each other's lists to duplicate the design.

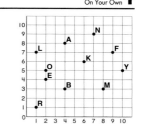

Chapter 3, Lesson 7, pages 104–105

Statistics

NCTM Standards

  Problem Solving
  Communication
✓ Reasoning
✓ Connections

ESL APPROPRIATE

Ordered Pairs

OBJECTIVE Use ordered pairs to identify and locate points on a grid.

Vocabulary ordered pair

1 Introduce

Talk about maps and giving directions. Ask students to name instances when they have been asked to give directions.

- **What terms are important when giving directions?**
- **What landmarks can you give to help people find where they are going?** [Answers may vary.]

2 Teach

Whole Class

▶ **LEARN** Read through the paragraph at the top of the page. Point out the grid map on the right. Have one student read the directions for how to locate a point on the grid while other students follow the directions on the grid. Have students answer the questions given, then ask:

- **To find a location on the grid, in which direction must you always travel first?** [to the right]
- **In which direction do you travel second?** [up]
- **Why is it important that the ordered pair always be written in the same way?** [If you are not consistent with directions, locations will not have distinct directions. You would not know if (3, 8) gave directions to Marcella's house or to Roberto's house.]
- **What other pair of houses could be hard to find if you didn't know which number represented up and which represented right?** [Marge's and Martin's houses]

3 Close

▶ **Check for Understanding** using items 1–5, page 104.

CRITICAL THINKING
Ask students where they think Tanya's house should be on the graph. They should realize that Tanya's house is at (0, 0). All the directions are from her house.

▶ **PRACTICE**
Materials have available: calculators

Options for assigning exercises:
A—Odd ex. 1–11; all ex. 13–16; **Mixed Review**
B—Even ex. 2–12; all ex. 13–16; **Mixed Review**

- Remind students to make sure their answers for ex. 1- 6 are written in the right order.

Mixed Review/Test Preparation In ex. 1- 4, students review estimating sums or differences, a skill learned in Chapter 2. You may suggest that students review range, median, and mode in Lesson 4 before attempting ex. 5 and 6.

STATISTICS

Ordered Pairs

L E A R N

Have you ever made a map to show where you live or where you need to go? This grid map uses both horizontal and vertical scale numbers to describe the locations of places on the map.

To locate a point on the grid, start at zero, go right, then go up.

To tell where Marge lives, Tanya starts at zero. She counts 5 blocks to the right and then 7 blocks up. The 5 and the 7 are an **ordered pair.** They are written as (5, 7).

▶ How would you find (3, 8)? Explain. **Start at zero, go right 3 blocks, then go up 8 blocks.**

▶ Is this location the same as (8, 3)? Explain. **No; (8, 3) would mean go right 8 blocks and then go up 3 blocks.**

▶ Why is the order of the numbers in a pair important?

> **ordered pair** A pair of numbers that gives the location of a point on a grid.

C H E C K

Check for Understanding

1️⃣ Give the ordered pairs for where Denise, Juan, and Julia live. **(5, 3), (5, 9), (9, 7)**

2️⃣ Tell who lives at (2, 4), (7, 5), and (8, 9). **Roy, Martin, Tony**

3️⃣ **What if** Justin lives a block away from Roy. Where could you place his house on the map? **Possible answers: (2, 3), (1, 4), (3, 4), (2, 5)**

Critical Thinking: Analyze **Explain your reasoning.**

4️⃣ What is similar and different about finding the locations (5, 3) and (5, 9)? (1, 7) and (9, 7)? **See below.**

5️⃣ What can you say about the locations of any group of ordered pairs that have the same first number? the same second number? **They are directly above one another; they are beside one another.**

Meeting Individual Needs

Early Finishers

Have students create a map of the school using graph paper. Ask them to use ordered pairs to identify the location of various rooms in the school. Students may present their map to the class.

ESL ▸ APPROPRIATE

Extra Support

Remind students to start at zero, go right, then go up when locating a point on the grid. Have students write *left, right, up* and *down* on the four sides of a grid.

Ongoing Assessment

Anecdotal Report Determine if students understand ordered pairs by observing if they find and name points on a grid. They should know that the first number indicates movement to the right and the second movement up.

Follow Up Students needing practice with ordered pairs can share the maps they created for exercise 15, or do **Reteach 27.**

Challenge students by asking them to compile the maps into a book with the answers given on the reverse side of the map, or assign **Extend 27.**

15. Students may show the location of their home, stores, school, friends' homes, and so on.

Practice

Use the map to find the ordered pair for the location.

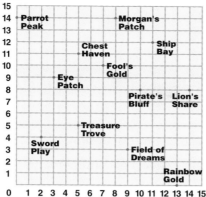

1. Pirate's Bluff (10, 8)

2. Parrot Peak (0, 14)

3. Ship Bay (11, 12)

4. Treasure Trove (5, 5)

5. Rainbow Gold (13, 0)

6. Morgan's Patch (8, 14)

Tell what is found at the location on the map.

7. (5, 11) **Chest Haven**
8. (14, 8) **Lion's Share**
9. (2, 4) **Sword Play**
10. (9, 3) **Field of Dreams**
11. (3, 9) **Eye Patch**
12. (7, 10) **Fool's Gold**

MIXED APPLICATIONS
Problem Solving

16. Possible answer: rectangle, parallelogram, trapezoid, rhombus

13. **Logical reasoning** Kettle Climb is directly above Rainbow Gold and to the right of Treasure Trove. What is the ordered pair that describes its location? (13, 5)

14. Tanya leaves Parrot Peak at 10:30 A.M. She arrives at Rainbow Gold at 1:45 P.M. How long did she take to get to Rainbow Gold? **3 h 15 min**

15. **Data Point** Use a grid to create a neighborhood of your own or draw a map of your neighborhood. Give coordinates for places on your map. Have others find the locations. See above.

16. **Spatial reasoning** You have two squares of the same size. You cut each square to get two equal triangles. What different shapes can you create with the four triangles? See above.

mixed review • test preparation

Estimate the sum or difference.

1. 67 + 43 **110**

2. 498 − 261 **200**

3. $4.93 + $2.38 **$7.00**

4. 78,967 − 21,638 **60,000**

Estimates may vary. Estimates given were found by rounding.

Find the range, median, and mode of the game scores.

5. 24, 59, 38, 26, 93, 26, 47
69, 38, 26

6. 75, 80, 82, 76, 95, 95, 95, 60, 70
35, 80, 95

Extra Practice, page 494

Time, Data, and Graphs **105**

Alternate Teaching Strategy

Refer to the graph on page 105. Write the ordered pairs shown below on the chalkboard.

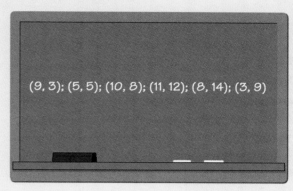

(9, 3); (5, 5); (10, 8); (11, 12); (8, 14); (3, 9)

Tell students that the buried treasure can be found by using these ordered pairs to locate the islands where other clues can be found. The clues must be collected in the exact order to find the buried treasure.

Tell students that to locate (13,1) start at 0, go 13 blocks right and 1 block up to the island of "Rainbow Gold."

Ask students to use the rest of the ordered pairs to find the islands at which they must stop for clues and list them in order. [Rainbow Gold, Field of Dreams, Treasure Trove, Pirate's Bluff, Ship Bay, Morgan's Patch, Eye Patch]

PRACTICE • 27

Name: _____

Practice 27

ORDERED PAIRS

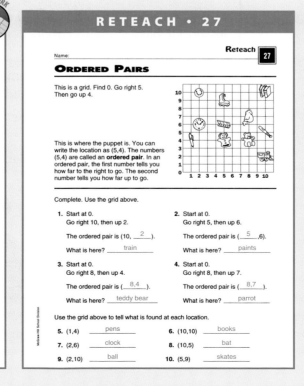

Hill, Jill, Will, and Gill are playing golf. Write the name of the player at each location.

1. (1,5) __Jill__ 2. (4,2) __Gill__ 3. (1,10) __Hill__ 4. (9,2) __Will__

The friends play past different objects. Write the ordered pair for the location of each object.

5. cow __4,8__ 6. birdhouse __3,9__ 7. windmill __4,6__

8. sunflower __8,4__ 9. rooster __9,9__ 10. tunnel __9,6__

11. waterfall __3,5__ 12. bridge __2,3__ 13. mountain __5,3__

Solve. Use the grid of the golf course above.

14. The owners of the course decide to add a 10th bonus hole 3 spaces down from the sunflower. What ordered pair names this location?
(8,1)

15. On her second shot, Jill is between the waterfall and her original position. What ordered pair names her new location on the grid?
(2,5)

RETEACH • 27

Name: _____

Reteach 27

ORDERED PAIRS

This is a grid. Find 0. Go right 5. Then go up 4.

This is where the puppet is. You can write the location as (5,4). The numbers (5,4) are called an **ordered pair**. In an ordered pair, the first number tells you how far to the right to go. The second number tells you how far up to go.

Complete. Use the grid above.

1. Start at 0.
Go right 10, then up 2.
The ordered pair is (10, __2__).
What is here? __train__

2. Start at 0.
Go right 5, then up 6.
The ordered pair is (__5__,6).
What is here? __paints__

3. Start at 0.
Go right 8, then up 4.
The ordered pair is (__8,4__).
What is here? __teddy bear__

4. Start at 0.
Go right 8, then up 7.
The ordered pair is (__8,7__).
What is here? __parrot__

Use the grid above to tell what is found at each location.

5. (1,4) __pens__ 6. (10,10) __books__

7. (2,6) __clock__ 8. (10,5) __bat__

9. (2,10) __ball__ 10. (5,9) __skates__

EXTEND • 27

Name: _____

Extend 27

ORDERED PAIRS

Making Connections
You need: graph paper

Find the secret drawing. Connect the dots in the order described by each ordered pair.

1. (7,13)   2. (5,12)   3. (3,12)   4. (4,11)
5. (4,9)   6. (2,6)   7. (0,9)   8. (0,6)
9. (2,5)   10. (3,3)   11. (1,1)   12. (2,0)
13. (5,2)   14. (5,5)   15. (7,7)   16. (8,6)
17. (10,9)   18. (9,9)   19. (8,8)   20. (6,9)
21. (7,10)   22. (8,10)   23. (8,11)   24. (6,11)
25. (7,12)   26. (7,13)

Think Critically

27. Is there a way to create a list of ordered pairs that would make a curve? How?
Answers may vary. Possible answer: No, any figure you make will be made up of straight lines. If you made the dots close enough together, your figure might look more and more like a curve.

LESSON 3.8

EXPLORE ACTIVITY
Line Graphs

OBJECTIVE Explore reading and making line graphs.

Teaching with Technology
See alternate computer lesson, pp. 109A–109B.

RESOURCE REMINDER
Math Center Cards 28
Practice 28, Reteach 28, Extend 28

SKILLS TRACE

GRADE 3	• Introduced at grade 4.
GRADE 4	• Explore reading and making line graphs.
GRADE 5	• Read and make line graphs. (Chapter 3)

WARM-UP

Cooperative Pairs   **Visual/Spatial**

OBJECTIVE Make a dot-to-dot design.

Materials per pair: 2 sheets of centimeter graph paper (TA 7); color pencil

▶ Ask pairs of students to decide on an object or design for a simple dot-to-dot drawing. Tell students that the drawing should be made up of straight lines that meet where grid lines intersect.

▶ Have students draw their design on the first sheet of graph paper. On the second sheet students should place only the dots.

▶ Instruct students to select a point at the bottom left of their drawings to be (0, 0), then make a list of the ordered pairs for each point in the dot-to-dot in the order the dots will be connected.

▶ Students exchange their dot designs and list of ordered pairs and solve each others' dot designs.

ESL APPROPRIATE

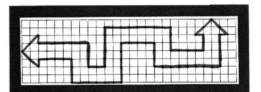

REAL-LIFE CONNECTION

Cooperative Pairs   **Visual/Spatial**

OBJECTIVE Explore how many graphs can be made from the same data.

Materials: graphing software (optional)

▶ Give each pair a set of data they collected for an activity in a previous lesson. Or, have students conduct another in-class survey and organize the results in a table.

▶ Using graphing software, students input the data on a bar graph and a line graph. Have students print the graphs.

▶ Instruct students to compare the two graphs and write a paragraph describing what they find.

▶ If graphing software is not available, students can draw the bar and line graphs on graph paper.

Daily Review

PREVIOUS DAY QUICK REVIEW

Determine what time it was:
1. 2 h 10 min before 3:20 *[1:10]*
2. 1 h 30 min before 6:15 *[4:45]*
3. 5 h 5 min before 11:00 *[5:55]*

FAST FACTS

1. 16 − 9 *[7]*
2. 11 − 3 *[8]*
3. 7 − 5 *[2]*
4. 8 − 7 *[1]*

Problem of the Day • 28

Kera has $4.00 to buy several 23¢ and 32¢ stamps. She wants at least five 23¢ stamps. She wants to use the rest of her money for 32¢ stamps, but will buy another 23¢ stamp if she has money left over. How many 23¢ and 32¢ stamps will Kera buy? *[eight 32¢ stamps and six 23¢ stamps]*

TECH LINK

MATH VAN

Activity You may wish to use *Here's the Scoop!* to teach this lesson.

MATH FORUM

Management Tip Graphs can be difficult and time-consuming to check. I let pairs of students compare their graphs to the one I draw on the board. My students point out any differences and correct their graphs.

Visit our Resource Village at http://www.mhschool.com to see more of the Math Forum.

MATH CENTER

Practice

OBJECTIVE Make and interpret a line graph.

Materials per student: Math Center Recording Sheet (TA 31 optional)

Students make a line graph from given data and answer questions about what it shows. *[Possible answer: The plant grew very slowly at first, but starting at day 3 it grew quickly. From day 5 to 6, it grew the most—3 cm. On the last day, the growth slowed again.]*

PRACTICE ACTIVITY 28

MATH CENTER
On Your Own

Number Sense • Growing Graphs

For a science project, Alana planted a bean seed at home. She measured its height every day, and recorded her results. Her table is shown at the right.

- Make a line graph to show this data. Label the bottom of the graph "Days" and the left side "Centimeters."
- Describe how the plant grew. On which day did it grow the most? What happened at the end of the week?

YOU NEED
graph paper

Growth of Alana's Bean Seed

Day	Height (cm)
1	0
2	1
3	1
4	3
5	5
6	8
7	8

NCTM Standards
- ✓ Problem Solving
- ✓ Communication
- ✓ Reasoning
- Connections

Chapter 3, Lesson 8, pages 106–109   Statistics

Problem Solving

OBJECTIVE Interpret line graphs.

Materials per student: Math Center Recording Sheet (TA 31 optional)

Students match 3 line graphs to possible news stories that they represent. Then they title and label the graphs and write short news stories for each. *[Graph A, headline 2; Graph B, headline 3; Graph C, headline 1]*

PROBLEM-SOLVING ACTIVITY 28

MATH CENTER
On Your Own

Logical Reasoning • Headline Reporting

Draw each of these graphs on a separate piece of paper.

Then match each of these newspaper headlines with the appropriate graph.

1. Temperature Keeps Rising
2. Fewer People With Flu This Winter
3. After Slow Start, Song Hits Charts

Give each graph a title and label its horizontal and vertical sides. Then use your imagination to write 3 short news paragraphs to explain each headline and graph.

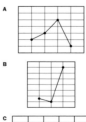

NCTM Standards
- Problem Solving
- ✓ Communication
- ✓ Reasoning
- Connections

Chapter 3, Lesson 8, pages 106–109   Statistics

Lesson 3.8 continued

EXPLORE ACTIVITY
Line Graphs

> **OBJECTIVE** Explore reading and making line graphs.
>
> **Materials** per pair: centimeter graph paper (TA 7)
>
> **Vocabulary** line graph

1 Introduce

Ask students if they subscribe to any newsletters or magazines. Invite them to talk about the types of newsletters or magazines they like to read and why. Have students cover the line graph and look at the table on page 106. Ask students:
- **Between which two months did the number of subscribers increase the most?** *[months 1 and 2]*

Then have students uncover the line graph. Ask students:
- **Would it be easier to answer the question using the line graph? Explain.** *[Yes; it's easier to compare the lengths of the lines than to subtract.]*

2 Teach   *Cooperative Pairs*

▶ **LEARN** Read the information about how to make a line graph. Make sure all students understand what is meant by scale. Point out the scale on the partial graph shown and discuss what it means.

Work Together Point out the line graph. Ask students the following questions:
- **What is the ordered pair for the first point on the graph?** *[(1, 24)]*
- **What data does this point refer to?** *[number of individual subscribers for 1 month.]*
- **What ordered pair represents the number of subscribers for 3 months?** *[(3, 30)]*
- **Will the graph contain an ordered pair with 36 as the second number? Why?** *[No; the number of subscribers during the 8 months never reached 36.]*

Ask each pair to finish the graph shown on graph paper.

Talk It Over After discussing the graph as a class ask:
- **What other information can be found by using the graph?** *[Possible answer: how quickly the number of subscribers increased from Month 1 to Month 2]*

Have each student write one question that could be answered by referring to the graph.

Line Graphs

The *EcoSphere* children research, interview, draw, and photograph for each issue of the magazine. You can show the number of new *EcoSphere* subscribers in a line graph.

Work Together
Work with a partner. Copy and complete the line graph. Then answer the questions.

> **line graph** A graph that uses lines to show changes in data.

IN THE WORKPLACE
Susannah Druck is the program coordinator of *EcoSphere*, a conservation magazine produced by children.

Month	Number of New Subscribers
1	24
2	30
3	30
4	34
5	33
6	32
7	32
8	28

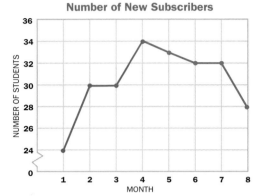

Number of New Subscribers

Talk It Over
▶ How did you show the number of new subscribers for months 5, 6, 7, and 8? **See page T17.**

▶ Which month had the fewest new subscribers? the most?
month 1; month 4

▶ Which months had the same number of new subscribers?
months 2 and 3, and months 6 and 7

106 Lesson 3.8

Meeting Individual Needs

Extra Support

Create a bulletin board of line graphs. Display various line graphs cut from newspapers, magazines, or made by students. You may call on students to interpret the line graphs during the class.

Ongoing Assessment

Anecdotal Report Make notes on students' ability to make and read line graphs. Students should be able to determine the ordered pairs needed to represent given data, and write and answer questions based on a line graph.

Follow Up Students who need more practice with line graphs may try **Reteach 28.**

For students who need a greater challenge, have them draw line graphs using the coordinates off street maps, or assign **Extend 28.**

Q 1. Possible answer: The attendance was greater in month 2; a higher point on the line shows a greater number.

Make Connections

To make a line graph:

▶ choose scale numbers and label the graph. You can use a broken graph to make a scale shorter.

▶ plot points that show the data and connect them with a line.

▶ write a title.

How do you choose a scale for the graph? What do you have to think about? **Possible answer: Look at the numbers that need to be shown and**

A line graph helps you to see changes that **consider how far apart they are.**
happen over time.

▶ The line on the line graph rises between months 1 and 2. What can you say about the number of new subscribers for month 1 compared with month 2? How do you know? **See above.**

▶ What does it mean when the line goes down? when the line is flat? Give examples. **See page T17.**

▶ What does this graph tell you about the number of new subscribers for the first eight months? How do you know?
Possible answer: The number of new subscribers increased, stayed the same for the third month, then increased again; the rise of the line shows this.

Check for Understanding

Use the line graph for problems 1–4.

1 In which month is the depth of the river the greatest? the least?
March, August

2 Between which two months does the depth of the river change the most?
August and September

Critical Thinking: Analyze
Explain your reasoning.

3 What statements can you make based on the data in the graph?
Possible answer: The river was 25 feet deep in March.

4 Why do you think a line graph is a good way to show data?

Possible answer: Data can be compared quickly by looking at whether the line rises, falls, or is flat, and by looking at how steep the line is.

Depth of Burlington River

Turn the page for Practice. ➡

C H E C K

MAKE CONNECTIONS

Read through the text, letting students point out the places in the line graph to which the text refers. Ask students:

- **In what month was the number of subscribers the least? When was it the greatest?** [Month 1; Month 4]
- **In what month(s) was the number of subscribers 30?** [Month 2 and Month 3]
- **Between what two months did the number of subscribers increase the most?** [between Month 1 and Month 2]

Give students the opportunity to discuss the advantages of a line graph over a bar graph or pictograph.

3 Close

▶ **Check for Understanding** using items 1–4, page 107.

CRITICAL THINKING

JOURNAL   Have students write a paragraph comparing the graphing techniques they have learned in this chapter. They could compare the types of data that are best shown by each kind of graph.

Practice See pages 108 –109.

Language Support

Have students write the words *increase, decrease,* and *no change* on separate index cards. Then have them draw lines going up, down, and straight across to show the meaning of the words as they relate to line graphs. Have an English-speaking student check the completed cards.

ESL **APPROPRIATE**

Inclusion

Encourage students with poor handwriting to use a ruler when creating graphs. A ruler will help them draw straight lines. In addition, students can use a ruler to make a scale with regular increments when not using graph paper.

▶ PRACTICE

Materials have available: graph paper, calculators

Assign ex. 1–14 and **More to Explore** as independent work.

- For ex. 7, encourage students to use graph paper. This will make it easier for them to make straight lines and regular scale increments. Students should use rulers to connect the points.
- Ex. 9 asks students to find the difference between the highest and lowest temperatures. They should recognize that they are finding the range.
- For **Make It Right** (ex. 11), see Common Error below.
- For ex. 13, tell students to connect the points in order and to connect the last point to the first point.

More to Explore Give students time to read the introductory information and the time line. Ask students:

- **In what year did Benjamin Banneker build a wooden clock?** *[1751]*
- **What happened in Benjamin Banneker's life in 1792?** *[He published the first almanac.]*

Let students answer the questions given. Then have students create time lines for their lives.

P
R
A
C
T
I
C
E

Practice

Use the line graph for problems 1–6.

1 How tall was Colleen when she was 4? **100 cm**

2 Between which two ages did Colleen grow the most? **birth and age 1**

3 How much did Colleen grow between the ages of 5 and 6? **10 cm**

4 How old was Colleen when she was 120 cm tall? **7 y old**

5 What was Colleen's height at age 1? How do you know? **See right.**

6 What does this graph tell you about how Colleen grew? Possible answer: **Colleen grew steadily.**

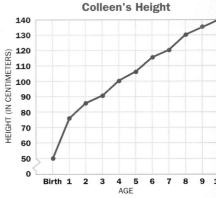

Colleen's Height

75 cm; possible answer: the point on the line directly above age 1 is directly across from height of 75 cm on the vertical scale.

Use the table for problems 7–11.

7 Make a line graph using the data in the table. **Check students' work.**

8 Tell how you chose the scale you used. **Check students' work.**

9 What was the difference between the highest and lowest temperatures? What does this tell you about the school day? **See below.**

10 Write a short paragraph describing what the weather was like on that school day. **See below.**

Temperature During Schooltime

Time	Temperature (in degrees Celsius, °C)
A.M.	
8	4
9	8
10	10
11	12
Noon 12	12
P.M.	
1	12
2	16
3	20

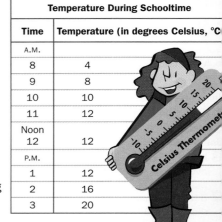

················· **Make It Right** ·················

11 Tyler wrote this statement. Explain what mistake was made, then correct it. **Possible answer: Did not realize that the temperature remained the same—the line would be flat.**

If the temperature at 4:00 P.M. is 20°C. the line in the graph will fall because the line rises only if the temperature increases.

9. 16°; possible answer: the temperature did not vary more than 16° throughout the day.

10. Possible answer: The temperature was low in the morning but warmed up to 20°C by the end of the day.

108   Lesson 3.8

Meeting Individual Needs

Early Finishers

Give students the class attendance record for at least the last five days. Have them make a graph showing the data. Ask students to write a paragraph describing the information they conclude from the graph.

COMMON ERROR

As in the **Make It Right,** students can often confuse what information they can derive from lines that rise, fall, or stay horizontal.

Have students look at the data that cause the line to change as it does. Let students make the discovery that lines that rise coincide with increasing data, lines that fall coincide with decreasing data, and lines that are flat coincide with data that remain the same.

12. Title b; neither the numbers of hats nor a puppy's weight would increase as sharply as the line shows in June to August.

MIXED APPLICATIONS
Problem Solving
Pencil & Paper · Calculator · Mental Math

12 **Make a decision** Match the graph to a title. Explain your decision.
a. The Numbers of Hats We Owned Last Year
b. Numbers of Hours Spent Swimming Each Month Last Year
c. My Puppy's Weight Each Month Last Year **See above.**

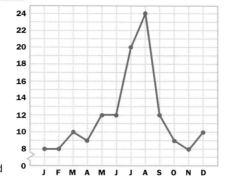

13 **Spatial reasoning** If you drew lines to connect the ordered pairs (1, 1), (4, 1), and (2, 4), what shape would you get? **triangle**

14 **Data Point** Use the table on page 535 in the Databank to make a line graph. Write a sentence about what the graph tells you. **Students' graphs show Kim's weight from 1 year old to 10 years old.**

more to explore

Time Lines

Benjamin Banneker was a well-known African American mathematician, astronomer, and writer. This time line shows some of the important events in his life.

Life of Benjamin Banneker

Born 1731 — Built wooden clock 1751 — Predicted eclipse 1789 — First published almanac 1792

1730 1750 1770 1790 1810

Began survey for Washington, D.C. 1791 — Died 1806

Possible answer: Alike—they both show numbers in order along a line;
different—a time line shows dates and has labels that tell what happened on those dates.

1 How is a time line like a number line? How is it different? **See above right.**

2 How many years are between each mark on the time line? **20 y**

3 How old was Banneker when he first published an almanac? **61 y old**

4 Make a time line that shows some important events in your own life.

Extra Practice, page 495

4. Students may start with their dates of birth, then show first day of school, first time to ride a bike, birth of siblings, and so on.

Time, Data, and Graphs **109**

Alternate Teaching Strategy

Resources graphing program, or Math Van Tools

Have students show the data in the table on Student Book page 106 using a line graph of a graphing program.

Ask them to tell how they would set up the horizontal and vertical axes and how they would plot the points.

Have students compare their line graphs. Then have them compare how making a line graph using a computer is different from making a line graph using pencil and paper. *[Possible answer: When making a line graph using a graphing program, the computer adjusts the scale of the vertical axis for you automatically; when making a line graph using pencil and paper, you have to decide on the scale of the vertical axis first.]*

You may have students make more line graphs on a computer using the data in other tables of this lesson.

PRACTICE · 28

HOMEWORK

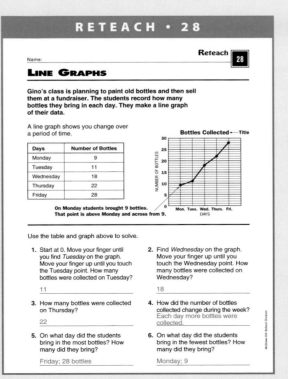

Practice 28

Name: ____

LINE GRAPHS

Use the line graph for problems 1–4.

People in the Card Store Each Hour

1. In which hour were the most people in the card store? How many people were there?
   1–2 P.M.; 25

2. In which hours were there the fewest people in the card store?
   7–8 A.M. and 10–11 A.M.

3. How many people were in the card store between 8 and 9 A.M.?
   15 people

4. Between which two periods was there the greatest increase in the number of people in the card store?
   between 12–1 P.M. and 1–2 P.M.

Use the table for problems 5–8.

PIZZAS SOLD EACH DAY							
Day	M	T	W	T	F	S	S
Number Sold	9	6	14	18	20	19	12

5. Make a line graph from the data given.
   Check students' work.

6. Between which two days was there the greatest increase in the number of pizzas sold?
   between Tuesday and Wednesday

7. Between which two days was there the greatest decrease in the number of pizzas sold?
   between Saturday and Sunday

RETEACH · 28

Reteach 28

Name: ____

LINE GRAPHS

Gino's class is planning to paint old bottles and then sell them at a fundraiser. The students record how many bottles they bring in each day. They make a line graph of their data.

A line graph shows you change over a period of time.

Days	Number of Bottles
Monday	9
Tuesday	11
Wednesday	18
Thursday	22
Friday	28

Bottles Collected ← Title

On Monday students brought 9 bottles. That point is above Monday and across from 9.

Use the table and graph above to solve.

1. Start at 0. Move your finger until you find *Tuesday* on the graph. Move your finger up until you touch the Tuesday point. How many bottles were collected on Tuesday?
   11

2. Find *Wednesday* on the graph. Move your finger up until you touch the Wednesday point. How many bottles were collected on Wednesday?
   18

3. How many bottles were collected on Thursday?
   22

4. How did the number of bottles collected change during the week?
   Each day more bottles were collected.

5. On what day did the students bring in the most bottles? How many did they bring?
   Friday; 28 bottles

6. On what day did the students bring in the fewest bottles? How many did they bring?
   Monday; 9

EXTEND · 28

Extend 28

Name: ____

LINE GRAPHS

Deli Doings

Use the clues and points given on the graphs to complete each line graph.

Colby's Deli is keeping track of sandwich sales.

1. Colby's sold 5 fewer sandwiches on Monday than on Tuesday.

2. Colby's sold twice as many sandwiches on Wednesday as on Monday.

Sandwich Sales

3. On Thursday Colby's sold 15 more sandwiches than the day before.

4. On Friday they sold as many sandwiches as on Monday and Tuesday combined.

Colby's Deli also keeps track of new customers.

5. Colby's had 10 fewer new customers in November than in October.

New Customers

6. In August Colby's had 15 fewer new customers than they had in November.

7. In September Colby's had as many new customers as in August and November combined.

8. In December 15 more new customers came than in November.

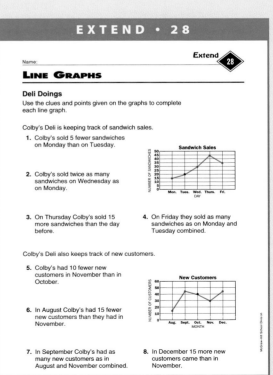

109

Teaching With Technology

Line Graphs

OBJECTIVE Students learn how to transfer data from a table to a line graph and how to read a line graph to make predictions.

Resource Math Van Activity: *Here's the Scoop*

SET UP
Provide students with the activity card for *Here's the Scoop.* Start **Math Van** and click the *Activities* button. Click the *Here's the Scoop* activity on the Fax Machine.

USING THE MATH VAN ACTIVITY

1 Getting Started Students help Wanda create a Line Graph so she can easily figure out when she needs the most workers and supplies at her ice cream booth.

2 Practice and Apply Students create and label a Line Graph to help predict the number of ice cream sales that will take place at the booth in May and June.

3 Close You may wish to discuss the meaning of ascending and descending lines in line graphs and how they help in making educated predictions.

Extend Students collect data such as daily rainfall or monthly temperature and place it in a Line Graph. They label, title, and take a photo of the graph and describe it in their Notes.

TIPS FOR TOOLS

Students can check the accuracy of their Line Graphs by turning on the Show Point Values option in Graph Setup.

Here's the Scoop!

SCREEN 1

Students label and set a scale for the Line Graph to help Wanda predict her needs for the booth.

SCREEN 2

Students plot the sales using data from the chart on the activity card. Then they title the graph and check their work.

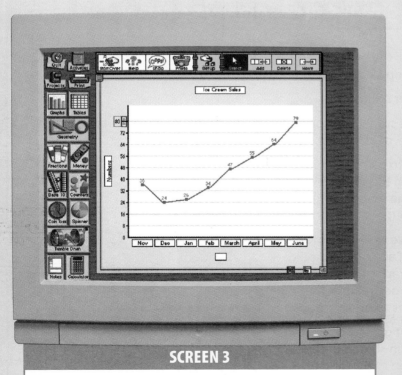

SCREEN 3

Students change the graph to reflect ice cream sales changes and make predictions about future sales.

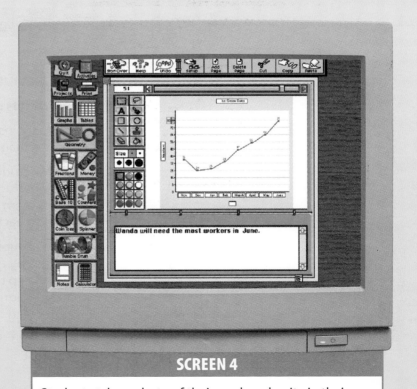

SCREEN 4

Students take a photo of their work and write in their Notes about using the Line Graph to predict sales.

LESSON 3.9

Problem Solvers at Work

OBJECTIVES Solve/write problems by interpreting data from different graphs.

RESOURCE REMINDER
Math Center Cards 29
Practice 29, Reteach 29, Extend 29

SKILLS TRACE

GRADE 3	• Formulate and solve problems involving collecting, displaying, and interpreting data and choosing the best display. *(Chapter 5)*
GRADE 4	• Formulate and solve problems involving finding needed information from different graphs.
GRADE 5	• Formulate and solve problems involving the best way to represent data. *(Chapter 3)*

WARM-UP

Cooperative Pairs   **Visual/Spatial**

OBJECTIVE Make a graph to describe data.

Materials per pair: 0–9 spinner (TA 2), centimeter graph paper (TA 7)

► Tell each pair to spin the spinner 30 times. The result of each spin should be recorded.

► Using the data recorded from the spins, have each pair make a bar graph. Tell each pair to compare their graph with two or three other graphs made by other pairs of students.

► Ask students how they would change their graph to make it similar to one of the other graphs. Have them explain their steps to their group.

► Ask each group to write one or two paragraphs describing the data in their graph and comparing their results to those of others.

STATISTICS CONNECTION

Cooperative Groups   **Linguistic**

OBJECTIVE Compare types of graphs and their uses.

Materials poster boards

Prepare Instruct students to bring to class two or three graphs from a newspaper, magazine, or any other source.

► Ask students to name the types of graphs studied in this chapter as you write them on the board. Assign one type to each group for their poster.

► In groups, have students sort the graphs by type. Each group should then keep the graphs that match their assigned type and give the remaining graphs to other groups.

► Groups mount graphs on poster board. Each graph should be labeled with a description of the kind of information it displays.

Daily Review

PREVIOUS DAY QUICK REVIEW

If it is 2:00 P.M. now, determine what time it will be:

1. in 45 min. *[2:45 P.M.]*
2. in 2 h 10 min. *[4:10 P.M.]*
3. in 6 h 15 min. *[8:15 P.M.]*
4. in 5 h 10 min. *[7:10 P.M.]*

FAST FACTS

1. 4 − 3 *[1]*
2. 13 − 5 *[8]*
3. 13 − 6 *[7]*
4. 11 − 7 *[4]*

Problem of the Day • 29

Tim and Sarah are saving money to buy the same CD. Tim has to save $22 more and Sarah needs to save $3 more. If they combine their savings, they need $1 more to buy one copy of the CD. What is the cost of the CD? *[$24]*

TECH LINK

MATH VAN

Tool You may wish to use the Table tool and the graph tool with this lesson.

MATH FORUM

Combination Classes My older students find data, make graphs, and write two or more problems that can be solved by my younger students.

Visit our Resource Village at http://www.mhschool.com to see more of the Math Forum.

MATH CENTER

Practice

OBJECTIVE Interpret a bar graph.

Materials Math Center Recording Sheet (TA 31 optional)

Students interpret data from the graph to answer questions and write a question of their own. *[1. 7:35; 2. Possible answer: Around 8:00 A.M., since most students arrive at or before that time; 3. 35 minutes; 4. 20; students' questions may vary.]*

PRACTICE ACTIVITY 29
MATH CENTER On Your Own

Number Sense • Get to School on Time

Miss Marcoux's students collected data about what time they arrived at school. Then they arranged their data in a bar graph.

1. What time did the first student arrive at school?
2. Around what time do you think school starts? Why?
3. How much time was there between the first student's arrival and the last student's arrival?
4. How many students came to Miss Marcoux's class that day?
• Write another question that can be answered from this graph.

Chapter 3, Lesson 9, pages 110–113   Problem Solving

NCTM Standards
✓ Problem Solving
  Communication
✓ Reasoning
✓ Connections

Problem Solving

OBJECTIVE Create a divided-bar graph.

Materials per student: Math Center Recording Sheet (TA 31 optional)

Students make a divided bar graph to represent the activities of a hypothetical student over 24 hours. They make up problems based on the graphs and exchange them with a classmate.

PROBLEM-SOLVING ACTIVITY 29
MATH CENTER On Your Own

Formulating Problems • A Day in the Life of . . .

A divided-bar graph uses one bar to represent a whole. The bar is then divided to show how much belongs to each part. For example, you could represent a 24-hour day with a divided-bar graph with 24 divisions like this:

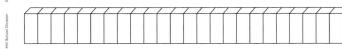

• Make up data about a day in the life of a student your age. You might include time spent sleeping, eating, going to school, exercising, and so on.
• Organize your data in a table. Use your data to make a divided-bar graph. Write problems based on your graph. Give your problems to a classmate to solve.

Chapter 3, Lesson 9, pages 110–113   Problem Solving

NCTM Standards
✓ Problem Solving
✓ Communication
✓ Reasoning
✓ Connections

Problem Solvers at Work

OBJECTIVE Solve/write problems by interpreting data from different graphs.

1 Introduce

Ask students about the organizations or clubs to which they belong. Make a list of these groups on the chalkboard with tally marks for the number of students in each group. Have students compare the data collected to the data given in the graphs in the text. Ask students:

- **How are the data in the bar graph different from the data we've collected?** *[The bar graph shows the total number of members in each group, not just the number of members in one class or one grade.]*

2 Teach

Cooperative Pairs

PART 1 INTERPRET DATA

▶ **LEARN** Point out the graphs at the top of the page. Ask students the following:

- **If the data collected on the chalkboard were displayed on a graph, which graph in the book would it look like?** *[the bar graph]*
- **Could you create a graph similar to the line graph with the data collected? Explain.** *[No; the data collected is only for the present time.]*
- **What further information would you need to make a graph similar to the line graph?** *[the number of members in one or more groups for the past eight years]*

Work Together Let students work in pairs to answer the questions. Tell students that they will be expected to explain their answers for at least one of the questions. If some pairs finish before others, have them write problems that can be solved using the data displayed in one or both of the graphs.

Write: Compare/Contrast As students share their paragraphs, note additional ways that the graphs are similar and different. For example, both graphs have numbers along the left side labeled "Number of Students," but the numbers differ. Both have titles. One graph shows color bars while the other shows a colored line. Both graphs show data and labels along the bottom.

Encourage students to observe the graphs closely and find other ways to compare and contrast them.

Problem Solvers at Work

Read | Plan | Solve | Look Back

Part 1 Interpret Data

Mikel gathered data on membership in the after-school clubs in his school.

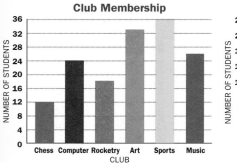

Work Together

Solve. Tell which graph you used.

1 How many more students belong to the Sports Club than belong to the Chess Club? **24 students; bar graph**

2 When was the greatest increase in membership in the Computer Club? How much was the increase? **between 1995 and 1996; 5 students; line graph**

3 If 12 members of the Rocketry Club also belong to the Sports Club, how many students are in both clubs in all? **42 students; bar graph**

4 **What if** membership in the Computer Club continues to increase each year by the same amount as it increased between 1996 and 1997. In what year would there be at least 40 members? **2003; line graph**

5 **Write: Compare/Contrast** Compare the data on each graph. Write a paragraph to compare and contrast the data shown. **Possible answer: Bar graph shows number of students in 6 different clubs; line graph shows membership in the computer club over time. Both graphs show computer club membership in 1997.**

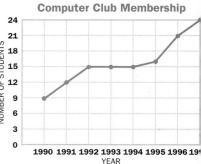

110 Lesson 3.9

Meeting Individual Needs

Early Finishers

Have students choose bar graphs and line graphs used in previous lessons. Ask them to write three questions for each graph. Exchange problems with others.

Ongoing Assessment

Interview Determine if students understand how to use a graph to solve problems by referring to the graphs on page 110 and asking:

- **Which year's membership does the bar graph represent?** *[1997]*

Follow Up For more practice solving problems, assign **Reteach 29.**

Student pairs may write answers and challenge their partners to find the question and the graph that represents them, or complete **Extend 29.**

Language Support

Students may wish to make a picture or write a phrase in their language next to the unknown words to help them go back and solve the assigned problems.

ESL **APPROPRIATE**

Part 2 Write and Share Problems

Chris Wellman used the data in the line graph to write a problem.

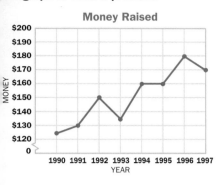

Money Raised

6 Explain how to solve Chris's problem using only words. **See below.**

7 **Write a problem** of your own that uses information from the graph. Explain how your problem and Chris's problem are alike and different. **For problems 7-9, see Teacher's Edition.**

8 Trade problems. Solve at least three problems written by your classmates.

9 What was the most interesting problem that you solved? Why?

Each year, the PTA raises money for science equipment. Which years did they raise the same amount of money?

Chris Wellman
Mandarin Oaks Elementary School
Jacksonville, FL

6. Possible answer: Compare the years to find which years of the graph have the line at the same height, then read the amount of money at that height on the graph.

Turn the page for Practice Strategies. ➡
Time, Data, and Graphs **111**

PART 2 WRITE AND SHARE PROBLEMS

Check Let students work in pairs to answer the questions given. For item 6, students may compare the slopes of the line segments between points. The line segment having the greatest slope will occur between two years where the increase in the amount of money earned is the greatest.

For item 7, have each student, rather than each pair, write a problem. Have pairs trade and solve each other's problems first. If necessary, students should revise their problems before trading them with other pairs.

Give students time to share some of the interesting problems they solved. Encourage them to describe what made the problems interesting.

3 Close

Have students discuss how they write their own problems. Have them compare the methods they used to solve each other's problems.

Practice See pages 112–113.

Gifted And Talented

Ask students to describe appropriate uses for each type of graph. Encourage students to generalize the types of data that could be displayed on each graph.

Inclusion

Some students may have difficulty reading across a graph. They may not be able to compare accurately the vertical scale to a point or a bar in the graph.

Have students use a ruler to guide their line of vision. The ruler can be placed so that it lines up a point or top of a bar with the vertical scale. This will allow students to make fewer mistakes when reading the value of a point or bar.

▶ **PART 3 PRACTICE STRATEGIES**
Materials have available: calculators

Students have the option of choosing any five problems from ex. 1–8, and any two problems from ex. 9–12.

- You may have students work in pairs to solve the problems. Tell students that they must solve at least one problem that their partner did not.
- Ex. 10 can be altered so that it describes the requirements of your state or school.
- For ex. 12, encourage students to use the graphing program to create more than one graph. After printing out the graphs, have students decide which graph best represents the data. Ask students to describe how they made their choices.

a **Algebra: Patterns** In ex. 8, students explore algebraic thinking by finding the pattern in money collected over consecutive months.

At the Computer If computers are not available, students may draw their graphs on poster board. You may wish to display their graphs around the classroom.

Math Van Students may use the Graph tool to create graphs of their survey.

---

2. No; possible answer: overestimate to get $3 1 $4 1 $1 5 $8, which is more than the actual amount.

Part 3 Practice Strategies

Choose five problems and solve them. Explain your methods.

1 Desmond caught the train at 10:34 A.M. He rode on the train for 1 hour 40 minutes. At what time did Desmond get off the train? **12:14 P.M.**

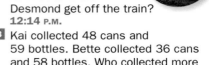

2 Tara buys a pen for $2.75, a notebook for $3.65, and a ruler for $0.98. Does she spend over $8.00? How do you know? **See above.**

3 Kai collected 48 cans and 59 bottles. Bette collected 36 cans and 58 bottles. Who collected more cans and bottles? How many more?

4 Hallie spends $9.53 on school supplies. She gives the clerk a $1 bill. What is the least number of coins she can receive as change?

5 coins—1 quarter, 2 dimes, 2 pennies

Kai; 12 cans and 1 bottle more

5 Joel's game scores are 1,243; 2,765; 3,142; 2,541; and 3,689. Pam's game scores are 2,165; 1,978; 3,047; 3,156; and 3,002. Who has the higher median score? By how much? **Pam; 237**

6 In Rio de Janeiro, Brazil, a crowd of 199,854 attended a World Cup soccer game in 1950. In 1990, about 180,000 attended a rock concert there. Which event had the greater attendance? By about how many more people? **soccer game; about 20,000 people**

7 Rory bought a coat for $160. He paid for it with 1 hundred-dollar bill and 6 ten-dollar bills. What other combinations of one-, ten-, and hundred-dollar bills could he have used? **Possible answer: 1 hundred-dollar bill, 60 one-dollar bills**

a **8** ALGEBRA: PATTERNS Rhonda collected $15 for a charity in the first month, $20 in the second month, and $25 in the third month. If she continues with this pattern, how much should she expect to collect in the fifth month? Explain. **$35; she collects $5 more each month.**

112 Lesson 3.9

Meeting Individual Needs

Early Finishers	**Gender Fairness**
As a way of reviewing the skills taught in this chapter, ask students to list the numbers of the exercises where a skill taught in Chapter 3 could be used to solve the problem. Have students describe the skills used.	Have girls read aloud their word problems, and then have boys solve them. Then alternate the roles.

Choose two problems and solve them. Explain your methods. Explanations may vary.

9 In the Chinese calendar, a year is named for one of 12 animals. After 12 years, the calendar starts at the first animal again. At the right is a chart of two 12-year cycles.

a. Which years between 1900 and 1999 are named after the monkey? **See above.**

b. For which animal is the year 2000 named? **dragon**

c. Karen was 14 years old in 1996. She was born in the year of the Dog. Tell how old she will be when it is the year of the Dog again. What year is that? **24 y old; 2006**

Rat	1864	1876
Ox	1865	1877
Tiger	1866	1878
Rabbit	1867	1879
Dragon	1868	1880
Snake	1869	1881
Horse	1870	1882
Goat	1871	1883
Monkey	1872	1884
Rooster	1873	1885
Dog	1874	1886
Pig	1875	1887

10 Plan the next school week for your class. Include the following in the schedule: **Check students' work.**
- ▶ at least 4 hours of mathematics classes
- ▶ 3 hours at most of reading and spelling every day
- ▶ at least two science classes
- ▶ two gym classes

Your schedule must have at least lunch and four classes on any day. No two classes can be scheduled for the same time in a day.

11 Suppose you have 26¢. Can you spend exactly this amount in the school store? How? Is there more than one way to spend exactly 26¢? If so, tell how.

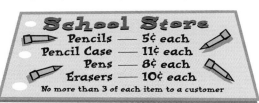

School Store
Pencils — 5¢ each
Pencil Case — 11¢ each
Pens — 8¢ each
Erasers — 10¢ each
No more than 3 of each item to a customer

11. Yes; possible answer: 1 eraser and 2 pens, 2 pencils and 2 pens, 1 pencil and 1 pencil case and 1 eraser, 3 pencils and 1 pencil case; yes; see list above.

12 **At the Computer** Choose a question to ask your classmates about some feature or topic that interests you. Ask ten classmates your question. Then use a graphing program to display their responses. Write a paragraph describing what the data tells you about your classmates.
Students may ask about favorite foods, sports, games, and so on.

Extra Practice, page 495

Alternate Teaching Strategy

Materials have available: graph paper

As a class, collect data on students' involvement in various clubs and groups. Ask each student to guess the number of members in each group to which he or she belongs. Invite several students to work together to make a graph on the chalkboard to display these data.

Ask students to get the necessary data and make a graph that shows the change in membership for their groups over five to ten years. Have the students draw their graphs on the chalkboard.

Have each member of the class write two or three problems using the data in the graphs on the chalkboard. Students should write the answers for the problems on another sheet of paper.

Collect all the problems and redistribute them so that no student receives his or her own questions. Students solve the problems they receive and check their answers with the authors of the problems when they are finished.

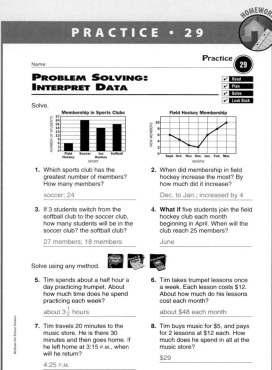

PRACTICE • 29

Name:

Practice **29**

PROBLEM SOLVING: INTERPRET DATA

☑ Read ☑ Plan ☑ Solve ☑ Look Back

Solve.

1. Which sports club has the greatest number of members? How many members?
soccer; 24

2. When did membership in field hockey increase the most? By how much did it increase?
Dec. to Jan.; increased by 4

3. If 3 students switch from the softball club to the soccer club, how many students will be in the soccer club? the softball club?
27 members; 18 members

4. What if five students join the field hockey club each month beginning in April. When will the club reach 25 members?
June

Solve using any method.

5. Tim spends about a half hour a day practicing trumpet. About how much time does he spend practicing each week?
about 3½ hours

6. Tim takes trumpet lessons once a week. Each lesson costs $12. About how much do his lessons cost each month?
about $48 each month

7. Tim travels 20 minutes to the music store. He is there 30 minutes and then goes home. If he left home at 3:15 P.M., when will he return?
4:25 P.M.

8. Tim buys music for $5, and pays for 2 lessons at $12 each. How much does he spend in all at the music store?
$29

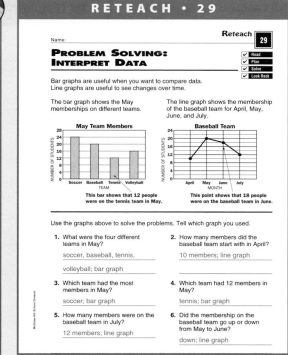

RETEACH • 29

Name:

Reteach **29**

PROBLEM SOLVING: INTERPRET DATA

☑ Read ☑ Plan ☑ Solve ☑ Look Back

Bar graphs are useful when you want to compare data.
Line graphs are useful to see changes over time.

The bar graph shows the May memberships on different teams.

The line graph shows the membership of the baseball team for April, May, June, and July.

This bar shows that 12 people were on the tennis team in May.

This point shows that 18 people were on the baseball team in June.

Use the graphs above to solve the problems. Tell which graph you used.

1. What were the four different teams in May?
soccer, baseball, tennis, volleyball; bar graph

2. How many members did the baseball team start with in April?
10 members; line graph

3. Which team had the most members in May?
soccer; bar graph

4. Which team had 12 members in May?
tennis; bar graph

5. How many members were on the baseball team in July?
12 members; line graph

6. Did the membership on the baseball team go up or down from May to June?
down; line graph

EXTEND • 29

Name:

Extend **29**

PROBLEM SOLVING

Nine to a Side

You need: 32 counters

This is what a square made up of 32 counters with 9 counters to a side would look like.

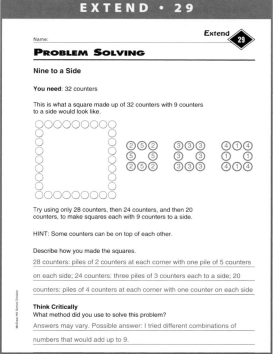

Try using only 28 counters, then 24 counters, and then 20 counters, to make squares each with 9 counters to a side.

HINT: Some counters can be on top of each other.

Describe how you made the squares.
28 counters: piles of 2 counters at each corner with one pile of 5 counters on each side; 24 counters: three piles of 3 counters each to a side; 20 counters: piles of 4 counters at each corner with one counter on each side

Think Critically
What method did you use to solve this problem?
Answers may vary. Possible answer: I tried different combinations of numbers that would add up to 9.

PURPOSE Review and assess the concepts, skills, and strategies that students have learned in the chapter.

Materials per student: calculator (optional)

Chapter Objectives

3A   Estimate, tell, and write time

3B   Find elapsed time and use a calendar or schedule

3C   Find the range, median, and mode of a set of data

3D   Read, interpret, organize, and display data

3E   Solve problems, including those that involve time, data, graphs, and working backward

Using the Chapter Review

The **Chapter Review** can be used as a review, practice test, or chapter test.

THINK CRITICALLY Ask students to compare the table and pictograph. Have students list ways in which the table and pictograph are similar or different. Students should compare the ease of using each of the graphs and describe the information that stands out in the graphs.

Language and Mathematics

Complete the sentence. Use a word in the chart. (pages 82–109)

1 An ■ describes the location of a point on a grid.
ordered pair

2 You can use a ■ to show changes in data over time.
line graph

3 The ■ is the middle number in an ordered set of data.
median

4 Five minutes after 12 noon is 12:05 ■. **P.M.**

Vocabulary

median

A.M.

P.M.

line plot

ordered pair

line graph

Concepts and Skills

8. 87, 368, none; difference between highest and lowest score is 87 points, 368 falls in the middle of the scores when ordered, no score is repeated

Complete. (page 84)

5 Start time: 2:15 P.M.
Elapsed time: 3 h 50 min
End time: ■ 6:05 P.M.

6 Start time: ■ 9:30 A.M.
Elapsed time: 4 h
End time: 1:30 P.M.

7 Start date: April 22
Elapsed time: ■ 23 d
End date: May 14

Find the range, median, and mode for the set of data. Tell how each number describes the data. (page 90)

8 Math scores
325   352   368   375   412
See above.

9 Height of seven students (in inches)
49   50   55   61   50   53   54
See below.

Use the map for ex. 10–15.

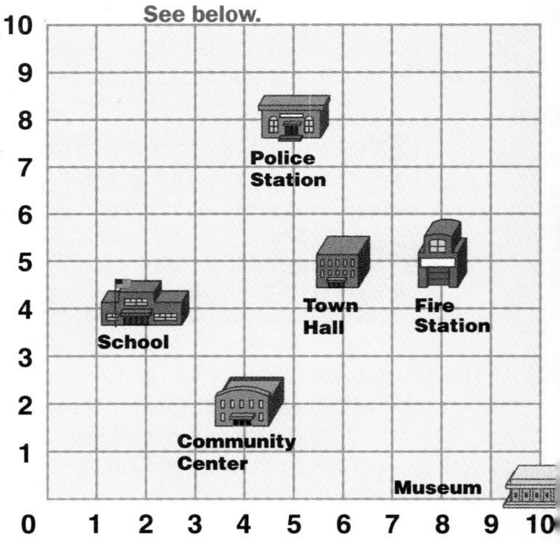

Find the ordered pair for the location. (page 104)

10 Town Hall **(6, 5)**

11 Museum **(10, 0)**

12 School **(2, 4)**

Tell what is found at the location. (page 104)

13 (4, 2) **Community Center**

14 (5, 8) **Police Station**

15 (8, 5) **Fire Station**

9. 12, 53, 50; the tallest student is 12 in. taller than the shortest student, at least half the students are 53 in. or taller, more students are 50 in. tall.

114 Chapter 3 Review

Reinforcement and Remediation

CHAPTER OBJECTIVES	CHAPTER REVIEW ITEMS	STUDENT BOOK PAGES		TEACHER'S EDITION PAGES		TEACHER RESOURCES
		Lesson	Midchapter Review	Activities	Alternate Teaching Strategy	Reteach
3A	4	82–83	96	81A	83	21
3B	5–7	84–87	96	83A	87	22
3C	3, 8–9	90–93	96	89A	93	24
3D	1, 2, 10–15	94–95, 100–109	96	93A, 99A, 103A, 105A	95, 103, 105, 109	25, 26, 27, 28
3E	16–20	88–89, 110–113		87A, 109C	89, 113	23, 29

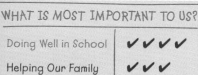

WHAT IS MOST IMPORTANT TO US?	
Doing Well in School	✔ ✔ ✔ ✔
Helping Our Family	✔ ✔ ✔
Staying Healthy	✔ ✔

✔ Stands for 3 votes

Two students voted for Staying Healthy.

Think critically. (page 110)

16 Analyze. Explain what mistake was made, then correct it. **See below.**

16. Possible answer: Did not use the key for the pictograph—6 students voted for staying healthy.

MIXED APPLICATIONS
Problem Solving Pencil & Paper / Calculator / Mental Math

(pages 88, 110)

Use the line graph for problems 17–20.

17 Which question can you *not* answer? Tell why.
  a. Was there any change in price of Super Digidisc from 1994 to 1999?
  b. In which year were the most number of Super Digidiscs sold?
  c. In which year was the price of Super Digidisc the greatest? the least? **b; the graph shows the price of the Digidisc, not the sales.**

18 Describe what happened to the price between 1994 and 1999. **See below.**

19 Between which two years was the greatest change in price? What was the change? Was it an increase or decrease? **1995 and 1996; $7; decrease**

Price of Super Digidisc

20 In 1998 Doreen bought a Digidisc. She used a coupon good for $2.50 off the price. How much did she pay? **$11.50**

18. Possible answer: The price rose between 1994 and 1995, fell to $19 in 1996, stayed at $19 until 1998, and then fell and kept falling after that.

Time, Data, and Graphs **115**

CHAPTER TEST

chapter test

PURPOSE Assess the concepts, skills, and strategies students have learned in this chapter.

Chapter Objectives
3A Estimate, tell, and write time
3B Find elapsed time and use a calendar or schedule
3C Find the range, median, and mode of a set of data
3D Read, interpret, organize, and display data
3E Solve problems, including those that involve time, data, graphs, and working backward

Using the Chapter Test

The **Chapter Test** can be used as a practice test, a chapter test, or as an additional review. The **Performance Assessment** on Student Book page 117 provides an alternate means of assessing students' understanding of time, data, and graphs.

Assessment Resources

TEST MASTERS

The Testing Program Blackline Masters provide three forms of the Chapter Test to assess students' understanding of the chapter concepts, skills, and strategies. Form C uses a free-response format. Forms A and B use a multiple-choice format.

COMPUTER TEST GENERATOR

The Computer Test Generator supplies abundant multiple-choice and free-response test items, which you may use to generate tests and practice work sheets tailored to the needs of your class.

TEACHER'S ASSESSMENT RESOURCES

Teacher's Assessment Resources provides resources for alternate assessment. It includes guidelines for Building a Portfolio, page 6, and the Holistic Scoring Guide, page 27.

Write each time in two ways.

1 Possible answers: 1:07, seven minutes after one

2 Possible answer: quarter to eight, seven forty-five

3  Possible answer: thirty minutes after four, four-thirty

Complete.

Start Time	Elapsed Time	End Time
4 1:15 P.M.	2 hours 55 minutes	■ 4:10 P.M.
5 9:55 A.M.	■ 1 h 20 min	11:15 A.M.
6 ■ May 15	30 days	June 13
7 September 13	29 days	■ October 11

Find the range, median, and mode for the set of data.

8 25, 15, 15
10, 15, 15

9 2, 3, 9, 3, 9
7, 3, 3 and 9

10 4, 4, 4, 4, 0
4, 4, 4

11 10, 15, 10, 18, 2
16, 10, 10

12 11, 6, 3, 3, 1
10, 3, 3

13 2, 49, 37, 19, 1, 11, 8
48, 11, none

Use the bar graph for ex. 14–16.

14 How many students were surveyed?
46 students

15 Which pet did students like least?
rat

16 How many more students chose the rat than chose the fish? **5 students**

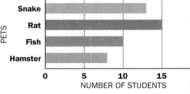

My Least Favorite Pet

Solve.

17 Sean wants to be at a party at 4 P.M. He takes 3 h to mow the lawn and 40 min to walk to the party. What is the latest time he can start mowing the lawn?
12:20 P.M.

18 If each ● stands for 4 balls in a pictograph, how many ● would you draw to show 38 balls?
$9\frac{1}{2}$ ●

19 Vern entered a number in his calculator. He added 23 and then subtracted 10 to get 28. What number did he start with? **15**

20 Rita bought a camera originally priced at $139.65. Because it was on sale, she saved $13.96. How much did she pay for the camera?
$125.69

116 Chapter 3 Test

Test Correlation

CHAPTER OBJECTIVES	TEST ITEMS	TEXT PAGES
3A	1–3	82–83
3B	4–7	84–87
3C	8–13	90–93
3D	14–16	94–95 100–109
3E	17–20	88–89 110–113

See Teacher's Assessment Resources for samples of student work.

What Did You Learn?   Check students' work.

Help Seymour write a report to his teacher about how he spends his time after school. Include the following:

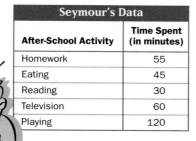

▶ A graph to display the data. Tell why you chose that type of graph. **See below.**

▶ At least three statements about the data and the graph that use the terms *range*, *median*, and *mode* when appropriate. **See below.**

▶ A description of how you spend your time after school. Tell how you would collect and display your data. **Check students' answers.**

Seymour's Data	
After-School Activity	Time Spent (in minutes)
Homework	55
Eating	45
Reading	30
Television	60
Playing	120

You will need
• graph paper

Question 1. Graphs may vary. Possible answer: A pictograph or bar graph shows the data most clearly.

•••••••••• **A Good Answer** ••••••••••
• includes an appropriate graph that is labeled correctly and shows the data accurately
• clearly describes the data using the terms *range*, *median*, or *mode* correctly

 You may want to place your work in your portfolio.

What Do You Think ❓
See Teacher's Edition.

1 Are you able to read and make graphs successfully? Why or why not?

2 What do you need to think about when you make a graph?
• What kind of graph is best for the data? **Question 2. Possible answer:**
• Is a symbol or key needed?   **The difference between the time spent**
• What scale will you use?   **playing and reading is 90 min—this is the**
• Other. Explain.   **range of Seymour's data, the median time Seymour spends on after-school activities is 55 min, Seymour spends a different amount of time doing each activity—there is no mode.**

Time, Data, and Graphs   **117**

Reviewing A Portfolio

Have students review their portfolios. Consider including these items:
• Finished work on the Chapter Project (p. 79F) or **Investigation** (pp. 98–99).
• Selected math journal entries, pp. 81, 91, 96, 107.
• Finished work on the nonroutine problem in **What Do You Know?** (p. 81) and problems from the Menu (pp. 112–113).
• Each student's self-selected "best piece" from work completed during the chapter. Have each student attach a note explaining why he or she chose that piece.
• Any work you or an individual student wishes to keep for future reference.

You may take this opportunity to conduct conferences with students. The Portfolio Analysis Form can help you report their progress. See Teacher's Assessment Resources, p. 33.

PURPOSE Review and assess the concepts, skills, and strategies learned in this chapter.

Materials have available: centimeter graph paper (TA 7)

Using the Performance Assessment

Have students read the problem and restate it in their own words. Make sure that they realize that the first and third problems have two parts.

Point out the section on the student page headed "A Good Answer." Make sure students understand that you use these points to evaluate their answers. Also, point out that they need to describe how they spend their time after school and tell how they would collect data about that time and display it.

Evaluating Student Work

As you read students' papers, look for the following:
• *Can the student select an appropriate graph to represent Seymour's data?*
• *Does the graph accurately represent Seymour's data?*
• *Can the student draw conclusions about Seymour's data, including conclusions about the range, median, and mode?*
• *Can the student create a good plan for collecting data about how he or she spends time after school?*

The Holistic Scoring Guide and annotated samples of students' work can be used to assess this task. See pages 27–32 and 37–72 in Teacher's Assessment Resources.

Using the Self-Assessment

What Do You Think? Assure students that there are no right or wrong answers. Tell them the emphasis is on what they think and how they justify their answers.

Follow-Up Interviews

These questions can be used to gain insight into students' thinking:
• **Why did you choose that type of graph?**
• **What would be a good title for your graph?**
• **What is your basis for this statement? (Ask as you point to one of the students' statements.)**
• **How did you find the range for the data? the median? the mode?**
• **What type of graph would be inappropriate for displaying Seymour's data? Why?**

OBJECTIVE Investigate heart rates in a math and science context.

Materials stopwatch or clock with a second hand

Resources graphing software, or Math Van Tools

Science

Cultural Connection Read the **Cultural Note.** Have students share experiences they have had in which they were examined with a stethoscope.

Explain that the word *aerobic* comes from a Greek word that means "with air." Aerobic exercise lasting for more than a few minutes allows the blood to supply increased amounts of oxygen (air) to the muscles and heart.

Discuss how exercise and heart rate are related. Ask:
- **How do you exercise?** *[Answers may vary.]*
- **How do you think your heart rate changes when you exercise?** *[Possible answer: It gets faster.]*

Point out that this happens because the muscles need more oxygen when working hard so the heart pumps more blood to deliver the oxygen.

Math

Divide the class into pairs. Each pair will be measuring heart rates for a total of 12 minutes.

Students will do the activity twice. First, one partner exercises and rests while the other takes his or her pulse and records the data. Then partners switch roles and repeat the activity.

Students can either make a double-line graph showing the results for both partners, or two different line graphs showing each partner's results.

For item 2 students may notice that their heart rates increase dramatically after a minute of exercise and then decrease during the rest periods.

Keeping the Beat

Aerobic exercise helps keep your muscles and heart in shape. Your heart pumps blood throughout your body. Each beat is a pumping action.

Your pulse matches each beat of your heart. By counting your pulse, you can discover how fast your heart beats. You can also see how exercise and rest affect your heart rate.

Flow of blood through the heart

▶ How does your breathing change when you exercise? your temperature? What other changes do you notice?
Possible answer: You breathe more rapidly; your temperature increases; you perspire and you feel tired.

2 ways to find your pulse (a) neck (b) wrist

118 Math • Science • Technology Connection

Extending The Activity

1. Have students experiment with how many minutes of exercise they need to reach their target heart rate. The target heart rate for 10-year-old children is between 163 and 194 beats per minute. Partners can work together to take each other's pulse after 1, 2, and 3 minutes of exercise, with intervals of rest between each period of timed exercise.

2. Students can experiment with exercise of different intensity to learn how it affects their heart rate. Make sure students are warmed up before attempting strenuous exercise.

2. Possible answer: Pulse increases right after exercise, slows down after a short rest, and returns to a steady rate after resting for a while.

Measure Your Heart Rate

Work with a partner to record your heart rates at rest and exercising.

Get Ready
- What exercises will you do?
- How will you keep time?
- How will you record your heart rates?

Rest for 2 minutes, then take your pulse for 10 seconds. After you take your pulse, do the following steps. Take your pulse for 10 seconds after each step.

Step 1 Exercise for 1 minute.
Step 2 Rest for 1 minute.
Step 3 Rest for another minute.

Repeat Steps 1, 2, and 3 two more times. Remember to take your pulse after each step.

When you are done, rest for a minute one final time. Then take your pulse for 10 seconds.

Use the data you collected for problems 1–2. Check students' work.

1 Make a line graph that shows your heart rate during the 10 minutes of exercise and rest.

2 Write about what your graph shows. **See above.**

At the Computer

3 Heart rates are usually given in beats per minute. Use a spreadsheet to change the heart rates for 10 seconds to heart rates for each minute. Then graph the data. (Hint: 60 seconds = 1 minute) **Check students' work.**

4 How is this graph similar to the one you made earlier? How is it different? **Similar—lines rise and fall together; different—labels and scales are different.**

Heart Rate During Exercise and Rest

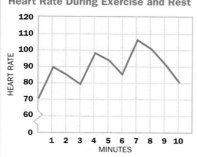

Technology

Students can multiply the heart rate by 6 to find the heart rate per minute. Have students use the data from the spreadsheet to create their graphs.

Students can use a graphing program to create their graphs.

 Math Van For problem 1, students may use the Graph tool to create line graphs of their heart rates. A project electronic teacher aid has been provided.

Interesting Facts

- **Heart rates vary widely among animals.** Animals with high heart rates include canaries (1,000 beats per minute) and shrews (1,200 beats per minute). Animals with low heart rates include elephants (25 beats per minute) and gray whales (8 beats per minute).

- **Whale's blood** can absorb more oxygen than the blood of mammals that live on land.

Bibliography

The Heart: Our Circulatory System, by Seymour Simon. New York: Morrow Junior Books, 1996. ISBN 0–688–11407–5.

Running a Race: How You Walk, Run, and Jump, by Steve Parker. New York: Franklin Watts, 1991, ISBN 0–531–14096–2.

Sportsworks: More Than Fifty Fun Games and Activities That Explore the Science of Sports, by Ontario Science Centre Staff. Reading, MA: Addison-Wesley Publishing Co., Inc., 1989, ISBN 0–201–15296–7.

CUMULATIVE REVIEW

PURPOSE Review and assess the concepts, skills, and strategies that students have learned this chapter.

Materials per student: calculators (optional)

Using the Cumulative Review

The **Cumulative Review** is presented in a multiple-choice format to provide practice in taking a standardized test.

Assessment Resources

TEST MASTERS

There are multiple-choice Cumulative Tests and a Year-End Test that provide additional opportunities for students to practice taking standardized tests.

COMPUTER GENERATOR

The Computer Generator supplies abundant multiple-choice and free-response test items, which you may use to generate tests and practice work sheets tailored to the needs of your class.

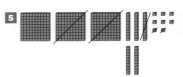

T E S T   P R E P A R A T I O N

Choose the letter of the best answer.

1 Which names the same number as 2,037? **B**

- **A** 200 + 30 + 7
- **B** 2,000 + 30 + 7
- **C** 2,000 + 300 + 7
- **D** 20,000 + 30 + 7

2 Which statement describes the graph on the number line below? **G**

50 51 52 53 54 55 56 57 58 59

- **F** All whole numbers greater than 55 and less than 57
- **G** All whole numbers greater than 54 and less than 58
- **H** All whole numbers greater than 54
- **J** All whole numbers less than 58

3 Pablo leaves home for school at 8:25 A.M. He arrives at school at 9:05 A.M. How long does it take Pablo to get to school from his home? **C**

- **A** 25 min
- **B** 30 min
- **C** 40 min
- **D** 35 min

4 What is Δ? **J**

$$3\Delta4$$
$$- 287$$
$$\overline{17}$$

- **F** 9
- **G** 5
- **H** 3
- **J** 0

5

Which subtraction is shown? **C**

- **A** 212 2 146
- **B** 358 2 146
- **C** 358 2 212
- **D** not here

6 Ian collects 179 cans. Sal collects 131 cans. Which is the best estimate of how many cans they both collect? **J**

- **F** 30
- **G** 100
- **H** 200
- **J** 300

7 Marsha has an hour to use her computer before bedtime. She plays a game for 10 minutes. Then, she writes a math report for 25 minutes. How much computer time does she have left? **C**

- **A** 15 min
- **B** 35 min
- **C** 25 min
- **D** 30 min

8 If each * stands for 2 dogs, how can you show 12 dogs? **H**

- **F** * *
- **G** * * *
- **H** * * * * * *
- **J** * * * * * * * * * * * *

Cumulative Review Correlation

REVIEW ITEMS	TEXT PAGES	REVIEW ITEMS	TEXT PAGES
1	8–11	11	44–45
2	12–13	12	88–89
3	84–87	13	90–93
4	58–59	14	20–23
5	62–63	15, 16	100–103
6	46–47		
7	66–67		
8	94–95		
9	40–41		
10	8–11		

★ ★

9 Paul has $0.77. Which group of coins can he *not* have? **B**

A 7 dimes, 1 nickel, 2 pennies
B 6 dimes, 4 nickels, 2 pennies
C 1 quarter, 5 dimes, 2 pennies
D 3 quarters, 2 pennies

10 Which number is 1 thousand more than 565,400? **H**

F 665,400
G 575,400
H 566,400
J not given

11 Complete the sentence.
96 + ■ = 163 **C**

A 259
B 76
C 67
D 29

12 Lea has $15 at the end of the week. During the week she took out $5 and put in $3. Which method could you use to find how much money she had at the beginning of the week? **H**

F Add $3 to $15 then subtract $5
G Subtract $5 from $15 then add $3
H Subtract $3 from $15 then add $5
J Add $5 and $3 to $15

13 Which set of data has a mode of 54? **C**

A 50, 89, 104, 54, 76
B 49, 51, 55, 56, 54
C 23, 54, 67, 54, 58
D 48, 60, 53, 55, 54

14 What is 75,514 rounded to the nearest thousand? **G**

F 80,000
G 76,000
H 75,000
J 70,000

Use the bar graph for problems 15–16.

Number of Visitors to the Sports Center

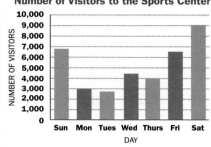

15 Which statement describes the bar graph? **B**

A The Sports Center is more popular than the mall.
B More visitors go to the center on Saturday than on any other day.
C Most children enjoy the center.
D Discount tickets are sold on Wednesdays.

16 How many more visitors were there on Friday than on Monday? **F**

F 3,500
G 3,000
H 6,500
J 9,500

Time, Data, and Graphs **121**

T E S T P R E P A R A T I O N

CHAPTER 4 AT A GLANCE:

Theme: Sports   Suggested Pacing: 14–17 Days

Multiplication and Division Facts

WEEK ONE

DAY 1 — PREASSESSMENT

Introduction pp. 122

What Do You Know? p. 123

CHAPTER OBJECTIVES: 4A–C, 4D, 4E

RESOURCES   Read-Aloud Anthology pp. 18–19
Pretest: Test Master Form A, B, or C
Diagnostic Inventory

Portfolio   Journal   **NCTM STANDARDS:** 1, 2, 3, 4, 7, 8

DAY 2 — LESSON 4.1

EXPLORE ACTIVITY

Meaning of Multiplication pp. 124–127

CHAPTER OBJECTIVES: 4A

MATERIALS   spinners (TA 2), counters (TA 13), centimeter graph paper (TA 7), number lines (TA 14)

RESOURCES   Reteach/Practice/Extend: 30
Math Center Cards: 30
Extra Practice: 496

Daily Review TE p. 123B

Algebraic Thinking

Technology Link   **NCTM STANDARDS:** 4, 7, 8

DAY 3 — LESSON 4.2

MENTAL MATH

2 Through 5 as Factors pp. 128–131

CHAPTER OBJECTIVES: 4A

MATERIALS   centimeter graph paper (TA 7), number lines (TA 14)

RESOURCES   Reteach/Practice/Extend: 31
Math Center Cards: 31
Extra Practice: 496

Daily Review TE p. 127B

Algebraic Thinking

Technology Link   **NCTM STANDARDS:** 8

WEEK TWO

LESSON 4.5

PROBLEM-SOLVING STRATEGY

Find a Pattern pp. 138–139

CHAPTER OBJECTIVES: 4E

MATERIALS   connecting cubes

RESOURCES   Reteach/Practice/Extend: 34
Math Center Cards: 34
Extra Practice: 497

Daily Review TE p. 137B

Algebraic Thinking

Technology Link   **NCTM STANDARDS:** 1, 2, 3, 4, 8, 13

LESSON 4.6

Three Factors pp. 140–141

CHAPTER OBJECTIVES: 4A, 4C

MATERIALS   counters (TA 13), calculators (opt.)

RESOURCES   Reteach/Practice/Extend: 35
Math Center Cards: 35
Extra Practice: 497

Daily Review TE p. 139B

Algebraic Thinking

Technology Link   **NCTM STANDARDS:** 8

MIDCHAPTER ASSESSMENT

Midchapter Review p. 142

CHAPTER OBJECTIVES: 4A, 4C, 4E

MATERIALS   calculators (opt.)

Developing Algebra Sense p. 143

MATERIALS   counters (TA 13), number lines (TA 14)

REAL-LIFE INVESTIGATION:

Applying Multiplication Facts pp. 144–145

Portfolio   Journal   **NCTM STANDARDS:** 1, 2, 3, 4, 8, 13

WEEK THREE

LESSON 4.9

6 Through 9 as Divisors pp. 152–153

CHAPTER OBJECTIVES: 4B

MATERIALS   balls, calculators (opt.)

RESOURCES   Reteach/Practice/Extend: 38
Math Center Cards: 38
Extra Practice: 498

Daily Review TE p. 151B

Technology Link   **NCTM STANDARDS:** 8

LESSON 4.10

Fact Families pp. 154–155

CHAPTER OBJECTIVES: 4D

MATERIALS   calculators (opt.)

RESOURCES   Reteach/Practice/Extend: 39
Math Center Cards: 39
Extra Practice: 499

TEACHING WITH TECHNOLOGY
Alternate Lesson TE pp. 155A–155B

Daily Review TE p. 153B

Algebraic Thinking

Technology Link   **NCTM STANDARDS:** 4, 8, 13

LESSON 4.11

EXPLORE ACTIVITY

Remainders pp. 156–157

CHAPTER OBJECTIVES: 4B

MATERIALS   counters (TA 13), cm graph paper (TA 7), geoboard (TA 15)

RESOURCES   Reteach/Practice/Extend: 40
Math Center Cards: 40
Extra Practice: 499

Daily Review TE p. 155D

Technology Link   **NCTM STANDARDS:** 4, 8

LESSON 4.3

MENTAL MATH

6 and 8 as Factors pp. 132–133

CHAPTER OBJECTIVES: 4A, 4C

MATERIALS counters (TA 13), calculators (opt.)

RESOURCES Reteach/Practice/Extend: 32
Math Center Cards: 32
Extra Practice: 496

Daily Review TE p. 131B

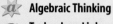 Algebraic Thinking

Technology Link

NCTM STANDARDS:
8

LESSON 4.7

EXPLORE ACTIVITY

Meaning of Division pp. 146–149

CHAPTER OBJECTIVES: 4B

MATERIALS counters (TA 13), pennies, connecting cubes, cm graph paper (TA 7), cm dot paper (TA 9)

RESOURCES Reteach/Practice/Extend: 36
Math Center Cards: 36
Extra Practice: 498

Daily Review TE p. 145B

 Algebraic Thinking

Technology Link

NCTM STANDARDS:
4, 7, 8

LESSON 4.12

PROBLEM SOLVERS AT WORK

Choose the Operation pp. 158–161

CHAPTER OBJECTIVES: 4E

MATERIALS calculators (opt.)

RESOURCES Reteach/Practice/Extend: 41
Math Center Cards: 41
Extra Practice: 499

Daily Review TE p. 157B

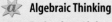 Algebraic Thinking

Technology Link

NCTM STANDARDS:
1, 2, 3, 4, 8

LESSON 4.4

MENTAL MATH

7 and 9 as Factors pp. 134–137

CHAPTER OBJECTIVES: 4A

MATERIALS calculators (opt.)

RESOURCES Reteach/Practice/Extend: 33
Math Center Cards: 33
Extra Practice: 497

Daily Review TE p. 133B

 Algebraic Thinking

 Journal

Technology Link

NCTM STANDARDS:
8

LESSON 4.8

2 Through 5 as Divisors pp. 150–151

CHAPTER OBJECTIVES: 4B

MATERIALS counters (TA 13), pennies, connecting cubes, calculators (opt.)

RESOURCES Reteach/Practice/Extend: 37
Math Center Cards: 37
Extra Practice: 498

Daily Review TE p. 149B

 Journal

 Technology Link

NCTM STANDARDS:
8

CHAPTER ASSESSMENT

Chapter Review pp. 162–163

MATERIALS calculators (opt.)

Chapter Test p. 164

RESOURCES Posttest: Test Master Form A, B, or C

Performance Assessment p. 165

RESOURCES Performance Task: Test Master

Math • Science • Technology Connection pp. 166–167

Technology Link

 Portfolio

NCTM STANDARDS:
1, 4, 8

Assessment Options

FORMAL

Chapter Tests

STUDENT BOOK
- Midchapter Review, p. 142
- Chapter Review, pp. 162–163
- Chapter Test, p. 164

BLACKLINE MASTERS
- Test Master Form A, B, or C
- Diagnostic Inventory

COMPUTER TEST GENERATOR
- Available on disk

Performance Assessment
- What Do You Know? p. 123
- Performance Assessment, p. 165
- Holistic Scoring Guide, Teacher's Assessment Resources, pp. 27–32
- Follow-Up Interviews, p. 165
- Performance Task, Test Masters

Teacher's Assessment Resources
- Portfolio Guidelines and Forms, pp. 6–9, 33–35
- Holistic Scoring Guide, pp. 27–32
- Samples of Student Work, pp. 37–72

INFORMAL

Ongoing Assessment
- Observation Checklist, pp. 124, 132, 134, 146, 156
- Interview, pp. 128, 140, 152
- Anecdotal Report, pp. 138, 150, 154, 158

Portfolio Opportunities
- Chapter Project, p. 121F
- What Do You Know? p. 123
- Investigation, pp. 144–145
- Journal Writing, pp. 123, 135, 142, 150
- Performance Assessment, p. 165
- Self-Assessment: What Do You Think? p. 165

Chapter Objectives		Standardized Test Correlations
4A	Multiply, facts to 81	MAT, CAT, SAT, ITBS, CTBS, TN*
4B	Divide, facts to 81	MAT, CAT, SAT, ITBS, CTBS, TN*
4C	Use the Order, Identify, Zero, and Grouping properties	MAT, CAT, SAT, ITBS, CTBS, TN*
4D	Use inverse operations to identify fact families and find missing factors	SAT, TN*
4E	Solve problems, including those that involve multiplication and division and patterns	MAT, CAT, SAT, ITBS, CTBS, TN*

*Terra Nova

NCTM Standards Grades K–4

1 Problem Solving	8 Whole Number Computation
2 Communication	9 Geometry and Spatial Sense
3 Reasoning	10 Measurement
4 Connections	11 Statistics and Probability
5 Estimation	12 Fractions and Decimals
6 Number Sense and Numeration	13 Patterns and Relationships
7 Concepts of Whole Number Operations	

MULTIPLICATION AND DIVISION FACTS

Meeting Individual Needs

LEARNING STYLES

- **AUDITORY/LINGUISTIC**
- LOGICAL/ANALYTICAL
- **VISUAL/SPATIAL**
- **MUSICAL**
- **KINESTHETIC**
- **SOCIAL**
- **INDIVIDUAL**

Students who are talented in art, language, and physical activity may better understand mathematical concepts when these concepts are connected to their areas of interest. Use the following activity to stimulate the different learning styles of some of your students.

Logical/Analytical Learners

Make up logic puzzles with multiplication and division.

What is my product?
My product is an odd number.
It is between 50 and 60.
One of my factors is 11.
The other factor is 5.

What is my quotient?
My quotient is less than 15.
My divisor is 5.
My dividend is 50.

See Lesson Resources, pp. 123A, 127A, 131A, 133A, 137A, 139A, 145A, 149A, 151A, 153A, 155C, 157A.

GIFTED AND TALENTED

Students who are able can do comparison problems involving multiplication and division. This will help them review the facts and develop thinking skills.

8×4	4×9
$24 \div 8$	4×5
7×6	3×9

Problems on each line can be either multiplication, division, or a combination of both. Have students circle the problem that has the larger product or quotient. If the products or quotients are the same, students can circle both. Encourage students to see if they can guess which answer is larger without having to solve either side. Ask them to explain their thinking.

See also Meeting Individual Needs, pp. 124, 135, 147.

EXTRA SUPPORT

Some students may need to use counters or to draw arrays throughout the chapter activities. As students gain confidence in their recall of multiplcation facts, they will rely less and less frequently on these concrete and pictorial models.

Specific suggestions for ways to provide extra support to students appear in every lesson in this chapter.

See Meeting Individual Needs, pp. 124, 128, 132, 134, 138, 140, 146, 150, 152, 154, 156, 158.

EARLY FINISHERS

Students who finish their class work early can create practice timed tests to help players prepare for the Math Tournament. Students write tests that can be completed in one minute by another student. Tests can be written on index cards with the answers on the back of the card which can be left in a central place for practice. (See *Chapter Project*, p. 121F.)

See also Meeting Individual Needs, pp. 126, 130, 132, 136, 138, 140, 148, 150, 152, 154, 156, 158, 160.

LANGUAGE SUPPORT

When reading word problems, be sure to speak slowly and clearly. Use pictures, drawings, actions, or gestures to help students understand the content of the problems.

Pair students acquiring English with fluent speakers to work on word problems. Encourage students to verbalize multiplication and division facts.

See also Meeting Individual Needs, pp. 128, 146, 160.

ESL ▸ APPROPRIATE

INCLUSION

- **For inclusion ideas, information, and suggestions, see pp. 125, 129, 136, T15.**
- **For gender fairness tips, see pp. 159, T15.**

USING MANIPULATIVES

Building Understanding Students can use multiplication and division fact cards to practice facts and develop thinking skills. Cards can be used to play games, such as "Fact Families."

Students can work in pairs. Separate and sort the multiplication and division cards. Students have to find multiplication and division cards that are related. When they find the matches, they say "Fact Family." Students playing will write the related facts on a recording sheet.

Easy-to-Make Manipulatives Have students write out multiplication and division facts on blank index cards. Store cards in plastic bags for easy distribution and collection.

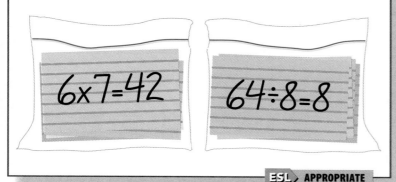

$6 \times 7 = 42$ $64 \div 8 = 8$

ESL APPROPRIATE

USING COOPERATIVE LEARNING

Pairs Compare This strategy develops teamwork by bringing students together to compare their work.

- **Students work individually to solve a problem.**
- **Students meet with a partner to compare ideas.**
- **Two sets of partners (pairs) join together to compare their strategies, methods, or answers.**

USING LITERATURE

Use the article *Amazing Kids!* to introduce the chapter theme, Sports. This article is reprinted on pages 18–19 of the Read-Aloud Anthology.

Also available in the Read-Aloud Anthology is the story *Sea Squares*, page 20.

MULTIPLICATION AND DIVISION FACTS

Linking Technology

This integrated package of programs and services allows students to explore, develop, and practice concepts; solve problems; build portfolios; and assess their own progress. Teachers can enhance instruction, provide remediation, and share ideas with other educational professionals.

CD-ROM ACTIVITY

In *Sports Day*, students use counters to help organize players into sports teams. Students can use the online notebook to write about the different ways to divide numbers. To extend the activity, students use the Math Van tools to formulate their own division problems. **Available on CD-ROM.**

CD-ROM TOOLS

Students can use Math Van's counters to explore multiplication and division facts. The Tech Links on the Lesson Resources pages highlight opportunities for students to use this and other tools such as graphs, tables, online notes, and calculator to provide additional practice, reteaching, or extension. **Available on CD-ROM.**

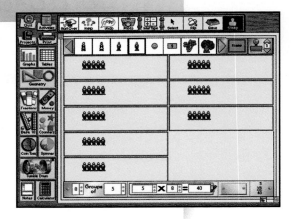

WEB SITE   http://www.mhschool.com

Teachers can access the McGraw-Hill School Division World Wide Web site for additional curriculum support at http://www.mhschool.com. Click on our Resource Village for specially designed activities linking Web sites to multiplication and division. Motivate children by inviting them to explore Web sites that develop the chapter theme of "Sports." Exchange ideas on classroom management, cultural diversity, and other areas in the Math Forum.

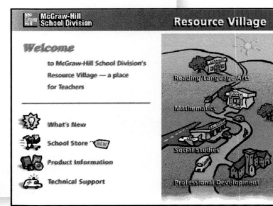

Chapter Project TOURNAMENT TIME

Highlighting the Math

- design a schedule
- create a scoring system
- reinforce multiplication and division facts

1 Starting the Project ESL APPROPRIATE

Introduce the idea of a Math Tournament, explaining that students will play Math Baseball using game boards they make. A flash-card captain will display multiplication and division flash cards and the batter will try to complete them correctly.

Sample rules: Each batter gets one chance for a hit. An incorrect answer is an out. After two outs, the next team is up. After five innings, the team with the most runs wins. In case of a tie, play another inning.

Assign students to teams of 4 or 5 and designate a score keeper and a flash-card captain for each team. Consider how family or community members may participate.

2 Continuing the Project

- Students work in groups, creating baseball-diamond game boards on pieces of sturdy paper. Each group member obtains a button to use as a marker. Within a group, colors of buttons should not be duplicated.
- Each group chooses a name and creates its own scoring chart.

3 Finishing the Project

Hold the Math Baseball Tournament. The flash-card captain stands beside his or her team and displays the multiplication and division fact cards, one at a time. Decide upon a way to determine the order in which teams play each other. After the first round, the winning teams play each other. Continue in this manner until one team is declared the grand winner.

BUILDING A PORTFOLIO

Each student's portfolio should include a photograph of the schedule display and a summary of his or her role in playing the game. The portfolio should also contain any facts that the student needs to study more.

To assess students' work, refer to the Holistic Scoring Guide on page 27 in the Teacher's Assessment Resources.

PURPOSE Introduce the theme of the chapter.

Resources Read-Aloud Anthology, pages 18–19

Using Literature

Read "Amazing Kids!" from the Read-Aloud Anthology to introduce the chapter theme, "Sports."

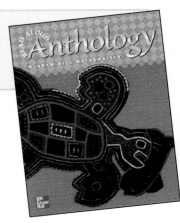

Developing the Theme

Encourage students to tell about the sports they participate in or enjoy watching. Students may describe school sports, after-school activities, or professional sports.

Ask students to suggest ways of organizing a class list of different sports. Students may suggest grouping the sports into team and individual sports; by professional and amateur sports; or by Olympic and non-Olympic sports.

These sports are discussed in this chapter:

Street hockey	pp. 124–127
Basketball	pp. 128–131, 138–139
Field hockey	pp. 132–133
Ice hockey	pp. 132–133
Gymnastics	pp. 134–137
Table tennis	pp. 138–139
Football	pp. 138–139
Soccer	pp. 138–139, 156–157
Baseball	pp. 140–141, 149
Running	pp. 146–149, 152–153, 158–161
Rafting	pp. 150–151
Swimming	pp. 154–155

On pages 144–145, students will explore rules in sports.

CHAPTER 4

MULTIPLICATION AND DIVISION FACTS

THEME   Sports

Different sports are played around the world. In this chapter, you will learn how you can use math to help solve sports problems and to understand sports rules.

122

Chapter Bibliography

Arnold's Fitness for Kids: A Guide to Health, Exercise, and Nutrition by Arnold Schwarzenegger with Charles Gaines. New York: Doubleday, 1993. ISBN 0–385–42267–9.

Jackie Joyner Kersee: Super Woman by Margaret J. Goldstein and Jennifer Larson. Minneapolis: Lerner Publications, 1993. ISBN 0–8225–0524–X.

Community Involvement

Have students make a map of the community that highlights sports arenas, ball fields, and other recreational facilities. Students can work in groups to research the recreational sites and make a poster that includes all sites and contact information. Then reproduce it and distribute it to community centers and/or to the facilities listed on the map.

2. Possible answers: List the racers in order of the time they started, show the time they finished and their race time.

What Do You Know

1. 3 Groups of 4 caps; 12 caps; possible answers: added 3 fours, found 3×4.

Michael collects sports caps and puts them on his wall.

1 How are the caps arranged? How many caps are there? Explain how you found the answer. See above.

2 **What if** the caps were arranged in two equal rows. How many caps would be in each row? Explain. 6 caps; 2 groups of 6 is 12.

3 Think about arranging 24 caps in equal rows on a wall. Draw as many different ways as you can to arrange them.

 Sequence of Events **Four runners begin a race at the same time. Tyler is the winner. Cora gets second prize, and Ana gets third. Ryan plans to do better next time. In what sequence did these runners finish?**

When you read, it helps to understand the sequence, or order, of the events. Sometimes authors give you sequence words to help you understand. Sometimes they don't.

1 What sequence word would you choose for each runner? Tyler—first; Cora—next or second; Ana—then or third; Ryan—last or fourth

2 How could you use a table or diagram to show race results? See above.

Vocabulary

array, p. 125	**Commutative**	**divisor,** p. 146
factor, p. 125	**Property,** p. 140	**quotient,** p. 146
product, p. 125	**Associative**	**fact family,** p. 154
skip-count, p. 128	**Property,** p. 140	**remainder,** p. 157
multiple, p. 128	**dividend,** p. 146	

Multiplication and Division Facts **123**

 ## Reading, Writing, Arithmetic

Sequence of Events Ask students to write five things they have done so far today. Once they have their list, have them go back and number the events in the order in which they happened. Have students relate the events in order to partners who record the sequence of the events and any signal words used by the students. Partners trade roles and continue.

Vocabulary

 Students may record new words in their journals. Encourage them to show examples and draw diagrams to help tell what the words mean.

• Draw a picture to show the product 2×3 and the quotient $8 \div 2$.

$2 \times 3 = 6$ $8 \div 2 = 4$

PURPOSE Assess students' ability to apply prior knowledge of the meaning of multiplication and division.

Materials have available: counters, calculators (optional)

Assessing Prior Knowledge

Ask students to give examples of problems that can be solved by multiplying or dividing. Include students' examples in a table like the one below.

PROBLEMS THAT CAN BE SOLVED BY

Multiplying	Dividing
Sue bought 5 books for $3 each. How much did they cost altogether?	I have 12 cookies. I am going to split them evenly among 4 children. How many will each get?
Ted has 6 shells. Maria has 4 times as many shells as Ted. How many does Maria have?	I have 20 cookies. How many children can I give 4 cookies to?
Suppose you plant 3 rows of tomato plants with 5 plants in each row. How many have you planted altogether?	Jim has $5. Mary has $15 dollars. How many times as much money as Jim does Mary have?

Encourage students to use whatever methods they wish to answer items 1–3. Observe them as they work. Look at the drawings that students make for item 3.

BUILDING A PORTFOLIO

 Item 3 can be used as a benchmark to show where students are in their understanding of multiplication and division.

A Portfolio Checklist for Students and a Checklist for Teachers are provided in Teacher's Assessment Resources, pp. 33–34.

Prerequisite Skills

• *Do students know when to add and when to multiply?*
• *Do students know when to subtract and when to divide?*
• *Can students recognize multiplication and division representations?*

Assessment Resources

DIAGNOSTIC INVENTORY

Use this blackline master to assess prerequisite skills that students will need in order to be successful in this chapter.

TEST MASTERS

Use the multiple choice format (form A or B) or the free response format (form C) as a pretest of the skills in this chapter.

LESSON 4.1

EXPLORE ACTIVITY

Meaning of Multiplication

OBJECTIVE Explore multiplication using models.

RESOURCE REMINDER
Math Center Cards 30
Practice 30, Reteach 30, Extend 30

SKILLS TRACE

GRADE 3	• Explore making equal groups to find a total and separating a total into equal groups. *(Chapter 6)*
GRADE 4	• Explore multiplication using models.
GRADE 5	• Use mental math strategies to multiply whole numbers and decimals by multiples of 10, 100, and 1,000. *(Chapter 4)*

WARM-UP

Cooperative Pairs   **Logical/Analytical**

OBJECTIVE Skip-count by twos, threes, fives, and tens.

Materials per group: calculator

► Each team sits in a circle. They determine the order and direction of play, and choose a referee.

► For the first round, students skip-count by twos to 100. The referee uses a calculator to count along with the team. He or she determines when a mistake is made and records the last number counted correctly.

► Teams repeat the game, counting by threes, then fives, then tens.

► After every team has completed the four rounds, have teams compare their results. Discuss which number was easiest to skip-count.

ART CONNECTION

Whole Class   **Visual/Spatial**

OBJECTIVE Represent a number by showing equal groups of objects.

Materials per student: macaroni, glue, construction paper

► Students count the macaroni by making equal groups of numbers less than 10.

► Students glue their groups on construction paper. Suggest that they arrange their groups to create a piece of art.

► On a separate sheet of paper, students describe how they grouped the items to make them easier to count and how they found the total.

► Students may repeat the activity, grouping a different way.

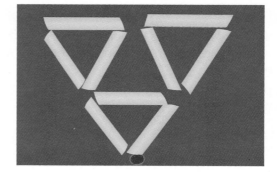

Daily Review

PREVIOUS DAY QUICK REVIEW

Heights (in inches) of students:
55, 39, 65, 35, 59, 46, 39.

1. What is the range? *[30]*

2. What is the median? *[46]*

3. What is the mode? *[39]*

FAST FACTS

1. 3 + 3 *[6]*

2. 5 + 7 *[12]*

3. 8 + 2 *[10]*

4. 5 + 6 *[11]*

Problem of the Day • 30

Penny's pet hamster had eight babies. How many possible combinations of male and female hamsters are there? *[9: all female; all male; 7 females, 1 male; 6 females, 2 males; 5 females, three males; 7 males, 1 female; 6 males, 2 females; 5 males, 3 females; 4 males, 4 females]*

TECH LINK

ONLINE EXPLORATION

Use our Web-linked activities and lesson plans to connect your students to the real world of sports.

MATH FORUM

Idea I have pairs of students use calculators to find products of greater numbers. Students record the multiplication sentence, look for patterns, and make and test their predictions.

Visit our Resource Village at http://www.mhschool.com to access the Online Exploration and the Math Forum.

MATH CENTER

Practice

OBJECTIVE Use counters to find a product.

Materials per student: number cube, counters, Math Center Recording Sheet (TA 31 optional)

Students generate factors by throwing a number cube. They put out sets of counters to find the product. *[Check students' work.]*

PRACTICE ACTIVITY 30

MATH CENTER
Partners

Manipulatives • Talking Times

YOU NEED
- number cube
- counters

1. One player rolls the number cube once to find how many groups to make and a second time to find the size of each group.
2. The second player makes the groups and says the multiplication sentence that describes the counters. Include the product.
3. Write the multiplication sentence.
4. Trade tasks and repeat the activity several times.

Chapter 4, Lesson 1, pages 124–127

Multiplication

NCTM Standards

✓ Problem Solving
✓ Communication
✓ Reasoning
Connections

ESL APPROPRIATE

Problem Solving

OBJECTIVE Use reasoning to unscramble multiplication facts.

Materials per student: slips of blank paper, Math Center Recording Sheet (TA 31 optional)

Students unscramble eight multiplication sentences, whose factors and products are all mixed up. Then they explain how they did it. *[8 × 3 = 24; 3 × 5 = 15; 6 × 7 = 42; 3 × 2 = 6; 2 × 9 = 18; 2 × 2 = 4; 4 × 2 = 8; 4 × 5 = 20. Possible answer: I wrote each number on a separate slip of paper and used the slips to test different number combinations.]*

PROBLEM-SOLVING ACTIVITY 30

MATH CENTER
On Your Own

Decision Making • Mix and Match

YOU NEED
- slips of blank paper
- counters

The factors in the 8 multiplication problems below are all jumbled up. Switch the factors around until they match the products.

3 × 7 = 6	5 × 9 = 15
2 × 2 = 8	2 × 2 = 20
3 × 4 = 42	6 × 5 = 24
4 × 2 = 4	8 × 3 = 18

Explain how you solved the problem. You may want to use counters to help you.

Chapter 4, Lesson 1, pages 124–127

Multiplication

NCTM Standards

✓ Problem Solving
✓ Communication
Reasoning
Connections

Lesson 4.1 *continued*

EXPLORE ACTIVITY
Meaning of Multiplication

OBJECTIVE Explore multiplication using models.

Materials per pair: 0–9 spinner (TA 2), counters, centimeter graph paper (TA 7)

Vocabulary array, factor, product

 **1 Introduce**

Present this problem:

> A sporting goods company packages table tennis balls in 3s. How many balls are in 2 packages?

- **How could you solve this problem?** *[Possible answers: Multiply 3 by 2, skip-count by 3.]*

 **2 Teach**   *Cooperative Pairs*

▶ **LEARN Work Together** Copy the table on page 124 onto the chalkboard. Ask a student to help you demonstrate the activity. Spin the spinner. Ask:
- **How many 1-packs were ordered?** *[Answers may vary according to the number on the spinner.]*

Have the volunteer write the number in the table.
- **What do you need to do to find the total number of hockey pucks that were ordered?** *[Multiply.]*
- **How many pucks were ordered?** *[Answers may vary.]*

Have the volunteer write the number of balls in the table.

Talk It Over Allow pairs to present their methods and tell why they prefer them. Then have pairs compare their choices for ease of use, accuracy, and efficiency.
- **Why is the total for three 5-packs the same as the total for five 3-packs?** *[Possible answer: Because you are using the same numbers to multiply each time—5 and 3.]*

Meaning of Multiplication

Some day, you may have your own business. Suppose your company custom packages brightly colored street-hockey pucks. You offer these five packages.

Work Together
Work with a partner to fill orders for hockey pucks.

Spin the spinner to get the number of 1-packs you need to fill. Your partner may use counters or graph paper to find the total number of pucks needed to fill the order.

You will need
- 0–9 spinner
- counters
- graph paper

Take turns spinning to fill two more orders for 1-packs. Then work together to fill three orders for 2-packs, 3-packs, 4-packs, and 5-packs.

Record your work in a table like the one shown.

Number of Packs Ordered	Number in Each Pack	Total
3	1	3
0	1	0

Talk It Over
- ▶ What method did you use to find the totals? Explain. **Methods may vary. Possible answers: Used counters to show pucks and added, skip-counted.**
- ▶ **What if** you have an order for three 5-packs and another order for five 3-packs. What do you notice about the totals? **The total for both orders is the same.**
- ▶ Find the total for six 4-packs. Predict the total for four 6-packs. Explain your reasoning. Then check your prediction. **24 pucks; 24 pucks; possible answer: switching the number of packs and the number in each pack does not change the total.**

124 Lesson 4.1

Meeting Individual Needs

Extra Support

Some students may wish to think of multiplication as repeated addition. Have them write the number of counters in each stack, put an addition sign between each stack, and then add to find the total.

ESL ▶ APPROPRIATE

Gifted And Talented

Challenge students to find patterns in multiplication sentences with 2, 5, and 10 as factors.

Ongoing Assessment

Observation Checklist Determine whether students understand how to write and find multiplication facts by observing them as they write facts for pictures that show multiplication.

Follow Up Encourage students having difficulty with multiplication to use counters to show packs of pucks, then to skip-count to find the totals. For more practice with finding products, assign **Reteach 30.**

Assign **Extend 30** to those students who need a challenge.

Possible answer: zero property—the product of any number and 0 is 0; property of one—the product of any number and 1 is the number

Make Connections
You can make an array to show 9 groups of 4.

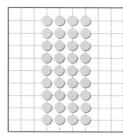

Number of Packs Ordered	Number in Each Pack	Total
9	4	36

You can also write a multiplication sentence.

Write: 9 × 4 = 36   9
             ↑   ↑   ↑   or × 4
          factor factor product   36

Read: 9 times 4 is equal to 36.

> Write number sentences that have 0 as a factor and 1 as a factor. Use the patterns you notice to write a definition of the Zero Property and the Property of One. See above.

array Objects displayed in rows and columns.

factor Numbers that are multiplied to give a product.

product The result of multiplication.

Check for Understanding
Write a multiplication sentence for the picture.

1
2 × 6 = 12

2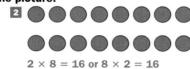
2 × 8 = 16 or 8 × 2 = 16

Multiply. You may use counters or graph paper.

3 5 × 4 20   **4** 2 × 7 14   **5** 3 × 2 6   **6** 5 × 6 30   **7** 8 × 3 24

8 6 × 6 36   **9** 9 × 4 36   **10** 9 × 8 72   **11** 8 × 0 0   **12** 5 × 5 25

Critical Thinking: Analyze

13 ALGEBRA: PATTERNS Find the products. What patterns do you see?
  a. 6 × 1   8 × 1   1 × 7   1 × 5
  b. 4 × 0   0 × 9   0 × 6   7 × 0
  c. 3 × 9   9 × 3   8 × 7   7 × 8

13a. 6; 8; 7; 5; the product of 1 and another number is the other number.

13b. 0; 0; 0; 0; the product of 0 and another number is 0.

13c. 27; 27; 56; 56; the order of the factors does not change the product.

14 Nicole finds 5 groups of 7 by adding 7 + 7 + 7 + 7 + 7. Can she use multiplication to find the total? Explain. Show the multiplication sentence if you can. **Yes; explanations may vary; 5 × 7 = 35.**

Turn the page for Practice.
Multiplication and Division Facts **125**

MAKE CONNECTIONS
Vocabulary Relate the terms *array, factor* and *product* to the student work on page 125. Have volunteers write multiplication sentences for several entries in their tables.

Talk about the Zero and Identity properties of multiplication.

- **Will a factor of zero always result in a product of zero? Explain.** [Possible answer: If you multiply something by zero, you get zero.]
- **When you multiply a number by 1, why do you always get that number?** [Possible answer: because you only have one of the number]

3 Close

> **Check for Understanding** using items 1–14, page 125.

CRITICAL THINKING
Algebra: Patterns In item 13, students rediscover the patterns they found for multiplying by 1 and by zero and for the Commutative Property.

In item 14, students show that multiplication is a faster way of finding a total. It is also another way to represent a problem.

Practice See pages 126–127.

▶ **PRACTICE**

Materials have available: calculators

Options for assigning exercises:
A—Even ex. 2–30; all ex. 32–43; **Mixed Review**
B—Odd ex. 1–31; all ex. 32–43; **Mixed Review**

- For ex. 1–4, accept answers with factors in any order. For example, for ex. 1, 3 × 6 = 18 is an acceptable answer.
- For ex. 5–9, accept arrays with rows and columns in any order.
- For ex. 10–30, remind students that problems written horizontally are the same as problems written vertically.
- For ex. 40, number sense and the Guess and Test strategy are two strategies students may use.

Mixed Review/Test Preparation Students practice addition and subtraction, skills learned in Chapter 2.

P
R
A
C
T
I
C
E

Practice

Write a multiplication sentence for the picture.

1

$3 \times 6 = 18$ or $6 \times 3 = 18$

2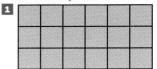

$4 \times 8 = 32$ or $8 \times 4 = 32$

3

$4 \times 5 = 20$

4

$4 \times 4 = 16$

Make or draw an array. Find the product Check students' arrays

5 2×7 14   **6** 3×4 12   **7** 6×5 30   **8** 7×3 21   **9** 4×6 24

Multiply using any method.

10 9×5 45   **11** 3×8 24   **12** 6×5 30   **13** 8×4 32   **14** 7×7 49

15 4×1 4   **16** 9×6 54   **17** 5×8 40   **18** 0×8 0   **19** 1×9 9

20 3×3 9   **21** 5×3 15   **22** 8×6 48   **23** 7×5 35   **24** 6×2 12

25
$$\begin{array}{r} 8 \\ \times 9 \\ \hline 72 \end{array}$$
26
$$\begin{array}{r} 2 \\ \times 5 \\ \hline 10 \end{array}$$
27
$$\begin{array}{r} 9 \\ \times 9 \\ \hline 81 \end{array}$$
28
$$\begin{array}{r} 7 \\ \times 0 \\ \hline 0 \end{array}$$
29
$$\begin{array}{r} 5 \\ \times 8 \\ \hline 40 \end{array}$$
30
$$\begin{array}{r} 6 \\ \times 7 \\ \hline 42 \end{array}$$

Write the letter of the factors with the same total.

31 $7 + 7 + 7 + 7 + 7 + 7$ d   **a.** 6×2

32 $4 + 4 + 4 + 4 + 4 + 4 + 4$ c   **b.** 7×9

33 $2 + 2 + 2 + 2 + 2 + 2 + 2 + 2$ e   **c.** 7×4

34 4×3 a   **d.** 6×7

35 9×7 b   **e.** 8×2

126 Lesson 4.1

Meeting Individual Needs

Early Finishers

Have students think of other objects that come in multi-packs. Have them create tables that show the number of objects in various number of packs. They can create problems, trade them with other students, and solve.

COMMON ERROR

Some students will find the sum instead of the product when given a multiplication sentence. Encourage them to draw pictures or diagrams to illustrate the multiplication sentence.

MIXED APPLICATIONS
Problem Solving

36 At a tennis competition, each of 6 schools brings a team of 6 tennis players. How many tennis players attend altogether? **36 players**

37 In a classroom, there are 5 tables with 5 students at each table. How many students are in the classroom? **25 students**

38 Skye is buying paddles for the table-tennis team. Each of the 7 players will get 3 paddles. How many paddles will Skye buy? **21 paddles**

39 Fifty-six students play soccer. Thirty-nine students play basketball. Which sport has more players? How many more? **soccer; 17 players**

40 Complete this problem using your own numbers.
■ students worked on school projects. They worked in ■ groups of ■ students.
Possible answer: 54; 9; 6.

41 Hanna lines up the hockey sticks in the supply closet after practice. She puts them in rows of 6. She makes 7 rows. How many hockey sticks are there? **42 hockey sticks**

42 Rule: The first two numbers are even. The third number is odd. Which does *not* follow the rule? **c**
a. 2, 200, 101
b. 10, 330, 207
c. 6, 63, 65

43 Ezra's school has 3 fourth-grade classes. One class has 22 students, another has 28 students, and a third has 31 students. How many students are in the fourth grade? **81 students**

mixed review • test preparation

1 24 + 16 40   **2** 52 − 49 3   **3** 57 + 109 166   **4** 1,280 − 1,053 227

5 45 + 86 = 131   **6** $5.35 − 2.75 = $2.60   **7** 728 + 93 = 821   **8** 375 + 468 = 843   **9** 1,205 − 896 = 309

10 2,637 − 598 = 2,039   **11** $63.45 + 79.39 = $142.84   **12** $5,108 − 965 = $4,143   **13** 5,253 − 4,557 = 696   **14** 72,005 + 9,997 = 82,002

Extra Practice, page 496

Multiplication and Division Facts **127**

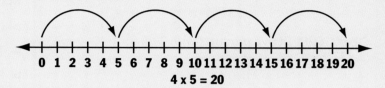

Alternate Teaching Strategy

Materials per student: number lines (TA 14)

Draw a number line on the chalkboard and demonstrate how to use it to show 4 × 5.

4 x 5 = 20

Write the following problem on the chalkboard:
Kesha picked apples in her family's apple orchard. She put the apples in trays of 6. Kesha filled 8 trays. How many apples did Kesha pick?

Ask a volunteer to show how to solve the problem using the number line.
- **What multiplication sentence can you write for this problem?** [8 × 6 = 48]
- **What are the factors? What is the product?** [8 and 6; 48]

Repeat the activity for other factors, such as 3 × 6 and 4 × 7. Have students use their number lines to find the products, then write the multiplication sentences.

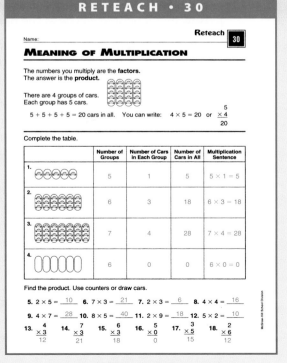

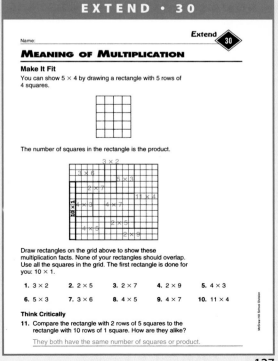

127

LESSON 4.2

MENTAL MATH

2 Through 5 as Factors

OBJECTIVE Derive products with 2 through 5 as factors.

RESOURCE REMINDER 31
Math Center Cards 31
Practice 31, Reteach 31, Extend 31

SKILLS TRACE

GRADE 3	• Use skip-counting, adding on a known fact, and doubling to find multiplication facts for 2 through 5. *(Chapter 6)*
GRADE 4	• Find products with 2 through 5 as factors.
GRADE 5	• Use mental math strategies to multiply whole numbers and decimals by multiples of 10, 100, and 1,000. *(Chapter 4)*

MANIPULATIVE WARM-UP

Cooperative Pairs   **Kinesthetic**

OBJECTIVE Explore multiplication with grouping.

Materials per pair: 30 counters

► One partner puts the counters in equal groups of 5 and counts the groups.

► The other partner writes the corresponding multiplication sentence.

► Partners switch roles and repeat the activity for equal groups of six.

► Have students discuss their results. Then ask:
  • **Do you write the same multiplication sentence for 5 groups of 6 and 6 groups of 5? Why or why not?** *[No, 5 × 6 = 30 means 5 groups of 6 and 6 × 5 = 30 means 6 groups of 5.]*

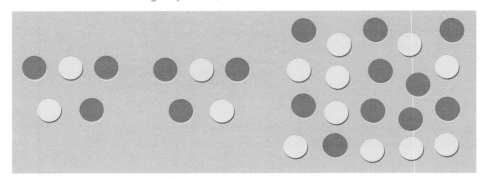

ESL APPROPRIATE

ALGEBRA CONNECTION

Cooperative Pairs   **Logical/Analytical**

OBJECTIVE Connect multiplication with grouping.

► Write the following problem on the chalkboard:

Eve is having a birthday party. She sets up 3 tables that can seat 4 people each. How many people will be at the party?

► Have students solve the problem by acting it out or drawing a picture, or both. Ask a volunteer to write the multiplication sentence for the problem on the chalkboard. *[3 × 4 = 12]*

► Have each pair write their own multiplication word problems. Allow time for several pairs to present their problems and act them out. Ask other students to write the multiplication sentence for each problem.

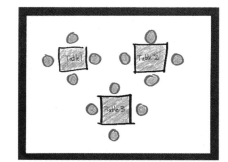

Daily Review

PREVIOUS DAY QUICK REVIEW

Multiply using any method.

1. 3 × 3 *[9]*
2. 2 × 4 *[8]*
3. 5 × 3 *[15]*
4. 1 × 9 *[9]*

FAST FACTS

1. 14 − 6 *[8]*
2. 7 − 7 *[0]*
3. 9 − 3 *[6]*
4. 16 − 7 *[9]*

Problem of the Day • 31

Pat earned $15 baby-sitting 4 hours on Friday night. She earned $3 per hour plus $1 per child. How many children did Pat baby-sit? *[3]*

TECH LINK

MATH VAN

Tools You may wish to use the Counters tool with this lesson.

MATH FORUM

Idea There are several rhymes based on skip-counting by twos. I encourage my students to create rhymes based on skip-counting by threes, fours and fives.

Visit our Resource Village at http://www.mhschool.com to see more of the Math Forum.

MATH CENTER

Practice

OBJECTIVE Use calculators to find products with factors 2–5 by skip-counting.

Materials per pair: calculator, counters; per student: Math Center Recording Sheet (TA 31 optional)

Students are introduced to the use of a calculator to skip-count to find products. This activity prepares students for a comprehensive use of calculators to find products and quotients in Lesson 8, page 151, *More to Explore*. *[15, 9, 25, 10]*

Problem Solving

OBJECTIVE Solve problems about total price of a group of items.

Materials per pair: two sets of index cards with numbers 2–5; per student: Math Center Recording Sheet (TA 31 optional)

Students are given a price list. They choose an item to buy and pick a number from 2–5 at random. They multiply the price of a single item by the random number to find the total. *[Check students' answers]*

PRACTICE ACTIVITY 31

MATH CENTER
On Your Own

Calculator • Calculator Skip-Counting

YOU NEED
calculator

You can practice skip-counting with a calculator. Follow these steps.

- Enter a number from 2 to 5. This is the number by which you will skip-count.

- Press ⊞ .

- Press ⊟ . Each time you press ⊟ , the display shows the next skip-counted number. For example, to find 3 × 2, press 2 , and then press ⊟ 3 times. The display should show 6.

Try this method to find the products 3 × 5, 3 × 3, 5 × 5, and 2 × 5. Record your work.

Chapter 4, Lesson 2, pages 128–131

Multiplication

NCTM Standards

Problem Solving
✓ Communication
✓ Reasoning
Connections

ESL APPROPRIATE

PROBLEM-SOLVING ACTIVITY 31

MATH CENTER
Partners

Using Data • Product Prices

YOU NEED
8 index cards—2 sets numbered 2 through 5

- Put the 2 sets of cards together and mix them up.
- Take turns being the customer and buying things from the following list of items.

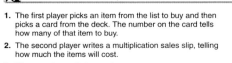

baseball	$4	baby doll	$8	model car	$3
paint set	$5	knit-a-rug	$7	jump rope	$2
toy boat	$6	trivia game	$9	pick-up sticks	$4
lunch box	$8	model plane	$3	doll stroller	$9

1. The first player picks an item from the list to buy and then picks a card from the deck. The number on the card tells how many of that item to buy.

2. The second player writes a multiplication sales slip, telling how much the items will cost.

3. Change roles and play again.

Chapter 4, Lesson 2, pages 128–131

Multiplication

NCTM Standards

✓ Problem Solving
Communication
✓ Reasoning
Connections

MENTAL MATH
2 Through 5 as Factors

OBJECTIVE Derive products with 2 through 5 as factors.

Materials have available: number line (TA 14)

Vocabulary multiple, skip-count

Write the following on the chalkboard:

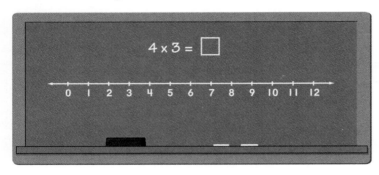

$4 \times 3 = \square$

0 1 2 3 4 5 6 7 8 9 10 11 12

- **How can you use a picture or models to show 4 × 3?**
[Possible answers: Show 4 groups of 3 counters, draw 4 groups of 3, show 4 "skips" of 3 on a number line.]

Have a volunteer come to the board and show 4 × 3 on the number line. Repeat the activity with other multiplication exercises, such as 2 × 6, 3 × 3, and 2 × 4.

 **Teach** *Whole Class*

Cultural Connection Read the **Cultural Note**. Point out that the Naismith Memorial Basketball Hall of Fame is located in Springfield, Massachusetts. The Basketball Hall of Fame was founded in 1959 to honor those who have made great contributions to the sport of basketball. Encourage students who have visited the Hall of Fame or another place that honors athletes to share their experiences.

▶ **LEARN** Read the introductory problem and discuss why multiplication is used to solve both parts. Students should realize that there are 3 baskets worth 2 points each in the first part, and 4 equal teams of 5 students in the second part. Multiplication can be used to find the total of a given number of equal groups.

As you look at the method used to solve the problem, discuss how jumps on a number line compare to skip-counting mentally.

Talk It Over After students discuss the question, ask:
- **What strategy could you use to find 7 × 3?** *[Answers may vary. Possible answer: Double 3 × 3, and add on one more group of 3—(3 × 3) + (3 × 3) + 3 = 9 + 9 + 3 = 21.]*

---

2 Through 5 as Factors

"There were four teams of five players in the Fourth Grade Basketball tournament. The only points made in the final minute were by three players on the winning team!"

In the final minute of the semifinal game, your team made its third 2-point shot to win the game. How many points did your team get in the final minute? How many fourth graders played in the tournament?

Skip-counting is a strategy that can help you find products.

To find the total number of points, you can skip-count by twos 3 times.

Cultural Note
Basketball was invented in 1891 in Springfield, Massachusetts, by Dr. James Naismith. Today, the game is played all over the world.

Think: Each of 3 players scores 2 points.

$3 \times 2 = 6$

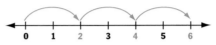

0 1 2 3 4 5 6

2, 4, and 6 are **multiples** of 2. Your team got 6 points.

skip-count Counting by twos, threes, and so on.

multiple The product of a number and any whole number.

To find the total number of players, you can skip-count by fives 4 times.

0 1 2 3 4 5 6 7 8 9 10 11 12 13 14 15 16 17 18 19 20

5, 10, 15, and 20 are multiples of 5.

There were 20 fourth graders in the tournament.

Think: 4 teams of 5 players

$4 \times 5 = 20$

Talk It Over
▶ **ALGEBRA: PATTERNS** Name other multiples of 2 and 5. What pattern do you see in the multiples of 2? the multiples of 5? *Possible answers: Multiples of 2—8, 10, 12, 14, 16, 18; multiples of 5—25, 30, 35, 40, 45; multiples of 2 are all even numbers; multiples of 5 have either a 0 or a 5 in the ones place.*

Meeting Individual Needs

Extra Support

Some students may need to continue to use counters to model multiplication facts. Have these students use counters to model the examples on page 128.

ESL APPROPRIATE

Language Support

Make certain that all students make the connection between the newspaper clipping and the introductory problem. Also discuss unfamiliar words in the clipping.

ESL APPROPRIATE

Ongoing Assessment

Interview Determine if students understand finding products with factors of 2 to 5 by asking:
- **What two multiplication facts can you find by skip-counting by 3 five times?** *[Possible answers: 5 × 3 = 15, 3 × 5 = 15]*

Follow Up Students having difficulty finding the product can use number lines showing multiples of 2, 3, 4, and 5, and complete **Reteach 31**.

For students who can multiply using 2 through 5 as factors, assign **Extend 31**.

Here are some strategies to help you find products when 3 and 4 are factors.

Multiply: 3×6

You can find a known fact then add on.

Think: 2 groups of 6 plus 6 more

$$\underbrace{2 \times 6}$$
$$12 \quad + \quad 6 = 18 \quad \text{So } 3 \times 6 = 18.$$

Multiply: 4×7

You can double a known fact.

Think: 2 groups of 7 plus 2 groups of 7

$$\underbrace{2 \times 7} \qquad + \qquad \underbrace{2 \times 7}$$
$$14 \qquad + \qquad 14 \quad = 28 \qquad \text{So } 4 \times 7 = 28.$$

Check for Understanding
Multiply.

1 3×5	**2** 7×5	**3** 6×5	**4** 8×5	**5** 5×3
15	35	30	40	15
6 6×3	**7** 4×2	**8** 9×2	**9** 7×2	**10** 8×2
18	8	18	14	16
11 3×3	**12** 4×4	**13** 4×9	**14** 3×7	**15** 5×5
9	16	36	21	25

Critical Thinking: Analyze   **Explain your reasoning.**

16 ALGEBRA: PATTERNS What is 2×3? 3×2? What is 4×5?
5×4? What pattern do you see? 6; 6; 20; 20; if the order of the factors is
changed, the product remains the same.

17 If you know 3×7, what other fact do you know? 7×3

Turn the page for Practice.
Multiplication and Division Facts **129**

CHECK

As a class, read through the examples of how students can use facts they know to find products of other facts. Ask:
- **How can you use 7 × 3 = 21 to find the product of 8 × 3?**
  [We already know that seven 3s are 21. We need one more 3, so add 3 to 21. 8 × 3 = 21 + 3]
- **How can you use 4 × 4 = 16 to find the product of 8 × 4?**
  [We need twice as many 4s, so we can double the product of 4 × 4. 8 × 4 = 16 + 16 = 32]

You may also wish to introduce an additional strategy which is similar to those introduced in the lesson.
- **How can you use 5 × 3 = 15 to find the product of 4 × 3?**
  [We already know that five 3s are 15. We need one less 3. Subtract 3 from 15. 4 × 3 = 15 − 3 = 12]

3 Close

Check for Understanding using items 1–17, page 129.

CRITICAL THINKING
Algebra: Patterns After students discuss item 16, ask:
- **How can you use this pattern to help increase the number of multiplication facts you know?** *[Possible answer: You can take a fact that you know, change the order of the factors, and find a new fact that you know.]*

Practice See pages 130–131.

Inclusion

Let students circle groups of dots on dot paper to show the multiplication exercises in the lesson. Students can use the pictures to check products found by using other methods. You can also have them use the pictures to explore and explain the other strategies in the lesson.

ESL APPROPRIATE

129

▶ **PRACTICE**

Materials have available: calculators; play money—nickels

Options for assigning exercises:
A—Odd ex. 1–31; all ex. 32–43; **More to Explore**
B—Even ex. 2–30; all ex. 32–43; **More to Explore**

- For ex. 1–5 accept answers with factors in any order.
- For ex. 6–10 accept arrays with rows and columns in any order.
- For ex. 11–31, you may wish to choose several exercises and have volunteers explain the methods they used to multiply.
- For **Make It Right** (ex. 39), see Common Error below.
- For ex. 40–43, students may use the strategies of getting information from a table and choosing the operation.

a **Algebra** Ex. 32 and 33 introduce the idea of a function. Students should understand that a function is a basic algebraic concept that shows the relationship between numbers.

More to Explore Students can draw nickels or use play nickels for this activity. The activity reinforces students' knowledge of multiples of 5.

Practice

Write a multiplication sentence for the picture.

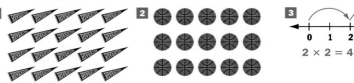

1 $4 \times 5 = 20$ or $5 \times 4 = 20$

2 $3 \times 5 = 15$ or $5 \times 3 = 15$

3 $2 \times 2 = 4$

4 $4 \times 2 = 8$

5 $3 \times 4 = 12$

Draw an array. Find the product. Check students' arrays.

6 9×2 18	**7** 1×5 5	**8** 2×5 10	**9** 6×3 18	**10** 7×4 28

Multiply using any method.

11 7×2 14	**12** 5×3 15	**13** 2×6 12	**14** 5×9 45	**15** 5×8 40
16 4×7 28	**17** 3×8 24	**18** 3×9 27	**19** 4×2 8	**20** 4×8 32
21 2×8 16	**22** 3×7 21	**23** 4×6 24	**24** 2×5 10	**25** 5×7 35

26 $\begin{array}{r}4\\ \times 8\\ \hline 32\end{array}$	**27** $\begin{array}{r}5\\ \times 4\\ \hline 20\end{array}$	**28** $\begin{array}{r}9\\ \times 2\\ \hline 18\end{array}$	**29** $\begin{array}{r}7\\ \times 4\\ \hline 28\end{array}$	**30** $\begin{array}{r}6\\ \times 5\\ \hline 30\end{array}$	**31** $\begin{array}{r}9\\ \times 5\\ \hline 45\end{array}$

a **ALGEBRA Find the rule. Then complete the table.**

32 Rule: ▓ Multiply by 3.

0	1	2	3	4	5	6
0	3	6	9	12	15	18

33 Rule: ▓ Multiply by 4.

0	1	2	3	4	5	6
0	4	8	12	16	20	24

Tell if the number is a multiple of both 2 and 5.

34 12 No. **35** 15 No. **36** 20 Yes. **37** 25 No. **38** 40 Yes.

········· **Make It Right** ·········

39 Here is how Linda found 3×8. Tell what the mistake is, then give the correct answer.

$$3 \times 8 = \underline{2 \text{ groups of } 8} + \underline{1 \text{ group of } 3}$$
$$= \underline{\quad 16 \quad} + \underline{\quad 3 \quad} = 19$$

She separated the groups incorrectly—$3 \times 8 = 2$ groups of $8 + 1$ group of $8 = 16 + 8 = 24$.

Meeting Individual Needs

Early Finishers

Present the problems below. After students solve them, they can create similar problems.

Sam scored 4 two-point baskets and 3 three-point baskets. How many points did he score in all? *[17 points]*

Rachel made at least one 2-point and one 3-point shot during the game. She scored 12 points in all. How many of each type of shot did she make? *[3 2-point, 2 3-point]*

COMMON ERROR

As in **Make It Right** (ex. 38), some students may confuse the number of groups with the number in each group. Have these students use pictorial representations to determine the groupings.

Let students circle groups of dots on dot paper to show the multiplication exercises in the lesson. Students can use the pictures to check products found by using other methods. You can also have them use the pictures to explore and explain the other strategies in the lesson.

MIXED APPLICATIONS
Problem Solving

42. Yes; possible answer: by rounding down, the estimated sum of Jordan's points is 17,000.

National Basketball Association Scoring Champion

Season	Player	Games	2-point Field Goals	3-point Field Goals	Free Throws	Total Number of Points
1986–1987	Michael Jordan	82	1,086	12	833	3,041
1987–1988	Michael Jordan	82	1,062	7	723	2,868
1988–1989	Michael Jordan	81	939	27	674	2,633
1989–1990	Michael Jordan	82	942	92	593	2,753
1990–1991	Michael Jordan	82	961	29	571	2,580
1991–1992	Michael Jordan	80	916	27	491	2,404
1992–1993	Michael Jordan	78	911	81	476	2,541
1995–1996	Michael Jordan	82	805	111	548	2,491

Use the table for problems 40–43.

40 In the 1987–1988 season, how many points did Michael Jordan score with 3-point field goals? **21 points**

41 Which is worth more points: five 3-point field goals or seven 2-point field goals? Explain. **See below.**

42 Did Michael Jordan score more than 17,000 points from the 1986–1987 season through the 1995–1996 season? Explain how you used estimation to find the answer. **See above.**

43 The scoring leader for the 1994–1995 season was Shaquille O'Neal with 2,315 points. Did Michael Jordan score more points in the 1986–1987 season? If he did, how many more points? **Yes; 3,041 − 2,315 = 726 points.**

more to explore

Counting Nickels

You can use nickels to find products with 5 as a factor.

To find 6 × 5, think of 6 nickels.

Think: 6 nickels is 30¢.   6 × 5 = 30

Tell how to find the product using nickels.

1 2 × 5 10; 2 nickels   **2** 3 × 5 15; 3 nickels   **3** 5 × 5 25; 5 nickels   **4** 7 × 5 35; 7 nickels   **5** 8 × 5 40; 8 nickels

41. Five 3-pointers is 15 points, which is more than 14 points for the seven 2-pointers.

Extra Practice, page 496

Multiplication and Division Facts   **131**

Materials per group: 30 beans or macaroni noodles

Each group uses beans to show 3 × 6.

Have students use the model to answer the question:
- **How many beans are in one group? two groups?** [6, 12]
- **How would you find the number of beans in three groups?** [Possible response: add the number of beans in one group and the number of beans in two groups.]

Have each group use beans to model 4 × 7.

Pose the question:
- **How many beans are in two groups?** [14]
- **How many two groups are in four groups?** [two]
- **How would you find the number of beans in four groups?** [Possible response: find the sum of the number of beans in each of the two groups.]

Continue the activity using other multiplication expressions. Possible examples are: 3 × 8, 3 × 9, 4 × 6, 4 × 8.

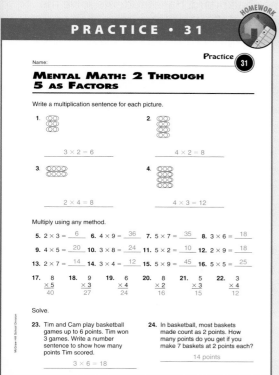

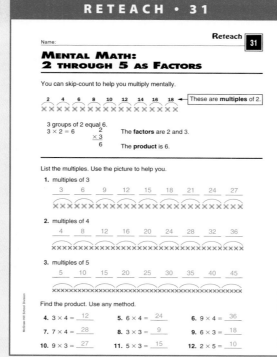

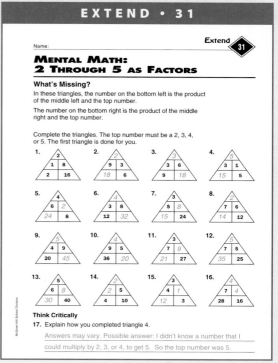

LESSON 4.3

MENTAL MATH
6 and 8 as Factors

OBJECTIVE Derive products with 6 and 8 as factors.

RESOURCE REMINDER
Math Center Cards 32
Practice 32, Reteach 32, Extend 32

SKILLS TRACE

GRADE 3	• Use strategies of doubling a known fact and adding on a known fact to find multiplication facts for 6, 7, 8, and 9. *(Chapter 7)*
GRADE 4	• Find products with 6 and 8 as factors.
GRADE 5	• Use mental math strategies to multiply whole numbers and decimals by multiples of 10, 100, and 1,000. *(Chapter 4)*

MANIPULATIVE WARM-UP

Cooperative Pairs   **Visual/Spatial**

OBJECTIVE Find multiples of 6.

Materials per pair: 9 hexagon pattern blocks (TA 17), number cube, calculator

▶ One partner tosses the number cube to see how many pattern blocks to use. The second partner cuts out that number of hexagons and writes the corresponding number sentence to show the total number of sides. The first partner uses a calculator to check the sentence.

▶ Partners switch roles and continue finding multiples of 6.

▶ When students have finished, ask:
  • **How did you find the multiples of 6 using the pattern blocks?** *[Possible answers: counting, repeated addition, using multiplication facts]*

CONSUMER CONNECTION

Cooperative Pairs   **Kinesthetic**

OBJECTIVE Grouping numbers to solve a problem.

▶ Write the following problem on the chalkboard. Have students solve the problem using what they know about multiplication. *[3 packages of hot dogs and 4 packages of buns]* Encourage students to draw pictures if they have any trouble getting started.

> Patrice is having a party. She has invited 24 people. She wants to buy enough hot dogs and buns so that each guest can have one. Hot dogs come in packages of 8. Buns come in packages of 6. How many packages of hot dogs and buns should Patrice purchase?

Daily Review

Math Van

PREVIOUS DAY QUICK REVIEW

Multiply using any method.

1. 2 × 5 *[10]*
2. 3 × 4 *[12]*
3. 7 × 2 *[14]*
4. 5 × 3 *[15]*

FAST FACTS

1. 18 − 9 *[9]*
2. 13 − 6 *[7]*
3. 15 − 9 *[6]*
4. 11 − 7 *[4]*

Problem of the Day • 32

Kevin took a survey. He asked his friends how many hours each week they spent studying. The data he collected is shown below. Find the median, range, and mode of these data: 2, 7, 3, 6, 1, 5, 2, 7, 3, 9, 10, 5, 4, 7, 8, 4, 7. *[median– 5, range– 9, mode– 7]*

TECH LINK

MATH VAN

Tools You may wish to use the Counters tool with this lesson.

MATH FORUM

Management Tip Have students keep track of the facts they know in a multiplication table.

Visit our Resource Village at http://www.mhschool.com to see more of the Math Forum.

MATH CENTER

Practice

OBJECTIVE Use counters to explore the order property of multiplication.

Materials per pair: counters, 0-9 spinner (TA 2); per student: Math Center Recording Sheet (TA 31 optional)

Students find two ways of grouping counters to solve a multiplication problem involving 6 and 8 as factors. The two ways illustrate the order property of multiplication. *[Check students' multiplication sentences to see that they show the Order Property of multiplication.]*

PRACTICE ACTIVITY 32

MATH CENTER
Partners 👥

Number Sense • What Is the Product?

- One partner selects one factor. It must be either 6 or 8. The same partner spins for the other factor, any number from 1–9. (If you spin zero, spin again.)
- The other partner shows two ways to find the product using counters. For instance, to find the product of 6 and 2, you could put out 2 groups of 6 counters and 6 groups of 2 counters.
- Record the multiplication sentence.
- Switch roles and try the activity again.

YOU NEED
counters
spinner (0–9)

Chapter 4, Lesson 3, pages 132–133

Multiplication

NCTM Standards

Problem Solving
✓ Communication
✓ Reasoning
Connections

Problem Solving

OBJECTIVE Solve a multistep problem.

Materials per student: Math Center Recording Sheet (TA 31 optional)

Students use multiples of 6 and 8 to find out how many pencils were purchased. *[There are 4 possible answers: 12 six-cent pencils and 1 eight-cent pencil; 4 eight-cent pencils and 8 six-cent pencils; 7 eight-cent pencils and 4 six-cent pencils; 10 eight-cent pencils. Possible answers: I guessed ; I worked backwards; I made a list.]*

PROBLEM-SOLVING ACTIVITY 32

MATH CENTER
On Your Own 👤

Logical Reasoning • Pencils

Pencils at the store cost 6¢ or 8¢. You spend a total of 80¢ on pencils.

1. How many of each kind of pencil do you buy?
2. Explain how you solved the problem.
3. Find other ways to answer the question.
4. Pick another amount less than $1.00. Tell what pencils you might buy to spend that amount or close to it without going over $1.00.

Chapter 4, Lesson 3, pages 132–133

Multiplication

NCTM Standards

✓ Problem Solving
✓ Communication
✓ Reasoning
Connections

Lesson 4.3 *continued*

MENTAL MATH
6 and 8 as Factors

OBJECTIVE Derive products with 6 and 8 as factors.

1 Introduce

Materials per pair: 20 counters

Have each pair of students show 4 groups of 5 counters.
- **What multiplication fact did you show?** [4 × 5 = 20]
- **How can this fact help you find 8 × 5?** [You can double 4 × 5. 8 × 5 = 4 × 5 + 4 × 5 = 20 + 20 = 40]
- **Can you use 8 × 5 to help you find 5 × 8? Explain.** [Yes; the Order Property says that 8 × 5 = 5 × 8.]

2 Teach
Whole Class

▶ **LEARN** After reading the introductory problem, discuss the strategy of doubling a known fact.
- **How many groups of 4 are in 6 × 4?** [6]
- **Why does doubling 3 × 4 give you the same product as 6 × 4?** [3 × 4 means 3 groups of 4. Doubling 3 × 4 gives you 6 groups of 4, which is 6 × 4.]
- **What other strategies could you use to find the product for 6 × 4?** [Possible answers: skip-counting, drawing a picture, using the Order Property and 4 × 6]

3 Close

▶ **Check for Understanding** using items 1–6, page 132.

CRITICAL THINKING
The strategies presented give students tools to find most facts to 9 × 9, except those in which each factor is a 7 or 9.

▶ **PRACTICE**
Materials have available: calculators

Options for assigning exercises:
A—Odd ex. 1–21; ex. 23–33; **Mixed Review**
B—Even ex. 2–20; ex. 22–33; **Mixed Review**

- For ex. 1–21, you may want students to describe the methods they used for several exercises.
- For ex. 33, Make a Table and the Guess and Test strategy may be used.

a **Algebra** Missing factor ex. 22–29 explore the connection between multiplication and division. Ex. 26 and 27 is an informal example of the Distributive Property. Ex. 28 and 29 are an informal introduction to variables.

Mixed Review/Test Preparation Students review *range, median, mode,* and *elapsed time,* introduced in Chapter 3.

---

6 and 8 as Factors

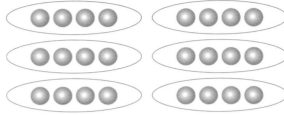

LEARN

You can use strategies to find products when 6 and 8 are factors. You can double a known fact.

Multiply: 6 × 4   **Think:** 3 groups of 4 plus 3 groups of 4

$$\underbrace{3 \times 4}_{12} \quad + \quad \underbrace{3 \times 4}_{12} = 24 \quad \text{So } 6 \times 4 = 24.$$

Multiply: 8 × 3   **Think:** 4 groups of 3 plus 4 groups of 3

$$\underbrace{4 \times 3}_{12} \quad + \quad \underbrace{4 \times 3}_{12} = 24 \quad \text{So } 8 \times 3 = 24.$$

CHECK

Check for Understanding
Multiply. Show your methods. Methods may vary.
1 6 × 3 18   **2** 8 × 8 64   **3** 6 × 6 36   **4** 7 × 6 42   **5** 3 × 8 24

Critical Thinking: Analyze
6 Find two ways to double a known fact to solve 4 × 8 = ■.

(2 × 8) + (2 × 8) = 32; (4 × 4) + (4 × 4) = 32

132 Lesson 4.3

Meeting Individual Needs

Early Finishers
Have each student create a problem whose solution is a product with a factor of 6 or 8.

Extra Support
Have students continue to use counters to help them with their multiplication facts.

Ongoing Assessment
Observation Checklist Determine if students understand how to derive products with 6 and 8 as factors by observing them solve 6 × 8. Students should be able to use products with 2, 3, 4, or 5 as factors to help find the product.

Follow Up If students need further practice with this skill, assign **Reteach 32.**

If students need a greater challenge, assign **Extend 32.**

Practice

Multiply using any method.

1 6 × 2 **12**　　**2** 8 × 4 **32**　　**3** 6 × 5 **30**　　**4** 6 × 7 **42**　　**5** 7 × 8 **56**

6 8 × 1 **8**　　**7** 6 × 0 **0**　　**8** 8 × 7 **56**　　**9** 2 × 8 **16**　　**10** 9 × 6 **54**

11 8 × 0 **0**　　**12** 3 × 6 **18**　　**13** 6 × 6 **36**　　**14** 5 × 8 **40**　　**15** 6 × 8 **48**

16 1	**17** 2	**18** 8	**19** 4	**20** 8	**21** 9
× 6	× 8	× 6	× 6	× 8	× 8
6	**16**	**48**	**24**	**64**	**72**

ALGEBRA Complete the multiplication sentence.

22 8 × ■ = 56 **7**　　**23** ■ × 5 = 30 **6**　　**24** 6 × ■ = 0 **0**　　**25** ■ × 8 = 32 **4**

26 8 × 9 = (4 × 9) + (■ × 9) **4**　　　**27** 8 × 7 = (4 × 7) + (4 × ■) **7**

28 If △ = 7, then how much is △△△? **21**

29 If □ = 5, then how much is □□□□□□? **30**

MIXED APPLICATIONS

Problem Solving

30 In the fourth-grade hockey game, there were three periods, each 10 minutes long. How long was the playing time? **30 min**

31 In the 1995–1996 season, the Philadelphia Flyers won 45 games, lost 24 games, and tied 13. How many games did they play in all? **82 games**

32 Logical reasoning "I am a 2-digit number between 20 and 30. I am a multiple of 3 and 4. My ones digit is two more than my tens digit. What number am I?" **24**

33 The Howe family went to a hockey game. They bought 3 adult tickets at $7 each and 6 children's tickets at $3 each. How much did they spend in all? **$39**

mixed review • test preparation

Find the range, median, and mode of the data.

1 26, 23, 26, 18, 21　　**8, 23, 26**

2 85, 80, 60, 90, 75　　**30, 80, none**

3 98, 100, 92, 80, 100　　**20, 98, 100**

4 143, 387, 288, 143, 288, 648, 322　　**505, 288, 143 and 288**

Tell the time that is 15 minutes before the time shown.

5 11:15 A.M.　　**11:00 A.M.**

6 6:30 P.M.　　**6:15 P.M.**

7 8:08 A.M.　　**7:53 A.M.**

8 12 noon　　**11:45 A.M.**

Alternate Teaching Strategy

Materials per pair: connecting cubes—54 red and 54 blue

Ask one partner to use red connecting cubes to model 3 groups of 4.

- **What multiplication sentence can you write to represent the model?** *[3 × 4 = 12]*

Ask the other partner to use blue connecting cubes to model 3 groups of 4.

- **What multiplication sentence can you write to represent the model?** *[3 × 4 = 12]*

Have the partners connect their models by alternating the colors of the trains.

- **What multiplication sentence can you write to represent the model?** *[6 × 4 = 24]*

Have students continue to use cubes to represent other multiples of 6 by building two equal groups of cubes.

Then extend the activity to develop multiples of 8.

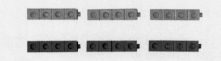

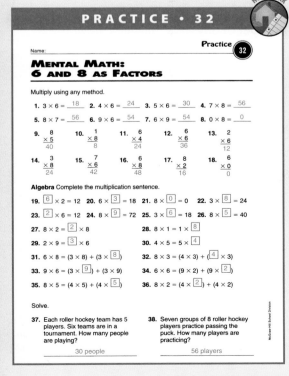

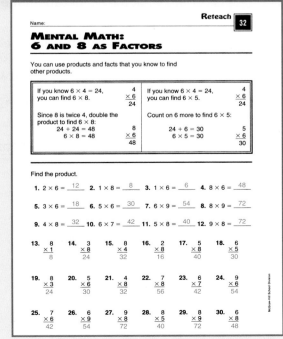

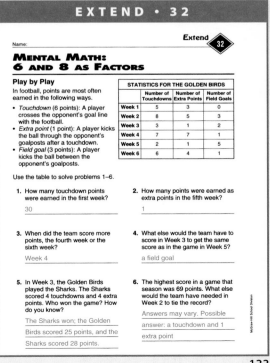

LESSON 4.4

MENTAL MATH

7 and 9 as Factors

OBJECTIVE Derive products with 7 and 9 as factors.

RESOURCE REMINDER
Math Center Cards 33
Practice 33, Reteach 33, Extend 33

SKILLS TRACE

GRADE 3
• Use strategies of doubling a known fact and adding on a known fact to find multiplication facts for 6, 7, 8, and 9. *(Chapter 7)*

GRADE 4
• Find products with 7 and 9 as factors.

GRADE 5
• Use mental math strategies to multiply whole numbers and decimals by multiples of 10, 100, and 1,000. *(Chapter 4)*

WARM-UP

Cooperative Pairs   **Logical/Analytical**

OBJECTIVE Find multiples of 9.

▶ Have each pair of students draw a 3-by-3 grid on a sheet of paper. Then have them write one of the following numbers in each square: 0, 9, 18, 27, 36, 45, 54, 63, 72. Each square contains a different number.

27	63	72
36	54	9
18	45	0

▶ Write a multiplication exercise on the chalkboard with 9 as a factor. Students find the product and mark it on their grid. Then write another multiplication exercise with 9 as a factor.

▶ Have the first pair of students who complete a row, column, or diagonal present their grid to the class.

72	54	18
36	45	9
0	63	27

REAL-LIFE CONNECTION

Whole Class   **Auditory/Linguistic**

OBJECTIVE Connect multiples of 7 with everyday events.

▶ Begin by having students consider a familiar "seven" in their lives: the length of a (full) week.

▶ Using what they know about the number of days in a full week, have them calculate the following:

• the number of days in a two-week vacation *[14 days]*
• a "4–6 weeks for delivery" promise *[28–42 days]*
• a comet that will be visible for 8 weeks *[56 days]*

▶ Then have students create and solve other problems that relate to their everyday life, using 7 as a factor.

❄ DECEMBER ❄						
SUNDAY	MONDAY	TUESDAY	WEDNESDAY	THURSDAY	FRIDAY	SATURDAY
		1	2	3	4	5
6	7	8	9	10	11	12
13	14	15	16	17	18	19
20	21	22	23	24	25	26
27	28	29	30	31		

Daily Review

PREVIOUS DAY QUICK REVIEW

Multiply using any method.

1. 2 × 8 *[16]*
2. 0 × 3 *[0]*
3. 4 × 7 *[28]*
4. 6 × 8 *[48]*

FAST FACTS

1. 9 + 4 *[13]*
2. 5 + 7 *[12]*
3. 6 + 8 *[14]*
4. 5 + 6 *[11]*

Problem of the Day • 33

Morgan ran around the school track in 89 sec. Taylor ran around in 1 min 32 sec. Who completed the lap faster? by how much?

[Morgan; 3 sec]

TECH LINK

MATH VAN

Tools You may wish to use the Counters tool with this lesson.

MATH FORUM

Combination Classes I teach both younger and older students the strategies for deriving products because it is a skill that is helpful at all levels.

Visit our Resource Village at http://www.mhschool.com to see more of the Math Forum.

MATH CENTER

Practice

OBJECTIVE Find products with factors 7 or 9.

Materials per student: counters, Math Center Recording Sheet (TA 31 optional)

Students solve multiplication problems about the number of items for a party. They are encouraged to use mental math strategies and to use counters to check their work. *[1. 36; 18; 72; 2. 35; 21]*

PRACTICE ACTIVITY 33

MATH CENTER
On Your Own 👤

Number Sense • The Party

YOU NEED
: counters

1. Use products with 10 as a factor and then subtract to solve. Use counters to check if you wish.
   There are 9 people at your party.
   If each person at the party gets 4 balloons, how many balloons should you buy? If each person will use 2 plates, how many plates should you buy? If you want to give 8 streamers to each person, how many streamers do you need?

2. Count on from known facts to find each answer.
   You go to a party where there are 7 people.
   If each person at the party gets 5 prizes, how many prizes will be given? If each person uses 3 cups, how many cups will be used?

NCTM Standards
✓ Problem Solving
  Communication
✓ Reasoning
✓ Connections

Chapter 4, Lesson 4, pages 134–137

Multiplication

Problem Solving

OBJECTIVE Discover a pattern for multiples of 9.

Materials per student: Math Center Recording Sheet (TA 31 optional)

Students explore a pattern for products with 9 as a factor. *[Answers may vary. Possible answer: When you multiply any number from 1 to 10 by 9, the sum of the product's digits add up to 9. 9 − 5 = 4; 4 + 3 = 7]*

PROBLEM-SOLVING ACTIVITY 33

MATH CENTER
Partners 👥

Formulating Problems • Number Riddle

• Have your partner think of a number between 1 and 10.

• Ask your partner to:
   a. Multiply the number by 9.
   b. Find the sum of the digits in the product.
   c. Subtract 5 from the sum.
   d. Add 3.

• Your partner should get a final number of 7.

• Repeat this activity with several different numbers. Explain why you get 7 each time.

• Try to come up with other steps that always lead to the same answer. (It doesn't have to be 7.) Write out the steps and ask your partner to try them.

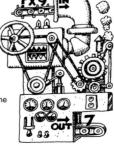

NCTM Standards
✓ Problem Solving
  Communication
✓ Reasoning
  Connections

Chapter 4, Lesson 4, pages 134–137

Multiplication

Lesson 4.4 *continued*

MENTAL MATH
7 and 9 as Factors

1 Introduce

Present the following problem to students:

At a gymnastics competition, Luis scored 9 points in each of 4 events. How many points did he score? *[36 points]*

- **What multiplication fact would you use to solve this problem?** *[4 × 9]*
- **How could you use the Commutative Property and 9 × 4 to find the product?** *[Since the order of the factors doesn't matter, 4 × 9 = 9 × 4.]*

2 Teach
Whole Class

LEARN Discuss the introductory problem and the two strategies used to solve the problem by asking:
- **From which known fact can you count back? Explain.** *[8 × 5; 7 × 5 = 5 less than 8 groups of 5 = 40 − 5 = 35.]*

Talk It Over Encourage students to present as many different ways as they can of breaking apart 7 × 9. Students should recognize that (4 × 9) + (3 × 9) and (3 × 9) + (4 × 9) show the same multiplication situation. Ask:
- **What other ways can you break apart 7 × 9?** *[1 group of 9 + 6 groups of 9, 2 groups of 9 + 5 groups of 9]*

---

7 and 9 as Factors

L E A R N

Seven members of the Cypress Academy gymnastics club made it to the 1996 Women's Junior National Team. If each member competed in 5 events at the Junior Olympics, how many times did the club compete?

Multiply: 7 × 5

You can use different strategies to find the product.

You can add to a known fact.

Think: 6 groups of 5 + 5 more

$$\underbrace{6 \times 5}_{30} \quad + \quad 5$$
$$30 \quad + \quad 5 = 35$$

The Junior National Team
Cypress Academy, Houston, TX

You can also break apart a factor to get known facts.

Think: 5 groups of 5 + 2 groups of 5

$$\underbrace{5 \times 5}_{25} \quad + \quad \underbrace{2 \times 5}_{10}$$
$$25 \quad + \quad 10 = 35$$

The club competed 35 times.

What if 9 members from Cypress Academy had made the team. If each member competed in 5 events, how many times would the club have competed?

Multiply: 9 × 5

To find products with 9 as a factor, you can first find products with 10 as a factor and then subtract.

Think: 10 groups of 5 − 1 group of 5

$$\underbrace{10 \times 5}_{50} \quad - \quad \underbrace{1 \times 5}_{5}$$
$$50 \quad - \quad 5 = 45$$

Talk It Over
▶ In what ways can you break apart 7 to find 7 × 9? How can you use 10 as a factor to find the product? Show your methods. **Possible answer: (4 × 9) + (3 × 9), (5 × 9) + (2 × 9), (6 × 9) + (1 × 9); (10 × 7) − (1 × 7)**

134 Lesson 4.4

Meeting Individual Needs

Extra Support

You may wish to review basic addition facts to 9 in order for students to break apart a factor when multiplying.

COMMON ERROR

Some students may add instead of multiplying. Have them use dot paper to review the meaning of multiplication: for example, 7 × 9 means 7 groups of 9, not 7 + 9.

Ongoing Assessment

Observation Checklist Determine if students can derive new facts from known facts by asking them to identify the strategies used to find the facts in this lesson.

Follow Up If students have difficulty deriving new facts, let them work with others who can explain strategies as they use them. Assign **Reteach 33.**

Assign **Extend 33** to students who understand multiplication using 7 and 9 as factors.

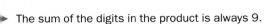

ALGEBRA: PATTERNS You can also use a pattern to find 9 × 5. Look at these products with 9 as a factor.

▶ The tens digit of the product is always 1 less than the second factor.

$$\overset{2-1}{\downarrow} \qquad \overset{3-1}{\downarrow} \qquad \overset{4-1}{\downarrow} \qquad \overset{5-1}{\downarrow}$$
$$9 \times 2 = \underset{1+8}{\underbrace{18}} \qquad 9 \times 3 = \underset{2+7}{\underbrace{27}} \qquad 9 \times 4 = \underset{3+6}{\underbrace{36}} \qquad 9 \times 5 = \underset{4+5}{\underbrace{45}}$$

▶ The sum of the digits in the product is always 9.

The club would have competed 45 times.

More Examples

A 7 × 8
 Think: 5 groups of 8 + 2 groups of 8
         40   +   16   =   56

B 9 × 8
 Think: 10 groups of 8 − 1 group of 8
         80   −   8   =   72

C 9 × 7
 Think: 7 − 1 = 6
         6 + ■ = 9
         6 + 3 = 9
         9 × 7 = 63

D 9 × 6
 Think: 6 − 1 = 5
         5 + ■ = 9
         5 + 4 = 9
         9 × 6 = 54

Check for Understanding

Multiply using any method.

1 3 × 7 21   **2** 6 × 9 54   **3** 7 × 9 63   **4** 4 × 7 28   **5** 3 × 9 27

6 7 × 1 7   **7** 9 × 9 81   **8** 6 × 7 42   **9** 9 × 1 9   **10** 2 × 7 14

11 7 × 3 21   **12** 4 × 9 36   **13** 2 × 9 18   **14** 7 × 0 0   **15** 5 × 7 35

Critical Thinking: Analyze   **Explain your reasoning.** Explanations may vary.

16 How can you find 7 × 4 if you know 6 × 4?
 Possible answer: Add on another group of 4.

17 Is 9 a factor of each product below?
 a. 54 Yes.   **b.** 48 No.   **c.** 81 Yes.   **d.** 72 Yes.   **e.** 91 No.

18 How can you break apart 9 to find 9 × 8?
 Possible answer: (4 × 8) + (5 × 8)

Turn the page for Practice. ➡
Multiplication and Division Facts   **135**

In the discussion that follows the **What If** question, students are shown two strategies for finding a product.

 **Algebra: Patterns** Students may also note that when the multiples of 9 are listed in a column, the ten digits go 1–8 and the ones go in reverse order, 8–1.

More Examples As students discuss Examples A, B, C, and D, remind them that there are other ways of finding each product. For Examples C and D, students can first find a product with a factor of 10, and then subtract.

3 Close

▶ **Check for Understanding** using items 1–18, page 135.

CRITICAL THINKING
As you discuss item 16, encourage volunteers to give as many different strategies as possible for using a known fact to find 7 × 4. It is important to reinforce the understanding that there are many ways to derive any one fact.

JOURNAL For item 18, ask students to compare this method for finding a product with 9 as a factor to the method using multiples of 10.

Practice See pages 136–137.

Gifted And Talented

Challenge students to use facts they know to find products when one of the factors is greater than 10, such as 13 × 5.

▶ **PRACTICE**

Materials have available: calculators

Options for assigning exercises:
A—Odd ex. 1–33; all ex. 34–51; **Cultural Connection**
B—Even ex. 2–32; all ex. 34–51; **Cultural Connection**

• In ex. 50, students may use the strategies Choose the Operation and Solving a Multistep Problem.

Algebra In ex. 38, 39, and 41 students will use known facts to find the factor. In ex. 40 and 43, they will use the Commutative Property. In ex. 42, they will use the rule for multiplying by 1. In ex. 44–47, they will show different ways of breaking apart a multiplication sentence.

Cultural Connection Ahmes was required to complete twelve years of school to qualify as a scribe. He wrote about basic operations, algebra, and geometry. He wrote on a paper-like material made from papyrus reeds. The contents of the Ahmes Papyrus have helped us to understand the level of mathematical thinking of the Egyptians.

While students are solving the puzzle, make sure they realize that to find the answer to each part, they must use the answer to the previous part. Solving a simpler problem, with only 2 houses, cats, and so on, may help students see how to solve the more complex problem.

---

28. 1×9, 3×3
29. 2×6, 6×2, 4×3
30. 3×6, 6×3, 2×9
31. 4×6, 8×3
32. 1×72, 8×9
33. 4×0, 6×0, 8×0, 1×0, 3×0, 2×0, 5×0

Practice

Multiply mentally.

1. 7 3 2 14
2. 9 3 3 27
3. 9 3 0 0
4. 9 3 5 45
5. 7 3 6 42
6. 1 3 9 9
7. 4 3 4 16
8. 7 3 8 56
9. 8 3 9 72
10. 9 3 9 81
11. 7 3 7 49
12. 1 3 7 7
13. 6 3 6 36
14. 9 3 8 72
15. 7 3 8 56

16. 6 / 3 5 / 30
17. 7 / 3 9 / 63
18. 3 / 3 7 / 21
19. 5 / 3 3 / 15
20. 9 / 3 2 / 18
21. 7 / 3 6 / 42
22. 7 / 3 7 / 49
23. 1 / 3 5 / 5
24. 4 / 3 6 / 24
25. 6 / 3 3 / 18
26. 5 / 3 0 / 0
27. 8 / 3 5 / 40

Show at least two ways to get the product. See above.

28. 9   29. 12   30. 18   31. 24   32. 72   33. 0

Complete the order form.

	Title of Book	Price	Number Ordered	Total	
34	Women in Gymnastics	$9	7	■	$63
35	How to Tumble	$5	1	■	$5
36	Getting to the Olympics	$7	2	■	$14
37	All About the Parallel Bars	$3	8	■	$24

ALGEBRA Complete the sentence.

38. 7 3 ■ 5 28 4
39. ■ 3 6 5 54 9
40. 5 3 ■ 5 7 3 5 7
41. 3 3 ■ 5 6 3 4 8
42. 11 3 ■ 5 11 1
43. 23 3 14 5 ■ 3 23 14

44. 6 3 6 5 ■ groups of 6 1 ■ groups of 6 Possible answers: 1, 5; 2, 4; 3, 3

45. 9 3 4 5 ■ groups of 4 1 ■ groups of 4 Possible answers: 1, 8; 2, 7; 3, 6; 4, 5

46. 8 3 7 5 ■ groups of 7 1 ■ groups of 7 Possible answers: 1, 7; 2, 6; 3, 5; 4, 4

47. 7 3 4 5 ■ groups of 7 1 ■ groups of 7 Possible answers: 1, 3; 2, 2

136 Lesson 4.4

Meeting Individual Needs

Early Finishers

Have students write a multiplication expression with a factor of 7 or 9. Challenge them to find all the ways to break apart the expression.

ESL APPROPRIATE

Inclusion

Continue to provide students with visual models that help clarify strategies such as doubling a known fact, breaking apart a known factor, or counting on from a known fact. Talk students through the models.

48. Possible answer: Each row is like a group, so 4 rows is the same as 4 groups of 7 counters (or 4 × 7)—the grid shows (4 × 7) + (4 × 7) = 28 + 28 = 56.

Problem Solving

48 Tsung uses the area model at the right to find 8 × 7. He says that multiplication using the area model is the same as grouping counters. Explain how this is so. **See above.**

49 **Spatial reasoning** What shape can you not get by combining four equal-sized triangles?
a. circle   **b.** square   **c.** triangle **a**

50 There are four events in the Olympic women's gymnastics competition. If a gymnast scores a 9 in three events and a 7 in one event, what is her total number of points? **34 points**

51 The Olympics is held every 4 years. How many team gold medals in a row did the USSR win in the Olympics? **SEE INFOBIT. 8 team gold medals in a row**

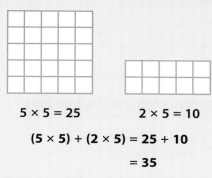

INFOBIT
The USSR Olympic gymnastics team won team gold medals in every Olympics from 1952 until 1980.

Cultural Connection Egyptian Math Puzzle

The Ahmes Papyrus was written by a scribe named Ahmes. He recorded discoveries that Egyptians made about 4,000 years ago. Here is a part of a mathematical puzzle he wrote.

In each of seven houses, there are seven cats.
Each cat eats seven mice.
Each mouse eats seven ears of grain.
Each ear holds seven measures of grain.

Use a calculator to find the number of:

1 cats.
49

2 mice eaten.
343

3 ears of grain eaten. **2,401**

4 measures of grain eaten. **16,807**

Extra Practice, page 497

Multiplication and Division Facts   **137**

Alternate Teaching Strategy

Materials per student: centimeter graph paper (TA 7), scissors

Have students make a rectangle on the grid paper that is 7 units high and 5 units across. Ask students what multiplication fact they think this shows. *[7 × 5]*

Demonstrate how students can find the total number of squares by cutting the rectangle into two smaller rectangles.

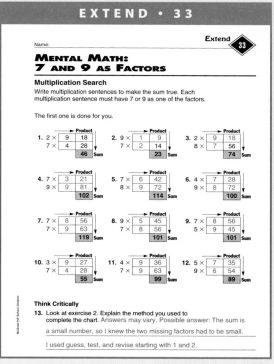

5 × 5 = 25   2 × 5 = 10

(5 × 5) + (2 × 5) = 25 + 10

= 35

Ask students to create their own smaller rectangles and then find the total number of squares in the original rectangle. Have them write a multiplication sentence for each smaller rectangle and explain how they found the total number of small squares in the original rectangle.

Have students compare their results. List all the different ways they broke apart the larger rectangles.

Continue the activity using other multiplication exercises with 7 and 9 as factors, such as 9 × 6 and 7 × 8.

ESL APPROPRIATE

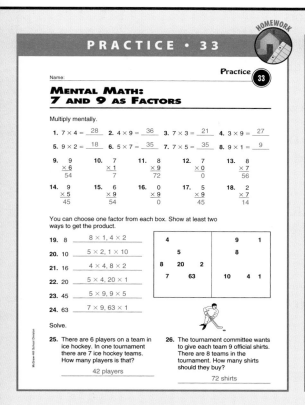

HOMEWORK

Name: _____   Practice **33**

MENTAL MATH: 7 AND 9 AS FACTORS

Multiply mentally.

1. 7 × 4 = **28**   2. 4 × 9 = **36**   3. 7 × 3 = **21**   4. 3 × 9 = **27**

5. 9 × 2 = **18**   6. 5 × 7 = **35**   7. 7 × 5 = **35**   8. 9 × 1 = **9**

9. 9 ×6 = **54**   10. 7 ×1 = **7**   11. 8 ×9 = **72**   12. 8 ×0 = **0**   13. 8 ×7 = **56**

14. 9 ×5 = **45**   15. 6 ×9 = **54**   16. 0 ×9 = **0**   17. 5 ×9 = **45**   18. 2 ×7 = **14**

You can choose one factor from each box. Show at least two ways to get the product.

19. 8   **8 × 1, 4 × 2**
20. 10 **5 × 2, 1 × 10**
21. 16 **4 × 4, 8 × 2**
22. 20 **5 × 4, 20 × 1**
23. 45 **5 × 9, 9 × 5**
24. 63 **7 × 9, 63 × 1**

4			9	1
	5			8
8	20	2		
7	63		10	4	1

Solve.

25. There are 6 players on a team in ice hockey. In one tournament there are 7 ice hockey teams. How many players is that? **42 players**

26. The tournament committee wants to give each team 9 official shirts. There are 8 teams in the tournament. How many shirts should they buy? **72 shirts**

Name: _____   Reteach **33**

MENTAL MATH: 7 AND 9 AS FACTORS

You can use known facts to find other products.

| If you know 4 × 9 = 36, you can find 8 × 9. | 9 ×4 ——— 36 | If you know 4 × 9 = 36, you can find 5 × 9. | 9 ×4 ——— 36 |
| Since 8 is twice 4, double the product to find 8 × 9: 36 + 36 = 72   8 × 9 = 72 | 9 ×8 ——— 72 | Count on 9 more to find 5 × 9: 36 + 9 = 45   5 × 9 = 45 | 9 ×5 ——— 45 |

Find the product.

1. 7 × 2 = **14**   2. 3 × 9 = **27**   3. 8 × 3 = **24**
   Count on 7 more.   Double the product.   Count on 3 more.
   7 × 3 = **21**   6 × 9 = **54**   9 × 3 = **27**
4. 8 × 9 = **72**   5. 7 × 7 = **49**   6. 3 × 7 = **21**
   9 × 9 = **81**   8 × 7 = **56**   6 × 7 = **42**
7. 9 × 5 = **45**   8. 8 × 4 = **32**   9. 9 × 7 = **63**
10. 7 × 5 = **35**   11. 1 × 9 = **9**   12. 9 × 6 = **54**
13. 9 × 4 = **36**   14. 7 × 9 = **63**   15. 7 × 8 = **56**
16. 7 × 4 = **28**   17. 1 × 7 = **7**   18. 2 × 9 = **18**

19. 9 ×3 ——— **27**   20. 5 ×9 ——— **45**   21. 2 ×7 ——— **14**   22. 9 ×1 ——— **9**   23. 3 ×7 ——— **21**   24. 4 ×9 ——— **36**

25. 7 ×9 ——— **63**   26. 5 ×7 ——— **35**   27. 6 ×9 ——— **54**   28. 9 ×9 ——— **81**   29. 9 ×7 ——— **63**   30. 8 ×9 ——— **72**

Name: _____   Extend **33**

MENTAL MATH: 7 AND 9 AS FACTORS

Multiplication Search

Write multiplication sentences to make the sum true. Each multiplication sentence must have 7 or 9 as one of the factors.

The first one is done for you.

1. 2 × **9** = 18   → Product
   7 × **4** = 28
   46 Sum

2. 9 × **1** = 9
   7 × **2** = 14
   23 Sum

3. 2 × **9** = 18
   8 × **7** = 56
   74 Sum

4. 7 × **3** = 21
   9 × **9** = 81
   102 Sum

5. 7 × **6** = 42
   8 × **9** = 72
   114 Sum

6. 4 × **7** = 28
   9 × **8** = 72
   100 Sum

7. 7 × **8** = 56
   7 × **9** = 63
   119 Sum

8. 9 × **5** = 45
   7 × **8** = 56
   101 Sum

9. 7 × **8** = 56
   5 × **9** = 45
   101 Sum

10. 3 × **9** = 27
    7 × **4** = 28
    55 Sum

11. 4 × **9** = 36
    7 × **9** = 63
    99 Sum

12. 5 × **7** = 35
    9 × **6** = 54
    89 Sum

Think Critically

13. Look at exercise 2. Explain the method you used to complete the chart. Answers may vary. Possible answer: The sum is a small number, so I knew the two missing factors had to be small. I used guess, test, and revise starting with 1 and 2.

137

LESSON 4.5

Problem-Solving Strategy: Find a Pattern

OBJECTIVE Solve problems by finding and using a pattern.

RESOURCE REMINDER
Math Center Cards 34
Practice 34, Reteach 34, Extend 34

SKILLS TRACE

GRADE 3	• Solve problems by finding and using a pattern. *(Chapter 10)*
GRADE 4	• Solve problems by finding and using a pattern.
GRADE 5	• Solve problems by finding and using a pattern. *(Chapter 7)*

WARM-UP

Cooperative Groups   Logical/Analytical

OBJECTIVE Explore square numbers.

▶ Show the following on the chalkboard:

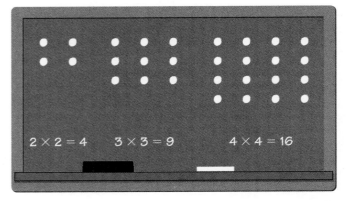

$2 \times 2 = 4$ $3 \times 3 = 9$ $4 \times 4 = 16$

▶ Students discuss the pattern shown by these three arrays and multiplication sentences. Then groups draw the next five arrays and write the multiplication sentences. *[5 × 5 = 25, 6 × 6 = 36, 7 × 7 = 49, 8 × 8 = 64, 9 × 9 = 81]*

▶ Groups compare their results, and work together to create a description of the pattern. Explain that the numbers in this pattern are called *square numbers*. Discuss how this name describes these numbers.

SCIENCE CONNECTION

Cooperative Pairs   Logical/Analytical

OBJECTIVE Connect identifying patterns in data with science.

Materials have available: calculators

Prepare Make a time line on a large sheet of paper.

▶ Present the time line and the problem below on the chalkboard.

Dr. Kerry Stuart has discovered a new star. She records the star's distance from Earth on a time line. What can Dr. Stuart conclude from her data? How far will the star be from Earth on March 27th?

▶ Pairs work together to analyze the data and describe the pattern in the table. *[The star is moving away from Earth at a rate of 2,025 miles per day.]*

▶ Pairs work together to predict the star's distance from Earth on March 27th. *[1,312,600 miles]*

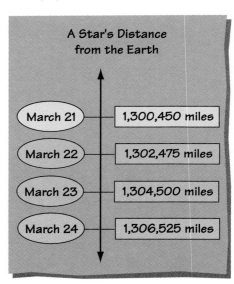

A Star's Distance from the Earth

March 21	1,300,450 miles
March 22	1,302,475 miles
March 23	1,304,500 miles
March 24	1,306,525 miles

Daily Review

PREVIOUS DAY QUICK REVIEW

Multiply mentally.
1. 7 × 6 [42]
2. 9 × 5 [45]
3. 7 × 6 [42]
4. 9 × 9 [81]

FAST FACTS

1. 5 − 5 [0]
2. 10 − 2 [8]
3. 9 − 6 [3]
4. 12 − 4 [8]

Problem of the Day • 34

Which number makes the most sense?
Use the numbers below to complete the
paragraph.
The Empire State Building is ___ ft tall. Over
___ million people visit the building each
year. Some climb the ___ steps to the top.
1,238   1,860   2 [1,238; 2; 1,860]

TECH LINK

MATH VAN

Tools You may wish to use the Table
and Graph for Data Point in this lesson.

MATH FORUM

Combination Classes I encourage my
older students to write problems
involving two or more steps.

**Visit our Resource Village at
http://www.mhschool.com to see
more of the Math Forum.**

MATH CENTER

Practice

OBJECTIVE Identify and continue patterns.

Materials poster paper, crayons, markers

Students draw three shirts to extend a pattern and
they explain the pattern in words. Students make up
their own patterns. They ask classmates to identify
and continue their patterns. [1. *4th shirt: 3 chest stripes
and 4 stripes on each sleeve; 5th shirt: 4 chest stripes and 5
stripes on each sleeve; 6th shirt: 5 chest stripes and 6 stripes
on each sleeve; 2. Check students' descriptions.*]

PRACTICE ACTIVITY 34

MATH CENTER
Partners

Spatial Sense • Designing Uniforms

YOU NEED
poster paper
crayons or markers

1. Find the pattern in the shirts.
   • Draw the next 3 shirts.
   • Explain the pattern with words.
2. Make up a different pattern.
   • Draw the first 3 pictures in your pattern.
   • Trade patterns with your partner.
   • See if your partner can figure out your
     pattern and draw the next 3 pictures in
     the pattern.

Chapter 4, Lesson 5, pages 138–139

Problem Solving

NCTM Standards

✓ Problem Solving
✓ Communication
  Reasoning
  Connections

ESL APPROPRIATE

Problem Solving

OBJECTIVE Solve problems by identifying patterns.

Materials per student: calculator, Math Center
Recording Sheet (TA 31 optional)

Students explore patterns to answer questions.
[1. *blue—101, green—81; blue increases by 25 every week,
green multiplies by 3 every week; 2. blue—126, green—
243*]

PROBLEM-SOLVING ACTIVITY 34

MATH CENTER
On Your Own

Patterning • Bugs

YOU NEED
calculator

Blue bugs increase in this pattern:

BLUE BUGS			
Week 1	Week 2	Week 3	Week 4
Total bugs 1	Total bugs 26	Total bugs 51	Total bugs 76

Green bugs increase in this pattern:

GREEN BUGS			
Week 1	Week 2	Week 3	Week 4
Total bugs 1	Total bugs 3	Total bugs 9	Total bugs 27

Look at the patterns shown above. Use a calculator to help you
answer these questions.
1. What will each population be in Week 5? Explain your answer.
2. What will each population be in Week 6?

Chapter 4, Lesson 5, pages 138–139

Problem Solving

NCTM Standards

✓ Problem Solving
✓ Communication
✓ Reasoning
  Connections

Problem-Solving Strategy: Find a Pattern

OBJECTIVE Solve problems by finding and using a pattern.

1 Introduce

Materials connecting cubes—4 blue, 4 red, 2 yellow

Display a cube train that shows the following pattern.

- **What pattern does the cube train show?** *[2 blue cubes, 2 red cubes, 1 yellow cube]*
- **Suppose this pattern continues to repeat. How could you use the pattern to find the color of the 25th cube?** *[Possible answer: You can predict that since the pattern repeats after every 5 cubes, and 25 is a multiple of 5, the 25th cube will be the same color as the 5th cube, yellow.]*

2 Teach
Whole Class

▶ **LEARN** Have students read the problem on page 138, restate it in their own words, and make a plan for solving it. Ask:
- **What are you trying to find?** *[who serves next]*
- **How can you find this out?** *[Answers may vary, but students should mention finding and using a pattern.]*

After students identify the pattern, ask:
- **Who serves the 8th point? the 13th point?** *[Amy; Pedro]*

3 Close

▶ **Check for Understanding** using items 1 and 2, page 138.

CRITICAL THINKING
For item 2, ask students if another possible answer is 3 touchdowns and 8 placekicks. Students should realize that a placekick cannot be attempted unless a team scores a touchdown. So, the number of placekicks has to be less than or equal to the number of touchdowns.

▶ **PRACTICE**
Have students choose three exercises from ex. 1–5 and complete all ex. 6–11.
- In ex. 1, remind students that the diagonals are the numbers that go from the upper left corner to the lower right corner, and the upper right corner to the lower left corner.
- For ex. 7–10, students use the strategy of interpreting data from a graph.

Problem-Solving Strategy

Read
Plan
Solve
Look Back

Find a Pattern

LEARN

Read Amy and Pedro are playing a game of table tennis. Each player changes serve after serving 5 points. When the game began, Pedro served first. They have played for 17 points so far. Who will serve the next ball?

Plan To solve the problem, you can find a pattern.

Solve Find the serving pattern.
Pedro serves points 1 to 5.
Amy serves points 6 to 10.
Pedro serves points 11 to 15.
Amy serves points 16 to 20.
Pedro serves points 21 to 25.

Think: 17 points have been served.

The next ball is the 18th point. Amy serves the 18th point.

Look Back Has the question been answered? Yes—Amy serves the 18th point, which is the next ball.

CHECK

Check for Understanding

1 **What if** the score was 5 to 18 in favor of Amy. What is the next point? Who will serve the ball? Explain your reasoning. $5 + 18 = 23$, so the next point is the 24th point; Pedro will serve next; he serves points 21 through 25

Critical Thinking: Analyze **Explain your reasoning.** Explanations may vary.

2 In American football, a touchdown is worth 6 points. A placekick over the crossbar following a touchdown is worth 1 point. If a team scores 26 points in a game, what combination of touchdowns and placekicks did they make? **4 touchdowns and 2 placekicks**

138 Lesson 4.5

Meeting Individual Needs

Early Finishers

Have students continue the pattern to find the tenth triangular number: *[30]*

3   6   9

ESL APPROPRIATE

Extra Support

Some students may find the pattern but forget to go back and answer the question. Remind students to look back to see if they have answered the question.

Ongoing Assessment

Anecdotal Report Make notes on students' ability to recognize patterns. If they choose other strategies to solve problems that could be solved with patterns, ask them to describe another way to solve the problems.

Follow Up If students need more practice working with patterns, assign **Reteach 34.**

If they need a greater challenge, assign **Extend 34.**

1 A magic square has rows, columns, and diagonals that add to the same number. The total is called the magic number. Complete the magic square below.

7	■	3	17
■	9	■	5; 13
■	■	11	15; 1

2 **Spatial reasoning** A football field is lined with chalk every 5 yards. How many chalk lines are there from goal line to goal line? **21 lines**

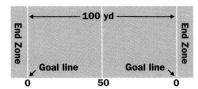

3 There are five Olympic speed-skating events for men: 500 m; 1,000 m; 1,500 m; 5,000 m; and 10,000 m. If a skater competes in all five events, what is his total distance? **18,000 m**

4 In the 1996 NCAA Women's Basketball Tournament championship game, Tennessee scored 5 more points than Connecticut in overtime. Their combined scores were 171. How many points did each team score? **Tennessee—88, Connecticut—83**

5 Keith Gledhill won a table-tennis championship in 1926. He won another championship in 1987. How many years had passed? **61 y**

6 There are 16 cans in the 8th row, 14 in the 7th row, and 12 in the 6th row. If the pattern continues, how many cans will be in the 1st row? **2 cans**

Use the graph for problems 7–10.

7 Which ball weighs the most? the least? **basketball; table-tennis ball**

8 Which of the balls shown weigh more than 4 ounces? **baseball, basketball, football, lacrosse ball**

9 **What if** soccer were listed in the graph. A soccer ball weighs about 16 ounces. How many balls would you use to show the weight of a soccer ball? **8 balls**

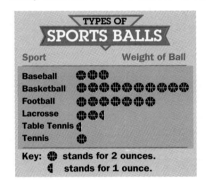

TYPES OF
SPORTS BALLS

Sport	Weight of Ball

Baseball
Basketball
Football
Lacrosse
Table Tennis
Tennis

Key: ● stands for 2 ounces.
◐ stands for 1 ounce.

10 **Write a problem** using the data in the pictograph. Solve it and have others solve it. **Students should compare problems and solutions.**

11 **Data Point** Find how many different types of sports balls you have at home. Create a pictograph. **Students may create a pictograph with a soccer ball, volleyball, racquetball, and so on.** Multiplication and Division Facts **139**

Extra Practice, page 497

Alternate Teaching Strategy

Present the following problem:

A golf store is giving away 2 golf tees for every $4.00 spent, 4 tees for every $8.00, and 6 tees for every $12.00. If you get 10 free tees, how much did you spend?

Demonstrate how using a table can help students find a pattern. Write the following on the board:

tees	2	4	6
money spent	$4	$8	$12

Ask:
- **Do you see a pattern in the top row?** [Possible answer: Yes, the numbers are multiples of 2.]
- **Do you see a pattern in the bottom row?** [Possible answer: Yes, the amounts are multiples of 4.]

Have students use the pattern in the table to find the amount spent to get 8 tees. [$16] Then have them complete the table for 10 tees. [$20]

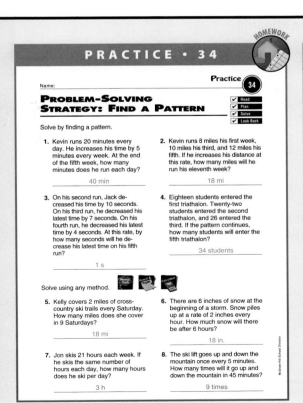

Practice 34

Name: _____

PROBLEM-SOLVING STRATEGY: FIND A PATTERN

☑ Read
☑ Plan
☑ Solve
☑ Look Back

Solve by finding a pattern.

1. Kevin runs 20 minutes every day. He increases his time by 5 minutes every week. At the end of the fifth week, how many minutes does he run each day?
40 min

2. Kevin runs 8 miles his first week, 10 miles his third, and 12 miles his fifth. If he increases his distance at this rate, how many miles will he run his eleventh week?
_18 mi_

3. On his second run, Jack decreased his time by 10 seconds. On his third run, he decreased his latest time by 7 seconds. On his fourth run, he decreased his latest time by 4 seconds. At this rate, by how many seconds will he decrease his latest time on his fifth run?
_1 s_

4. Eighteen students entered the first triathalon. Twenty-two students entered the second triathalon, and 26 entered the third. If the pattern continues, how many students will enter the fifth triathalon?
34 students

Solve using any method.

5. Kelly covers 2 miles of cross-country ski trails every Saturday. How many miles does she cover in 9 Saturdays?
_18 mi_

6. There are 6 inches of snow at the beginning of a storm. Snow piles up at a rate of 2 inches per hour. How much snow will there be after 6 hours?
_18 in._

7. Jon skis 21 hours each week. If he skis the same number of hours each day, how many hours does he ski per day?
_3 h_

8. The ski lift goes up and down the mountain once every 5 minutes. How many times will it go up and down the mountain in 45 minutes?
9 times

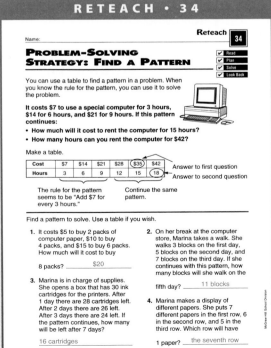

Reteach 34

Name: _____

PROBLEM-SOLVING STRATEGY: FIND A PATTERN

☑ Read
☑ Plan
☑ Solve
☑ Look Back

You can use a table to find a pattern in a problem. When you know the rule for the pattern, you can use it to solve the problem.

It costs $7 to use a special computer for 3 hours, $14 for 6 hours, and $21 for 9 hours. If this pattern continues:
- How much will it cost to rent the computer for 15 hours?
- How many hours can you rent the computer for $42?

Make a table.

Cost	$7	$14	$21	$28	$35	$42
Hours	3	6	9	12	15	18

Answer to first question
Answer to second question

The rule for the pattern seems to be "Add $7 for every 3 hours."

Continue the same pattern.

Find a pattern to solve. Use a table if you wish.

1. It costs $5 to buy 2 packs of computer paper, $10 to buy 4 packs, and $15 to buy 6 packs. How much will it cost to buy 8 packs?
_$20_

2. On her break at the computer store, Marina takes a walk. She walks 3 blocks on the first day, 5 blocks on the second day, and 7 blocks on the third day. If she continues with this pattern, how many blocks will she walk on the fifth day?
11 blocks

3. Marina is in charge of supplies. She opens a box that has 30 ink cartridges for the printers. After 1 day there are 28 cartridges left. After 2 days there are 26 left. After 3 days there are 24 left. If the pattern continues, how many will be left after 7 days?
16 cartridges

4. Marina makes a display of different papers. She puts 7 different papers in the first row, 6 in the second row, and 5 in the third row. Which row will have 1 paper?
the seventh row

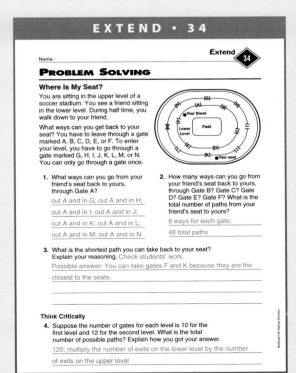

Extend 34

Name: _____

PROBLEM SOLVING

Where Is My Seat?

You are sitting in the upper level of a soccer stadium. You see a friend sitting in the lower level. During half time, you walk down to your friend.

What ways can you get back to your seat? You have to leave through a gate marked A, B, C, D, E, or F. To enter your level, you have to go through a gate marked G, H, I, J, K, L, M, or N. You can only go through a gate once.

1. What ways can you go from your friend's seat back to yours, through Gate A?
out A and in G; out A and in H;
out A and in I; out A and in J;
out A and in K; out A and in L;
out A and in M; out A and in N

2. How many ways can you go from your friend's seat back to yours, through Gate B? Gate C? Gate D? Gate E? Gate F? What is the total number of paths from your friend's seat to yours?
8 ways for each gate;
48 total paths

3. What is the shortest path you can take back to your seat? Explain your reasoning. Check students' work.
Possible answer: You can take gates F and K because they are the
closest to the seats.

Think Critically

4. Suppose the number of gates for each level is 10 for the first level and 12 for the second level. What is the total number of possible paths? Explain how you got your answer.
120; multiply the number of exits on the lower level by the number
of exits on the upper level

139

LESSON 4.6

Three Factors

OBJECTIVE Find the product of three factors.

RESOURCE REMINDER
Math Center Cards 35
Practice 35, Reteach 35, Extend 35

SKILLS TRACE

GRADE 3 • Explore finding the product of three or more factors. *(Chapter 7)*

GRADE 4 • Find the product of three or more factors.

GRADE 5 • Find the product of three or more factors. *(Chapter 4)*

MANIPULATIVE WARM-UP

Cooperative Groups   **Visual/Spatial**

OBJECTIVE Multiply 3 factors.

Materials per group: 24 connecting cubes

► Have students make a shape that is 2 cubes by 4 cubes. Then have them make two more shapes that are the same.

► Have students make a box by stacking the three shapes.

► Have students write a multiplication sentence using 2 or 3 factors to show each of the following:
  • The number of cubes in the bottom layer $[2 \times 4 = 8]$
  • The number of cubes in the bottom two layers $[2 \times 2 \times 4 = 16]$
  • The number of cubes in all 3 layers $[3 \times 2 \times 4 = 24]$

► Have students build other boxes to continue multiplying 3 factors such as $2 \times 2 \times 2$, $2 \times 3 \times 2$, and $3 \times 2 \times 4$.

ESL APPROPRIATE

CONSUMER CONNECTION

Whole Class   **Logical/Analytical**

OBJECTIVE Connect finding the product of three factors to consumerism.

► Draw the table below on the chalkboard:

► Have students complete the following:

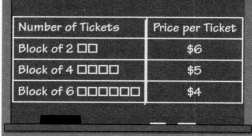

Number of Tickets	Price per Ticket
Block of 2 ☐☐	$6
Block of 4 ☐☐☐☐	$5
Block of 6 ☐☐☐☐☐☐	$4

  • **You want to buy 12 tickets. How many blocks of 2 would you need to buy? How many blocks of 4? How many blocks of 6?** *[6 blocks of 2; 3 blocks of 4; 2 blocks of 6]*
  • **What is the least expensive way to buy 12 tickets? Write multiplication sentences that show the cost of each possible way. Then find the difference in cost between the least and most expensive ways.** *[2 blocks of 6 tickets; $6 \times 2 \times \$6 = \$72$; $3 \times 4 \times \$5 = \$60$; $2 \times 6 \times \$4 = \$48$; $\$72 - \$48 = \$24$]*

► Extend the problem by having students find the least expensive way to buy 20 tickets. *[3 blocks of 6 tickets and 1 block of 2 tickets; $\$72 + \$12 = \$84$]*

Daily Review

Problem of the Day • 35

Donna's relay team won a relay race. Each member's time is shown below. How long did it take for the team to complete the race?

Donna: 1 min 20 sec   Kara: 1 min 25 sec
Martin: 1 min 41 sec   Becca: 1 min 16 sec

[5 min 42 sec]

TECH LINK

MATH VAN

Tools You may wish to use Table and Graph for datapoint with this lesson.

MATH FORUM

Cultural Diversity I encourage students from different cultures to share the ways they have learned addition, subtraction, and multiplication facts.

Visit our Resource Village at http://www.mhschool.com to see more of the Math Forum.

MATH CENTER

Practice

OBJECTIVE Write multiplication sentences with three factors.

Materials per pair: 0-9 spinner (TA 2), number cube; per student: Math Center Recording Sheet (TA 31 optional)

Students use a spinner and number cubes to generate factors for multiplication sentences. Facts do not exceed 9 × 3 × 3. *[Check students' work.]*

PRACTICE ACTIVITY 35

MATH CENTER
Partners 👥

Manipulatives • Product of Three

- One player spins for one number.
- The other player rolls the cube. Write two numbers that add up to the number on the cube. (If you roll 5, you might write 2 and 3—or 4 and 1.)
- Together use the three numbers as factors to write a multiplication sentence. Show grouping. Then write another sentence with the same factors.
- Play again several times.

YOU NEED
- spinner (0–9)
- number cube

2

2 3

$2 \times (2 \times 3) = 12$

NCTM Standards

  Problem Solving
✓ Communication
✓ Reasoning
✓ Connections

Chapter 4, Lesson 6, pages 140–141   Multiplication

Grade Level 4   *McGraw-Hill School Division*

ESL APPROPRIATE

Problem Solving

OBJECTIVE Solve multistep problems involving money and making a decision.

Materials per student: Math Center Recording Sheet (TA 31 optional)

Students compare the amount of money Elaine will earn depending on how she is paid. *[$2 an hour pays $24 in four weeks, but students may chose either method based on weekly work hours. Sample problem: Elaine's parents offer $3 an hour for 3 hours per week or $15 every other week for working 3 hours per week. Which way earns her more money?]*

PROBLEM-SOLVING ACTIVITY 35

MATH CENTER
On Your Own 👤

Decision Making • Earning Money

Elaine will do a household job for 4 weeks to earn extra money. By which method will she earn more money? Which method would you choose? Explain.

Elaine's parents have offered her a choice of how she gets paid. One choice is to earn $2 an hour and work 3 hours a week. Her other choice is to earn $8 every other week by working 2 hours a week.

Write another problem like this one. Solve it. Give it to other students to solve.

$2 an hour

$8 every other week

NCTM Standards

  Problem Solving
  Communication
✓ Reasoning
  Connections

Chapter 4, Lesson 6, pages 140–141   Multiplication

Grade Level 4   *McGraw-Hill School Division*

Lesson 4.6 continued

Three Factors

OBJECTIVE Find the product of three factors.

Vocabulary Associative Property, Commutative Property

 Introduce

Materials per pair: 20 two-color counters

Review the Commutative Property with students. Have pairs of students use counters to make a 3 by 5 array. Ask:
- **What two multiplication facts do the counters show? Write the facts.** [$3 \times 5 = 15, 5 \times 3 = 15$]
- **What multiplication property is shown by these two multiplication facts?** [the Commutative Property]

2 Teach
Whole Class

▶ **LEARN** Read the introductory problem aloud. Ask:
- **What expression represents the number of outs for 1 team?** [9×3]
- **What expression represents the number of outs for 2 teams?** [$2 \times (9 \times 3)$]

Read through the solution with students. Ask:
- **Why are the numbers ordered and grouped this way?** [Sample answer: to make it easier to multiply]

More Examples Elicit that in Examples A and B, only the Associative Property, not the Commutative Property, is used.

3 Close

▶ **Check for Understanding** using items 1–9, page 140.

CRITICAL THINKING
Remind students of the Associative Property of Addition. For example: $(2 + 3) + 4 = 2 + (3 + 4)$.

In item 9, students should show examples to support their explanations.

▶ **PRACTICE**
Materials have available: calculators

Options for assigning exercises:
A—Ex. 1–15; ex. 18–22; **Mixed Review**
B—Ex. 9–22; **Mixed Review**

- In ex. 20 and 21, students can use estimation and number sense.

a **Algebra** In ex. 13–17, students use the Commutative and Associative properties, as well as their knowledge of multiplication facts, to find products and missing factors.

Mixed Review/Test Preparation Students review place value, a concept that they learned in Chapter 1.

Three Factors

IN THE WORKPLACE
Rich Garcia, major league umpire, American League

Have you ever watched a baseball gam that goes on and on? Rich Garcia rules whether a batter is out. If there are 9 complete innings and 3 outs per inning for each of the two teams, it takes a long time to see all those outs. How many outs are there?

You can multiply $2 \times (9 \times 3)$ to find the number of outs. Using properties may keep the factors easy to multiply.

$$
\begin{aligned}
2 \times (9 \times 3) &= 2 \times (3 \times 9) \longleftarrow \text{Use the Commutative Property.} \\
&= (2 \times 3) \times 9 \longleftarrow \text{Use the Associative Property.} \\
&= 6 \times 9 \qquad \longleftarrow \text{Multiply.} \\
&= 54 \qquad \quad \text{There are 54 outs.}
\end{aligned}
$$

Commutative Property
You can change the order of two factors without changing the product. $9 \times 3 = 3 \times 9$

Associative Property
You can change the grouping of three or more factors without changing the product. $2 \times (3 \times 9) = (2 \times 3) \times$

More Examples

A $(8 \times 2) \times 5 = 8 \times (2 \times 5)$
$= 8 \times 10$
$= 80$

B $3 \times (2 \times 7) = (3 \times 2) \times 7$
$= 6 \times 7$
$= 42$

Check for Understanding
Multiply.

1 $(3 \times 6) \times 2$ 36   **2** $3 \times (5 \times 3)$ 45   **3** $(8 \times 4) \times 2$ 64   **4** $2 \times (7 \times 4)$

5 $5 \times (9 \times 2)$ 90   **6** $(2 \times 7) \times 3$ 42   **7** $(5 \times 7) \times 2$ 70   **8** $2 \times (8 \times 4)$

Critical Thinking: Analyze   Explain your reasoning.

9 How are the Commutative and Associative Properties for multiplication similar to those for addition?

Possible answer: The way addends and factors are ordered or grouped does not affect their answers.

Meeting Individual Needs

Early Finishers
Challenge students to write a rule for finding the product of 3 factors if one of the factors is 1.

Extra Support
For students having difficulty you may wish to have them use place-value models to find the product in the development.

ESL APPROPRIATE

Ongoing Assessment
Interview Determine if students understand the Commutative and Associative properties. Ask:
- **Use the Commutative and Associative properties to solve $3 \times 8 \times 3$.**
  [$3 \times 8 \times 3 = (3 \times 8) \times 3$
  $= (8 \times 3) \times 3 = 8$
  $\times (3 \times 3) = 8 \times 9 = 72$]

Follow Up If students need more practice multiplying three factors, have groups spin three 1–5 spinners and find the product of the numbers. You may also assign **Reteach 35**.

Assign **Extend 35** to those students who need a challenge.

Practice

Multiply.

1 $(5 \times 2) \times 2$ **20** **2** $(9 \times 3) \times 2$ **54** **3** $8 \times (7 \times 1)$ **56** **4** $(6 \times 3) \times 3$ **54**

5 $(2 \times 6) \times 4$ **48** **6** $2 \times (5 \times 4)$ **40** **7** $(3 \times 5) \times 2$ **30** **8** $(2 \times 9) \times 3$ **54**

9 $3 \times (4 \times 3)$ **36** **10** $(8 \times 3) \times 2$ **48** **11** $9 \times (0 \times 8)$ **0** **12** $(7 \times 1) \times 7$ **49**

ALGEBRA Complete the multiplication sentence.

13 $(7 \times 4) \times 1 = \blacksquare$ **28** **14** $6 \times (5 \times 0) = \blacksquare$ **0** **15** $8 \times 2 = \blacksquare \times 8$ **2**

16 $6 \times 9 = 6 \times (\blacksquare \times 3)$ **3** **17** $(2 \times 3) \times 4 = (2 \times 4) \times \blacksquare$ **3**

MIXED APPLICATIONS
Problem Solving

18 Tori runs 2 miles each day on 5 days of each week. About how many miles does she run during February? **about 40 mi**

19 **Logical reasoning** Find as many ways as you can to show the number 90 using three numbers and at least two operations.

Answers may vary. Possible answer: $50 \times 2 - 10$

20 **Make a decision** Look at the dartboard at the right. What sections should you aim for to get a score of 50 using the fewest number of darts? Why? **Aim for 35 and 15; explanations may vary.**

dartboard: 10 5 17 35 23 24 15 29

21 Estimate which of these products will be between 50 and 100. Explain your reasoning.
a. 15×3 b. 25×10
c. 9×8 d. 16×4
The products of c and d; explanations may vary.

22 **Data Point** Survey your classmates to find the different types of exercises they do. Use a bar graph to show your data. Write a sentence about your graph.
Students may list jogging, playing sports, dancing, and so on.

---

mixed review • test preparation

Write in standard form.

1 $5{,}000 + 200 + 90 + 3$ **5,293**

2 $70{,}000 + 800 + 50$ **70,850**

3 $300{,}000 + 40 + 2$ **300,042**

4 six thousand, eleven **6,011**

5 eighty thousand, four hundred four **80,404**

Compare. Write >, <, or =.

6 $8{,}742 \blacksquare 8{,}800$ **<**

7 $20{,}306 \blacksquare 20{,}360$ **<**

8 5 million $\blacksquare$ 500,000 **>**

Extra Practice, page 497

Multiplication and Division Facts **141**

Alternate Teaching Strategy

Write the following on the board:

$$4 \times (6 \times 2)$$

Have students use the Commutative Property to rewrite what is in the parentheses. $[4 \times (2 \times 6)]$

Then have them use the Associative Property to rewrite the 3 factors so that the product in the parentheses is easier to multiply. $[(4 \times 2) \times 6]$

Continue with other examples such as $4 \times (8 \times 2)$ and $(3 \times 9) \times 2$, having students use the Commutative Property and the Associative Property to help them multiply the 3 factors.

PRACTICE • 35

Name: _____ **Practice 35**

THREE FACTORS

Multiply.

1. $4 \times (2 \times 5) = \underline{40}$
2. $4 \times (2 \times 3) = \underline{24}$
3. $7 \times (2 \times 5) = \underline{70}$
4. $(3 \times 2) \times 8 = \underline{48}$
5. $(4 \times 3) \times 2 = \underline{24}$
6. $6 \times (3 \times 2) = \underline{36}$
7. $4 \times (4 \times 2) = \underline{32}$
8. $(2 \times 2) \times 2 = \underline{8}$
9. $(3 \times 0) \times 9 = \underline{0}$
10. $(5 \times 2) \times 4 = \underline{40}$
11. $8 \times (2 \times 2) = \underline{32}$
12. $7 \times (3 \times 3) = \underline{63}$
13. $6 \times (2 \times 2) = \underline{24}$
14. $(2 \times 7) \times 2 = \underline{28}$
15. $(4 \times 3) \times 0 = \underline{0}$
16. $5 \times (4 \times 2) = \underline{40}$
17. $9 \times (2 \times 4) = \underline{72}$
18. $5 \times (3 \times 3) = \underline{45}$
19. $4 \times (6 \times 1) = \underline{24}$
20. $2 \times (5 \times 0) = \underline{0}$
21. $7 \times (3 \times 2) = \underline{42}$
22. $9 \times (2 \times 3) = \underline{54}$
23. $(8 \times 1) \times 9 = \underline{72}$
24. $5 \times (2 \times 3) = \underline{30}$

Algebra Complete the multiplication sentence.

25. $5 \times 6 = 5 \times (3 \times \boxed{2})$
26. $3 \times (5 \times \boxed{4}) = 60$
27. $(\boxed{0} \times 8) \times 7 = 0$
28. $9 \times (\boxed{3} \times 1) = 27$
29. $(2 \times 4) \times \boxed{3} = 24$
30. $(3 \times 5) \times \boxed{3} = 9 \times 5$
31. $3 \times 6 = 3 \times (3 \times \boxed{2})$
32. $3 \times 8 = 3 \times (2 \times \boxed{4})$
33. $3 \times 16 = 3 \times (4 \times \boxed{4})$
34. $4 \times 6 = (3 \times 4) \times \boxed{2}$

Solve.

35. The school gives each tennis player a blue shirt and a white shirt. Each shirt costs the school $9. What is the total cost of shirts for 5 players? **$90**

36. Two cans of tennis balls are needed for each tennis match. There are 3 tennis balls in each can. How many balls are needed for 5 matches? **30 balls**

RETEACH • 35

Name: _____ **Reteach 35**

THREE FACTORS

Compare these multiplication sentences.

$2 \times 3 \quad 2 \times 3 \quad 2 \times 3 \quad 2 \times 3$

$(2 \times 3) \times 4 = 24$

$3 \times 4 \quad 3 \times 4$

$2 \times (3 \times 4) = 24$

The **grouping property** of multiplication means that the way you group the factors does not matter.

Complete.

1. $(4 \times 6) \times 3 = 4 \times (\boxed{6} \times 3)$
2. $7 \times (5 \times 2) = (\boxed{7} \times 5) \times 2$
3. $(1 \times 3) \times 5 = 1 \times (3 \times \boxed{5})$
4. $4 \times (6 \times 1) = (4 \times 6) \times \boxed{1}$
5. $2 \times (3 \times 4) = (2 \times 3) \times 4 = \boxed{24}$
6. $4 \times (2 \times 8) = (\boxed{4} \times 2) \times 8 = \boxed{64}$
7. $5 \times (4 \times 3) = (5 \times \boxed{4}) \times 3 = \boxed{60}$
8. $(8 \times 1) \times 7 = 8 \times (1 \times \boxed{7}) = \boxed{56}$

Find the product.

9. $(2 \times 4) \times 3 = \underline{24}$
10. $2 \times (2 \times 3) = \underline{12}$
11. $(1 \times 6) \times 2 = \underline{12}$
12. $(4 \times 3) \times 1 = \underline{12}$
13. $(5 \times 2) \times 3 = \underline{30}$
14. $(7 \times 1) \times 3 = \underline{21}$
15. $(4 \times 8) \times 1 = \underline{32}$
16. $3 \times (3 \times 2) = \underline{18}$
17. $5 \times (3 \times 2) = \underline{30}$
18. $(5 \times 4) \times 2 = \underline{40}$
19. $9 \times (2 \times 3) = \underline{54}$
20. $3 \times (3 \times 3) = \underline{27}$
21. $(2 \times 7) \times 2 = \underline{28}$
22. $(5 \times 6) \times 1 = \underline{30}$
23. $(1 \times 5) \times 2 = \underline{10}$
24. $(2 \times 7) \times 1 = \underline{14}$

EXTEND • 35

Name: _____ **Extend 35**

THREE FACTORS

Spinners Times Three

Suppose you are playing a game. You are supposed to spin each spinner three times and multiply the numbers you spin.

Spinner A: 1, 2, 3, 3   Spinner B: 0, 1, 3, 2

Answer these questions about your spins.

1. What is the greatest product you can get on spinner A? on B?
   27 on A; 27 on B

2. What is the least product you can get on spinner B? on A?
   0 on B; 1 on A

Suppose that the rules change. If you spin a number already spun, spin again until you get 3 different factors.

Spinner C: 1, 2, 4, 3   Spinner D: 2, 3, 1, 3

3. What is the greatest product you can get on spinner C? on D?
   24 on C; 6 on D

4. What is the least product you can get on spinner D? on C?
   6 on D; 6 on C

Think Critically

5. Look back at problem 1. Explain how you got your answer.
   Answers may vary. Possible answer: I could get 3 on each spin: $3 \times 3 \times 3 = 27$.

MIDCHAPTER REVIEW

PURPOSE Maintain and review concepts, skills, and strategies that students have learned thus far in the chapter.

Materials per student: calculator (optional)

Using the Midchapter Review

Have students complete the **Midchapter Review** independently or use it with the whole class.

If students have trouble remembering basic facts, remind them of the strategies they have used to find products.

 Algebra Ex. 30–36 develop algebra sense by having students find missing factors and find the rule that describes a function.

Students can approach this problem at their own levels. Most students should be able to explain two or three strategies.

Possible strategies include:
- using pictorial representations
- using a number line
- skip-counting
- using manipulatives
- using known facts
- using the Commutative Property

Vocabulary Review

Write the following words on the chalkboard:

array
factor   multiple
Associative Property   Commutative Property
product   skip-count

Ask for volunteers to explain, show, or act out the meaning of these words.

Write a multiplication sentence for the picture.

1  $4 \times 3 = 12$

2  $3 \times 9 = 27$

3  $4 \times 7 = 28$ or $7 \times 4 = 2$

Multiply. Draw an array or use counters if you wish.

4 6×1 6 **5** 1×7 7 **6** 0×4 0 **7** 8×0 0 **8** 5×3 15

9 0×1 0 **10** 2×3 6 **11** 5×6 30 **12** 2×8 16 **13** 8×8 64

14 3×5 15 **15** 4×3 12 **16** 6×5 30 **17** 3×8 24 **18** 6×7 42

19 4×4 16 **20** 9×3 27 **21** 9×8 72 **22** 7×7 49 **23** 5×9 45

24 $3 \times 5 \times 3$ 45 **25** $8 \times 5 \times 2$ 80 **26** $2 \times 9 \times 3$ 54

27 $4 \times 6 \times 2$ 48 **28** $2 \times 7 \times 4$ 56 **29** $8 \times 3 \times 3$ 72

ALGEBRA Complete the sentence.

30 $4 \times 8 \times 0 = \blacksquare$ 0 **31** $7 \times 6 \times 1 = \blacksquare$ 42 **32** $4 \times 9 = 9 \times \blacksquare$ 4

33 $3 \times \blacksquare \times 9 = 9 \times 9$ 3 **34** $6 \times 4 = \blacksquare \times 3 \times 4$ 2

ALGEBRA Find the rule. Then complete the table.

35

Rule: ■ Multiply by 8.					
0	1	2	3	4	5
0	■	16	■	32	■

8   24   40

36

Rule: ■ Multiply by 7.					
0	1	2	3	4	5
0	7	■	21	■	■

14   28   35

Solve. Use any method.

37 At the basketball game, 7 rows of 8 seats were set aside for students. How many seats were set aside? **56 seats**

38 The band marches across the football field in 9 rows. Each row has 6 students. How many students are in the band? **54 students**

39 Sybil bought a box of golf balls. The box had 2 layers of balls. Each layer had 5 rows of 4 balls. How many balls were in the box? **40 balls**

40 Explain two different ways you can find 9×3. **Possible answers: Use counters or a number line, use the Commutative Property and find $3 \times 9 = 27$, find 10×3 then subtract $3 = 30 - 3 = 27$.**

Reinforcement and Remediation

CHAPTER OBJECTIVE	MIDCHAPTER REVIEW ITEMS	STUDENT BOOK PAGES	TEACHER'S EDITION PAGES		TEACHER RESOURCES
			Activities	Alternate Teaching Strategy	Reteach
*4A	1–29	124–137	123A, 127A, 131A, 133A	127, 131, 133, 137	30–33
*4C	6, 7, 9, 24–34	140–141	139A	141	35
*4E	35–39	138–139	137A	139	34

*4A Multiply, facts to 81
*4C Use the Commutative, Identity, Zero, and Associative properties
*4E Solve problems, including those that involve multiplication and division and patterns

developing algebra sense
MATH CONNECTION

Patterns and Properties

e product
always
ual to the
ctor for the
lumn; the
oduct is
ways equal
the factor
the row.

2. The product of
zero and another
number is zero,
so the products
in the first
column and row
are all zeros.

3. Possible answer:
The numbers in
Row 4 are double
the numbers in
Row 2.

Complete the multiplication table below. The number 20 is
placed in Row 5 and in Column 4 because 20 is the product
of 5 and 4. What is the product of 9 and 6? 54

COLUMN

×	0	1	2	3	4	5	6	7	8	9	10	11	12
0	0	0	0	0	0	0	0	0	0	0	0	0	0
1	0	1	2	3	4	5	6	7	8	9	10	11	12
2	0	2	4	6	8	10	12	14	16	18	20	22	24
3	0	3	6	9	12	15	18	21	24	27	30	33	36
4	0	4	8	12	16	20	24	28	32	36	40	44	48
5	0	5	10	15	20	25	30	35	40	45	50	55	60
6	0	6	12	18	24	30	36	42	48	54	60	66	72
7	0	7	14	21	28	35	42	49	56	63	70	77	84
8	0	8	16	24	32	40	48	56	64	72	80	88	96
9	0	9	18	27	36	45	54	63	72	81	90	99	108
10	0	10	20	30	40	50	60	70	80	90	100	110	120
11	0	11	22	33	44	55	66	77	88	99	110	121	132
12	0	12	24	36	48	60	72	84	96	108	120	132	144

ROW

ALGEBRA: PATTERNS Solve. Use the multiplication table.

1. What pattern do you see in Row 1?
in Column 1? See above.

2. What property can you use to
complete Row 0 and Column 0?
See above.

3. Look at the products in Row 2.
Compare these products with the
products in Row 4. What pattern
do you see? See above.

4. If you complete Columns 0–3,
which rows can you complete?
Why? Rows 0–3; possible answer:
use the Commutative Property.

5. Square numbers can be shown as
squares. Where are these numbers
in the table? What can you say
about their factors? From the
upper left corner down the diagonal
to the lower right corner; both
factors are the same number.

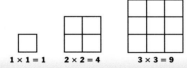

$1 \times 1 = 1$ $2 \times 2 = 4$ $3 \times 3 = 9$

Multiplication and Division Facts **143**

OBJECTIVE Recognize and use patterns in a multiplication table.

Materials have available: counters, graph paper, number lines, and other materials that students can use to find products

Using Algebra Sense

Math Connection In Lessons 1 and 2, students used patterns to help them find products. Here students use a multiplication table to find more patterns and to discuss properties of multiplication.

After students have read the opening paragraph, ask:
- **Where else can you place 20 in the table?** [Possible answer: in row 4 and column 5 since 4 × 5 = 20]
- **Where else can you place 54 in the table?** [in row 6 and column 9 since 6 × 9 = 54]

Algebra: Patterns: Have students talk about the methods they use to complete the table. Ask them to describe any patterns they see. Discuss how they can use those patterns to complete the rows and columns for 10, 11, and 12. Ask:
- **What pattern do you see in row 10? 11? 12?** [Possible answers: row 10: there is a 0 next to the number being multiplied by 10; row 11: the number being multiplied by 11 is in both the tens and the ones place; row 12: the product is equal to the number being multiplied by 12 times 10 plus twice that number]

Students may work in pairs or on their own to complete the table and ex. 1–5.

Applying Multiplication Facts

OBJECTIVE Use multiplication facts to find total scores for an invented sport.

Materials per group: poster board, markers, balls of various sizes and types

1 Engage

Lead a brief discussion about favorite sports. Then focus on sports in which points increase in multiples, such as basketball and football.

- **How can you use multiplication facts to help keep score in these games?** *[Possible answer: In basketball, a basket is worth two points. If the shot comes from behind the three-point line, it earns three points. A team with seven baskets made from behind the three-point line—3 × 7 = 21 points.]*

2 Investigate *Cooperative Groups*

Using the Pairs Compare Strategy, have students work individually to think of ideas for a new sport. Students meet with a partner to compare ideas. Two sets of partners (pairs) join together to compare their ideas for a new sport.

Suggest that students use the questions on page 144 of the Student Book as a checklist to help them organize their investigation.

Creating Your Sport

 Sequence of Events Suggest that groups choose one member to be the recorder for their group. After informally listing the rules for their sport, give groups time to try out the game by following the rules just as they are written. Students may need to adjust or simplify the rules to make it easier to understand and play.

3 Reflect and Share

Materials have available: calculators

Report Your Findings As the class compares the new sports, ask a volunteer to make a list of multiplication facts needed in each sport to find total scores.

Students can complete a table of possible scores for one team, then check their work on a calculator. Remind them that the goal is to gain between 40 and 50 points.

Revise your work Students can work toward clarity in their written rules by eliminating unnecessary words. You might also suggest that they use other students' reactions to their rules as a guideline for revision.

real-life investigation
APPLYING MULTIPLICATION FACTS

changing the Rules

Rules in sports are very important. They tell how many people should play and what equipment they should use. They also tell how to play the sport and who the winner should be. In this activity, you will work in teams to create a sport of your own. That way you make all the rules!

- ▶ What do you need to think about when you create your sport?

- ▶ Will you create an entirely new sport or change one that you already know?

- ▶ How many players will there be? What roles will they play? What will they use or wear?

- ▶ When will players score points? How will they score points? What events should get a higher score?

- ▶ How will players know that they have won the game?

144 Real-life Investigation

More To Investigate

Predict Possible approach: Imagine a game that already has a winner. How did the winner accumulate the points to win? You can either change the number of points each player scored or change the number of successful plays made by one or more players.

Explore Possible approach: Make winning easier. You may also need to think about the size, strength, and skill levels of younger children and their ability to understand the rules of the game.

Find Possible approach: Students can use reference books or an online computer service to look up the history of their favorite sport.

Bibliography Students interested in reading more about sports can try:

Multicultural Portrait of Professional Sports, by David Paul Press. New York: Marshall Cavendish Pub., 1994. ISBN 1–854–35661–5.

DECISION MAKING

Creating Your Sport

1 Work with a small group. Think of different ideas for sports.

2 Decide what your sport will be. Choose one that your classmates will enjoy playing at school. Make up a catchy name for your sport.

3 **Sequence of Events** Write the rules of your sport using sequence words. Make sure that your sport is safe.

4 Play your sport with the members of your group. Revise the sport or the rules if you need to make them simple and easy to understand.

Reporting Your Findings

5 Prepare a poster that explains your sport. Include the following:

► Explain the rules and show drawings or photographs that help others understand how to play.

► Show some possible ways to get between 40 and 50 points. Use multiplication when you find the totals.

► Explain how you would group your entire class to play.

6 Compare your poster with those of other groups.

Revise your work.
► Does your poster include all the information that players need?
► Are your rules and scoring clear and easy to understand?
► Did you proofread your work?

MORE TO INVESTIGATE

See Teacher's Edition.

PREDICT all the different ways to win the game by getting a score you choose.

EXPLORE ways to change your sport so that younger children can play. What do you need to think about to do this step?

FIND out who invented your favorite sport and what changes have been made to the sport since it was invented.

Multiplication and Division Facts **145**

Building A Portfolio

This investigation will allow you to evaluate students' ability to create and organize data and to use multiplication facts to find a total.

Allow students to revise their work for the portfolio. Each student's portfolio piece should consist of a copy of the rules for the sport his or her group invented, the scoring procedure, as well as strategies and skills the student believes are needed to play the sport successfully.

The portfolio should also include the student's opinion about the sport including any changes that were made after trying out the game and why the changes were necessary. Place any notes you made about a student's work in his or her portfolio.

You may use the Holistic Scoring Guide to assess this task. See page 27 in Teacher's Assessment Resources.

Students' Work

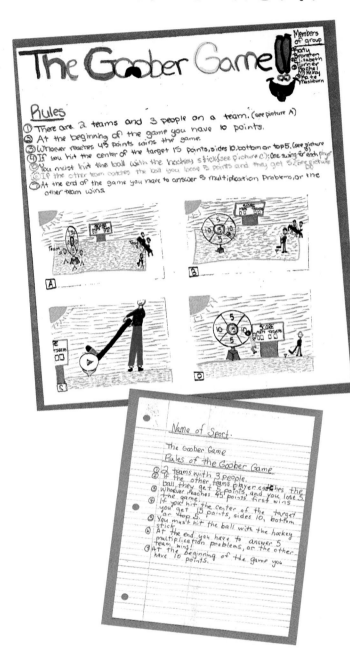

LESSON 4.7

EXPLORE ACTIVITY
Meaning of Division

OBJECTIVE Explore the two meanings of division.

RESOURCE REMINDER
Math Center Cards 36
Practice 36, Reteach 36, Extend 36

SKILLS TRACE

GRADE 2	• Use counters to explore "How many groups?" and "How many in each group?" *(Chapter 8)*
GRADE 3	• Explore the two meanings of division.
GRADE 4	• Review the language and meaning of division through basic facts. *(Chapter 5)*

WARM-UP

Cooperative Pairs   **Visual/Spatial**

OBJECTIVE Review the distinction between the number of groups and the number of items in each group.

▶ Have students write down the following multiplication facts: $7 \times 8 = 56$, $8 \times 7 = 56$

▶ Ask each student in a pair to illustrate one of the two facts. Have students share their drawings and describe the differences between 7×8 and 8×7. For each fact, ask students to identify the factor that tells how many groups, and the factor that tells how many in each group.

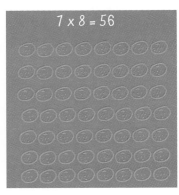
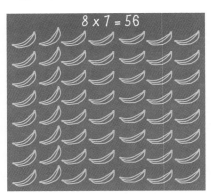

LOGICAL REASONING CONNECTION

Whole Class   **Logical/Analytical**

OBJECTIVE Identify and extend patterns involving division facts.

Materials have available: calculators, 42 counters

▶ Write the following on the chalkboard:

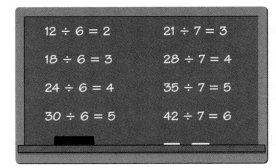

▶ In each column, students look for a pattern, then write the next three division sentences in each pattern. Let students use calculators, place-value models, or counters to check their work. *[36 ÷ 6 = 6, 42 ÷ 6 = 7, 48 ÷ 6 = 8; 49 ÷ 7 = 7; 56 ÷ 7 = 8; 63 ÷ 7 = 9]*

▶ Students share their work and discuss the methods they used.

Daily Review

PREVIOUS DAY QUICK REVIEW

Multiply.

1. $(2 \times 9) \times 3$ *[54]*
2. $3 \times (6 \times 2)$ *[36]*
3. $5 \times (2 \times 8)$ *[80]*
4. $(6 \times 5) \times 2$ *[60]*

FAST FACTS

1. 4×5 *[20]*
2. 3×6 *[18]*
3. 5×2 *[10]*
4. 6×8 *[48]*

Problem of the Day • 36

Michael bought three pairs of shorts for $30, two T-shirts for $18, and a hat for $17. How much will it cost Ken to buy one pair of shorts and 3 T-shirts? *[$37]*

TECH LINK

MATH VAN

Tools You may wish to use Counters and Division Mat with this lesson.

MATH FORUM

Cultural Diversity Students from other cultures may have learned other methods of division. I ask these students to share their methods.

Visit our Resource Village at http://www.mhschool.com to see more of the Math Forum.

MATH CENTER

Practice

OBJECTIVE Use manipulatives to identify dividends and divisors.

Materials per student: 64 counters, pennies, or connecting cubes, Math Center Recording Sheet (TA 31 optional)

Working with counters, students find all the factor pairs of 64. Students then write division sentences to explain the different groups of counters. *[Answers show the number of groups, the number in each group, and the division sentence: $64 \div 2 = 32$; $64 \div 4 = 16$; $64 \div 8 = 8$; $64 \div 16 = 4$; $64 \div 32 = 2$; $64 \div 64 = 1$]*

PRACTICE ACTIVITY 36

MATH CENTER
Partners

Manipulatives • Groups

1. Divide the counters into equal groups with your partner. Copy the table and record your data.
2. Repeat step 1 until you have found all the possible ways that you can group 64 counters.
3. Now repeat with 50 counters.

YOU NEED
64 counters (pennies or connecting cubes)

Number of counters	Number of groups	Number of counters in each group	Division sentence
64	1	64	$64 \div 1 = 64$
64			
64			

Chapter 4, Lesson 7, pages 146–149

Division

NCTM Standards
✓ Problem Solving
✓ Communication
✓ Reasoning
Connections

ESL APPROPRIATE

Problem Solving

OBJECTIVE Use graph paper to make a model of a division problem.

Materials per student: centimeter graph paper (TA 9), Math Center Recording Sheet (TA 31 optional)

Students outline an 8×8 square on graph paper to determine how many ways they can divide it into equal-sized plots. *[64 one-acre plots, 32 two-acre plots, 16 four-acre plots, 8 eight-acre plots, 4 sixteen-acre plots, 2 thirty-two acre plots]*

PROBLEM-SOLVING ACTIVITY 36

MATH CENTER
On Your Own

Spatial Reasoning • Splitting the Land

What if you own 64 acres of land. How many ways could you split the land into smaller plots all the same size?

To find out, draw an 8-by-8 box square on a piece of graph paper. If you count, you will find that you have 64 small squares. Let each small square stand for 1 acre.

YOU NEED
graph paper

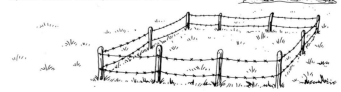

Chapter 4, Lesson 7, pages 146–149

Division

NCTM Standards
✓ Problem Solving
Communication
✓ Reasoning
✓ Connections

EXPLORE ACTIVITY
Meaning of Division

OBJECTIVE Explore the two meanings of division.

Materials per pair: 64 counters, pennies, connecting cubes or other countable items

Vocabulary dividend, divisor, quotient

 **Introduce**

Materials per pair: 64 counters or other countable items; centimeter graph paper (TA 7); centimeter dot paper (TA 9)

Display 18 counters. Tell students that the counters need to be separated into groups of 6. Have a volunteer show how to group the counters, as pairs of students do so at their desks. Ask:

• **How many groups of 6 counters are there?** *[3]*

2 Teach   *Cooperative Pairs*

▶ **LEARN Work Together** To help students think creatively about different ways to solve the introductory problem, ask:

• **How could you show the 24 runners?** *[Answers may vary. Possible answers: showing 24 counters, finding 24 on a number line, shading 24 squares on graph paper, circling 24 dots on dot paper]*

• **How can you show making teams of 4 from the 24 runners?** *[Answers may vary. Possible answers: showing making groups of 4 counters until all 24 counters are used, skip counting by 4 on the number line until 24 is reached, circling groups of 4 squares or dots on grid paper or dot paper until all 24 squares or dots have been circled]*

Encourage students to try a different method to answer the Work Together questions. Students' answers will provide an informal introduction to the concept of remainders.

Talk It Over Allow pairs to present their methods and tell which method they prefer.

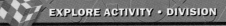

Meaning of Division

L E A R N

Do you ever run relay races in gym class? With 4 runners on each team, how many teams can you make with 24 runners?

Work Together
Work with a partner. Use any method you want to model the problem. Record your work in a table like the one shown.

Total Number	Number in Each Team	Number of Teams
24	4	

How many teams of 3, 4, 5, and 6 can you make from your class?

You will need
• counters
• graph paper

Talk It Over
▶ Explain your method for finding the number of teams.
 Students may use models, subtract, or divide to find the number of teams.

Make Connections
You used a table to record your work. You can also write a division sentence to record how you found the number of teams.

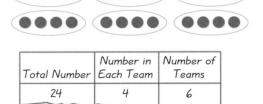

dividend A number to be divided.

divisor A number by which the dividend is divided.

quotient The result of division.

Total Number	Number in Each Team	Number of Teams
24	4	6

Write:

	Total		Number in each group		Number of groups		
	24	÷	4	=	6	or	$4\overline{)24}$ with quotient 6

↑ dividend   ↑ divisor   ↑ quotient

Read: 24 divided by 4 is equal to 6.

146 Lesson 4.7

Meeting Individual Needs

Extra Support

For some students it may be helpful to use paper cups to separate groups of counters to show division. This approach makes it easier to see the number of groups that resulted from the total.

Ongoing Assessment

Observation Checklist Determine if students understand the meaning of division by observing the methods they use to solve problems. Make sure students can show a group of items divided into equal groups.

Follow Up For more practice with division, assign **Reteach 36.**

For a greater challenge, assign **Extend 36.**

Language Support

As students use models to show division, circulate among them. Ask them how many groups there are, and how many items are in each group.

ESL APPROPRIATE

You can also divide to find the number in each group.

	Total		Number of groups		Number in each group
Write:	24	÷	6	=	4
	↑		↑		↑
	dividend		divisor		quotient

- Compare the multiplication sentence $6 \times 4 = 24$ to the division sentences above. Why do you think they are called related sentences? **Possible answer: They use the same numbers—6, 4, and 24.**
- **What if** you divide 32 students into 4 teams. How many students will be on each team? Is the quotient the number of groups or the number in each group? **8 students; the number in each group**

Check for Understanding

Complete the division sentence. Tell whether you divided to find: *the number of groups* or *the number in each group*.

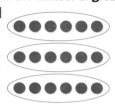
1 $18 \div 6 = \blacksquare$
3; the number of groups

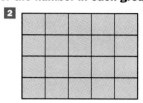
2 $20 \div 4 = \blacksquare$
5; the number in each group

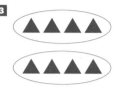
3 $8 \div 4 = \blacksquare$
2; the number of groups

Divide. Draw a picture to show the division. **Check students' drawings.**

4 $9 \div 3$
3

5 $12 \div 6$
2

6 $18 \div 9$
2

7 $25 \div 5$
5

8 $28 \div 4$
7

9 $12 \div 3$
4

10 $21 \div 7$
3

11 $18 \div 3$
6

12 $32 \div 8$
4

13 $48 \div 6$
8

Critical Thinking: Analyze

14 What does *division* mean? Use the words *separate* and *group* in your explanation. **Possible answer: Division separates a total into groups of equal size, although there may be leftovers if there are not enough to form another group.**

15 Allie found $24 \div 6$ using the method below. Explain why her method works.

$24 - 6 = 18$ $18 - 6 = 12$ $12 - 6 = 6$ $6 - 6 = 0$

I subtracted 6 four times, so $24 \div 6 = 4$.

Possible answer: She subtracted 4 groups of 6, which is the same as separating 24 into groups of 6 and finding the number of groups.

Turn the page for Practice. ➡
Multiplication and Division Facts **147**

MAKE CONNECTIONS

The symbolic method of recording division facts is shown on page 146. Students should connect each number in the division sentence to the appropriate column in the table. Students should understand that a total can be divided by the number of groups to find the number in each group, or that a total can be divided by the number in each group to find the number of groups.

Have students look at the two division sentences and write an explanation of why these two sentences are called *related sentences*. This will prepare them for a later lesson on *fact families*.

3 Close

Check for Understanding using items 1–15, page 147.

CRITICAL THINKING
Have students who are having trouble writing a definition for item 14 use pictorial representations.

Practice See pages 148–149.

Gifted And Talented

Ask students to discuss and explain why a number cannot be divided by zero. If students are unable to explain, help them see that a quantity of objects cannot be divided into zero groups—the items always form at least one group.

▶ **PRACTICE**

Materials have available: centimeter graph paper (TA 7), counters, index cards, number cubes

Options for assigning exercises:
A—Ex. 1–3, even 4–28; 30–32; **Dividing the Bases Game!; Mixed Review**
B—Ex. 1–3; odd 5–29; 30–32; **Dividing the Bases Game!; Mixed Review**

• Point out to students that they can use the drawings in ex. 1–3 to determine if the answer is the number of groups or the number in each group.
• For **Make It Right** (ex. 30), see Common Error below.

ɑ **Algebra** In ex.19–22, students find quotients. In ex. 23–26, students use their understanding of the meaning of division to find missing dividends and divisors. Ex. 27–29 pair multiplication and division and provide an opportunity for students to explore and develop their understanding of the relationship between division and multiplication.

Dividing the Bases Game! Students can use the game board in their books or trace the board on a separate sheet of paper. Before students begin the game, you may wish to demonstrate a turn. Toss a number cube and ask:
• **Which number is the dividend?** *[the number on the game board]* **divisor?** *[the number on the number cube]*
• **Into how many groups are you trying to divide the number on the card?** *[the number on the number cube]*
• **How can you tell if you can divide the number into equal groups?** *[Answers may vary. Sample answers may include any of the methods used in this lesson.]*

Mixed Review/Test Preparation Students review rounding and elapsed time skills they learned in Chapters 1 and 3.

Practice

Complete the division sentence. Tell whether you divided to find *the number of groups* or *the number in each group*.

1 5; the number of groups or the number in each group
$30 \div 6 = \blacksquare$

2 $35 \div 7 = \blacksquare$ 5; the number of groups

3 $24 \div 3 = \blacksquare$ 8; the number in each group

Draw an array. Find the quotient. Check students' arrays.

4 $12 \div 4$ 3 **5** $15 \div 3$ 5 **6** $21 \div 7$ 3 **7** $28 \div 4$ 7 **8** $18 \div 2$ 9

Divide using any method.

9 $12 \div 6$ 2 **10** $30 \div 5$ 6 **11** $24 \div 3$ 8 **12** $27 \div 9$ 3 **13** $32 \div 8$ 4

14 $2\overline{)16}$ 8 **15** $5\overline{)35}$ 7 **16** $6\overline{)30}$ 5 **17** $4\overline{)32}$ 8 **18** $7\overline{)28}$ 4

ɑ **ALGEBRA** Find the missing number.

19 $8 \div 4 = \blacksquare$ 2 **20** $16 \div 2 = \blacksquare$ 8 **21** $20 \div 5 = \blacksquare$ 4 **22** $36 \div 9 = \blacksquare$ 4

23 $\blacksquare \div 6 = 6$ 36 **24** $42 \div \blacksquare = 7$ 6 **25** $40 \div \blacksquare = 8$ 5 **26** $\blacksquare \div 7 = 8$ 56

27 $8 \div 2 = \blacksquare \times 4$ 1 **28** $4 \times \blacksquare = 40 \div 5$ 2 **29** $24 \div \blacksquare = 21 \div 7$ 8

····················· Make It Right ·····················
30 Here is how Calvin found $12 \div 3$. Explain what the mistake is, then give the correct answer.

$12 \div 3 = 3$

Possible answer: He counted the number of groups instead of the number in each group—$12 \div 3 = 4$.

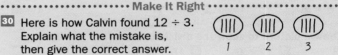

MIXED APPLICATIONS
Problem Solving

31 Your gym class has 35 students. For each basketball game you need two teams of 5 players each. Can your class play 4 basketball games on different courts at the same time? Why or why not? No; 40 players are needed

32 Your 6-player hockey team is playing another team in the semi-finals. Two other 6-player teams are also in the semi-finals. How many players are in the semi-finals? 24 players

148 Lesson 4.7

Meeting Individual Needs

Early Finishers

Have students create their own baseball diamond for a "Dividing the Bases Game!" Students should choose 2-digit numbers for the baseline spaces and boxes. They can create their own rules that use division.

COMMON ERROR

Some students may use the number of groups as a divisor, then incorrectly use that number again as the answer, as Calvin did in ex. 30.

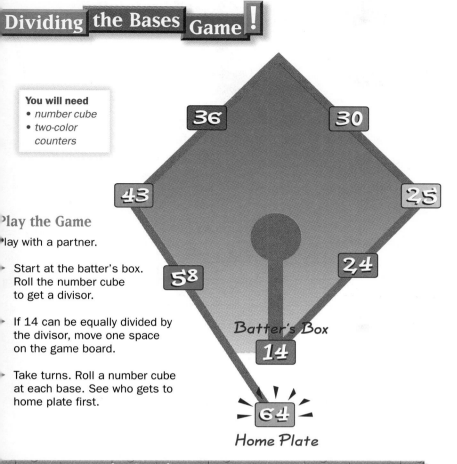

Dividing the Bases Game!

You will need
- *number cube*
- *two-color counters*

36   30

43   25

58   24

Batter's Box

14

64

Home Plate

Play the Game

Play with a partner.

▶ Start at the batter's box. Roll the number cube to get a divisor.

▶ If 14 can be equally divided by the divisor, move one space on the game board.

▶ Take turns. Roll a number cube at each base. See who gets to home plate first.

mixed review · test preparation

Tell the time.

1 2 h 30 min after 3:15 P.M. **5:45 P.M.**　**2** 5 h 15 min after 9 A.M. **2:15 P.M.**

3 4 h 30 min before 5:30 P.M. **1:00 P.M.**　**4** 3 h 45 min before 1:00 P.M. **9:15 A.M.**

Round to the nearest hundred.

5 374　　　**6** 2,536　　　**7** 5,027　　　**8** 12,360
400　　　　**2,500**　　　　**5,000**　　　　**12,400**

Extra Practice, page 498

Multiplication and Division Facts　**149**

Alternate Teaching Strategy

Have a group of 12 students stand up. Ask them to form groups of 3.

Write the division sentence 12 ÷ 3 = 4 on the chalkboard. Read it aloud and explain that it represents what the students who are standing up just did. Then ask volunteers to explain what each number in the division sentence represents. *[the total number of students, the number of students in each group, the number of equal groups]*

Have the 3 groups come together. Then have them split into 4 equal groups.

Write the division sentence 12 ÷ 4 = 3 on the chalkboard. Ask volunteers to explain what each number in the division sentence represents. *[the total number of students, the number of equal groups, the number of students in each group]*

Have the 12 students form groups of 5.

Write the division sentence 12 ÷ 5 = 2R2 on the chalkboard. Ask volunteers to explain what each number in the division sentence represents. *[the total number of students, the number of equal groups, the number of students in each group, the number of students left out]*

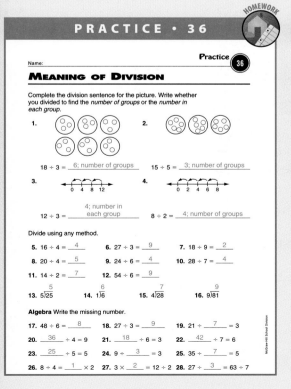

PRACTICE · 36

Name: _____　　　Practice **36**

MEANING OF DIVISION

Complete the division sentence for the picture. Write whether you divided to find the *number of groups* or the *number in each group*.

1.　　　　　　　　　**2.**

18 ÷ 3 = ___6; number of groups　　15 ÷ 5 = ___3; number of groups

3.　　　　　　　　　**4.**

12 ÷ 3 = ___4; number in each group　　8 ÷ 2 = ___4; number of groups

Divide using any method.

5. 16 ÷ 4 = __4__　**6.** 27 ÷ 3 = __9__　**7.** 18 ÷ 9 = __2__

8. 20 ÷ 4 = __5__　**9.** 24 ÷ 6 = __4__　**10.** 28 ÷ 7 = __4__

11. 14 ÷ 2 = __7__　**12.** 54 ÷ 6 = __9__

13. 5)25 = 5　**14.** 1)6 = 6　**15.** 4)28 = 7　**16.** 9)81 = 9

Algebra Write the missing number.

17. 48 ÷ 6 = __8__　**18.** 27 ÷ 3 = __9__　**19.** 21 ÷ __7__ = 3

20. __36__ ÷ 4 = 9　**21.** __18__ ÷ 6 = 3　**22.** __42__ ÷ 7 = 6

23. __25__ ÷ 5 = 5　**24.** 9 ÷ __3__ = 3　**25.** 35 ÷ __7__ = 5

26. 8 ÷ 4 = __1__ × 2　**27.** 3 × __2__ = 12 ÷ 2　**28.** 27 ÷ __3__ = 63 ÷ 7

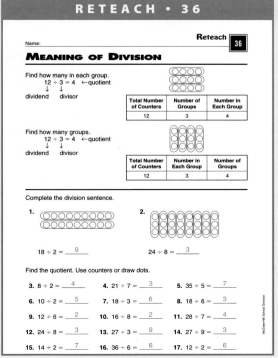

RETEACH · 36

Name: _____　　　Reteach **36**

MEANING OF DIVISION

Find how many in each group.
12 ÷ 3 = 4　←quotient
↓　　↓
dividend　divisor

Total Number of Counters	Number of Groups	Number in Each Group
12	3	4

Find how many groups.
12 ÷ 3 = 4　←quotient
↓　　↓
dividend　divisor

Total Number of Counters	Number in Each Group	Number of Groups
12	3	4

Complete the division sentence.

1.　　　　　　　　　**2.**

18 ÷ 2 = __9__　　　　24 ÷ 8 = __3__

Find the quotient. Use counters or draw dots.

3. 8 ÷ 2 = __4__　**4.** 21 ÷ 7 = __3__　**5.** 35 ÷ 5 = __7__

6. 10 ÷ 2 = __5__　**7.** 18 ÷ 3 = __6__　**8.** 18 ÷ 6 = __3__

9. 12 ÷ 6 = __2__　**10.** 16 ÷ 8 = __2__　**11.** 28 ÷ 7 = __4__

12. 24 ÷ 8 = __3__　**13.** 27 ÷ 3 = __9__　**14.** 27 ÷ 9 = __3__

15. 14 ÷ 2 = __7__　**16.** 36 ÷ 6 = __6__　**17.** 12 ÷ 2 = __6__

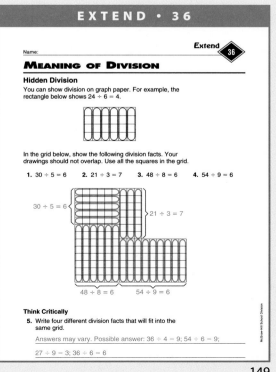

EXTEND · 36

Name: _____　　　Extend **36**

MEANING OF DIVISION

Hidden Division

You can show division on graph paper. For example, the rectangle below shows 24 ÷ 6 = 4.

In the grid below, show the following division facts. Your drawings should not overlap. Use all the squares in the grid.

1. 30 ÷ 5 = 6　**2.** 21 ÷ 3 = 7　**3.** 48 ÷ 8 = 6　**4.** 54 ÷ 9 = 6

30 ÷ 5 = 6　　　　　　　　21 ÷ 3 = 7

48 ÷ 8 = 6　　　54 ÷ 9 = 6

Think Critically

5. Write four different division facts that will fit into the same grid.

Answers may vary. Possible answer: 36 ÷ 4 = 9; 54 ÷ 6 = 9;

27 ÷ 9 = 3; 36 ÷ 6 = 6

149

LESSON 4.8

2 Through 5 as Divisors

OBJECTIVE Use related multiplication facts to find division facts for 2 through 5.

RESOURCE REMINDER
Math Center Cards 37
Practice 37, Reteach 37, Extend 37

SKILLS TRACE

GRADE 2
- Use related multiplication facts to find division facts for 2, 3, 4, and 5. *(Chapter 8)*

GRADE 3
- Solve division problems with 2 through 5 as divisors.

GRADE 4
- Review the language and meaning of division through basic facts. *(Chapter 5)*

LESSON 4.8 RESOURCES

MANIPULATIVE WARM-UP

Cooperative Groups   **Kinesthetic**

OBJECTIVE To find all the equal groups that can be formed from a given total.

Materials per group: 12 counters

▶ Give each group 12 counters. Ask them to separate the counters into as many equal groups as they can. Have them record their results in a table like the one below:

Total	Number of Equal Groups	Number in Each Group	Division Sentence
12	4	3	$12 \div 4 = 3$

▶ Have groups share their results and make a class list of all the division sentences with 12 as the dividend. *[$12 \div 1 = 12$, $12 \div 2 = 6$, $12 \div 3 = 4$, $12 \div 4 = 3$, $12 \div 6 = 2$, $12 \div 12 = 1$]*

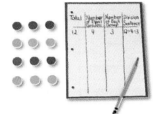

ESL APPROPRIATE

MUSIC CONNECTION

Whole Class   **Logical/Analytical**

OBJECTIVE Connect division to music.

▶ Draw the following:

1 whole note   2 half notes

▶ Ask students who play musical instruments to explain what the notes mean. Make sure that students understand the notes indicate how long a tone should be held, and that one whole note has the same time value as two half notes.

▶ Draw 8 half notes and circle each pair of notes. Write the division sentence $8 \div 2 = 4$. Ask questions such as:
- **How many whole notes make the same time value as 8 half notes?**
  [4 whole notes—$8 \div 2 = 4$]
- **How many whole notes make the same time value as 12 half notes?**
  [6 whole notes—$12 \div 2 = 6$]

Daily Review

PREVIOUS DAY QUICK REVIEW

Divide using any method.

1. 18 ÷ 9 *[2]*
2. 9 ÷ 3 *[3]*
3. 24 ÷ 4 *[6]*
4. 12 ÷ 6 *[2]*

FAST FACTS

1. 2 + 2 *[4]*
2. 3 + 3 *[6]*
3. 4 + 4 *[8]*
4. 5 + 5 *[10]*

Problem of the Day • 37

The product of two numbers is 24; their sum is 10. What are the two numbers? *[6 and 4]*

TECH LINK

MATH FORUM

Management Tip I have each student make a list of division facts without answers. Once a student can solve a fact I have him or her circle it. This helps students know which facts they need to practice.

Visit our Resource Village at http://www.mhschool.com to see more of the Math Forum.

MATH CENTER

Practice

OBJECTIVE Use division to solve a problem involving 2–5 as divisors.

Materials per student: Math Center Recording Sheet (TA 31 optional)

Students use the number line to help them decide whether numbers are divisible by 2, 3, 4, and 5. *[Red group: 15 cans; Blue group: 32 cans; Green group: 21 cans; Orange group: 16 cans]*

PRACTICE ACTIVITY 37

MATH CENTER
On Your Own 🚶

Number Sense • Collecting Cans

- Four groups of students in Ms. Tienou's class collected cans for the town's recycling project. The total numbers of cans collected by the groups were 32, 16, 15, and 21. Use the clues below to find out how many cans each group collected. Skip-count on the number line.

Each of the 5 students in the Red group collected the same number of cans. Both the students in the Orange group collected the same number of cans. Each of 3 students in the Green group collected the same number of cans. Each of the 4 students in the Blue group collected the same number of cans as each student in the Orange group.

Chapter 4, Lesson 8, pages 150–151   Division

NCTM Standards

✓ **Problem Solving**
✓ **Communication**
✓ **Reasoning**
✓ **Connections**

Problem Solving

OBJECTIVE Find a pattern for multiples of 3.

Materials per student: calculator, Math Center Recording Sheet (TA 31 optional)

Students look at all the numbers from 1 to 100 that are divisible by 3. They find the sum of the digits for each 2-digit number and look for a pattern. *[The sum of the digits is divisible by 3.]*

PROBLEM-SOLVING ACTIVITY 37

MATH CENTER
On Your Own 🚶

Patterning • The Wonder Number 3

On your recording sheet, list all the numbers from 1 to 100.

- Circle every number divisible by 3. If you need help, use your calculator.
- Find the sum of the digits for any of the 2-digit numbers you circle.

Look for patterns. Explain any that you see.

YOU NEED
⋮ calculator

1
2
③
4
5
⑥
7
8

Chapter 4, Lesson 8, pages 150–151   Division

NCTM Standards

✓ **Problem Solving**
✓ **Communication**
✓ **Reasoning**
  Connections

Lesson 4.8 *continued*

2 Through 5 as Divisors

OBJECTIVE Use related multiplication facts to find division facts for 2 through 5.

 **Introduce**

Materials per pair: 28 counters, pennies, connecting cubes or other countable items

Present the following problem to students:

Four people can fit in each boat at an amusement park ride. How many boats are needed for 28 people? *[7]*
- **How could you use a multiplication sentence with a missing factor to represent this problem?** *[Since you don't know the number of groups, but know the number in each group and the total (28), you can write ___ × 4 = 28.]*
- **What division sentence could you use to represent this problem?** *[28 ÷ 4 = ___]*

Have pairs of students use counters to solve the problem.

 **Teach** **Whole Class**

▶ **LEARN** Read the problem and discuss why division is used to solve it. *[20 people are divided into equal groups of 5.]* Ask:
- **How is skip-counting to show division different from skip-counting to show multiplication?** *[In division, you skip backward from a number to zero and in multiplication, you skip forward from zero to a number.]*

The second method for solving the problem uses the relationship between multiplication and division. Students who know multiplication facts may prefer this method.

 **Close**

▶ **Check for Understanding** using items 1–11, page 150.

> **CRITICAL THINKING**
> Have each student write a definition in his or her own words, with examples, of inverse operations.

▶ **PRACTICE**
Materials have available: calculators

Each student chooses twelve exercises from ex. 1–17, all exercises 18–21, and **More to Explore.**
• In ex. 21, students can use the strategy of interpreting data.

More to Explore Explain that to skip-count they can push (+) or (−), the number added or subtracted, and (=), repeatedly.

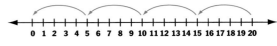 **DIVISION**

2 Through 5 as Divisors

L E A R N

Whitewater rafting is exciting! A group of 20 people is rafting. If each raft has 5 people, how many rafts are there?

Divide: 20 ÷ 5

To find the number of rafts, you can skip-count backward on a number line.

```
 ⤸   ⤸   ⤸   ⤸
+-+-+-+-+-+-+-+-+-+-+-+-+-+-+-+-+-+-+-+-+-+→
0 1 2 3 4 5 6 7 8 9 10 11 12 13 14 15 16 17 18 19 20
```

Think: 15, 10, 5, 0
So 20 ÷ 5 = 4.

You can also use a related multiplication sentence to find the quotient.

   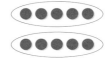

Think: What number times 5 is 20?
■ × 5 = 20
4 × 5 = 20
So 20 ÷ 5 = 4.

There are 4 rafts.

C H E C K

Check for Understanding
Divide.

1 10 ÷ 2 *5*	**2** 6 ÷ 3 *2*	**3** 12 ÷ 4 *3*	**4** 15 ÷ 5 *3*	**5** 9 ÷ 3 *3*
6 16 ÷ 4 *4*	**7** 21 ÷ 3 *7*	**8** 8 ÷ 2 *4*	**9** 4 ÷ 4 *1*	**10** 5 ÷ 1 *5*

Critical Thinking: Generalize **Explain your reasoning.**

11 Addition and subtraction are called *inverse* operations because one operation undoes the other. Are multiplication and division inverse operations? Give an example. *Yes; 4 × 2 = 8 and 8 ÷ 2 = 4.*

150 Lesson 4.8

Meeting Individual Needs

Early Finishers
Have students find the missing numbers:

◇ × ◇ = 9

18 ÷ ♥ = ◇
[◇ = 3, ♥ = 6]

Extra Support
For students confusing the terms in a division sequence, you may wish to have them label the dividend, divisor, and quotient for several exercises.

Ongoing Assessment
Anecdotal Report Make notes on students' methods of solving division problems. Students who can use multiplication facts to solve division problems have progressed further in their understanding of multiplication and division.

Follow Up If students need more practice, have pairs make up division problems for each other to solve. You may also assign **Reteach 37.**

Assign **Extend 37** to students who need more of a challenge.

Practice

Write a division sentence for each picture.

1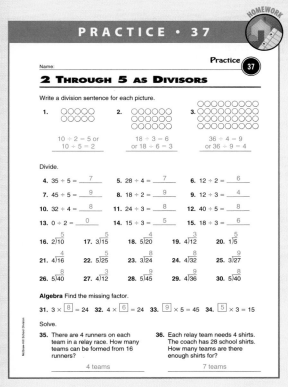

2
```
  ←─────────────────────────────→
  0  1  2  3  4  5  6  7  8  9  10
```
$10 \div 2 = 5$ or $10 \div 5 = 2$

$32 \div 4 = 8$ or $32 \div 8 = 4$

Divide.

3 $25 \div 5$ **5** **4** $8 \div 4$ **2** **5** $0 \div 3$ **0** **6** $14 \div 2$ **7** **7** $36 \div 4$ **9**

8 $4\overline{)24}$ **6** **9** $3\overline{)12}$ **4** **10** $5\overline{)35}$ **7** **11** $4\overline{)28}$ **7** **12** $5\overline{)5}$ **1**

13 $5\overline{)30}$ **6** **14** $6\overline{)18}$ **3** **15** $2\overline{)16}$ **8** **16** $7\overline{)21}$ **8** **17** $4\overline{)36}$ **9**

MIXED APPLICATIONS
Problem Solving

18 **What if** there are 4 rafts and 28 people. How many people can ride each raft if each raft has the same number of people? **7 people**

19 A life jacket at the Outdoor Store costs $23.00. Shani has a store coupon for $5.45. How much will she pay for the jacket? **$17.55**

20 **Write a problem** where you divide to make groups of the same size. Solve your problem and have others solve it. **Students should compare problems and solutions.**

21 **Data Point** Use the Databank on page 536. Which tree is higher: the coconut palm or the western hemlock? By how many feet? **western hemlock; 135 ft**

more to explore

Using a Calculator to Skip-Count

Multiply: 5×9

Enter: [0] [+] [5]

Press [=] nine times. Display: **45.**

Starting at 0 and counting by 5s nine times gives 45. So $5 \times 9 = 45$.

Divide: $36 \div 4$

Enter: [3] [6] [−] [4]

Press [=] until you reach 0. Count the number of times.

Starting at 36 and counting back by 4s nine times gives 0. So $36 \div 4 = 9$.

Multiply or divide. Use your calculator to skip-count.

1 3×8 **24** **2** $27 \div 3$ **9** **3** $30 \div 5$ **6** **4** 9×6 **54** **5** $16 \div 2$ **8**

Extra Practice, page 498

Multiplication and Division Facts **151**

Alternate Teaching Strategy

Materials per pair: 32 counters or centimeter graph paper (TA 7)

Write the following incomplete division and multiplication facts on the chalkboard:

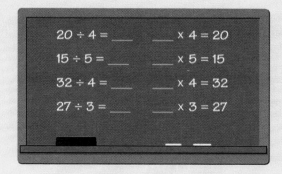

$20 \div 4 = \_\_\_$ $\_\_\_ \times 4 = 20$

$15 \div 5 = \_\_\_$ $\_\_\_ \times 5 = 15$

$32 \div 4 = \_\_\_$ $\_\_\_ \times 4 = 32$

$27 \div 3 = \_\_\_$ $\_\_\_ \times 3 = 27$

Have pairs of students work on one row of number sentences at a time. They can use counters or grid paper to find the answers. As students complete each row, encourage them to look for patterns.

Make sure students see the connections between each pair of sentences. The quotient is the same as the missing factor.

The sentences are related sentences.

Multiplying undoes division. Encourage them to use the pattern and the quotients to help them find the rest of the missing factors.

Give students one more division problem. Ask them to write and solve a related multiplication problem, then solve the division problem. Let students share their work with the class.

ESL APPROPRIATE

PRACTICE • 37

Practice 37

Name:

2 THROUGH 5 AS DIVISORS

Write a division sentence for each picture.

1. (5 rows of circles) **2.** (rows of circles) **3.** (rows of circles)

$10 \div 2 = 5$ or $10 \div 5 = 2$

$18 \div 3 = 6$ or $18 \div 6 = 3$

$36 \div 4 = 9$ or $36 \div 9 = 4$

Divide.

4. $35 \div 5 = $ **7** **5.** $28 \div 4 = $ **7** **6.** $12 \div 2 = $ **6**

7. $45 \div 5 = $ **9** **8.** $18 \div 2 = $ **9** **9.** $12 \div 3 = $ **4**

10. $32 \div 4 = $ **8** **11.** $24 \div 3 = $ **8** **12.** $40 \div 5 = $ **8**

13. $0 \div 2 = $ **0** **14.** $15 \div 3 = $ **5** **15.** $18 \div 3 = $ **6**

16. $2\overline{)10}$ **5** **17.** $3\overline{)15}$ **5** **18.** $5\overline{)20}$ **4** **19.** $4\overline{)12}$ **3** **20.** $1\overline{)5}$ **5**

21. $4\overline{)16}$ **4** **22.** $5\overline{)25}$ **5** **23.** $3\overline{)24}$ **8** **24.** $4\overline{)32}$ **8** **25.** $3\overline{)27}$ **9**

26. $5\overline{)40}$ **8** **27.** $4\overline{)12}$ **3** **28.** $5\overline{)45}$ **9** **29.** $4\overline{)36}$ **9** **30.** $5\overline{)40}$ **8**

Algebra Find the missing factor.

31. $3 \times \boxed{8} = 24$ **32.** $4 \times \boxed{6} = 24$ **33.** $\boxed{9} \times 5 = 45$ **34.** $\boxed{5} \times 3 = 15$

Solve.

35. There are 4 runners on each team in a relay race. How many teams can be formed from 16 runners? **4 teams**

36. Each relay team needs 4 shirts. The coach has 28 school shirts. How many teams are there enough shirts for? **7 teams**

RETEACH • 37

Reteach 37

Name:

2 THROUGH 5 AS DIVISORS

You have 10 connecting cubes. How many groups of 5 cubes can you make?

(diagram of cubes) **Think: 2 groups of 5 cubes.**

You can write
$10 \div 5 = 2$ or $5\overline{)10}^{\,2}$

How many groups of 2 cubes can you make?

(diagram of cubes) **Think: 5 groups of 2 cubes.**

$10 \div 2 = 5$ or $2\overline{)10}^{\,5}$

Complete the division sentence.

1. (circles) $15 \div 3 = $ **5**

2. (circles) $27 \div 3 = $ **9**

Find the quotient.

3. $24 \div 4 = $ **6** **4.** $24 \div 3 = $ **8** **5.** $12 \div 4 = $ **3**

6. $8 \div 2 = $ **4** **7.** $45 \div 5 = $ **9** **8.** $32 \div 4 = $ **8**

9. $9 \div 3 = $ **3** **10.** $21 \div 3 = $ **7** **11.** $28 \div 7 = $ **4**

12. $5\overline{)20}$ **4** **13.** $5\overline{)15}$ **3** **14.** $5\overline{)35}$ **7** **15.** $2\overline{)16}$ **8**

16. $2\overline{)18}$ **9** **17.** $2\overline{)12}$ **6** **18.** $5\overline{)40}$ **8** **19.** $4\overline{)20}$ **5**

EXTEND • 37

Extend 37

Name:

2 THROUGH 5 AS DIVISORS

Pack 'Em

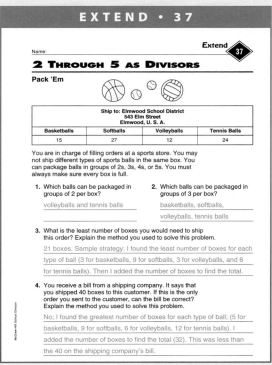

Ship to: Elmwood School District 543 Elm Street Elmwood, U. S. A.			
Basketballs	**Softballs**	**Volleyballs**	**Tennis Balls**
15	27	12	24

You are in charge of filling orders at a sports store. You may not ship different types of sports balls in the same box. You can package balls in groups of 2s, 3s, 4s, or 5s. You must always make sure every box is full.

1. Which balls can be packaged in groups of 2 per box?

volleyballs and tennis balls

2. Which balls can be packaged in groups of 3 per box?

basketballs, softballs, volleyballs, tennis balls

3. What is the least number of boxes you would need to ship this order? Explain the method you used to solve this problem.

21 boxes. Sample strategy: I found the least number of boxes for each type of ball (3 for basketballs, 9 for softballs, 3 for volleyballs, and 6 for tennis balls). Then I added the number of boxes to find the total.

4. You receive a bill from a shipping company. It says that you shipped 40 boxes to this customer. If this is the only order you sent to the customer, can the bill be correct? Explain the method you used to solve this problem.

No; I found the greatest number of boxes for each type of ball; (5 for basketballs, 9 for softballs, 6 for volleyballs, 12 for tennis balls). I added the number of boxes to find the total (32). This was less than the 40 on the shipping company's bill.

151

6 Through 9 as Divisors

OBJECTIVE Use related multiplication facts to find division facts for 6 through 9.

RESOURCE REMINDER
Math Center Cards 38
Practice 38, Reteach 38, Extend 38

SKILLS TRACE

GRADE 3
- Use related multiplication facts to find division facts for 6, 7, 8, and 9. *(Chapter 8)*

GRADE 4
- Solve division problems with 6 through 9 as divisors.

GRADE 5
- Review the language and meaning of division through basic facts. *(Chapter 5)*

WARM-UP

Cooperative Pairs   **Logical/Analytical**

OBJECTIVE Review multiplication facts.

▶ To prepare students for using related multiplication facts to solve division problems, write the following list of numbers on the board:

12, 18, 24, 30, 36, 48, 56, 64, 72, 81

▶ Tell students that these are products. Have pairs of students write all the multiplication facts that they can think of that have these products.

STATISTICS CONNECTION

Cooperative Pairs   **Logical/Analytical**

OBJECTIVE Connect division to graph scales.

▶ Write the following on the chalkboard:

LUNCHES SOLD BY THE SNACK SHACK IN ITS FIRST FOUR DAYS				
Day	Mon.	Tues.	Wed.	Thurs.
Lunches Sold	8	16	24	32

▶ Ask students to make a bar graph of the data. Have them use a scale in which each line equals 8 lunches.
  • **How many lines high is the highest bar? How do you know?** *[4 lines; $32 \div 8 = 4$]* **If each line equals 2 lunches, how many lines high is each bar?** *[4, 8, 12, 16]*

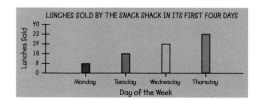

Daily Review

PREVIOUS DAY QUICK REVIEW

Divide.

1. 35 ÷ 5 *[7]*
2. 28 ÷ 4 *[7]*
3. 9 ÷ 9 *[1]*
4. 42 ÷ 7 *[6]*

FAST FACTS

1. 3 × 7 *[21]*
2. 4 × 9 *[36]*
3. 6 × 8 *[48]*
4. 4 × 8 *[32]*

Problem of the Day • 38

Of the median, mode, and range of this data, which is the greatest? *[the range]*

Points Scored

```
      x
      x     x           x
x  x  x           x           x
2  4  6  8  10  12  14  16  18  20
```

TECH LINK

MATH VAN

Tools You may wish to use Counters and Division Mat with this lesson.

MATH FORUM

Idea If my students have difficulty with division facts, I give them more practice with multiplication facts and with identifying related facts.

Visit our Resource Village at http://www.mhschool.com to see more of the Math Forum.

MATH CENTER

Practice

OBJECTIVE Use counters to explore divisors 6–9.

Materials per pair: 50 counters, paper bag, spinner (TA 2); per student: Math Center Recording Sheet (TA 31 optional)

Prepare Have students label a 4-part spinner 6 through 9.

Students use counters and a spinner to generate dividends and divisors. Then they use counters to check their mental-math division.

Problem Solving

OBJECTIVE Find multiple solutions to a problem involving multiplication.

Materials per student: Math Center Recording Sheet (TA 31 optional)

Students generate multiples of 6, 7, 8, and 9 and look for combinations that add up to 88. *[Possible answers: Green: 24; Red: 21; Blue: 16; Yellow: 27]*

PRACTICE ACTIVITY 38

MATH CENTER
Partners

Manipulatives • How Many?

- One partner picks a handful of counters out of the bag and counts them.
- The other partner spins the spinner for a number from 6 to 9. That number will be the divisor.
- The first partner figures out mentally whether the number of counters can be divided evenly by the divisor.
- The second partner checks the answer using the counters.
- Change roles and continue playing. Be sure to record all your work.

YOU NEED
50 counters
paper bag
spinner (6–9)

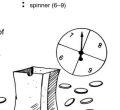

NCTM Standards
✓ Problem Solving
✓ Communication
  Reasoning
✓ Connections

Chapter 4, Lesson 9, pages 152–153

Division

PROBLEM-SOLVING ACTIVITY 38

MATH CENTER
Small Group

Logical Reasoning • Survey Says

Toys-Galore took a survey to decide what color to make their new toy. They surveyed 88 students. The surveyor lost the original data but had the following notes:

- The number for green could be divided evenly by 6.
- The number for red could be divided evenly by 7.
- The number for blue could be divided evenly by 8.
- The number for yellow could be divided evenly by 9.

Find out how many students picked each color. Work with your group to find as many solutions as you can.

NCTM Standards
✓ Problem Solving
  Communication
✓ Reasoning
✓ Connections

Chapter 4, Lesson 9, pages 152–153

Division

Lesson 4.9 *continued*

6 Through 9 as Divisors

OBJECTIVE Use related multiplication facts to find division facts for 6 through 9.

1 Introduce

Write the following on the board:

30 ÷ 6 = ■   48 ÷ 8 = ■   42 ÷ 7 = ■

Have students write a related multiplication sentence with a missing factor for each division sentence.
[■ × 6 = 30; ■ × 8 = 48; ■ × 7 = 42]

2 Teach   *Whole Class*

Materials per group: 7 balls

Cultural Connection Have teams of 7 students play the Coconut Shell Relay. To begin, the leader (Player 1) throws one shell at a time, represented by a ball, to the person on the left (Player 2), who throws it to the next person (Player 3), and so on until Player 7 has all the shells. Player 7 places the shells at his or her feet. Player 7 then becomes the leader. Play continues until Player 6 has all 7 shells. Repeat for each player until Player 1 has all the shells. The first team to complete the relay wins.

▶ **LEARN** After reading the problem on page 152, ask:
 - **Why is division used to solve this problem?** *[21 students need to be separated into groups of 7.]*
 - **Are you finding the number of groups or the number in each group?** *[the number of groups]*

3 Close

▶ **Check for Understanding** using items 1–11, page 152.

CRITICAL THINKING
Accept all reasonable methods of division for item 11.

▶ **PRACTICE**
Materials have available: calculators

Options for assigning exercises:
A—Odd ex. 1–17; all ex. 18–21; **Mixed Review**
B—Even ex. 2–16; all ex. 18–21; **Mixed Review**

 - To solve ex. 18 and 20, students use the strategy of choosing the operation.
 - To solve ex. 21, students can use estimation or mental math.

Mixed Review/Test Preparation Students interpret a pictograph, a skill learned in Chapter 3, and practice multiplication facts from Chapter 4.

---

6 Through 9 as Divisors

LEARN

A fourth-grade class wants to play the Coconut Shell Relay. There are 21 students. They need to form teams of 7 students. How many teams can they make?

Divide: 21 ÷ 7

Cultural Note
The Coconut Shell Relay is played by the Aborigines, a group of people native to Australia.

You can use a multiplication fact to find the quotient.

Think: What number times 7 is 21?
 ■ × 7 = 21
 3 × 7 = 21
 So 21 ÷ 7 = 3.

You can also use a related division fact to find the quotient.

Think: 21 divided by what number is 7?
 21 ÷ ■ = 7
 21 ÷ 3 = 7
 So 21 ÷ 7 = 3.

The class can make 3 teams.

CHECK

Check for Understanding
Divide.

1. 14 ÷ 7 2   2. 24 ÷ 8 3   3. 12 ÷ 6 2   4. 18 ÷ 6 3   5. 27 ÷ 9 3

6. 40 ÷ 8 5   7. 21 ÷ 7 3   8. 36 ÷ 6 6   9. 72 ÷ 9 8   10. 8 ÷ 8 1

Critical Thinking: Summarize

11. Explain the method you would use to find each quotient. *Check students' methods.*
 a. 24 ÷ 6 4   **b.** 56 ÷ 7 8   **c.** 16 ÷ 8 2   **d.** 81 ÷ 9

Meeting Individual Needs

Early Finishers

Challenge students to solve division problems where the divisor or quotient is greater than 10, such as 39 ÷ 13 and 56 ÷ 4. Have them describe the methods or strategies they use.

Ongoing

Interview Determine if students understand how to use related facts by asking them the following:
 - **How can you use a related fact to solve 56 ÷ 8?** *[Possible answers: Use 8 × 7 = 56, 7 × 8 = 56, or 56 ÷ 7 = 8.]*

Follow Up If students need further practice with divisors of 6 through 9, assign **Reteach 38**.

For a greater challenge, assign **Extend 38**.

Extra Support

For students having difficulty, you may wish to have them use a number line for the exercises.

9. Possible answer: Form 3 teams of 7 students, the remaining 3 students can rotate in after each round.

Practice

Write a division sentence for the picture.

1

$24 \div 4 = 6$ or $24 \div 6 = 4$

2

$35 \div 5 = 7$ or $35 \div 7 = 5$

Divide.

3 $18 \div 9$ **2** **4** $28 \div 7$ **4** **5** $7 \div 7$ **1** **6** $32 \div 8$ **4** **7** $45 \div 9$ **5**

8 $54 \div 6$ **9** **9** $56 \div 8$ **7** **10** $49 \div 7$ **7** **11** $0 \div 9$ **0** **12** $48 \div 6$ **8**

13 $6\overline{)30}$ **5** **14** $9\overline{)36}$ **4** **15** $8\overline{)48}$ **6** **16** $7\overline{)42}$ **6** **17** $7\overline{)63}$ **9**

MIXED APPLICATIONS
Problem Solving

Pencil & Paper · Calculator · Mental Math

18 In a game of Coconut Shell Relay, there are 5 teams of 7 players. How many players are there in all?
35 players

19 Make a decision Your class has 24 students. How would you arrange the teams to play the Coconut Shell Relay?
See above.

20 How many tickets can be bought with $64 if each ticket costs $8?
8 tickets

21 About how many coconuts grow on a tree? **SEE INFOBIT. Possible answer: about 100–200 coconuts**

INFOBIT
About ten clusters of coconuts may be on a tree. There are 10 to 20 coconuts in a cluster.

mixed review · test preparation

Use the pictograph to answer questions 1 and 2.

1 If 21 life jackets were rented on Monday, what is the key?
👕 **stands for 7 life jackets**

2 How many jackets were rented on Tuesday? on Wednesday?
35 life jackets; 7 life jackets

Number of Jackets Rented	
Monday	👕 👕 👕
Tuesday	👕 👕 👕 👕 👕
Wednesday	👕

Multiply.

3 9×4 **36** **4** 6×8 **48** **5** 4×5 **20** **6** 7×7 **49** **7** 3×9 **27**

Extra Practice, page 498

Multiplication and Division Facts **153**

Alternate Teaching Strategy

Separate the class into two groups.

Tell one group that you will write a division problem on the board and that they are to solve the problem using a multiplication fact.

The other group has to solve the problem using a related division fact.

Once both groups agree on their answers, write answers on the board.

Continue with several examples.

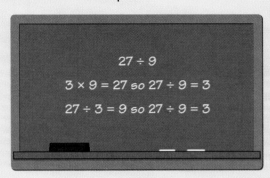

$27 \div 9$
$3 \times 9 = 27$ so $27 \div 9 = 3$
$27 \div 3 = 9$ so $27 \div 9 = 3$

PRACTICE · 38

HOMEWORK

Name: _____ Practice **38**

6 THROUGH 9 AS DIVISORS

Write a division sentence for each picture.

1. $54 \div 9 = 6$ or $54 \div 6 = 9$

2. $40 \div 8 = 5$ or $40 \div 5 = 8$

3. $49 \div 7 = 7$

Divide.

4. $54 \div 9 = \underline{6}$ 5. $35 \div 7 = \underline{5}$ 6. $0 \div 7 = \underline{0}$

7. $36 \div 9 = \underline{4}$ 8. $63 \div 9 = \underline{7}$ 9. $6 \div 6 = \underline{1}$

10. $42 \div 6 = \underline{7}$ 11. $48 \div 8 = \underline{6}$ 12. $72 \div 8 = \underline{9}$

13. $64 \div 8 = \underline{8}$ 14. $9 \div 9 = \underline{1}$ 15. $0 \div 8 = \underline{0}$

16. $7\overline{)28}$ **4** 17. $6\overline{)24}$ **4** 18. $6\overline{)18}$ **3** 19. $8\overline{)64}$ **8** 20. $7\overline{)49}$ **7**

21. $6\overline{)36}$ **6** 22. $9\overline{)27}$ **3** 23. $9\overline{)81}$ **9** 24. $6\overline{)54}$ **9** 25. $9\overline{)72}$ **8**

Algebra Find the missing factor.

26. $7 \times \boxed{4} = 28$ 27. $9 \times \boxed{9} = 81$ 28. $8 \times \boxed{5} = 40$ 29. $\boxed{5} \times 6 = 30$

30. $5 \times \boxed{6} = 30$ 31. $3 \times \boxed{7} = 21$ 32. $2 \times \boxed{9} = 18$ 33. $\boxed{5} \times 7 = 35$

Solve.

34. There are 54 students in all of the fourth grade classes. How many baseball teams can you form with 9 players on each team?
_____ 6 teams

35. Pete's swim team has 24 members. One school van can take 8 swimmers to the swim meet. How many vans are needed?
_____ 3 vans

RETEACH · 38

Name: _____ Reteach **38**

6 THROUGH 9 AS DIVISORS

You can skip-count to find quotients that all have the same divisor.

$48 \div 8 = ?$

Start at 0 and skip-count by 8. You are finding products that have 8 as a factor.

It takes 6 steps to get from 0 to 48.

It takes 6 steps back to get from 48 to 0. When you divide 48 by 8 the quotient is 6.

1	2	3	4	5	6			
0	8	16	24	32	40	48	56	64	72

$48 \div 8 = 6$ $8\overline{)48}$ **6**

Use the number line above to find the quotient.

1. $16 \div 8 = \underline{2}$ 2. $24 \div 8 = \underline{3}$ 3. $32 \div 8 = \underline{4}$

4. $40 \div 8 = \underline{5}$ 5. $56 \div 8 = \underline{7}$ 6. $72 \div 8 = \underline{9}$

7. $64 \div 8 = \underline{8}$ 8. $8 \div 8 = \underline{1}$

Find the quotient.

1	2	3	4	5	6	7	8	9
0	7	14	21	28	35	42	49	56	63

9. $21 \div 7 = \underline{3}$ 10. $56 \div 7 = \underline{8}$ 11. $63 \div 7 = \underline{9}$

12. $49 \div 7 = \underline{7}$ 13. $35 \div 7 = \underline{5}$ 14. $42 \div 7 = \underline{6}$

15. $7 \div 7 = \underline{1}$ 16. $28 \div 7 = \underline{4}$ 17. $14 \div 7 = \underline{2}$

1	2	3	4	5	6	7	8	9
0	9	18	27	36	45	54	63	72	81

18. $63 \div 9 = \underline{7}$ 19. $45 \div 9 = \underline{5}$ 20. $27 \div 3 = \underline{9}$

21. $18 \div 2 = \underline{9}$ 22. $36 \div 9 = \underline{4}$ 23. $54 \div 9 = \underline{6}$

EXTEND · 38

Name: _____ Extend **38**

6 THROUGH 9 AS DIVISORS

Stampede!
Lucy has a stamp collection.
Here are the stamps in her collection.

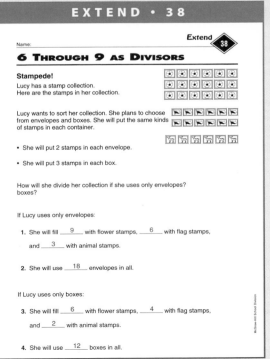

Lucy wants to sort her collection. She plans to choose from envelopes and boxes. She will put the same kinds of stamps in each container.

- She will put 2 stamps in each envelope.
- She will put 3 stamps in each box.

How will she divide her collection if she uses only envelopes? boxes?

If Lucy uses only envelopes:

1. She will fill _____ 9 with flower stamps, _____ 6 with flag stamps, and _____ 3 with animal stamps.

2. She will use _____ 18 envelopes in all.

If Lucy uses only boxes:

3. She will fill _____ 6 with flower stamps, _____ 4 with flag stamps, and _____ 2 with animal stamps.

4. She will use _____ 12 boxes in all.

153

LESSON 4.10

Fact Families

OBJECTIVE Develop fact families to solve division problems.

RESOURCE REMINDER
Math Center Cards 39
Practice 39, Reteach 39, Extend 39

SKILLS TRACE

GRADE 2	• Develop fact families and use them as a strategy to solve division problems. *(Chapter 8)*
GRADE 3	• Develop fact families and use them as a strategy to solve division problems.
GRADE 4	• Review the language and meaning of division through basic facts. *(Chapter 5)*

MANIPULATIVE WARM-UP

Cooperative Pairs   **Logical/Analytical**

OBJECTIVE Review fact families.

Materials per pair: 20 two-color counters, or other countable objects

► Write 10, 20, 30, and 40 on chalkboard.

► Tell each pair to pick a number and write down as many multiplication sentences as they can that have the number as a product. Also ask them to write down as many division sentences as they can that have the number as a dividend.

► Encourage them to use models to show each sentence.

► Allow time to have some students present their work to the class.

ESL APPROPRIATE

REAL-LIFE CONNECTION

Cooperative Pairs   **Linguistic**

OBJECTIVE Explore families.

► Discuss families of people with your students. Talk about what makes a family and ways in which you can tell people are related. Then have students write about families.

► Tell students to write their own definition of a family and compare that to their definition of a fact family. Students can also write about ways in which they can tell families of people are related and compare that to ways in which they know basic facts are related.

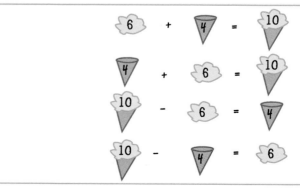

Daily Review

PREVIOUS DAY QUICK REVIEW

Divide
1. $0 \div 5$ [0]
2. $63 \div 7$ [9]
3. $56 \div 8$ [7]
4. $81 \div 9$ [9]

FAST FACTS

1. $9 + 7$ [16]
2. $4 + 8$ [12]
3. $6 + 4$ [10]
4. $5 + 6$ [11]

Problem of the Day • 39

Draw all possible lines connecting two corners. How many lines can you draw? [5]

TECH LINK

MATH VAN

Activity You may wish to use Sports Day to teach this lesson.

MATH FORUM

Combination Classes Some of my younger students find that drawing a picture helps them find all of the facts in a fact family.

Visit our Resource Village at http://www.mhschool.com to see more of the Math Forum.

MATH CENTER

Practice

OBJECTIVE Identify fact families.

Materials per student: 0-9 spinner (TA 2); Math Center Recording Sheet (TA 31 optional)

Students use a spinner to generate random numbers. Then they write multiplication/division fact families for those numbers. [Check students' work.]

PRACTICE ACTIVITY 39

MATH CENTER
On Your Own

Number Sense • Fact Families

- Spin the spinner twice. If you spin 0, spin again to get another number.
- Write a multiplication/division fact family that has the two numbers you spin.
- Repeat for five more fact families.

YOU NEED
- spinner (0–9)

NCTM Standards
✓ Problem Solving
  Communication
✓ Reasoning
  Connections

Chapter 4, Lesson 10, pages 154–155

Division

ESL APPROPRIATE

Problem Solving

OBJECTIVE Identify the number sentences in specific fact families.

Materials per pair: 40 index cards; per student: Math Center Recording Sheet (TA 31 optional)

Students play a card game with fact families. On each turn, they must decide whether to pick a new card or guess that their partner has one of the cards they need.

PROBLEM-SOLVING ACTIVITY 39

MATH CENTER
Partners

Decision Making • Fact Rummy

- On 4 separate cards, write each fact of a fact family, such as:

| $2 \times 7 = 14$ | $7 \times 2 = 14$ | $14 \div 7 = 2$ | $14 \div 2 = 7$ |

YOU NEED
- 40 index cards (or 10 sheets of paper folded twice and cut apart to make 4 slips per sheet)

Make cards for 10 fact families in all.
- Mix up the cards into 1 big deck. Put it facedown. Each player chooses 7 cards.
- On your turn, lay down any complete fact families you have in your hand. Ask your partner for a missing member of a fact family.
- If the player has the card you want, he or she must give it to you. If your partner doesn't have the card you want, draw a card from the pile in the center. Now let the next player take a turn. The first player to get rid of all his or her cards is the winner.

Chapter 4, Lesson 10, pages 154–155

Division

NCTM Standards
  Problem Solving
✓ Communication
✓ Reasoning
  Connections

Fact Families

OBJECTIVE Develop fact families to solve division problems.

Vocabulary fact family

1 Introduce

Review related facts with students. Present this problem:

40 students enter a basketball tournament. There are 5 students on each team. How many teams are there?

Ask:

- **What division fact must you use to solve this problem?** [40 ÷ 5 = 8]
- **What are the related multiplication facts for 40 ÷ 5 = 8?** [5 × 8 = 40, 8 × 5 = 40]
- **What is the related division fact for 40 ÷ 5 = 8?** [40 ÷ 8 = 5]

2 Teach   *Whole Class*

▶ **LEARN** Read the introductory problem aloud. Remind students that they can use related facts to solve a division problem. Ask:

- **How many related facts do you need to solve the problem?** [1]

Students should realize that if they know one fact in a fact family, they can find the rest.

3 Close

▶ **Check for Understanding** using items 1–8, page 154.

CRITICAL THINKING
Materials per student: 6 counters

Students may have difficulty understanding why dividing by zero is impossible. Give them 6 counters, and ask them to illustrate how to divide the counters into zero groups. Then ask them to show how to divide the counters into groups of zero.

▶ **PRACTICE**

Materials have available: calculators

Each student completes all exercises and the **Mixed Review** as independent work.
- In ex. 23, students can use the Guess and Test strategy.

a **Algebra** In ex. 13–20, students develop algebraic thinking by using related facts to help them find missing factors, dividends, divisors, and quotients.

Mixed Review/Test Preparation Students review subtraction and show combinations of coins and bills, a skill they learned in Chapter 2.

 **DIVISION**

Fact Families

At the medal ceremony for synchronized swimming, 24 swimmers crowded the platform for the awarding of the 3 team medals. How many swimmers were on each team?

You can use a **fact family** to find the number of swimmers on each team.

fact family Related facts using the same numbers.	$3 \times 8 = 24$ $8 \times 3 = 24$ $24 \div 8 = 3$ $24 \div 3 = 8$

There were 3 teams with a total of 24 swimmers. There were 8 swimmers on each team.

More Examples

A
$2 \times 4 = 8$
$4 \times 2 = 8$
$8 \div 2 = 4$
$8 \div 4 = 2$

B
$9 \times 1 = 9$
$1 \times 9 = 9$
$9 \div 1 = 9$
$9 \div 9 = 1$

C
$3 \times 3 = 9$
$9 \div 3 = 3$

6. No; possible answer: any numbe multiplied by 0 is always 0, so 6 ÷ 0 has no quotient.

Check for Understanding
Find the fact family for the numbers. See page T17.

1. 16, 8, 2   2. 4, 5, 20   3. 6, 1, 6   4. 4, 9, 36   5. 8, 8, 64

Critical Thinking: Analyze   Explain your reasoning.

6. Can you find 6 ÷ 0 using a fact family? Why or why not? See above.

7. What can you say about any number divided by zero?

a 8. **ALGEBRA: PATTERNS** Divide. What patterns do you see?
a. $0 \div 3$ 0 $0 \div 4$ 0 $0 \div 6$ 0 $0 \div 9$ 0
b. $3 \div 3$ 1 $7 \div 7$ 1 $8 \div 8$ 1 $1 \div 1$ 1
c. $4 \div 1$ 4 $5 \div 1$ 5 $7 \div 1$ 7 $9 \div 1$ 9

7. Possible answer It is not possible to find the quotient becaus there is no number times zero that gives a number other than zero.

a. Zero divided by any number is zero.   b. Any number divided by itself is 1.
c. Any number divided by 1 is that number.

154   Lesson 4.10

Meeting Individual Needs

Early Finishers

Challenge students to find all the numbers between 1 and 81 that have only 2 sentences in their fact family. *[1, 2, 3, 7, 11, 13, 17, 23, 29, 31, 37, 41, 43, 47, 53, 61, 67, 71, 73, 79]*

Extra Support

When finding the fact family for a set of numbers, students may find it helpful to write the three numbers on cards. They can then arrange those cards, operation cards, and an equals card to find the fact family.

Ongoing Assessment

Anecdotal Report Make notes on students' ability to write fact families for a given problem. Students should be able to pick the appropriate numbers from a problem and write a fact family based on those numbers.

Follow Up If students need more practice with fact families, let them use a multiplication or division chart to help them complete **Reteach 39**.

For students who need more of a challenge, assign **Extend 39**.

Practice

Find the fact family for the numbers. See page T17.

1 3, 6, 18   **2** 4, 7, 28   **3** 5, 25, 5   **4** 72, 8, 9

5 9, 45, 5   **6** 14, 7, 2   **7** 63, 9, 7   **8** 1, 8, 8

9 4, 8, 32   **10** 7, 49, 7   **11** 7, 56, 8   **12** 9, 81, 9

ALGEBRA **Find the missing number.**

13 $\blacksquare \div 9 = 4$ **36**   **14** $48 \div 6 = \blacksquare$ **8**   **15** $6 \times \blacksquare = 54$ **9**   **16** $64 \div \blacksquare = 8$ **8**

17 $8 \times \blacksquare = 16$ **2**   **18** $42 \div \blacksquare = 7$ **6**   **19** $\blacksquare \div 8 = 5$ **40**   **20** $\blacksquare \div 9 = 6$ **54**

23. Possible answers: 10 gold,
5 gold and 10 silver, 3 gold
and 6 silver and 10 bronze

MIXED APPLICATIONS
Problem Solving
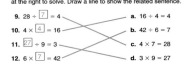

One scoring system in the Olympics gives 10 points for each gold, 5 points for each silver, and 4 points for each bronze.

21 What is the total score for Cuba? **162 points**

22 Which nation has the greatest score? the least score? **United States; Ukraine**

23 Suppose a nation has a score of 100. What are possible medals its athletes could have won? **See above.**

24 **Write a problem** using information from the table. Trade problems with other students. Solve. **Students check each other's work by comparing problems and solutions.**

Medals by Country 1996 Summer Olympics			
Nation	**Gold**	**Silver**	**Bronze**
Australia	9	9	23
China	16	22	12
Cuba	9	8	8
France	15	7	15
Germany	20	18	27
Hungary	13	10	12
Italy	33	21	28
Korea	7	15	5
Russian Federation	26	21	16
Ukraine	9	2	12
United States	44	32	25

mixed review · test preparation

Subtract. Answers may vary. Possible answers given.

1 $5 - \$1.98$ **2** $2 - \$1.15$ **3** $10 - \$5.75$ **4** $5.02 - \$1.27$
$3.02   **$0.85**   **$4.25**   **$3.75**

Show the change in two different ways. Answers may vary. Possible answers given.

5 86¢   **6** 29¢   **7** $1.94   **8** $7.33   **9** $15.75
3 Q, 1 D,   29 P; 5N,   1 $1,   1 $5, 2 $1, 3 D,   1 $10, 1 $5, 3 Q;
1 P; 8 D, 6 P   4 P   9D, 4 P;   3 P; 7 $1, 33 P   15 $1, 7 D, 1 N
               19 D, 4 P

Extra Practice, page 499   Multiplication and Division Facts **155**

Alternate Teaching Strategy

Name a product, like 30, and have students develop multiplication and division fact families. [$6 \times 5 = 30, 5 \times 6 = 30$, [$30 \div 6 = 5, 30 \div 5 = 6$]

Then make copies of each fact family for each student to compile into their own book. This book can be used as a reference and a learning tool for learning multiplication and division facts.

ESL **APPROPRIATE**

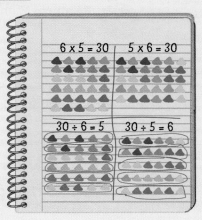

PRACTICE · 39

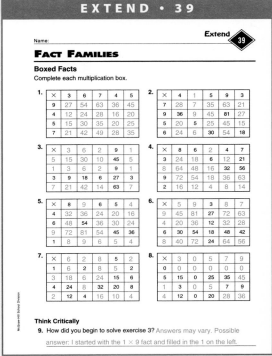

RETEACH · 39

EXTEND · 39

Teaching With Technology

Fact Families

OBJECTIVE Students use counters to explore fact families and create models of related facts.

Resource Math Van Activity: *Sports Day*

SET UP
Provide students with the activity card for *Sports Day*. Start **Math Van** and click the *Activities* button. Click the *Sports Day* activity on the Fax Machine.

USING THE MATH VAN ACTIVITY

1 Getting Started Students use Counters to help Jackie organize a Sports Day with four events for 24 of her classmates.

2 Practice and Apply Students use Counters to help Jackie organize 24 students who signed up for volleyball into even teams.

3 Close You may wish to have students discuss the two different ways to divide a number. Students can share how the division and multiplication facts are related.

Extend Students write word problems that use four related facts. A partner shows the word problem on the Open Mat within the Counters tool.

TIPS FOR TOOLS

Remind students that they can draw a box around a group of Counters using the *Select* button and drag them as a group to arrange them more easily on the mat.

Sports Day

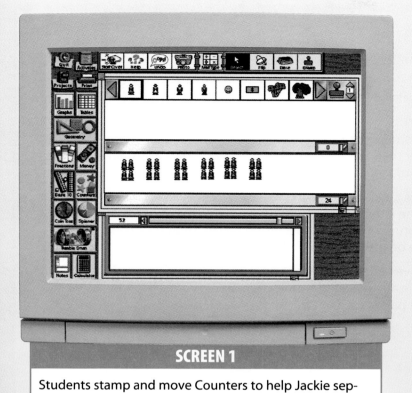

SCREEN 1

Students stamp and move Counters to help Jackie separate students into equal teams.

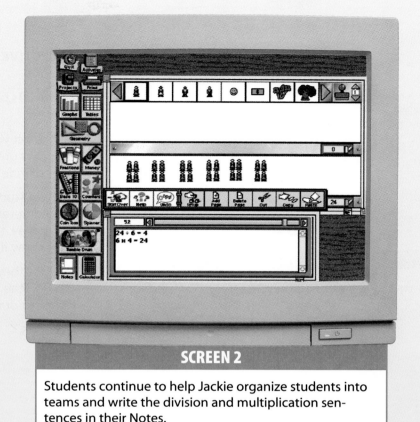

SCREEN 2

Students continue to help Jackie organize students into teams and write the division and multiplication sentences in their Notes.

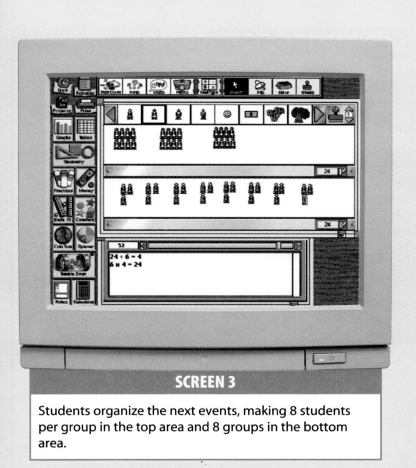

SCREEN 3

Students organize the next events, making 8 students per group in the top area and 8 groups in the bottom area.

SCREEN 4

Students take a photo of their work and answer questions in their Notes about related facts.

LESSON 4.11

EXPLORE ACTIVITY
Remainders

OBJECTIVE Explore the concept of remainder.

RESOURCE REMINDER
Math Center Cards 40
Practice 40, Reteach 40, Extend 40

SKILLS TRACE

GRADE 3	• Explore the concept of remainder. *(Chapter 8)*
GRADE 4	• Explore the concept of remainder.
GRADE 5	• Divide 2-and 3-digit numbers by 1-digit numbers. *(Chapter 5)*

WARM-UP

Cooperative Pairs   **Logical/Mathematical**

OBJECTIVE Determine if an amount can be divided evenly by another amount.

Materials per pair: 15 index cards—36, 42, 56, 21, 54, 37, 25, 64, 35, 63, 9, 8, 7, 6, and 5

► Instruct your students to sort the index cards into two piles—one pile of numbers greater than ten and the other pile of numbers less than ten. The piles of index cards should be placed face down on the table.

► Have students take turns drawing one card from each stack. Students should determine if the smaller number can divide the larger number evenly. Either way, the student should show (using any method they choose) how they know if the greater number drawn can or cannot be divided evenly.

► Once they have convinced their partner, the pair of index cards can be put back on the table and mixed in with the remaining cards. Then the other student can draw a pair of cards.

CONSUMER CONNECTION

Cooperative Pairs   **Social**

OBJECTIVE Connect remainders with making consumer decisions.

► Copy the following information onto the chalkboard:

> Suzanna is planning a party for 15 people. She is trying to decide what food to serve. She has $25. Suzanna wants to get the most for her money without having too many leftovers.
>
> | | | |
> |---|---|---|
> | Pizza | Serves 6 | $9.95 |
> | Hamburgers | Serves 10 | $7.89 |
> | Foot-long Sandwich | Serves 4 | $5.19 |

► Ask students to consider the information given and decide what they would serve at the party. Students will have to determine the cost and the number of left over servings for each item. Accept any answer that includes a reasonable explanation.

Daily Review

PREVIOUS DAY QUICK REVIEW

Find the fact family.

1. 3, 21, 7 *[3 × 7 = 21, 7 × 3 = 21, 21 ÷ 7 = 3, 21 ÷ 3 = 7]*
2. 40, 8, 5 *[8 × 5 = 40, 5 × 8 = 40, 40 ÷ 8 = 5, 40 ÷ 5 = 8]*

FAST FACTS

1. 4 × 8 *[32]*
2. 6 × 6 *[36]*
3. 3 × 5 *[15]*
4. 5 × 9 *[45]*

Problem of the Day • 40

When December 6th is on a Friday, on what day of the week was the previous November 13th? *[Wednesday]*

TECH LINK

MATH VAN

Tools You may wish to use the Counters and Division Mat tools with this lesson.

MATH FORUM

Management Tip I keep number lines, dot paper, grid paper, and countable objects available at a work station where children can come to use them throughout math class.

Visit our Resource Village at http://www.mhschool.com to see more of the Math Forum.

MATH CENTER

Practice

OBJECTIVE Solve division problems with remainders.

Materials per student: counters, Math Center Recording Sheet (TA 31 optional)

Given the total number of pieces in a game, students calculate the number of pieces each player would get. They divide numbers that sometimes have remainders and tell the remainder. *[a. 42; b. 28; c. 21; d. 16, with 4 left over; e. 14; f. 12; g. 10, 4 left over; h. 9, 3 left over]*

Problem Solving

OBJECTIVE Relate geometric patterns to remainders of division problems.

Students examine a pattern of squares that repeats itself every four times. They explain how to find any square in the pattern without having to see that part of the pattern. *[1. square A; 2. square B; 3. Answers may vary. Possible answer: Divide the number by 4 and look at the remainder. A is R1, B is R2, C is R3, and D is R0.]*

PRACTICE ACTIVITY 40

MATH CENTER
Partners

Number Sense • How Many?

A toy manufacturer designed a new board game. It contains 84 pieces. To play the game, the pieces must be divided evenly among the players. Any extra pieces will not be used in the game.

YOU NEED
counters

How many pieces would each player get if there were:

a. 2 players? **b.** 3 players? **c.** 4 players? **d.** 5 players?
e. 6 players? **f.** 7 players? **g.** 8 players? **h.** 9 players?

If there are pieces left over, tell how many. Use counters to help. Work with your partner to redesign the game for another total number of pieces.

Chapter 4, Lesson 11, pages 156–157

Division

NCTM Standards

✓ Problem Solving
✓ Communication
✓ Reasoning
✓ Connections

PROBLEM-SOLVING ACTIVITY 40

MATH CENTER
On Your Own

Spatial Reasoning • What's Next?

A.   B.   C.   D.

Look at the pattern.
1. What will the next square look like?
2. What will the 30th square look like?
3. How can you figure out what any square in the pattern will look like without seeing it? Explain.

Chapter 4, Lesson 11, pages 156–157

Division

NCTM Standards

✓ Problem Solving
✓ Communication
✓ Reasoning
✓ Connections

Lesson 4.11 continued

EXPLORE ACTIVITY
Remainders

OBJECTIVE Explore the concept of remainder.

Materials per pair: 64 counters, or other countable items; centimeter graph paper (TA 7); geoboard

Vocabulary divisible by, remainder

 **Introduce**

Materials per pair: 32 counters, or other countable items

Have pairs of students divide 32 counters into groups of 6.
- **How many groups of 6 are there?** *[5 groups]*
- **How many counters are not in a group of 6?** *[2]*

 **Teach**   Cooperative Pairs

Cultural Connection Have students share what they know about soccer. Explain that the World Cup is a tournament in which 24 countries compete for the world championship.

▶ **LEARN Work Together** Have two students demonstrate the activity to the class. The first student chooses a 2-digit number. Ask:
- **How many students are in the class?** *[the 2-digit number]*

The second student chooses a 1-digit number. Ask:
- **How many students are in each group?** *[the 1-digit number]*
- **What are you asked to find?** *[the number of groups and the number of students left]*

Have partners use counters to solve the problem. Then discuss their entry for each column in the table.

MAKE CONNECTIONS
Make sure that students can identify each part of a division sentence, and can explain what it means to say that one number is divisible by another.

 **Close**

▶ **Check for Understanding** using items 1–11, page 157.

CRITICAL THINKING
After students answer item 11, ask:
- **Why must the remainder be less than the divisor?** *[If the remainder was greater than or equal to the divisor it could be divided again.]*

▶ ## PRACTICE
Materials have available: calculators

Options for assigning exercises:
A—Odd ex. 1–25
B—Even ex. 2–24

Remainders

A class is going to a soccer game. Your job is to decide how many cars are needed to take the students to the game.

Cultural Note
Some historians trace soccer to the Japanese game of *kemari* which was played as early as 600 B.C.

You will need
- *counters*
- *graph paper*

Work Together
Work with a partner.

Take turns. Your partner chooses a 2-digit number for the total number of students. You choose a 1-digit number for the number in each group.

KEEP IN MIND
▶ Check your work to make sure that your answer is correct.
▶ Be ready to explain your methods to the class.

Use any method you want to find the number of equal groups and the number left over.

Record your results in a table.

Total Number of Students	Number in Each Group	Number of Equal Groups	Number Left Over	Number of Cars
23	5			

▶ How did you decide how many cars are needed?
Possible answer: the same number of cars as the number of equal groups, plus 1 if there are any students left over

156 Lesson 4.11

Meeting Individual Needs

Early Finishers
Challenge students to make up a word problem that involves division with a remainder. Have them share their problems with the class.

Extra Support
Students may forget to note the remainder. Remind them that when using the division housing and the computation method, they should circle any difference that is not zero to show the remainders.

Ongoing Assessment
Observation Checklist
Determine if students understand division housing by observing if they write the quotient above the bar and subtract the product to find the remainder.

Follow Up If students need more practice using division housing, have them rewrite ex. 1–10 in this form.

For students who need more practice with division, assign **Reteach 40.**

For students who need a challenge, assign **Extend 40.**

Make Connections

Sometimes when you divide, the numbers do not come out evenly. They have a **remainder.**

$$\begin{array}{r} 4\text{ R}3 \\ 5\overline{)23} \\ -20 \\ \hline 3 \end{array}$$

Think: $5 \times 4 = 20 \qquad 20 < 23$
$5 \times 5 = 25 \qquad 25 > 23$

So $23 \div 5 = 4$ R3.

▶ When there is no remainder, we say that the dividend is **divisible by** the divisor. What numbers in your table are divisible by 2? by 3? by 6?
Possible answer: 24; 27; 30.

▶ If a number is divisible by 2 and by 3, is it also divisible by 6? **Yes.**

▶ What happens when the dividend is not divisible by the divisor? **There is a remainder.**

> **remainder** the number left over when dividing.

> **Check Out the Glossary**
> **divisible by**
> See page 544.

Check for Understanding
Divide.

1 $9 \div 2$ **4 R1** **2** $11 \div 3$ **3 R2** **3** $15 \div 4$ **3 R3** **4** $13 \div 5$ **2 R3** **5** $25 \div 4$ **6 R1**

6 $7\overline{)37}$ **5 R2** **7** $2\overline{)17}$ **8 R1** **8** $5\overline{)47}$ **9 R2** **9** $9\overline{)26}$ **2 R8** **10** $3\overline{)29}$ **9 R2**

Critical Thinking: Analyze   Explain your reasoning.

11 Compare the remainder and divisor in several division problems. Is the remainder always equal to, greater than, or less than the divisor? **less than**

Practice
Divide.

1 $22 \div 5$ **4 R2** **2** $13 \div 3$ **4 R1** **3** $25 \div 7$ **3 R4** **4** $36 \div 9$ **4** **5** $38 \div 6$ **6 R2**

6 $44 \div 8$ **5 R4** **7** $50 \div 7$ **7 R1** **8** $45 \div 6$ **7 R3** **9** $55 \div 9$ **6 R1** **10** $56 \div 8$ **7**

11 $3\overline{)19}$ **6 R1** **12** $6\overline{)35}$ **5 R5** **13** $7\overline{)28}$ **4** **14** $8\overline{)60}$ **7 R4** **15** $5\overline{)34}$ **6 R4**

16 $9\overline{)87}$ **9 R6** **17** $4\overline{)18}$ **4 R2** **18** $2\overline{)19}$ **9 R1** **19** $5\overline{)34}$ **6 R4** **20** $3\overline{)22}$ **7 R1**

21 $8\overline{)77}$ **9 R6** **22** $9\overline{)83}$ **4 R2** **23** $5\overline{)41}$ **9 R1** **24** $3\overline{)26}$ **6 R4** **25** $7\overline{)48}$ **7 R1**

Extra Practice, page 499

Multiplication and Division Facts **157**

Alternate Teaching Strategy

Materials per pair: 23 two-color counters

Demonstrate dividing 23 counters into 5 equal groups.

Write the division sentence $23 \div 5 = 4$R3 on the chalkboard.

Have volunteers explain how each number in the division sentence describes the counters. Explain to students that the number left over is called the remainder. It is indicated by the number after the "R" in the division sentence.

Have students repeat the activity with groups of 5 and 3. Pairs write a division sentence to represent the grouping and explain how each number describes the counters.

Ask students what they notice about the remainders and the divisors. Students should see that the remainder is always less than the divisor.

ESL APPROPRIATE

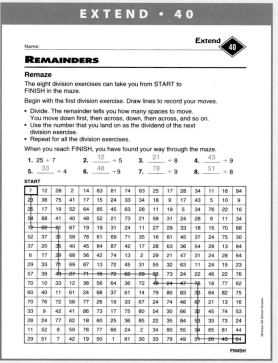

LESSON 4.12

Problem Solvers at Work: Choose the Operation

OBJECTIVE Solve and write problems by choosing the operation.

RESOURCE REMINDER
Math Center Cards 41
Practice 41, Reteach 41, Extend 41

SKILLS TRACE

GRADE 3	• Formulate and solve problems involving choosing the operation (all four operations). *(Chapter 8)*
GRADE 4	• Formulate and solve problems involving choosing the operation (all four operations).
GRADE 5	• Formulate and solve problems involving choosing the operation (all four operations). *(Chapter 5)*

WARM-UP

Cooperative Groups   Logical/Analytical

OBJECTIVE Solve basic addition, subtraction, multiplication, and division problems.

Materials per group: operation cube, 0 - 9 spinner (TA 2)

▶ Students take turns rolling the operation cube and spinning the spinner twice. Each student combines the two numbers on the spinner using the operation rolled on the operation cube.

▶ If the student gives the correct answer, he or she earns one point. If the answer is incorrect, the first person to the right can earn a point by giving the correct answer.

▶ Play continues around the group until time is called. The person who has earned the most points is the winner.

CONSUMER CONNECTION

Whole Class   Logical/Analytical

OBJECTIVE Connect choosing the operation with consumer situations.

Materials per student: catalog or store advertisement, number cube, calculator (optional)

▶ Each student brings in a store ad or catalog. The student chooses four items with prices of less than $10, rounds each price to the nearest dollar, and records it.

Item Description	Price	Quantity	Total Cost

▶ The student tosses the number cube to find the number of each item to buy, and writes these numbers in the table. The student completes the table and finds the total cost of all the purchases.

Daily Review

PREVIOUS DAY QUICK REVIEW

Divide
1. 24 ÷ 5 *[4 R4]*
2. 17 ÷ 4 *[4 R1]*
3. 32 ÷ 7 *[4 R4]*
4. 29 ÷ 9 *[3 R2]*

FAST FACTS

1. 35 ÷ 5 *[7]*
2. 48 ÷ 6 *[8]*
3. 27 ÷ 3 *[9]*
4. 36 ÷ 6 *[6]*

Problem of the Day • 41

Sally has 1 black shirt, 1 white shirt, 1 black skirt, 1 white skirt, and 1 gray skirt. How many different combinations of shirt and skirt can she make? *[6– black-black, black-white, black gray, white-black, white-white, white-gray]*

TECH LINK

MATH VAN

Aid You may wish to use the Electronic Teacher Aid in the Math Van with this lesson.

MATH FORUM

Cultural Diversity I encourage my students to write problems with themes that help other students understand their culture.

Visit our Resource Village at http://www.mhschool.com to see more of the Math Forum.

MATH CENTER

Practice

OBJECTIVE Solve problems by choosing the operation.

Materials per student: Math Center Recording Sheets (TA 31 optional)

Students solve a problem in which they must decide what operations to use. *[$2.00; $4 × 3 = $12, $20 − $12 = $8; $8 + $10 = $18; 8 × $.25 = $2; $18 − $2 = $16; $16 ÷ 4 = $4; $4 − $2 = $2]*

PRACTICE ACTIVITY 41

MATH CENTER
On Your Own 👤

Using Data • What's Left?

Mrs. Choi starts the day with $20.00.
• She buys 4 greeting cards for $3.00 each.
• She finds a wallet and turns it in at the store counter. The clerk gives her a $10.00 reward.
• She buys 8 holiday stickers for 25¢ each.
• She divides the rest of her money with 3 friends. She and her friends go out for lunch. Her lunch costs $2.00.

How much money does she have left after lunch? Record your work.

NCTM Standards

✓ Problem Solving
  Communication
✓ Reasoning
✓ Connections

Chapter 4, Lesson 12, pages 158–161   Problem Solving

Problem Solving

OBJECTIVE Write number sentences for given answers.

Materials per student: Math Center Recording Sheet (TA 31 optional)

Students use the different operations and explore basic facts for 1 through 20. *[Answers may vary. Possible answers: 20 − 19 = 1; 18 ÷ 9 = 2; 6 − 3 = 3;16 − 12 = 4; 13 − 8 = 5; 17 − 11 = 6; 14 − 7 = 7; 4 × 2 = 8; 10 − 1 = 9; 15 − 5 = 10.]*

PROBLEM-SOLVING ACTIVITY 41

MATH CENTER
On Your Own 👤

Logical Reasoning • What Is the Problem?

The table shows the answers to ten math problems.

= 1	= 2	= 3	= 4	= 5
= 6	= 7	= 8	= 9	= 10

• For each problem use any operation you want.
• Try and use the numbers from 1 through 20 *only* once (except for the answers).

NCTM Standards

✓ Problem Solving
  Communication
✓ Reasoning
  Connections

Chapter 4, Lesson 12, pages 158–161   Problem Solving

Problem Solvers at Work

OBJECTIVE Solve and write problems by choosing the operation.

Resources spreadsheet program, or Math Van Tools

1 Introduce

Ask students to give examples of problem-solving strategies they have used in the past. Tell them that interpreting data, using tables, finding patterns, and choosing the operation are among the strategies that can be applied in this lesson.

2 Teach *Whole Class*

Cultural Connection Read the **Cultural Note.** The 100th running of the Boston Marathon took place on April 15, 1996. The top three runners were Kenyans, who ran most of the race together. Ask if students know anyone who has competed in a marathon.

Ask:

- **How do you find each runner's time for the race?** *[Subtract the starting time from the ending time.]*

PART 1 CHOOSE THE OPERATION

▶ **LEARN** Read over the introductory information and have students review the table. Make sure students understand that the time is given in hours, minutes, and seconds. Review elapsed time if necessary. Then ask:
- **Which runner started the race at 7 minutes after 11:00?** *[Paul Malloy]*
- **Which runner completed the race in 30 minutes and 46 seconds?** *[Pedro Arcy]*

Work Together For item 2, students should realize that they are assuming Jane can maintain her 2-km pace for 10 km and for 30 min. Her pace may be slower for longer distances, though.

Students may just divide 24 by 3 in item 3. Remind them that the question asks how many times Tim stops before the end of the race.

Sequence of Events Have students explain how they determined the sequence of the racers' starts and finishes for item 5.

Problem Solvers at Work

Read	Plan
Solve	Look Back

Part 1 Choose the Operation

2. Answers may vary. Possible answer: more than 50 min since she will become tired the longer she runs; about 6 km; multiplication

The town of Woodside sponsored a 10-km run for marathon runners. The top six runners are listed below.

Name of Runner	Starting Time	Ending Time
Fouz Alaoyi	11:00:00	11:31:48
Pedro Arcy	11:05:00	11:35:46
Stacy Flynn	11:00:00	11:40:45
Paul Malloy	11:07:00	11:37:59
Trevor Reed	11:08:00	11:49:28
Lena Wicks	11:05:00	11:42:16

Note: 11:31:48 stands for 11 hours 31 minutes 48 seconds.

Work Together

Solve. Tell which operation you used.

1. Which runner ran the race in the shortest time? the longest time? **Pedro Arcy; Trevor Reed; subtraction**

2. **What if** Jane ran 2 km in 10 min. If she continues at about this pace, how long will it take her to run 10 km? About how far can she run in 30 min? **See above.**

3. Tim stops to drink water every 3 km. In a 24-km run, how often will he stop to drink water before finishing the race? **7 times; possible answer: division**

4. **ALGEBRA: PATTERNS** To train for a race, Russell runs 30 min each day of the first week, 45 min each day of the second week, 60 min each day of the third week, and 75 min each day of the fourth week. If he continues this pattern, how long will he run each day of the fifth week? the sixth week? **90 min; 105 min; possible answer: addition**

5. **Sequence of Events** Write a paragraph for the Woodside newspaper giving the results of the race. Describe the race in the order of the events that happened. **Check students' work. It should have the correct sequence at the start and at the finish; start: FA and SF, PA, LW, PM, TR; finish from first to sixth: PA, PM, FA, LW, SF, TR.**

158 Lesson 4.12

Meeting Individual Needs

Extra Support

For students having difficulty deciding on which operation to use to solve problems, review problems with simpler numbers to reinforce the use of each of the four operations to solve problems.

Gifted And Talented

Encourage students to write problems requiring more than one step and more than one operation. Challenge students to write the difficult problems. Then let students share their problems with each other.

Ongoing Assessment

Anecdotal Report Note if students can solve problems in an organized way.

Follow Up Help students who are having difficulty write a plan for solving each problem. Assign **Reteach 41.**

For students who successfully complete the lesson, assign **Extend 41.**

Part 2 Write and Share Problems

Matthew used information about a runner to write the problem.

Bob runs 5 miles every day for 6 weeks. He needs a new pair of running shoes every 6 months. A pair of his running shoes costs $45.

6 Solve Matthew's problem. What operation did you use to solve the problem? **Possible answer: 5 × 7 × 6 = 210 mi; multiplication**

7 Change Matthew's problem so that you need information to solve it. **For problems 7–11, see Teacher's Edition.**

8 Explain what type of information is needed and how you might be able to collect the information.

9 **Write a problem** of your own about running. You should be able to solve the problem using multiplication or division.

10 Trade problems. Solve at least three problems written by your classmates.

11 What was the most interesting problem that you solved? Why?

> **STUDENT TO STUDENT**
>
> If Bob runs 5 miles every day for 6 weeks, how many miles will Bob run altogether?

Matthew Niemi
Latson Road Elementary School
Howell, MI

CHECK

Cultural Note

The marathon is named in honor of the famous Greek messenger from the plains of Pheidippides (fī-DIP-uh-deez), who ran from Marathon to Athens.

Turn the page for Practice Strategies. ➡
Multiplication and Division Facts **159**

COMMON ERROR

Some students may have trouble choosing the correct operation. Have them check their answers to ensure that they make sense.

Gender Fairness

Respond enthusiastically to answers given by both girls and boys. You may try giving a positive comment to girls and boys who participate in a discussion.

PART 2 WRITE AND SHARE PROBLEMS

▶ **Check** Ask students to explain how they chose the operation to solve Matthew's problem. Item 7 allows students to change the given problem to create another problem. This prepares students to write problems of their own. For item 8, students may suggest taking a survey or using an encyclopedia or other reference books to collect information.

For item 9, some students will paraphrase Matthew's problem, others will write simple one-step problems, and some will write complicated multistep problems.

Encourage students' creativity by suggesting other contexts or questions that can be used in problems.

For items 10 and 11, encourage students to discuss the problems they solved and their reasons why a problem was most interesting.

3 Close

Have students discuss how they write their own problems. Have them compare the methods they used to solve each other's problems.

Practice See pages 160–161.

Lesson 4.12 *continued* **PRACTICE**

▶ **PART 3 PRACTICE STRATEGIES**
Materials have available: calculators

Students have the option of choosing any five problems from ex. 1–8, and any two problems from ex. 9–12. They may choose to do more problems if they wish. Have students describe how they made their choices.

- For ex. 5, encourage students to record a guess first and then check it on the calculator. If students work too quickly, they may forget what they have entered to produce a result of 24.
- Tell students not to give up too quickly on ex. 9. Ask them to be certain they have thought of all possible ways to set up the teams before going on to another problem.
- In ex. 11, tell students that they will act as scientists to find patterns and make predictions.

At the Computer If computers are not available, students can record the data in a table and use a calculator to find the totals.

 Math Van Students may use the Table tool to create a spreadsheet.

---

5. Answers may vary. Possible answers: 2 4, $2 \times 3 \times 4 =$, $2 \times 2 \times 2 \times 3 =$, $4 + 4 + 4 + 4 + 4 + 4 =$, $4 \times 4 + 4 + 4 =$, $4 \times 4 \times 3 \div 2 =$

Part 3 Practice Strategies

Menu
Choose five problems and solve them. Explain your methods. Explanations may vary.

1 A sports drink comes in 8-ounce bottles. How many ounces are in 4 bottles?
32 oz

2 Charlie's school day starts at 8:15 A.M. and ends at 2:45 P.M. How long is his school day?
6 h 30 min

3 Ace in-line skates have 4 wheels on each skate. The stockroom has 75 wheels. How many pairs of in-line skates can the company make? How many wheels will be left over? **9 pairs; 3 wheels**

4 Students use the gym for basketball every night from 5:00 P.M. to 8:00 P.M. How many hours each week is the gym used for basketball? **21 h**

5 Use only the following keys on a calculator: 2 3 4 + − × ÷ = .
Show five different ways to get 24.
See above.

6 The tennis teacher wants to buy at least 25 tennis balls. The store sells tennis balls in containers of 3 balls for $4. How many containers does she need to buy? What is the total cost?
9 containers; $36

7 How many times does the digit 2 appear on the March calendar? Explain your answer.

8 **Write a problem** about baseball that can be solved by finding 9×12. Solve it. Have others solve it. Did you use mental math, pencil and paper, or a calculator? Why? **Students should compare problems and solutions.**

13 times; on the following dates: 2nd, 12th, and 20th through 29th

160 Lesson 4.12

Meeting Individual Needs

Early Finishers
Challenge students to write four problems that can be solved by each of the four operations. Have them explain why the operation they chose was used to solve each problem.

Language Support
Pair students acquiring English with those who are good readers. Have the good readers help the others understand what is being asked.

ESL APPROPRIATE

9. 6 ways; 2 teams of 15 students, 3 teams of 10 students, 5 teams of 6 students, 15 teams of 2 students, 10 teams of 3 students, 6 teams of 5 students

Choose two problems and solve them. Explain your methods. *Explanations may vary.*

9 You want to have a relay race with 30 students. Each team has the same number of students. There are at least 2 students on a team. How many different ways can you form teams? Name them. **See above.**

10 Each letter stands for a digit. Find the numbers that match this addition problem.

$$\begin{array}{r} \text{ANT} \\ + \text{ANT} \\ \hline \text{TEEN} \end{array} \qquad \begin{array}{r} 721 \\ + 721 \\ \hline 1{,}442 \end{array}$$

11 **ALGEBRA: PATTERNS** On your calculator, find products of two odd numbers, products of two even numbers, and products of one even and one odd number. Record each multiplication sentence and look for a pattern in the three cases.
a. What is the product of two odd numbers—odd or even? **odd**
b. What is the product of two even numbers—odd or even? **even**
c. What is the product of an even number and an odd number? **even**

Use patterns to predict if the product is even or odd.
d. 7×8 **even**
e. 9×7 **odd**
f. 15×7 **odd**
g. 18×14 **even**
h. 57×16 **even**

Use patterns to help you tell whether the product is correct or incorrect.
i. $6 \times 8 = 47$ **incorrect**
j. $9 \times 7 = 63$ **correct**
k. $15 \times 12 = 185$ **incorrect**
l. $21 \times 11 = 232$ **incorrect**

12 **At the Computer** Create a spreadsheet that can record the points scored in a basketball game. Watch a game and record the number of 2-point shots, 3-point shots, and free throws that are made for each team. Use the spreadsheet to calculate the total number of points for each team and compare your total to the total shown at the end of the game. **Check students' work.**

Basketball Scores

Player	Number of 2-point Shots	Number of 3-point Shots	Number of Free Throws	Total Points

Extra Practice, page 499

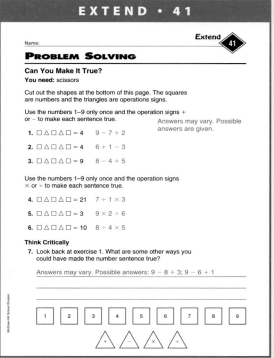

Alternate Teaching Strategy

Copy the table below onto the chalkboard:

Addition	Subtraction	Multiplication	Division

As they solve problems, have students describe how they know which operation to use to solve each type of problem. Generate a list of characteristics for each operation in the table. Have students keep this same list in their notebooks.

After completing the table, have students compare the operations.

Students should see that if the answer involves combining, adding onto groups, or finding the total created by equal groups, it requires addition or multiplication; if it involves taking away from a group, or dividing a group into parts, it requires subtraction or division.

Ask students how they distinguish addition from multiplication and subtraction from division.

PRACTICE • 41

Name: _____   **Practice 41**

PROBLEM SOLVING: CHOOSE THE OPERATION

☑ Read ☑ Plan ☑ Solve ☑ Look Back

Solve. Tell which operation you used.

1. There are 3 softball teams. There are 9 students on each team. How many students play softball?
27 students; multiplication

2. Tyrone forms 4 teams for a relay race. There are 24 students. How many students will there be on each team?
6 students; division

3. Ellen ran the first leg of a 4-leg relay race in 3 minutes. If the others on her team run just as fast, about how long will it take the team to finish the race?
about 12 min; multiplication

4. The students started playing a softball game at 1:20 P.M. The game lasted 1 hour and 50 minutes. What time did the game end?
3:10 P.M.; addition

Solve using any method.

5. A standard soccer field is 100 yards long and 50 yards wide. On a scale drawing, 1 inch represents 10 yards. How long is the field on the scale drawing?
10 in.

6. It takes Veronica 25 minutes to get to soccer practice. If practice starts at 4:00, what time should she leave home? On Friday, she needs an extra 15 minutes before practice to buy socks. What time should she leave home on Friday?
3:35; 3:20

7. Veronica has soccer practice for 2 hours 3 times a week. How many hours does she practice in 4 weeks?
24 h

8. **Logical Reasoning** The fourth grade chooses sides for kickball by counting off "1, 2, 1, 2. . ." Will the 29th student be on the 1s' team or the 2s' team?
the 1s' team

RETEACH • 41

Name: _____   **Reteach 41**

PROBLEM SOLVING: CHOOSE THE OPERATION

☑ Read ☑ Plan ☑ Solve ☑ Look Back

There are 36 connecting cubes.

Jan uses all of the cubes to make 4 equal groups. How many cubes are in each group?
Use **division** because you are separating into equal groups.
$36 \div 4 = 9$ cubes

Raul makes 7 cube trains with 4 cubes in each train. How many cubes does he use?
Use **multiplication** because you are combining equal groups.
$7 \times 4 = 28$ cubes

There are 7 red cubes. How many of the cubes are not red?
Use **subtraction** because you know one part and the whole, and you are finding the missing part.
$36 - 7 = 29$ cubes

A set of 8 cubes is added to the set of 36. How many connecting cubes are there in all?
Use **addition** because you are combining unequal groups.
$36 + 8 = 44$ cubes

First write which operation to use. Then solve.

1. A class of 24 breaks into groups of 3 for throwing practice. How many groups are there?
division; 8 groups

2. The class practices for 1 hour every day after school. How many hours is that in 1 week?
multiplication; 5 hours

3. Last week 78 people came to the game in vans. Another 43 people walked to the game. How many people came to the game?
addition; 121 people

4. At the start of the day, there was $48 in the cash register. At the end, there was $823. How much money did the food stand take in?
subtraction; $775

EXTEND • 41

Name: _____   **Extend 41**

PROBLEM SOLVING

Can You Make It True?
You need: scissors

Cut out the shapes at the bottom of this page. The squares are numbers and the triangles are operations signs.

Use the numbers 1–9 only once and the operation signs + or − to make each sentence true.
Answers may vary. Possible answers are given.

1. □ △ □ △ □ = 4 $9 - 7 + 2$
2. □ △ □ △ □ = 4 $6 + 1 - 3$
3. □ △ □ △ □ = 9 $8 - 4 + 5$

Use the numbers 1–9 only once and the operation signs × or ÷ to make each sentence true.

4. □ △ □ △ □ = 21 $7 \div 1 \times 3$
5. □ △ □ △ □ = 3 $9 \times 2 \div 6$
6. □ △ □ △ □ = 10 $8 \div 4 \times 5$

Think Critically
7. Look back at exercise 1. What are some other ways you could have made the number sentence true?
Answers may vary. Possible answers: $9 - 8 + 3$; $9 - 6 + 1$

1	2	3	4	5	6	7	8	9

△+ △− △× △÷

PURPOSE Review and assess the concepts, skills, and strategies that students have learned in the chapter.

Materials per student: calculator, optional

Chapter Objectives

4A Multiply, facts to 81

4B Divide, facts to 81

4C Use the Commutative, Identity, Zero, and Associative properties

4D Use inverse operations to identify fact families and find missing factors

4E Solve problems, including those that involve multiplication and division, and patterns

Using the Chapter Review

The **Chapter Review** can be used as a review, practice test, or chapter test.

Think Critically Students' explanations for ex. 31 will indicate whether they understand the relationship between the divisor and the remainder.

Language and Mathematics

Complete the sentence. Use a word in the chart. (pages 124–157)

1 The ■ of 15 divided by 5 is 3. **quotient**

2 When a number does not divide another number evenly, there will be a ■. **remainder**

3 Since $7 \times 9 = 63$, 63 is a ■ of 7. **multiple**

4 The number sentence $4 \times 8 = 8 \times 4$ shows the ■ Property. **Commutative**

> **Vocabulary**
> factor
> multiple
> quotient
> remainder
> Commutative
> Associative

Concepts and Skills

Write a multiplication sentence for the picture. (page 124)

5

6

7

$2 \times 5 = 10$ **or** $5 \times 2 = 10$

$5 \times 6 = 30$

$3 \times 4 = 12$ **or** $4 \times 3 = 12$

Draw an array. Find the product or quotient. (page 124, 146)

8 2×7 **14**　　**9** 8×3 **24**　　**10** $36 \div 9$ **4**　　**11** $8 \div 1$ **8**　　**12** 6×7 **42**

Check students' arrays.

Find the product or quotient. (page 124)

13 8×6 **48**　　**14** 9×5 **45**　　**15** 4×4 **16**　　**16** 6×0 **0**　　**17** $7 \div 7$ **1**

18 $35 \div 5$ **7**　　**19** $28 \div 4$ **7**　　**20** $10 \div 3$ **3 R1**　　**21** $25 \div 9$ **2 R7**　　**22** $27 \div 3$ **9**

α ALGEBRA Complete the sentence. (pages 124, 146, 154)

23 $6 \times ■ = 24$ **4**　　　　**24** $■ \times 7 = 49$ **7**　　　　**25** $8 \times 9 = ■$ **72**

26 $■ \div 4 = 8$ **32**　　　　**27** $50 \div 8 = ■$ R2 **6**　　　　**28** $40 \div ■ = 6$ R4 **6**

α ALGEBRA Find the rule. Then complete the table. (page 124) **Multiply by 5.**

29

Multiply by 3.	Rule: ■					
	0	1	2	3	4	5
	0	■	6	9	■	■

3　　　　12　15

30

Rule: ■						
1	2	3	4	5	6
■	10	15	20	■	■

5　　　　25　30

162 Chapter 4 Review

Reinforcement and Remediation

CHAPTER OBJECTIVES	CHAPTER REVIEW ITEMS	STUDENT BOOK PAGES		TEACHER'S EDITION PAGES		TEACHER RESOURCES
		Lesson	Midchapter Review	Activities	Alternate Teaching Strategy	Reteach
4A	3, 5–14	124–137	142	123A, 127A, 131A, 133A	127,131, 133,137	30–33
4B	1, 2, 15–22	146–153, 156–157	142	145A, 149A, 151A 155C	149, 151, 153, 157	36–38, 40
4C	4, 11, 16	140–141	142	139A	141	35
4D	23–28 31–32	154–155		153A	155	39
4E	29–30 33–40	138–139, 158–161	142	137A, 157A	139, 161	34, 41

32b. Multiplication is like repeated addition;
$3 + 3 + 3 + 3 = 4 \times 3$.

Think critically. (page 156)

31 Analyze. Explain what mistake was made, then correct it. Did not find the multiple of 6 that was closest to $6 \times 6 = 36 < 39$, $39 \div 6 = 6$ R3.

$39 \div 6 = 5 R9$

32 Generalize. How are the operations related to each other? Give examples to show your answer. (page 158) See below.

a. addition and subtraction inverse operations; $3 + 4 = 7, 7 - 4 = 3$

b. addition and multiplication See above.

c. multiplication and division inverse operations; $4 \times 7 = 28, 28 \div 7 = 4$

d. division and subtraction Division is like repeated subtraction; you can find $6 \div 3$ or the number of times you can subtract 3 from 6.

MIXED APPLICATIONS

Problem Solving (pages 138, 158)

33 Eric plans to bike 75 miles. If he bikes 8 miles each hour, will he travel this distance in less than 9 hours? How do you know? No, $8 \times 9 = 72$, which is less than 75.

35 In 1924, the Olympic 100-meter freestyle was won in under a minute. It took 52 more years for it to be won in under 50 seconds. In what year did this happen? 1976

34 ALGEBRA: PATTERNS A group of 18 people is waiting for tables at a diner. If each table seats 6 people, how many tables do they need? 3 tables

36 To prepare for a bicycle tour, Jerry wants to buy a helmet for $34.89, a pair of gloves for $16.29, and a jacket for $45.99. If he has $100, does he have enough money? Yes, $35 + 17 + 46 = 98 < 100$.

Use the table for problems 37–40.

37 Who biked the longest distance? the shortest distance? John Hathaway; Tal Burt

38 What is the difference between the longest and shortest distances? 37,077 mi

39 Who took the most time to complete the bike tour? John Hathaway

40 About how many days did it take for the Slaughters to complete their bike tour? Possible answer: about 600 d

Bike Tours		
Who?	**When?**	**Distance (miles)**
Jay Aldous and Matt DeWaal	Apr. 2 to July 16, 1987	14,290
Tal Burt	June 1 to Aug. 17, 1992	13,523
John Hathaway	Nov. 10, 1974, to Oct. 6, 1976	50,600
Ronald and Sandra Slaughter	Dec. 30, 1989, to July 28, 1991	18,077

32. Answers may vary. Possible answers are given.

Multiplication and Division Facts **163**

CHAPTER TEST

PURPOSE Assess the concepts, skills, and strategies students have learned in this chapter.

Chapter Objectives

4A Multiply, facts to 81

4B Divide, facts to 81

4C Use the Commutative, Identity, Zero, and Associative properties

4D Use inverse operations to identify fact families and find missing factors

4E Solve problems, including those that involve multiplication and division and patterns

Using the Chapter Test

The **Chapter Test** can be used as a practice test, a chapter test, or as an additional review. The **Performance Assessment** on Student Book page 165 provides an alternate means of assessing students' understanding of time, data, and graphs.

Assessment Resources

TEST MASTERS

The Testing Program Blackline Masters provide three forms of the Chapter Test to assess students' understanding of the chapter concepts, skills, and strategies. Form C uses a free-response format. Forms A and B use a multiple-choice format.

COMPUTER TEST GENERATOR

The Computer Test Generator supplies abundant multiple-choice and free-response test items, which you may use to generate tests and practice worksheets tailored to the needs of your class.

TEACHER'S ASSESSMENT RESOURCES

Teacher's Assessment Resources provides resources for alternate assessment. It includes guidelines for Building a Portfolio, page 6, Holistic Scoring Guide, page 27, and samples of students' work, page 37.

Write a multiplication sentence for the picture.

1

2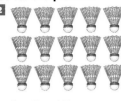

3

$4 \times 4 = 16$ $3 \times 5 = 15$ $2 \times 4 = 8$

Draw an array. Find the product or quotient. Check students' arrays.

4 3×6 **18**   **5** 9×5 **45**   **6** $25 \div 5$ **5**   **7** $54 \div 6$ **9**

Find the product or quotient.

8 $36 \div 4$ **9**   **9** $30 \div 6$ **5**   **10** 8×6 **48**   **11** 7×7 **49**

Complete the sentence.

12 $8 \times \blacksquare = 81$ **1**   **13** $\blacksquare \times 2 = 0$ **0**

14 $4 \times 7 = 7 \times \blacksquare$ **4**   **15** $(3 \times 5) \times 2 = 3 \times (\blacksquare \times 2)$ **5**

Write the fact family. See below.

16 2, 3, 6   **17** 6, 7, 42   **18** 8, 8, 64

19 4, 9, 36   **20** 4, 4, 16   **21** 5, 6, 30

Solve.

22 Mario bakes 28 cookies. He has 7 friends over. How many cookies does each friend get if he shares the cookies equally among them? **4 cookies**

23 Kelsey bought 3 tickets for the Olympics. Two cost $52.50 each, and the other one cost $38. How much did he spend? **$143**

24 Isabelle has a scarf. Each foot of her scarf has the following colored stripes on it: red, black, black, white. If there are 8 black stripes on the entire scarf, how long is the scarf? **4 ft**

25 Totsi rides her bike 1 mile on Monday, 1 mile on Tuesday, 2 miles on Wednesday, 3 miles on Thursday, and 5 miles on Friday. If she continues this pattern, how far will she ride on Saturday and Sunday? **8 mi; 13 mi**

16. $2 \times 3 = 6$, $3 \times 2 = 6$, $6 \div 3 = 2$, $6 \div 2 = 3$
17. $6 \times 7 = 42$, $7 \times 6 = 42$, $42 \div 6 = 7$, $42 \div 7 = 6$
18. $8 \times 8 = 64$, $64 \div 8 = 8$
19. $4 \times 9 = 36$, $9 \times 4 = 36$, $36 \div 4 = 9$, $36 \div 9 = 4$
20. $4 \times 4 = 16$, $16 \div 4 = 4$
21. $5 \times 6 = 30$, $6 \times 5 = 30$, $30 \div 5 = 6$, $30 \div 6 = 5$

164 Chapter 4 Test

Test Correlation		
CHAPTER OBJECTIVES	**TEST ITEMS**	**TEXT PAGES**
4A	1–5, 10–11	124–137
4B	6–9	146–153, 156–157
4C	12–15	140–141
4D	16–21	154–155
4E	22–25	138–139, 158–161

What Did You Learn? Check students' work.

See Teacher's Assessment Resources for samples of student work.

Mr. Jefferson works for a sporting goods store. He spilled some ink on this order form and cannot read some of the numbers.

► There can be from 1 through 9 items in each box. Name as many ways as you can think of to complete the bottom two rows of the form.

► For each row, explain your strategy for selecting numbers that might be under the ink spots.

ORDER FORM

Item	Number of Items in a Box	Number of Boxes Ordered	Total Number of Items Ordered
Hockey Pucks	6	5	30
Baseballs		4	
Table Tennis Paddles			24

··············· • A Good Answer • ···············

• shows different ways to complete the order form correctly
• clearly describes the reasons for choosing possible missing numbers

 You may want to place your work in your portfolio.

What Do You Think ?
See Teacher's Edition.

1 Can you find answers to multiplication and division facts easily? Why or why not?

2 List some methods you might use to multiply and some you might use to divide.

3 What would you do if you could not decide whether to multiply or divide to solve a problem?
• Use counters to model the problem.   • Draw a picture.
• Other. Explain.

Multiplication and Division Facts   **165**

Reviewing A Portfolio

Have students review their portfolios. Consider including these items:
• Finished work on the Chapter Project (p. 121F) or **Investigation** (pp. 144–145).
• Selected math journal entries, pp. 125, 135, 142, 150.
• Finished work on the nonroutine problem in **What Do You Know?** (p. 123) and problems from the Menu (pp. 160–161).
• Each student's self-selected "best piece" from work completed during the chapter. Have each student attach a note explaining why he or she chose that piece.
• Any work you or an individual student wishes to keep for future reference.

You may take this opportunity to conduct conferences with students. The Portfolio Analysis Form can help you report students' progress. See Teacher's Assessment Resources, p. 33.

PERFORMANCE ASSESSMENT   Pages 164–165

PURPOSE Review and assess the concepts, skills, and strategies learned in this chapter.

Materials have available: counters, calculators (optional)

Using the Performance Assessment

Have students read and restate the problems in their own words. Make sure they understand there is more than one way to complete each of the bottom two rows. Point out that they need to explain how they got each pair of numbers that they name for each of those rows.

Point out the section on the student page headed "A Good Answer." Make sure students understand that you will use these points to evaluate their answers.

Evaluating Student Work

As you read students' papers, look for the following:
• *Can the student name at least one way to complete each of the bottom two rows?*
• *Can the student name more than one way to complete each of the bottom two rows?*
• *Can the student explain how she or he found numbers to complete the middle row? the bottom row?*

The Holistic Scoring Guide and annotated samples of students' work can be used to assess this task. See pages 27–32 and 37–72 in Teacher's Assessment Resources.

Using the Self-Assessment

What Do You Think? Assure students that there are no right or wrong answers. Tell them the emphasis is on what they think and how they justify their answers.

Follow-Up Interviews

These questions can be used to gain insight into students' thinking:
• **What clues did you use in solving these problems?**
• **How did you find a pair of numbers that completed the middle row? Explain how you know those numbers work.**
• **How could you use multiplication to find a pair of numbers that completes the middle row?**
• **How did you find a pair of numbers that completed the bottom row? Explain how you know those numbers work.**

OBJECTIVE Learn different ways animals protect themselves, and use multiplication in a science context.

Resources word-processing and graphing programs, or Math Van Tools

Science

Cultural Connection Read the **Cultural Note.** Have students share descriptions of the armor mentioned on page 166 of the Student Book that they may have seen in movies, television programs, or in museums.

Read and discuss the remainder of the page with the class. Discuss how methods of protection vary depending upon what the person or animal is protecting against. Ask:

- **How do people protect themselves from the cold? the heat? insects?** *[Answers vary. Possible responses: clothing; staying in the shade; bug repellent.]*

Math

Complete items 1 through 3 together with the class. Have volunteers explain how they arrived at each answer. Then ask questions which require division facts to answer. For example, ask:

- **How many miles can a human being run in 12 minutes? How can you calculate it?** *[5 miles; 12 minutes is $\frac{1}{5}$ of an hour, and $25 \div 5 = 5$]*
- **How can you use the same method to find out how far a grizzly bear and Cape hunting dog can run in 12 minutes?** *[$30 \div 5 = 6$ miles; $45 \div 5 = 9$ miles]*

math science technology
CONNECTION

Nature's Protection

Cultural Note
Throughout history, humans have protected themselves using armor made from soft materials such as feathers and quilting, or hard materials such as bone, leather, and metal. Armor of crocodile skin was made in Egypt, helmets of porcupine fish skin were worn in the Pacific Islands, and covering made from short rods of wood were used by Native American tribes from the northwest coast of America.

Animals have different ways of protecting themselves against other animals that hunt them. The animals that hunt are called *predators*. The animals that are hunted are called *prey*.

The chameleon changes its color so that it blends in with the things around it. This makes it difficult for predators to find it.

The squid discharges a brownish-black substance called ink. The ink clouds the water and dulls the sense of smell in fishes that pursue the squid by scent.

The porcupine uses its quills to defend itself against predators. It turns its back and stiffens its quills, rushing backward toward the enemy.

▶ How do the animals you know protect themselves from predators? **Possible answer: Bees sting their enemies, snakes bite their enemies and discharge venom, deer run away quickly.**

166 Math • Science • Technology Connection

Extending The Activity

Have students measure how many times they would have to run around the gym to run $\frac{1}{4}$ mile or 1,320 feet. First have them calculate $\frac{1}{4}$ mile in feet: $5{,}280 \div 4 = 1{,}320$. Then have partners time each other to see how long it takes them to run $\frac{1}{4}$ mile. Students can use this information to calculate how many miles they can run in an hour (mph).

1. Possible answer: Cheetahs; they can run faster, so they can catch the gazelles— the gazelles would outrun the coyotes.

Comparing Speeds

Some animals' protection is their speed or agility. The table below shows the greatest speeds of some animals.

Animal	Speed (in miles per hour)
Chicken	9
Human	25
Grizzly bear	30
Coyote	43
Cape hunting dog	45
Lion	50
Gazelle	50
Cheetah	70

1 Which do you think hunt gazelles for food, coyotes or cheetahs? Explain. **See above.**

2 Which animals are more than three times faster than a chicken? **See below.**

3 **What if** you were told that a predator of the chicken is more than five times faster. If the predator is not the gazelle, what animal could it be? **Possible answer: lion or cheetah**

At the Computer
Check students' work.

4 Research to find other animals to add to the table. Use a graphing program to make a bar graph of the running speeds of the different animals.

5 Prepare a report that compares the speeds of the animals. Tell which animals are two times, three times, or four times faster than a chicken.

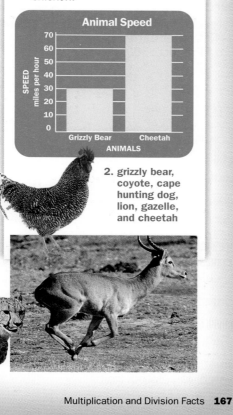

Animal Speed

2. grizzly bear, coyote, cape hunting dog, lion, gazelle, and cheetah

Multiplication and Division Facts **167**

Bibliography

Animal Camouflage: A Closer Look, by Joyce Powzyk. New York: Bradbury Press, 1990. ISBN 0–02–774980–0.

Feathers, by Dorothy Hinshaw Patent. New York: Cobblehill Books, 1992. ISBN 0–525–65081–4.

Why Mammals Have Fur, by Dorothy Hinshaw Patent. New York: Cobblehill Books, 1995. ISBN 0–525–65141–1.

Technology

Other animals students can include in their graphs are:

Pig	11 mph
Squirrel	12 mph
Wild turkey	15 mph
Cat	30 mph
Rabbit	35 mph
Zebra	40 mph

You may wish to have students use a word-processing program to write their reports.

Math Van Students may use the Graph tool to create bar graphs. A project electronic teacher aid has been provided.

Interesting Facts

- **A chameleon's tongue is longer than its body.** It traps prey on the sticky tip and then pulls both back into its mouth.

- **Horned toads spurt blood from their eyes** when frightened. This may be a defense mechanism, but its purpose remains unclear.

- **When in danger a beaver slaps the water with its tail** as it dives in order to warn other beavers.

- **Camels have long eyelashes,** hair-covered ear openings, and slit-like nostrils for protection from wind and sand.

Chapter 5 Organizer

Chapter 5

CHAPTER 5 AT A GLANCE:

Theme: Factories   Suggested Pacing: 10–13 days

Multiply by 1-Digit Numbers

WEEK ONE

DAY 1

PREASSESSMENT

Introduction   pp. 168

What Do You Know? p. 169
CHAPTER OBJECTIVES: 5A, 5B, 5C, 5D
MATERIALS   place-value models (TA 22)
RESOURCES   Read-Aloud Anthology
pp. 22–24
Pretest: Test Master Form A,
B, or C
Diagnostic Inventory

Portfolio   Journal   **NCTM STANDARDS:**
1, 2, 3, 4, 6, 8

DAY 2

LESSON 5.1

MENTAL MATH
Multiplication Patterns   pp. 170–171

CHAPTER OBJECTIVES: 5A
MATERIALS   calculators (opt.)
RESOURCES   Reteach/Practice/Extend: 42
Math Center Cards: 42
Extra Practice: 500

Daily Review   TE p. 169B

Algebraic Thinking
Technology Link   **NCTM STANDARDS:**
6, 8, 13

DAY 3

LESSON 5.2

MENTAL MATH
Estimate Products   pp. 172–173

CHAPTER OBJECTIVES: 5B
MATERIALS   calculators (opt.)
RESOURCES   Reteach/Practice/Extend: 43
Math Center Cards: 43
Extra Practice: 500

Daily Review   TE p. 171B

Algebraic Thinking
Technology Link   **NCTM STANDARDS:**
5, 8

WEEK TWO

LESSON 5.5

PROBLEM-SOLVING STRATEGY
Solve Multistep Problems   pp. 182–183

CHAPTER OBJECTIVES: 5D
RESOURCES   Reteach/Practice/Extend: 46
Math Center Cards: 46
Extra Practice: 502

Daily Review   TE p. 181B

Technology Link   **NCTM STANDARDS:**
1, 2, 3, 4, 8

MIDCHAPTER ASSESSMENT

Midchapter Review   p. 184
CHAPTER OBJECTIVES: 5A, 5B, 5C, 5D
MATERIALS   calculators (opt.)

Developing Number Sense   p. 185

REAL-LIFE INVESTIGATION:
Applying Multiplication   pp. 186–187
MATERIALS   sheets of paper, clock or
watch, calculators (opt.)

Algebraic Thinking
Portfolio
Journal   **NCTM STANDARDS:**
1, 2, 3, 5, 6, 8, 9

LESSON 5.6

Multiply Greater Numbers   pp. 188–191

CHAPTER OBJECTIVES: 5C
MATERIALS   place-value models (TA 22),
calculators (opt.)
RESOURCES   Reteach/Practice/Extend: 47
Math Center Cards: 47
Extra Practice: 502

Daily Review   TE p. 187B

Algebraic Thinking
Technology Link   **NCTM STANDARDS:**
4, 8

WEEK THREE

CHAPTER ASSESSMENT

Chapter Review   pp. 198–199
MATERIALS   calculators (opt.)

Chapter Test   p. 200
RESOURCES   Posttest: Test Master Form A,
B, or C

Performance Assessment   p. 201
RESOURCES   Performance Task: Test Master

Math • Science • Technology Connection
pp. 202–203

Technology Link
Portfolio   **NCTM STANDARDS:**
1, 4, 8, 11

DAY 4

LESSON 5.3

EXPLORE ACTIVITY

Use Models to Multiply pp. 174–177

CHAPTER OBJECTIVES: 5C

MATERIALS graph paper (TA 7), place-value models (TA 22), index cards, calculators (opt.)

RESOURCES Reteach/Practice/Extend: 44
Math Center Cards: 44
Extra Practice: 501

 TEACHING WITH TECHNOLOGY
Alternate Lesson for Use Models to Multiply, TE
pp. 177A–177B

Daily Review TE p. 173B

📓 Journal

🖱 Technology Link

NCTM STANDARDS: 4, 8

LESSON 5.7

Multiply Money pp. 192–193

CHAPTER OBJECTIVES: 5C

MATERIALS calculators (opt.)

RESOURCES Reteach/Practice/Extend: 48
Math Center Cards: 48
Extra Practice: 503

Daily Review TE p. 191B

📓 Journal

🖱 Technology Link

NCTM STANDARDS: 4, 8

DAY 5

LESSON 5.4

Multiply 2-Digit Numbers pp. 178–181

CHAPTER OBJECTIVES: 5C

MATERIALS place-value models (TA 22), calculators (opt.)

RESOURCES Reteach/Practice/Extend: 45
Math Center Cards: 45
Extra Practice: 501

Daily Review TE p. 177D

⭐ Algebraic Thinking

🖱 Technology Link

NCTM STANDARDS: 4, 8

LESSON 5.8

PROBLEM SOLVERS AT WORK

Interpret Data pp. 194–197

CHAPTER OBJECTIVES: 5D

MATERIALS calculators (opt.), computer spreadsheet program (opt.), drawing program (opt.)

RESOURCES Reteach/Practice/Extend: 49
Math Center Cards: 49
Extra Practice: 503

Daily Review TE p. 193B

🖱 Technology Link

NCTM STANDARDS: 1, 2, 3, 4, 8

Assessment Options

FORMAL

Chapter Tests

STUDENT BOOK
- Mdchapter Review, p. 184
- Chapter Review, pp. 198–199
- Chapter Test, p. 200

BLACKLINE MASTERS
- Test Master Form A, B, or C
- Diagnostic Inventory

COMPUTER TEST GENERATOR
- Available on disk

Performance Assessment
- What Do You Know? p. 169
- Performance Assessment, p. 201
- Holistic Scoring Guide, Teacher's Assessment Resources, pp. 27–32
- Follow-Up Interviews, p. 201
- Performance Task, Test Masters

Teacher's Assessment Resources
- Portfolio Guidelines and Forms, pp. 6, 33–35
- Holistic Scoring Guide, pp. 27–32
- Samples of Student Work, pp. 37–72

INFORMAL

Ongoing Assessment
- Observation Checklist, pp. 170, 172, 174, 182, 192
- Interview, p. 178
- Anecdotal Report, pp. 188, 194

Portfolio Opportunities
- Chapter Project, p. 167F
- What Do You Know? p. 169
- Investigation, pp. 186–187
- Journal Writing, pp. 169, 175, 184
- Performance Assessment, p. 201
- Self-Assessment: What Do You Think? p. 201

Chapter Objectives	Standardized Test Correlations
5A Multiply multiples of 10, 100, and 1,000 by a 1-digit factor	MAT, CAT, SAT, ITBS, CTBS,TN*
5B Estimate products, including money amounts	MAT, CAT, SAT, ITBS, CTBS,TN*
5C Multiply by 1-digit factors, including money amounts	MAT, CAT, SAT, ITBS, CTBS,TN*
5D Solve problems, including those that involve multiplication and solving a multistep problem	CTBS,TN*

*Terra Nova

NCTM Standards Grades K–4

1 Problem Solving	**8** Whole Number Computation
2 Communication	**9** Geometry and Spatial Sense
3 Reasoning	**10** Measurement
4 Connections	**11** Statistics and Probability
5 Estimation	**12** Fractions and Decimals
6 Number Sense and Numeration	**13** Patterns and Relationships
7 Concepts of Whole Number Operations	

Meeting Individual Needs

LEARNING STYLES

- AUDITORY/LINGUISTIC
- LOGICAL/ANALYTICAL
- VISUAL/SPATIAL
- MUSICAL
- KINESTHETIC
- SOCIAL
- INDIVIDUAL

Students talented in areas such as art, music, language, and physical activity may better understand mathematical concepts when these concepts are connected to their areas of interest. Use the following activity to stimulate the different learning styles of some of your students.

Visual/Spatial Learners

Have students draw pictures or make diagrams to show multiplication.

See Lesson Resources, pp. 169A, 171A, 173A, 177C, 181A, 187A, 191A, 193A.

GIFTED AND TALENTED

Cultural Connection Some students might be interested in seeing how twelfth-century Hindu mathematicians in India used the lattice method to multiply 5×876.

Encourage students to tell where the numbers inside and outside the lattices came from. (The inside numbers are the products 5×8, 5×7, and 5×6. The outside numbers are the factors, and the sums of the numbers are written on the diagonals.) Have students find the products and relate this method of recording to their methods.

See also Meeting Individual Needs, pp. 174, 178, 194.

EXTRA SUPPORT

Have available place-value models for students to use throughout the chapter. Specific suggestions for ways to provide extra support to students appear in every lesson in this chapter.

See Meeting Individual Needs, pp. 170, 172, 174, 178, 182, 188, 192, 194.

EARLY FINISHERS

Students who finish their class work early may spend time collecting and/or organizing data for the class project.

See also Meeting Individual Needs, pp. 170, 172, 176, 180, 182, 190, 192, 196.

LANGUAGE SUPPORT

Have students draw diagrams to illustrate multiplication concepts. Keep their diagrams posted throughout the chapter.

See also Meeting Individual Needs, pp. 176, 196.

ESL APPROPRIATE

INCLUSION

- For **inclusion** ideas, information, and suggestions, see pp. 180, 188, T15.
- For **gender fairness** tips, see pp. 196, T15.

USING MANIPULATIVES

Building Understanding Graph-paper models and place-value models will help students understand multiplication by a 1-digit number.

- Graph-paper models help students visualize partial products. (See Lesson 5.3) Note: The activities in this chapter work best with standard 4-square-per-inch graph paper rather than with centimeter or inch graph paper.

- Place-value models provide students with a hands-on opportunity to regroup. (See Lesson 5.4)

Easy-to-Make Manipulatives Make place-value models by gluing graph paper onto cardboard. Then cut into blocks of hundreds (10 units by 10 units), tens (1 unit by 10 units), and ones (1 unit by 1 unit).

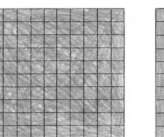
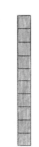

ESL APPROPRIATE

USING COOPERATIVE LEARNING

Triads Practice Strategy This strategy groups 3 students together to support learning and to reinforce practice.

- Students take note of and discuss one another's ideas.

- Students share their work and may revise one another's work.

In this chapter, you can use this strategy effectively in Lessons 3, 4, and 5.

USING LITERATURE

How Is a Crayon Made? is reprinted on pages 22–24 in the Read-Aloud Anthology. Use this selection to introduce the chapter theme, Factories.

The Read-Aloud Anthology selection *The Rajah's Rice,* pp. 25–28, is the basis for a multiplication activity. (See Lesson 5.6)

The Read-Aloud Anthology selection "Good Hot Dogs," pp. 29–30, is used to introduce multiplication with money. (See Lesson 5.7)

MULTIPLY BY 1-DIGIT NUMBERS

Linking Technology

This integrated package of programs and services allows students to explore, develop, and practice concepts; solve problems; build portfolios; and assess their own progress. Teachers can enhance instruction, provide remediation, and share ideas with other educational professionals.

CD-ROM ACTIVITY

In *Fun Factory Functions* students use place-value models to help a boy fill toy orders involving 1-digit multiplication. Students can use the online notebook to write about the process they develop. To extend the activity, students use the Math Van tools to complete an open-ended problem related to the concept. **Available on CD-ROM.**

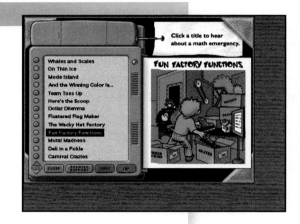

CD-ROM TOOLS

Students can use Math Van's place-value models to explore the concept of multiplying 1-digit numbers. The Tech Links on the Lesson Resources pages highlight opportunities for students to use this and other tools such as money models, tables, graphs, drawings, online notes, and calculators to provide additional practice, reteaching, or extension. **Available on CD-ROM.**

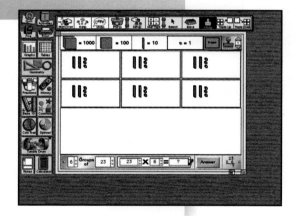

WEB SITE   http://www.mhschool.com

Teachers can access the McGraw-Hill School Division World Wide Web site for additional curriculum support at http://www.mhschool.com. Click on our Resource Village for specially designed activities linking Web sites to multiplication. Motivate students by inviting them to explore Web sites that develop the chapter theme of factories and manufacturing. Exchange ideas on classroom management, cultural diversity, and other areas in the Math Forum.

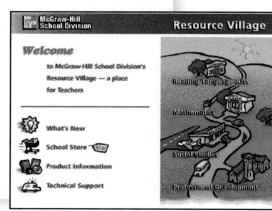

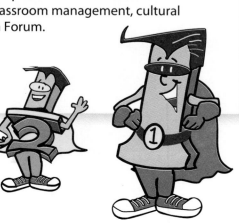

Chapter Project FACTORY NUMBERS

1 Starting the Project

Working together in groups, students will find out about a factory in their community or state and assemble a book on it.

To familiarize students with factories, read and discuss the newspaper article with your class. Have students jot down math problems to solve using the numbers in the article. Example: At the rate of 56 vehicles an hour, how long does it take to produce all the vans and minivans?

Brainstorm ways to gather information and collect data: tour a local factory, invite guests into the class, write letters to factory officials, search the Internet. Consider how family or community members can participate.

Discuss data that could be shown in a chart, table, or graph, such as sales figures and numbers of products manufactured over five years.

2 Continuing the Project

Have students work in small groups to gather information and data for their books. Encourage them to:
• include the location of the factory and what the factory produces
• arrange their data in charts, tables, and/or graphs
• create math problems that can be answered using the data
• describe one thing the group learned and one thing the group liked

3 Finishing the Project

Have the students in each group solve the problems they wrote, then arrange the information and the data they collected in the form of a book. If they wish, students may cut out the cover and the pages of their books to resemble the shape of the item whose manufacture they have been studying.

Community Involvement
• Display students' reports as part of a Parents' Night Presentation.
• Visit the McGraw-Hill School Division Web site for connections to factories.

Highlighting the Math
• collect data
• use numbers to quantify and compare
• write and solve real-life problems involving addition, subtraction, and multiplication

New Vehicle Assembly Plant Head Hired

DETROIT, MICHIGAN
In September, at age 41, Ms. Kent became the first woman to head a vehicle assembly plant at the Ford Motor Company, and the only African-American woman ever to rise to that post. Her duties include managing two shifts with a total of 3,746 workers, as well as 420 robots, and overseeing the annual production of 216,035 Ford Econoline vans and 115,184 Mercury Villager and Nissan Quest mini-vans at a pace of up to 56 vehicles an hour on an assembly line that stretches

Deborah S. Kent

19.5 miles. The plant, the third largest of the company's 38 United States facilities, is the only one to manufacture those models.
(continued on page 8)

The New York Times, February 5, 1995

BUILDING A PORTFOLIO

Each student's portfolio piece should include a copy of the group's book, along with an explanation of how data was collected, a statement of the problems posed, conclusions that the student reached, and calculations to support the conclusions. A videotape of the presentation may also serve as an entry.

To assess the work, refer to the Holistic Scoring Guide on page 27 in Teacher's Assessment Resources.

PURPOSE Introduce the theme of the chapter.

Resource Read-Aloud Anthology, pages 35–39.

Using Literature

Read *How Is a Crayon Made?* from the Read-Aloud Anthology to introduce the chapter theme "Factories."

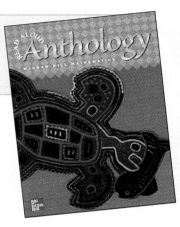

Developing the Theme

Encourage students to tell what they think a factory is like. Students may describe a factory building, different factory jobs, or assembly lines.

Create a class list by asking students to name various products they use that are manufactured in factories. Then ask them to suggest ways of organizing the list. Students may suggest grouping by place of manufacture or by type of product.

Students may wish to research the rise of factories in the United States and present an oral report to the class.

These factory-made products are discussed in this chapter:

Crayons	pp. 168–169	Games	p. 185
Computers	pp. 170–171	Bottles	pp.188–189
Bicycles	pp. 172–173	Clothing	pp. 192–193
Piñatas	pp. 178–181	Chocolate bars	pp. 202–203
Skateboards	pp. 182–183		

On pages 186–187, students will explore working on an assembly line.

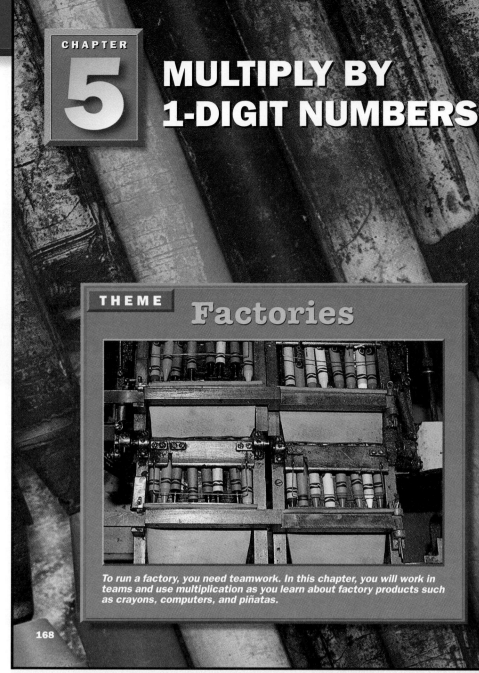

CHAPTER

5 MULTIPLY BY 1-DIGIT NUMBERS

THEME Factories

To run a factory, you need teamwork. In this chapter, you will work in teams and use multiplication as you learn about factory products such as crayons, computers, and piñatas.

168

Chapter Bibliography

How a Doll Is Made, by Susan Kuklin. New York: Hyperion Books for Children, 1994. ISBN 1–56282–667–0.

Ice Cream, by William Jaspersohn. New York: Simon & Schuster Books for Young Readers, 1988. ISBN 0–02–747821–1.

Field Trip Video: *Our Class Visits the Nabisco Factory.* Macmillan/McGraw-Hill Social Studies Videodisc: *Regions Near and Far.*

Community Involvement

Discuss what factory-made products students use. Invite relatives or community members who have worked in factories to share their experiences with the class. If possible, arrange for students to tour a factory in the community.

Left Page

2. Answer depends on the number of students in the class.

What Do You Know ?

1 How many crayons are there altogether in 3 boxes of 8 crayons? **24 crayons**

2 If each person in your class got a box of 8 crayons, how many crayons would there be altogether? Explain your method. **See above.**

3 Find the total number of crayons for as many orders in the table as you can. Explain your methods. **Answers may vary. Possible answers: 10 groups of 8 can be shown as $10 \times 8 = 8 \times 10 =$ 8 tens = 80, find $16 + 16 + 16 + 16 = 64$; use models to show 6 groups of 32 and find the total, 192.**

Number of Crayons in Each Box	Number of Boxes Ordered	Total Number of Crayons
8	10	
16	4	
32	6	

 Draw Conclusions A carton arrives from the crayon factory for your class. The carton holds **30 boxes of crayons.**

To draw a conclusion, you use information that the writer provides. You also use what you already know.

1 What did you already know about crayons? **Possible answers: Crayons are used to draw; They usually come in boxes of 8, 16, 32, or 64.**

2 What conclusion can you draw about the box? **Possible answers: The carton contains boxes of crayons for the class; The class will use the crayons to draw.**

Vocabulary

estimate, p. 172   **factor**, p. 172   **regroup**, p. 178
product, p. 172   **round**, p. 172

 Reading, Writing, Arithmetic

Draw Conclusions Discuss students' conclusions. Point out that usually math problems do not tell which operation to use. Therefore, students must draw conclusions based on the information given and what they already know.

Vocabulary

Students may record new words in their journals. Encourage them to draw pictures or diagrams to help them tell what the words mean.

• **Draw a picture to show the factors and the product for 3 × 5; for 3 × 11.** *[Possible answers on right.]*

Right Page

PURPOSE Assess students' ability to apply prior knowledge of using strategies to multiply.

Materials have available: place-value models

Assessing Prior Knowledge

Ask volunteers to give examples of times when they add, subtract, multiply, or divide. Have students discuss when they choose to add and when they choose to multiply.

WHEN DO YOU . . .

Add?	Multiply?
unequal groups equal groups	equal groups

Encourage students to use whatever methods they wish to answer items 1–3. Observe students as they work. They may draw a picture or use skip-counting, repeated addition, models, or multiplication.

BUILDING A PORTFOLIO

 Item 3 can be used as a benchmark to show where students are in their understanding of multiplication strategies.

A Portfolio Checklist for Students and a Checklist for Teachers are provided in Teacher's Assessment Resources, pp. 33–34.

Prerequisite Skills

• *Do students recognize situations that involve equal groups?*
• *Do students know basic multiplication facts?*

Assessment Resources

DIAGNOSTIC INVENTORY

Use this blackline master to assess prerequisite skills that students will need in order to be successful in this chapter.

TEST MASTERS

Use the multiple choice format (form A or B) or the free response format (form C) as a pretest of the skills in this chapter.

Possible Vocabulary answers:

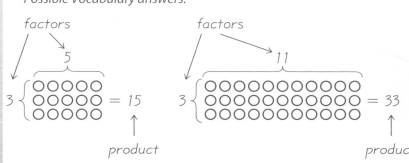

LESSON 5.1

MENTAL MATH
Multiplication Patterns

OBJECTIVE Use mental math strategies to multiply multiples of 10 by 1-digit numbers.

RESOURCE REMINDER
Math Center Cards 42
Practice 42, Reteach 42, Extend 42

SKILLS TRACE

GRADE 3 • Explore patterns found by multiplying by 10 and 100. *(Chapter 12)*

GRADE 4 • Use patterns found by multiplying by 10, 100, and 1,000 to multiply mentally.

GRADE 5 • Multiply mentally whole numbers and decimals by multiples of 10, 100, and 1,000. *(Chapter 4)*

WARM-UP

Cooperative Pairs   Logical/Analytical

OBJECTIVE Generate and analyze patterns.

Materials per pair: calculator

► Working together, one student selects a multiplication fact, uses a calculator to find the product, and multiplies repeatedly by 10. The other student records the products on paper as they are displayed.

► Students take turns using other multiplication facts to create patterns. Ask students to describe their number patterns.

$4 \times 8 =$ 　32.

$\times 10 =$ 　320.

$\times 10 =$ 　3200.

$\times 10 =$ 　32000.

ESL APPROPRIATE

SOCIAL STUDIES CONNECTION

Whole Class   Visual/Spatial

OBJECTIVE Interpret data from a pictograph.

Materials map of United States

► Draw the pictograph below on the chalkboard. Have students use a map of the United States to locate each state named in the pictograph. Ask volunteers to tell how they can determine the number of classroom teachers in a state. *[Multiply the number of symbols by 1,000.]*

CLASSROOM TEACHERS

State	Number of Classroom Teachers
Alaska	👤👤👤👤👤👤
Hawaii	👤👤👤👤👤👤👤👤
North Dakota	👤👤👤👤👤👤👤👤
Rhode Island	👤👤👤👤👤👤👤👤👤👤
Vermont	👤👤👤👤👤👤👤
Wyoming	👤👤👤👤👤👤

Each 👤 stands for 1,000 teachers

► Have students determine the number of classroom teachers in each state. Then have each student write a problem that uses information from the graph. Have students trade problems and share their solutions.

Daily Review

PREVIOUS DAY QUICK REVIEW

Divide.
1. 26 ÷ 7 [3 R5]
2. 42 ÷ 8 [5 R2]
3. 9)76 [8 R4]
4. 4)38 [9 R2]

FAST FACTS

1. 6 + 8 [14]
2. 9 + 5 [14]
3. 8 + 5 [13]
4. 4 + 9 [13]

Problem of the Day • 42

Warren and Kim have after-school jobs. Warren works 2 hours a day and Kim works 3 hours a day. Last year Warren worked 100 days and Kim worked 80 days. Who worked the greater number of hours? How do you know? [Kim; 240 h > 200 h]

TECH LINK

ONLINE EXPLORATION

Use our Web-linked activities and lesson plans to connect your students to the real world of factories.

MATH FORUM

Idea My students benefited from seeing how the mental math strategy in this lesson uses the Associative Property.

Visit our Resource Village at http://www.mhschool.com to access the Online Exploration and the Math Forum.

MATH CENTER

Practice

OBJECTIVE Multiply mentally.

Materials per group: 15 index cards; per student: Math Center Recording Sheet (TA 31 optional)

Prepare Label the index cards with the following numbers: 60; 70; 80; 90; 200; 300; 400; 500; 700; 900; 2,000; 3,000; 4,000; 6,000; 8,000.

Students play a game by mentally multiplying the numbers on number cards by 3. The student with the highest sum of products wins. Students repeat the game by mentally multiplying by other 1-digit numbers.

Problem Solving

OBJECTIVE Formulate word problems.

Materials per student: number cards for 2–9 (TA 29); 8 index cards; Math Center Recording Sheet (TA 31 optional)

Prepare Label the index cards with the following dollar amounts: $200; $300; $400; $500; $600; $700; $800; $900.

Students use cards showing dollar amounts and numbers to formulate multiplication problems and solve them mentally.

PRACTICE ACTIVITY 42

MATH CENTER
Small Group

Game • Triple the Draw
- Place the number cards in a pile facedown.
- Take turns drawing a number card.
- Mentally multiply your number by 3. Record the product.
- Explain to your group how you found the product mentally.
- Play until all the cards are gone. Add your products. The player with the highest total is the winner.

Play again by multiplying mentally other numbers between 2 and 9.

300, 700, 4,000, 80, 60, 200, 90, 400, 70, 6,000, 3,000, 2,000, 900, 8,000, 500

Chapter 5, Lesson 1, pages 170–171

Multiplication

NCTM Standards
- Problem Solving
- ✓ Communication
- ✓ Reasoning
- Connections

ESL APPROPRIATE

PROBLEM-SOLVING ACTIVITY 42

MATH CENTER
On Your Own

Formulating Problems • Out-Shopping Bargain Betty
- Pick a card showing a dollar amount and a number card.
- Use the numbers to fill in the blanks in the problem below.
- Solve the problem mentally. Write a number sentence to show your work.

    Bargain Betty spends $ _____ at the mall.

    Spend-It-Sam spends _____ times as much as Betty.

    How much does Spend-It-Sam spend?

Repeat the activity.

YOU NEED
- number cards (2–9)
- cards showing dollar amounts

Chapter 5, Lesson 1, pages 170–171

Multiplication

NCTM Standards
- ✓ Problem Solving
- ✓ Communication
- Reasoning
- ✓ Connections

Lesson 5.1 continued

MENTAL MATH
Multiplication Patterns

OBJECTIVE Use mental math strategies to multiply multiples of 10 by 1-digit numbers.

 **Introduce**

Have students describe and complete these patterns which are similar to those found on page 170.

a. 1, 10, 100, 1,000, _____ *[10,000]*

b. 9, 90, 900, _____ *[9,000]*

c. 24, 240, 2,400, _____ *[24,000]*

 **Teach**　　　　　　　*Whole Class*

▶ **LEARN** Students should see that there is a relationship between how the factors and products are increasing.

a **Algebra: Patterns** As students describe patterns in the examples on page 170, list them on the board. Patterns they may suggest include:
–first factors are all 6
–second factors and products are 10 times previous ones
–all use a basic fact: $6 \times 1 = 6$ or $6 \times 3 = 18$
–same number of zeros in factors and products

More Examples For Example B, students see that changing the order of the factors does not change the patterns.

3 Close

▶ **Check for Understanding** using items 1–14, page 170.

　　CRITICAL THINKING
a **Algebra: Patterns** In item 13, students understand the relationship between numbers by finding patterns when multiplying by 10, 100, and 1,000.

▶ **PRACTICE**
Materials have available: calculators

Options for assigning exercises:
A—Ex. 1–12, 21–27; **More to Explore**
B—Ex. 9–27; **More to Explore**

• For ex. 1–20, remind students to use multiplication facts to find the product mentally.

a **Algebra** An understanding of the concept of variables is essential to the study of algebra. In ex. 21–24, the variables are placeholder boxes instead of letters.

More to Explore
a **Algebra** Students use the important algebraic concept of exponents to write powers of 10. Have students write the number represented by 10×10, or 10^2. *[100]*

Multiplication Patterns

IN THE WORKPLACE
Tom Rittenberry, sales representative, Sun Microsystems, Knoxville, TN

Sales representatives sell products to people or companies. A Java Internet device costs about $1,000, and an Ultra Sparc desktop computer costs about $3,000. About how much do 6 of each product cost?

a **ALGEBRA: PATTERNS** You can use patterns to find products mentally. What patterns do you see below?

$6 \times 1 = 6$	$6 \times 3 = 18$
$6 \times 10 = 60$	$6 \times 30 = 180$
$6 \times 100 = 600$	$6 \times 300 = 1,800$
$6 \times 1,000 = 6,000$	$6 \times 3,000 = 18,000$

Six Internet devices cost about $6,000.

Six desktop computers cost about $18,000.

More Examples

A	B	C
$8 \times 1 = 8$	$9 \times 7 = 63$	$5 \times 4 = 20$
$8 \times 10 = 80$	$90 \times 7 = 630$	$5 \times 40 = 200$
$8 \times 100 = 800$	$900 \times 7 = 6,300$	$5 \times 400 = 2,000$
$8 \times 1,000 = 8,000$	$9,000 \times 7 = 63,000$	$5 \times 4,000 = 20,000$

Check for Understanding
Multiply mentally.

1. 7×100　700
2. $1,000 \times 3$　3,000
3. 7×200　1,400
4. 8×50　400
5. 4×80　320
6. $8,000 \times 3$　24,000
7. 5×20　100
8. 400×9　3,600
9. 3×700　2,100
10. $6 \times 1,000$　6,000
11. $5,000 \times 8$　40,000
12. 90×9　810

Critical Thinking: Analyze　**Explain your reasoning.**

a 13. **ALGEBRA: PATTERNS** How can you use patterns to multiply mentally? Start with a multiplication fact and then write zeros in the product equal to the number of zeros in the factors.

14. Why does the product of 5 and 600 have one more zero than the product of 4 and 600? There is a zero in the product of 5 and 6, 30.

Meeting Individual Needs

Early Finishers

Tell students that a googol is 1 followed by a hundred zeros. Then have them describe the product of numbers such as 4, 10, 20, or 100 times a googol. *[4 with 100 zeros, 1 with 101 zeros, 2 with 101 zeros, 1 with 102 zeros]*

Extra Support

For students who have difficulty remembering multiplication facts to 10, post a chart of multiplication facts and review these facts daily.

Ongoing Assessment

Observation Checklist Determine if students understand how to multiply 1-digit numbers by multiples of 10, 100, 1,000 by observing if they use the basic fact and then write the correct number of zeros.

Follow Up Have students who need additional help multiplying multiples of 10, 100, 1,000 use **Reteach 42.**

Have students who are adept at mental math try **Extend 42.**

27. Yes; possible answer: by overestimating, the computer is about
$4,000, the modem is about $110, and the CD-ROM drive is about
$300—$4,000 + $110 + $300 = $4,410, which is less than $4,500.

Practice

Multiply mentally.

1 4 × 100
400

2 100 × 5
500

3 2 × 1,000
2,000

4 1,000 × 4
4,000

5 3 × 80
240

6 4 × 7,000
28,000

7 40 × 4
160

8 5 × 200
1,000

9 6 × 900
5,400

10 1,000 × 5
5,000

11 60 × 6
360

12 5 × 6,000
30,000

13 4 × 800
3,200

14 30 × 4
120

15 7 × 1,000
7,000

16 8,000 × 5
40,000

17 8 × 90
720

18 900 × 9
8,100

19 8 × 4,000
32,000

20 6,000 × 6
36,000

ALGEBRA Find the missing number.

21 7 × ■ = 350
50

22 3 × ■ = 900
300

23 4 × ■ = 8,000
2,000

24 ■ × 3 = 2,100
700

Problem Solving

25 HAL, Inc., makes computer chips and
packs 300 in each box. How many chips
are in 9 boxes? **2,700 chips**

26 How many more additions in a second
could the microcomputer do in 1987
than the ENIAC could in 1946?
SEE INFOBIT. 395,000 more additions

27 **Data Point** Use the Databank on page
537. Can you buy an Orange X610 laptop
computer, a Z14 external modem, and a
3.8Y CD-ROM drive if you do not want to
spend more than $4,500? Explain.
See above.

INFOBIT
In 1946, the ENIAC, the
earliest digital machine,
could do 5,000 additions
in one second. By 1987 a
microcomputer could do
400,000 additions in
one second.

more to explore

Exponents

ALGEBRA You can write powers of 10 using exponents.

$10 \times 10 \times 10 = 1,000 = 10^3$ Read: 10 to the third power

Think: 10 is used as a factor 3 times. The exponent is 3.

Write the power of 10 using an exponent.

1 $10 \times 10 \times 10 \times 10$
10^4

2 $10 \times 10 \times 10 \times 10 \times 10$
10^5

3 10×10
10^2

Extra Practice, page 500   Multiply by 1-Digit Numbers **171**

Alternate Teaching Strategy

Materials place-value models—40 ones, 4 tens, 4 hundreds,
and 4 thousands (if available)

Present this problem:

Frozen yogurt bars are sold in individual packets, in
boxes of 10, in cartons of 100, and in crates of 1,000.
How many bars are ordered if Max's Deli owner asks for
4 individual packets? 4 boxes? 4 cartons? 4 crates?

Have students model the problem, draw pictures, and write
multiplication sentences.

Let students continue working in the same way using different
numbers for the amount ordered.

ESL APPROPRIATE

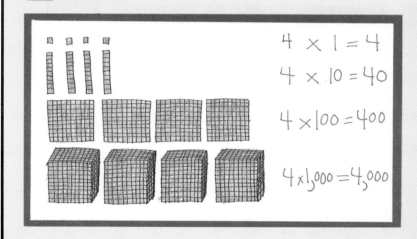

$4 \times 1 = 4$

$4 \times 10 = 40$

$4 \times 100 = 400$

$4 \times 1,000 = 4,000$

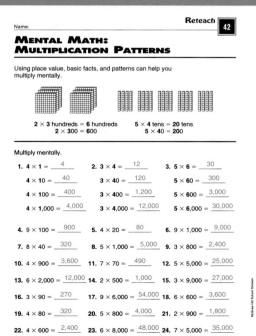

PRACTICE · 42

Name: _____

Practice 42

MENTAL MATH: MULTIPLICATION PATTERNS

Multiply mentally.

1. 2 × 100 = **200**   2. 2 × 600 = **1,200**   3. 2 × 3,000 = **6,000**

4. 2 × 30 = **60**   5. 4,000 × 2 = **8,000**   6. 20 × 3 = **60**

7. 40 × 3 = **120**   8. 30 × 7 = **210**   9. 3 × 7,000 = **21,000**

10. 3,000 × 7 = **21,000**   11. 300 × 2 = **600**   12. 800 × 5 = **4,000**

13. 200 × 4 = **800**   14. 8 × 5,000 = **40,000**   15. 5 × 400 = **2,000**

16. 6 × 8,000 = **48,000**   17. 3 × 600 = **1,800**   18. 6 × 5,000 = **30,000**

19. 7 × 600 = **4,200**   20. 5,000 × 7 = **35,000**   21. 9 × 200 = **1,800**

22. 9,000 × 4 = **36,000**   23. 6,000 × 4 = **24,000**   24. 6 × 700 = **4,200**

Algebra Find the missing number.

25. 5 × **90** = 450   26. 8 × **200** = 1,600

27. **300** × 9 = 2,700   28. **3,000** × 6 = 18,000

29. 4 × **7,000** = 28,000   30. **6** × 30 = 180

Solve.

31. At 8 A.M., each of LMO Limousine
Company's 40 vans was carrying
7 passengers. How many
passengers were in LMO vans
at 8 A.M.?

280 passengers

32. There were 2,000 people who
rode LMO vans yesterday. Each
person bought a ticket for $8.
How much money did LMO take
in yesterday?

$16,000

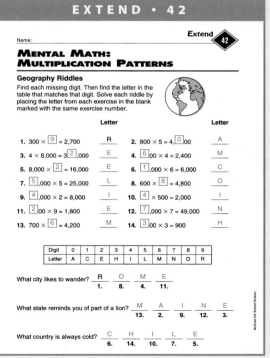

RETEACH · 42

Name: _____

Reteach 42

MENTAL MATH: MULTIPLICATION PATTERNS

Using place value, basic facts, and patterns can help you
multiply mentally.

2 × 3 hundreds = 6 hundreds   5 × 4 tens = 20 tens
2 × 300 = 600   5 × 40 = 200

Multiply mentally.

1. 4 × 1 = **4**   2. 3 × 4 = **12**   3. 5 × 6 = **30**
   4 × 10 = **40**   3 × 40 = **120**   5 × 60 = **300**
   4 × 100 = **400**   3 × 400 = **1,200**   5 × 600 = **3,000**
   4 × 1,000 = **4,000** 3 × 4,000 = **12,000** 5 × 6,000 = **30,000**

4. 9 × 100 = **900**   5. 4 × 20 = **80**   6. 9 × 1,000 = **9,000**

7. 8 × 40 = **320**   8. 5 × 1,000 = **5,000**   9. 3 × 800 = **2,400**

10. 4 × 900 = **3,600**   11. 7 × 70 = **490**   12. 5 × 5,000 = **25,000**

13. 6 × 2,000 = **12,000**   14. 2 × 500 = **1,000**   15. 3 × 9,000 = **27,000**

16. 3 × 90 = **270**   17. 9 × 6,000 = **54,000**   18. 6 × 600 = **3,600**

19. 4 × 80 = **320**   20. 5 × 800 = **4,000**   21. 2 × 900 = **1,800**

22. 4 × 600 = **2,400**   23. 6 × 8,000 = **48,000**   24. 7 × 5,000 = **35,000**

EXTEND · 42

Name: _____

Extend 42

MENTAL MATH: MULTIPLICATION PATTERNS

Geography Riddles
Find each missing digit. Then find the letter in the
table that matches that digit. Solve each riddle by
placing the letter from each exercise in the blank
marked with the same exercise number.

	Letter			Letter
1. 300 × **9** = 2,700	R	2. 800 × 5 = 4,**0**00	A
3. 4 × 8,000 = 3**2**,000	E	4. **6**00 × 4 = 2,400	M
5. 8,000 × **2** = 16,000	E	6. **1**,000 × 6 = 6,000	C
7. **5**,000 × 5 = 25,000	L	8. 600 × **8** = 4,800	O
9. **4**,000 × 2 = 8,000	I	10. **4** × 500 = 2,000	I
11. **2**00 × 9 = 1,800	E	12. **7**,000 × 7 = 49,000	N
13. 700 × **6** = 4,200	M	14. **3**00 × 3 = 900	H

Digit	0	1	2	3	4	5	6	7	8	9
Letter	A	C	E	H	I	L	M	N	O	R

What city likes to wander? R O M E
                            1. 8. 4. 11.

What state reminds you of part of a lion? M A I N E
                                          13. 2. 9. 12. 3.

What country is always cold? C H I L E
                              6. 14. 10. 7. 5.

171

LESSON 5.2

MENTAL MATH
Estimate Products

OBJECTIVE Estimate products by rounding.

RESOURCE REMINDER
Math Center Cards 43
Practice 43, Reteach 43, Extend 43

SKILLS TRACE

GRADE 3	• Explore estimating products by rounding. *(Chapter 12)*
GRADE 4	• Use rounding to estimate products.
GRADE 5	• Estimate products using rounding. *(Chapter 4)*

LESSON 5.2 RESOURCES

WARM-UP

Cooperative Pairs Logical/Analytical

OBJECTIVE Estimate products using mental math and logical reasoning.

Materials per pair: calculator

▶ Write $6 \times 70 = \square$ on the board. Have a volunteer give the product. *[420]*

▶ Working in pairs, each partner writes four multiplication sentences whose products are close to the product of 6 and 70. Partners exchange lists and use mental math or calculators to check each other's sentences.

▶ Partners compare how they chose the factors, and what they mean when they say that the products are close to 420.
Repeat the activity.

ALGEBRA CONNECTION

Cooperative Pairs Visual/Spatial

OBJECTIVE Connect multiplication and algebra.

Materials per pair: balance, 18 connecting cubes, 0–9 spinner (TA 2)

▶ Have students work in pairs. One student spins the spinner until two different numbers are generated and records the two numbers. The other student puts the first number of cubes on the left side of the balance and the second number of cubes on the right side. They record which side has more cubes.

▶ Then one student spins again to determine the number of groups to be made. The other student makes that many groups of the first and second numbers and returns them to their respective sides of the balance.

▶ The pair compares the side that is greater now with the side that was greater before. Repeat the activity five times. Ask students to describe what they observed. *[The side that was greater before remains greater.]*

5 > 3

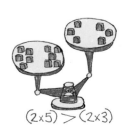

(2×5) > (2×3)

Daily Review

PREVIOUS DAY QUICK REVIEW

Multiply mentally.
1. 3 × 1,000 *[3,000]*
2. 6 × 300 *[1,800]*
3. 7,000 × 7 *[49,000]*
4. 4 × 5,000 *[20,000]*

FAST FACTS

1. 7 + 8 *[15]*
2. 5 + 7 *[12]*
3. 3 + 9 *[12]*
4. 6 + 5 *[11]*

Problem of the Day • 43

Zack wants to buy a CD for $13.85, a magazine for $1.75, and a cassette tape on sale for $2.50. He has $20. Does he have enough money? How do you know? *[Yes; estimate: $14 + $2 + $3 = $19, which is less than 20 and greater than the exact cost.]*

TECH LINK

MATH FORUM

Combination Classes Students may have different levels of experience in rounding and estimating products. Pair inexperienced students with experienced students.

Visit our Resource Village at http://www.mhschool.com to see more of the Math Forum.

MATH CENTER

Practice

OBJECTIVE Estimate products.

Materials per pair: blank spinner (TA 3)

Prepare Make a spinner with eight sections labeled 2 through 9.

Students take turns generating factors and estimating the products. Then they check each other's answers. If there is a discrepancy, they discuss whether this is due to different methods of rounding or a computational error.

PRACTICE ACTIVITY 43

MATH CENTER
Partners 👥

Number Sense • Round and Estimate!

Take turns.
• Spin the spinner.
• Your partner writes a 2-, 3-, or 4-digit number.
• Estimate the product of that number and the number you spun.
• See whether your partner agrees with your answer. If not, explain to each other how you got your answers. Did you use different methods of rounding?

YOU NEED
spinner (2–9)

2 × 4,586

7 × 2,595

279 × 3

Chapter 5, Lesson 2, pages 172–173   Multiplication

NCTM Standards

Problem Solving
✓ Communication
✓ Reasoning
Connections

Problem Solving

OBJECTIVE Make a decision by estimating costs.

Materials per group: Math Center Recording Sheet (TA 31 optional), calculator

Students are told they have $1,800 to spend on specified office supplies. As a group, they decide at which store they would buy each item and estimate the total cost of the supplies.

PROBLEM-SOLVING ACTIVITY 43

MATH CENTER
Small Group 👥👥

Decision Making • Setting Up Office

Ms. Fong has $1,800 to set up an office. She needs to buy these office supplies:

| 2 computers | 6 telephones | 3 fans |
| 4 printers | 3 staplers | 5 desk calendars |

Work with your group.
• Decide at what store you would buy which items.
• Discuss how you would estimate the cost of buying all the items. Then estimate the total cost.
• Does Ms. Fong have enough money to buy all these supplies? Use a calculator to check.

YOU NEED
calculator

DISCOUNT PRODUCTS

Computer	$599.00
Telephone	$28.99
Fan	$14.95
Printer	$121.50
Stapler	$14.10
Desk Calendar	$9.39

SAVER'S MART

Computer	$515.00
Telephone	$21.99
Fan	$22.15
Printer	$123.80
Stapler	$19.89
Desk Calendar	$6.49

Chapter 5, Lesson 2, pages 172–173   Multiplication

NCTM Standards

✓ Problem Solving
✓ Communication
✓ Reasoning
✓ Connections

Lesson 5.2 *continued*

MENTAL MATH
Estimate Products

OBJECTIVE Estimate products by rounding.

Vocabulary estimate, factor, product, round

① Introduce

Present this problem.

> **Li has $15. She wants to buy 3 cans of tennis balls. Each can costs $4.75. Does she have enough money? How much will she spend in all?**

Have students decide which question can be answered using estimation and which question requires an exact answer. *[first question, estimation; second question, exact answer]*

② Teach   *Whole Class*

▶ **LEARN** After the problem on page 172 is read, discuss how 725 was rounded to 700, a number that could be multiplied mentally.

Lead students to understand that: (a) since the exact number, 6 × 725, is greater than the estimate, 6 × 700, the factory can make more than 4,200 bicycles; and (b) since 4,200 is greater than the 4,000 needed, the factory can complete the order.

More Examples As students discuss Examples A and B, review the convention of rounding up when there is a 5 (45 rounds to 50).

③ Close

▶ **Check for Understanding** using items 1–10, page 172.

CRITICAL THINKING
For item 10, have students give examples of numbers that round to 10, 100, and 1,000.

▶ **PRACTICE**
Materials have available: calculators

Options for assigning exercises:
A—Odd ex. 1–19; **Mixed Review**
B—Even ex. 2–20; **Mixed Review**

- Students can use measurement sense and their own experiences to answer ex. 15.

⭐ **Algebra** Students practice algebraic thinking as they use inequality symbols to complete ex. 10–12.

Mixed Review/Test Preparation In ex. 1–4, students review estimating sums or differences, a skill learned in Chapter 2. In ex. 5–9, students review writing numbers in expanded form, a skill learned in Chapter 1.

MENTAL MATH • MULTIPLICATION

Estimate Products

The Acme Bicycle Factory makes 725 racing bicycles ea **day. Will Acme be able to complete this order in time?**

Date	December 5, 1997
Item	Racing Bicycle
Number of items	4,000
Due Date	December 10, 1997
Ship To	Smith Bicycle

From December 5 to December 10 is 6 days.

You can **estimate** to solve this problem.

To estimate a **product, round** the greater **factor** so you can multiply mentally.

Estimate: 6 × 725
Think: 6 × 700 = 4,200

> **Check Out the Glossary**
> For vocabulary words
> See page 544.

Compare this number with the number of items ordered.

Since 4,200 is greater than 4,000, you can predict that the order will be completed in time.

More Examples
A 3 × 45   **Think:** 3 × 50 = 150   **B** 8 × $4,612   **Think:** 8 × $5,000 = $40,000

Check for Understanding
Estimate the product. Tell how you rounded.

1 4 × 19   80   **2** 3 × 251   900   **3** 9 × $667   **4** 7 × 2,408
                                               $6,300   14,000

5	**6**	**7**	**8**	**9**
79	332	$589	3,641	$4,39
× 6	× 5	× 8	× 2	×
480	1,500	$4,800	8,000	$12,00

Critical Thinking: Generalize   **Explain your reasoning.**

10 How does knowing how to multiply multiples of 10, 100, and 1,000 help you estimate? **Estimate by rounding a factor to the nearest multiple of 10, 100, or 1,000 and then multiplying mentally.**

172 Lesson 5.2

Meeting Individual Needs

Early Finishers

Have students estimate using only the front digits and compare their results with using rounding. *[Front-end estimation and rounding are the same when the greatest digit of the rounded factor is not changed.]*

Extra Support

For students having difficulty rounding, draw a number line from 0 to 100 marked in intervals of ten. Have students locate numbers such as 43, 87, and 25 and round each to the nearest ten. *[40, 90, 30]*

Ongoing Assessment

Observation Checklist Determine if students are correctly estimating products, including money amounts, by observing if they round and multiply correctly.

Follow Up If students are unsure of how to round, have them work with number lines. For additional help, assign **Reteach 43.**

Students who are ready to attempt more difficult problems may want to try **Extend 43.**

15. Possible answer: Disagree; it should take two people less time to clean up the yard than one person.

Practice

Estimates may vary depending on the method used. Estimates shown are by rounding the greater factor to its greatest place.

Estimate the product.

1 6 × 25 **180**   **2** 5 × $153 **$1,000**   **3** 3 × 775 **2,400**   **4** 6 × 981 **6,000**

5
```
  5,029
×     7
35,000
```
6
```
  3,642
×     8
32,000
```
7
```
  $4,882
×      4
$20,000
```
8
```
  7,730
×     5
40,000
```
9
```
  $3,498
×      9
$27,000
```

ALGEBRA Estimate. Write > or <.

10 4 × 284 ● 645 **>**   **11** 6 × 309 ● 2,400 **<**   **12** 21,000 ● 3 × 7,857 **<**

MIXED APPLICATIONS
Problem Solving

13 **Spatial reasoning** The tallest unicycle ever made is about 101 feet high. It is about as tall as a: **c**
a. child   **b.** chair   **c.** building

14 The bicycle race attracted about 1,890 people each day. The race lasted 5 days. About how many people watched the race?
about 10,000 people

15 **Logical reasoning** Katie takes 20 minutes to sweep the yard. She says that if her brother helps her, they should take 40 minutes. Do you agree or disagree? Why?
See above.

16 **Make a decision** Wang's Bicycle Shop has $6,000. They can buy folding bicycles for $1,788 each or deluxe models for $2,100 each. What should they do?
See page T17.

Estimate the cost.

17 7 pairs of gloves **$70**

18 8 helmets **$320**

19 4 jackets **$400**

20 5 speedometers and 2 helmets **$230**

Bicycle Price List	
Bicycle Supplies	**Price**
Helmet	$36
Gloves	$14
Speedometer	$25
Jacket	$109

mixed review • test preparation

Estimate the sum or difference. Estimates may vary. Estimates given were found by rounding.

1 51 + 67
120
2 859 − 601
300
3 $6.03 + $1.81
$8.00
4 57,937 − 11,836
50,000

Write the expanded form.

5 29
20 + 9
6 304
300 + 4
7 3,445
3,000 + 400 + 40 + 5
8 60,085
60,000 + 80 + 5
9 560,100
500,000 + 60,000 + 100

Extra Practice, page 500

Multiply by 1-Digit Numbers **173**

Alternate Teaching Strategy

Have students reread the problem on Student Book page 172. Then have them make and complete a table such as this one:

Number of Days	1	2	3	4	5	6
Approximate Number of Bicycles	700	[1,400]	[2,100]	[2,800]	[3,500]	[4,200]

Ask the following questions.

• **How did you complete the table?** [Possible answers: Add 700 to each previous day's total; multiply 700 by the number of days.]

• **How does the exact amount compare with the number under Day 6?** [Since 725 > 700, the exact amount, 6 × 725, is greater than the estimate, 6 × 700 = 4,200.]

PRACTICE • 43

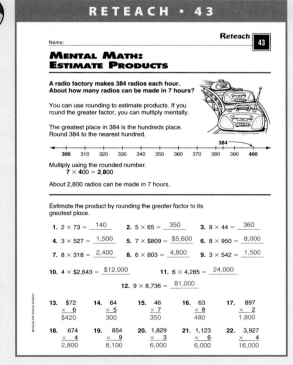

RETEACH • 43

EXTEND • 43

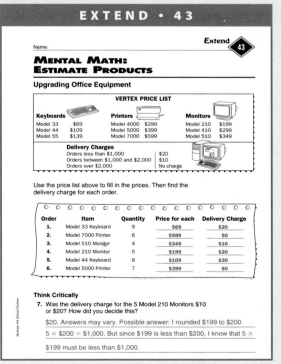

LESSON 5.3

EXPLORE ACTIVITY
Use Models to Multiply

OBJECTIVE Explore multiplying 2-digit numbers by 1-digit numbers.

Teaching with Technology
See alternate computer lesson, pp. 177A–177B.

RESOURCE REMINDER
Math Center Cards 44
Practice 44, Reteach 44, Extend 44

SKILLS TRACE

GRADE 3	• Explore multiplication by 1-digit factors using models. *(Chapter 12)*
GRADE 4	• Use models to multiply 2-digit numbers by 1-digit numbers.
GRADE 5	• Multiply 2-digit numbers. *(Chapter 4)*

MANIPULATIVE WARM-UP

Cooperative Pairs   **Visual/Spatial**

OBJECTIVE Review partitioning a factor using graph paper.

Materials per pair: scissors, centimeter graph paper (TA 7)

► One partner chooses a multiplication fact with 4, 6, or 8 as a factor and writes it down. The second partner cuts out a rectangle to show the fact and cuts the rectangle into two equal parts.

► Both partners then write down the facts for the two equal parts, and add the products. Have them compare these facts and the total to the original fact. Partners change roles and continue with other facts, listing any patterns they see.

$4 \times 6 = 24$

$4 \times 3 = 12$ $4 \times 3 = 12$

ALGEBRA CONNECTION

Cooperative Pairs   **Kinesthetic**

OBJECTIVE Explore multiplication and the Distributive Property.

Materials per pair: red and blue connecting cubes

► Working in pairs, one student builds a two-color cube train with fewer than 10 cubes. The other makes from 2 to 9 duplicate trains.

one student's method
$3 \times 6 = 18$

► Then one student uses multiplication to find the total number of cubes. The other student uses multiplication to find the total number of red cubes, the total number of blue cubes, and then adds these products. Both students write number sentences and compare their work.

► Students repeat the activity by building different trains. Ask students to explain how multiplication facts can be related to one another.

3×2 3×4

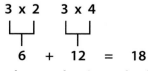

$6 \quad + \quad 12 \quad = \quad 18$

other student's method

Daily Review

PREVIOUS DAY QUICK REVIEW

Estimate the product.
1. 5×25 *[150]*
2. 3×68 *[210]*
3. 7×132 *[700]*
4. 9×678 *[6,300]*

FAST FACTS

1. $15 - 8$ *[7]*
2. $13 - 7$ *[6]*
3. $9 - 6$ *[3]*
4. $10 - 3$ *[7]*

Problem of the Day • 44

Find the values of ●, ■, and ◆.

● + ■ = ◆

■ + ■ = ■ × ■

● + ● + ● = ● × ●

[● = 3, ■ = 2, ◆ = 5]

TECH LINK

MATH VAN

Activity You may wish to use *Fun Factory Functions* to teach this lesson.

MATH FORUM

Management Tip As students play the **Greatest Product Game** on page 177, I have them use different variations like finding the least product or the product closest to 250.

Visit our Resource Village at http://www.mhschool.com to see more of the Math Forum.

MATH CENTER

Practice

OBJECTIVE Multiply by a 1-digit number.

Materials per student: 0–9 spinner (TA 3), centimeter graph paper (TA 7), Math Center Recording Sheet (TA 31 optional)

Students use a spinner to randomly generate two factors and graph paper to find the products. They cumulatively add the products and continue multiplying until they reach a total score of 5,000.

PRACTICE ACTIVITY 44

MATH CENTER
On Your Own 👤

Manipulatives • Target 500

- Spin the spinner two times. Write one digit in the square and one digit in the triangle to complete the multiplication exercise.
- Use graph paper to help you find the product.
- Record the product as the number of points you earn for that turn.
- Keep a running total of your products for each turn.
- Repeat until you reach 500 points.

YOU NEED
- spinner (0–9)
- graph paper

4×16

NCTM Standards
- Problem Solving
- ✓ Communication
- ✓ Reasoning
- ✓ Connections

Chapter 5, Lesson 3, pages 174–177 — Multiplication

ESL APPROPRIATE

Problem Solving

OBJECTIVE Use logical reasoning to find pairs of factors between 95 and 100.

Materials per student: Math Center Recording Sheet (TA 31 optional)

Students use a strategy such as guess, test, and revise to find pairs of factors with products between 95 and 105. *[Factor pairs: 2, 52; 3, 34; 4, 26; 5, 20; 6, 17; 7, 14; 8, 12; 9, 11]*

PROBLEM-SOLVING ACTIVITY 44

MATH CENTER
On Your Own 👤

Logical Reasoning • Make a Pair

- Find as many pairs of numbers as you can from the list below that have a product greater than 95 but less than 105.
- Record each pair and its product.
- Write about the strategy or strategies you used to find the pairs of numbers.

2	3	4	5	6	7	8	9
11	12	14	17	20	26	34	52

NCTM Standards
- ✓ Problem Solving
- ✓ Communication
- ✓ Reasoning
- Connections

Chapter 5, Lesson 3, pages 174–177 — Multiplication

Lesson 5.3 *continued*

EXPLORE ACTIVITY
Use Models to Multiply

OBJECTIVE Explore multiplying 2-digit numbers by 1-digit numbers.

Materials per group: centimeter graph paper (TA 7); per pair: 9 index cards; have available: place-value models—18 tens and 42 ones

Introduce

To give a context to the numbers on page 174, present this problem:

> **An assembly line produces 26 pet collars in a minute. How many will it produce in 7 minutes?**

Then ask:

- **How could you solve this problem?** *[Possible answers: Multiply 7 × 26, add 26 seven times, model it using a rectangular grid or place-value models.]*

Teach   *Cooperative Groups*

▶ **LEARN Work Together** Have students work in groups of three. Encourage members of each triad to take note of each other's work to find 7 × 26 in at least three different ways. To help students think creatively about different ways to find 7 × 26, ask:

- **What are some ways to rename 26?** *[Possible answers: 20 + 6, 10 + 10 + 6, 5 + 5 + 5 + 5 + 6, 13 + 13, 12 + 14]*

- **Which of these ways give parts of 26 that are easy to multiply mentally by 7? Tell why.** *[Possible answers: 20 + 6, 10 + 10 + 6, and 5 + 5 + 5 + 5 + 6 because you can use basic facts or a pattern.]*

- **What are some ways to rename 7?** *[Possible answers: 6 + 1, 5 + 2, 3 + 4]*

- **Do any of these ways help you find 7 × 26 mentally? Why or why not?** *[Possible answers: No; while parts like 1 × 26 or 2 × 26 can be easily found mentally, you cannot easily mentally multiply parts like 6 × 26 or 5 × 26.]*

Have students practice the cooperative skill of explaining to each other the method or strategy they used.

Talk It Over Allow triads to present their methods and tell why they prefer them. Have students compare their choices for ease of use, accuracy, and efficiency.

Observe whether students recognize that breaking up 26 into 20 + 6 or 10 + 10 + 6 allows them to use the mental math patterns from Lesson 1.

Use Models to Multiply

You can use what you know about place value and facts to multiply greater numbers.

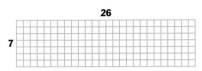
You will need
• *graph paper*

Work Together
Work in a group to find 7 × 26.

On graph paper draw a rectangle that is 7 squares high and 26 squares long. The number of squares in the rectangle is the product of 7 × 26.

KEEP IN MIND
▶ Think creatively and logically.
▶ Be prepared to present one of your methods to the class.

26

7

Use your rectangle to find 7 × 26 in at least three different ways.

182 squares; possible answers: counted the small squares individually, added seven 2
Talk It Over   added twenty-six 7s, separated the rectangle into parts that were

▶ How many squares are there inside the rectangle? easier to work with, su How did you find the number of squares? as 7 × 20 + 7 × 6 or 7 × 10 + 7 × 10 + 7

▶ How could you use estimation to know if your answer is reasonable?
Estimate: 7 × 30 = 210—the answer, 182, is close to the estimate.

174 Lesson 5.3

Meeting Individual Needs

Extra Support

Some students may benefit from folding or cutting their 7-by-26 grids into smaller parts to model other multiplication sentences they can solve.

 **ESL** APPROPRIATE

Gifted And Talented

Challenge students to extend their methods of multiplying by finding the product of 3-digit numbers and 1-digit numbers.

ESL APPROPRIATE

Ongoing Assessment

Observation Checklist
Observe if students are explaining the methods or strategies they used for solutions to each other.

Follow Up For students having difficulty explaining their methods to others, ask them to make a list of the steps they used to solve the problem, or assign **Reteach 44.**

For students who can multiply, assign **Extend 44.**

Make Connections

Here is how two students found 7×26.

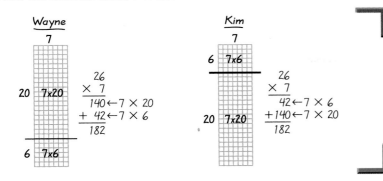

Wayne

$$\begin{array}{r} 26 \\ \times\ 7 \\ \hline 140 \leftarrow 7 \times 20 \\ +\ 42 \leftarrow 7 \times 6 \\ \hline 182 \end{array}$$

Kim

$$\begin{array}{r} 26 \\ \times\ 7 \\ \hline 42 \leftarrow 7 \times 6 \\ +140 \leftarrow 7 \times 20 \\ \hline 182 \end{array}$$

▸ How are Wayne's and Kim's methods the same? How are they different? **Possible answer: Same—factors and grid; different—the way the grid is divided and the order of the multiplication**

▸ How did they use place value, multiplication, and addition? **Possible answer: Thought of 26 as 2 tens and 6 ones, divided the grid so they could multiply 7 by 2 tens and then 7 by 6 ones, added the products.**

Check for Understanding

Find the total number of squares in the rectangle without counting all the squares.

1

84 squares

2

108 squares

3

112 squares

Find the product. You may use graph paper if you wish.

4 $\begin{array}{r} 23 \\ \times\ 3 \\ \hline 69 \end{array}$
5 $\begin{array}{r} 16 \\ \times\ 4 \\ \hline 64 \end{array}$
6 $\begin{array}{r} 43 \\ \times\ 7 \\ \hline 301 \end{array}$
7 $\begin{array}{r} 38 \\ \times\ 4 \\ \hline 152 \end{array}$
8 $\begin{array}{r} 35 \\ \times\ 5 \\ \hline 175 \end{array}$

9 4×37 148
10 6×25 150
11 7×42 294
12 9×19 171

Critical Thinking: Analyze

13 Tell how you could use tens and ones models to find 4×34. Draw a picture to show your model.
Possible answer: Find the total, 136, for four sets of 3 tens and 4 ones models; check students' drawings.

Turn the page for Practice. ➡

MAKE CONNECTIONS

The models show how the Distributive Property can be used to multiply greater numbers. Students should connect each partial product in the symbolic recordings to the appropriate parts of the models.

Either method of recording (tens first or ones first) is acceptable as long as students can justify their partial products.

Developing Algebra Sense An understanding of the Distributive Property will help students solve equations. As students multiply 2-digit numbers, they use the Distributive Property to find the partial products. You may wish to model the Distributive Property for students:

$$7 \times 26 = 7 \times (20 + 6) = (7 \times 20) + (7 \times 6) =$$
$$140 + 42 = 182$$

Encourage students to compare Wayne's and Kim's methods to their own. Help them see that using place value to break apart the numbers will allow them to use mental math patterns and basic facts.

Interested students can try this method with greater numbers. Give students exercises such as 3×123, 4×213, and 2×325. Have students record the partial products they find.

$$\begin{array}{r} 123 \\ \times\ \ \ 3 \\ \hline 300 \leftarrow 3 \times 100 \\ 60 \leftarrow 3 \times 20 \\ +\ \ \ 9 \leftarrow 3 \times 3 \\ \hline 369 \end{array} \quad \text{or} \quad \begin{array}{r} 123 \\ \times\ \ \ 3 \\ \hline 9 \leftarrow 3 \times 3 \\ 60 \leftarrow 3 \times 20 \\ +300 \leftarrow 3 \times 100 \\ \hline 369 \end{array}$$

3 Close

▸ **Check for Understanding** using items 1–13, page 175.

CRITICAL THINKING

JOURNAL Accept a wide variety of modeling strategies for finding 4×34 as long as students can justify their methods. Students will see place-value models used in Lesson 4.

Practice See pages 176–177.

▶ PRACTICE

Materials have available: calculators

Options for assigning exercises:
A—Ex. 1–8; odd ex. 9–31; ex. 32; **Greatest Product Game!; Mixed Review**
B—Ex. 1–8; even ex. 10–32; **Greatest Product Game!; Mixed Review**

• Students should check to see if they can solve ex. 9–31 using mental math.

Greatest Product Game! As student pairs play this game, they may develop the strategy of using the greatest digit as the 1-digit factor and using the next greatest digit as the tens digit in the 2-digit factor. You may want to place the game in a Math Corner so that students have easy access to it. Repeatedly playing the game will provide practice in multiplying. It will also help students develop more efficient strategies for arranging the factors.

Mixed Review/Test Preparation Students practice addition and subtraction, learned in Chapter 2, and multiplication and division facts, a skill learned in Chapter 4. Have students try to solve the problems mentally.

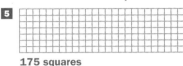

Practice

Find the total number of squares in the rectangle without counting.

1 68 squares

2 108 squares

3 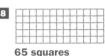 126 squares

4 176 squares

5 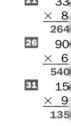 175 squares

6 99 squares

7 128 squares

8 65 squares

Find the product using any method.

9 6 × 38 228   **10** 6 × 37 222   **11** 9 × 42 378   **12** 8 × 60 480

13 8 × 13 104   **14** 9 × 16 144   **15** 8 × 23 184   **16** 4 × 60 240

17 28 × 2 = 56	**18** 17 × 5 = 85	**19** 36 × 7 = 252	**20** 40 × 5 = 200	**21** 33 × 8 = 264
22 23 × 4 = 92	**23** 25 × 8 = 200	**24** 60 × 8 = 480	**25** 18 × 4 = 72	**26** 90 × 6 = 540
27 33 × 7 = 231	**28** 44 × 5 = 220	**29** 19 × 3 = 57	**30** 17 × 4 = 68	**31** 15 × 9 = 135

32 Tell which of ex. 9–31 you can solve mentally. Explain how you would solve three of them. **Possible answer: ex. 12, 16, 20, 24, 26; explanations may vary.**

176 Lesson 5.3

Meeting Individual Needs

Early Finishers

Have students repeat the activity on page 174 with different rectangles.

ESL APPROPRIATE

Language Support

As students explain their methods for multiplying, help them by recording the process that each student describes. Use labeled diagrams as an aid.

ESL APPROPRIATE

COMMON ERROR

Some students multiply incorrectly, especially when one or both factors have zeros in them. Encourage students to use their number sense to find the correct magnitude of a product.

Greatest Product Game!

First, make one card for each of the numbers 1 through 9.

Next, on a sheet of paper, make a game sheet like the one at the right for each player.

You will need
• index cards
• sheet of paper

Play the Game

► Mix up the cards. Place them facedown. Pick two cards. Each player writes the two numbers in the boxes for Round 1.

► Find your product. Compare it with your partner's. The player with the greater product scores 1 point.

► If the products are the same, no one gets any points.

► Mix up the cards. Play Round 2 and Round 3. Continue playing, starting again at Round 1 until a player has 5 points.

What strategies did you use to place the numbers? **Used the greater number as the 1-digit factor and the other number as the ones digit in the 2-digit factor.**

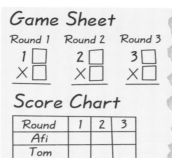

Game Sheet

Round 1   Round 2   Round 3

1 ☐   2 ☐   3 ☐
×☐   ×☐   ×☐

Score Chart

Round	1	2	3
Afi			
Tom			

Sample

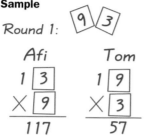

Round 1: [9] [3]

Afi   Tom

1 [3]   1 [9]
× [9]   × [3]
─────   ─────
117   57

Score: 1 point

---

mixed review • test preparation

1	2	3	4	5
7 ×9 **63**	6 ×3 **18**	544 +183 **727**	947 −540 **407**	239 +403 **642**

6 49 ÷ 7 **7**   **7** 32 ÷ 4 **8**   **8** 45 ÷ 5 **9**   **9** 72 ÷ 9 **8**

Extra Practice, page 501

Multiply by 1-Digit Numbers **177**

Alternate Teaching Strategy

Materials place-value models—10 tens and 30 ones

Present this problem:

Each car on the Fantasy Ferris Wheel holds 6 people. There are 14 cars on the Ferris wheel. How many people can ride the Ferris wheel when all of the cars are full?

Have students use tens and ones models to make 6 groups of 14.

• **How many tens are there?** *[6 tens]* **How many ones are there?** *[24 ones]*

• **How can you use the numbers of tens and ones to find the number of people that can ride the Ferris wheel?**
[Possible answers: add 6 groups of 10 to 6 groups of 4 to get 60 + 24, or 84 people; use mental math to find 6 × 10 and a basic fact to find 6 × 4 (or find 3 × 4 and double it).]

Continue the activity with other problems.

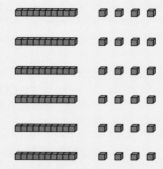

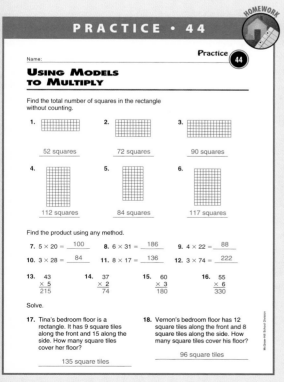
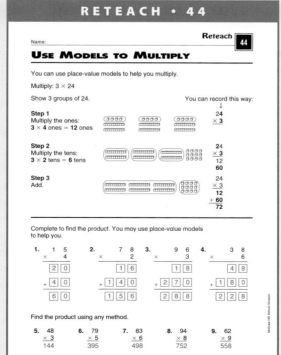
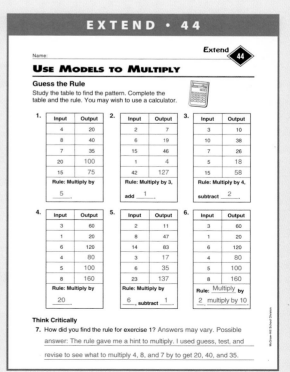
177

Teaching With Technology

Use Models to Multiply

OBJECTIVES Students use models to multiply 2-digit numbers by 1-digit numbers. Students solve multiplication problems.

Resource Math Van Activity: *Fun Factory Functions*

SET UP

Launch the **Math Van** program. Choose the Fax machine. Students may work in pairs. Tell them to click *Fun Factory Functions* activity.

USING THE MATH VAN ACTIVITY

1 Getting Started Students learn to use place-value models to multiply. They find the total number of toys needed to fill orders.

2 Practice and Apply Students use what they have learned to solve new multiplication problems to match orders with boxes of toys.

3 Close You may wish to have students compare how they used place-value models to multiply to solve problems. Have students tell how they know when to regroup.

Extend Students can continue the activity by creating their own orders. Partners take turns formulating and solving multiplication problems.

TIPS FOR TOOLS

If students have difficulty regrouping, have them click *Help* to be shown how to use the *Trade Up* and *Trade Down* buttons.

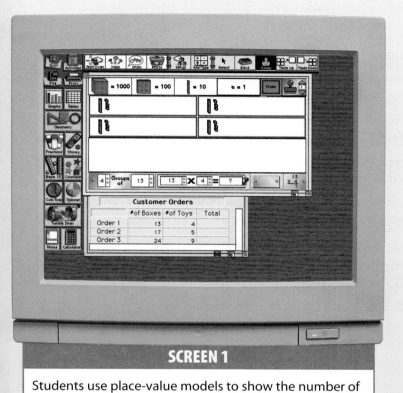

SCREEN 1

Students use place-value models to show the number of groups and the number in each group.

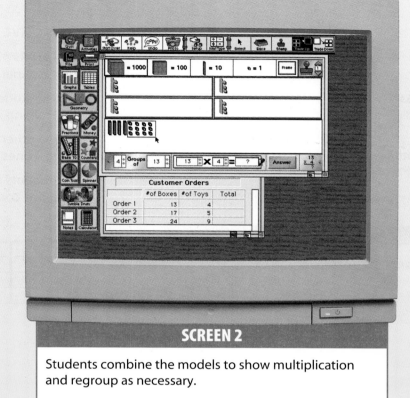

SCREEN 2

Students combine the models to show multiplication and regroup as necessary.

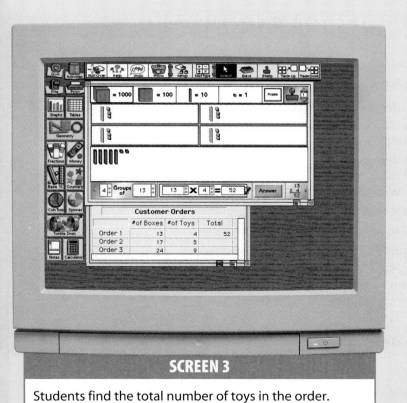

SCREEN 3

Students find the total number of toys in the order.

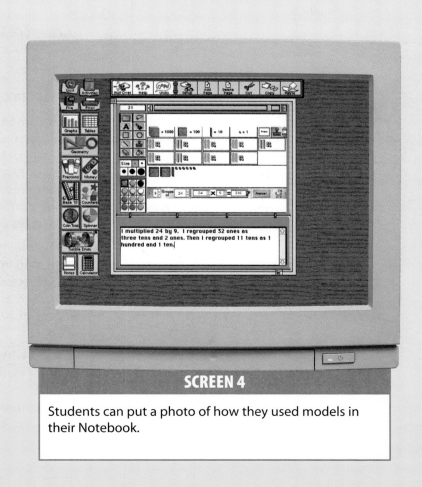

SCREEN 4

Students can put a photo of how they used models in their Notebook.

LESSON 5.4

Multiply 2-Digit Numbers

OBJECTIVE Multiply 2-digit numbers by 1-digit numbers.

RESOURCE REMINDER
Math Center Cards 45
Practice 45, Reteach 45, Extend 45

SKILLS TRACE

GRADE 3
- Explore multiplication by 1-digit factors using models. *(Chapter 12)*

GRADE 4
- Multiply 2-digit numbers by 1-digit numbers.

GRADE 5
- Apply multiplying 2-digit numbers by 1-digit numbers. *(Chapter 4)*

MANIPULATIVE WARM-UP

Cooperative Pairs   **Logical/Analytical**

OBJECTIVE Compare two models for finding products.

Materials per pair: place-value models—4 tens and 12 ones, centimeter graph paper (TA 7), scissors

▶ One student finds 4 × 13 by cutting a 4-by-13 rectangle out of graph paper and folding it into a 4-by-10 rectangle and a 4-by-3 rectangle.

▶ The other uses place-value models to find 4 × 13 by using 4 groups of 1 ten 3 ones and then regrouping the ones to get 5 tens 2 ones.

▶ Students repeat the activity using different multiplication examples. Have students compare the uses of the two models.

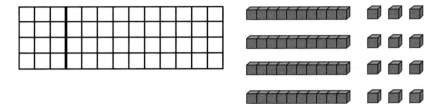

ESL APPROPRIATE

CULTURAL CONNECTION

Whole Class   **Auditory/Linguistic**

OBJECTIVE Explore the role of mental math in the Yoruba number system.

▶ Explain to students that the Yoruba (YOH-roo-bah) of Nigeria use a number system that requires mental math to name numbers. Write these rules on the board:

> Numbers 1 to 10 and 20 have their own names.
> Numbers 11 to 14 are expressed as "10 plus one," and so on.
> Numbers 15 to 19 are expressed as "20 less five," and so on.
> Numbers 21 to 24 are expressed as "20 plus one," and so on.

▶ All other numbers are expressed in groups of 20. For example, 45 is expressed as three groups of 20, minus 10, minus 5; 31 is expressed as two groups of 20, minus 10, plus 1.

▶ Work with students to help them express numbers up to 100 in the Yoruba number system. Then have them play a game in which one student calls out a number expressed in the Yoruba number system and other students try to be first to express the number using the Hindu-Arabic numbers commonly used in the United States.

Daily Review

PREVIOUS DAY QUICK REVIEW

Find the product.
1. 17 × 3 [51]
2. 40 × 8 [320]
3. 9 × 13 [117]
4. 6 × 47 [282]

FAST FACTS

1. 13 − 4 [9]
2. 11 − 5 [6]
3. 10 − 2 [8]
4. 15 − 6 [9]

Problem of the Day • 45

Jill is stacking boxes of skates for a display. She places 35 boxes on the bottom, 30 boxes on the second row, and 25 boxes on the third row. If she follows the same pattern for the rest of the stack, how many rows are in the finished stack? How many boxes are there in all? [7 rows; 140 boxes]

TECH LINK

MATH VAN

Activity You may wish to use *Fun Factory Functions* to practice and extend skills and concepts.

MATH FORUM

Idea I allow my students to continue to use place-value models until they demonstrate an understanding of the pencil-and-paper process.

Visit our Resource Village at http://www.mhschool.com to see more of the Math Forum.

MATH CENTER

Practice

OBJECTIVE Multiply 2-digit numbers.

Materials per student: number cube, Math Center Recording Sheet (TA 31 optional)

Students use a number cube to randomly generate factors. To begin, they roll the cube twice and find the product of the numbers rolled. They roll again, and multiply the first product by the number rolled. They continue in this fashion, multiplying the previous product by the number rolled, until they get a 3-digit product.

PRACTICE ACTIVITY 45

MATH CENTER
On Your Own

Number Sense • Roll for Products

YOU NEED
number cube

- Roll the number cube twice. Find the product of the two numbers you rolled. Record the product.
- Roll the cube again. Multiply the number rolled by your first product. Record the new product.
- Continue rolling the cube and multiplying the number rolled by the product you got the turn before.
- Stop when you get a 3-digit product.

Repeat.

Chapter 5, Lesson 4, pages 178–181

Multiplication

ESL APPROPRIATE

NCTM Standards

Problem Solving
Communication
✓ Reasoning
Connections

Problem Solving

OBJECTIVE Use logical reasoning to solve multiplication riddles.

Materials per student: Math Center Recording Sheet (TA 31 optional)

Students solve riddles that involve multiplication using a strategy such as guess, test, and revise. Then they formulate their own riddles. [1. 23; 2. 44]

PROBLEM-SOLVING ACTIVITY 45

MATH CENTER
Partners

Logical Reasoning • What's the Number?

Solve these riddles by yourself. Then compare your answers with your partner's answers.

1. I am a 2-digit number. The sum of my digits is 5. My product with 4 is 92. What number am I?
2. I am a 2-digit number. I am between 40 and 50. My product with 5 is 220. What number am I?

Write two of your own riddles using multiplication. Have your partner solve them.

Chapter 5, Lesson 4, pages 178–181

Multiplication

NCTM Standards

✓ Problem Solving
✓ Communication
✓ Reasoning
Connections

Multiply 2-Digit Numbers

OBJECTIVE Multiply 2-digit numbers by 1-digit numbers.

Materials per student: place-value models—at least 5 tens and 24 ones (optional)

Vocabulary regroup

 Introduce

Ask students to listen carefully as you read these two problems. Then have them tell you how to solve them.

Erin is packing stuffed animals. She puts 87 in one box, 83 in another box, and 52 in another box. How many animals does she pack in all? *[222 animals; use addition.]*

José is packing stuffed animals. He puts 86 in each box. He packs 3 boxes. How many animals does he pack in all? *[258 animals; use multiplication.]*

❷ Teach   *Whole Class*

Cultural Connection Read the **Cultural Note**. Point out that piñatas are used in birthday celebrations in many Spanish-speaking countries and are becoming increasingly popular in the United States. Encourage students to share their birthday celebration traditions.

▶ **LEARN** Read the introductory problem and discuss why multiplication is used to solve it. *[because there are 3 equal groups of 18 piñatas]* Then discuss how mental math was used to estimate the product.

As you look at the first method for solving this problem, review the relationship between the parts of the grid and the partial products.

Developing Algebra Sense In this lesson, students continue to explore algebraic concepts as they informally use the Distributive Property to determine partial products.

Have students go through each step of the second method and explain how the models illustrate each step.
- **In Step 1, why does thinking of 24 as 2 tens 4 ones help you record what you're doing?** *[Possible answer: It shows that the 2 goes above the tens place.]*
- **In Step 2, where did the 2 new tens come from?** *[Possible answer: The 2 new tens are the 2 tens regrouped in Step 1.]*

Talk It Over To encourage discussion, ask students to describe how the partial products are recorded in each method.

When discussing reasonableness and estimation, ask students whether they prefer to estimate before or after finding an exact answer and tell why.

MULTIPLICATION

Multiply 2-Digit Numbers

Cultural Note Piñatas are used in birthday celebrations in Mexico.

A factory worker is packing piñatas to be shipped. There are 18 piñatas on each of 3 shelves. How many piñatas are there?

To estimate the number of piñatas, use mental math.

Think: $3 \times 20 = 60$

In the last lesson, you used this method to find the exact answer.

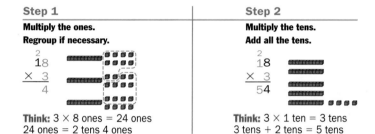

$$\begin{array}{r} 18 \\ \times\ 3 \\ \hline 24 \leftarrow 3 \times 8 \\ +\ 30 \leftarrow 3 \times 10 \\ \hline 54 \end{array}$$

Here is another method. Place-value models help you see the **regrouping.**

Step 1	Step 2
Multiply the ones. **Regroup if necessary.**	**Multiply the tens.** **Add all the tens.**
$\begin{array}{r} \overset{2}{1}8 \\ \times\ 3 \\ \hline 4 \end{array}$	$\begin{array}{r} \overset{2}{1}8 \\ \times\ 3 \\ \hline 54 \end{array}$
Think: 3×8 ones = 24 ones 24 ones = 2 tens 4 ones	**Think:** 3×1 ten = 3 tens 3 tens + 2 tens = 5 tens

There are 54 piñatas.

Talk It Over
▶ In what ways are these two methods alike? In what ways are they different? **Possible answer: both numbers are the same; the ways of recording are different.**
▶ How did estimation help you know that 54 piñatas is a reasonable answer? **Possible answer: 54 is close to 60.**

> **Check Out the Glossary** regroup See page 544.

Meeting Individual Needs

Extra Support

Some students may need to use place-value models or graph paper to complete items 1–5 of **Check for Understanding.**

Gifted And Talented

Challenge students to use each digit 1–9 only once to complete the following. *[Possible answer: 359 + 127 = 486]*

$$\begin{array}{r} \square\square\square \\ +\ \square\square\square \\ \hline \square\square\square \end{array}$$

ESL APPROPRIATE

Ongoing Assessment

Interview Determine if students understand how and when to regroup by asking:
- **Do you regroup when multiplying 4 × 67? Explain.** *[Yes; 4 × 7 ones = 28 ones, so you have to regroup ones.]*
- **Do you regroup when multiplying 3 × 32? Explain.** *[No; 2 × 3 ones = 6 ones, 3 × 3 tens = 9 tens.]*

Follow Up For students who need additional help, assign **Reteach 45.**

For students who understand how to regroup when multiplying, assign **Extend 45.**

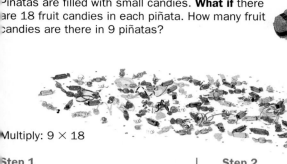

Piñatas are filled with small candies. **What if** there are 18 fruit candies in each piñata. How many fruit candies are there in 9 piñatas?

Multiply: 9 × 18

Step 1	Step 2
Multiply the ones. **Regroup if necessary.**	**Multiply the tens.** **Add all the tens** **Regroup if necessary.**

$\begin{array}{r} {}^{7} \\ 18 \\ \times\ 9 \\ \hline 2 \end{array}$ **Think:** 9 × 8 ones = 72 ones
            72 ones = 7 tens 2 ones
	$\begin{array}{r} {}^{7} \\ 18 \\ \times\ 9 \\ \hline 162 \end{array}$ **Think:** 9 × 1 ten = 9 tens
	            9 tens + 7 tens = 16 tens

There are 162 fruit candies.

More Examples

A $\begin{array}{r} 21 \\ \times\ 4 \\ \hline 84 \end{array}$ **B** $\begin{array}{r} {}^{3} \\ 16 \\ \times\ 5 \\ \hline 80 \end{array}$ **C** $\begin{array}{r} 63 \\ \times\ 3 \\ \hline 189 \end{array}$ **D** $\begin{array}{r} {}^{2} \\ 47 \\ \times\ 3 \\ \hline 141 \end{array}$

Check for Understanding

Find the product using any method. Estimate to check the reasonableness of your answer. Estimates may vary. Estimates given are by rounding.

1 $\begin{array}{r} 32 \\ \times\ 3 \\ \hline \end{array}$ 96; 90   **2** $\begin{array}{r} 20 \\ \times\ 6 \\ \hline \end{array}$ 120; 120   **3** $\begin{array}{r} 24 \\ \times\ 4 \\ \hline \end{array}$ 96; 80   **4** $\begin{array}{r} 43 \\ \times\ 3 \\ \hline \end{array}$ 129; 120   **5** $\begin{array}{r} 38 \\ \times\ 5 \\ \hline \end{array}$ 190; 200

Critical Thinking: Generalize   **Explain your reasoning.**

6 When you multiply 2-digit numbers, how do you use facts? How do you use place value? Possible answer: to multiply the digits; to know the values of the digits

7 If you multiply a 2-digit number by a 1-digit number, what is the least product you can get? What is the greatest product you can get? (any 2-digit number) × 0 = 0; 99 × 9 = 891

Turn the page for Practice. ➡
Multiply by 1-Digit Numbers   **179**

Have students compare how they computed 3 × 18 and 9 × 18. Elicit that in the second example they regrouped the ones and the tens.

- **Why does 9 × 18 result in a 3-digit product?** *[Possible answer: because 16 tens are equal to 1 hundred 6 tens]*

More Examples For each example, ask students to tell if they need to regroup and why. Point out that in Example B they need to write a zero in the product since they can regroup all of the ones as tens.

3 Close

Check for Understanding using items 1–7, page 179.

Encourage students to estimate to check their answers for reasonableness in ex. 1–5.

CRITICAL THINKING
For item 7, discuss the fact that zero is the least 1-digit factor, so the least product is also zero.

- **What is the least nonzero product?** *[1 × 10 = 10]*

Practice See pages 180–181.

▶ **PRACTICE**

Materials have available: calculators

Options for assigning exercises:
A—Choice of ten exercises from ex. 1–20; all ex. 21–52; **More to Explore**
B—Choice of five exercises from ex. 1–10; all ex. 16–52; **More to Explore**

- Students may wish to write ex. 11–24 in vertical form before multiplying.
- Encourage students to use estimation to complete the sentences in ex. 35–38 correctly.
- For **Make It Right** (ex. 45), see Common Error below.
- In ex. 46, students need to visualize the boxes that cannot fully be seen to understand that there are 12 boxes in all.
- In ex. 50, students are given the opportunity to solve a problem that has many solutions.

 Algebra Equations and inequalities are essential algebraic concepts. In ex. 39–44, students use algebraic thinking as they explore the relationships between two expressions. Such informal algebraic experiences will help students develop confidence in using algebra to solve problems.

More to Explore Have pairs of students work together. For each exercise, have them identify the number that the addends cluster about.

Practice

Find the product using any method. Remember to estimate.

1	2	3	4	5
13	37	15	50	61
× 3	× 3	× 5	× 8	× 5
39	111	75	400	305

6	7	8	9	10
65	14	90	86	48
× 6	× 4	× 4	× 7	× 5
390	56	360	602	240

11 3 × 17 51   **12** 55 × 8 440   **13** 52 × 7 364   **14** 5 × 20 100   **15** 70 × 210

16 8 × 23 184   **17** 23 × 4 92   **18** 6 × 40 240   **19** 45 × 6 270   **20** 8 × 616

21 Find the product of 32 and 7. 224   **22** Find the product of 8 and 46. 368

23 Find the product of 81 and 4. 324   **24** Find the product of 7 and 30. 210

**Find only the products that are greater than 400.
Use estimation to help you decide.**

25	26	27	28	29
36	67	97	89	75
× 4	× 8	× 8	× 9	× 6
less than 400	536	776	801	450

30	31	32	33	34
49	69	45	35	63
× 4	× 3	× 7	× 8	× 7
less than 400	less than 400	less than 400	less than 400	441

 ALGEBRA Find the missing digit.

35	36	37	38
15	■3	2■	■8
× ■	× 4	× 7	× ■
45	132	1■2	882
3	3	6; 8	9; 9

 ALGEBRA Write >, <, or =.

39 7 × 34 ● 897 <   **40** 210 ● 45 × 8 <   **41** 47 × 5 ● 78 >

42 7 × 45 ● 588 <   **43** 774 ● 86 × 9 =   **44** 42 × 9 ● 353 >

···················· **Make It Right** ····················
45 Here is how John found 6 × 54. Explain to a third grader what the mistake is. Write steps that show the correct answer.

$$\begin{array}{r} 54 \\ \times\ 6 \\ \hline 3{,}024 \end{array} \qquad \begin{array}{r} {}^{2} \\ 54 \\ \times\ 6 \\ \hline 324 \end{array}$$

He did not regroup the tens and hundreds. Step 1: Multiply the ones—6 × 4 ones = 24 ones; regroup—24 ones = 2 tens 4 ones. Step 2: Multiply the tens—6 × 5 tens = 30 tens; add all the tens—30 tens + 2 tens = 32 tens.

180 Lesson 5.4

Meeting Individual Needs

Early Finishers

Have pairs play the **Greatest Product Game!** on page 177. Change the rules so that students try to get the least product.

ESL APPROPRIATE

Inclusion

Help students who have trouble aligning digits with the same place value by asking them to turn their papers sideways so that the lines are vertical.

COMMON ERROR

Some students regroup incorrectly or add incorrectly. As in the **Make It Right** on page 180, students may forget to regroup at all. Encourage them to write out each step of the multiplication separately so it is easier for them to check their own work. They should also identify the place values of the digits in each partial product or step.

50. *Possible answer: 2 smalls, 2 mediums, 1 large, 1 extra large*

MIXED APPLICATIONS
Problem Solving

46 There are 8 dolls in each box shown at the right. How many dolls are there altogether in the boxes? **96 dolls**

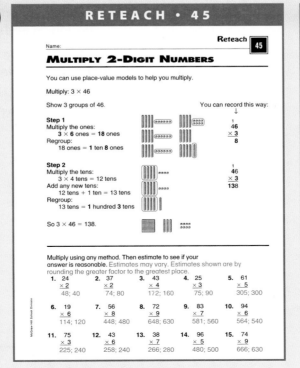

47 A machine can fill 7 bottles of soda in a minute. How many bottles can it fill in an hour? (Hint: 1 hour = 60 minutes.) **420 bottles**

48 A factory packs 8 pencils in each package. How many packages will 24 pencils fill? **3 packages**

Use the information below to solve problems 49–51.

 *Small $8.00*
 *Medium $12.00*
 *Large $19.00*
 *Extra Large $37.00*

49 How much would it cost to buy 3 medium piñatas and 6 large piñatas? **$150**

50 How many different ways can you buy the piñatas to spend exactly $96? Show all your answers. **See above.**

51 Write a problem about piñatas. Use the prices of the piñatas in the picture or make up prices of your own. **Students should check each other's work by comparing problems and solutions.**

52 Data Point Survey your classmates about their favorite toy. Make a pictograph of the data. What is the most popular toy? **Students may make a graph showing video games, stuffed animals, board games, and so on.**

more to explore

Estimating Sums by Clustering

You can use multiplication to help you estimate certain sums.

Estimate: 62 + 57 + 52 + 66   **Think:** Each number is about 60.

$$4 \times 60 = 240$$

Estimate the sum. Explain your thinking.

1 43 + 39 + 41
120; about 3 × 40

2 79 + 82 + 84 + 74
320; about 4 × 80

3 311 + 295 + 308 + 302
1,200; about 4 × 300

4 58 + 62 + 63
180; about 3 × 60

5 199 + 203 + 201
600; about 3 × 200

6 88 + 91 + 86
270; about 3 × 90

Extra Practice, page 501

Multiply by 1-Digit Numbers **181**

Alternate Teaching Strategy

Materials place-value models—9 hundreds, 19 tens, 19 ones

Present this problem:

> A box holds 36 toy spider rings. A store orders 4 boxes. How many spider rings does the store order?

Have students model four groups of 3 tens 6 ones.

- **How many ones are there?** *[24 ones]* **Regroup to make tens. How many ones do you have now?** *[4 ones]*

- **How many tens are there?** *[14 tens]* **Regroup to make hundreds. How many tens do you have now?** *[4 tens]* **How many hundreds do you have?** *[1 hundred]*

- **What number do you have?** *[144]* **How many spider rings did the store order?** *[144 spider rings]*

Continue the activity with other problems.

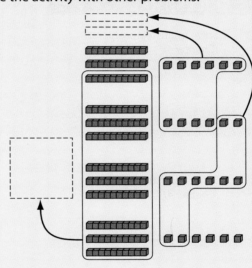

PRACTICE • 45

Name: _____

Practice 45

MULTIPLYING 2-DIGIT NUMBERS

Find only the products that are greater than 300.
Use estimation to help you decide.

1. 42 × 6   **less than 300**
2. 53 × 7   **371**
3. 51 × 4   **less than 300**
4. 48 × 8   **384**
5. 65 × 9   **585**

6. 14 × 5   **less than 300**
7. 76 × 8   **608**
8. 88 × 4   **352**
9. 91 × 3   **less than 300**
10. 37 × 9   **333**

11. 42 × 9   **378**
12. 45 × 5   **less than 300**
13. 74 × 8   **592**
14. 88 × 2   **less than 300**
15. 59 × 9   **531**

16. 63 × 8   **504**
17. 37 × 6   **less than 300**
18. 58 × 6   **348**
19. 96 × 4   **384**
20. 85 × 9   **765**

21. 5 × 87 = **435**
22. 74 × 6 = **444**
23. 6 × 93 = **558**
24. 8 × 63 = **504**
25. 9 × 57 = **513**
26. 4 × 28 = **less than 300**
27. 56 × 7 = **392**
28. 9 × 18 = **less than 300**
29. 7 × 96 = **672**

Algebra Find the missing digit.

30. 23 × **4** = 92
31. 5**8** × 6 = 348
32. 4**7** × 5 = 235
33. 3**7** × 2 = 74

Solve.

34. Buses from Tours, Inc. hold 54 passengers. How many passengers will 6 of these buses hold? **324 passengers**

35. A bus traveled at a speed of 55 miles per hour for 3 hours. How many miles did it travel in that time? **165 miles**

RETEACH • 45

Name: _____

Reteach 45

MULTIPLY 2-DIGIT NUMBERS

You can use place-value models to help you multiply.

Multiply: 3 × 46

Show 3 groups of 46.   You can record this way:

Step 1
Multiply the ones:
3 × 6 ones = 18 ones
Regroup:
18 ones = 1 ten 8 ones

46 × 3 = 8

Step 2
Multiply the tens:
3 × 4 tens = 12 tens
Add any new tens:
12 tens + 1 ten = 13 tens
Regroup:
13 tens = 1 hundred 3 tens

46 × 3 = 138

So 3 × 46 = 138.

Multiply using any method. Then estimate to see if your answer is reasonable. Estimates may vary. Estimates shown are by rounding the greater factor to the greatest place.

1. 24 × 2   **48; 40**
2. 37 × 4   **74; 80**
3. 43 × 4   **172; 160**
4. 25 × 3   **75; 90**
5. 61 × 5   **305; 300**

6. 19 × 6   **114; 120**
7. 56 × 8   **448; 480**
8. 72 × 9   **648; 630**
9. 83 × 7   **581; 560**
10. 94 × 6   **564; 540**

11. 75 × 3   **225; 240**
12. 43 × 6   **258; 240**
13. 38 × 7   **266; 280**
14. 96 × 5   **480; 500**
15. 74 × 9   **666; 630**

EXTEND • 45

Name: _____

Extend 45

MULTIPLY 2-DIGIT NUMBERS

Let Your Fingers Do the Measuring

Here is a way to estimate distances on a map.

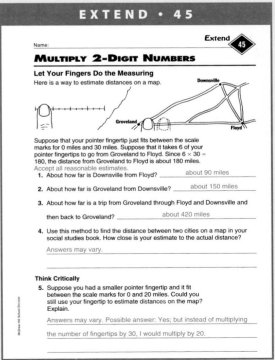

Suppose that your pointer fingertip just fits between the scale marks for 0 miles and 30 miles. Suppose that it takes 6 of your pointer fingertips to go from Groveland to Floyd. Since 6 × 30 = 180, the distance from Groveland to Floyd is about 180 miles. Accept all reasonable estimates.

1. About how far is Downsville from Floyd? _____ **about 90 miles**

2. About how far is Groveland from Downsville? _____ **about 150 miles**

3. About how far is a trip from Groveland through Floyd and Downsville and then back to Groveland? _____ **about 420 miles**

4. Use this method to find the distance between two cities on a map in your social studies book. How close is your estimate to the actual distance?
Answers may vary.

Think Critically

5. Suppose you had a smaller pointer fingertip and it fit between the scale marks for 0 and 20 miles. Could you still use your fingertip to estimate distances on the map? Explain.
Answers may vary. Possible answer: Yes; but instead of multiplying the number of fingertips by 30, I would multiply by 20.

LESSON 5.5

Problem-Solving Strategy: Solve Multistep Problems

OBJECTIVE Solve multistep problems.

RESOURCE REMINDER
Math Center Cards 46
Practice 46, Reteach 46, Extend 46

SKILLS TRACE

GRADE 3	• Solve multistep problems. *(Chapter 4)*
GRADE 4	• Solve multistep problems.
GRADE 5	• Solve multistep problems. *(Chapter 4)*

WARM-UP

Cooperative Pairs   **Logical/Analytical**

OBJECTIVE Use tree diagrams to find all of the possible combinations.

▶ Have students in each group create lists of their 3 favorite lunch foods and 2 favorite beverages. Each group draws a tree diagram to show all of the possible combinations for lunch if one item is chosen from each category.

▶ You may need to start a tree diagram to help students organize their work. Interested students can extend the activity by changing the number of items in each category or by changing the number of categories.

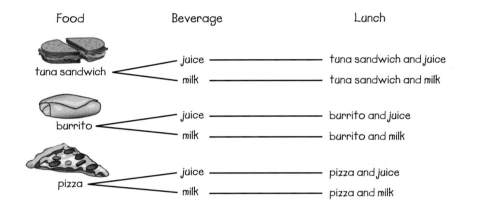

DISCRETE MATH CONNECTION

Whole Class   **Visual/Spatial**

OBJECTIVE Use manipulatives to solve combination problems.

Materials per pair: red marker, blue marker

▶ Students draw a blank T-shirt on three pieces of paper. Then they draw a different geometric design on each one.

▶ Tell students each T-shirt can be colored red or blue. Ask them to show all possible combinations of T-shirt designs and colors. *[6 combinations]*

▶ They repeat the activity with a different number of designed T-shirts or with three or four different colors. Ask students to explain how they found the number of combinations.

ESL **APPROPRIATE**

Daily Review

Problem of the Day • 46

On January 1, Brandon was asked, "How old are you?" He answered "The day before yesterday, I was 9. Next year, I'll be 12." Explain how this can be true. *[His birthday is Dec. 31. He was 9 on Dec. 30 and 10 on Dec. 31 of the previous year. He will be 11 on Dec. 31 of the present year, and 12 on Dec. 31 of the following year.]*

TECH LINK

MATH VAN

Tool You may wish to use the Table tool with this lesson.

MATH FORUM

Idea My students often do not complete all the steps in a multistep problem. I suggest that they make a plan and ask themselves, "Did I answer the question?"

Visit our Resource Village at http://www.mhschool.com to see more of the Math Forum.

MATH CENTER

Practice

OBJECTIVE Formulate and solve multistep problems involving multiplication and subtraction.

Materials per student: Math Center Recording Sheet (TA 31 optional)

Students plan how to solve a multistep problem involving multiplication and subtraction. They supply their own numbers and solve their problems.

PRACTICE ACTIVITY 46

MATH CENTER
On Your Own

Formulating Problems • Super Saver

Tomás is paid $ [2-digit number] an hour.

He works [1-digit number] hours each week.

Each week he spends $ [3-digit number] and saves the rest.

How much money will he save in 4 weeks?

- First make a plan for solving the problem.
- Then fill in the first two boxes with numbers.
- Think carefully about what 3-digit number to use in the third box. Fill in the third box.
- Solve your problem.

Repeat with different numbers.

Chapter 5, Lesson 5, pages 182–183   Multiplication

NCTM Standards
- ✓ Problem Solving
- ✓ Communication
- ✓ Reasoning
- ✓ Connections

Problem Solving

OBJECTIVE Use data in a table to solve problems.

Materials per student: Math Center Recording Sheet (TA 31 optional)

Students work with their partner to solve multistep problems by using data in a road mileage chart. They then use the data to formulate their own problem for their partner to solve. *[1. 1,366 miles; 2. Yes.]*

PROBLEM-SOLVING ACTIVITY 46

MATH CENTER
On Your Own

Using Data • Take a Trip!

Use the table to answer these questions.
1. How many miles would you travel if you went from Boston to New York and back to Boston, and then went to Indianapolis?
2. Ms. Simon makes 5 round trips in November between Chicago and Philadelphia. If she travels 5,000 miles in a month, she gets a bonus. Will she get a bonus in November?

ROAD MILEAGES BETWEEN U.S. CITIES (IN MILES)					
Cities	Boston	Chicago	Philadelphia	Indianapolis	New York
Boston	—	983	304	940	213
Chicago	983	—	758	189	840
Philadelphia	304	758	—	647	93
Indianapolis	940	189	647	—	739
New York	213	840	93	739	—

Chapter 5, Lesson 5, pages 182–183   Multiplication

NCTM Standards
- ✓ Problem Solving
- ✓ Communication
- ✓ Reasoning
- ✓ Connections

Lesson 5.5 *continued*

Problem-Solving Strategy: Solve Multistep Problems

OBJECTIVE Solve multistep problems.

Ask students to create two-step problems that involve addition and subtraction. Tell students that some problems with two or more steps can involve multiplication as well.

 *Whole Class*

LEARN After reading aloud the problem on page 182, have students restate it in their own words and make a plan for solving it.

Explain that the tree diagram shows all the possible combinations the company could choose for a pattern on a color.

- **What are the different choices that the company can make?** [red deck with lightning pattern, purple deck with lightning pattern, green deck with lightning pattern, red deck with wavy pattern, purple deck with wavy pattern, green deck with wavy pattern]

After students identify the steps in the problem, ask:

- **Does the order of the steps in this problem matter? Why or why not?** [Yes; you need to find the number of combinations before finding the total number of different skateboards.]

Check for Understanding using items 1–2, page 182.

CRITICAL THINKING
After discussing item 2, ask:

- **After reading a problem, how can you tell whether it involves more than one step?** [You have to find some missing information before finding the complete solution to the problem.]

▶ **PRACTICE**

Materials have available: calculators

Assign ex. 1–10 as independent work.

- You may want to have a volunteer explain how to read the table and what makes up a $3 cone before assigning ex.1 and 3–6.
- If students are having trouble with ex. 2, suggest that they find triangles made from 1 small triangle, then from 2 small triangles.
- For ex. 4, students may use the Make a List or Draw a Picture strategy.

Solve Multistep Problems   Look Back

Read Action Sports makes skateboards with decks in 2 different patterns and 3 different colors. The company makes 8,000 of each type. How many skateboards will the company make?

Plan You need to think about two questions to solve the problem.

Step 1 How many types of skateboards are possible?

Step 2 What is the total number of skateboards?

Solve **Step 1** Use a tree diagram.

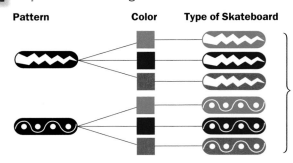

Pattern	Color	Type of Skateboard

$3 \times 2 = 6$

There are 6 possible combinations.

Step 2 Use mental math. $6 \times 8,000 = 48,000$
The company will make 48,000 skateboards.

Look Back How could you solve this problem in a different way? **Possible answer: Make a list of the types of skateboards and then multiply mentally.**

Check for Understanding
Solve. Tell the steps you used.

1 **What if** Action Sports makes skateboard decks in 2 colors and 4 patterns. What is the cost to buy one of each type at $42 each? What two questions did you answer to solve the problem? **$336; possible answer: How many types of skateboards are there? How much do that many skateboards cost?**

Critical Thinking: Analyze   Show two different ways to solve.

2 Stickers for short decks sell for $1. Stickers for long decks sell for $2 more. How much does it cost to buy 2,000 stickers for short decks and 3,000 stickers for long decks?

$11,000; possible answer: (2,000 × $1) + (3,000 × $3) or (2,000 × $1) + (3,000 × $1) + (3,000 × $2)
182 Lesson 5.5

Meeting Individual Needs

Early Finishers

Challenge students to find the digits A, B, C, and D that make the following true.

$$\begin{array}{r} ABCD \\ \times\quad 4 \\ \hline DCBA \end{array}$$

[A = 2, B = 1, C = 7, D = 8]

ESL APPROPRIATE

Extra Support

Students may not see the hidden question in a multistep problem. Have students continue to write the questions needed to solve multistep problems.

Ongoing Assessment

Observation Checklist
Observe if students can make a plan identifying the steps needed to solve a multistep problem that involves multiplication.

Follow Up For students who are having trouble solving multistep problems, make a flowchart or a list showing a sequence of steps. For additional help, assign **Reteach 46.**

For students who are able to do multistep problems accurately, assign **Extend 46.**

MIXED APPLICATIONS
Problem Solving

Pencil & Paper · Calculator · Mental Math

Yogurt Delight serves one fruit topping with either vanilla or chocolate yogurt on a sugar cone.

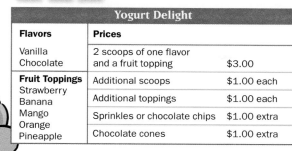

Yogurt Delight	
Flavors	**Prices**
Vanilla Chocolate	2 scoops of one flavor and a fruit topping $3.00
Fruit Toppings Strawberry Banana Mango Orange Pineapple	Additional scoops $1.00 each
	Additional toppings $1.00 each
	Sprinkles or chocolate chips $1.00 extra
	Chocolate cones $1.00 extra

1 Draw a diagram or make a table that shows all the possible flavor and fruit topping combinations at Yogurt Delight. **Check students' work.**

2 **Spatial reasoning** How many triangles can you find in Yogurt Delight's logo? **12 triangles**

YOGURT DELIGHT

3 Yogurt Delight has 3 cases of 600 cones in the storeroom. The rest are behind the counter on 4 shelves. Each shelf holds 46 cones. How many cones are there in all? **1,984 cones**

4 **What if** your class saves $120 to buy yogurt for a class party. How many toppings, different-type cones, and scoops of each flavor can your class buy? How much money will be left over?
Answers may vary depending on class size.

5 Caleb closes the Yogurt Delight store at 7 P.M. He works 8 hours a day. At what time does he start work? **11 A.M.**

6 **Write a problem** using the information from Yogurt Delight's price list. Solve it and have others solve it. **Students should compare problems and solutions.**

Use the graph for problems 7–10.

7 Which hobby is the most popular? **drawing**

8 How many more students preferred baseball to reading? **3 more students**

9 How many students were surveyed? **20 students**

10 **What if** listening to music was added to the survey. How do you think the graph would change?
Answers may vary. Possible answer: Height of given bars may decrease to accommodate the new category.

Favorite Hobby of Students

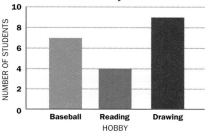

Extra Practice, page 502

Multiply by 1-Digit Numbers **183**

Alternate Teaching Strategy

Materials have available: strips of red, purple and green construction paper, markers

Read the problem on Student Book page 182. To help students build up to two patterns, start with a simpler problem of one pattern and two colors, then two patterns and two colors. Encourage students to make or draw models to show the number of possible combinations with red, purple and green skateboards.

Have students complete the rows of the table one at a time and explain their reasoning.

	Number of possible combinations with lightning and wavy patterns	Number of types of skateboards
For 1 color	$1 \times 2 = 2$	$2 \times 8{,}000 = 16{,}000$
For 2 colors	$2 \times 2 = 4$	$4 \times 8{,}000 = 32{,}000$
For 3 colors	$3 \times 2 = 6$	$6 \times 8{,}000 = 48{,}000$

PRACTICE · 46

HOMEWORK

Name: _____ Practice **46**

PROBLEM-SOLVING STRATEGY:
SOLVE MULTISTEP PROBLEMS

☑ Read ☑ Plan ☑ Solve ☑ Look Back

Solve.

1. It is 22 miles between Ms. Castro's home and her office. She drives to and from work 5 days a week. How many miles does she make today to and from work each week?
220 miles

2. Ms. Cata earns $9 an hour. She works 35 hours each week. She sets aside $70 a week to pay for rent. How much does she have left a week to spend?
$245

3. Mr. Schwab works 22 hours a week at one job, earning $8 an hour. He works 16 hours a week at another job, earning $6 an hour. How much does he earn altogether each week?
$272

4. During 4 weeks in May, Jesse put $29 a week in his savings account. He already had $378 in his account. How much does he have at the end of May?
$494

Solve using any strategy.

5. Becky needs to leave at 3 P.M. She began painting at 9:00 A.M. How many hours can she paint?
6 hours

6. Ann sold 172 dolls for $8 each. How much money did she make?
$1,376

7. Ann sewed buttons on the three dolls she made today. She sewed 6 buttons on one doll, 5 buttons on another doll, and 4 buttons on a third doll. At the end of the day, she had 14 buttons left. How many did she start out with?
29 buttons

8. **Logical Reasoning** Alex, Betty, and Cara make crafts. One paints, another knits, and the third carves wood. Alex does not work with wood. Betty likes to knit. Cara does not knit. Who does what?
Alex—paints; Betty—knits; Cara—carves

RETEACH · 46

Name: _____ Reteach **46**

PROBLEM-SOLVING STRATEGY:
SOLVE MULTISTEP PROBLEMS

☑ Read ☑ Plan ☑ Solve ☑ Look Back

Some problems take more than one step to solve. First, make a plan that tells what the steps are. Then find the answer for each step to solve the problem.

Ramona buys 4 sweatshirts for $15 each and a sweater for $23. How much does she pay altogether?

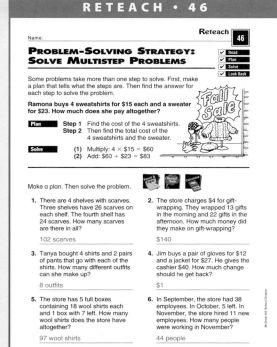

Plan
Step 1 Find the cost of the 4 sweatshirts.
Step 2 Then find the total cost of the 4 sweatshirts and the sweater.

Solve
(1) Multiply: $4 \times \$15 = \$60$
(2) Add: $\$60 + \$23 = \$83$

Make a plan. Then solve the problem.

1. There are 4 shelves with scarves. Three shelves have 26 scarves on each shelf. The fourth shelf has 24 scarves. How many scarves are there in all?
102 scarves

2. The store charges $4 for gift-wrapping. They wrapped 13 gifts in the morning and 22 gifts in the afternoon. How much money did they make on gift-wrapping?
$140

3. Tanya bought 4 shirts and 2 pairs of pants that go with each of the shirts. How many different outfits can she make up?
8 outfits

4. Jim buys a pair of gloves for $12 and a jacket for $27. He gives the cashier $40. How much change should he get back?
$1

5. The store has 5 full boxes containing 18 wool shirts each and 1 box with 7 left. How many wool shirts does the store have altogether?
97 wool shirts

6. In September, the store had 38 employees. In October, 5 left. In November, the store hired 11 new employees. How many people were working in November?
44 people

EXTEND · 46

Name: _____ Extend **46**

PROBLEM SOLVING

Three-Cube Puzzle

You need: scissors, clear tape

Cut out the three patterns. Fold along the dotted lines and tape the patterns into cubes. Use the cubes to solve this puzzle.

Place the cubes next to each other in a row so that along the top, front, and bottom, there is a row of different shapes. **Possible answers are given.**

Draw what you see.

1. Row of cubes from the top.

2. Row of cubes from the front.

3. Turn the cubes so you can see the row of cubes on the bottom. Draw what you see.

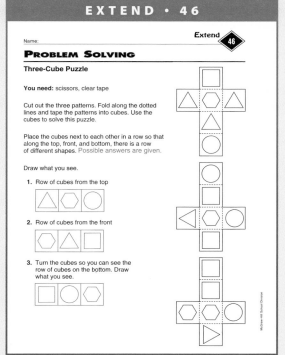

MIDCHAPTER REVIEW

Using the Midchapter Review

Have students complete the **Midchapter Review** independently, or use it with the whole class.

 Algebra: Patterns In ex. 1–3, students understand the relationship between numbers by finding patterns when multiplying by 10, 100, and 1,000.

For ex. 4–7, students need to get information from the table before estimating. Students round either the number of packs/cartons or the number in each pack/carton.

JOURNAL Students can approach this open-ended problem at their own levels. Most students should be able to explain two or three methods.

Possible methods include using:
–repeated addition to add eight 62s
–a model (area or place-value)
–a paper-and-pencil method
–a calculator

Vocabulary Review

Write the following words on the board:

estimate	factor	product
reasonable	regroup	round

Ask for volunteers to explain the meanings of these words and to give examples.

ALGEBRA: PATTERNS Copy and complete.

1 $6 \times 9 = $ ■ 54
$6 \times 90 = $ ■ 540
$6 \times 900 = $ ■ 5,400
$6 \times 9,000 = $ ■ 54,000

2 $5 \times 60 = $ ■ 300
$5 \times 600 = $ ■ 3,000
$5 \times 6,000 = $ ■ 30,000

3 $8 \times 20 = $ ■ 160
$8 \times 200 = $ ■ 1,600
$8 \times 2,000 = $ ■ 16,000

Estimate how many. Estimates may vary. Possible estimates are given.

4 4 cartons of tea bags **80 tea bags**

5 28 packs of soda **180 sodas**

6 42 packs of hot dogs **320 hot dogs**

7 6 cartons of eggs **60 eggs**

Item	Number of Items in Each Pack/Carton
Soda	6
Eggs	12
Hot dogs	8
Tea bags	18

Find the product. Use graph paper if you need to.

8 $\begin{array}{r} 22 \\ \times 4 \\ \hline 88 \end{array}$
9 $\begin{array}{r} 34 \\ \times 5 \\ \hline 170 \end{array}$
10 $\begin{array}{r} 37 \\ \times 6 \\ \hline 222 \end{array}$
11 $\begin{array}{r} \$29 \\ \times 7 \\ \hline \$203 \end{array}$
12 $\begin{array}{r} 38 \\ \times 8 \\ \hline 304 \end{array}$

13 3×200 **600**
14 $5 \times \$8,000$ **$40,000**
15 7×78 **546**
16 65×3 **195**

17 8×500 **4,000**
18 $3,000 \times 8$ **24,000**
19 4×83 **332**
20 52×7 **364**

Solve. Use mental math when you can.

21 A machine can make 3 doll arms each minute. How many can it make each hour? (Hint: 1 hour = 60 minutes.) **180 arms**

22 A machine makes about 26 earrings each hour. Estimate how many earrings 6 of the machines can make in an hour. **about 180 earrings**

23 A toy company is selling stuffed dinosaurs for $7 each. A toy store orders 500. The shipping charge is $60 extra. What is the total bill? **$3,560**

24 A factory packs 9 model space shuttles in each box. How many models are in 54 boxes? **486 models**

25 Journal Explain as many different ways as you can how to find 8×62. **Check students' work.**

Reinforcement and Remediation

CHAPTER OBJECTIVES	MIDCHAPTER REVIEW ITEMS	STUDENT BOOK PAGES	TEACHER'S EDITION PAGES		TEACHER RESOURCES
			Activities	Alternate Teaching Strategy	Reteach
*5A	1–3, 13–14, 17–18	170–171	169A	171	42
*5B	4–7	172–173	171A	173	43
*5C	8–12, 15–16, 19–20	174–177, 178–181	173A, 177C	177, 181	44, 45
*5D	21–25	182–183	181A	183	46

*5A Multiply multiples of 10, 100, 1,000 by a 1-digit factor
*5B Estimate products, including money amounts
*5C Multiply numbers by 1-digit factors, including money amounts
*5D Solve problems, including those that involve multiplication and solving a multistep problem

Compare Exact Answers to Estimates

[G]arcía Products donated 8 boxes of games to the hospital. [E]ach box holds 32 games. Are there enough games to give [a]s gifts to the 240 children at the hospital?

[E]stimate to solve this problem.

[E]xact [N]umbers	Estimate	Compare
[8] x 32	8 × 30 = 240	Since 32 > 30, the exact answer is greater than 240.

[Y]es, there are enough games. [T]here are more than 240 of them.

[E]stimate to solve the problem. Is the exact answer [g]reater than or less than your estimate? **Tell why.** See page T17.

1 The 4-H Club has $3,000. The members voted to buy 3 wheelchairs that cost $1,397 each for a hospital. Does the club have enough money? No; exact cost is greater.

2 The Key Club is saving money to donate a $320 television set to charity. The club can save $42 a month for 8 months. Will it have enough money? Yes; exact amount is greater.

3 Circus Products packs 48 toy clowns in a box. Are there enough clowns in 6 boxes for 300 children if each child gets 1 toy? No; exact number is less.

4 Ms. Kim works 34 hours a week in a hospital lab. She earns $9 an hour. Does she earn at least $270 a week? Yes; exact earnings are greater.

5 The Computer Club washes cars to raise money for charity. They charge $7 for each car. They wash 47 cars. Have they raised $350? No; exact amount is less.

6 The Grin and Bear It Company packages 24 toy bears in a box. Are there enough bears in 5 boxes for 100 children? Yes; exact number is greater.

7 The staff at Children's Hospital is having a holiday party for 180 children. They have 9 packages of cups with 15 cups in a package. Are there enough cups for the party? No; exact amount is less.

8 Kareem works 12 hours a week as a hospital volunteer. If he volunteers at least 40 hours a month, he gets free lunch in the cafeteria. Does he get his lunch free? Yes; exact number is greater.

Multiply by 1-Digit Numbers **185**

OBJECTIVE Solve problems by estimating products.

Using Number Sense

Math Connection In Lesson 2, students used rounding to estimate products. Here students decide whether the exact products are greater than or less than the estimated products.

After students read the opening problem and solution, reinforce the comparison by asking:
- **What two multiplication examples are being compared?** [8 × 32 and 8 × 30]
- **How does knowing that 32 > 30 help you know that the exact product is greater than 240?** [Since 32 is greater than 30, the exact answer for 8 × 32 (256) is greater than 8 × 30 (240).]
- **In what situations do you want to know if your estimate is greater than the exact answer? less than the exact answer?** [Possible answers: saving for a particular goal; fundraising for a certain amount]

Students may work in small groups or on their own to complete ex. 1–8.

Applying Multiplication

OBJECTIVE Collect data and use multiplication in a social studies context.

Materials per group: 50 sheets of paper, clock or watch, calculators

1 Engage

Make sure students understand how an assembly line operates. For example, in a car assembly line, people, robots, and machines work beside a moving belt that carries the unfinished car past them. Each worker or machine does a special job such as connecting the radio or framing the windshield.

- **What is an example of an assembly line that you use at home?** [Possible answers: doing the dishes]

2 Investigate

Demonstrate how to follow the diagrams to fold an $8\frac{1}{2}$-inch-by-11-inch piece of paper into a paper airplane. Then ask students to do the same.

Making Paper Airplanes Form teams of three students. Using the Triad Practice Strategy, have team members speak aloud to each other as they plan how they will divide the tasks to set up their assembly lines. On their first attempt, some teams may discover that certain tasks on the assembly line take longer to complete and cause congestion at points on the assembly line.

To increase production, students could recommend reassigning tasks so that each task will take approximately the same amount of time to complete. Teams should be able to make about 8 airplanes in 5 minutes.

3 Reflect and Share

Materials have available: calculators

Report Your Findings As you discuss student reports, demonstrate the cumulative effect of multiplying the number of planes made in 5 minutes by 12 (an hour), then by 7 (a work day), and then by 5 (a week). For example:

8 planes in 5 min = $8 \times 12 \times 7 \times 5$ = 3,360 planes a wk

9 planes in 5 min = $9 \times 12 \times 7 \times 5$ = 3,780 planes a wk

Note that increasing the 5-minute output by just 1 airplane is significant.

- **Do you think that your team could produce 8 airplanes every 5 minutes for 7 hours a day? Why or why not?** [Fewer would probably be made because people get tired, paper runs out, and people take breaks.]

Paper Plane Factory

Assembly lines are used in many factories to increase the number of items made. In this activity, you will work in teams to make paper planes on an assembly line.

You will need
- *sheets of paper*

steps:

1 Fold in half and open up.

2 Fold corners A and B to center line.

3 Fold corners C and D to center line.

4 Fold in half.

5 Fold the wings down to complete.

More To Investigate

Predict Sample approaches: Add the number of planes each group predicted they could make in a day and multiply by the number of weekdays in the month; add the number of planes each group predicted that they could make in a week and multiply by 4.

Explore Sample answer: Throwing the plane produces thrust, a forward force. Air traveling over and under the wings causes lift.

Find According to the *1995 Guinness Book of Records,* the world record is 18.8 seconds, set by Ken Blackburn on February 17, 1994.

Bibliography Students who wish to learn more about paper airplanes can read *The World Record Paper Airplane Book,* by Ken Blackburn. New York: Workman Publishing, 1994. ISBN 1–56305–631–3.

DECISION MAKING

Making Paper Airplanes

1 Form an assembly line to make paper planes. Use the design on the left. Let each person make one or more of the folds.

2 How many planes can your assembly line make in 5 minutes?

3 Decide how you can change your assembly line to increase the number of planes that your team can make. Make a new plan for your assembly line.

4 How many planes can your new assembly line make in 5 minutes?

Reporting Your Findings

5 Prepare a report on what you learned. Include the following:

▶ Describe how your assembly line workers shared the work to make the greatest number of planes in 5 minutes. How many planes did they make?

▶ Predict the number of planes your assembly line could make in:
  a. one hour.
  b. a 7-hour day.
  c. a 5-day week.

Explain how you made your predictions.

6 Compare your report with the reports of other teams.

Revise your work.
▶ Are your calculations correct?
▶ Is your report clear and organized?
▶ Did you proofread your work?

MORE TO INVESTIGATE

See Teacher's Edition.

PREDICT the number of paper planes your entire class could make in a month.

EXPLORE why paper planes fly.

FIND the world record for indoor flight-time of a paper plane.

Building A Portfolio

This investigation will allow you to evaluate students' ability to organize data and to multiply in order to solve a problem.

Allow students to review their work for the portfolio. Each student's portfolio piece should consist of a copy of her or his written report about the team's findings, which includes their predictions for the output of their assembly line in one hour, a 7-hour day, and a 5-day week.

You may use the Holistic Scoring Guide to assess this task. See page 27 in Teacher's Assessment Resources.

Student's Work

LESSON 5.6

Multiply Greater Numbers

OBJECTIVE Multiply greater numbers by 1-digit numbers.

RESOURCE REMINDER
Math Center Cards 47
Practice 47, Reteach 47, Extend 47

SKILLS TRACE

GRADE 3	• Multiply 2-digit numbers by 1-digit numbers. *(Chapter 12)*
GRADE 4	• Multiply 3- and 4-digit numbers by 1-digit numbers.
GRADE 5	• Apply multiplying 4-digit numbers by 1-digit numbers. *(Chapter 4)*

MANIPULATIVE WARM-UP

Cooperative Pairs   **Logical/Analytical**

OBJECTIVE Multiply 3-digit numbers by 1-digit numbers.

Materials per pair: place-value models—at least 4 hundreds, 17 tens, 21 ones

▶ In pairs, students use place-value models to show 3 groups of 147. They combine the models and regroup to find 3 × 157. *[471]*

▶ Students repeat the activity with different 3-digit numbers. Have students explain how the models help them find the products.

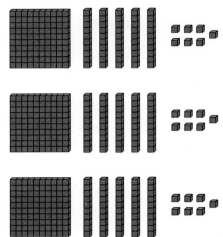

ESL APPROPRIATE

LITERATURE CONNECTION

Whole Class   **Logical/Analytical**

OBJECTIVE Use manipulatives to solve combination problems.

Materials per student: inch graph paper (TA 8), calculator

Resource Read-Aloud Anthology, pp. 25–28

▶ Students will use the story *The Rajah's Rice* to create a multiplication pattern. First, have students draw an 8-by-8 grid on graph paper.

▶ Then, read the story, stopping when the two servants place 256 grains of rice on the eighth square of the Rajah's chessboard. Have students write 2 in the first box and write each successive product in the boxes to model the Rajah's use of the chessboard to record how much rice he owes. Have students use calculators to find the number of grains of rice owed by the sixteenth day. *[65,536]*

2	4	8	16	32	64	128	258

Daily Review

Math Van

PREVIOUS DAY QUICK REVIEW

Write >, <, or =.

1. 23 × 6 _____ 150 [<]
2. 5 × 42 _____ 210 [=]
3. 326 _____ 72 × 6 [<]
4. 157 _____ 34 × 4 [>]

FAST FACTS

1. 7 × 3 [21]
2. 6 × 5 [30]
3. 9 × 2 [18]
4. 3 × 4 [12]

Problem of the Day • 47

Find the products: 9 × 11, 9 × 22, 9 × 33, and 9 × 44. Then use patterns to find 9 × 55 and 9 × 66. Tell which patterns you used. *[99, 198, 297, 396; 495; 594; possible pattern: hundreds increase by 1, tens remain 9, ones decrease by 1, hundreds and ones add up to 9.]*

TECH LINK

MATH VAN

Tool You may wish to use the Calculator with this lesson.

MATH FORUM

Idea When my students use the computer to formulate problems, I also encourage them to use the computer as a calculator to find answers.

Visit our Resource Village at http://www.mhschool.com to see more of the Math Forum.

MATH CENTER

Practice

OBJECTIVE Multiply greater numbers.

Materials per pair: number cards for 2–9; per student: Math Center Recording Sheet (TA 31 optional), calculator

Students complete multiplication function tables. They use calculators to check their partner's work, and score a point for each correct answer. After five games, the partner with the greater number of points wins.

PRACTICE ACTIVITY 47

MATH CENTER
Partners 👥

Algebra Sense • Multiplication Machines

- One of you copies Machine A, and the other copies Machine B.
- One of you picks a number card from the stack to determine the rule for the machine. Both of you then find the products to complete your machines.
- Use a calculator to check each other's work. You get one point for each correct product.

Repeat the activity five times. The person with the greater number of points wins.

YOU NEED

number cards (2–9)
calculators

MACHINE A
Rule: Multiply by _____

Input	Output
345	
607	
1,458	
6,070	

MACHINE B
Rule: Multiply by _____

Input	Output
527	
790	
2,072	
7,169	

Chapter 5, Lesson 6, pages 188–191

Multiplication

NCTM Standards

Problem Solving
✓ Communication
✓ Reasoning
Connections

Problem Solving

OBJECTIVE Use logical reasoning to solve problems.

Materials per student: Math Center Recording Sheet (TA 31 optional)

Students find different combinations of coins that total 55¢. Students may make a list, use patterns, or use the Guess, Test, and Revise strategy. *[2 Q, 1 N; 1 Q, 3 D; 1 Q, 2 D, 2 N; 1 Q, 1 D, 4 N; 1 Q, 6 N; 5 D, 1 N; 4 D, 3 N; 3 D, 5 N; 2 D, 7 N; 1 D, 9 N; 11 N]*

PROBLEM-SOLVING ACTIVITY 47

MATH CENTER
On Your Own 🧍

Logical Reasoning • Exact Change Only

This juice machine takes only quarters, dimes, and nickels. You must use exact change. What coins could you use to buy a can of juice? List all the possible coins.

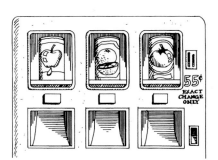

Chapter 5, Lesson 6, pages 188–191

Multiplication

NCTM Standards

✓ Problem Solving
Communication
✓ Reasoning
✓ Connections

Lesson 5.6 *continued*

Multiply Greater Numbers

OBJECTIVE Multiply greater numbers by 1-digit numbers.

Materials per student: place-value models—at least 3 hundreds, 10 tens, 6 ones; calculator

1 Introduce

Write place-value clues on the chalkboard and have students list numbers that match each clue.

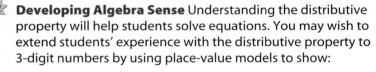

a. 4 in the hundreds place

b. 6 in the thousands place

c. 2 in the hundreds place and 8 in the thousands place

Have students pick a number from each list and write the expanded form, for example:

$$485 = (4 \times 100) + (8 \times 10) + (5 \times 1) \text{ or}$$
$$4 \text{ hundreds } 8 \text{ tens } 5 \text{ ones}$$

2 Teach
Whole Class

▶ **LEARN** Discuss the estimate and how the place-value models show the steps.

- **In Step 3, where did the 1 new hundred come from?** [*Possible answer: The 1 is the hundred that was regrouped from Step 2.*]

- **In Step 3, why do you multiply the hundreds before adding the new hundred?** [*There are 2 groups of 1 hundred plus an additional hundred formed by regrouping the tens.*]

Developing Algebra Sense Understanding the distributive property will help students solve equations. You may wish to extend students' experience with the distributive property to 3-digit numbers by using place-value models to show:

$$2 \times 163 = (2 \times 100) + (2 \times 60) + (2 \times 3)$$
$$= 200 + 120 + 6 = 326$$

Have students work through an example, such as 4×621, that involves regrouping hundreds to thousands. Have them compare regrouping hundreds to thousands and regrouping tens to hundreds.

Talk It Over To help students answer the second question, ask:

- **How are finding 3×242 and 3×42 alike? different?** [*Possible answer: Steps 1 and 2 are the same in both cases, but for 3×242, another step is needed for hundreds.*]

Multiply Greater Numbers

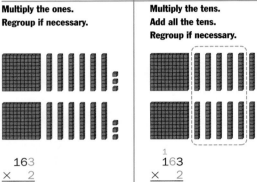

An old bottling machine puts 163 caps on bottles each hour. The factory bought a new robot that is 2 times as fast. How many bottles can the robot cap each hour?

To estimate the number of bottles the robot can cap each hour, use mental math.

Think: $2 \times 200 = 400$

To find the exact answer, use pencil and paper.

Step 1	Step 2	Step 3
Multiply the ones. Regroup if necessary.	**Multiply the tens. Add all the tens. Regroup if necessary.**	**Multiply the hundreds. Add all the hundreds. Regroup if necessary.**

$$\begin{array}{r} 163 \\ \times\ \ 2 \\ \hline 6 \end{array}$$

$$\begin{array}{r} 1\ \ \ \\ 163 \\ \times\ \ 2 \\ \hline 26 \end{array}$$

$$\begin{array}{r} 1\ \ \ \\ 163 \\ \times\ \ 2 \\ \hline 326 \end{array}$$

Think: 2×3 ones $= 6$ ones

Think:
2×6 tens $= 12$ tens
12 tens $= 1$ hundred 2 tens

Think:
2×1 hundred $= 2$ hundreds
2 hundreds $+ 1$ hundred $= 3$ hundreds

The robot can cap 326 bottles each hour.

Talk It Over
▶ How do you know the answer is reasonable? It is close to the estimate, 400.

▶ How is multiplying 3-digit numbers the same as multiplying 2-digit numbers? How is it different?
Possible answer: Same—the digits are multiplied, and place value is used to record properly; different—more digits are multiplied for 3-digit numbers.

188 Lesson 5.6

Meeting Individual Needs

Extra Support

Some students may fail to record the regrouped digit after each step. Have students make a small circle above each digit to the left of the ones place as a reminder before beginning to multiply.

Inclusion

Have students who are having trouble with the sequence of multiplying, regrouping, and adding find each partial product as a separate problem. Then they can add to find the final product.

Ongoing Assessment

Anecdotal Report Note if students know how and when to regroup when multiplying 3-digit numbers by 1-digit numbers.

Follow Up Have students who are multiplying incorrectly try turning lined paper vertically. This helps them align the digits correctly. For additional help, assign **Reteach 47**.

For students who are multiplying accurately, assign **Extend 47**.

What if a machine labels 2,342 bottles each hour. How many bottles can the machine label in 7 hours?

Multiply: 7 × 2,342

You can use paper and pencil to find the product.

$$\begin{array}{r} {\scriptstyle 2\ 21} \\ 2{,}342 \\ \times\ \ \ \ 7 \\ \hline 16{,}394 \end{array}$$

 You can also use a calculator.

7 × 2,342 = *16394.*

The machine can label 16,394 bottles in 7 hours.

More Examples

A
$$\begin{array}{r} {\scriptstyle 4} \\ 107 \\ \times\ \ 6 \\ \hline 642 \end{array}$$

B
$$\begin{array}{r} {\scriptstyle 3\ 4} \\ 356 \\ \times\ \ 7 \\ \hline 2{,}492 \end{array}$$

C
$$\begin{array}{r} {\scriptstyle 2} \\ 1{,}009 \\ \times\ \ \ \ 3 \\ \hline 3{,}027 \end{array}$$

D
$$\begin{array}{r} {\scriptstyle 2\ 21} \\ \$2{,}563 \\ \times\ \ \ \ 4 \\ \hline \$10{,}252 \end{array}$$

Check for Understanding

Multiply. Estimate to check that your answer is reasonable. Estimates may vary. Estimates given are by rounding.

1
$$\begin{array}{r} 401 \\ \times\ 3 \\ \hline \end{array}$$
1,203; 1,200

2
$$\begin{array}{r} 997 \\ \times\ 2 \\ \hline \end{array}$$
1,994; 2,000

3
$$\begin{array}{r} 1{,}750 \\ \times\ \ \ \ 4 \\ \hline \end{array}$$
7,000; 8,000

4
$$\begin{array}{r} 8{,}002 \\ \times\ \ \ \ 3 \\ \hline \end{array}$$
24,006; 24,000

5
$$\begin{array}{r} \$8{,}765 \\ \times\ \ \ \ \ 9 \\ \hline \end{array}$$
$78,885; $81,000

6 6 × 115
690; 600

7 9 × 843
7,587; 7,200

8 2 × 3,472
6,944; 6,000

9 8 × 7,183
57,464; 56,000

Critical Thinking: Analyze **Explain your reasoning.**

10 You use a calculator to find 6 × 3,336. The display reads *200016.* . Is the answer reasonable?
No; 200,016 is much greater than the estimate, 18,000.

11 What error might you make when using a calculator to multiply? Possible answer: Push wrong numbers or keys.

12 Is it always easier to multiply greater numbers using a calculator? Give an example to support your reasons.
No; sometimes using mental math is easier, for example, finding 9 × 8,000.

Turn the page for Practice.
Multiply by 1-Digit Numbers **189**

The example on Student Book page 189 involves the final step of the paper-and-pencil method for a 4-digit factor. Multiply the thousands, add any new thousands, regroup if necessary. Show students that this step is just an extension of earlier steps.

Review the procedures for using a calculator to multiply. Have students use their calculators to multiply 7 × 2,342. Ask:

- **Where does the comma go in the product?** *[between the 6 and 3]*
- **How could you check the reasonableness of your answer?** *[Use estimation: 7 × 2,000 = 14,000, so 16,394 is reasonable.]*

More Examples For each example, ask students to tell what was regrouped.

You may want to discuss with students the various methods they can use to multiply. Draw out the reasoning they would use to decide on a specific method. It may be helpful to create a chart like the one below.

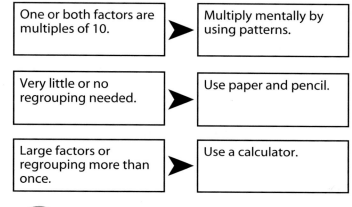

One or both factors are multiples of 10.	Multiply mentally by using patterns.
Very little or no regrouping needed.	Use paper and pencil.
Large factors or regrouping more than once.	Use a calculator.

3 Close

Check for Understanding by assigning items 1–12, page 189.

CRITICAL THINKING
After discussing item 12, have students take another look at items 1–9 and indicate which are especially suited for a calculator and explain why.

Practice See pages 190–191.

189

▶ **PRACTICE**

Materials have available: calculators

Options for assigning exercises:
A—Odd ex. 1–33; all ex. 35–39; **Cultural Connection**
B—Even ex. 2–34; all ex. 35–39; **Cultural Connection**

- Encourage students to use number sense and estimation to eliminate choices in ex. 17–28.
- For **Make It Right** (ex. 35) see Common Error below.

 Algebra In ex. 29–31, students apply their knowledge of multiplication to interpreting and completing function tables. In ex. 32–34, students explore the concept of variables. Students use algebraic thinking to find the missing factor.

Draw Conclusions For ex. 38, have students explain what information they used to draw a conclusion about replacing the machines. Then ask students if they would replace a Becker machine with an Adams machine. Point out that conclusions sometimes differ. Encourage students to use the data and prior information to explain their conclusions.

Cultural Connection Ask volunteers to read the introduction and problem. Point out that much of our knowledge of Egyptian mathematics comes from a document called the Ahmes (AH-mus) papyrus, after the scribe who wrote it. Scribes were among the few people who learned to read and write at the time. They kept records about every part of Egyptian social and economic life. Discuss how records about our society are kept today.

After students have worked through the example, help them see that products can be added in more than one way to find the final product. Demonstrate by using ex. 12:

$$7 \times 333 = (1 \times 333) + (2 \times 333) + (4 \times 333)$$

or

$$= (1 \times 333) + (2 \times 333) + (2 \times 333) + (2 \times 333)$$

or

$$= (1 \times 333) + (1 \times 333) + (1 \times 333) + (2 \times 333)$$
$$+ (2 \times 333)$$

Have groups solve a problem in as many ways as they can.

Practice

Multiply. Remember to estimate.

1	**2**	**3**	**4**	**5**
123	181	206	437	$961
× 4	× 5	× 7	× 2	× 3
492	905	1,442	874	$2,883

6	**7**	**8**	**9**	**10**
1,172	$4,903	5,092	9,238	$8,24_
× 3	× 8	× 4	× 9	× _
3,516	$39,224	20,368	83,142	$16,49_

11 4 × 612 2,448　**12** 7 × 333 2,331　**13** 6 × 6,553 39,318　**14** 8 × $7,423 $59,384

15 Find the product of 3 and 278. 834　**16** What is 7 times 5,594? 39,158

Find only products between 1,200 and 60,000.
Use estimation to help you decide.

17 2 × 415　less than 1,200　**18** 2 × 671 1,342　**19** 5 × 222　less than 1,200　**20** 5 × 4,716 23,580

21 8 × 5,864 46,912　**22** 9 × 6,018 54,162　**23** 4 × 1,789 7,156　**24** 3 × 4,881 14,643

25 7 × 9,011　more than 60,000　**26** 9 × 6,123 55,107　**27** 2 × 4,760 9,520　**28** 8 × 8,007　more than 6_

 ALGEBRA Complete the table.

29 Rule: Multiply by 3.		**30** Multiply by 2. Rule: ▪		**31** Multiply by 5. Rule: ▪	
Input	**Output**	**Input**	**Output**	**Input**	**Output**
27	▪ 81	91	182	21	105
403	▪ 1,209	403	806	301	1,505
5,010	▪ 15,030	3,700	7,400	2,005	10,025

 ALGEBRA Write the letter of the missing number.

32 ▪ × 333 = 999 b　　a. 5　b. 3　c. 2　d. 4

33 ▪ × 876 = 3,504 c　　a. 9　b. 2　c. 4　d. 5

34 5 × ▪ = 11,110 a　　a. 2,222　b. 2,111　c. 1,111　d. 5,555

┅┅┅┅┅┅┅┅┅ **Make It Right** ┅┅┅┅┅┅┅┅┅

35 Helen multiplied 2,135 by 4.
Explain what the mistake is.
Show the correct answer.

$$\begin{array}{r} {}^{1\,22} \\ 2{,}135 \\ \times\ \ \ 4 \\ \hline 12{,}200 \end{array}$$

$$\begin{array}{r} {}^{12} \\ 2{,}135 \\ \times\ \ \ 4 \\ \hline 8{,}540 \end{array}$$

She added the regrouped number before multiplying.

Meeting Individual Needs

Early Finishers

Extend the **Greatest Product Game!** on page 177 by having students try to find the greatest product of a 3-digit number and a 1-digit number. Let students use calculators to develop number-sense strategies.

ESL **APPROPRIATE**

COMMON ERROR

As in the **Make It Right** (ex. 35), some students may add a regrouped number before multiplying. If this happens, point out that adding 3 + 2 and then multiplying by 4 means that 4 groups of 5 were regrouped. Have students model this error and compare it to multiplying 3 by 4 and then adding 2.

8. Possible answer: She needed to produce more umbrellas so she chose the Croy machine that makes 1,200 umbrellas.

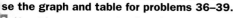

MIXED APPLICATIONS
Problem Solving

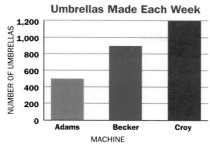

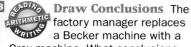
Use the graph and table for problems 36–39.

36 About how many umbrellas does the Adams machine make in 7 weeks? **about 3,500 umbrellas**

37 How much would it cost to buy 3 Adams machines and 6 Croy machines? **$36,438**

38 **Draw Conclusions** The factory manager replaces a Becker machine with a Croy machine. What conclusions can you draw about her decision? **See above.**

39 **Write a problem** that can be solved using the graph or the table. Solve it and have others solve it. **Students should compare problems and solutions.**

Umbrellas Made Each Week

(bar graph, NUMBER OF UMBRELLAS on y-axis from 0 to 1,200; MACHINE on x-axis: Adams, Becker, Croy)

Machine	Cost of Each Machine
Adams	$798
Becker	$1,453
Croy	$5,674

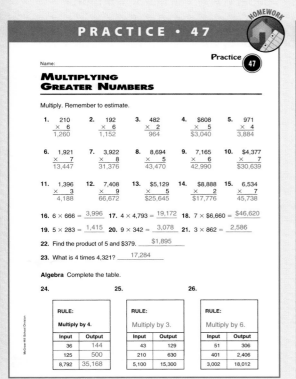

Cultural Connection
Egyptian Multiplication

In ancient Egypt, scribes kept records of payments to the pharaoh. As we do today, they used a number system based on ten. They used a line for 1 (|), a heel bone for 10 (∩), and a snare for 100 (ꝯ). The number 142 would be ꝯ∩∩∩∩||.

What if 5 people paid 142 baskets of wheat each? Here is how the scribes would find 5×142.

Start with 142 and double the numbers.	Find those that add up to 5.	Add their products.
$1 \times 142 = 142$	$1 \times 142 = 142$	142
$2 \times 142 = 284$	$2 \times 142 = 284$	$+568$
$4 \times 142 = 568$	$4 \times 142 = 568$	$5 \times 142 = 710$

Use this method to solve ex. 17, 19, 23, and 25 on page 190. **Check students' work.**

Extra Practice, page 502

Multiply by 1-Digit Numbers **191**

Alternate Teaching Strategy

Write these two examples on the board.

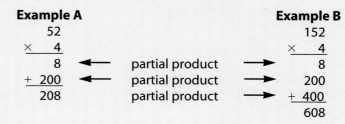

Example A		Example B
52		152
$\times\ 4$		$\times\ 4$
8	← partial product →	8
$+\ 200$	← partial product →	200
208	partial product →	$+\ 400$
		608

Ask students to explain what is the same and what is different about the examples.

• **Why does Example B have three different products?**
[There is a hundred in 152 that needs to be multiplied by 4.]

Continue the activity with other multiplication examples, including those with 4-digit factors.

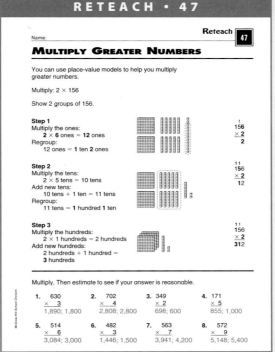

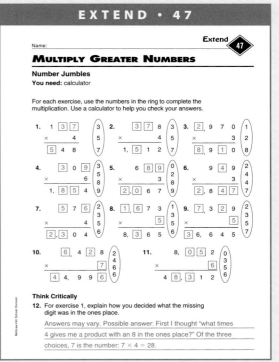

Multiply with Money

OBJECTIVE Multiply money amounts by 1-digit numbers.

RESOURCE REMINDER
Math Center Cards 48
Practice 48, Reteach 48, Extend 48

SKILLS TRACE

GRADE 3
• Multiply 2-digit money amounts by 1-digit numbers. (*Chapter 12*)

GRADE 4
• Multiply money amounts by 1-digit numbers.

GRADE 5
• Apply multiplying money amounts. (*Chapter 4*)

MANIPULATIVE WARM-UP

Cooperative Pairs   **Kinesthetic**

OBJECTIVE Multiply money amounts by 1-digit numbers.

Materials per pair: play money—9 ten-dollar bills, 20 one-dollar bills, 20 dimes, 30 pennies

► Each pair of students uses play money to show 3 × $1.41.

► Students repeat the activity with different 3- and 4-digit money amounts.

► Ask them to explain how the models help them find the products.

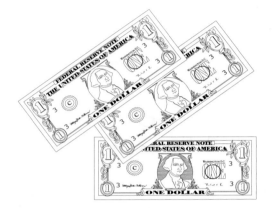

ESL APPROPRIATE

STATISTICS CONNECTION

Cooperative Pairs   **Visual/Spatial**

OBJECTIVE Use a line graph to show change in savings over time.

Materials per pair: centimeter graph paper (TA 7), calculator, computer graphing program (optional)

► Have partners choose an amount of money they might want to save each week. Check to see that a variety of amounts is chosen.

► Partners create tables to show the total saved each week for 2 months. Then they use this data to make a line graph.

► Have pairs of students compare their graphs, then determine how much they would save in 6 months, 1 year, and so on.

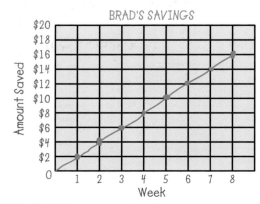

BRAD'S SAVINGS

Daily Review

Math Van

PREVIOUS DAY QUICK REVIEW

Multiply.
1. 246 × 6 [1,476]
2. $481 × 3 [$1,443]
3. 5 × 3,438 [17,190]
4. 4 × $6,821 [$27,284]

FAST FACTS

1. 6 ÷ 3 [2]
2. 8 ÷ 2 [4]
3. 7 ÷ 1 [7]
4. 12 ÷ 6 [2]

Problem of the Day • 48

You have 30¢. You have 6 coins. What coins do you have? [Possible answers: 1 quarter, 5 pennies; 6 nickels]

TECH LINK

MATH VAN

Tool You may wish to use the Money tool with this lesson.

MATH FORUM

Idea I have my students collect catalogs, sales flyers, menus, and ads so that they can use real prices when they write problems.

Visit our Resource Village at http://www.mhschool.com to see more of the Math Forum.

MATH CENTER

Practice

OBJECTIVE Multiply money amounts.

Materials per student: calculator, Math Center Recording Sheet (TA 31 optional)

Students take turns being the salesperson who finds the total cost of purchases.

PRACTICE ACTIVITY 48

MATH CENTER
Partners 👥

Number Sense • The Price Is Right!

One of you acts as a salesperson. The other acts as a customer.

- The customer chooses from 1 to 9 of each item to buy.
- The salesperson writes a sales slip for the customer's order. The sales slip should show the cost per item, how many of each item is being bought, the total cost for each product, and the grand total.
- The customer checks the total on a calculator.

Trade roles and repeat the activity.

YOU NEED
: calculators

Shine Toothpaste	$2.59 a tube
Best Soap	$0.95 a bar
Glint Shampoo	$2.75 a bottle
Whoosh Mouthwash	$1.78 a bottle

SALES SLIP

Item	Cost per item	Quantity	Total Cost
Shine Toothpaste	$2.59	3	$7.77
		GRAND TOTAL:	

Grade Level 4   McGraw-Hill School Division

Chapter 5, Lesson 7, pages 192–193

Multiplication

NCTM Standards
- ✓ Problem Solving
- ✓ Communication
- ✓ Reasoning
- ✓ Connections

Problem Solving

OBJECTIVE Solve multistep problems involving money.

Materials per student: Math Center Recording Sheet (TA 31 optional)

Students use a price list to calculate the costs of printing various words or phrases on a T-shirt.

PROBLEM-SOLVING ACTIVITY 48

MATH CENTER
On Your Own 👤

Using Data • Words Worth

Suppose you are buying three different T-shirts.
1. How much would it cost to print your name on a T-shirt?
2. Choose a city or country that you like. How much would it cost to print its name on a T-shirt?
3. What would you like your third T-shirt to say? How much would it cost to print that?

Words Are Us

Print words at a reasonable price! Cost includes T-shirt!

Vowel	$2.27
R	$1.29
T	$1.30
S	$1.32
Other consonants	$3.35

Take $2.50 off if your purchase is more than $10.

Grade Level 4   McGraw-Hill School Division

Chapter 5, Lesson 7, pages 192–193

Multiplication

NCTM Standards
- ✓ Problem Solving
- ✓ Communication
- ✓ Reasoning
- ✓ Connections

Lesson 5.7 *continued*

Multiply Money

OBJECTIVE Multiply money amounts by 1-digit numbers.

Materials per student: calculator

 **Introduce**

Resource Read-Aloud Anthology, pp. 29–30

Read "Good Hot Dogs" from the Read-Aloud Anthology to present a situation that involves multiplying money amounts. If $0.50 is the cost of one lunch, have students write number sentences to show how to find the costs of 2, 3, and 4 lunches. *[2 × $0.50 = $1.00; 3 × $0.50 = $1.50; 4 × $0.50 = $2.00]*

2 Teach *Whole Class*

Cultural Connection Read the **Cultural Note** on page 192. Point out that a chipao (also spelled ch'i-p'ao) is a modified form of a traditional fashion from the Manchu Ch'ing Dynasty. Have students share what they know of traditional clothing.

▶ **LEARN** Read the introductory problem. Review how the estimate was found by rounding to the greatest place.

As you review the methods shown for multiplying money amounts, discuss the placement of the decimal point.
  • **How do you know where to place the dollar sign and decimal point in the product?** *[$317 is close to the estimate of $300, so the decimal point is between 7 and 9.]*

More Examples Point out that there is no need to enter a zero before the decimal point when using a calculator.

 **Close**

▶ **Check for Understanding** by assigning items 1–7, page 192.

CRITICAL THINKING
For item 6, explain that calculators do not display unnecessary zeros to the right of the decimal point.

▶ **PRACTICE**
Materials have available: calculators

Options for assigning exercises:
A—Choice of fifteen exercises from ex. 1–23; all ex. 24–28; **Mixed Review**
B—Choice of eight exercises from ex. 1–15; all ex. 16–28; **Mixed Review**
• For ex. 1–23, encourage students to use estimation to check the reasonableness of their answers.

Mixed Review/Test Preparation Students review addition and subtraction of greater numbers, learned in Chapter 2.

Multiply Money

Cultural Note
A chipao is a traditional Chinese dress.

Mrs. Hsu is buying 6 yards of silk to make *chipaos* (CHEE-powz). Each yard costs $52.99. What will be the total cost?

To estimate the cost, use mental math.

Think: 6 × $50 = $300

You can use pencil and paper to find the exact answer.

$$\begin{array}{r} {\scriptstyle 1\,5\ 5} \\ \$52.99 \\ \times\ \ \ \ \ 6 \\ \hline \$317.94 \end{array}$$

 You can also use a calculator.
6 × 52.99 = *317.94*

↑ ↑
Write a dollar sign and a decimal point in the product.

The total cost will be $317.94.

More Examples

A
$$\begin{array}{r} {\scriptstyle 5} \\ \$0.47 \\ \times\ \ \ \ 8 \\ \hline \$3.76 \end{array}$$
8 × 0.47 = *3.76*

B
$$\begin{array}{r} {\scriptstyle 2} \\ \$6.03 \\ \times\ \ \ \ 9 \\ \hline \$54.27 \end{array}$$
9 × 6.03 = *54.27*

Check for Understanding
Multiply. Estimate to check the reasonableness of your answer. Estimates may vary. Estimates given are by rounding.

1	**2**	**3**	**4**	**5**
$0.09	$0.64	$7.32	$36.12	$94.7
× 8	× 7	× 5	× 2	×
$0.72; $0.80	$4.48; $4.20	$36.60; $35.00	$72.24; $80.00	$379.0 $360.0

Critical Thinking: Analyze **Explain your reasoning.**

6 You use a calculator to find 6 x $3.45. The display reads *20.7* . What is the answer? Explain how you know that the answer is reasonable. **$20.70; it is close to the estimate of $18 (6 × $3).**

7 How does finding the product of 4 and 5,482 help you to find the product of 4 and $54.82? **The digits in the product of 4 × $54.82 are the same as the digits in the product of 4 × 5,482, but a decimal point has to be put in the money prod**

192 Lesson 5.7

Meeting Individual Needs

Early Finishers
Have students try this problem:
Suppose that a candy bar costs 15¢ in 1980 and that the price tripled every 5 years. What will be the price of the candy bar in the year 2000? *[$12.15]*

Extra Support
Some students may forget to place the decimal point in the answer when multiplying money amounts. Have these students write a decimal point directly below the decimal point in the factor before multiplying.

Ongoing Assessment
Observation Checklist
Observe if students make the connection between multiplying whole numbers and multiplying money amounts. Have them compute 5 × $46.79 and explain each step.

Follow Up Have students who are not recording correctly write the examples on graph paper. For additional help, assign **Reteach 48**.

For students who are multiplying accurately, assign **Extend 48**.

Practice

Multiply. Remember to estimate.

1 $0.52 × 6 $3.12	**2** $0.93 × 7 $6.51	**3** $7.04 × 8 $56.32	**4** $0.58 × 4 $2.32	**5** $6.19 × 5 $30.95
6 $3.19 × 2 $6.38	**7** $63.86 × 5 $319.30	**8** $0.76 × 3 $2.28	**9** $9.84 × 3 $29.52	**10** $0.47 × 9 $4.23
11 $43.09 × 6 $258.54	**12** $8.21 × 9 $73.89	**13** $56.87 × 2 $113.74	**14** $25.49 × 8 $203.92	**15** $81.79 × 6 $490.74

16 3 × $0.84
 $2.52

17 8 × $24.95
 $199.60

18 2 × $4.75
 $9.50

19 $70.39 × 6
 $422.34

20 7 × $6.93
 $48.51

21 9 × $0.19
 $1.71

22 $7.82 × 5
 $39.10

23 4 × $85.85
 $343.40

MIXED APPLICATIONS
Problem Solving

Use the table to solve problems 24–27.

24 How many chipaos can Mrs. Hsu make with the 6 yards of silk fabric that she bought?
3 chipaos

25 Mr. Li plans to make 5 vests and 4 jackets. How much fabric does he need?
13 yd of fabric

26 **Make a decision** Mei can make a chipao in 6 hours. How much should she charge for selling it? Explain your reasoning. **Students' decisions should reflect data provided.**

27 **Write a problem** that uses information from the table. Solve it and ask others to solve it. **Students should compare problems and solutions.**

28 A weaver uses the silk from 10 cocoons. About how many yards of thread does the weaver use? **SEE INFOBIT.** **Possible answer: up to 10,000 yd of thread**

COST OF HANDMADE CLOTHING

Item	Fabric	Yards Needed	Cost for each Yard
Chipao	Silk	2	$52.99
Vest	Satin	1	$23.45
Jacket	Cotton	2	$31.89

INFOBIT
Silk fabric is made from the cocoons of silkworms. When unwrapped, the strands from each cocoon yield up to 1,000 yards of silk thread.

mixed review · test preparation

1 13,467
 − 12,836
 631

2 5,083
 + 795
 5,878

3 19,726
 + 53,027
 72,753

4 3,791
 − 298
 3,493

5 $4,002
 − 3,145
 $857

Extra Practice, page 503

Multiply by 1-Digit Numbers **193**

Alternate Teaching Strategy

Materials play money—bills and coins

Write these examples on the chalkboard:

Example A	**Example B**
$3.46 × 4	346 cents × 4 24 cents 160 cents + 1200 cents 1,384 cents = $13.84

First, have students use play money to show the multiplication for Example A. Then have them explain how each partial product is found in Example B.

Continue the activity with other examples, including those involving multiplying 4-digit money amounts.

ESL APPROPRIATE

PRACTICE · 48

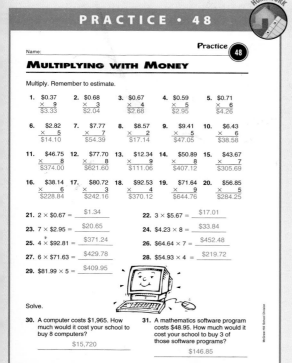

Practice 48

Name:

MULTIPLYING WITH MONEY

Multiply. Remember to estimate.

1. $0.37 × 9 $3.33	2. $0.68 × 3 $2.04	3. $0.67 × 4 $2.68	4. $0.59 × 5 $2.95	5. $0.71 × 6 $4.26
6. $2.82 × 5 $14.10	7. $7.77 × 7 $54.39	8. $8.57 × 2 $17.14	9. $9.41 × 5 $47.05	10. $6.43 × 6 $38.58
11. $46.75 × 8 $374.00	12. $77.70 × 8 $621.60	13. $12.34 × 9 $111.06	14. $50.89 × 8 $407.12	15. $43.67 × 7 $305.69
16. $38.14 × 6 $228.84	17. $80.72 × 3 $242.16	18. $92.53 × 4 $370.12	19. $71.64 × 9 $644.76	20. $56.85 × 5 $284.25

21. 2 × $0.67 = __$1.34__

22. 3 × $5.67 = __$17.01__

23. 7 × $2.95 = __$20.65__

24. $4.23 × 8 = __$33.84__

25. 4 × $92.81 = __$371.24__

26. $64.64 × 7 = __$452.48__

27. 6 × $71.63 = __$429.78__

28. $54.93 × 4 = __$219.72__

29. $81.99 × 5 = __$409.95__

Solve.

30. A computer costs $1,965. How much would it cost your school to buy 8 computers?
$15,720

31. A mathematics software program costs $48.95. How much would it cost your school to buy 3 of those software programs?
$146.85

RETEACH · 48

Reteach 48

Name:

MULTIPLY MONEY

Hector bought 4 pounds of tomatoes that cost $1.69 for each pound. How much did Hector pay for the tomatoes?

Multiply: 4 × $1.69

Step 1
Multiply the same way you multiply whole numbers.

Think: 4 × $2 is $8. The product should be about $8.

2 3
 $1.69
 × 4
 676

Step 2
Then write the dollar sign and the decimal point in the product.

2 3
 $1.69
 × 4
 $6.76

Hector paid $6.76 for the tomatoes.   Line up the decimal points.

Multiply. Then estimate to see if your answer is reasonable. Estimates may vary. Estimates given are by rounding to the greatest place.

1. $0.82 × 4 $3.28; $3.20	2. $0.16 × 5 $0.80; $1	3. $0.47 × 9 $4.23; $4.50	4. $0.26 × 8 $2.08; $2.40
5. $0.95 × 6 $5.70; $6	6. $3.09 × 2 $6.18; $6	7. $5.17 × 5 $25.85; $25	8. $2.98 × 4 $11.92; $12
9. $9.42 × 7 $65.94; $63	10. $6.74 × 9 $60.66; $63	11. $10.08 × 6 $60.48; $60	12. $31.79 × 8 $254.32; $240
13. $47.25 × 7 $330.75; $350	14. $62.20 × 9 $559.80; $540	15. $86.54 × 3 $259.62; $270	16. $72.63 × 5 $363.15; $350

EXTEND · 48

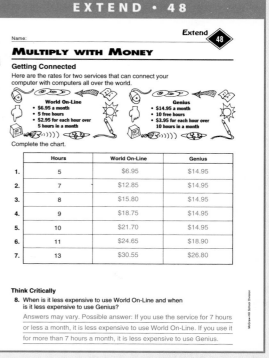

Extend 48

Name:

MULTIPLY WITH MONEY

Getting Connected

Here are the rates for two services that can connect your computer with computers all over the world.

World On-Line
• $6.95 a month
• 5 free hours
• $2.95 for each hour over 5 hours in a month

Genius
• $14.95 a month
• 10 free hours
• $3.95 for each hour over 10 hours in a month

Complete the chart.

	Hours	World On-Line	Genius
1.	5	$6.95	$14.95
2.	7	$12.85	$14.95
3.	8	$15.80	$14.95
4.	9	$18.75	$14.95
5.	10	$21.70	$14.95
6.	11	$24.65	$18.90
7.	13	$30.55	$26.80

Think Critically

8. When is it less expensive to use World On-Line and when is it less expensive to use Genius?
Answers may vary. Possible answer: If you use the service for 7 hours or less a month, it is less expensive to use World On-Line. If you use it for more than 7 hours a month, it is less expensive to use Genius.

Problem Solvers at Work

OBJECTIVE Write and solve problems by interpreting data.

RESOURCE REMINDER
Math Center Cards 49
Practice 49, Reteach 49, Extend 49

SKILLS TRACE

GRADE 3	• Use a graph or display to formulate and solve problems, including those that involve addition and subtraction. *(Chapter 5)*
GRADE 4	• Use a graph or display to formulate and solve problems, including those that involve multiplication.
GRADE 5	• Use a graph or display to formulate and solve problems, including those that involve multiplication. *(Chapter 4)*

WARM-UP

Cooperative Pairs   Logical/Analytical

OBJECTIVE Explore solving a problem using more than one method.

Materials have available: place-value models

▶ Present this problem to the class.
If you buy 4 full-price tickets to the museum theater you get 1 ticket free. What is the least number of tickets you must buy so that everyone in your class can go? *[Answers must include both full-price and free tickets.]*

▶ Groups work together to solve the problem using modeling, drawing a picture, finding a pattern, making a table, and using operations.

ALGEBRA CONNECTION

Cooperative Pairs   Logical/Analytical

OBJECTIVE Explore finding the rule in a function table.

▶ In pairs, have students draw a two-column table. One student decides on a rule such as "subtract 3" or "multiply by 1" without telling the other student. The second student writes a number in the first column of the table.

▶ The first student applies the rule to that number without revealing what was done and writes the answer in the second column.

▶ The second student tries to guess the rule. If unsuccessful, the partner writes and then operates on new numbers until the rule is found. Students switch roles, draw another table, and repeat the activity until each student has guessed five rules.

Rule: multiply by 7	
input	output
2	14
4	28
1	7

Rule: multiply by 6	
input	output
5	30
3	18
9	54

Daily Review

Problem of the Day • 49

Gail colors 4 squares red and 3 squares yellow. She colors 32 copies of this design in all. How many squares does she color altogether? How do you know? [224 squares; 4 + 3 = 7; 7 × 32 = 224]

FAST FACTS

1. 5 ÷ 1 [5]
2. 10 ÷ 2 [5]
3. 8 ÷ 4 [2]
4. 4 ÷ 2 [2]

TECH LINK

MATH VAN

Aid You may wish to use the Electronic Teacher Aid in the Math Van with this lesson.

MATH FORUM

Idea I use current events to spark ideas for writing problems. I ask my students to read, watch, or listen to the daily news.

Visit our Resource Village at http://www.mhschool.com to see more of the Math Forum.

MATH CENTER

Practice

OBJECTIVE Use and interpret data.

Materials per student: Math Center Recording Sheet (TA 31 optional)

Students use data from a chart and table to solve problems. [1. January, April; 2. action; 3. January]

PRACTICE ACTIVITY 49
MATH CENTER
On Your Own

Using Data • Video Madness

The table below shows Popcorn Video's rentals for the first four months of the year.

1. In which months did Popcorn Video make more than $900 in rentals?

2. Which type of video was most popular?

3. In which month did Popcorn Video make the most in rentals?

Write two problems of your own using the data in the table. Give them to a classmate to solve.

	Action	Comedy	Romance
Jan.	138	96	57
Feb.	102	74	61
March	115	50	77
April	96	89	85

Popcorn Video Rentals	
Action	$4
Comedy	$3
Romance	$3

Chapter 5, Lesson 8, pages 194–197

Multiplication

NCTM Standards
- ✓ Problem Solving
- ✓ Communication
- ✓ Reasoning
- ✓ Connections

Problem Solving

OBJECTIVE Make decisions using data in a map and table.

Materials per student: Math Center Recording Sheet (TA 31 optional)

Students identify and consider various factors before deciding which route to take. [1. 110 miles; 2. $4; 3. Route 26; 4. Answers may vary. Possible response: need to eat or to get gas; whether or not you are in a hurry; 5. Answers may vary.]

PROBLEM-SOLVING ACTIVITY 49
MATH CENTER
On Your Own

Decision Making • Which Way to Go?

You and your family are driving from Appleton to Cherryville.

1. How many miles is it between Appleton and Cherryville if you go along routes 118 and 5?

2. How much more would you pay in tolls if you used Route 26?

3. Which is the shorter route?

4. What other things should you think about in choosing a route?

5. If traffic on all routes was the same, which route would you take? Why?

TOLL CHART	
Route	Cost
26	$6
118	$1
5	$1

Cherryville

Route 5
Speed Limit:
40 miles per hour

Route 26
Speed Limit:
60 miles per hour

90 miles

40 miles

Appleton

Route 118
Speed Limit:
35 miles per hour

70 miles

Berryberg

Restaurant and gas station

Chapter 5, Lesson 8, pages 194–197

Multiplication

NCTM Standards
- ✓ Problem Solving
- ✓ Communication
- ✓ Reasoning
- ✓ Connections

Problem Solvers at Work

OBJECTIVE Write and solve problems by interpreting data.

Materials have available: calculators; computer spreadsheet program (optional); computer drawing program (optional)

 Introduce

Ask students to give examples of problem-solving methods they have used in the past. Tell them that interpreting data, using tables, working backward, guessing, testing, and revising, and solving multistep problems are among the methods that can be applied in this lesson.

Teach *Cooperative Groups*

PART 1 INTERPRET DATA

▶ **LEARN** Assign students to groups of three. Allow students to use calculators or a spreadsheet program as they solve items 1–5.

- **How do you find the value of the tickets sold each day?**
  [Multiply the number of adult tickets by $6, multiply the number of children's tickets by $4, and then add the two products.]

Draw Conclusions Invite volunteers to share their conclusions for item 2. Extend the concept by asking:
- **If the mill puts on another play, on what days can they expect to earn the most money?** *[Possible conclusion: Fridays and Saturdays, because the attendance will most likely be greater on these days.]*

For item 4, students may use a guess-test-and-revise strategy to find possible combinations of adult and children tickets. You may wish to record their responses in an organized list.

Item 5 is an enhanced problem as students need to make their own assumptions and decisions about a situation that has many different interpretations. Students may assume, for example, that senior citizens may take their grandchildren with them if they have a discount. Have students list any assumptions they make when they explain their reasoning.

Problem Solvers at Work

Part 1 Interpret Data

To keep the mill open for visitors, the mill needs to collect $500 worth of tickets each day.

The spreadsheet shows the number of people who bought tickets during a week in February.

	Adult	Children
Sunday	94	63
Monday	105	39
Tuesday	35	46
Wednesday	63	79
Thursday	34	65
Friday	57	86
Saturday	74	88

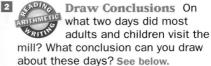

Mill Tour Admissions
Adults $6.00
Children (under 18) $4.00

4. Answers may vary. Possible answers: 70 adult, 80 children's, or 65 adult, 85 children's; yes.

Work Together
Solve. Use the information in the spreadsheet.

1 On which days were more than $500 worth of tickets sold? Sunday, Monday, Wednesday, Friday, Saturday

2 **Draw Conclusions** On what two days did most adults and children visit the mill? What conclusion can you draw about these days? See below.

3 On which day did the mill collect the most money for tours? Sunday

4 What if one day the mill sells 150 tickets and collects between $700 and $750. How many children's tickets are sold? How many adult tickets are sold? Is there more than one possible answer? See above.

5 **Make a decision** The mill manager can offer a discount either to schools or to senior citizens on Sundays, Mondays, or Tuesdays. Which discount would you choose? Which day? Why? See page T17.

194 Lesson 5.8   2. Friday and Saturday: Possible conclusions: People have more free time on weekends; people prefer to go out on weekends.

Meeting Individual Needs

Extra Support

Remind students that a pictograph uses a symbol to represent a number. Emphasize what number the symbol represents and what a partial symbol represents.

Gifted And Talented

Students who want an additional challenge can write a series of problems. The answer to each problem should provide information needed to solve the problem that follows.

Ongoing Assessment

Anecdotal Report Note if students can solve problems in an organized way.

Follow Up Help students who are having difficulty write a plan for solving each problem. Assign **Reteach 49.**

For students who successfully complete the lesson, assign **Extend 49.**

7. Problems may vary. Possible answer: How many more people attended on Saturday than on Thursday? How much more money was collected?

Part 2 Write and Share Problems

Josh used the data in the pictograph to write a problem.

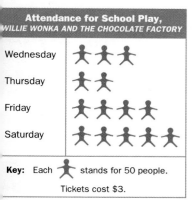

Attendance for School Play, *WILLIE WONKA AND THE CHOCOLATE FACTORY*	
Wednesday	🚶🚶🚶
Thursday	🚶🚶
Friday	🚶🚶🚶🚶
Saturday	🚶🚶🚶🚶🚶

Key: Each 🚶 stands for 50 people.
Tickets cost $3.

6 Solve Josh's problem. **Wednesday**

7 Change Josh's problem so that it is either easier or harder to solve. Do not change any of the data in the pictograph. **See above.**

8 Solve the new problem and explain why it is easier or harder to solve than Josh's. **See below.**

9 Write a problem of your own that uses information from the graph.
For problems 9–11, see Teacher's Edition.

10 Trade problems. Solve at least three problems written by your classmates.

11 What was the most interesting problem that you solved? Why?

8. Possible answer for sample answer given in problem 7: 150 people; $450; the problem is harder than Josh's problem because it is necessary to compare the attendance on different days.

On which day did they make $450?

Josh Watson
Hawthorne School
Indianapolis, IN

Turn the page for Practice Strategies. ➡

Multiply by 1-Digit Numbers **195**

PART 2 WRITE AND SHARE PROBLEMS

▶ **Check** Ask students to explain how they obtained and compared data from the graph.

Items 7 and 8 allow students to change the given problem to create another problem. This prepares students to write problems of their own.

For item 9, some students will paraphrase Josh's problem, others will write simple one-step problems, and some will write complicated multistep problems.

For items 10 and 11, encourage students to discuss the problems they solved and their reasons why a problem was most interesting.

Encourage students' creativity by suggesting other contexts or questions that can be used in word problems.

③ Close

Have students discuss how they go about writing their own problems. Have them compare the methods they used to solve each other's problems.

Practice See pages 196–197.

▶ **PART 3 PRACTICE STRATEGIES**
Materials have available: calculators

Students have the option of choosing any five problems from ex. 1–8, and any two problems from ex. 9–12.

- Ex. 5, 6, and 8 are multistep problems. Students may need to write a plan for each step of the problem.
- Encourage students to choose well-balanced meals for ex. 9. Sample responses:

MEAL 1	
Food	Calories
Orange juice (8 oz)	110
Egg (1)	80
Toast, buttered (2 slices)	210
Milk (8 oz)	160
Total	560

MEAL 2	
Food	Calories
Grapefruit (half)	45
Muffins (2)	240
Cornflakes (1 cup)	100
Milk (8 oz)	160
Total	545

At the Computer If computers are not available, students may use graph paper to do ex. 12. Make sure that they understand that rectangles such as 1-by-2 and 2-by-1 are considered the same when they are counting.

Math Van Have students use the Drawing tool to build different rectangles. They can record their data on a table provided as a project electronic teacher aid.

Part 3   Practice Strategies

Menu
Choose five problems and solve them. Explain your methods. Explanations may vary.

1 Barth, Inc., makes mouse pads. They pack 400 in each box. How many are in 6 boxes?
2,400 pads

2 Betty Sue bought a CD that cost $13.95. She paid $14.79, with tax. How much was the tax?
$0.84

3 Steve earns $8.50 an hour for baby-sitting. How much does he earn by baby-sitting for 5 hours?
$42.50

4 You are about 12 miles from your camp. You can walk about 2 miles every hour. How long will it take you to get back to your camp?
about 6 h

5 There are 24 dolls in each carton. There are 4 cartons in each box. How many dolls are in 5 boxes?
480 dolls

6 Joe has about 150 baseball cards. His sister has twice as many. About how many cards do they have altogether?
about 450 cards

7 Each day an airline has 8 flights from Chicago to Dallas. Each flight can carry up to 245 people. What is the greatest number of people that can fly each day on those flights?
1,960 people

8 Ana wants to roast a 9-pound turkey. The directions say that the turkey must be roasted 20 minutes for each pound. If she wants the turkey to be done at 2:00 P.M., what time should she start roasting?
11:00 A.M.

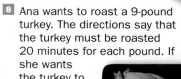

Meeting Individual Needs

Early Finishers

Have students solve this problem: **The sum of the digits in a 2-digit number is 13. If the digits are reversed, the new number is 27 more than the original number. What is the original number?** *[58]*

Gender Fairness

Alternate calling on girls and boys to solve words problems of equal difficulty until all students have participated.

Language Support

Before assigning the Menu items, pair students acquiring English with English-speaking students to ensure that students understand what the word problems are about.

Point out to students that all of the word problems on page 196 have pictures to help them with unfamiliar vocabulary.

ESL APPROPRIATE

11. Headlines may vary. Possible answers: Video Game Roller Coaster, Video Game Sales Move into High Gear
9. Students should plan a balanced breakfast with a variety of food items.

Explanations may vary.
Choose two problems and solve them. Explain your methods.

9 Use the charts to plan two different breakfasts that have between 500 and 700 calories. **See above.**

Food	Calories
Orange juice (8 ounces)	110
Grapefruit (half)	45
Orange	65
Egg	80
Whole milk (8 ounces)	160

Food	Calories
Toast (one slice) unbuttered	70
buttered	105
Muffin	120
Cornflakes (1 cup, with no milk)	100

10 **Spatial reasoning** How many squares are there in this figure? Count squares of any size. (Hint: There are more than 10.)

14 squares; nine 1-by-1 squares, four 2-by-2 squares, and one 3-by-3 square

11 Write at least three possible newspaper headlines for the graph below. **See above.**

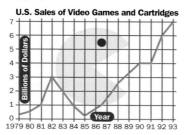

U.S. Sales of Video Games and Cartridges

1979 80 81 82 83 84 85 86 87 88 89 90 91 92 93

12 **At the Computer** You can make two different rectangles containing 4 squares, as shown on the right.

Use a drawing program to build as many different rectangles as possible containing 5 squares, 6 squares, and so on, up to 14 squares. Make a table like the one below. Then write about what you notice. **See below.**

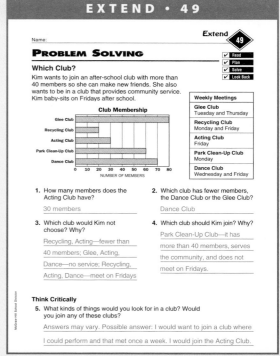

Number of Squares	1	2	3	4
Number of Different Rectangles	1	1	1	2

Possible answer: There is only one rectangle for the prime numbers but more than one rectangle for all other numbers greater than 2.

Extra Practice, page 503

Multiply by 1-Digit Numbers **197**

Alternate Teaching Strategy

Materials have available: spreadsheet and graphing program (optional)

Have students expand the spreadsheet on page 194. Ask them to tell how they set up the columns and cells to find the total number and value of the tickets sold each day of the week. *[Possible spreadsheet shown below.]*

Have students compare their spreadsheets. Then have them write, solve, and share problems using information from their spreadsheets. Students should discuss how they solved these problems.

Day	Number of Adult Tickets [A]	Number of Children Tickets [C]	Total Number of Tickets [A + C]	Value of Adult Tickets [A × 6 = D]	Value of Children Tickets [C × 4 = E]	Total Value of Tickets [D + E]
Sunday	94	63	157	564	252	816
Monday	105	39	144	630	156	786
Tuesday	35	46	81	210	184	394
Wednesday	63	79	142	378	316	694
Thursday	34	65	99	204	260	464
Friday	57	86	143	342	344	686
Saturday	74	88	143	444	352	796

PRACTICE • 49

Practice **49**

☑ Read
☑ Plan
☑ Solve
☑ Look Back

PROBLEM SOLVING: INTERPRET DATA

Use the pictograph to solve problems 1–4.

98th STREET PET STORE GOLDFISH SALES

March	🐟🐟🐟🐟
April	🐟🐟🐟🐟🐟🐟
May	🐟🐟
June	🐟🐟🐟

🐟 = 25 goldfish   Each goldfish sold for $2.

1. In which month did the pet store sell the least goldfish?

   May

2. In which months were at least $200 worth of goldfish sold?

   March and April

3. Were more goldfish sold in April, or in May and June combined?

   April

4. **What if** the pet store sold 100 goldfish in July. How much money would the store have made in the months March through July?

   $950

Solve.

5. A pet store sells 4 cans of cat food for $2, 8 cans for $4, and 12 cans for $6. How many cans would you get for $10?

   20 cans

6. Keira has $7 left after going to the pet store. She bought 3 toys for her kitten for $3 each. How much money did she start out with?

   $16

7. Pets for You has 48 parakeets. There are twice as many female parakeets as male parakeets. How many parakeets are female? male?

   32 female parakeets; 16 male parakeets

8. Nick buys a fish tank through a TV ad. He makes 3 payments of $39.95 each to pay for it. He also pays $7.50 for shipping. What is the total cost of the fish tank?

   $127.35

RETEACH • 49

Name: _____

Reteach **49**

☑ Read
☑ Plan
☑ Solve
☑ Look Back

PROBLEM SOLVING: INTERPRET DATA

A table organizes data to help you find information quickly.

The title tells you what the table is about.

These labels tell you that the first column gives data on adults and the second column gives data on children.

MOVIE ATTENDANCE

	Adults	Children
Sunday	46	12
Monday	33	16
Tuesday	57	8
Wednesday	29	11
Thursday	35	4
Friday	93	7
Saturday	36	53

These labels tell you that each row gives data for one day of the week.

To find out how many children went to the movie on Wednesday, put your finger on *Wednesday* in the table. Move your finger to the right along the row until you come to the *Children* column. There were 11 children who went to the movie on Wednesday.

Use the table above to answer these questions.

1. How many adults went to the movie on Wednesday?

   29 adults

2. How many children went to the movie on Friday?

   7 children

3. On Saturday, did more children or more adults go to the movie?

   children

4. How many people went to the movie on Sunday?

   58 people

5. On which day was attendance at the movie the highest?

   Friday

6. On which day was attendance the lowest?

   Thursday

EXTEND • 49

Name: _____

Extend **49**

☑ Read
☑ Plan
☑ Solve
☑ Look Back

PROBLEM SOLVING

Which Club?

Kim wants to join an after-school club with more than 40 members so she can make new friends. She also wants to be in a club that provides community service. Kim baby-sits on Fridays after school.

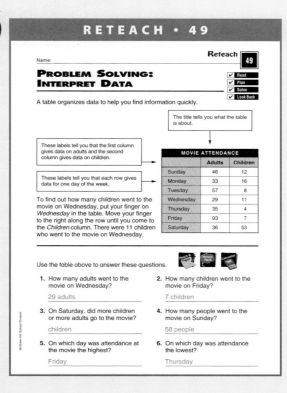

Club Membership

Glee Club
Recycling Club
Acting Club
Park Clean-Up Club
Dance Club

0 10 20 30 40 50 60 70 80
NUMBER OF MEMBERS

Weekly Meetings

Glee Club
Tuesday and Thursday

Recycling Club
Monday and Friday

Acting Club
Friday

Park Clean-Up Club
Monday

Dance Club
Wednesday and Friday

1. How many members does the Acting Club have?

   30 members

2. Which club has fewer members, the Dance Club or the Glee Club?

   Dance Club

3. Which club would Kim not choose? Why?

   Recycling, Acting—fewer than 40 members; Glee, Acting, Dance—no service; Recycling, Acting, Dance—meet on Fridays

4. Which club should Kim join? Why?

   Park Clean-Up Club—it has more than 40 members, serves the community, and does not meet on Fridays.

Think Critically

5. What kinds of things would you look for in a club? Would you join any of these clubs?

   Answers may vary. Possible answer: I would want to join a club where I could perform and that met once a week. I would join the Acting Club.

197

PURPOSE Review and assess the concepts, skills, and strategies that students have learned in this chapter.

Materials per student: calculator (optional)

Chapter Objectives

5A   Multiply multiples of 10, 100, and 1,000 by a 1-digit factor

5B   Estimate products, including money amounts

5C   Multiply numbers by 1-digit factors, including money amounts

5D   Solve problems, including those that involve multiplication and solving a multistep problem

Using the Chapter Review

The **Chapter Review** can be used as a review, practice test, or chapter test.

Think Critically Students' explanations for ex. 31 will indicate whether they understand the steps of and regrouping involved in multiplying greater numbers. In ex. 32, students use number sense to make generalizations about products.

Language and Mathematics

Complete the sentence. Use a word in the chart. (pages 170–193)

1 The ■ of 8 and 20 is 160. product

2 You ■ to change 36 tens to 3 hundreds 6 tens. regroup

3 To estimate 7 × 382, you can ■ 382 and then multiply. round

4 If you change the order of the ■, the product is the same. factors

Vocabulary
regroup
factors
product
sum
round
addends

Concepts and Skills

Find the product mentally. (page 170)

5 7 × 1,000   **6** 6 × 900 5,400   **7** 4 × $70 $280   **8** 5 × 8,000
7,000   40,000

Estimates may vary depending on the

Estimate the product. (page 172) method used. Estimates shown are by rounding.

9 5 × 63 300   **10** 9 × 451 4,500   **11** 8 × 1,070   **12** 4 × $6,553
                                          8,000 $28,000

Find the total number of squares in the rectangle without counting all the squares. (page 174)

13 72 squares   **14** 78 squares   **15** 54 squares

Multiply. (pages 178, 188, 192)

16 97
     × 3
     291

17 406
     × 5
     2,030

18 $6.34
     × 2
     $12.68

19 8,199
     × 4
     32,796

20 58
     × 8
     464

21 18 × 5
     90

22 6 × 22
     132

23 3 × 514
     1,542

24 7 × 399
     2,793

25 9 × $857
     $7,713

26 9 × 82
     738

27 4 × 79
     316

28 2 × $56.05
     $112.10

29 8 × 634
     5,072

30 6 × 2,007
     12,042

Reinforcement and Remediation

CHAPTER OBJECTIVES	REVIEW ITEMS	STUDENT BOOK PAGES		TEACHER'S EDITION PAGES		TEACHER RESOURCES
		Lessons	Midchapter Review	Activities	Alternate Teaching Strategy	Reteach
5A	1, 5–8,	170–171	184	169A	171	42
5B	3 9–12, 32	172–173	184	171A	173	43
5C	2, 4 13–15, 16–32	174–177, 178–181, 188–191, 192–193	184	173A, 177C, 187A, 191A	177, 181, 191, 193	44, 45, 47, 48
5D	33–40	182–183, 194–197	184	181A, 193A	183, 197	46, 49

32a. sometimes; 3 × 23 → 3 × 20 = 60, exact product > estimate,
but 3 × 28 → 3 × 30 = 90, exact product < estimate

Think critically. (page 178)

31 Analyze. Explain what mistake was made, then correct it.
Added the regrouped number before multiplying.

$$\begin{array}{r} \overset{11}{456} \\ \times\ \ 3 \\ \hline 1{,}588 \end{array}$$

$$\begin{array}{r} \overset{1\ 1}{456} \\ \times\ \ 3 \\ \hline 1{,}368 \end{array}$$

32 Generalize. Write *always*, *sometimes*, or *never*. Give examples to support your answer.

a. When you round one of two factors to find an estimate, the exact product is less than the estimate. See above.

b. A 3-digit number multiplied by a 1-digit number has a 4-digit product. sometimes; 2 × 333 = 666, 2 × 501 = 1,002

c. The product of an odd number and an even number is an even number. always; 4 × 31 = 124, 3 × 12 = 36, and so on

---

MIXED APPLICATIONS

Problem Solving

(pages 182, 194)

33 A machine prints 8,000 copies of a newsletter each hour. How many copies can the machine print in 7 hours? 56,000 copies

34 Ruth's company needs to buy 3 printers. Each printer costs $1,876. Estimate about how much they will cost altogether. See below.

35 What is the mystery number? It is an even number. The number is greater than the product of 2 and 23 but less than the sum of 17 and 33. 48

36 *The Sun Newspaper* has 758 more workers this year than last year. There are 1,742 workers this year. How many workers were there last year? 984 workers

Use the information in the ad to solve problems 37–40.

37 What is the cost of 2 floor lamps and 3 sets of cookware? $499

38 What is the cost of 3 bunk beds? $2,007

39 Pedro has $2,200. Does he have enough to buy 3 bunk beds and 3 chairs? Yes.

40 You give the clerk $50 to pay for a chair and a radio alarm. How much change should you get? $4.41

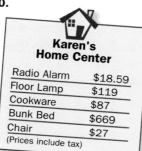

Karen's Home Center

Radio Alarm	$18.59
Floor Lamp	$119
Cookware	$87
Bunk Bed	$669
Chair	$27

(Prices include tax)

34. Answers may vary. Possible answer:
3 × $2,000 = $6,000

Multiply by 1-Digit Numbers **199**

PURPOSE Assess the concepts, skills, and strategies students have learned in this chapter.

Chapter Objectives

5A Multiply multiples of 10, 100, and 1,000 by a 1-digit factor

5B Estimate products, including money amounts

5C Multiply numbers by 1-digit factors, including money amounts

5D Solve problems, including those that involve multiplication and solving a multistep problem

Using the Chapter Test

The **Chapter Test** can be used as a practice test, a chapter test, or as an additional review. The **Performance Assessment** on Student Book page 201 provides an alternate means of assessing students' understanding of multiplication by 1-digit numbers. The table below correlates the test items to the chapter objectives and to the Student Book pages on which the skills are taught.

Assessment Resources

TEST MASTERS

The Testing Program Blackline Masters provide three forms of the Chapter Test to assess students' understanding of the chapter concepts, skills, and strategies. Form C uses a free-response format. Forms A and B use a multiple-choice format.

COMPUTER TEST GENERATOR

The Computer Test Generator supplies abundant multiple-choice and free-response test items, which you may use to generate tests and practice worksheets tailored to the needs of your class.

TEACHER'S ASSESSMENT RESOURCES

Teacher's Assessment Resources provides resources for alternate assessment. It includes guidelines for Building a Portfolio, p. 83 and the Holistic Scoring Guide.

Estimate the product. Estimates may vary. Possible estimates are given.

1 8 × 72 **560**   **2** 4 × $19 **$80**   **3** 9 × 37 **360**   **4** 6 × 832 **4,800**

5 3 × 154 **600**   **6** 7 × 108 **700**   **7** 5 × 2,089 **10,000**   **8** 3 × $5,592 **$18,000**

Multiply. Use mental math when you can.

9
$$\begin{array}{r} 38 \\ \times\ 4 \\ \hline 152 \end{array}$$

10
$$\begin{array}{r} 80 \\ \times\ 9 \\ \hline 720 \end{array}$$

11
$$\begin{array}{r} 57 \\ \times\ 6 \\ \hline 342 \end{array}$$

12
$$\begin{array}{r} \$29 \\ \times\ 4 \\ \hline \$116 \end{array}$$

13
$$\begin{array}{r} 60 \\ \times\ 8 \\ \hline 480 \end{array}$$

14
$$\begin{array}{r} 712 \\ \times\ 5 \\ \hline 3,560 \end{array}$$

15
$$\begin{array}{r} \$300 \\ \times\ 8 \\ \hline \$2,400 \end{array}$$

16
$$\begin{array}{r} 406 \\ \times\ 2 \\ \hline 812 \end{array}$$

17
$$\begin{array}{r} 600 \\ \times\ 7 \\ \hline 4,200 \end{array}$$

18
$$\begin{array}{r} \$25.88 \\ \times\ 3 \\ \hline \$77.64 \end{array}$$

19 8 × 86 **688**   **20** 5 × $60 **$300**   **21** 9 × 72 **648**

22 6 × 324 **1,944**   **23** 8 × 100 **800**   **24** 7 × $6.39 **$44.73**

25 2 × 700 **1,400**   **26** 3 × 228 **684**   **27** 9 × 4,000 **36,000**

28 4 × $3,856 **$15,424**   **29** 5 × 5,983 **29,915**

Solve. Use the table for problems 30–33.

30 Sean's employees each work 2,000 hours each year. How many hours each year do all Sean's employees work? **16,000 h**

31 The Rainbow factory in Mayville has 3,600 employees. How many more employees are in the Mayville factory than in the Rogerville factory? **2,724 employees**

Companies in Rogerville	
Company	Number of Employees
Big Foot Shoe Co.	3,246
Rainbow Mfg.	876
Big Top Tents	2,141
Sean's Bicycles	8

32 The total number of employees in all locations of these companies is 19,835. How many people outside Rogerville are employed at these companies? **13,564 people**

33 Big Top Tents needs to buy 6 computers that cost $2,164 each and 4 printers that cost $420 each. How much will they spend in all? **$14,664**

Test Correlation

CHAPTER OBJECTIVES	TEST ITEMS	TEXT PAGES
5A	10, 13, 15, 17, 20, 23, 25, 27	170–171
5B	1–8	172–173
5C	9–29	174–177, 178–181, 188–191, 192–193
5D	30–33	182–183, 194–197

See Teacher's Assessment Resources for samples of student work.

What Did You Learn? Check students' work.

Lynne and Zoe calculated how many loaves of wheat bread to order for February. Lynne usually orders 8 loaves a day. There are 28 days in February.

$$
\text{Lynne} \quad \begin{array}{r} 28 \\ \times\ 8 \\ \hline 64 \\ +160 \\ \hline 224 \end{array}
\qquad
\text{Zoe} \quad \begin{array}{r} 28 \\ \times\ 8 \\ \hline 160 \\ +\ 64 \\ \hline 224 \end{array}
$$

▶ Explain how the multiplication methods are different and why the answers are the same. Use graph paper or pictures of place-value models if you wish. See below.

You will need
• graph paper
• place-value models

▶ Explain how you could find the answer a different way.
Answers may vary. Possible answers: Use a pattern, use a table, add 8 twenty-eight times.

················· A Good Answer ·················
• clearly explains Lynne's and Zoe's methods and how they are alike and different
• tells another way to find the answer

 You may want to place your work in your portfolio.

What Do You Think
See Teacher's Edition.

1 Can you recognize problems that can be solved by multiplying? Why or why not?

2 List all the ways you might use to solve a multiplication problem:
• Use place-value models.   • Use paper and pencil.
• Use mental math.   • Other. Explain.

3 Explain when you would use mental math to solve a multiplication problem.

Question 1. Answers may vary. Possible answer: Different—Lynne multiplied 8 ones by 8 and then 2 tens by 8, while Zoe multiplied the 2 tens before the 8 ones; same—both added 160 and 64 to find the total of 224.   Multiply by 1-Digit Numbers **201**

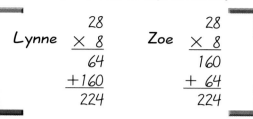

Reviewing A Portfolio

Have students review their portfolios. Consider including these items:
• Finished work on the Chapter Project (p. 167F) or **Investigation** (pp. 186–187).
• Selected math journal entries, pp. 175, 184, 192.
• Finished work on the nonroutine problem in **What Do You Know?** (p. 169) and problems from the Menu (pp. 196–197).
• Each student's self-selected "best piece" from work completed during the chapter. Have each student attach a note explaining why he or she chose that piece.
• Any work you or an individual student wishes to keep for future reference.

You may take this opportunity to conduct conferences with students. The Portfolio Analysis Form can help you report students' progress. See Teacher's Assessment Resources, p. 33.

PURPOSE Review and assess the concepts, skills, and strategies learned in this chapter.

Materials have available: centimeter graph paper (TA 7), place-value models

Using the Performance Assessment

Have students read and restate the problem in their own words. Make sure they understand that Lynne and Zoe have solved the same problem in two different ways.

Evaluating Student Work

As you read students' papers, look for the following:
• *Does the student recognize that the problem involves multiplication?*
• *Does the student understand how the multiplication methods are different, and why the answers are the same?*
• *Does the student correctly interpret the problem and show the information correctly using graph paper or models?*
• *Can the student use an alternate method of solving the problem?*
• *Does the student multiply and regroup accurately?*

The Holistic Scoring Guide and annotated samples of students' work can be used to assess this task. See pages 27–32 and 37–72 in Teacher's Assessment Resources.

Using the Self-Assessment

What Do You Think? Assure students that there are no right or wrong answers. Tell students the emphasis is on what they think and how they justify their answers.

Follow-Up Interviews

These questions can be used to gain insight into students' thinking:
• **How do Lynne's and Zoe's multiplication methods differ? How are their methods alike?**
• **How did using graph paper or place-value models help you?**
• **How did you determine that you could find the answer a different way?**

OBJECTIVE Collect and analyze data, use graphing software, and solve problems in a science context.

Materials have available: calculators; computer graphing program (optional)

Science

Cultural Connection Read the **Cultural Note.** Discuss with students other foods that were originally grown in the Western Hemisphere and are now grown elsewhere, such as corn and potatoes. Interested students can research the effect that growing new types of crops has had on various cultures.

Let students read page 202 independently. Then discuss the steps in producing candy bars from cocoa beans and the questions about seeds.

Other information you can discuss with the class is given in the Interesting Facts on page 203 of this Teacher's Edition.

Math

Students should work in small groups to conduct the class survey on page 203, organize the data, and answer items 1–3. Then let groups share their results and their methods with the class.

Students can find the answers to items 1 and 2 by multiplying:

6 × number of bars in a month = number of bars in 6 months

9 × number of bars in 6 months = number of beans for 6 months

For item 3, alert students to the fact that the answer will be a range. One way to find the range is to use a guess-test-and-revise strategy.

Another way to find the range is to use a calculator to divide the number of beans for 6 months by 50 to find the number of pods needed. Then divide the number of pods by 20 to find the maximum number of trees needed and divide the number of pods by 40 to find the minimum number of trees needed.

math science technology
C O N N E C T I O N

FROM SEED TO CANDY BAR
The Cocoa Story

Cultural Note
Over 500 years ago, the Maya of Central America and the Aztec of Mexico cultivated cocoa beans. Now the Ivory Coast in Africa and Brazil in South America produce the most cocoa beans.

1 Today, cocoa beans come from South America, Central America, and Africa. They grow in pods on cacao trees.

2 The cacao tree has 20 to 40 pods growing on it at a time. The trees are 25 to 40 feet tall.

3 Each pod has about 50 beans.

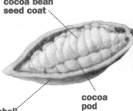

cocoa bean
seed coat

shell   cocoa pod

4 The beans are separated from the pod, kept dry, and shipped to the chocolate factory.

5 At the factory, the beans are roasted, ground, and made into a liquid.

6 About 9 beans are needed to make a 2-ounce milk chocolate bar.

▶ What other seeds do we use for food? **Possible answer: lima beans, peas, corn kernels, walnuts, pecans, sunflower seeds**

▶ Why are cocoa beans kept dry? What happens to seeds when they are kept moist? **Possible answer: Dryness keeps them from spoiling; they can mold or sprout.**

Extending The Activity

1. Have students find the amount of each ingredient needed to make chocolate for 2 people. Then have them rewrite the recipe to serve 6 people and then again to serve their entire class. Encourage interested students to make the recipe at home for family and friends and to report on the results.

2. Students can survey another class or do a home survey on the number of 2-ounce candy bars eaten in a month and use graphing software to make another bar graph.

5. Possible answer: More than half the students eat 3 or more chocolate bars, more students eat 4 chocolate bars than any other number, no student eats more than 5.

How Much Chocolate Do You Eat?

Survey your class to find out how much chocolate is eaten in a month.

Class Survey

Do you eat chocolate?

yes ☐ no ☐

If yes, about how many 2-ounce chocolate bars do you eat in a month?

Answers are given for data in the graph.

Use the data you collected to answer these questions.

1 About how many 2-ounce milk chocolate bars does your class eat in a month? in 6 months? *about 68 in 1 mo; about 408 in 6 mo*

2 About how many cocoa beans would it take to supply milk chocolate bars to your class for 6 months? *about 3,672 cocoa beans*

3 **What if** you grow your own cocoa beans. About how many cacao trees will you need to supply chocolate bars to your class for 6 months? *It takes 2 to 4 trees to produce the 74 pods needed.*

At the Computer

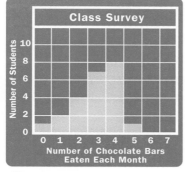

Class Survey

(Bar graph: vertical axis "Number of Students" marked 0, 2, 4, 6, 8, 10; horizontal axis "Number of Chocolate Bars Eaten Each Month" marked 0 1 2 3 4 5 6 7)

4 Use graphing software. Enter data from your survey to make a bar graph. **Check students' graphs.**

5 Write three statements about your class based on the graph. **See above.**

203

Technology

Have pairs of students from the same group work together to produce a bar graph of their survey data. Check that students have labeled their graphs and their scales.

Some students may set up their bar graph like the one at the top of page 203. Others may show the number of chocolate bars eaten in a month on a vertical scale.

Math Van Students may use the Graph tool to create their own bar graphs. A project electronic teacher aid has been provided.

Interesting Facts

• **Cocoa beans** come from the cacao tree. Many years ago, a spelling mistake was made. From that time, cacao beans have often been called cocoa beans by people who speak English.

• **Cocoa beans** are about 2 centimeters long, the width of two small paper clips side-by-side.

• **Special chocolate bars** that resist heat were developed for soldiers in the Persian Gulf War in 1992. For people stranded in cold weather, "survival" bars are now under development.

• **Food scientists** are developing chocolate with less fat and fewer calories, as well as chocolate for people on sugar-restricted diets.

Bibliography

The Chocolate Book: A Sampler for Boys and Girls by Michael Patrick Hearn. New York: Caedmon, 1983. IBSN 0–89845–163–9.

Chocolate by Hershey: A Story about Milton S. Hershey by Betty Burford. Minneapolis: Carolrhoda Books, Inc., 1994. ISBN 0–87614–641–8.

"Chocolate." Science Weekly 11, no. 1 (1994).

CHAPTER 6 AT A GLANCE: Theme: Earth Watch   Suggested Pacing: 10–13 days

Multiply by 2-Digit Numbers

CHAPTER 6 ORGANIZER

	DAY 1	DAY 2	DAY 3

WEEK ONE

PREASSESSMENT

Introduction pp. 204

What Do You Know? p. 205
CHAPTER OBJECTIVES: 6A, 6B, 6C, 6D
RESOURCES Read-Aloud Anthology
pp. 31–32
Pretest: Test Master
Form A, B, or C
Diagnostic Inventory

📁 Portfolio   📓 Journal   **NCTM STANDARDS:** 1, 2, 3, 4, 6, 8

LESSON 6.1

MENTAL MATH
Multiplication Patterns pp. 206–207

CHAPTER OBJECTIVES: 6A
MATERIALS calculators (opt.)
RESOURCES Reteach/Practice/Extend: 50
Math Center Cards: 50
Extra Practice: 504

Daily Review TE p. 205B
⭐ Algebraic Thinking
🖱 Technology Link   **NCTM STANDARDS:** 6, 8, 13

LESSON 6.2

MENTAL MATH
Estimate Products pp. 208–209

CHAPTER OBJECTIVES: 6B
MATERIALS newspapers, scissors, tape, calculators (opt.)
RESOURCES Reteach/Practice/Extend: 51
Math Center Cards: 51
Extra Practice: 504

Daily Review TE p. 207B
🖱 Technology Link   **NCTM STANDARDS:** 5, 8

WEEK TWO

MIDCHAPTER ASSESSMENT

Midchapter Review p. 218
CHAPTER OBJECTIVES: 6A, 6B, 6C, 6D
MATERIALS calculators (opt.)

Developing Number Sense p. 219

REAL-LIFE INVESTIGATION:
Applying Multiplication pp. 220–221

📁 Portfolio   📓 Journal   **NCTM STANDARDS:** 1, 2, 3, 4, 8, 10

LESSON 6.5

PROBLEM-SOLVING STRATEGY
Use Alternate Methods pp. 222–223

CHAPTER OBJECTIVES: 6D
MATERIALS calculators (opt.)
RESOURCES Reteach/Practice/Extend: 54
Math Center Cards: 54
Extra Practice: 506

Daily Review TE p. 221B
🖱 Technology Link   **NCTM STANDARDS:** 1, 2, 3, 4, 8

LESSON 6.6

Multiply 3-Digit Numbers pp. 224–225

CHAPTER OBJECTIVES: 6C
MATERIALS calculators (opt.)
RESOURCES Reteach/Practice/Extend: 55
Math Center Cards: 55
Extra Practice: 506

Daily Review TE p. 223B
🖱 Technology Link   **NCTM STANDARDS:** 8

WEEK THREE

CHAPTER ASSESSMENT

Chapter Review pp. 232–233
MATERIALS calculators (opt.)

Chapter Test p. 234
RESOURCES Posttest: Test Master
Form A, B, or C

Performance Assessment p. 235
RESOURCES Performance Task: Test Master

Math · Science · Technology Connection
pp. 236–237

Cumulative Review
pp. 238–239
MATERIALS calculators (opt.)
📁 Portfolio   **NCTM STANDARDS:** 1, 4, 8

DAY 4

LESSON 6.3

EXPLORE ACTIVITY

Multiply 2-Digit Numbers pp. 210–213

CHAPTER OBJECTIVES: 6C
MATERIALS 4-part spinners (TA 3), centimeter graph paper (TA 7), scissors
RESOURCES Reteach/Practice/Extend: 52
Math Center Cards: 52
Extra Practice: 505

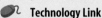 Daily Review TE p. 209B

 Technology Link | NCTM STANDARDS: 4, 8 |

LESSON 6.7

Multiply Greater Numbers pp. 226–227

CHAPTER OBJECTIVES: 6C
MATERIALS calculators (opt.)
RESOURCES Reteach/Practice/Extend: 56
Math Center Cards: 56
Extra Practice: 507

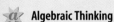 Daily Review TE p. 225B

 Algebraic Thinking
 Journal
 Technology Link | NCTM STANDARDS: 8 |

DAY 5

LESSON 6.4

Multiply 2-Digit Numbers pp. 214–217

CHAPTER OBJECTIVES: 6C
MATERIALS counters (TA 13) or connecting cubes, calculators (opt.)
RESOURCES Reteach/Practice/Extend: 53
Math Center Cards: 53
Extra Practice: 505

TEACHING WITH TECHNOLOGY
Alternate Lesson TE pp. 217A–217B

Daily Review TE p. 213B

 Algebraic Thinking
Journal
Technology Link | NCTM STANDARDS: 4, 8 |

LESSON 6.8

PROBLEM SOLVERS AT WORK

Use an Estimate or an Exact Answer pp. 228–231

CHAPTER OBJECTIVES: 6D
MATERIALS calculators (opt.), graph paper (TA 7), place-value models (TA 22)
RESOURCES Reteach/Practice/Extend: 57
Math Center Cards: 57
Extra Practice: 507

Daily Review TE p. 227B

Algebraic Thinking
Technology Link | NCTM STANDARDS: 1, 2, 3, 4, 5, 8 |

Assessment Options

FORMAL

Chapter Tests

STUDENT BOOK
- Midchapter Review, p. 218
- Chapter Review, pp. 232–233
- Chapter Test, p. 234
- Cumulative Review, pp. 238–239

BLACKLINE MASTERS
- Test Master Form A, B, or C
- Diagnostic Inventory

COMPUTER TEST GENERATOR
- Available on disk

Performance Assessment
- What Do You Know? p. 205
- Performance Assessment, p. 235
- Holistic Scoring Guide, Teacher's Assessment Resources, pp. 27–32
- Follow-Up Interviews, p. 235
- Performance Task, Test Masters

Teacher's Assessment Resources
- Portfolio Guidelines and Forms, pp. 6–9, 33–35
- Holistic Scoring Guide, pp. 27–32
- Samples of Student Work, pp. 37–72

INFORMAL

Ongoing Assessment
- Observation Checklist, pp. 210, 224, 228
- Interview, pp. 206, 222
- Anecdotal Report, pp. 208, 214, 226

Portfolio Opportunities
- Chapter Project, p. 203F
- What Do You Know? p. 205
- Investigation, pp. 220–221
- Journal Writing, pp. 205, 215, 218, 226
- Performance Assessment, p. 235
- Self-Assessment: What Do You Think? p. 235

Chapter Objectives		Standardized Test Correlations
6A	Multiply multiples of 10, 100, and 1,000 by multiples of 10	MAT, CAT, SAT, ITBS, CTBS,TN*
6B	Estimate products, including money amounts	MAT, CAT, SAT, ITBS, CTBS,TN*
6C	Multiply by 2-digit factors, including money amounts	MAT, CAT, SAT, ITBS, CTBS,TN*
6D	Solve problems, including those that involve multiplication and using alternate solution methods	MAT, CAT, SAT, ITBS, CTBS,TN*

*Terra Nova

NCTM Standards Grades K–4

1 Problem Solving	**8** Whole Number Computation
2 Communication	**9** Geometry and Spatial Sense
3 Reasoning	**10** Measurement
4 Connections	**11** Statistics and Probability
5 Estimation	**12** Fractions and Decimals
6 Number Sense and Numeration	**13** Patterns and Relationships
7 Concepts of Whole Number Operations	

CHAPTER 6 ORGANIZER

Meeting Individual Needs

LEARNING STYLES

- AUDITORY/LINGUISTIC
- **LOGICAL/ANALYTICAL**
- **VISUAL/SPATIAL**
- **MUSICAL**
- **KINESTHETIC**
- SOCIAL
- **INDIVIDUAL**

Students who are talented in art, language, and physical activity may better understand mathematical concepts when these concepts are connected to their areas of interest. Use the following activities to stimulate the different learning styles of some of your students.

Social Learners

Some students may enjoy working with a partner or in small groups. Give them a word problem to solve together. Have them compare their strategies and solution.

Auditory/Linguistic Learners

Some students can easily verbalize how problems are solved. Give more verbal students opportunities to explain how they solved a particular problem. Students can write and make an audio tape of their explanations. Other students can read and listen to the recordings.

See Lesson Resources, pp. 205A, 207A, 209A, 213A, 221A, 223A, 225A, 227A.

GIFTED AND TALENTED

Students can develop flexible thinking and number sense by playing a game called Place the Digits. Provide each student with a recording sheet like the following, with five frames:

Place the Digits

$$
\begin{array}{ccc}
\_ & \_ & \_ \\
\times & \_ & \_ \\
\hline
\end{array}
$$

Use a zero to nine spinner. Have students work in pairs, taking turns spinning. Each student will record the digit spun on one of their frame spaces. Explain to students that they are to place the digits on spaces to try to get the highest product. After recording five digits, students solve their problems. The student with the highest product wins.

See also Meeting Individual Needs, pp. 210, 214.

ESL **APPROPRIATE**

EXTRA SUPPORT

Some students may benefit from having samples of algorithms when multiplying. They may use the samples as guides until they are more comfortable multiplying greater numbers. Specific suggestions for ways to provide extra support to students appear in every lesson in this chapter.

See Meeting Individual Needs, pp. 206, 208, 214, 222, 224, 226, 228.

EARLY FINISHERS

Students who finish their class work early may design and color a commemorative stamp honoring earth-wise endeavors. Display all the commemorative stamps on a bulletin board. (See *Chapter Project*, p. 203F.)

See also Meeting Individual Needs, pp. 206, 208, 210, 212, 216, 222, 224, 226, 230.

ESL **APPROPRIATE**

LANGUAGE SUPPORT

Students may benefit from hearing brief stories to help them understand word problems. Make up short stories for some of the word problems and write them on chart paper. Have students read the story along with you. Point out and emphasize key words in the story.

See also Meeting Individual Needs, pp. 212, 215, 228.

ESL **APPROPRIATE**

INCLUSION

- For **inclusion** ideas, information, and suggestions, see pp. 215, 230, T15.
- For **gender fairness** tips, see pp. 212, T15.

USING MANIPULATIVES

Building Understanding Place-value models can be used to model problems as students solve them. Have students model one of the factors.

Students can also model each part of the number as you multiply. Write the number on the board and have students manipulate the blocks as you multiply. Refer to the blocks when you multiply the ones and tens parts. Have students organize and count up the blocks.

Easy-to-make Manipulatives If place-value models are not available, glue centimeter graph paper onto cardboard. Cut into blocks of hundreds (10 by 10), tens (1 by 10), and ones (1 by 1).

ESL APPROPRIATE

USING COOPERATIVE LEARNING

Partners Brainstorm This strategy develops teamwork by having partners work together to list ideas about a topic.

- Students work individually to list as many ideas as they can.
- Students work with a partner to compare and combine lists.
- Partners work together to add more ideas to their list.

USING LITERATURE

Use the selection *50 Simple Things Kids Can Do To Recycle* to introduce the chapter theme, Earth Watch. This selection is reprinted on pages 31–32 of the Read-Aloud Anthology.

Also available in the Read-Aloud Anthology is the poem "Multiplication," page 33.

MULTIPLY BY 2-DIGIT NUMBERS

Linking Technology

This integrated package of programs and services allows students to explore, develop, and practice concepts; solve problems; build portfolios; and assess their own progress. Teachers can enhance instruction, provide remediation, and share ideas with other educational professionals.

CD-ROM ACTIVITY

In *Earth Day Plans,* students explore the concept of multiplying by 2-digit numbers by using a table as a spreadsheet to help them in the planting of a garden. Students can use the online notebook to explain how they solved the problem. To extend the activity, students use the Math Van tools to complete an open-ended problem related to the concept. **Available on CD-ROM.**

CD-ROM TOOLS

Students can use Math Van's place-value models and tables to explore the concept of multiplying by 2-digit numbers. The Tech Links on the Lesson Resources pages highlight opportunities for students to use these and other tools such as counters, graphs, online notes, and calculator to provide additional practice, reteaching, or extension. **Available on CD-ROM.**

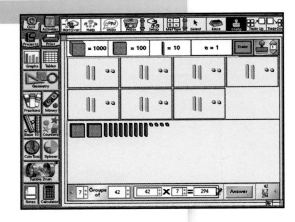

WEB SITE   http://www.mhschool.com

Teachers can access the McGraw-Hill School Division World Wide Web site for additional curriculum support at http://www.mhschool.com. Click on our Resource Village for specially designed activities linking Web sites to multiplication. Motivate children by inviting them to explore Web sites that develop the chapter theme of "Earth Watch." Exchange ideas on classroom management, cultural diversity, and other areas in the Math Forum.

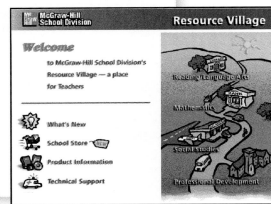

Chapter Project EARTH WISE

1 Starting the Project

Discuss various areas of environmental concern; for example, recycling, clean air, conserving water, packaging. Explain that students will work in groups to create Earth Wise Multiplication Booklets. Divide the class into working groups. As the project progresses, discuss how family and community members can participate.

Highlighting the Math

- collect, organize, and display data
- use data to predict effects over greater length of time
- write and solve real-world multiplication problems from data students have collected

2 Continuing the Project

- Using $4\frac{1}{4}$ in. $\times 5\frac{1}{2}$ in. paper, each group makes up, writes, and solves three multiplication problems focusing on one of the environmental topics discussed earlier. Example: "A leaky faucet wastes 73 gallons of water in 1 month. How much water would the faucet waste in 14 months? in 2 years?"
- Each group assembles its problem pages into a booklet and creates a cover for it.

3 Finishing the Project

Have each group present two of its problems to the class. Have the class solve the problems individually. Then have a volunteer come to the chalkboard to demonstrate the multiplication.

Community Involvement

Display the booklets on a bookshelf and allow students to check them out to take home for two nights.

Invite a speaker from a recycling center to visit the class.

BUILDING A PORTFOLIO

Have each student write a paragraph about his or her role in developing the group booklet. Take photographs of the booklets if possible.

Each student's portfolio should include the written paragraph, photos (if possible), and any notes you made about the student's work.

To assess students' work, refer to the Holistic Scoring Guide on page 27 in the Teacher's Assessment Resources.

PURPOSE Introduce the theme of the chapter.

Resource Read-Aloud Anthology, pages 31–32

Using Literature

Read "50 Simple Things Kids Can Do to Recycle" from the Anthology to introduce the chapter theme "Earth Watch."

Developing the Theme

This chapter explores ways that students can help better the world around them. Many problem-solving situations are based on recycling programs and how such a program can earn money while cleaning up the community and reducing landfills.

Students may find it interesting to learn that Kids Against Pollution (KAP), an organization to fight pollution, was founded in Closter, New Jersey by the fifth-grade class at Tenakill School. They were successful in getting polystyrene banned from their school district and then from their town. (Polystyrenes release CFCs, a major air pollutant, when they are produced and thrown away.) KAP is now at least 800 chapters strong in the United States and other countries.

Encourage students to participate in recycling programs in the community. If students want to do more, suggest that they read some of the books in the Chapter Bibliography.

These various ways to help the environment are discussed in this chapter:

Recycling	204–205, 208–209, 228–229
Collecting litter	206–207
Conservation programs	214–215
Conserving water	224–225
Conserving electricity	226–227

On pages 220–221, students will explore recycling paper.

CHAPTER 6 MULTIPLY BY 2-DIGIT NUMBERS

THEME Earth Watch

Have you ever thought of what you can do to help the environment? In this chapter you will see how multiplication is used in projects that help keep our earth a nice place to live.

Chapter Bibliography

Antonio's Rain Forest by Anna Lewington. Minneapolis: Carolrhoda Books, Inc., 1993. ISBN 0–87614–749–X.

Earthwise at School: A Guide to the Care and Feeding of Your Planet by Linda Lowery and Marybeth Lorbiecki. Minneapolis: Carolrhoda Books, Inc., 1993. ISBN 0–87614–587–X.

The Kids' Earth Handbook by Sandra Markle. New York: Atheneum Books for Young Readers, 1991. ISBN 0–689–31707–7.

Community Involvement

Have students create a newsletter which highlights ways that fourth graders can help prevent pollution. Students can work in groups based on the kind of pollution they feel most concerned about. Every student can help distribute the newsletter to fourth graders in other classes and at other schools.

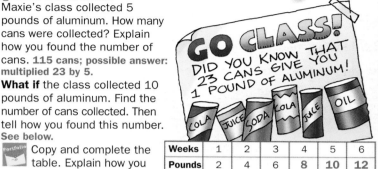

1. Possible answer: Step 1: Find two boxes; Step 2: Mark one box for aluminum cans and the other for plastic bottles; Step 3: Take the cans and bottles to the recycling center once a month.

What Do You Know ?

 Maxie's class collected 5 pounds of aluminum. How many cans were collected? Explain how you found the number of cans. **115 cans; possible answer: multiplied 23 by 5.**

2 **What if** the class collected 10 pounds of aluminum. Find the number of cans collected. Then tell how you found this number. **See below.**

3 Copy and complete the table. Explain how you completed it. **Possible answer: multiply 23 by each number.**

Weeks	1	2	3	4	5	6
Pounds	2	4	6	8	10	12
Cans	46	92	138	184	230	276

Steps in a Process Maxie's class plans to recycle. They need boxes for cans and plastic bottles. They also need to take the cans to the recycling center once a month.

Paying attention to each step in a process helps you follow directions or understand information you read.

1 List the steps Maxie's class can follow to recycle their cans. **See above.**

2 Why does it help to list the steps in order? **to understand what to do first, second, and last**

2. **230 cans; possible answer: multiplied 23 by 70.**

Vocabulary

product, p. 206   **round,** p. 208   **regroup,** p. 214
estimate, p. 208   **factor,** p. 208

Multiply by 2-Digit Numbers   **205**

Reading, Writing, Arithmetic

Steps in a Process Discuss the steps to recycle cans. Then ask students what steps they might take to find the product of two 1-digit numbers. Work with students to list a set of steps on the chalkboard. Encourage students to use and modify these steps as they practice multiplying 2-digit numbers.

Vocabulary

 Students may record new words in their journals. Encourage them to show examples and draw diagrams to help them tell what the words mean.

PURPOSE Assess students' ability to apply prior knowledge of multiplying by 1- and 2-digit numbers.

Materials have available: place-value models, calculators (optional)

Assessing Prior Knowledge

Ask students to give examples of strategies for multiplying. List their examples on the board.

STRATEGIES FOR MULTIPLYING

1. Use repeated addition.
2. Use place-value models.
3. Multiply tens and ones separately, and then add.
4. Make an array and count the number of objects in it.
5. Multiply with pencil and paper in the usual way.
6. Use a calculator.

Tell students to assume that in item 3, the pattern in the second row continues.

Encourage students to use whatever methods they wish to answer items 1–3. Observe students as they work. To complete the bottom row of item 3, some students may keep adding 46 cans to the previous number to get the next number. Some may use repeated addition, adding 23 to itself the number of times that there are pounds. Others may multiply the number of pounds by 23.

BUILDING A PORTFOLIO

Item 3 can be used as a benchmark to show where students are in their understanding of multiplying by 1- and 2-digit numbers.

A Portfolio Checklist for Students and a Checklist for Teachers are provided in Teacher's Assessment Resources, pp. 33–34.

Prerequisite Skills

- *Can students round numbers to the nearest 10 and 100?*
- *Can students multiply by 1-digit numbers?*

Assessment Resources

DIAGNOSTIC INVENTORY

Use this blackline master to assess prerequisite skills that students will need in order to be successful in this chapter.

TEST MASTERS

Use the multiple choice format (form A or B) or the free response format (form C) as a pretest of the skills in this chapter.

LESSON 6.1

MENTAL MATH

Multiplication Patterns

OBJECTIVE Use mental math strategies to multiply multiples of 10, 100, and 1,000 by multiples of 10.

RESOURCE REMINDER
Math Center Cards 50
Practice 50, Reteach 50, Extend 50

SKILLS TRACE

GRADE 3	• Multiply multiples of 10 and 100 mentally. *(Chapter 12)*
GRADE 4	• Multiply mentally multiples of 10, 100, and 1,000 by multiples of 10.
GRADE 5	• Multiply mentally whole numbers and decimals by multiples of 10, 100, and 1,000. *(Chapter 4)*

WARM-UP

Cooperative Pairs   Logical/Analytical

OBJECTIVE Explore a pattern using calculators.

Materials per student: calculator

► Write the following on the chalkboard:

1×1

11×11

111×111

► Ask pairs to find the products using a calculator, and describe the pattern in their own words.

► Ask a volunteer to tell the pattern and have the class adjust and/or correct it. Then have students complete the pattern based upon the discussion. *[1; 121; 12,321]*

► Challenge students to predict the next element in the pattern. *[1,111 × 1111 = 1,234,321]*

► You may choose to have students continue the pattern with other numbers.

SCIENCE CONNECTION

Cooperative Pairs   Visual/Spatial

OBJECTIVE Connect using factors and multiples to science.

► Write the following chart on the chalkboard:

Animal	Life-Size Length
1. bee hummingbird	6 inches
2. white-fronted falconet	6 inches
3. thread snake	4 inches
4. namaqua dwarf snake	8 inches
5. Mozambique marine toad	1 inch
6. long-tailed planigale mouse	5 inches

► Tell students that life-size photos of the animals are going to be enlarged to make posters. The poster paper comes in lengths of 30 inches, 40 inches, and 60 inches.

► Have pairs decide how much each photo should be enlarged and the length of the paper to be used. Then have pairs fill in their decisions in the table and share them with other pairs. *[Possible answers: 1. 10 times on 60 in. paper; 2. 10 times on 60 in. paper; 3. 10 times on 40 in. paper; 4. 5 times on 40 in. paper; 5. 60 times on 60 in. paper; 6. 12 times on 60 in. paper]*

Daily Review

PREVIOUS DAY QUICK REVIEW

1. 4 × 622 [2,488]
2. 5 × 863 [4,315]
3. 2 × 1,209 [2,418]
4. 6 × 3,153 [18,918]

FAST FACTS

1. 3 × 4 [12]
2. 2 × 6 [12]
3. 9 × 5 [45]
4. 8 × 7 [56]

Problem of the Day • 50

Lee entered a number in a calculator, divided by 8, and the result was 516 with a remainder of 3. Lee has forgotten the first number he entered. What can Lee do to calculate the number? What was the number? *[Since multiplication is the opposite of division, Lee can multiply 8 by 516 and add 3 to find the number—4,131.]*

TECH LINK

ONLINE EXPLORATION

Use our Web-linked activities and lesson plans to connect your students to the real world of Earth watch.

MATH FORUM

Management Tip When teaching a key skill, I have students describe their solution to the problem.

Visit our Resource Village at http://www.mhschool.com to access the Online Exploration and the Math Forum.

MATH CENTER

Practice

OBJECTIVE Identify multiplication patterns.

Materials per student: Math Center Recording Sheet (TA 31 optional)

Students complete a table to sort factors by the number of zeros added to the end of basic-fact products. *[1. 4,800; 2. 180,000; 3. 320,000; 4. 18,000; 5. 1,800; 6. 1,500,000; 7. 4,900,000; 8. 240,000; 9. 1,200; 10. 36,000; 2 zeros: ex. 1, 5, 9; 3 zeros: ex. 4, 10; 4 zeros: ex. 2, 3, 8; 5 zeros: ex. 6, 7]*

PRACTICE ACTIVITY 50

MATH CENTER
On Your Own

Number Sense • Oodles of Zeros

How many zeros are in each product? First find products mentally. Then sort them by the number of zeros you add to the basic fact product. Make a chart like the one shown.

1. 800 × 6
2. 6,000 × 30
3. 40 × 8,000
4. 20 × 900
5. 6 × 300
6. 300 × 5,000
7. 70 × 70,000
8. 60 × 4,000
9. 40 × 30
10. 400 × 90

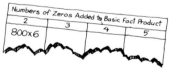

Numbers of Zeros Added to Basic Fact Product			
2	3	4	5
800×6			

NCTM Standards

- Problem Solving
- ✓ Communication
- ✓ Reasoning
- Connections

Chapter 6, Lesson 1, pages 206–207   Multiplication

Problem Solving

OBJECTIVE Find factor pairs for given products.

Materials per student: Math Center Recording Sheet (TA 31 optional)

Starting with basic facts, students manipulate powers of 10 to form different factor pairs for given products. *[Answers may vary. Possible answers: 1. 800 × 80, 8 × 8,000; 2. 6 × 700, 70 × 60, 7 × 600; 3. 3 × 9,000, 9 × 3,000, 30 × 900, 90 × 300; 4. 5 × 2,000, 2 × 5,000, 20 × 500, 50 × 200; 5. 3 × 600, 6 × 300, 30 × 60, 2 × 900, 9 × 200, 90 × 20; 6. 3,000 × 8, 8,000 × 3, 30 × 800, 80 × 300, 6 × 4,000, 4 × 6,000, 60 × 400, 40 × 600]*

PROBLEM-SOLVING ACTIVITY 50

MATH CENTER
On Your Own

Logical Reasoning • Factors to Consider

How many different factor pairs have the same product? Find factor pairs for each product below. Find the number of factor pairs indicated in the parentheses. For example:

Product: 21,000 (4 factor pairs)
30 × 700   70 × 300   7,000 × 3   3,000 × 7

1. Product: 64,000 (2)
2. Product: 4,200 (3)
3. Product: 27,000 (4)
4. Product: 10,000 (4)
5. Product: 1,800 (6)
6. Product: 24,000 (8)

? × ? = 24,000

NCTM Standards

- ✓ Problem Solving
- Communication
- ✓ Reasoning
- ✓ Connections

Chapter 6, Lesson 1, pages 206–207   Multiplication

MENTAL MATH
Multiplication Patterns

OBJECTIVE Use mental math strategies to multiply multiples of 10, 100, and 1,000 by multiples of 10.

Vocabulary product

1 Introduce

Discuss recycling with students. Generate a list of the amount of trash generated by the class and the amount that could be recycled.

2 Teach
Whole Class

▶ **LEARN** Read through the problem with students. Then ask:
- **What possible litter may be found on a beach?** *[Possible answers: soda bottles, paper wrappers, and so on.]*

a **Algebra: Patterns** Before going on, ask students:
- **What are you asked to find?** *[Possible answer: gallons of litter on the first day and on the remaining 4 days]*

Have the class find the pattern. Students should see that to find the product, you multiply the front digits and attach the number of zeros in each factor.

More Examples Point out that in Example B there is a zero in the product of 4 and 5, but the pattern is the same.

3 Close

▶ **Check for Understanding** using items 1–13, page 206.

CRITICAL THINKING
Students should realize the pattern of multiplying the basic fact and adding zeros to the product is equivalent to the number of zeros in the factors.

▶ **PRACTICE**
Materials have available: calculators

Options for assigning exercises:
A—Even ex. 2–30; **Mixed Review**
B—Odd ex. 1–29; **Mixed Review**

- For ex. 1–20, encourage students to use the patterns they found in the lesson.
- In ex. 12, 15, and 20, the product of the front digits ends in zero.
- Students can use the estimates they made during the Motivate activity to help them solve ex. 28.

Mixed Review/Test Preparation Students learned inequalities in Chapter 1.

a **Algebra** In ex. 21–26, a symbol is used in place of a variable to solve an equation.

Multiplication Patterns

L E A R N

Have you ever seen signs along a highway or beach that say that the land is adopted? This means volunteers care for it by cleaning up the litter.

Suppose volunteers fill 30-gallon bags at a beach. If they fill 1,000 bags each day, how many gallons of trash do they pick up in 1 day? in 4 days?

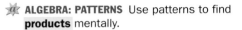

a **ALGEBRA: PATTERNS** Use patterns to find **products** mentally.

$3 \times 1 = 3$
$30 \times 1 = 30$
$30 \times 10 = 300$
$30 \times 100 = 3,000$
$30 \times 1,000 = 30,000$

$3 \times 4 = 12$
$30 \times 4 = 120$
$30 \times 40 = 1,200$
$30 \times 400 = 12,000$
$30 \times 4,000 = 120,000$

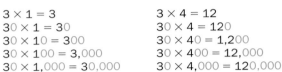
Check Out the Glossary
For vocabulary words
See page 544.

They pick up 30,000 gallons of trash in 1 day.

They pick up 120,000 gallons of trash in 4 days.

More Examples

A $2 \times 3 = 6$
$20 \times 3 = 60$
$20 \times 30 = 600$
$20 \times 300 = 6,000$
$20 \times 3,000 = 60,000$

B $4 \times 5 = 20$
$4 \times 50 = 200$
$40 \times 50 = 2,000$
$40 \times 500 = 20,000$
$40 \times 5,000 = 200,000$

C $6 \times 8 = 48$
$60 \times 8 = 480$
$60 \times 80 = 4,800$
$600 \times 80 = 48,000$
$6,000 \times 80 = 480,000$

C H E C K

Check for Understanding
Multiply mentally.

1 60×10 600

2 $80 \times 1,000$
80,000

3 50×30 1,500

4 100×40
4,000

5 60×50 3,000

6 300×30 9,000

7 700×40
28,000

8 $2,000 \times 50$
100,000

9 90×700 63,000

10 $20 \times 8,000$
160,000

11 $5,000 \times 80$
400,000

12 $6,000 \times 90$
540,000

Critical Thinking: Summarize   **Explain your reasoning.**

13 How does knowing basic facts help you find a product mentally?
Possible answer: Start with a basic fact and then, at the end of the product, write zeros equal to the number of zeros in the factors.

Meeting Individual Needs

Early Finishers

Challenge these students to find the products of greater numbers such as $50 \times 70,000$ and $80 \times 50,000$. *[3,500,000; 4,000,000]*

ESL **APPROPRIATE**

Extra Support

Ask students having difficulty seeing the pattern to write the patterns down. Have them use one color to identify the basic fact and a color to identify the zeros in the factors and in the product.

Ongoing Assessment

Interview Determine if students understand how to multiply multiples of 10 by asking them to describe the pattern and how they use it to solve $40 \times 8,000$. Student responses should include multiplying the nonzero digits and attaching zeros. *[320,000]*

Follow Up If students need further practice multiplying multiples of 10, assign **Reteach 50**.

For students who need a challenge, assign **Extend 50**.

Practice

Multiply mentally.

1 20 × 100
2,000

2 70 × 50
3,500

3 60 × 300
18,000

4 1,000 × 90
90,000

5 80 × 60
4,800

6 600 × 40
24,000

7 50 × 5,000
250,000

8 80 × 4,000
320,000

9 900 × 30
27,000

10 2,000 × 40
80,000

11 70 × 600
42,000

12 5,000 × 40
200,000

13 8,000 × 30
240,000

14 60 × 1,000
60,000

15 800 × 50
40,000

16 90 × 90
8,100

17 70 × 70
4,900

18 2,000 × 90
180,000

19 70 × 800
56,000

20 5,000 × 60
300,000

ALGEBRA Find the missing number.

21 40 × ■ = 1,200
30

22 60 × ■ = 36,000
600

23 ■ × 1,000 = 80,000
80

24 80 × ■ = 80,000
1,000

25 ■ × 200 = 8,000
40

26 ■ × 50 = 40,000
800

MIXED APPLICATIONS
Problem Solving

Answers may vary. Possible answer for a 10-year-old: over 10,000 lb

27 Every month the Carter twins collect 30 newspapers from each of 70 homes. How many newspapers do they collect in a month? **2,100 newspapers**

28 On the average each American throws out over 1,000 pounds of trash each year. How much trash has just one American thrown out on the average in your lifetime?

29 Logical reasoning The product of two numbers is 2,400. One number is 20 more than the other. What are the two numbers? **60 and 40**

30 A restaurant threw out 143 pounds of garbage in Week 1 and 251 pounds in Week 2. How many more pounds of garbage were thrown out in Week 2? **108 lb**

mixed review • test preparation

Complete. Write >, <, or =.

1 685 + 34 ● 719 **=**

2 456 − 189 ● 377 **<**

3 $549 ● $246 + $189 **>**

4 3,004 − 95 ● 2,119 **>**

5 2 × 8 ● 3 × 9 **<**

6 6 × 4 ● 5 × 5 **<**

7 24 ÷ 4 ● 36 ÷ 6 **=**

8 40 ÷ 5 ● 63 ÷ 9 **>**

Extra Practice, page 504

Multiply by 2-Digit Numbers **207**

Alternate Teaching Strategy

Show students the following method to multiply by multiples of 10, 100, and 1,000. To multiply 5,000 × 80:

- Have students circle the front digits and then find the product. 5 × 8 = 40
- Count the total number of zeros in the factors and find the sum.

  5,000 ⟶ 3 zeros

  80 ⟶ 1 zero

  ⎯⎯⎯⎯⎯

  4 zeros

- Attach the total number of zeros onto the product. 40 with 4 zeros is 400,000.

Have students follow the steps for other examples.

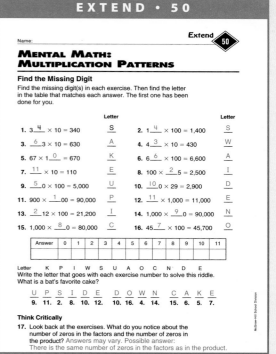

PRACTICE • 50

Name: _____

Practice **50**

MENTAL MATH: MULTIPLICATION PATTERNS

Multiply mentally.

1. 40 × 10 = __400__
2. 20 × 80 = __1,600__
3. 12 × 10 = __120__
4. 90 × 40 = __3,600__
5. 80 × 200 = __16,000__
6. 30 × 300 = __9,000__
7. 30 × 70 = __2,100__
8. 50 × 300 = __15,000__
9. 80 × 80 = __6,400__
10. 400 × 30 = __12,000__
11. 600 × 20 = __12,000__
12. 40 × 1,000 = __40,000__
13. 500 × 20 = __10,000__
14. 300 × 80 = __24,000__
15. 700 × 90 = __63,000__
16. 600 × 30 = __18,000__
17. 60 × 700 = __42,000__
18. 40 × 700 = __28,000__
19. 800 × 60 = __48,000__
20. 600 × 60 = __36,000__
21. 5,000 × 20 = __100,000__

Algebra Find the missing number.

22. 200 × __40__ = 8,000
23. __40__ × 400 = 16,000
24. 90 × __1,000__ = 90,000
25. __30__ × 700 = 21,000
26. 80 × __600__ = 48,000
27. 500 × __50__ = 25,000
28. 800 × __40__ = 32,000
29. __300__ × 90 = 27,000
30. 30 × __800__ = 24,000
31. 90 × __400__ = 36,000

Solve.

32. A company puts 30 cans of tennis balls in a box. How many cans are in 200 boxes? in 1,000 boxes?

    6,000 cans; 30,000 cans

33. A tennis club uses 5,000 balls in a year. How many does it use in 10 years? in 20 years?

    50,000 balls; 100,000 balls

RETEACH • 50

Name: _____

Reteach **50**

MENTAL MATH: MULTIPLICATION PATTERNS

You can use patterns to multiply mentally. Start with the basic fact.

2 × 4 = 8

20 × 40 = 800
| 1 zero + 1 zero | 2 zeros |

20 × 400 = 8,000
| 1 zero + 2 zeros | 3 zeros |

20 × 4,000 = 80,000
| 1 zero + 3 zeros | 4 zeros |

5 × 4 = 20

50 × 40 = 2,000
| 1 zero + 1 zero | 2 zeros |

50 × 400 = 20,000
| 1 zero + 2 zeros | 3 zeros |

50 × 4,000 = 200,000
| 1 zero + 3 zeros | 4 zeros |

Complete the pattern.

1. 3 × 2 = __6__
   30 × 20 = __600__
   30 × 200 = __6,000__
   30 × 2,000 = __60,000__

2. 5 × 2 = __10__
   50 × 20 = __1,000__
   50 × 200 = __10,000__
   50 × 2,000 = __100,000__

Multiply mentally.

3. 2 × 6 = __12__
4. 20 × 60 = __1,200__
5. 20 × 600 = __12,000__
6. 5 × 9 = __45__
7. 50 × 90 = __4,500__
8. 50 × 900 = __45,000__
9. 70 × 30 = __2,100__
10. 800 × 30 = __24,000__
11. 60 × 30 = __1,800__
12. 400 × 70 = __28,000__
13. 90 × 600 = __54,000__
14. 80 × 800 = __64,000__

EXTEND • 50

Name: _____

Extend **50**

MENTAL MATH: MULTIPLICATION PATTERNS

Find the Missing Digit

Find the missing digit(s) in each exercise. Then find the letter in the table that matches each answer. The first one has been done for you.

		Letter				Letter
1.	3 _4_ × 10 = 340	S	2.	1 _4_ × 100 = 1,400	S
3.	_6_ 3 × 10 = 630	A	4.	4 _3_ × 10 = 430	W
5.	67 × 1 _0_ = 670	K	6.	6 _6_ × 100 = 6,600	A
7.	_11_ × 10 = 110	E	8.	100 × _2_ 5 = 2,500	I
9.	_5_ 0 × 100 = 5,000	U	10.	_10_ 0 × 29 = 2,900	D
11.	900 × _1_ 00 = 90,000	P	12.	_11_ × 1,000 = 11,000	E
13.	_2_ 12 × 100 = 21,200	I	14.	1,000 × _9_ 0 = 90,000	N
15.	1,000 × _8_ 0 = 80,000	C	16.	45 _7_ × 100 = 45,700	O

Answer	0	1	2	3	4	5	6	7	8	9	10	11

Letter	K	P	I	W	S	U	A	O	C	N	D	E

Write the letter that goes with each exercise number to solve this riddle. What is a bat's favorite cake?

U P S I D E   D O W N   C A K E
9. 11. 2. 8. 10. 12.   10. 16. 4. 14.   15. 6. 5. 7.

Think Critically

17. Look back at the exercises. What do you notice about the number of zeros in the factors and the number of zeros in the product? Answers may vary. Possible answer: There is the same number of zeros in the factors as in the product.

207

MENTAL MATH

Estimate Products

OBJECTIVE Estimate products by rounding.

RESOURCE REMINDER
Math Center Cards 51
Practice 51, Reteach 51, Extend 51

SKILLS TRACE

GRADE 3	• Estimate products of 2- to 3-digit numbers by rounding. *(Chapter 12)*
GRADE 4	• Estimate products of 2- to 5-digit numbers by rounding.
GRADE 5	• Estimate products of whole numbers and decimals by rounding. *(Chapter 4)*

MANIPULATIVE WARM-UP

Cooperative Pairs   Social

OBJECTIVE Review rounding a number to the greatest place.

Materials per pair: one bag, 10 paper slips.

Prepare Write one digit from 0 to 9 on each paper slip.

▶ Tell each student to draw three boxes that will show a 3-digit number on their papers. Tell students their goal is to get the greatest (or least) number when it is rounded.

▶ Each player in the pair draws 3 numbers from the bag and decides which box he or she wants to place the digit in.

▶ Students round their numbers. Then they compare whose rounded number is greater or less.

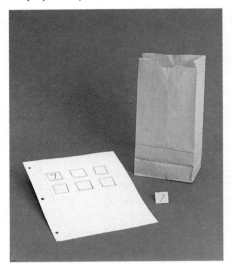

ESL APPROPRIATE

CONSUMER CONNECTION

Cooperative Groups   Logical/Analytical

OBJECTIVE Connect estimation of two-digit products to consumerism.

Materials per group: 2 number cubes

▶ Write the following items and their prices on the chalkboard.

Jeans–$23   **Sneakers–$35**   **Shirt–$18**   **Baseball cap–$12**

▶ Have one person in the group toss one number cube to find the tens digit. Then toss the second cube to find the ones digit.

▶ Tell students that the number represents the number of each item on the board that were sold in a store. They need to estimate how much each item is sold for and the total sale for all the items.

Daily Review

PREVIOUS DAY QUICK REVIEW

1. 50 × 30 [1,500]
2. 100 × 50 [5,000]
3. 400 × 300 [120,000]
4. 20 × 4,000 [80,000]

FAST FACTS

1. 1 × 3 [3]
2. 2 × 4 [8]
3. 3 × 6 [18]
4. 5 × 8 [40]

Problem of the Day • 51

The houses on Pat's side of the street are all even numbers. The first house on the street is numbered 100 and the last one is numbered 400. Pat noticed that no even number is skipped. How many houses are there on one side of the street? [151 houses]

TECH LINK

MATH VAN

Tools You may wish to use the Table and Graph tool for the Data Point in this lesson.

MATH FORUM

Combination Classes I use estimation activities for multiplying by 2-digit numbers with my younger students while my older students find exact products and check with calculators.

Visit our Resource Village at http://www.mhschool.com to see more of the Math Forum.

MATH CENTER

Practice

OBJECTIVE Estimate products.

Materials per pair: number cards (0–9); per student: Math Center Recording Sheet (TA 31 optional)

Students practice estimating. They compare the answers for two estimation methods. Students find that when factors are rounded up the estimate differs from the front-end estimate.

PRACTICE ACTIVITY 51

MATH CENTER
Partners

Number Sense • Estimation Sort

YOU NEED
number cards (0–9)

- Pick four number cards to make two 2-digit factors. Estimate the product by rounding. Write the factors and estimated product in a table. Your partner uses the same factors, estimates the product using front digits, and writes the factors and the estimated product in the same table.
- Mix up the cards and repeat, each of you using the other estimation method. When are the estimates alike? When are they different? Repeat the activity, picking five number cards to make 3-digit and 2-digit factors.

Factors	Rounded Factors and Product	Front-end Factors and Product

Chapter 6, Lesson 2, pages 208–209

Multiplication

NCTM Standards

Problem Solving
Communication
✓ Reasoning
Connections

Problem Solving

OBJECTIVE Decide on a method of estimation.

Materials per student: Math Center Recording Sheet (TA 31 optional)

Students decide on which method of estimating products—front-end or rounding—gives a more exact answer to questions about buying sports equipment. [Estimates may vary. Possible answers: 1. $900, 2. $800, 3. $1,800, 4. No. $500 is not enough money.]

PROBLEM-SOLVING ACTIVITY 51

MATH CENTER
On Your Own

Decision Making • Product Estimate

- Use the price list from Sports Specials to tell about how much each club will spend. Use estimation.
1. The Bowling Club needs 26 pairs of bowling shoes.
2. The Snorkel Society needs 42 pairs of fins.
3. Gliders Ice Rink wants 30 pairs of ice skates.
4. Hamilton Hikers needs a dozen pairs of hiking boots. Will $500 be enough money?
- Use the price list to make up a problem. Exchange problems with a classmate.

SPORTS SPECIALS
SWIM FINS $17.99
ICE SKATES $58.88
BOWLING SHOES $32.00
HIKING BOOTS $52.29

Chapter 6, Lesson 2, pages 208–209

Multiplication

NCTM Standards

✓ Problem Solving
Communication
✓ Reasoning
Connections

Lesson 6.2 *continued*

MENTAL MATH
Estimate Products

OBJECTIVE Estimate products by rounding.

Materials per group: newspapers, tape, scissors

Vocabulary estimate, factor, round

❶ Introduce

Ask students to name a few of the plastic things they throw away. Then ask students to estimate the amount of plastic items they throw away or recycle in a week and in a month. Have them record their estimates. *[Accept any reasonable unit of quantity, such as number of items, pounds, or trash bags full.]*

❷ Teach   *Whole Class*

▶ **LEARN** After reading through the problem as a class, ask students to describe how they think they could find the estimate.

- **Why do you round 765 to 800 and 88 to 90?** *[Possible answer: Round each to its greatest place.]*
- **How does multiplying by multiples of 10, 100, and 1,000 help you solve this problem?** *[After rounding the numbers, the problem involves multiplying two numbers with multiple zeros. The pattern taught in the previous lesson applies.]*

More Examples Ex. A shows a 2-digit × 2-digit and Example B shows a 2-digit × 4-digit with money.

❸ Close

> **Check for Understanding** using items 1–11, page 208.
>
> **CRITICAL THINKING**
> Students may need to use a calculator to explore the possibilities and give examples for item 11.

▶ **PRACTICE**
Materials have available: calculators

Options for assigning exercises:
A—Ex. 1–8, 17–23; **More to Explore**
B—Ex. 9–16, 17–23; **More to Explore**

- In ex. 7 and 10, one factor ends in zero. Some students may work too quickly and write too many or too few zeros.
- For ex. 17–19, remind students to use the conclusions they reached in the **Critical Thinking** items to help them determine which symbol is used to complete the sentence.

More to Explore Have students read through and complete this activity on their own. Then ask students to do items 1–4 using rounding and then compare their estimates.

Estimate Products

L E A R N

On the average, an American family throws out about 88 pounds of plastic each year. About how many pounds of plastic would a town of 765 families throw out?

You can **estimate** to solve this problem.

Round each **factor** so you can multiply mentally.

Estimate: 88 3 765   **Think:** 88 3 765
                                          ↓   ↓
                                          90 3 800 5 72,000

A town of 765 families throws out about 72,000 pounds of plastic each year.

More Examples

A Estimate: 73 3 89   **Think:** 70 3 90 5 6,300

B Estimate: 24 3 $3,258   **Think:** 20 3 $3,000 5 $60,000

10. Estimate by rounding each factor to the nearest multiple of 10, 100, or 1,000 and then multiply mentally.

C H E C K

Check for Understanding
Estimates may vary depending on the method used. Estimates shown are by rounding.

Estimate the product. Tell how you rounded.

1 56 3 18   **2** 84 3 371   **3** 49 3 $5,250   **4** 91 3 645
60 × 20; 1,200   80 × 400; 32,000   50 × $5,000; $250,000   90 × 600; 54,000

5   65   **6**   372   **7**   754   **8** $1,925   **9**   5,289
      3 14   3 48   3 34   3   25   3   78
10 × 70;   50 × 400;   30 × 800;   30 × $2,000;   80 × 5,000;
   700   20,000   24,000 $60,000   400,000

Critical Thinking: Generalize   **Explain your reasoning.**

10 How can multiplying tens, hundreds, and thousands mentally help you estimate? See above.

11 How does an exact product compare to an estimate found by rounding *up* both factors? rounding *down* both factors? Rounding up both factors gives an estimate greater than the exact product; rounding down both factors gives an estimate less than the exact product.

> **Check Out the Glossary**
> For vocabulary words
> See page 544.

208 Lesson 6.2

Meeting Individual Needs

Early Finishers

Have students redraw the pictograph on page 209 with each symbol representing 60 pounds of garbage.

 **ESL APPROPRIATE**

Extra Support

Some students may need to review the rules for rounding whole numbers. Have them explain how to round a 2-digit number to the nearest ten.

Ongoing Assessment

Anecdotal Report Make notes on students' ability to complete both steps of the problem— rounding to the greatest place and multiplying multiples of ten.

Follow Up If students have difficulty estimating products, you may want to assign **Reteach 51.**

For students who need a greater challenge, assign **Extend 51.**

Practice

Estimate the product. Estimates may vary depending on the method used. Estimates shown are by rounding.

1 72 × $39
70 × $40; $2,800

2 55 × 63
60 × 60; 3,600

3 85 × $29
90 × $30; $2,700

4 12 × 18
10 × 20; 200

5 91 × 432
90 × 400; 36,000

6 83 × 654
80 × 700; 56,000

7 35 × 950
40 × 1,000; 40,000

8 49 × $519
50 × $500; $25,000

9 45 × $1,925
50 × $2,000; $100,000

10 28 × 5,250
30 × 5,000; 150,000

11 74 × 2,915
70 × 3,000; 210,000

12 17 × 6,643
20 × 7,000; 140,000

13 58 × 92
60 × 90; 5,400

14 15 × $712
20 × $700; $14,000

15 44 × 854
40 × 900; 36,000

16 75 × $3,925
80 × $4,000; $320,000

Estimate to solve. Write > or <.

17 47 × 35 ● 2,000 <   **18** 57 × 32 ● 1,500 >   **19** 756 × 89 ● 72,000 <

MIXED APPLICATIONS
Problem Solving

What is in your garbage?
Amount produced by one person in one year

Food Yard
Glass
Metal
Paper
Plastic

Key: Each 🗑 stands for 30 pounds

Use the pictograph for problems 20–22.

20 About how many pounds of food/yard, glass, metal, paper, and plastic garbage does one person produce in one year?
Possible answer: about 1,300 lb

21 About how many times more paper is produced than plastic? about 7 times more

22 **Write a problem** using information from the pictograph. Exchange problems with a classmate and solve each other's problems.
Students should compare problems and solutions.

23 **Data Point** For one day, count the plastic items you throw away and recycle. Combine your list with others to make a class graph.
Students' class graph should reflect collected data.

---

more to explore

Use Front Digits to Estimate

Here is another way to estimate a product.

Use the first digit of each factor. Replace the other digits with zeros. Then multiply.

Estimate: 66 × 4,710
Think: 60 × 4,000 = 240,000

Estimate the product using front digits.

1 24 × 356 6,000   **2** 745 × 87 56,000   **3** 55 × 860 40,000   **4** 46 × 7,457 280,000

Extra Practice, page 504

Multiply by 2-Digit Numbers **209**

Alternate Teaching Strategy

Present the following problem:

> Local scout troops collect about 42 pounds of newspaper a day to recycle. About how many pounds of newspaper will they recycle in one year?

Ask:

- **What operation will you use to solve the problem?** *[multiplication]*
- **What is 42 rounded to the nearest ten?** *[40]*
- **How many days are in one year? What is the number rounded to the nearest hundred?** *[365 days; 400]*
- **You can use rounded factors to estimate the product. What is 40 × 400?** *[16,000]*
- **About how many pounds of newspaper will the scout troops recycle in one year?** *[about 16,000 lb]*

Have a volunteer show the solution on the chalkboard. Then repeat the activity using other numbers.

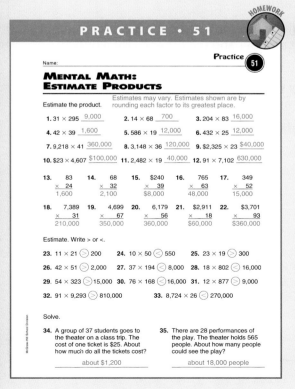

PRACTICE · 51

Name:

Practice **51**

MENTAL MATH: ESTIMATE PRODUCTS

Estimate the product. Estimates may vary. Estimates shown are by rounding each factor to its greatest place.

1. 31 × 295 9,000
2. 14 × 68 700
3. 204 × 83 16,000
4. 42 × 39 1,600
5. 586 × 19 12,000
6. 432 × 25 12,000
7. 9,218 × 41 360,000
8. 3,148 × 36 120,000
9. $2,325 × 23 $40,000
10. $23 × 4,607 $100,000
11. 2,482 × 19 40,000
12. 91 × 7,102 630,000

13. 83 × 24 = 1,600
14. 68 × 32 = 2,100
15. $240 × 39 = $8,000
16. 765 × 63 = 48,000
17. 349 × 52 = 15,000

18. 7,389 × 31 = 210,000
19. 4,699 × 67 = 350,000
20. 6,179 × 56 = 360,000
21. $2,911 × 18 = $60,000
22. $3,701 × 93 = $360,000

Estimate. Write > or <.

23. 11 × 21 > 200
24. 10 × 50 < 550
25. 23 × 19 > 300
26. 42 × 51 > 2,000
27. 37 × 194 < 8,000
28. 18 × 802 < 16,000
29. 54 × 323 > 15,000
30. 76 × 168 < 16,000
31. 12 × 877 > 9,000
32. 91 × 9,293 > 810,000
33. 8,724 × 26 < 270,000

Solve.

34. A group of 37 students goes to the theater on a class trip. The cost of one ticket is $25. About how much do all the tickets cost?
about $1,200

35. There are 28 performances of the play. The theater holds 565 people. About how many people could see the play?
about 18,000 people

RETEACH · 51

Name:

Reteach **51**

MENTAL MATH: ESTIMATE PRODUCTS

You can use rounding to estimate products. Round each number to the greatest place. Then multiply.

Estimate: 32 × 49

32
Think: The greatest place is the tens place. Round to the nearest ten. 32 rounds to 30.

49
Think: The greatest place is the tens place. Round to the nearest ten. 49 rounds to 50.

49 → 50
× 32 → × 30
1,500 estimate

Estimate: 54 × 117

54
Think: The greatest place is the tens place. Round to the nearest ten. 54 rounds to 50.

117
Think: The greatest place is the hundreds place. Round to the nearest hundred. 117 rounds to 100.

117 → 100
× 54 → × 50
5,000 estimate

Round to the greatest place.

1. 78
greatest place: tens
78 rounds to 80.

2. 423
greatest place: hundreds
423 rounds to 400.

Estimate the product by rounding.

3. 34 → 30
× 23 → × 20
600

4. 47 → 50
× 12 → × 10
500

5. 729 → 700
× 38 → × 40
28,000

EXTEND · 51

Name:

Extend **51**

MENTAL MATH: ESTIMATE PRODUCTS

Find the Factors Puzzle

This puzzle has all the answers, but needs clues.

- Each answer, across or down, is a product.
- The clues are two factors of that product.
- Possible clues are given for 1 Across and 1 Down.

Make up clues for each answer. Then copy the puzzle without the answers and give it to a friend to complete.

Clues may vary. Check students' work.

ACROSS
1. 9,000 × 70, or 70 × 9,000, or 7,000 × 90
2. _____
3. _____
4. _____
5. _____
6. _____

DOWN
1. 800 × 8,000, or 8,000 × 800, or 1,600 × 4,000
2. _____
3. _____
4. _____
5. _____
6. _____

209

LESSON 6.3

EXPLORE ACTIVITY

Multiply 2-Digit Numbers

OBJECTIVE Explore multiplying 2-digit numbers by 2-digit numbers.

RESOURCE REMINDER
Math Center Cards 52
Practice 52, Reteach 52, Extend 52

SKILLS TRACE

GRADE 3	• Multiply 2-digit numbers by 1-digit numbers with/without regrouping. *(Chapter 12)*
GRADE 4	• Explore multiplying 2-digit numbers by 2-digit numbers.
GRADE 5	• Multiply whole numbers by 2-digit numbers. *(Chapter 4)*

WARM-UP

Cooperative Groups   Logical/Analytical

OBJECTIVE Review multiplying by a 1-digit number.

Materials per group: 2 number cubes

▶ Have students draw the following several times on a sheet of paper:

▶ One student tosses a number cube until a 3, 4, or 5 is rolled to determine the number of digits in the first number. Have students cross out any unnecessary boxes as needed.

▶ The player to the right tosses both number cubes and each player writes the sum of the two numbers in one of the boxes (or two if the sum is a 2-digit number).

▶ Once all the boxes are filled, students find the product of the numbers they generated. The player with the greatest product is the winner of the round. The game can be altered by having players try for the least product, the product closest to 50,000, and so on.

ART CONNECTION

Cooperative Pairs   Logical/Analytical

OBJECTIVE Connect art to multiplication.

Materials per pair: 2 large index cards

▶ Have pairs of students write a multiplication word problem. One factor in the problem should be a one-digit number and the other factor a one- or two-digit number.

▶ Have each pair decide how they would draw the answer to their multiplication problem. Then they draw the answer on the other card.

▶ Display all the word problems and drawings of answers. Challenge students to match problems to answers.

Daily Review

PREVIOUS DAY QUICK REVIEW

Estimate the product. *[Estimates may vary.]*

1. 12 × 18 *[200]*
2. 36 × 207 *[8,000]*
3. 49 × 188 *[10,000]*
4. 32 × 2,135 *[60,000]*

FAST FACTS

1. 3 × 3 *[9]*
2. 5 × 5 *[25]*
3. 7 × 7 *[49]*
4. 8 × 8 *[64]*

Problem of the Day • 52

In an average day, 20,000 people write letters to the President of the United States. In 30 days should the President receive about a million letters, about a half million letters, or about 250,000 letters? *[about a half million letters]*

TECH LINK

MATH VAN

Activity You may wish to use *Earth Day Plans* to teach this lesson.

MATH FORUM

Cultural Diversity My students enjoy learning about holidays celebrated in other cultures. I have students research these celebrations. Then they use the information to write and illustrate a problem.

Visit our Resource Village at http://www.mhschool.com to see more of the Math Forum.

MATH CENTER

Practice

OBJECTIVE Use the distributive property to find factors and the product for a given model of a product.

Materials per pair: ruler, colored pencils, graph paper; per student: Math Center Recording Sheet (TA 31 optional)

Students model a product on graph paper. They exchange papers and each states the product of the model, "breaking apart" the factors to find the product without counting. They then find another pair of factors for the product. *[Answers may vary]*

Problem Solving

OBJECTIVE Solve area problems.

Materials per student: straightedge, graph paper, Math Center Recording Sheet (TA 31 optional)

Students draw a simple floor plan of one level in a house. They calculate the area of each room and of the total. *[Answers may vary. Check students' work.]*

PRACTICE ACTIVITY 52

MATH CENTER
Partners 👥

Spatial Sense • Mystery Factors

Both partners follow the same steps.

- Draw a rectangle or square on a sheet of graph paper. Make both the length and width at least 10 boxes long. Also be sure that either the length or the width is an even number of boxes.
- Exchange papers. Find the factors. Find the area by breaking apart the factors. Show your work on the graph paper rectangle. Find another pair of factors that will give you the same area.

YOU NEED
ruler
colored pencils
graph paper

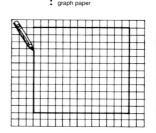

Chapter 6, Lesson 3, pages 210–213

Multiplication

NCTM Standards

✓ Problem Solving
  Communication
  Reasoning
✓ Connections

ESL APPROPRIATE

PROBLEM-SOLVING ACTIVITY 52

MATH CENTER
On Your Own 👤

Spatial Reasoning • Floor Plan

Andrew's classroom is 30 ft wide by 40 ft long. To find the area of the room, he multiplies 30 × 40. The area is 1,200 sq ft.

Draw a floor plan for one level in a house. Put at least four rooms on your plan.

- Label the length and width of each room.
- Calculate the area of each room in square feet.
- Find the total area by adding the areas of all the rooms.

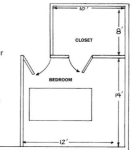

Chapter 6, Lesson 3, pages 210–213

Multiplication

NCTM Standards

✓ Problem Solving
  Communication
  Reasoning
✓ Connections

Lesson 6.3 *continued*

EXPLORE ACTIVITY
Multiply 2-Digit Numbers

OBJECTIVE Explore multiplying 2-digit numbers by 2-digit numbers.

Materials per pair: 1–4 spinner (TA 3), centimeter graph paper (TA 7), scissors

Have one or more students illustrate how to use graph paper to multiply by 1-digit numbers. Students can use the overhead and markers or draw the rectangles on the chalkboard.

   *Cooperative Pairs*

▶ **LEARN Work Together** Review the activity with the class. Give students time to solve a few more problems. Remind students that their graph paper has about 33 boxes across and 38 boxes down so that the numbers they choose must fit on the paper.

Talk It Over Let students share their methods with the class. Allow time for some students to illustrate their methods on the chalkboard.

Multiply 2-Digit Numbers

Grids can help you to multiply. You used grids to multiply by 1-digit numbers. You can also use grids to multiply by 2-digit numbers.

You will need
- *1–4 spinner*
- *centimeter graph paper*

Work Together
Work with a partner. Spin the spinner twice to get the tens and ones digits of a factor. Spin twice again to get the second factor.

Cut out or draw a rectangle on graph paper. Use the first factor as the length and the second factor as the width.

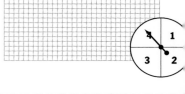

Find the product of the two factors without counting all the squares in the grid.

Record your results in a table.

First Factor	Second Factor	Product
32	14	

Repeat with two new factors.

Possible answer: Partitioned the rectangle into hundreds squares, te
Talk It Over   **strips, and ones, then counted, regrouped if necessary, and added.**
▶ Explain the method you used to find the totals.

▶ How can you tell if your products are reasonable?
Possible answer: Round each factor to the nearest ten and estimate—the estimated and exact products should be close.

210 Lesson 6.3

Meeting Individual Needs

Extra Support

Some students may need to review the rules for rounding whole numbers. Have them explain how to round a 2-digit number to the nearest ten.

Gifted And Talented

If students are using the multiplication algorithm, have them show how the algorithm relates to using graph paper. Students should show how place value is used in the algorithm to find the product of two numbers.

Ongoing Assessment

Observation Checklist Determine if students understand how to multiply by 2-digit numbers by observing them finding the product of 34 and 38. *[1,292]* Students should realize they can break the problem up into smaller problems. One possible way of breaking up the problem is $(34 \times 8) + (34 \times 30)$.

Follow Up For more practice with multiplication models, assign **Reteach 52.**

For students who are ready to move on, assign **Extend 52.**

Make Connections

Brian and Eileen broke the factors apart to find their products.

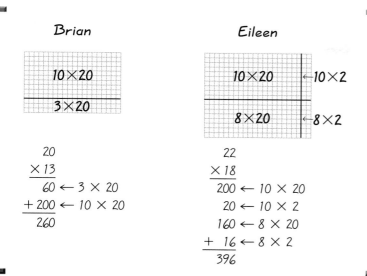

Brian

Eileen

$$
\begin{array}{r}
20 \\
\times\ 13 \\
\hline
60 \leftarrow 3 \times 20 \\
+\ 200 \leftarrow 10 \times 20 \\
\hline
260
\end{array}
$$

$$
\begin{array}{r}
22 \\
\times\ 18 \\
\hline
200 \leftarrow 10 \times 20 \\
20 \leftarrow 10 \times 2 \\
160 \leftarrow 8 \times 20 \\
+\ 16 \leftarrow 8 \times 2 \\
\hline
396
\end{array}
$$

▶ How did Brian and Eileen use place value when they broke apart the factors to find the products? **Possible answer: Brian broke one factor, 13, into 1 ten 3 ones, then multiplied the tens by 20 and the ones by 20; Eileen broke both factors into tens and ones and then multiplied each separately.**

▶ Why does Brian's method have two addends while Eileen's method has four addends? **Possible answer: In Brian's method, 20 does not have a digit in the ones place; in Eileen's method, both factors have tens and ones.**

Check for Understanding
Multiply using any method.

1	**2**	**3**	**4**	**5**
25	36	17	12	21
× 30	× 23	× 20	× 38	× 35
750	828	340	456	735

Critical Thinking: Analyze   Explain your reasoning.

6 Another way to find 13 × 20 is by thinking:
13 × 2 tens = 26 tens = 260. How is this method like Brian's method? How is it different? **Possible answer: Alike—both use multiplying by a multiple of ten to find the products more easily; different—Brian broke apart 13, while this method renamed 20 to 2 tens to multiply.**

Turn the page for Practice. ➡

Multiply by 2-Digit Numbers **211**

MAKE CONNECTIONS

Have students look at the methods Brian and Eileen used to find two products. Point out how Brian broke apart 1 factor and found the sum of 2 partial products. Point out how Eileen broke apart both factors and found the sum of 4 partial products.

Let students discuss their answers to the questions following Brian's and Eileen's methods. Ask students if any of the methods they used were similar to Brian's and Eileen's. Also ask students if they wrote their work in a similar way.

3 Close

▶ **Check for Understanding** using items 1–6, page 211.

CRITICAL THINKING
In item 6, extend students' thinking by asking:
- **How could you solve 743 × 20 by using place value?**
  [Possible answer: 743 × 2 tens = 1,486 tens = 14,860]

Practice See pages 212–213.

▶ PRACTICE

Materials have available: graph paper, scissors

Options for assigning exercises:
A—Odd ex. 1–19; all ex. 20–24; **Cultural Connection**
B—Even ex. 2–20; all ex. 21–24; **Cultural Connection**

• For ex. 1–4, have students draw a sketch of the rectangle on their paper and show how they would section the rectangle to find the product.
• For ex. 5–19, let students use any method they choose. Encourage students to show their method.
• For **Make It Right** (ex. 20), see Common Error below.

Cultural Connection Work through the steps using the lattice method. Point out to students that a 1-digit number would be written with a zero in the left most triangle. For example, 8 would be written 08. Students add columns of numbers diagonally starting with the first column on the far right. Sums are regrouped as needed.

Practice

Find the total number of squares in the rectangle without counting.

1   18
10
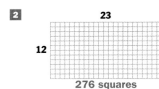
180 squares

2   23
12
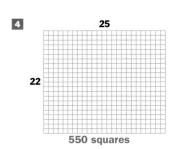
276 squares

3   16
20
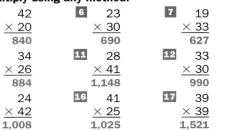
320 squares

4   25
22
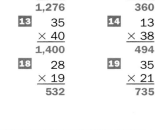
550 squares

Multiply using any method.

5	**6**	**7**	**8**	**9**
42	23	19	44	20
× 20	× 30	× 33	× 29	× 18
840	690	627	1,276	360

10	**11**	**12**	**13**	**14**
34	28	33	35	13
× 26	× 41	× 30	× 40	× 38
884	1,148	990	1,400	494

15	**16**	**17**	**18**	**19**
24	41	39	28	35
× 42	× 25	× 39	× 19	× 21
1,008	1,025	1,521	532	735

····················· **Make It Right** ·····················

20 Here is how Riley found 20 × 37. Explain what the mistake is, then correct it.
Possible answer: He multiplied 3 by 20 instead of 30 by 20.

```
        37
      × 20
       140   ← 20 × 7
    + 600    ← 20 × 30
      740
```

```
        37
      × 20
       140   ← 20 × 7
    +  60    ← 20 × 3
       200
```

Meeting Individual Needs

Early Finishers

Have students show alternate ways of finding the products in ex. 1–4. If they did not use place value the first time, require students to use this method the second time.

COMMON ERROR

Students can often forget the importance of place value. Remind students that 37 is 3 tens + 7 ones or 30 + 7. For students who make this error, review place value to re-emphasize its importance.

Gender Fairness

Give equal amounts of attention and feedback when girls or boys participate in a discussion.

Language Support

Encourage students acquiring English to answer the first question in the **Talk It Over** section using graph paper. They may feel more comfortable explaining their methods using this visual aid.

ESL APPROPRIATE

23. Possible answer: Buy the carton; if you need 10 packages of paper, then the carton is $2 cheaper; 3 × 10 = 30 and $30 − $28 = $2.

MIXED APPLICATIONS
Problem Solving
Pencil & Paper · Calculator · Mental Math

21 List all the pairs of numbers that have a product of 400. 20 and 20, 10 and 40, 25 and 16, 5 and 80

20	10	25	15
18	24	100	20
5	16	40	80

22 How many tiles will you use if you cover a floor that is 18 feet by 11 feet using 1-foot by 1-foot tiles? **198 tiles**

23 Make a decision A carton of computer paper has 10 packages of paper in it and sells for $28. You can also buy the same paper for $3 per package. You have $35 to buy computer paper. What would you buy? Explain. **See above.**

24 Were the trees along the path of the Great Wall of China planted more than or less than 25 years ago? **SEE INFOBIT. Students subtract 1976 from the current year.**

INFOBIT
In 1976, the people who live in Beijing, China, planted more than 300 million fast-growing trees along the path of the Great Wall of China.

Cultural Connection
Hindu Lattice Multiplication

Here is a method Hindu mathematicians in India used to multiply two numbers.

INDIA

To find 45 × 36:

Step 1 Write the factors on the outside of the lattice as shown.

Step 2 Write the product of each pair of digits inside the lattice as shown.

Step 3 Starting at the top right, add the numbers in each diagonal row. Be careful to carry numbers to the next row if needed.

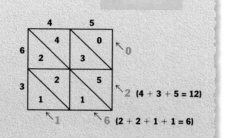

0

2 (4 + 3 + 5 = 12)

1   6 (2 + 2 + 1 + 1 = 6)

45 × 36 = 1,620

Use lattice multiplication to find the product. Check students' drawings.
1 12 × 18 **216**   **2** 25 × 19 **475**   **3** 32 × 39 **1,248**   **4** 56 × 44 **2,464**

Extra Practice, page 505

Multiply by 2-Digit Numbers **213**

Alternate Teaching Strategy

Materials per pair: 156 counters or place-value models

Write the problem 13 × 12 on the chalkboard. Have students use counters to show 13 groups of 12.

Tell students to find the number of counters there are altogether without counting them individually. Ask students to think of ways to group the counters. Students should group counters by tens and count the number of tens and the number of counters left. *[15 tens and 6 ones left]*

Then have students write the product in standard form. *[156]*

Have students work in pairs to find the product of another pair of 2-digit numbers. Choose relatively small numbers so that this method is easier for students to illustrate. Tell students they can make a drawing, use counters, or place-value models.

ESL APPROPRIATE

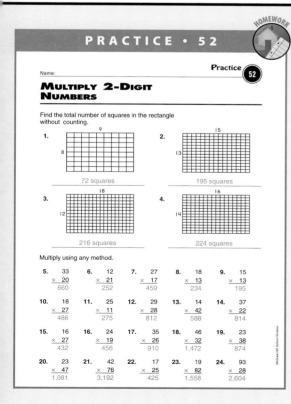

PRACTICE · 52

Name: _____   Practice **52**

MULTIPLY 2-DIGIT NUMBERS

Find the total number of squares in the rectangle without counting.

1. 9 / 8 — 72 squares
2. 15 / 13 — 195 squares
3. 18 / 12 — 216 squares
4. 16 / 14 — 224 squares

Multiply using any method.

5. 33 × 20 = 660	**6.** 12 × 21 = 252	**7.** 27 × 17 = 459	**8.** 18 × 13 = 234	**9.** 15 × 13 = 195
10. 18 × 27 = 486	**11.** 25 × 11 = 275	**12.** 29 × 28 = 812	**13.** 14 × 42 = 588	**14.** 37 × 22 = 814
15. 16 × 27 = 432	**16.** 24 × 19 = 456	**17.** 35 × 26 = 910	**18.** 46 × 32 = 1,472	**19.** 23 × 38 = 874
20. 23 × 47 = 1,081	**21.** 42 × 76 = 3,192	**22.** 17 × 25 = 425	**23.** 19 × 82 = 1,558	**24.** 93 × 28 = 2,604

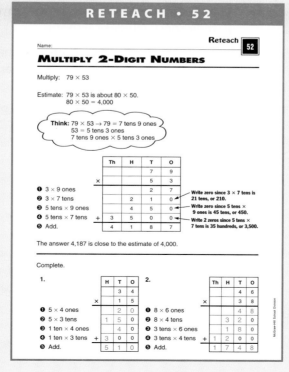

RETEACH · 52

Name: _____   Reteach **52**

MULTIPLY 2-DIGIT NUMBERS

Multiply: 79 × 53

Estimate: 79 × 53 is about 80 × 50.
80 × 50 = 4,000

Think: 79 × 53 → 79 = 7 tens 9 ones
53 = 5 tens 3 ones
7 tens 9 ones × 5 tens 3 ones

	Th	H	T	O
			7	9
×			5	3
❶ 3 × 9 ones			2	7
❷ 3 × 7 tens		2	1	0
❸ 5 tens × 9 ones		4	5	0
❹ 5 tens × 7 tens	3	5	0	0
❺ Add.	4	1	8	7

❷ Write zero since 3 × 7 tens is 21 tens, or 210.
❸ Write zero since 5 tens × 9 ones is 45 tens, or 450.
❹ Write 2 zeros since 5 tens × 7 tens is 35 hundreds, or 3,500.

The answer 4,187 is close to the estimate of 4,000.

Complete.

1.

	H	T	O
		3	4
×		1	5
❶ 5 × 4 ones		2	0
❷ 5 × 3 tens	1	5	0
❸ 1 ten × 4 ones		4	0
❹ 1 ten × 3 tens	3	0	
❺ Add.	5	1	0

2.

	Th	H	T	O
			4	6
×			3	8
❶ 8 × 6 ones			4	8
❷ 8 × 4 tens		3	2	0
❸ 3 tens × 6 ones		1	8	0
❹ 3 tens × 4 tens	1	2	0	
❺ Add.	1	7	4	8

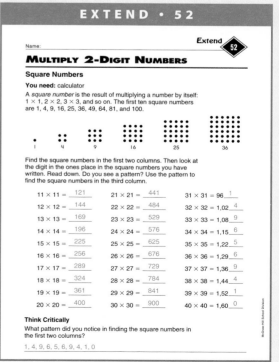

EXTEND · 52

Name: _____   Extend **52**

MULTIPLY 2-DIGIT NUMBERS

Square Numbers

You need: calculator

A *square number* is the result of multiplying a number by itself: 1 × 1, 2 × 2, 3 × 3, and so on. The first ten square numbers are 1, 4, 9, 16, 25, 36, 49, 64, 81, and 100.

• :: ⦂⦂ ⸬⸬ ⸭⸭ 36

Find the square numbers in the first two columns. Then look at the digit in the ones place in the square numbers you have written. Read down. Do you see a pattern? Use the pattern to find the square numbers in the third column.

11 × 11 = 121	21 × 21 = 441	31 × 31 = 96_1_
12 × 12 = 144	22 × 22 = 484	32 × 32 = 1,02_4_
13 × 13 = 169	23 × 23 = 529	33 × 33 = 1,08_9_
14 × 14 = 196	24 × 24 = 576	34 × 34 = 1,15_6_
15 × 15 = 225	25 × 25 = 625	35 × 35 = 1,22_5_
16 × 16 = 256	26 × 26 = 676	36 × 36 = 1,29_6_
17 × 17 = 289	27 × 27 = 729	37 × 37 = 1,36_9_
18 × 18 = 324	28 × 28 = 784	38 × 38 = 1,44_4_
19 × 19 = 361	29 × 29 = 841	39 × 39 = 1,52_1_
20 × 20 = 400	30 × 30 = 900	40 × 40 = 1,60_0_

Think Critically
What pattern did you notice in finding the square numbers in the first two columns?

1, 4, 9, 6, 5, 6, 9, 4, 1, 0

213

LESSON 6.4

Multiply 2-Digit Numbers

OBJECTIVE Multiply 2-digit numbers by 2-digit numbers, with and without regrouping.

Teaching with Technology
See alternate computer lesson, pp. 217A–217B.

RESOURCE REMINDER
Math Center Cards 53
Practice 53, Reteach 53, Extend 53

SKILLS TRACE

GRADE 3
• Multiply 2-digit numbers by 1-digit numbers with/without regrouping. (Chapter 12)

GRADE 4
• Multiply 2-digit numbers by 2-digit numbers with/without regrouping.

GRADE 5
• Multiply whole numbers by 2-digit numbers. (Chapter 4)

WARM-UP

Cooperative Pairs   **Logical/Analytical**

OBJECTIVE Explore using word names to find products.

► Review the standard form of word names for numbers. Then write problems like the following on the chalkboard using the word names:

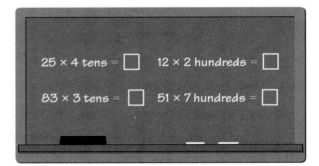

25×4 tens = ☐ 12×2 hundreds = ☐

83×3 tens = ☐ 51×7 hundreds = ☐

► Have students work in pairs to find each product. For example, 25×4 tens = 100 tens or 1,000. Then have them make up problems of their own to share.

ESL APPROPRIATE

LITERATURE CONNECTION

Cooperative Pairs   **Logical/Analytical**

OBJECTIVE Connect multiplication to word counting.

Materials per pair: social studies text

► Tell students to guess how many pages about 3,000 words would take up in their social studies textbook.

► Have students then determine an answer by counting the number of words in the longest line in a paragraph and multiplying by the number of lines on the page or column.

► Have them total individual page results to see how many pages are needed for 3,000 words.

Daily Review

Math Van

PREVIOUS DAY QUICK REVIEW

1. 42 × 20 *[840]*
2. 26 × 30 *[780]*
3. 25 × 14 *[350]*
4. 36 × 24 *[864]*

FAST FACTS

1. 9 + 8 *[17]*
2. 6 + 7 *[13]*
3. 5 + 9 *[14]*
4. 8 + 7 *[15]*

Problem of the Day • 53

Katie is twice as old as her little sister, Penny. In 5 years Katie will be 3 times as old as her sister is today. How old are Katie and Penny?
[Katie—10, Penny—5]

TECH LINK

MATH VAN

Activity You may wish to use *Earth Day Plans* to practice and extend skills and concepts.

MATH FORUM

Idea I encourage my students to create their own games involving the skill they are currently learning. They enjoy playing their own games and trying other students' games gives them a great amount of practice.

Visit our Resource Village at http://www.mhschool.com to see more of the Math Forum.

MATH CENTER

Practice

OBJECTIVE Multiply two 2-digit numbers.

Materials per group: inch ruler; per student: 2 counters or connecting cubes, Math Center Recording Sheet (TA 31 optional)

Students play a game in which they do 2-digit multiplication.

PRACTICE ACTIVITY 53
MATH CENTER Small Group

Game • Product Practice

- Each player makes a game sheet—a 4-by-5 rectangle with 20 boxes. Decide with your group on twenty 2-digit numbers to put in the boxes. Each player can put the numbers anywhere on the game sheet. Exchange game sheets with each other.
- On your turn, hold your hands about 2 ft above the game sheet. (Use a ruler.) In each hand have a counter or cube, which you drop onto the game sheet. Multiply the two numbers the counters land on to find your score. Play five rounds. The player with the greatest score wins.

YOU NEED
2 counters or connecting cubes
inch ruler

NCTM Standards
Problem Solving
Communication
✓ Reasoning
✓ Connections

Chapter 6, Lesson 4, pages 214–217   Multiplication

ESL APPROPRIATE

Problem Solving

OBJECTIVE Make predictions using multiplication.

Materials per student: 12 index cards, Math Center Recording Sheet (TA 31 optional)

Students multiply 2-digit factors and predict whether products will be odd or even. *[Two odd factors give an odd product; two even factors give an even product; one odd and one even give even products.]*

PROBLEM-SOLVING ACTIVITY 53
MATH CENTER On Your Own

Logical Reasoning • Odd or Even?

- Write the following factors on separate index cards: 10, 11, 12, 13, 20, 21, 22, 23, 30, 31, 32, 33.
- Mix up the cards and place them facedown. Then choose 2 cards. Find the product of the 2 factors. Record the multiplication sentence. Repeat until you have written 4 multiplication sentences.
- Look at the factors and the products. Notice which ones are odd and which ones are even. Repeat once more, but before you find the product, predict whether it will be odd or even.

YOU NEED
12 index cards

NCTM Standards
✓ Problem Solving
Communication
✓ Reasoning
✓ Connections

Chapter 6, Lesson 4, pages 214–217   Multiplication

Multiply 2-Digit Numbers

OBJECTIVE Multiply 2-digit numbers by 2-digit numbers, with and without regrouping.

Materials per pair: 16 counters or connecting cubes

Vocabulary regroup

Ask students:

- **Are there any tropical rain forests in the United States? If so, in which state?** *[Yes; in Hawaii.]*
- **How large do you think an acre might be?** *[Accept any reasonable estimate—1 acre = 4,840 square yards, a little smaller than a football field including the end zones.]*

Whole Class

Cultural Connection Read the **Cultural Note.** Have your students find Central America, South America, Asia, and Africa on a globe or map of the world. Ask students also to find the equator and note that these areas are near it.

▶ **LEARN** Read through the problem on page 214. First review how to estimate the product. You may wish to review the method from Lesson 3 to find the product. Then work through the steps to find the product using the new method in this lesson.

Talk It Over Have students compare the different methods of finding the product. Ask:

- **Why is it useful to have more than one method to multiply?** *[Possible answer: You can use one method to check the answer of another method.]*
- **Why do you estimate the product before you multiply?** *[Possible answer: to check the reasonableness of the answer you find]*

MULTIPLICATION

Multiply 2-Digit Numbers

To protect an acre of rain forest, you can send $35 to the Nature Conservancy's Adopt-an-Acre Program.

A fourth-grade class would like to protect 20 acres of rain forest. How much money does the class need to raise?

Estimate: 20 × $35   **Think:** 20 × $40 = $800

In the last lesson you used this method to find the exact answer.

$$
\begin{array}{r}
\$35 \\
\times\ \ 20 \\
\hline
100 \leftarrow 20 \times 5 \\
+\ \ \ 600 \leftarrow 20 \times 30 \\
\hline
\$700
\end{array}
$$

> **Cultural Note**
> Tropical rain forests are located to the north and south of the equator in Central America, South America, Asia, and Africa. Over 750,000 different kinds of plants grow in Earth's rain forests.

Here is another method.

Step 1	Step 2
Multiply by the ones.	**Multiply by the tens. Regroup if necessary.**
$$\begin{array}{r}\$35 \\ \times\ \ 20 \\ \hline 0\end{array}$$	$$\begin{array}{r}{}^{1} \\ \$35 \\ \times\ \ 20 \\ \hline \$700\end{array}$$
Think: 0 ones × 35 = 0	**Think:** 2 tens × 35 = 70 tens

Question 1. Similar—both use partial products; different—
The class needs to raise $700.   the first method breaks apart
35, while the second method breaks apart 20.

Talk It Over

▶ How are the two methods similar? different? See above.

▶ Describe how you could use a grid to find the product of 20 and 35.
Possible answer: Break up the grid to show 35 as 30 + 5, find 20 × 30 and 20 × 5, and add the products—600 + 100 = 700.

214 Lesson 6.4

Meeting Individual Needs

Extra Support

It may be helpful for students having difficulty to label each partial product as in the steps in the development. This assures that they are multiplying by the correct place value.

Gifted And Talented

Have students find the difference between the greatest and the least products of two 2-digit factors. They may repeat the task with two 3-digit factors.

Ongoing Assessment

Anecdotal Report Make notes on students' ability to solve a multiplication problem without using manipulatives. Watch students solve one of the practice ex. 1–23. Make sure students understand how to use the algorithm.

Follow Up For more practice with multiplying with 2-digit numbers, assign **Reteach 53**.

For students who need a challenge, assign **Extend 53**.

What if the class plants 26 rows of 35 seedlings. How many seedlings does the class plant?

Estimate: 26 × 35   **Think:** 30 × 40 = 1,200

Multiply: 26 × 35

Step 1	Step 2	Step 3
Multiply by the ones.	**Multiply by the tens.**	**Add the products.**
3 35 × 26 ——— 210	1 3̶ 35 × 26 ——— 210 700	1 3̶ 35 × 26 ——— 210 + 700 ——— 910
Think: 6 ones × 35 = 210 ones	**Think:** 2 tens × 35 = 70 tens	

The class plants 910 seedlings in all.

You can multiply money amounts the same way you multiply whole numbers.

> **Check Out the Glossary**
> For vocabulary words
> See page 544.

Multiply: 26 × $0.35

$0.35
×   26
————
$9.10
↑↑ Insert the dollar sign and decimal point.

Check for Understanding

Multiply using any method. Estimate to see if your answer is reasonable. Estimates may vary. Estimates shown are by rounding.

1	**2**	**3**	**4**	**5**
13 × 12 156; 100	25 × 11 275; 300	34 × 22 748; 600	29 × 30 870; 900	48 × 12 576; 500

Multiply.

6 16 × $53
$848

7 25 × $0.67
$16.75

8 34 × $0.59
$20.06

9 41 × $0.82
$33.62

Critical Thinking: Compare

10 If 5 × 45 = 225, what is 50 × 45? Explain your reasoning.
See page T17.

11 Why are there three steps to multiply 35 by 26 and only two steps to multiply 27 by 30? **Possible answer: For 35 × 26, both factors have digits in the tens and ones place, while for 27 × 30, one of the factors (30) has no ones, so you only need to multiply the tens.**

Turn the page for Practice. ➡

Multiply by 2-Digit Numbers **215**

C H E C K

Read through the problem at the top of the page and review the estimate. Work through each step of the algorithm with students. For Step 1, ask:
- **What does the little 3 mean in Step 1?** *[Possible answer: 6 × 5 = 30 and you want to add the 3 in the tens place.]*

Before students multiply by the tens in Step 2, ask:
- **Why is the 3 crossed out?** *[Possible answer: It was used in the product when you multiplied by the ones.]*

After reviewing Step 3, ask:
- **Why do you add the products?** *[Possible answer: To find the total product, you must add the products of the tens and the ones.]*

③ Close

Check for Understanding using items 1–11, page 215.

CRITICAL THINKING

 For item 11, ask students to describe 2-digit × 2-digit problems that can be solved in two steps. *[Possible answer: One of the numbers ends in a zero.]*

Practice See pages 216–217.

Inclusion

For students who have difficulty lining up columns of numbers, have them turn their paper sideways and use the lines to guide their columns.

Language Support

Help students focus on the multiplication algorithm by explaining terms in the problems that may be new to them. In the introductory problem explain that an acre is a unit of measurement for a square section of land. Conservancy means they want to take care of and protect, or conserve, the rain forest.

ESL APPROPRIATE

▶ **PRACTICE**

Materials per pair: 16 counters or connecting cubes; have
available: calculators

Options for assigning exercises:
A—Ex. 1–10, 20–29; **Hopscotch for Factors Game!;**
   Mixed Review
B—Ex. 6–19, 24–29; **Hopscotch for Factors Game!;**
   Mixed Review

• Students may use any method to solve ex. 1–23. Encourage
students to solve without using manipulatives or drawings if
possible.
• Students can use multiplying by multiples of 10, 100, and
1,000; guess and test; or number sense to choose the correct
answer in ex. 24–26.
• For **Make It Right,** see Common Error below.

 Algebra Variables are used extensively in the study of algebra. In ex. 24–26, students find the missing value of a variable
in a multiplication equation.

Hopscotch for Factors Game! Read the **Cultural Note.** Hopscotch is a children's game that is played by hopping around a
game board on one foot to retrieve an object on the board.

As students play the game, they develop strategies for choosing which space to mark as their own. You may wish to place
the game in the math center so that students have easy access
to it. Repeatedly playing the game will provide practice in estimating products.

Mixed Review/Test Preparation Students review estimating
sums, differences, and products, a skill learned in Chapters 2
and 3.

---

28. Possible answer: 50 lb; amount burned is 250, amount recycled
is 200 lb, 250 − 200 = 50 lb.

Practice

Multiply using any method. Remember to estimate.

1	**2**	**3**	**4**	**5**
17	31	26	$25	32
× 11	× 22	× 23	× 40	× 19
187	682	598	$1,000	608

6	**7**	**8**	**9**	**10**
24	$28	47	44	$60
× 35	× 12	× 30	× 29	× 18
840	$336	1,410	1,276	$1,080

11	**12**	**13**	**14**	**15**
24	35	29	35	64
× 18	× 23	× 42	× 58	× 19
432	805	1,218	2,030	1,216

16 25 × 50 **1,250**   **17** 54 × 12 **648**   **18** 36 × $27 **$972**   **19** 73 × 11 **803**

20 73 × 44 **3,212**   **21** 63 × $92 **$5,796**   **22** 88 × $0.36 **$31.68**   **23** 52 × $0.84 **$43.68**

✴ **ALGEBRA** Write the letter of the missing number.

24 ■ × 50 = 1,000 b   **a.** 6   **b.** 20   **c.** 15   **d.** 16

25 40 × ■ = 2,400 a   **a.** 60   **b.** 70   **c.** 6   **d.** 12

26 ■ × 32 = 960 c   **a.** 20   **b.** 15   **c.** 30   **d.** 25

**Use the bar graph on the right for
problems 27–28.**

27 How many pounds of a person's
trash are:
a. recycled? **200 lb**
b. placed in a landfill? **975 lb**

28 How many more pounds of trash
are burned than are recycled?
Explain how you know.
See above.

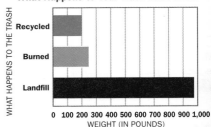

What Happens to Your Trash Each Year?

WEIGHT (IN POUNDS)

WHAT HAPPENS TO THE TRASH

····················· **Make It Right** ·····················

29 Here is how Luellen found 37 × 63.
Tell what the mistake is, then correct it.
**Possible answer: When multiplying 63 by 3 tens,
she did not record the partial product, 189,
in the correct position.**

```
    2                    2
   63                   63
 × 37                 × 37
  441                  441
+189               +1890
  630                2,331
```

Meeting Individual Needs

Early Finishers

Challenge students to make the
statements true by inserting a
multiplication sign.

1. 755 = 385 *[7 × 55 = 385]*
2. 548 = 432 *[54 × 8 = 432]*
3. 635 = 315 *[63 × 5 = 315]*

COMMON ERROR

Ask a student to write
the problem on the board and
show how to regroup when
multiplying by 7 ones. Then
show how to regroup when
multiplying by 3 tens. Suggest
that students write their
regrouping numbers small and
cross them out before multiplying by tens. Students may want
to erase the first set of marks,
but this will make it difficult for
them to check their work.

Hopscotch for Factors Game!

You will need
• 16 two-color counters

Play the Game

Work with a partner to find pairs of numbers whose product is between 400 and 500.

As you pick two numbers, place a counter on each one. Check the product. If it is between 400 and 500, keep both counters on the board. If not, remove the counters.

The object of the game is to cover all of the numbers with counters.

How did you decide if a product is between 400 and 500?

Possible answers: estimated the product, multiplied mentally

Cultural Note
This game board is similar to the hopscotch pattern used in France. The pattern is called escargot (es-kahr-GOH), which is the French word for "snail."

mixed review • test preparation

Estimate. Estimates may vary. Possible estimates are shown.

785 + 452 **1,300**	**2** $4,612 − 2,589 **$2,000**	**3** 25,460 + 72,950 **100,000**	**4** 90,180 − 84,300 **6,000**	**5** $31,980 + 19,652 **$50,000**

6 4 × 12 **40** **7** 8 × 68 **560** **8** 9 × $25 **$270** **9** 8 × $72 **$560** **10** 9 × 45 **450**

Extra Practice, page 505

Multiply by 2-Digit Numbers **217**

Alternate Teaching Strategy

Review the Distributive Property of Multiplication. Draw the following diagram on the chalkboard.

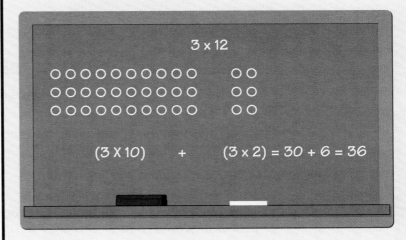

Explain to students that 3 groups of 12 is the sum of 3 groups of 10 and 3 groups of 2. Have students use the Distributive Property to find the product of 4 × 13. Encourage them to include a diagram in their work.

Write the following on a chalkboard:

$20 \times 35 = 20 \times (30 + 5)$

$= (20 \times 30) + (20 \times 5)$

$= 600 + 100$

$= 700$

Explain to students that 20 groups of 35 is the sum of 20 groups of 30 and 20 groups of 5. Challenge students to find the product of 26 × 35 using the Distributive Property. Have a volunteer explain how he or she finds the answer.

PRACTICE • 53

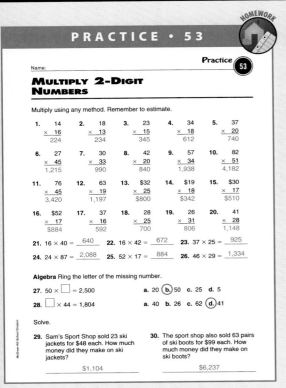

Name: _____

MULTIPLY 2-DIGIT NUMBERS

Multiply using any method. Remember to estimate.

1. 14 × 16 224	2. 18 × 13 234	3. 23 × 15 345	4. 34 × 18 612	5. 37 × 20 740
6. 27 × 45 1,215	7. 30 × 33 990	8. 42 × 20 840	9. 57 × 34 1,938	10. 82 × 51 4,182
11. 76 × 45 3,420	12. 63 × 19 1,197	13. $32 × 25 $800	14. $19 × 18 $342	15. $30 × 17 $510
16. $52 × 17 $884	17. 37 × 16 592	18. 28 × 25 700	19. 26 × 31 806	20. 41 × 28 1,148

21. 16 × 40 = **640** 22. 16 × 42 = **672** 23. 37 × 25 = **925**
24. 24 × 87 = **2,088** 25. 52 × 17 = **884** 26. 46 × 29 = **1,334**

Algebra Ring the letter of the missing number.

27. 50 × ☐ = 2,500 a. 20 (b.)50 c. 25 d. 5

28. ☐ × 44 = 1,804 a. 40 b. 26 c. 62 (d.)41

Solve.

29. Sam's Sport Shop sold 23 ski jackets for $48 each. How much money did they make on ski jackets? **$1,104**

30. The sport shop also sold 63 pairs of ski boots for $99 each. How much money did they make on ski boots? **$6,237**

RETEACH • 53

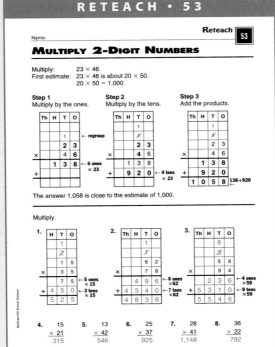

Name: _____

MULTIPLY 2-DIGIT NUMBERS

Multiply: 23 × 46
First estimate: 23 × 46 is about 20 × 50.
20 × 50 = 1,000

Step 1 Multiply by the ones.
Step 2 Multiply by the tens.
Step 3 Add the products.

The answer 1,058 is close to the estimate of 1,000.

Multiply.

4. 15 × 21 315	5. 13 × 42 546	6. 25 × 37 925	7. 28 × 41 1,148	8. 36 × 22 792

EXTEND • 53

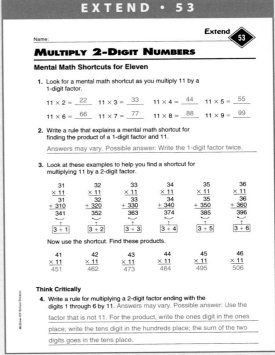

Name: _____

MULTIPLY 2-DIGIT NUMBERS

Mental Math Shortcuts for Eleven

1. Look for a mental math shortcut as you multiply 11 by a 1-digit factor.

   11 × 2 = **22**   11 × 3 = **33**   11 × 4 = **44**   11 × 5 = **55**

   11 × 6 = **66**   11 × 7 = **77**   11 × 8 = **88**   11 × 9 = **99**

2. Write a rule that explains a mental math shortcut for finding the product of a 1-digit factor and 11.

   Answers may vary. Possible answer: Write the 1-digit factor twice.

3. Look at these examples to help you find a shortcut for multiplying 11 by a 2-digit factor.

31 × 11 31 + 310 341	32 × 11 32 + 320 352	33 × 11 33 + 330 363	34 × 11 34 + 340 374	35 × 11 35 + 350 385	36 × 11 36 + 360 396
3 + 1	3 + 2	3 + 3	3 + 4	3 + 5	3 + 6

Now use the shortcut. Find these products.

41 × 11 451	42 × 11 462	43 × 11 473	44 × 11 484	45 × 11 495	46 × 11 506

Think Critically

4. Write a rule for multiplying a 2-digit factor ending with the digits 1 through 6 by 11. Answers may vary. Possible answer: Use the factor that is not 11. For the product, write the ones digit in the ones place; write the tens digit in the hundreds place; the sum of the two digits goes in the tens place.

Teaching With Technology

Multiply 2-Digit Numbers

OBJECTIVE Students estimate products of 2–digit numbers and use tables to verify estimations.

 Resource Math Van Activity: *Earth Day Plans*

SET UP

Provide students with the activity card for *Earth Day Plans*. Start **Math Van** and click the *Activities* button. Click the *Earth Day Plans* activity on the Fax Machine.

USING THE MATH VAN ACTIVITY

1 Getting Started Students estimate the total cost for the trees, benches, and bushes for the Nature Trail. Students create a formula in a Table to check their estimates.

2 Practice and Apply Students estimate how many plants will be needed for the flower garden based on how many plants in a row and how many rows available. Students create a formula in a Table to check if their estimations are close to the actual number. Students make changes and adjust their Table to reflect the change.

3 Close Discuss how estimation can help students to determine if their actual answers are reasonable.

Extend Students investigate how much paper is used in their classroom each day. They expand the Table to figure out how much the school uses in a day.

TIPS FOR TOOLS

Remind students that before they click the *Formula* button, they must highlight the blank column in the table where they want formula results to appear.

Earth Day Plans

SCREEN 1

Students estimate the total cost for each item and enter the figure into the Table.

SCREEN 2

Students set up a formula in the Table to calculate the total cost for each type of tree. Students check their estimated totals against the actual totals.

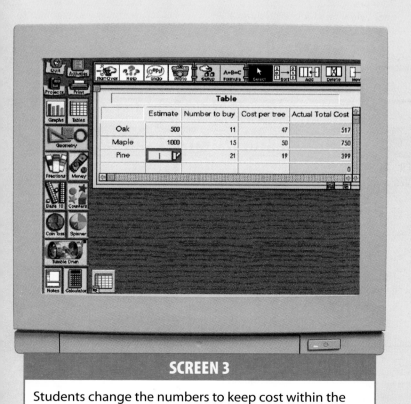

SCREEN 3

Students change the numbers to keep cost within the budget.

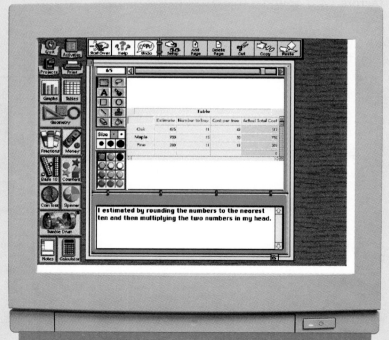

SCREEN 4

Students take a photo of their work and answer a question about their estimates.

PURPOSE Maintain and review concepts, skills, and strategies that students have learned thus far in the chapter.

Materials per student: calculators (optional)

Using the Midchapter Review

Have students complete the **Midchapter Review** independently or use it with the whole class.

For ex. 2–5, students need to get information from the table before estimating.

 Students should know several methods to find the product.

Possible methods include:
- draw pictures that represent place-value models.
- use graph paper to draw a rectangular shape 28 units wide and 34 units long, then break up the rectangle into smaller shapes that are easily counted.
- break the problem up into four parts—4 × 8, 4 × 20, 30 × 8, 30 × 20.
- use expanded form to break up the problem into two parts—28 × 4, 28 × 30.

Vocabulary Review

Write the following words on the chalkboard:

estimate	regroup
factors	round
product	

Ask for volunteers to explain, show, or act out the meaning of these words and give examples.

---

1 Find the total number of squares in the rectangle without counting. Explain your method.

280 square explanation may vary.

Estimates may vary depending on the method used. Estimates shown are by rounding.

Estimate the total amount.

2 12 boxes of detergent **1,000 oz**

3 376 bottles of shampoo **8,000 fl oz**

4 23 bags of dog food **800 lb**

5 32 bottles of soda **1,800 fl oz**

Item	Amount
Bag of dog food	40 pounds
Bottle of soda	64 fluid ounces
Box of detergent	128 ounces
Bottle of shampoo	22 fluid ounces

Multiply using any method.

6
$$\begin{array}{r} 12 \\ \times\ 14 \\ \hline 168 \end{array}$$

7
$$\begin{array}{r} 40 \\ \times\ 30 \\ \hline 1,200 \end{array}$$

8
$$\begin{array}{r} 24 \\ \times\ 42 \\ \hline 1,008 \end{array}$$

9
$$\begin{array}{r} 51 \\ \times\ 37 \\ \hline 1,887 \end{array}$$

10
$$\begin{array}{r} 2,00 \\ \times\ \ \ \ 6 \\ \hline 120,00 \end{array}$$

11
$$\begin{array}{r} \$0.52 \\ \times\ \ \ 38 \\ \hline \$19.76 \end{array}$$

12
$$\begin{array}{r} 25 \\ \times\ 39 \\ \hline 975 \end{array}$$

13
$$\begin{array}{r} \$0.46 \\ \times\ \ \ 16 \\ \hline \$7.36 \end{array}$$

14
$$\begin{array}{r} 8,000 \\ \times\ \ \ \ 70 \\ \hline 560,000 \end{array}$$

15
$$\begin{array}{r} 900 \\ \times\ 60 \\ \hline 54,000 \end{array}$$

Complete. Write >, <, or =.

16 4,000 ● 75 × 67 **<**

17 8,000 × 90 ● 500,000 **>**

18 38 × 45 ● 63 × 24 **>**

19 99 × 39 ● 97 × 72 **<**

Solve. Use mental math when you can.

20 A class collects 43 bags of litter. Each bag weighs 18 pounds. How many pounds of litter does the class collect? **774 lb**

21 A club needs 17 gallons of paint. Each gallon costs $23. About how much will the club pay? **about $4**

22 In a Green Day Parade, 30 groups marched through the town. Each group had about 40 people. About how many people marched in all? **Possible answer: about 1,200 people**

23 On Earth Day, each group of volunteers collected 14 pounds litter. If there were 23 groups, about how much litter was collected? **Possible answer: about 280 lb**

24 Banners for Earth Day cost $4.75 each. How much do 25 banners cost? **$118.75**

25 Explain two different methods you can use to find 28 × 34. **Check students' work. Possible answers include pencil and paper, and models.**

Reinforcement and Remediation

CHAPTER OBJECTIVES	MIDCHAPTER REVIEW ITEMS	STUDENT BOOK PAGES	TEACHER'S EDITION PAGES		TEACHER RESOURCES
			Activities	Alternate Teaching Strategy	Reteach
*6A	7, 10, 14, 15, 17	206–207	205A	207	50
*6B	2–5	208–209	207A	209	51
*6C	1, 6–19	210–217	209A, 213A	213, 217	52–53
*6D	20–25	206–217	205A, 207A, 209A, 213A	207, 209 213, 217	50–53

*6A Multiply multiples of 10, 100, and 1,000 by multiples of 10
*6B Estimate products, including money amounts
*6C Multiply by 2-digit factors, including money amounts
*6D Solve problems, including those that involve multiplication and using alternate solution methods

Use Calculators and Spreadsheets

You can use a calculator to add, subtract, multiply, and divide. You can also use computer spreadsheets.

Suppose 19 students signed up for a recycling drive in the first week of January, 14 in the second week, 23 in the third week, and 16 in the fourth week. To find the total number of students, you could use a calculator to add the four numbers.

Suppose you wanted to do this calculation every month for a year. It would be better to use a spreadsheet.

Number of Students

Month	Week 1	Week 2	Week 3	Week 4	Total
Jan.	19	14	23	16	Col 1+Col 2+ Col 3+Col 4
Feb.	6	12	15	0	
Mar.	18	7	9	14	

▶ Col 2 Row 3 has 12 in it. Why can you add Col 1, 2, 3, and 4 in each row to get the total?

▶ Work with a partner and enter the data above in a computer table to see what your Total column looks like.
Check students' work.

1 Create some other operations for your spreadsheet besides addition. Try the same operations on your calculator. Compare your work.
Check students' work.

Critical Thinking: Generalize

2 When might it be better to use a spreadsheet than a calculator? **Possible answer: when a lot of calculations have to be done or when the same calculations have to be done many times**

OBJECTIVE Create an electronic spreadsheet in which some cells are related to other cells by a formula.

Resource spreadsheet program or Math Van Tools

Using Technology Sense

Math Connection In prior lessons students have used tables to represent data. Computer tools allow students to create data tables so that the data in some cells is related to the data in other cells by a formula, change data in some of the cells and see how data in other cells is changed, and print the tables. Here, students enter data in a data table, make the last column the sum of the earlier columns, and then expand the spreadsheet.

At the Computer Allow students to explore the spreadsheet program before beginning the activities. Have a volunteer demonstrate how to make one of the columns the sum of the previous columns. Make sure students understand the table on Student Book page 219.

Extending the Activity Have students add a column to the table that automatically finds the average for the four weeks of each month.

Math Van Math Van Tools provide easy ways to make one row or column or cell in a table depend on others. For example, to make the sixth column the average of the first 4 columns, follow these steps. Click the top of the sixth column to highlight the column. Then click the *Formula* button on the Table toolbar and a dialog box will open up. Click the label at the top of the fourth column, click the division key on the calculator, and then click the 4 key on the calculator. You will see the mathematical expression *col 5 ÷ 4* appear in the window. Then click the *OK* button. A project electronic teacher aid has been provided.

REAL-LIFE INVESTIGATION

Applying Multiplication

OBJECTIVE Use multiplication and estimation in the context of recycling.

Materials have available: calculators

1 Engage

Make sure students understand what recycling means. Encourage them to share experiences they have had with recycling.

- **What materials does your town require households to recycle?** *[Possible answer: aluminum cans, newspaper, and plastic bottles]*
- **How do you participate in the recycling program in your neighborhood?** *[Possible answer: separate cans and plastics into different containers]*

2 Investigate   *Cooperative Groups*

You might start by listing students' responses to the questions on page 220. Then make a chart. Keep the chart displayed for students to refer to throughout their investigations.

Reusing and Recycling Each group can write a plan for collecting information about paper set aside to be recycled. Using the Partners Brainstorm Strategy, have students work individually to list as many ideas as they can. Students work with a partner to compare and combine lists. Partners work together to add more ideas to their list. Check each group's plan briefly before they begin collecting data.

Remind students to round and to use calculators as they estimate the amount thrown away in a month and in a year.

3 Reflect and Share

Materials have available: calculators

Report Your Findings

Steps in a Process Check students' lists to see that they put the steps in order. Discuss how these steps helped in collecting data.

Students should make a comparison between the total amount of paper thrown away and the amount recycled. They can use this comparison in their explanation of why recycling is important.

- **What do your results tell you about the need for recycling in your neighborhood?** *[Answers may vary. Possible answers: We need to recycle more because we throw away much more paper than we recycle, or our recycling rate is quite good when compared to other communities.]*

Revise Your Work Suggest that students use a strategy to check their calculations. For example, because they used multiplication to estimate the group's paper waste in a year, they can use division to check it on a calculator.

Be a Paper Recycler

Each year, paper is used to make millions of books, magazines, and newspapers and is turned into thousands of pounds of tissue paper in the United States.

How do you use paper?

Paper and paperboard make up most of the material that is thrown out as waste.

Why is recycling paper so important?

In 1994, more paper was recycled than was sent to landfills. The recycled paper could fill a space about one yard deep and the area of Washington, D.C.

What can you do to help reach the recycling goal?

Goal for the Year 2000
The nation's paper industry has set a goal. By the year 2000, they will recycle half of all the paper Americans use each year.

More To Investigate

Predict Possible approach: Multiply the number of families in the neighborhood by the amount of paper one group member's family threw away in a week.

Explore Students may wish to write to the U.S. Environmental Protection Agency's recycling department: EPA, Office of Solid Waste— 5306 W, 401 M Street S.W., Washington, D.C. 20460, phone: (703) 308-8300.

Find To complete this activity students can call local environmental groups, community groups, and sanitation departments or services.

Bibliography Students interested in learning more about recycling can read:

Cartons, Cans, and Orange Peels: Where Does Your Garbage Go? by Joanna Foster. Boston: Houghton Mifflin Company, 1993. ISBN 0–395–66504–3.

Recycle! A Handbook for Kids, by Gail Gibbons. Boston: Little, Brown and Company, Inc., 1992. ISBN 0–316–30943–5.

DECISION MAKING

Reusing and Recycling

1 Work in a group. Choose where you will collect data on paper use—at home, in your classroom, in the school office or cafeteria.

2 Decide on the following things:
a. what kinds of paper to include
b. how long you will collect paper
c. how you will measure the paper
d. how you will record your findings

3 Use your data to estimate how much paper is thrown away in a month and in a year.

4 Estimate how much paper and paper products are recycled in a week and in a month.

Reporting Your Findings

5 Prepare a report to persuade people to recycle paper. Include the following things:

► Explain why you think recycling is important.

► **Steps in a Process** List the steps your group followed to collect data.

► Write statements about the amount of paper your group members discovered was thrown away. Describe the math that you used.

6 Compare your report with the reports of other groups.

Revise your work.
► Have you checked your calculations?
► Is your report clear and organized?
► Did you proofread your work?

MORE TO INVESTIGATE

See Teacher's Edition.

PREDICT how much paper and paper products your neighborhood or community throws away in a week.

EXPLORE what kinds of paper are recycled by a recycling center near you. Find out how the paper is then used.

FIND projects that you can take part in to help increase the recycling of paper.

Multiply by 2-Digit Numbers **221**

Student's Work

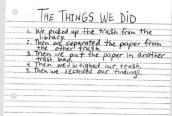

Group 1 chose to record the number of feet of paper used by the school office staff.

Length of paper

Types of paper	Day 1	Day 2	Day 3	Total
Standard Paper (illus)	4 4in 4 sheets	3 3in 3 sheets	2 2in 2 sheets	8 ft. 3 in
Index Cards (illus)	1 card 5 in	2 cards 10 in	4 cards 20 in	2 ft 11 in
Magazine (illus)	0 magazine 0 in	3 magazine 33 in	0 magazine 0 in	8 ft. 3 in.
Paper Towel	2 towels 20 in	4 towels 40 in	5 towels 50 in	9 ft 2 in
Computer paper Strips	2 strips 22 in	5 strips 55 in	6 strips 66 in	11 ft 11 in

Total trash for three days
1,398 in. or 116 ft 6 in

Daily Average 466 in or 38 ft 10 in

Estimated total per year (185 days)

40 x 185 = 7,400 ft.
rounded

Group 2 chose to investigate the number of kilograms of paper and paper products used by the people at the school library.

THE THINGS WE DID
1. We picked up the trash from the library.
2. Then we separated the paper from the other trash.
3. Then we put the paper in another trash bag.
4. Then we weighed our trash.
5. Then we recorded our findings.

Building A Portfolio

This investigation will allow you to evaluate a student's ability to collect and organize data and to use multiplication and estimation to find totals.

Allow students to revise their work for the portfolio. Each student's portfolio piece should consist of a copy of the group's data on paper thrown away and paper recycled, as well as a description of how the amounts were measured and how they are related to each other.

The portfolio should also include the student's opinion about her or his own contribution to recycling and any improvements she or he thinks can be made and how. Place any notes you made about a student's work in his or her portfolio.

You may use the Holistic Scoring Guide to assess this task. See page 27 in Teacher's Assessment Resources.

LESSON 6.5

Problem-Solving Strategy: Use Alternate Solution Methods

OBJECTIVE Solve the same problem using different strategies.

RESOURCE REMINDER
Math Center Cards 54
Practice 54, Reteach 54, Extend 54

SKILLS TRACE

GRADE 2	• Solve the same problem using different strategies. *(Chapter 6)*
GRADE 3	• Solve the same problem using different strategies.
GRADE 4	• Solve the same problem using different strategies. *(Chapter 5)*

WARM-UP

Cooperative Pairs   **Logical/Analytical**

OBJECTIVE Review guess and test strategy.

Materials per pair: calculator

► Present this problem:

> A textbook is opened and the product of the page numbers of the two facing pages is 812. What are the numbers of the pages?

► Have students use their calculators to solve the problem.

► Ask them the strategy they used to solve the problem. *[Possible answer: guess and test; since 30 × 30 is 900 we started guessing numbers less than 30—28 × 29 = 812.]*

REAL-LIFE CONNECTION

Cooperative Groups   **Visual/Spatial**

OBJECTIVE Connect estimating to problem solving.

► Have students work in small groups to estimate the number of cars that drive by their school in an hour. Direct them to develop a method for estimating the number of cars and to use their method to estimate.

► Have each group present their estimate and explain the strategy they used to make the estimate. *[Possible answer: Tally the number of cars that go by in a 10-minute period and multiply the total by 6.]*

► Discuss the strategies used to solve the problem.

Daily Review

PREVIOUS DAY **QUICK REVIEW**

1. 13 × 11 *[143]*
2. 12 × 18 *[216]*
3. 25 × 30 *[750]*
4. 27 × 41 *[1,107]*

FAST FACTS

1. 2 × 8 *[16]*
2. 3 × 7 *[21]*
3. 4 × 5 *[20]*
4. 5 × 7 *[35]*

Problem of the Day • 54

At Lickity Split Ice Cream, customers have a choice of 5 different flavors and 4 toppings. How many different choices of 1 flavor and 1 topping do you have? *[20]*

TECH LINK

MATH FORUM

Management Tip When teaching problem solving, I make sure to observe each student solving at least one problem. I talk individually with students about their solution and how they chose their method.

Visit our Resource Village at http://www.mhschool.com to see more of the Math Forum.

MATH CENTER

Practice

OBJECTIVE Solve a problem using various strategies.

Materials per student: ruler; graph paper; red, yellow, and blue markers; scissors; Math Center Recording Sheet (TA 31 optional)

Students try to color a cube with 3 colors so that no adjacent sides have the same color. They are encouraged to try a variety of strategies. *[Yes, it is possible if you color opposite sides of the cube the same color.]*

PRACTICE ACTIVITY 54

MATH CENTER
On Your Own

Spatial Sense • Cubic Thinking

Glyniss is going to color the sides of a cube using three colors. Is it possible for her to color them so that no touching sides are the same color?

Copy the net shown and use it to help you make a cube. Color the sides to check for possible solutions. Explain what you discover.

Before you color the cube, you might make another copy of the net and make a list or guess and test various possibilities.

YOU NEED
ruler
graph paper
red, yellow, and blue markers
scissors

Chapter 6, Lesson 5, pages 222–223

Problem Solving

NCTM Standards

✓ Problem Solving
Communication
✓ Reasoning
Connections

ESL APPROPRIATE

Problem Solving

OBJECTIVE Solve problems involving many steps and more than one possible method.

Materials per student: calculator, Math Center Recording Sheet (TA 31 optional)

Students calculate how many hours they have lived. Then they calculate how many years old they would be if they had lived 1,000,000 hours. *[Answers may vary. Possible answer: I have lived about 87,600 hours; I would be a little over 114 if I had lived 1 million hours.]*

PROBLEM-SOLVING ACTIVITY 54

MATH CENTER
On Your Own

Calculator • How Long Is 1 Million Hours?

How many hours have you lived? Write your guess.

• Write a plan to find out your age in hours. How many hours old are you?
• How many years old will you be when you have lived 1,000,000 hours?

YOU NEED
calculator

Chapter 6, Lesson 5, pages 222–223

Problem Solving

NCTM Standards

✓ Problem Solving
Communication
✓ Reasoning
Connections

Problem-Solving Strategy: Use Alternate Solution Methods

OBJECTIVE Solve the same problem using different strategies.

 Introduce

Ask students if there is more than one way to walk to school or to a friend's house. Talk about the different routes they can choose to take and ask if there is one "right" way. If they think there is, ask them to describe why they think it is the "right" way and help them see that the other ways are not "wrong." There may be good reasons for going the other ways.

 **Teach** *Whole Class*

▶ **LEARN** Read through the problem with the class. Before going on, ask students to describe ways they would solve this problem. List the ways they describe on the chalkboard.

Go over the Plan step with the class. Compare the methods described to the list written on the chalkboard. Ask students:
- **When using the guess and test method, what number would be your first guess?** *[Answers may vary.]*
- **Of the two methods listed, which method do you think is easier? Why?** *[Answers may vary.]*

 Close

▶ **Check for Understanding** using items 1 and 2, page 222.

CRITICAL THINKING
For item 2, have students explain how they identified the extra information in the riddle.

▶ **PRACTICE**
Materials have available: calculators

Assign exercises 1–9 as independent work.
- For ex. 1, students may solve the problem by drawing a diagram.

Problem-Solving Strategy

Read
Plan
Solve
Look Back

Use Alternate Methods

Read **Matt wants to solve this riddle.**

I am a number between 108 and 115. Each of my digits is less than 5. If you subtract 1 from me, you get a multiple of 5. What number am I?

Plan To find the answer, you can guess and test, or make a table.

Solve Guess and test.

Think: 110, 111, 112, 113, 114 have digits less than 5.

Try 110.
$110 - 1 = 109$ ← **not a multiple of 5**

Try 111.
$111 - 1 = 110$ ← **a multiple of**
So "I am 111."

Make a table.

Numbers from 109 to 114	109	110	111	112	113	114
Digits less than 5?	no	yes	yes	yes	yes	yes
Subtract 1. Multiple of 5?	no	no	yes	no	no	no

The only column in which each row has a *yes* is 111. So "I am 111."

Look Back How are the two methods alike? How are they different? Possible answer: Alike—they both use the hints to reduce choices; different—you don't need to show all the numbers when you guess and test

Check for Understanding

1 **What if** the riddle did not say that all the digits are less than 5. How would the two methods change? Possible answer: Guess and test would check all the numbers, and the table would have only two rows.

Critical Thinking: Analyze

2 Rewrite the riddle so that there is extra information but the answer is the same. Possible answer: I am a number between 108 and 115. My first digit is in the hundreds place. Each of my digits is less than 5. If you subtract 1 from me, you get a multiple of 5. What number am I?

222 Lesson 6.5

Meeting Individual Needs

Early Finishers

Have students go back and use a second method to solve one or more problems. Ask students to describe both methods and tell which method they liked better and why.

Extra Support

Have students review the problem-solving strategy lessons they have done thus far. You may want to keep a class list on display to remind students.

Ongoing Assessment

Interview Determine if students understand how to use different strategies by asking them to describe or show two ways to solve one of the problems.

Follow Up If students need more practice working with different strategies, assign **Reteach 54.**

If they need a greater challenge, assign **Extend 54.**

1. 16 mi; methods may vary; possible answer: draw a diagram and add the paths, 4 + 7 + 5 = 16 mi.

Problem Solving

8. Students' decisions should reflect data given on the price list.

1 On one field trip, students rode their bikes 4 miles to the beach, biked 7 miles along the beach path, and then rode 5 miles back to their starting positions. How far did they travel? Explain your method. What other method could you have used? **See above.**

2 A town recycles 30 tons of newspapers a week. About how many kilowatt-hours of electricity does the town save each week? **SEE INFOBIT. about 120,000 kWh**

INFOBIT
Recycling 1 ton of newspapers saves about 4,000 kilowatt-hours of electricity.

3 A recycling center received 81 pounds of cans the first day. The next day it received 72 pounds. The cans are packed in 9-pound bags. How many bags did the center receive altogether? **17 bags**

4 Logical reasoning Helen rolls two number cubes to get a 2-digit factor. She rolls the cubes again to get another 2-digit factor. What is the greatest product she can get? $66 \times 66 = 4,356$

Use the price list for problems 5–9.

5 The Center offers 3 one-hour field trips every week. Twelve people go on each trip. How much money do the field trips earn each week? **$324**

6 A club has 28 members. Is it cheaper for them to go to the Ecology Center or watch the wildlife film? **It is cheaper to watch the wildlife film as a group.**

7 Twenty-nine students plan to take a gardening class. What is the total cost for these students? **$90**

8 Make a decision Your class has $48 to spend at the Center. What should the class see and do? How much money will you spend? **See above.**

WETLANDS CENTER	
Ecology Center	$3 for each person
Birdwatching Tour	**FREE**
Gardening Class (6 week session)	$90 for each group* $12 for each person
Wildlife film	$75 for each group*
Field trip	$9 for each person

* A group has ten or more people.

9 Write a problem using at least two prices from the price list. Solve it using two methods. Have others solve it. **Students should compare problems and solutions.**

Extra Practice, page 506

Multiply by 2-Digit Numbers **223**

Alternate Teaching Strategy

Materials per group: play money—assorted coins

Ask students to describe several strategies they have used to solve problems and list them on the chalkboard. Then present the following problem:

> **A cashier only has quarters, dimes, and nickels left in her register. How many different ways can you get 70 cents in change if you get at least one coin of each kind?** *[4 ways: 25–25–10–5–5, 25–10–10–10–5–5–5, 25–10–10–5–5–5–5–5, 25–10–5–5–5–5–5–5–5]*

Have students work in cooperative groups to solve the problem. Allow them to use the chalkboard, if desired.

Have groups show their solution to the problem. Discuss the solution and methods. *[Possible answers: Make a table, make a list, use models, draw a picture.]*

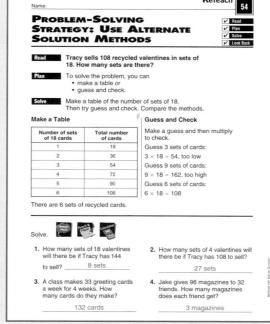
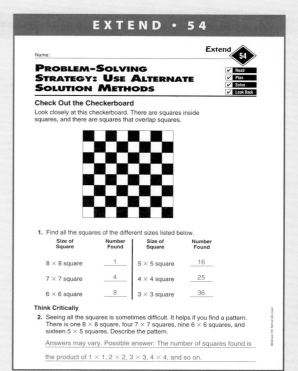

LESSON 6.6

Multiply 3-digit Numbers and Money

OBJECTIVE Multiply 3-digit numbers by 2-digit numbers with and without regrouping.

RESOURCE REMINDER
Math Center Cards 55
Practice 55, Reteach 55, Extend 55

SKILLS TRACE

GRADE 2
• Multiply 2-digit numbers by 1-digit numbers with/without regrouping. *(Chapter 12)*

GRADE 3
• Multiply 3-digit numbers by 2-digit numbers with/without regrouping.

GRADE 4
• Multiply whole numbers by 2-digit numbers. *(Chapter 4)*

MANIPULATIVE WARM-UP

Cooperative Pairs   **Visual/Spatial**

OBJECTIVE Explore multiplying 3-digit numbers.

Materials per pair: calculator

▶ Write the following on the chalkboard:

$15 \times 100 = ?$	$25 \times 100 = ?$	$12 \times 100 = ?$
$15 \times 200 = ?$	$25 \times 200 = ?$	$12 \times 200 = ?$
$15 \times 300 = ?$	$25 \times 300 = ?$	$12 \times 300 = ?$
$15 \times 400 = ?$	$25 \times 400 = ?$	$12 \times 400 = ?$

▶ Have pairs solve the problems using mental math or calculator. Ask volunteers to present their results to the class.

▶ Ask the following question:
• **Is it possible to get a product less than 1,000 when you multiply a 2-digit number by a 3-digit number? Explain.** *[No; [10 × 100 = 1,000]—this is the least product of a 2-digit number times a 3-digit number.]*

TECHNOLOGY CONNECTION

Cooperative Pairs   **Linguistic**

OBJECTIVE Connect writing steps to show how to multiply two 2-digit numbers to computer programming.

▶ Tell students that a particular computer knows: place value; multiplication facts; addition facts; multiplying by 10, 100, and 1,000; and how to add a column of numbers.

▶ Have students write arithmetic instructions for this computer to multiply a pair of 2-digit numbers. For example, 24 × 38.

▶ After each pair has developed a list of instructions for the computer, have the students test the instructions on each other. Then have pairs compare their instructions. *[Possible answer: 4 × 8 = 32, 4 × 30 = 120, 20 × 8 = 160, 20 × 30 = 600, 32 + 120 + 160 + 600 = 912]*

Daily Review

PREVIOUS DAY QUICK REVIEW

1. 24 × 16 *[384]*
2. 38 × 25 *[950]*
3. 62 × 17 *[1,054]*
4. 72 × 14 *[1,008]*

FAST FACTS

1. 5 + 7 *[12]*
2. 6 + 8 *[14]*
3. 9 + 4 *[13]*
4. 7 + 9 *[16]*

Problem of the Day • 55

Warren is saving money to buy a bicycle that costs $250. Warren saved $1 the first week, $2 the second week, $4 the third week, and $8 the fourth week. If he continues to save following the same pattern, how many weeks will it take Warren to save enough money to buy the bicycle? *[After 8 weeks, he will have saved $255, enough for the bicycle.]*

TECH LINK

MATH VAN

Tool You may wish to use Calculator with this lesson.

MATH FORUM

Multi-Age Classes Once my students start solving multiplication problems with more than one digit, I always have them check the products with a calculator.

Visit our Resource Village at http://www.mhschool.com to see more of the Math Forum.

MATH CENTER

Practice

OBJECTIVE Multiply 2- and 3-digit numbers.

Materials per group: number cards for 0–9 (TA29), number cube, play coins; per student: Math Center Recording Sheet (TA 31 optional)

Students generate a 3-digit money factor and multiply it by a 2-digit number. They earn a play dime if their product is odd, a nickel if their product is even, and no money if their product is wrong. *[Two odd factors give an odd product; two even factors give an even product; one odd and one even factor give an even product.]*

Problem Solving

OBJECTIVE Use logical reasoning to get close to a target number.

Materials per pair: 0–9 spinner (TA 2), calculator

Pairs of students play a game generating a five digit number closest to one of three target numbers.

PRACTICE ACTIVITY 55

MATH CENTER
Small Group 👥👥👥

Game • Money Multiplication

Take turns and see who earns the most money.

- The first player chooses three number cards and uses them to create a money factor.

Then he or she rolls the number cube twice for a 2-digit factor and multiplies that factor by the money factor.

- If the product is odd, the player earns a dime. If the product is even, the player earns a nickel. If the product is wrong, no money is awarded.
- The first player to earn 50¢ wins.

YOU NEED
- number cards (0–9)
- number cube
- play coins

YOUR PRODUCT EARNS A

$2.19 × 🎲🎲 = $176.65 *DON'T FORGET!*

Chapter 6, Lesson 6, pages 224–225

Multiplication

NCTM Standards
✓ Problem Solving
✓ Communication
   Reasoning
✓ Connections

ESL APPROPRIATE

PROBLEM-SOLVING ACTIVITY 55

MATH CENTER
Partners 👥👥

Logical Reasoning • How Close?

- One player spins the spinner five times. Record the numbers. (Some numbers may repeat.)
- Each player uses the five digits to make factors to get as close as possible to these targets:

A	B	C
20,000	50,000	80,000

- The player who gets closest to any target earns 1 point. Use a calculator to check the answers.
- Repeat with another set of five numbers. You may want to change the targets to other 5-digit numbers.

YOU NEED
- spinner (0–9)
- calculator

NCTM Standards
✓ Problem Solving
   Communication
✓ Reasoning
   Connections

Chapter 6, Lesson 6, pages 224–225

Multiplication

Lesson 6.6 *continued*

Multiply 3-Digit Numbers

OBJECTIVE Multiply 3-digit numbers by 2-digit numbers with and without regrouping.

1 Introduce

Ask students how their family has tried to conserve water. For example taking quick showers instead of baths, using a water-saving shower head, and so on.

2 Teach   *Whole Class*

▶ **LEARN** Read through the introductory problem. Then ask:
 • **Why do you estimate a product first?** *[Possible answer: to see if the product is reasonable]*

After going over the steps, ask:
 • **How is multiplying with a 3-digit number like multiplying two 2-digit numbers?** *[Answers may vary. Follow the same steps but also multiply hundreds.]*

3 Close

▶ **Check for Understanding** using items 1–6, page 224.

 CRITICAL THINKING
 To extend students' thinking, ask:
 • **If 23 × 1,879 = 43,217, what is 23 × $187.90?**
  [$4,321.70]

▶ **PRACTICE**
Materials have available: calculators

Each student chooses thirteen exercises from ex. 1–26, completes exercises 27 and 28, and the **More to Explore.**
• Tell students they may use whatever method they like to solve ex. 1–26. You may also want to point out that Ex. 3, 4, 18, 21 and 22 involve multiplying a number with a zero in the tens place.
.

More to Explore Solve a couple of problems as a class. Remind students that every leap year, or every four years, there is one extra day in the year: February 28. Even so, 365 days is used for the number of days in a year.

Multiply 3-Digit Numbers

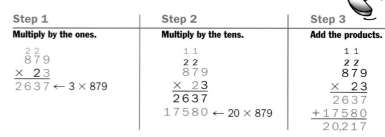

L E A R N

A leaky faucet dripping 1 drop each second wastes 879 gallons of water in a year. How many gallons of water can be saved by fixing the 23 faucets in an apartment building?

Estimate: 23 × 879

Think: 20 × 900 = 18,000

You can use pencil and paper to find the exact answer.

Multiply: 23 × 879

Step 1	Step 2	Step 3
Multiply by the ones.	**Multiply by the tens.**	**Add the products.**
2 2 8 7 9 × 2 3 ‾‾‾‾‾ 2 6 3 7 ← 3 × 879	1 1 2 2 8 7 9 × 2 3 ‾‾‾‾‾ 2 6 3 7 1 7 5 8 0 ← 20 × 879	1 1 2 2 8 7 9 × 2 3 ‾‾‾‾‾ 2 6 3 7 + 1 7 5 8 0 ‾‾‾‾‾‾‾ 2 0 , 2 1 7

 You can also use a calculator.   23 × 879 = **20217.**

20,217 gallons of water can be saved.

C H E C K

Check for Understanding
Multiply using any method. Estimate to see if your answer is reasonable.

1 153 × 12 1,836; 2,000	**2** 281 × 23 6,463; 6,000	**3** $3.54 × 17 $60.18; $80.00	**4** 359 × 44 15,796; 16,000	**5** 825 × 51 42,075; 40,

Critical Thinking: Generalize   **Explain your reasoning.**

6 If 23 × 879 = 20,217, what is 23 × $8.79 equal to? **$202.17**

224 Lesson 6.6

Meeting Individual Needs

Early Finishers

Challenge students to solve.

    3BA
  × C7
  ‾‾‾‾
  B303
 D64C0
 ‾‾‾‾‾
 D87C3

[B = 2; A = 9; C = 5; D = 1]

Extra Support

Students may write the regrouping but forget to add. Suggest that they draw a light slash mark through the number after they have added.

Ongoing Assessment

Observation Checklist Determine if students understand how to multiply a three-digit number by a two-digit number by observing them solve one of the problems in ex. 1–26. Make sure students are using a method that is accurate. If students use the multiplication algorithm, make sure they do all the steps.

Follow Up If students need more practice solving multiplication problems with three digits, assign **Reteach 55.**

For students who need a challenge, assign **Extend 55.**

28. Check that answers are based on a 2 minute shower that uses 20 gallons of water.

Practice

Multiply. Remember to estimate.

1 158 × 85 = **13,430**	**2** 430 × 42 = **18,060**	**3** 608 × 28 = **17,024**	**4** 706 × 28 = **19,768**	**5** 414 × 92 = **38,088**
6 $525 × 32 = **$16,800**	**7** $0.87 × 35 = **$30.45**	**8** $5.63 × 25 = **$140.75**	**9** $8.47 × 39 = **$330.33**	**10** $3.18 × 42 = **$133.56**

11 11 × 117 = **1,287** **12** 45 × $0.88 = **$39.60** **13** 13 × 239 = **3,107** **14** 22 × $3.01 = **$66.22**

15 64 × $7.86 = **$503.04** **16** 39 × $0.07 = **$2.73** **17** 31 × 754 = **23,374** **18** 37 × 306 = **11,322**

19 10 × 211 = **2,110** **20** 19 × $1.99 = **$37.81** **21** 41 × 309 = **12,669** **22** 45 × 807 = **36,315**

23 92 × 816 = **75,072** **24** 53 × 635 = **33,655** **25** 81 × $0.04 = **$3.24** **26** 74 × 560 = **41,440**

MIXED APPLICATIONS
Problem Solving

27 **What if** a toilet is flushed 25 times a day. An old toilet uses 5 gallons for each flush. A new toilet uses 2 gallons. How much water does the new toilet save? **75 gal**

28 **Data Point** Use the Databank on page 537. How long do you take to shower? About how much water do you use? Is this more than or less than the amount of water for a bath? **See above.**

more to explore

Changing Units of Time

This chart can help you show times in different units.

To show 3 hours in minutes, multiply.

Think: 1 hour = 60 minutes

3 hours = 3 × 60 minutes
        = 180 minutes

1 minute (min) = 60 seconds (s)
1 hour (h) = 60 minutes
1 day (d) = 24 hours
1 week (wk) = 7 days
1 year (y) = 52 weeks
1 year = 12 months (mo)
1 year = 365 days

Complete.

1 4 minutes = ■ seconds **240**
2 5 days = ■ hours **120**
3 14 hours = ■ minutes **840**
4 7 hours = ■ seconds **25,200**
5 15 weeks = ■ days **105**
6 6 years = ■ days **2,190**

Extra Practice, page 506

Multiply by 2-Digit Numbers **225**

Alternate Teaching Strategy

Materials have available: place-value mat (TA 5)

Have students multiply 3-digit numbers using partial products. Write on the chalkboard the steps of multiplying 3-digit numbers using partial products.

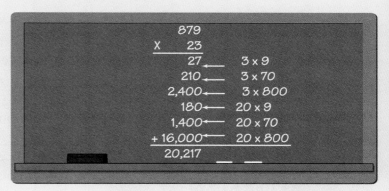

Discuss with students the advantage and disadvantage of multiplying greater numbers using partial products. *[Possible answer: Advantage: you see exactly where each partial product was from, you don't have to worry about regrouping or carry numbers; disadvantage: the algorithm gets very long when the numbers become greater.]*

Have students find the product of 12 × 153 using partial products. You may suggest students write the algorithm on a place-value mat.

PRACTICE • 55

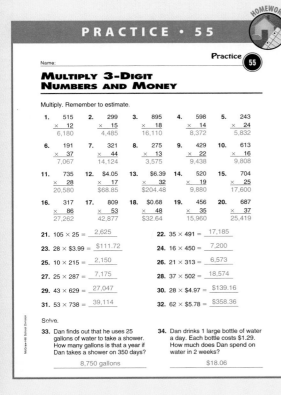

RETEACH • 55

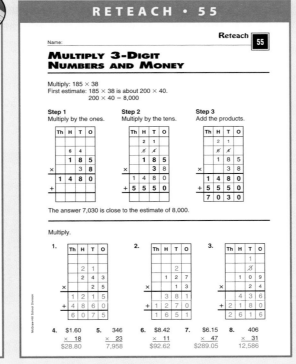

EXTEND • 55

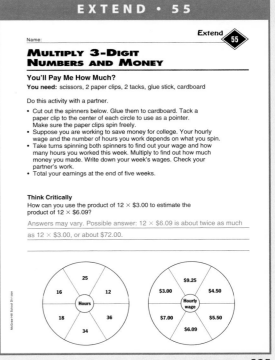

225

LESSON 6.7

Multiply Greater Numbers

OBJECTIVE Multiply up to 5-digit numbers, including money amounts, by 2-digit numbers.

RESOURCE REMINDER
Math Center Cards 56
Practice 56, Reteach 56, Extend 56

SKILLS TRACE

GRADE 3	• Multiply 2-digit numbers by 1-digit numbers with/without regrouping. *(Chapter 12)*
GRADE 4	• Multiply up to 5-digit numbers including money amounts by 2-digit numbers.
GRADE 5	• Multiply whole numbers by 2-digit numbers. *(Chapter 4)*

WARM-UP

Cooperative Pairs   **Visual/Spatial**

OBJECTIVE Review multiplying greater numbers.

Materials per group: centimeter graph paper (TA 7), markers

▶ Write the following on the chalkboard: 15 × 2,314

▶ Tell students to pick a color for each place value in 2,314. For example, green for thousands, red for hundreds, blue for tens, and yellow for ones.

▶ Ask students to shade the number of squares to represent the thousands in the partial products. *[30 green squares to show 15 × 2,000 = 30,000]* Have them continue to show the number of squares for each place value. *[45 red squares, 15 blue squares, and 60 yellow squares]*

▶ Ask students to add their squares, remembering the place value of each color, to find the product. *[34,710]* Continue with other examples.

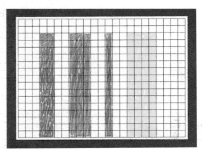

ESL ▶ APPROPRIATE

CONSUMER CONNECTION

Cooperative Groups   **Logical/Analytical**

OBJECTIVE Connect finding products to making purchases.

Materials per group: computer software advertisements; calculator

▶ Distribute the software advertisements to each group. Have students work together to write an order of educational computer software for their school. Tell students that they have a budget of $5,000 and must buy a minimum of 10 of each software program they order.

▶ Discuss the strategies and reasons students used to select the software and the number of each type ordered. Some groups may order fewer programs but have more variety while others may order more programs with less variety.

Daily Review

Math Van

PREVIOUS DAY QUICK REVIEW

1. 15 × 123 [1,845]
2. 28 × 308 [8,624]
3. 39 × 428 [16,692]
4. 62 × 319 [19,778]

Problem of the Day • 56

Consuela has a gymnastic class right after school that lasts 2 hours. On Tuesdays, she also has a club meeting right after gymnastics. Consuela's mother picks her up from the club meeting at 6:30. If Consuela got out of school at 3:00, how long was the club meeting? [1 h 30 min]

TECH LINK

MATH VAN

Tools You may wish to use the Calculator and the Table and Graph tools for the Data Point in this lesson.

MATH FORUM

Idea When working with problems with larger numbers, I assign fewer problems and emphasize that students solve each problem carefully and check their work again.

Visit our Resource Village at http://www.mhschool.com to see more of the Math Forum.

FAST FACTS

1. 8 × 6 [48]
2. 8 × 7 [56]
3. 8 × 8 [64]
4. 8 × 9 [72]

MATH CENTER

Practice

OBJECTIVE Write factors for the greatest possible product and the least possible product of 4-digit and 2-digit numbers.

Materials per pair: number cards 0–9 (TA 29), calculator; per student: Math Center Recording Sheet (TA 31 optional)

Students randomly select digits to form two sets of factors—one to make the greatest possible product, the other to make the least possible product. [Students check their answers using a calculator.]

PRACTICE ACTIVITY 56

MATH CENTER
Partners 👥

Calculator • Product Reasoning

Work together.

- Pick six number cards. Place them face up on the table. Then arrange them as a 2-digit and a 4-digit factor to get the greatest product.
- Try different arrangements. Discuss strategies. Use a calculator to help you. When you think that you have the greatest product, record it in a table like the one below.
- Rearrange the same digits to get the least product. Repeat the activity with a different set of digits.

YOU NEED
- number cards (0–9)
- calculator

Digits Picked	Factors for Greatest Product	Factors for Least Product

McGraw-Hill School Division   Grade Level 4

Chapter 6, Lesson 7, pages 226–227

Multiplication

NCTM Standards
✓ Problem Solving
  Communication
✓ Reasoning
✓ Connections

ESL APPROPRIATE

Problem Solving

OBJECTIVE Decide where to place randomly selected numbers to form factors to make a target product.

Materials per student: 2 number cubes, calculator, Math Center Recording Sheet (TA 31 optional)

In this activity, students use a number cube to generate numbers to make a 4-digit factor and a 2-digit factor. A number must be placed on a game sheet for each throw. The object is to get as close as possible to a given product. Students use calculators to check their work.

PROBLEM-SOLVING ACTIVITY 56

MATH CENTER
On Your Own 👤

Logical Reasoning • Product Solitaire

1. Make a copy of the game sheet below.

□ , □ □ □
× □ □

YOU NEED
- 2 number cubes
- calculator

2. Roll the cubes and choose either number to fill a space on the game sheet. The goal is to create factors that will give a product close to 100,000.

3. Keep rolling and filling in the grid. When it is complete, find the product. Use a calculator if you wish.
- How close were you? How might you have gotten closer if you had put the numbers in other boxes?
- Repeat with a new target number above 100,000.

McGraw-Hill School Division   Grade Level 4

Chapter 6, Lesson 7, pages 226–227

Multiplication

NCTM Standards
✓ Problem Solving
✓ Communication
  Reasoning
  Connections

ESL APPROPRIATE

Lesson 6.7 *continued*

Multiply Greater Numbers

OBJECTIVE Multiply up to 5-digit numbers, including money amounts, by 2-digit numbers.

 **Introduce**

Present the following information

During a beach cleanup along 300 miles of Texas shoreline in 1988, 15,600 plastic six-pack rings were found in 3 hours.

Tell students plastic six-pack rings have become a hazard to ocean birds and other marine life. Have students brainstorm things they can do to prevent such hazards from happening. *[Possible answers: Before tossing the rings, snip each circle with a pair of scissors; when you are on the beach, pick up any six-pack rings you can find.]*

 **Teach**   *Whole Class*

▶ **LEARN** Read aloud the problem given. Ask students to show on the chalkboard how to perform the steps needed to solve the multiplication problem. Remind students to find an estimate first as a way to check their answer.

 Close

▶ **Check for Understanding** using items 1–6, page 226.
CRITICAL THINKING
For item 6, students are asked to choose a computation method: mental math, paper and pencil, or a calculator. Suggest that students describe when they would choose each of the methods.

▶ **PRACTICE**
Materials have available: calculators

Options for assigning exercises:
A—Odd ex. 1–15; all ex. 16–19; **More to Explore**
B—Even ex. 2–14; all ex. 16–19; **More to Explore**

- For ex. 6–15, students may use any method they choose. If you prefer students to use paper and pencil for computation, you may wish to have them use a calculator to check their work.
- Remind students to place a dollar sign and decimal point in their answers if the problem involves money amounts.

More to Explore In this activity, students are introduced to a variable represented by a letter rather than by a symbol.

 **Algebra** A variable represents a value that is unknown or varies in an algebraic expression or equation. Items 1–4 are algebraic expressions and depend upon the value of a. Items 5–8 are equations, each with a unique solution for the variable.

Multiply Greater Numbers

L E A R N

To help fight pollution, some students decided to recycle rings from a six-pack of soda. So far they have 4,278 bundles of rings with 25 rings in each bundle. How many rings do they have?

IN THE WORKPLACE
Field ecologist, Jeff Mantu at work

Estimate: $25 \times 4,278$

Think: $30 \times 4,000 = 120,000$

You can use pencil and paper to find the exact answer.

Multiply: $25 \times 4,278$

Step 1	Step 2	Step 3
Multiply by the ones.	**Multiply by the tens.**	**Add the products.**
$\begin{array}{r} 1\,3\,4 \\ 4,278 \\ \times\ \ \ 25 \\ \hline 21390 \end{array}$ ←$5 \times 4,278$	$\begin{array}{r} 1\,1 \\ 1\,3\,4 \\ 4,278 \\ \times\ \ \ 25 \\ \hline 21390 \\ 85560 \end{array}$ ←$20 \times 4,278$	$\begin{array}{r} 1\,1 \\ 1\,3\,4 \\ 4,278 \\ \times\ \ \ 25 \\ \hline 21390 \\ +85560 \\ \hline 106,950 \end{array}$

 You can also use a calculator. $25 \times 4,278 = $ *106950.*

They have 106,950 rings.

C H E C K

Check for Understanding
Multiply using any method. Estimate to see if your answer is reasonable. $718.25; $800.00

1 2,584	**2** 3,285	**3** $42.25	**4** 12,045	**5** 51,00
× 37	× 21	× 17	× 62	×
95,608	68,985; 60,000		746,790; 600,000	1,479,2
				1,500,0

Critical Thinking: Generalize

6 Explain how you would find the following products.
   a. $40 \times 30,000$ **b.** $23 \times 3,216$ **c.** $72 \times 4,896$

mental math; 1,200,000   pencil and paper; 73,968   calculator; 352,512

Meeting Individual Needs

Early Finishers

Have students write word problems using ex. 11–15. Have them share their problems with the class.

Extra Support

Some students may have difficulty remembering what to do when multiplying numbers with a zero. Review examples such as 6×105 and 8×906 with these students.

Ongoing Assessment

Anecdotal Report Make notes on students' ability to find the product of greater numbers. Note whether or not students can choose an appropriate method to solve each problem.

Follow Up If students need more practice working with greater numbers, assign **Reteach 56.**

For students who need a challenge, assign **Extend 56.**

17. Possible answer: b; run and push the ball forward so that it rolls.

19. Possible answer: Students may find that on Saturdays and Sundays, they open the door more often because they are home.

Practice

Multiply mentally.

1	**2**	**3**	**4**	**5**
5,000	$7,000	8,000	46,000	25,000
× 60	× 30	× 80	× 20	× 30
300,000	$210,000	640,000	920,000	750,000

Multiply using any method. Remember to estimate.

6	**7**	**8**	**9**	**10**
957	$6.78	$18.15	6,029	7,060
× 98	× 19	× 75	× 19	× 87
93,786	$128.82	$1,361.25	114,551	614,220

11	**12**	**13**	**14**	**15**
$25.72	$84.14	3,225	21,400	43,200
× 24	× 9	× 51	× 33	× 42
$617.28	$757.26	164,475	706,200	1,814,400

MIXED APPLICATIONS
Problem Solving

16 What if there is an average of 4,074 students in each grade from kindergarten to grade 8 in your state. If each student recycles 5 bottles, how many bottles are recycled?
183,330 bottles

17 Spatial reasoning Which would be easiest to move if you were inside the shape? How would you move the shape?
a. a box   **b.** a ball   **c.** a cone
See above.

18 Tom and his brother spent $7.50 altogether at the Earth Day Festival. Tom spent $3.00 more than his brother. How much did each spend at the festival?
$2.25 and $5.25

19 Data Point Survey your classmates to see how many times they open the refrigerator in one day. Make a table of your results. What does your survey show?
See above.

more to explore

Using Variables

ALGEBRA You can use a letter to show an unknown amount.
Instead of writing $5 \times \blacksquare = 45$, you can write $5 \times a = 45$.

A Find $9 + b$ when $b = 7$.
Since $b = 7$, $9 + 7 = 16$.

B Find the value of z in $4 \times z = 12$.
Since $4 \times 3 = 12$, $z = 3$.

Find the answer when $a = 6$.

1 $5 + a$ 11   **2** $10 - a$ 4   **3** $7 \times a$ 42   **4** $a + 32$ 38

Find the value of the letter.

5 $6 + z = 25$ **6** $8 \times b = 32$ **7** $49 - t = 35$ **8** $y - 12 = 25$
  19   4   14   37

Extra Practice, page 507

Multiply by 2-Digit Numbers **227**

Alternate Teaching Strategy

Have students use expanded form to find the product of $46 \times 2,573$. Ask:

• **What is 2,573 in expanded form?** [2,000 + 500 + 70 + 3]

Have volunteers come to the chalkboard and find each of the following products in expanded form:

$$2,000 + 500 + 70 + 3$$
$$\times \qquad\qquad\qquad 6$$

[12,000 + 3,000 + 420 + 18]

$$2,000 + 500 + 70 + 3$$
$$\times \qquad\qquad\qquad 40$$

[80,000 + 20,000 + 2,800 + 120]

Have students write the expanded forms in standard form. [15,438; 102,920] Then have them find the sum of the partial products to find the product of $46 \times 2,573$. [118,358]

Repeat the activity with other products.

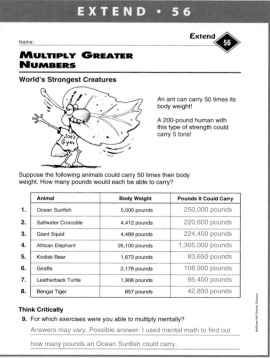

227

LESSON 6.8

Problem Solvers at Work

OBJECTIVE Solve and write problems by using an estimate or an exact answer.

RESOURCE REMINDER
Math Center Card 57
Practice 57, Reteach 57, Practice 57

SKILLS TRACE

GRADE 3	• Formulate and solve problems by determining if an estimate or exact answer is needed. *(Chapter 3)*
GRADE 4	• Formulate and solve problems by determining if an estimate or exact answer is needed.
GRADE 5	• Formulate and solve problems involving underestimates and overestimates. *(Chapter 2)*

WARM-UP

Cooperative Groups   **Logical/Analytical**

OBJECTIVE Write problems based on given information.

▶ Ask each group to write three multiplication problems based on the information given below. Tell students they may have to supply missing information to write their problems. Let each group present one of their problems for the rest of the class to solve.

> During one year an adult tree uses 13 pounds of carbon dioxide.
> Each day every person in the United States throws away about 4 pounds of garbage.
> About 17 trees are saved for every ton of recycled paper.
> You get 5 cents for recycling an aluminum can.

▶ Extend the activity by asking students whether they would use an estimate or find the exact answer to solve each problem.

SCIENCE CONNECTION

Cooperative Groups   **Visual/Spatial**

OBJECTIVE Connect using estimation in problem solving to science.

Materials per group: empty aluminum cans, paper bag

▶ Have students work in cooperative groups. Ask them how they would put the greatest number of aluminum cans in a paper bag. *[Crush the cans.]*

▶ Have them crush an aluminum can and use it to estimate how many crushed cans they could fit in the paper bag.

▶ Have each group present their estimates. Compare estimates and methods for the estimates. If enough cans are available, fill up paper bags and find the exact amount with students.

Daily Review

PREVIOUS DAY QUICK REVIEW

1. 30 × 4,000 *[120,000]*
2. 70 × 6,000 *[420,000]*
3. 82 × 359 *[29,438]*
4. 43 × 5,029 *[216,247]*

FAST FACTS

1. 2 × 7 *[14]*
2. 4 × 5 *[20]*
3. 6 × 6 *[36]*
4. 9 × 5 *[45]*

Problem of the Day • 57

Find a 3-digit number using the following clues:

–the sum of all three digits is 12;
–the sum of the ones digit and hundreds digit equals the tens digit;
–the tens digit is one greater than the ones digit. *[165]*

TECH LINK

MATH VAN

Aid You may wish to use the Electronic Teacher Aid in the Math Van with this lesson.

MATH FORUM

Idea Your students may be interested in planning and implementing a recycling program for your class or the school.

Visit our Resource Village at http://www.mhschool.com to see more of the Math Forum.

MATH CENTER

Practice

OBJECTIVE Solve multistep problems.

Materials per student: Math Center Recording Sheet (TA 31 optional)

Students solve multistep problems involving multiplication. *[The least number of mice is 60; the greatest is 192; the least number of bunnies is 36; the greatest is 75. Table should read: Mice 20, 40, 60–64, 128, 192; Bunnies 12, 24, 36–25, 50, 75.]*

PRACTICE ACTIVITY 57

MATH CENTER
On Your Own

Using Data • Pet Store

A pet-store owner has two parent rabbits and two parent mice. Each time there is a new litter, the owner sells all the baby bunnies or mice.

In three years, what's the least number of mice that could be sold? the greatest number? How about rabbits? Are you using estimates or exact answers?

Make a table to show the greatest/least number sold at the end of 1 year, 2 years, and 3 years. Your table should include all pets sold in each previous year.

Type of Animal	Litters Per Year	Usual Number in Litter
White Mouse	4–8	5–8 babies
Cottontail Rabbit	4–5	3–5 babies

Chapter 6, Lesson 8, pages 228–231

Problem Solving

NCTM Standards

✓ **Problem Solving**
   Communication
✓ **Reasoning**
✓ **Connections**

Problem Solving

OBJECTIVE Solve problems.

Materials paper cups, Math Center Recording Sheet (TA 31 optional)

Students find out amounts of ingredients they will need to make some Purple Pludge for everyone in school. They decide on a selling price and create a plan for making and selling Purple Pludge.

PROBLEM-SOLVING ACTIVITY 57

MATH CENTER
Small Group

Decision Making • Selling Purple Pludge

You have just invented a glue called Purple Pludge. Everyone wants to buy some.

• You can use paper cups for containers. It takes 5 cups of cornstarch, 3 cups of water, and 6 drops of food coloring to make 5 cups of Purple Pludge.

• You must sell 1 container to each person in your class. How much will each container hold? About how much cornstarch, water, and food coloring will you need?

• Decide how many paper cups you will need. Write your calculations. Decide on a selling price for Purple Pludge. Write a plan for making and selling Purple Pludge.

PLUDGE
Mix all ingredients in a bowl.
5 cups of cornstarch
3 cups of water
3 drops of blue food coloring
3 drops of red food coloring

Chapter 6, Lesson 8, pages 228–231

Problem Solving

NCTM Standards

✓ **Problem Solving**
   Communication
✓ **Reasoning**
✓ **Connections**

Problem Solvers at Work

OBJECTIVE Solve and write problems by using an estimate or an answer.

Resources spreadsheet program, or Math Van Tools.

1 Introduce

Discuss recycling projects in which your students may be involved. The school or a local organization may collect paper or cans as a fundraiser. Ask students to describe the projects of which they are aware. Ask students how much the group earns for their recyclables.

2 Teach
Cooperative Pairs

Cultural Connection Read the **Cultural Note.** In addition to using recycled copper to make the dome of the Massachusetts state house, Paul Revere used recycled copper for the bottom hull of the *Constitution,* a famous Revolutionary War ship. Revere collected other scrap metals to make cups, bowls, and other items.

PART 1 USE AN ESTIMATE OR FIND THE EXACT ANSWER

▶ **LEARN** Read aloud the opening information. Then ask students:

- **Will the truck driver be able to take all the recycled material in one trip? Explain how you know.** *[No. Answers may vary. Possible answer: The weight of the cardboard alone is too heavy to cross the bridge in one trip.]*

Work Together Let students work in cooperative pairs to solve each problem. For item 4, let students share their reasoning. For item 5, generate a list of answers including items carried and the amount of money earned.

Problem Solvers at Work

Read
Plan
Solve
Look Back

Part 1 Use an Estimate or an Exact Answer

LEARN

A recycling center trucks the materials it collects each week to a local processing plant. A truck can carry only 8,500 pounds of material on each trip.

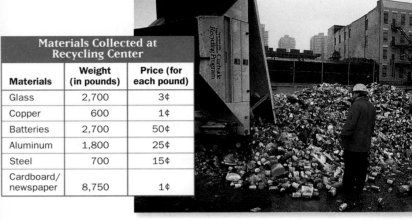

Materials Collected at Recycling Center		
Materials	**Weight (in pounds)**	**Price (for each pound)**
Glass	2,700	3¢
Copper	600	1¢
Batteries	2,700	50¢
Aluminum	1,800	25¢
Steel	700	15¢
Cardboard/ newspaper	8,750	1¢

Work Together
Use the table to solve. Tell whether you can solve without finding the exact answer. Explain your reasoning.

1 Will a truck be able to carry all the glass, cardboard, and newspaper in one truckload? **No—underestimate the sum of the weights, 2,00 + 8,000 = 10,000 lb > 8,500 lb; use an estimate to solve the problem.**

2 If a truck takes all the glass, batteries, and aluminum in one truckload, how much cardboard can it take on the trip? **8,500 − (2,700 + 2,700 + 1,800) = 1,300 lb; need to find the exact answer.**

3 The price list shows what the plant pays the center for each pound of material. Will the center get more than $1,500 for the batteries? **Overestimate to get 3,000 × 50¢ = $1,500.00, so the center w get less than $1,500; use an estimate to solve the problem.**

4 **What if** the center can get $400 for this week's aluminum by sending it out of the state. Should the center agree to this offer? Why or why not? **Possible answer: no; the center will get $450 from the processing plant; need to find the exact answer.**

5 **Make a decision** The truck can only make one trip this week. Which materials should the truck carry to earn the most money? **Possible answer: Take all the batteries, aluminum, steel, and glas and 600 lb of another material; need to find the exact answer.**

228 Lesson 6.8

Meeting Individual Needs

Extra Support

For some students you may need to review how to estimate a sum, difference, or product before they solve problems.

Language Support

Make sure students fully understand the difference between finding an estimate and finding the exact answer.

ESL APPROPRIATE

Ongoing Assessment

Observation Checklist Determine if students understand when estimates can be made by asking them if they would need an estimate or an exact answer to determine the number of packages of paper plates to buy for an all-school picnic. Students should be able to give reasons for their choices.

Follow Up For more practice with solving problems involving estimating and finding exact answers, assign **Reteach 57.**

For students who need a greater challenge, assign **Extend 57.**

Part 2 Write and Share Problems
....

Megan used the information on page 228 to write a problem.

6 Solve Megan's problem. Can you use estimation to solve the problem? Why or why not? **$6.00; no, need to find an exact answer.**

7 **Steps in a Process** How can you solve the problem in another way? List the steps you would follow. **For problems 7–12, see Teacher's Edition.**

8 **Write a problem** about recycling. You should be able to solve the problem using estimation.

9 Write a similar problem that needs an exact answer to solve it.

10 Solve both problems. Explain why they can or cannot be solved using estimation.

11 Trade problems. Solve at least three problems written by your classmates.

12 What was the most interesting problem that you solved? Why?

How much would the center get for all the copper?

Megan McAtee
Mandarin Oaks Elementary School
Jacksonville, FL

Cultural Note
Paul Revere used recycled copper metal to make parts of the dome of the Massachusetts statehouse.

Turn the page for Practice Strategies.
Multiply by 2-Digit Numbers **229**

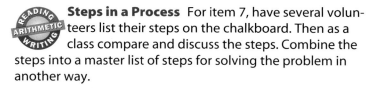

PART 2 WRITE AND SHARE PROBLEMS
▶ **Check** Let students work in pairs to complete items 6–12.

Steps in a Process For item 7, have several volunteers list their steps on the chalkboard. Then as a class compare and discuss the steps. Combine the steps into a master list of steps for solving the problem in another way.

For item 8, refer students to stories they have recently read or written. Encourage students to find the amount currently being paid for recycled materials or use the data given in the table on page 228.

For item 9, suggest that students can write a problem on a topic other than recycling. For item 10, students may suggest that problems requiring exact answers cannot be solved using estimation.

For items 11 and 12, encourage students to discuss the problems they solved and their reasons why a problem was most interesting.

3 Close

Let students discuss their answers for items 6, 7, and 12. Give time for several students to share what they wrote for items 8 and 9. Have students illustrate one of the problems they wrote for the classroom bulletin board. Write the answers on index cards and place them in a pocket on the bulletin board. Have students match the answers with the questions by writing on the card the number of the question they think it answers.

Practice See pages 230–231.

PART 3 PRACTICE STRATEGIES

Materials have available: calculators, graph paper, place-value models

Students have the option of choosing any five problems from ex. 1–8, and any two problems from ex. 9–12. They may choose to do more problems if they wish. Have students describe how they made their choices.

- For ex. 2, encourage students to write each number sentence before they enter it into a calculator. A guess-and-check strategy can be used to revise their number sentence each time.
- For ex. 10, encourage students to make a prediction before they begin adding or multiplying. Ask students if the result will be the same for any number they choose. Multiplying by 10 will always produce a greater result more quickly unless the starting number is 0 or 1.

 Algebra: Patterns Finding patterns helps develop algebraic thinking by showing the relationship between two factors.

At the Computer Ex. 12 suggests the use of a spreadsheet program, but students can still complete the exercise without the use of a computer. If computer time is limited, have students design their spreadsheet and formulas before going to the computer.

Have students use the Table tool to make a spreadsheet. A project electronic teacher aid has been provided.

---

1. No; 45 × 1,000 = 45,000, so 45 park benches use more than 45,000 milk jugs > 42,000 milk jugs.

2. Answers may vary. Possib answer: (2 + 3) × 24 = 2 × 3 =, 3 × 40 =, 30 + 30 + 30 =, 20 ÷ 2 × 3

Part 3 Practice Strategies

Menu Explanations may vary.
Choose five problems and solve them. Explain your methods.

1 It takes 1,022 milk jugs to make a plastic park bench. Can you make 45 park benches from 42,000 milk jugs? How do you know?
See above.

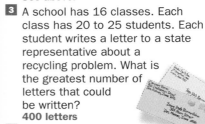

2 Use only the following keys on a calculator: 0 2 3 4 + − × ÷. Give five different ways to find 120.
See above.

3 A school has 16 classes. Each class has 20 to 25 students. Each student writes a letter to a state representative about a recycling problem. What is the greatest number of letters that could be written?
400 letters

4 **Write a problem** about recycling that can be solved by finding 365 × 25. Did you use mental math, pencil and paper, or a calculator? Why?
See page T17.

5 What is your age in weeks? How did you find the answer?
Possible answer:
489 weeks;
(9 × 52) +
(5 × 4) + 1 =
468 + 20 + 1 =
489

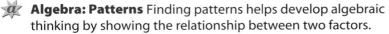

6 A town gives each of 6,750 families a recycling bin for aluminum cans. Each recycling bi costs 95¢. What is the total cost of the recycling bins?
$6,412.50

7 **Logical reasoning** Our class has two rules.
Rule 1: Use the computer if you finish your classwork early.
Rule 2: Use the computer for problems where you show graphs. Today I used the computer. Did I finish my classwork early? Explain.

8 The Morales family recycled 750 pounds of garbage last year. This year they recycled 3 times as much garbage. How many pounds of garbage did they recycle for both years? **3,000 lb**

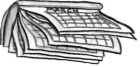

7. Maybe not; could have used the computer because there was a proble which needed a graph to be shown.

Meeting Individual Needs

Early Finishers

Ask students to show more than one way to solve one or more problems. This will tie together the problem-solving strategies taught in this chapter.

Inclusion

When assigning students to pairs, keep in mind the reading and mathematical abilities of each student. Match those with limited reading skills with good readers, but try to match students with close math abilities.

11. 10 rectangles; 240 × 1, 120 × 2, 80 × 3, 60 × 4, 48 × 5, 40 × 6, 30 × 8, 24 × 10, 20 × 12, 16 × 15

Choose two problems and solve them. Explain your methods.

ALGEBRA: PATTERNS Describe the pattern. Then find the next pair of factors. **Explanations may vary.**

16 × 20
18 × 18
20 × 16
22 × 14

Increase the first factor by 2 and decrease the second factor by 2; 24 × 12.

Think of a number other than 0. Compare adding 10 repeatedly to that number to multiplying that number by 10 repeatedly. Which way makes the number grow faster? Why? **See below.**

How many different rectangular grids can you make using 240 square units? What are they? **See above.**

At the Computer About how much water do you use in a day? in a week? Make a spreadsheet like the one shown here to estimate the amount of water you use each day, week, month, and year.
► Estimate the amount of water you use in a day for each entry.
► Have the computer calculate an estimate of the amount you use each week, month, and year.
► Predict the total amount of water you use in one month before using the computer to find it. Write about what you notice. **Check students' work.**

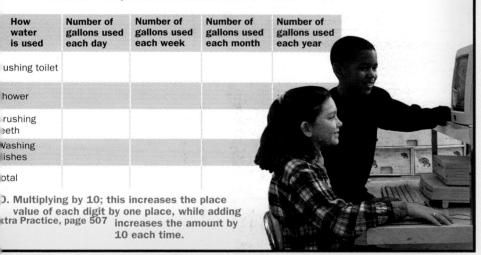

How water is used	Number of gallons used each day	Number of gallons used each week	Number of gallons used each month	Number of gallons used each year
Flushing toilet				
Shower				
Brushing teeth				
Washing dishes				
Total				

Multiplying by 10; this increases the place value of each digit by one place, while adding 10 increases the amount by 10 each time.

Extra Practice, page 507

Alternate Teaching Strategy

Materials per student: spreadsheet and graphing program

Have students copy the table on Student Book page 228 onto a spreadsheet program.

Ask them to tell how they would set up columns and cells to find the total value of the materials like the ones shown.

Have students compare their spreadsheets. Then have them write, solve, and share problems using the information from it. Students should discuss how they solved these problems.

You may wish to challenge students to use the spreadsheet to choose amounts of materials that come close to 15,000 pounds.

Processing Plant

Materials	Weight (in pounds)	Price (per pound)
glass	2,700	3¢
copper	600	1¢
batteries	2,700	50¢

PRACTICE • 57

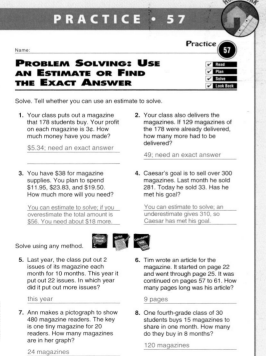

Name: _____ Practice **57**

PROBLEM SOLVING: USE AN ESTIMATE OR FIND THE EXACT ANSWER

☑ Read ☑ Plan ☑ Solve ☑ Look Back

Solve. Tell whether you can use an estimate to solve.

1. Your class puts out a magazine that 178 students buy. Your profit on each magazine is 3¢. How much money have you made?

   $5.34; need an exact answer

2. Your class also delivers the magazines. If 129 magazines of the 178 were already delivered, how many more had to be delivered?

   49; need an exact answer

3. You have $38 for magazine supplies. You plan to spend $11.95, $23.83, and $19.50. How much more will you need?

   You can estimate to solve; if you overestimate the total amount is $56. You need about $18 more.

4. Caesar's goal is to sell over 300 magazines. Last month he sold 281. Today he sold 33. Has he met his goal?

   You can estimate to solve; an underestimate gives 310, so Caesar has met his goal.

Solve using any method.

5. Last year, the class put out 2 issues of its magazine each month for 10 months. This year it put out 22 issues. In which year did it put out more issues?

   this year

6. Tim wrote an article for the magazine. It started on page 22 and went through page 25. It was continued on pages 57 to 61. How many pages long was his article?

   9 pages

7. Ann makes a pictograph to show 480 magazine readers. The key is one tiny magazine for 20 readers. How many magazines are in her graph?

   24 magazines

8. One fourth-grade class of 30 students buys 15 magazines to share in one month. How many do they buy in 8 months?

   120 magazines

RETEACH • 57

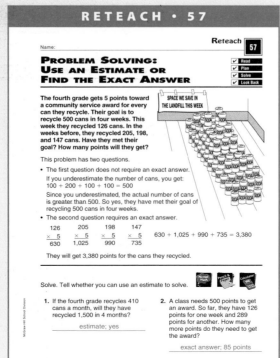

Name: _____ Reteach **57**

PROBLEM SOLVING: USE AN ESTIMATE OR FIND THE EXACT ANSWER

☑ Read ☑ Plan ☑ Solve ☑ Look Back

The fourth grade gets 5 points toward a community service award for every can they recycle. Their goal is to recycle 500 cans in four weeks. This week they recycled 126 cans. In the weeks before, they recycled 205, 198, and 147 cans. Have they met their goal? How many points will they get?

SPACE WE SAVE IN THE LANDFILL THIS WEEK

This problem has two questions.

• The first question does not require an exact answer.
If you underestimate the number of cans, you get:
100 + 200 + 100 + 100 = 500
Since you underestimated, the actual number of cans is greater than 500. So yes, they have met their goal of recycling 500 cans in four weeks.

• The second question requires an exact answer.

126	205	198	147	
× 5	× 5	× 5	× 5	630 + 1,025 + 990 + 735 = 3,380
630	1,025	990	735	

They will get 3,380 points for the cans they recycled.

Solve. Tell whether you can use an estimate to solve.

1. If the fourth grade recycles 410 cans a month, will they have recycled 1,500 in 4 months?

   estimate; yes

2. A class needs 500 points to get an award. So far, they have 126 points for one week and 289 points for another. How many more points do they need to get the award?

   exact answer; 85 points

EXTEND • 57

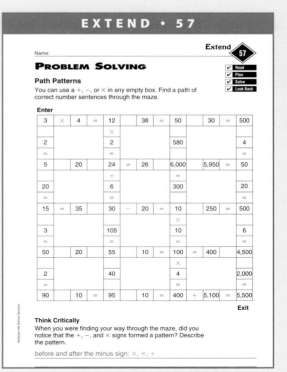

Name: _____ Extend **57**

PROBLEM SOLVING

☑ Read ☑ Plan ☑ Solve ☑ Look Back

Path Patterns

You can use a +, −, or × in any empty box. Find a path of correct number sentences through the maze.

Enter

3	×	4	=	12		38	=	50		30	=	500
		×										
2				2		580						4
=												
5		20		24	=	26		6,000		5,950	=	50
				+						=		
20				6				300				20
=				=								
15		35		30	=	20	=	10		250	=	500
				×								
3				105				10				6
=				=								
50		20		55		10	=	100	=	400		4,500
				×								
2				40				4				2,000
=				=								
90		10		95		10	=	400	+	5,100	=	5,500

Exit

Think Critically

When you were finding your way through the maze, did you notice that the +, −, and × signs formed a pattern? Describe the pattern.

before and after the minus sign: ×, ×, +

PURPOSE Review and assess the concepts, skills, and strategies that students have learned in the chapter.

Materials per student: calculator (optional)

Chapter Objectives
- **6A** Multiply multiples of 10, 100, and 1,000 by multiples of 10
- **6B** Estimate products, including money amounts
- **6C** Multiply by 2-digit factors, including money amounts
- **6D** Solve problems, including those that involve multiplication and using alternate solution methods

Using the Chapter Review

The **Chapter Review** can be used as a review, practice test, or chapter test.

Think Critically In ex. 33, the second partial product should only have one zero at its end, not two. Remind students how important it is to understand the place value of the partial products.

Language and Mathematics
Complete the sentence. Use a word in the chart. (pages 206–227)

1 The numbers 12 and 40 are ■ of 480. **factors**

2 To estimate 45 3 2,689, you can round 45 and 2,689 and then ■. **multiply**

3 If you change the order of the factors, the ■ is still the same. **product**

4 If you round up both factors, the exact product is less than the ■. **estimate**

Vocabulary
multiples
multiply
regroup
product
factors
estimate

Concepts and Skills
Without counting, find the total number of squares in the rectangle. (pages 210, 214)

5 21 / 15 — **315 squares**

6 23 / 19 — **437 squares**

Estimate the product. (page 208) Answers may vary. Estimates given are by round

7 78 3 17 **1,600**	**8** 51 3 $98 **$5,000**	**9** 52 3 $0.44 **$20**	**10** 47 3 113 **5,000**
11 52 3 $621 **$30,000**	**12** 11 3 $7.81 **$80**	**13** 81 3 2,079 **160,000**	**14** 19 3 27,10 **600,000**

Multiply. (pages 214, 224, 226)

15 20 3 30 **600**	**16** 32 3 11 **352**	**17** 50 3 30 **1,500**	**18** 35 3 $0.27 **$9.45**
19 25 3 $0.13 **$3.25**	**20** 42 3 98 **4,116**	**21** 56 3 $0.90 **$50.40**	**22** 77 3 58 **4,466**

23 30 3 90 **2,700**	**24** 48 3 42 **2,016**	**25** $0.45 3 62 **$27.90**	**26** 570 3 37 **21,090**	**27** 400 3 50 **20,000**
28 6,098 3 81 **493,938**	**29** $42.50 3 25 **$1,062.50**	**30** 9,604 3 54 **518,616**	**31** 13,800 3 70 **966,000**	**32** 52,00 3 18 **936,00**

Reinforcement and Remediation

CHAPTER OBJECTIVES	CHAPTER REVIEW ITEMS	STUDENT BOOK PAGES		TEACHER'S EDITION PAGES		TEACHER RESOURCES
		Lessons	Mid-chapter Review	Activities	Alternate Teaching Strategy	Reteach
6A	7, 9, 15, 19, 25	206–207	218	205A	207	50
6B	2, 4	208–209	218	207A	209	51
6C	1, 3, 5–6, 8, 10–14, 16–18, 20–24, 26–27	210–217; 224–227	218	209A, 213A, 223A, 225A	213, 217, 225, 227	52–53, 55–56
6D	28–33	222–223; 228–231	218	221A, 227A	223, 231	54, 57

3. The second partial product should only have one zero at its end, not two.
5. Possible answer: 40 people; 8 + (8 × 2) = 8 + 16 = 24, 1 × 16 = 16, 24 + 16 = 40

hink critically. (page 224)

3 Analyze. Explain what mistake was made, then correct it. **See above.**

$$\begin{array}{r} \overset{1\ 2}{\cancel{2\ 3}} \\ 247 \\ \times\ \ 35 \\ \hline 1235 \\ +74100 \\ \hline 75{,}335 \end{array}$$

$$\begin{array}{r} \overset{1\ 2}{\cancel{2\ 3}} \\ 247 \\ \times\ \ 35 \\ \hline 1235 \\ +7410 \\ \hline 8{,}645 \end{array}$$

4 Analyze. How can you find the product of 79 × 245 if you know that the product of 80 and 245 is 19,600? **Possible answer: Subtract 245 from 19,600 to get 19,355.**

Problem Solving Pencil & Paper · Calculator · Mental Math

(pages 222, 228)

35 The Interact Club has 8 members. Each member invited two friends to Cleanup Day. Each of these two friends invited one friend. How many people attended Cleanup Day? Explain your reasoning. **See above.**

36 The product of two mystery numbers is 280. The sum of these numbers is 47. What are the mystery numbers? **40 and 7**

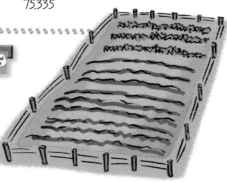

37 Spatial reasoning Students planted 91 tree seedlings in the field as shown above. About how many seedlings will fill the field? **See below.**

Use the sign for problems 38–40.

38 A large company recycles 19 tons of newspaper. How much money will the company collect? (Hint: 1 ton = 2,000 pounds) **$95**

39 A community collects 14 tons of aluminum cans and 24 tons of computer paper. How much money will the community collect? **$11,793.60**

40 How many tons of newspaper would a community have to collect to earn $100? **20 T**

Sal's Recycling Center
WE BUY FROM YOU!

newspaper	25¢ for 100 pounds
computer paper	7¢ for 100 pounds
aluminum cans	42¢ for 1 pound
cast aluminum	22¢ for 1 pound
copper	75¢ for 1 pound
steel	15¢ for 1 pound

HOURS

Monday through Friday	7 A.M. to 5 P.M.
Saturday	8 A.M. to 3 P.M.

37. Possible answer: about 4 × 100, or 400 seedlings

Multiply by 2-Digit Numbers **233**

PURPOSE Assess the concepts, skills, and strategies students have learned in this chapter.

Chapter Objectives

6A Multiply multiples of 10, 100, and 1,000 by multiples of 10

6B Estimate products, including money amounts

6C Multiply by 2-digit factors, including money amounts

6D Solve problems, including those that involve multiplication and using alternate solution methods

Using the Chapter Test

The **Chapter Test** can be used as a practice test, a chapter test, or as an additional review. The **Performance Assessment** on Student Book page 235 provides an alternate means of assessing students' understanding of multiplication by 2-digit numbers.

The table below correlates the test items to the chapter objectives and to the Student Book pages on which the skills are taught.

Assessment Resources

TEST MASTERS

The Testing Program Blackline Masters provide three forms of the Chapter Test to assess students' understanding of the chapter concepts, skills, and strategies. Form C uses a free-response format. Forms A and B use a multiple-choice format.

COMPUTER TEST GENERATOR

The Computer Test Generator supplies abundant multiple-choice and free-response test items, which you may use to generate tests and practice work sheets tailored to the needs of your class.

TEACHER'S ASSESSMENT RESOURCES

Teacher's Assessment Resources provides resources for alternate assessment. It includes guidelines for Building a Portfolio, page 6, and the Holistic Scoring Guide page 27.

Estimates may vary. Estimates shown are by rounding each number to its greatest

Estimate the product.

1 58 × 286	**2** 94 × 103	**3** 37 × 91	**4** 48 × $0.88
18,000	9,000	3,600	$45
5 18 × $7.66	**6** 68 × 335	**7** 22 × $58.19	**8** 28 × 3,053
$160	21,000	$1,200	90,000
9 81 × 457	**10** 77 × 915	**11** 43 × $629	**12** 15 × 2,057
40,000	72,000	$24,000	40,000

Multiply. Use mental math when you can.

13 90 × 70 6,300	**14** $5.73 × 28 $160.44	**15** 305 × 46 14,030	**16** $72.60 × 92 $6,679.20	**17** 8,0 × 640,40
18 68 × 41 2,788	**19** 50 × 20 1,000	**20** 68 × $0.41 $27.88	**21** 81 × 11 891	
22 56 × 35 1,960	**23** 80 × 500 40,000	**24** 20 × 80 1,600	**25** 30 × $100 $3,000	
26 63 × 67 4,221	**27** 48 × 7,052 338,496	**28** 87 × $39.04 $3,396.48	**29** 85 × $74,0 6,290,765	

Solve. Use the table for problems 30–31.

Average Content of 100 Pounds of Tras	
Paper products	39 pounds
Glass	6 pounds
Metals	8 pounds
Plastics	9 pounds
Wood	7 pounds
Food	7 pounds
Yard waste	15 pounds
Other	9 pounds

30 About how many times as many pounds of paper products are in the trash as metals? **about 5 times**

31 If your family throws away 5,200 pounds of trash, do you expect to throw away more than 550 pounds of plastics? Show two ways to solve. Explain your reasoning. **See below.**

32 Tara recycled 23 cans on Wednesday and 36 cans on Friday. She got 15¢ for each can. Does she have enough money to buy a book for $12.95? Explain. **No; possible answer: overestimati gives 60 × 20¢ = $12.00, which is still less than $12.95.**

33 Elle is 6 years older than Ming. The product of their ages is 216. Faye is 2 years younger than Elle. How old are Elle, Faye, and Ming? **18, 16, and 12**

31. No; possible answer: use an estimate—overestimating gives 520 lb of plastic, and 520 < 550; choose the operation—5,200 is 52 hundreds, so 9 × 52 = 468 lb plastics, and 468 < 550.

Test Correlation

CHAPTER OBJECTIVES	TEST ITEMS	TEXT PAGES
6A	13, 19, 23–25	206–207
6B	1–12	208–209
6C	13–29	210–217 224–227
6D	30–33	222–223 228–231

Check students' work. See Teacher's Assessment Resources for samples of student work.

What Did You Learn?

A cord of wood can make about:
- 1,500 pounds of paper.
- 942 books, each weighing a pound.
- 61,370 business envelopes.
- 1,200 copies of *National Geographic*.
- 2,700 copies of a daily newspaper.

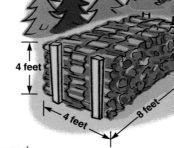

4 feet

4 feet

8 feet

A Cord of Wood

Tell what you can make with the following. Give one example for each. Show the method you used to solve each problem and explain why you chose that method.

1 10 cords of wood

2 17 cords of wood

3 29 cords of wood

4 40 cords of wood

··················· **A Good Answer** ···················
- includes a response for each amount of wood
- shows accurate calculations and clearly explains why each method was chosen

You may want to place your work in your portfolio.

What Do You Think ?
See Teacher's Edition.

1 How do you use what you know about multiplying by 1-digit numbers to help you multiply by 2-digit numbers?

2 If you want to find 13×356, which methods would you use?
- Use pencil and paper.
- Use a calculator.
- Use a diagram or model.
- Other. Explain.

3 Are you always able to break apart numbers to help you multiply? Why or why not?

Multiply by 2-Digit Numbers **235**

Reviewing A Portfolio

Have students review their portfolios. Consider including these items:
- Finished work on the Chapter Project (p. 203F) or **Investigation** (pp. 220–221).
- Selected math journal entries, pp. 205, 215, 218, 226.
- Finished work on the nonroutine problem in **What Do You Know?** (p. 205) and problems from the Menu (pp. 230–231).
- Each student's self-selected "best piece" from work completed during the chapter. Have each student attach a note explaining why he or she chose that piece.
- Any work you or an individual student wishes to keep for future reference.

You may take this opportunity to conduct conferences with students. The Portfolio Analysis Form can help you report students' progress. See Teacher's Assessment Resources, p. 33.

> **PURPOSE** Review and assess the concepts, skills, and strategies learned in this chapter.
>
> **Materials** have available: calculators (optional)

Using the Performance Assessment

Have students read and restate the problems in their own words. Make sure they understand what a cord of wood is and what they are to do. For example, for the first problem, they could find the number of pounds of paper (or the number of books, or the number of business envelopes, etc.) that can be made with 10 cords of wood.

Point out the section on the student page headed "A Good Answer." Make sure students understand that you will use these points to evaluate their answers.

Evaluating Student Work

As you read students' papers, look for the following:
- *Can the student multiply by 10? by 40?*
- *Can the student multiply by a 2-digit number?*
- *Does the student know basic multiplication facts or have strategies for finding them?*
- *How clearly can the student explain why she or he chose each method?*

The Holistic Scoring Guide and annotated samples of students' work can be used to assess this task. See pages 27–32 and 37–72 in Teacher's Assessment Resources.

Using the Self-Assessment

What Do You Think? Assure students that there are no right or wrong answers. Tell them the emphasis is on what they think and how they justify their answers.

Follow-Up Interviews

These questions can be used to gain insight into students' thinking:
- **What method did you use to show what you can make with 10 cords of wood? What is another way you could solve that problem?**
- **What method did you use to show what you can make with 40 cords of wood?**
- **What method did you use to show what you can make with 17 cords of wood? with 29 cords of wood?**

MATH · SCIENCE · TECHNOLOGY CONNECTION

OBJECTIVE Compare the cost and environmental effects of various types of batteries.

Materials flashlights and various batteries, such as regular, heavy duty, alkaline, and nicad

Resources spreadsheet program, or Math Van Tools

Science

Cultural Connection Read the **Cultural Note.** Tell students that before 1800 the only electricity that could be produced by people was static electricity which could not be stored or made useful.

Read and discuss the remainder of page 236 with the class. Then ask:
- **Which kind of battery do you prefer: non-rechargeable or rechargeable? Why?** [Answers may vary. Possible answers: rechargeable; it's better for the environment.]

You may also wish to have students test batteries in motorized toys or tape recorders. The batteries in these devices won't last as long as the batteries in a flashlight. Do the flashlight experiment as a whole class and display the lights so that the class can observe them periodically during the day.

Math

Have students work in pairs to complete items 1–4.

The following chart shows typical results for the flashlight experiment:

Battery Type	Cost (2 batteries)	Time
Regular	$1.00	1 hour
Heavy duty	$1.50	2 hours
Alkaline	$2.00	6 hours
Nicad (rechargeable)	$6.00	3 hours

Have partners share and compare their answers with the rest of the class.

BATTERY POWER

Cultural Note
An Italian scientist, Alessandro Volta, is believed to have invented the first working battery in 1800. The volt, a unit used to measure electrical energy, is named after him.

People use batteries to get energy for many things including radios, CD players, flashlights, cameras, and toys. The materials in batteries, however, can be harmful to the environment.

After they have been used up, regular and heavy-duty flashlight batteries are useless.

Alkaline batteries last longer than regular batteries but they also cost more.

Rechargeable batteries are expensive but they can be recharged as many as 1,000 times.

Batteries also come in different sizes.

Which battery is best? You can conduct your own experiment.
Place two of each type of size-D battery in a flashlight. Record the time it takes to use up each type of battery. Show your results in a table.

Type of Battery	Time	Cost of 2 Batteries
Regular	1 hour	$ 1.00
Heavy duty		
Alkaline		
Rechargeable		

▶ How else can you get energy besides using a battery?
Possible answers: windmills, solar energy, nuclear energy

You will need
- 4 flashlights
- 2 of each kind of size-D battery: regular, heavy duty, alkaline, rechargeable

Extending The Activity

Have students conduct a survey of the type and number of batteries their families use. Students can combine the results to create a table and graph showing the types and numbers of batteries used by the whole class. Volunteers can then calculate battery use for the entire year, based on this data.

Comparing Batteries

Use the results from your experiment.
Results may vary. Check students' work.

1. How many regular batteries would it take to get the same amount of energy as two alkaline batteries?

2. Find and compare the prices of the different types of size-D batteries. Is it better to buy the heavy-duty batteries or the regular batteries? Explain your reasoning.

3. **What if** a charger for the rechargeable batteries costs $20.00. What is the cost of two rechargeable batteries and the charger? How many alkaline batteries could you buy for this amount? How long would this number of alkaline batteries last?

4. Which battery would be best to use in a flashlight? Explain your reasoning.

At the Computer
Check students' work.

5. Write a lab report describing the experiment and the results. Tell which type of battery you think is best and explain why.

6. Make a spreadsheet that calculates the cost for each hour of use of each different type of battery.

Type of Size-D Battery	Cost of Batteries	Time Taken (hours)	Cost for each Hour of Use
Regular			
Alkaline			

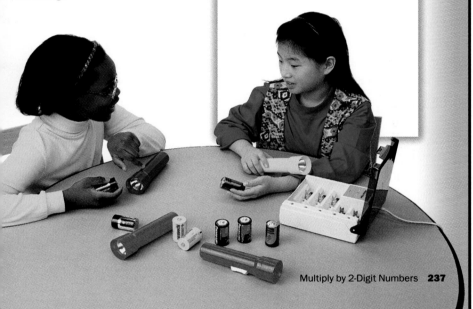

Multiply by 2-Digit Numbers **237**

Bibliography

Electricity, by Steve Parker. New York: Dorling Kindersley, 1992. ISBN 1-879-43182-3.

Energy, by Robert Snedden. New York: Chelsea House Publishers, 1996. ISBN 0-79-103-028-8.

Projects That Explore Energy, by Martin Gutnik and Natalie Browne-Gutnik. Brookfield, CT: The Millbrook Press, 1994. ISBN 1-56294-334-0.

Technology

Students may use a word-processing program to write their reports. They may also wish to write letters to a local recycling office or department of sanitation to ask questions about their policy on recycling batteries.

With access to the internet, students can email students in North Carolina to ask about their State's recycling policy for batteries. North Carolina recycles toxic batteries at the local level.

Math Van Students may use the Table tool to make their spreadsheets.

Interesting Facts

- **Batteries were first used in wristwatches in the 1950s.** Prior to that, "self winding" watches had a mainspring that could be wound from the motion of a person's wrist.

- **Most batteries are made up of a number of cells** connected in series in order to increase the voltage. Most cells produce about $1\frac{1}{2}$ volts.

- **Most small disk batteries contain mercury,** silver, cadmium, lithium, or other heavy metals and therefore cause damage to the environment when disposed of improperly. They are easily recycled since the materials can be recovered and reused.

CUMULATIVE REVIEW

PURPOSE Review and assess the concepts, skills, and strategies that students have already learned.

Materials per student: calculators (optional)

Using the Cumulative Review

The **Cumulative Review** is presented in a multiple-choice format to provide practice in taking a standardized test.

The table below correlates the review items to the text pages on which the skills are taught.

Assessment Resources

TEST MASTERS

There are multiple-choice Cumulative Tests and a Year-End Test that provides additional opportunities for students to practice taking standardized tests.

COMPUTER TEST GENERATOR

The Computer Test Generator supplies abundant multiple-choice and free-response test items, which you may use to generate tests and practice work sheets tailored to the needs of your class.

T E S T   P R E P A R A T I O N

Choose the letter of the best answer.

1 Choose the best estimate.
Seth can walk 4 miles in about ▮ minutes. **B**
- **A** 8
- **B** 80
- **C** 800
- **D** 8,000

2 All these numbers are: **G**

| 24 | 32 | 16 | 8 | 48 | 3 |

- **F** even.
- **G** less than 50.
- **H** odd.
- **J** 2-digit numbers.

3 Find the missing number. **C**

$$\begin{array}{r} 685 \\ + 14\blacksquare \\ \hline 831 \end{array}$$

- **A** 0
- **B** 4
- **C** 6
- **D** 7

4 Which names the same number as $(4 \times 5) \times 7$? **G**
- **F** $4 + (5 \times 7)$
- **G** $4 \times (5 \times 7)$
- **H** $4 \times (5 + 7)$
- **J** $(4 \times 5) + 7$

5 If June 8th is on a Saturday, on which day is June 27th? **D**
- **A** Saturday
- **B** Tuesday
- **C** Sunday
- **D** Thursday

6 Which statement is true? **G**
- **F** $34 \times 2,454 < 54 \times 1,414$
- **G** $\$6,000 - \$189 > \$5,900 - \$99$
- **H** $435 + 1,254 + 23 = 1,919$
- **J** $9 \times 689 > 6,300$

7 If one number is removed from each box and placed in the other, the products would be equal. Which numbers should be moved?

| 10×60 | | 5×30 |

- **A** 60, 30
- **B** 10, 30
- **C** 60, 5
- **D** 1, 3

8

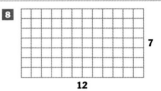

7

12

Find the total number of squares the rectangle. **F**
- **F** 84
- **G** 72
- **H** 70
- **J** 80

9 Find the difference between thes products:
21 × 37 and **27 × 31** **C**
- **A** 0
- **B** 40
- **C** 60
- **D** 80

238   Cumulative Review: Chapters 1–6

Cumulative Review Correlation

REVIEW ITEMS	TEXT PAGES	REVIEW ITEMS	TEXT PAGES
1	82	9	62, 214
2	12, 73	10	70
3	48	11	146
4	140	12	84
5	84	13	222
6	46, 208	14	128
7	170	15	40
8	174	16	94

You have saved $13 toward a bicycle. What other information is needed to determine how much more money you need to buy it? **G**

F The amount you save each day
G The cost of the bicycle
H The amount you started with
J The cost of a helmet

What is shown on the number line? **C**

0 1 2 3 4 5 6 7 8 9 10 11 12 13 14 15

A 15 − 5 = 3
B 5 + 3 = 15
C 15 ÷ 3 = 5
D 15 − 5 = 10

Mike leaves home at 3:00 P.M. and shops for 1 hour and 45 minutes. If he needs 40 minutes to travel to the school play, which starts at 5:30 P.M., he will be ■. **H**

F 10 minutes early
G on time
H 5 minutes early
J not given

Louise spent $4.60 on juice and fruit rolls. Juice sells for 35¢ a can, and fruit rolls are 50¢ each. How many of each did she buy? **C**

A 2 juice cans and 8 fruit rolls
B 5 juice cans and 6 fruit rolls
C 6 juice cans and 5 fruit rolls
D 8 juice cans and 2 fruit rolls

14 Which number comes next?
8, 16, 24, 32, ■ **H**

F 48
G 8
H 40
J 34

15 Ty pays for a $0.99 book cover and a $1.75 pen with 3 one-dollar bills. What change might she get back? **C**

A a quarter and a dime
B three dimes and a penny
C five nickels and a penny
D four nickels and four pennies

Use the graph for problem 16.

Paper Products at the Recycling Center	
Cardboard	■■■■■■
Newspaper	■■■■■
Office/commerical paper	■■■
Books and magazines	■■■

Key: Each ■ stands for 2,000 pounds.

16 Which statement does *not* describe the data in the graph? **H**

F The recycling center has 50,000 pounds of paper products.
G There is more cardboard than any other kind of paper material at the recycling center.
H Recycling paper saves trees!
J There is about twice as much cardboard as newspaper at the recycling center.

T E S T   P R E P A R A T I O N

Multiply by 2-Digit Numbers   **239**

Chapter 1 — EXTRA PRACTICE

PURPOSE Provide another opportunity for review and practice.

Materials have available: calculators

Using the Extra Practice

The Extra Practice can be used to provide further practice during a lesson or as a review later in the chapter.

Using the Additional Practice

The sections below provide additional practice that you can assign. You may wish to write these exercises on the chalkboard or put them on a reproducible master.

---

10. date—to order or measure, time—to measure, age—to count, address—to name and order, phone—to name

Numbers in Your World page 3

Write a sentence in which the number is used in the way given. Answers may vary. Possible answers are shown.

1 Number: 6
Used: to show order
Jan was 6th in line.

2 Number: 8
Used: to count
There are 8 bananas.

3 Number: 16
Used: to show order
Don placed 16th in the

4 Number: 24
Used: to measure
The mat is 24 in. long.

5 Number: 31
Used: to name
Marcia has class in room 31.

6 Number: 91
Used: to measure
The football player ran 91 yd.

7 Number: 57
Used: to name
Mel used school calculator 57.

8 Number: 25
Used: to count
There are 25 students in class.

9 Number: 36
Used: to measure
The material is 36 in. wide.

Solve.

10 Tell how each number on Sam's birthday invitation is used. See above.

11 Jan's birthday is 5 days later than Sam's. What is the date of her birthday? September 24

> Birthday Party
> You're invited!
> Sam Nelson will be 9.
>
> September 19
> 1:00 P.M.
> 1056 First Street
> RSVP: 888-8888

Building to Thousands page 7

Write the number.

1 9 hundreds 2 tens
920

2 7 hundreds 9 tens 8 ones
798

3 29 tens 8 ones
298

4 84 tens 3 ones
843

5 76 tens 4 ones
764

6 100 tens 9 ones
1,009

7 1 thousand 5 hundreds 6 ones
1,506

8 5 thousands 3 tens 9 ones
5,039

Solve.

9 Write the greatest 3-digit number using the cards at the right. Then, give the number that is 1,000 more. 976; 1,976

10 Write the least 3-digit number using the cards at the right. Then, give the number that is 100 less. 136; 36

Additional Practice

p. 3 **Write a sentence in which the number is used in the way given.** *[Answers may vary. Possible responses are shown.]*

1. Number: 7
Used: to show order
[The 7th month is July.]

2. Number: 15
Used: to measure
[The room is 15 feet long.]

3. Number: 32
Used: to count
[There are 32 students on the bus.]

4. Number: 43
Used: to measure
[My friend lives 43 miles away.]

5. Number: 5
Used: to name
[The club's name is The 5 Friends.]

6. Number: 25
Used: to show order
[The 25th of the month is a Sunday.]

7. Number: 43
Used: to name
[The football player wears 43.]

8. Number: 18
Used: to measure
[The can holds 18 ounces.]

9. Number: 52
Used: to count
[Ed bought 52 stamps.]

p. 7 **Write the number.**

1. 8 hundreds 6 ones *[806]*
2. 42 tens 3 ones *[423]*
3. 1 thousand 6 tens *[1,060]*
4. 5 hundreds 4 tens *[540]*
5. 1 thousand 2 ones *[1,002]*
6. 8 hundreds 7 ones *[807]*
7. 57 tens 2 ones *[572]*
8. 80 tens 3 ones *[803]*
9. 3 hundreds 9 tens 4 ones *[394]*
10. 4 thousands 8 tens 2 ones *[4,082]*
11. Find 10 more than 552. *[562]*
12. Find 10 less than 649. *[639]*
13. Find 100 more than 1,092. *[1,192]*
14. Find 100 less than 1,745. *[1,645]*

Thousands page 11

Write the number in standard form and in expanded form.

1 eight thousand, six
8,006; 8,000 + 6

2 nine thousand, sixty-four 9,064; 9,000 + 60 + 4

3 six thousand, two hundred ten 6,210; 6,000 + 200 + 10

4 four thousand, six hundred thirty-five 4,635; 4,000 + 600 + 30 + 5

5 nineteen thousand, fifty 19,050; 10,000 + 9,000 + 50

6 two hundred thousand, four hundred 200,400; 200,000 + 400

7 eighty-three thousand, six hundred seventy-two 83,672; 0,000 + 3,000 + 600 + 70 + 2

8 two hundred six thousand, three hundred forty-five 206,345; 200,000 + 6,000 + 300 + 40 + 5

9 eight hundred ten thousand, five hundred twenty 810,520; 800,000 + 10,000 + 500 + 20

Solve.

0 Tell what number this model would represent if you added 4 more thousands, 2 more hundreds, and 9 more ones. **7,803**

- -

Compare and Order Numbers page 13

Compare. Write >, <, or =.

1 962 ● 926 **>**   **2** 3,916 ● 3,691 **>**   **3** 7,019 ● 7,901 **<**

4 12,934 ● 21,934 **<**   **5** 405,196 ● 405,196 **=**   **6** 801,359 ● 891,530 **<**

Order the numbers from least to greatest.

7 568; 856; 658 **568; 658; 856**

8 4,925; 49,250; 49,025 **4,925; 49,025; 49,250**

9 7,092; 9,207; 9,389 **7,092; 9,207; 9,389**

10 94,210; 9,421; 94,021 **9,421; 94,021; 94,210**

11 14,281; 8,365; 14,821 **8,365; 14,281; 14,821**

12 17,392; 17,923; 1,732 **1,732; 17,392; 17,923**

Solve.

13 Postage stamps come in sheets of 100. How many full sheets of stamps can you receive if you purchase 513 stamps? **5 full sheets**

14 You purchase 345 stamps and receive as many full sheets of stamps as possible. How many stamps are on the partial sheet? **45 stamps**

15 Carolee has $35. Earlier, she bought a pair of gloves for $20 and socks for $10. How much money did she start with? **$65**

16 Logical reasoning Pat is creating his own secret code. The letter *A* is 1, *B* is 3, *C* is 5, and *D* is 7. What pattern is he using?
Possible answer: Add 2 after the first letter to get the code for the next letter.

Extra Practice **485**

ⓐ DEVELOPING ALGEBRA SENSE

This section provides another opportunity for students to reinforce algebraic ideas.

Find the missing number.

1. 3,605 = 3,000 + ◆ + 5 *[600]*

2. 4,000 + 200 + ◆ = 4,250 *[50]*

3. 17,207 = ◆ + 7,000 + 200 + 7 *[10,000]*

4. 5,000 + ◆ + 8 = 5,208 *[200]*

5. 23,100 = 20,000 + ◆ + 100 *[3,000]*

6. 60,000 + 300 + ◆ = 60,370 *[70]*

- -

p. 11 Write the number in standard form and in expanded form.

1. seventy thousand, two hundred fifty-seven
[70,257; 70,000 + 200 + 50 + 7]

2. three hundred thousand, twelve
[300,012; 300,000 + 10 + 2]

3. sixteen thousand seventy-four
[16,074; 10,000 + 6,000 + 70 + 4]

4. six thousand, two hundred forty-two
[6,242; 6,000 + 200 + 40 + 2]

5. fifteen thousand, one hundred thirty-five
[15,135; 10,000 + 5,000 + 100 + 30 + 5]

6. thirty-four thousand, one hundred seven
[34,107; 30,000 + 4,000 + 100 + 7]

p. 13 Compare. Write >, <, or =.

1. 274 ◆ 247 *[>]*   **2.** 4,124 ◆ 4,183 *[<]*

3. 101,325 ◆ 11,325 *[>]*   **4.** 52,210 ◆ 52,379 *[<]*

5. 670,123 ◆ 670,123 *[=]*   **6.** 8,264 ◆ 6,248 *[>]*

Order the numbers from least to greatest.

7. 257; 238; 285 *[238; 257; 285]*

8. 34,712; 3,472; 3,742 *[3,472; 3,742; 34,712]*

9. 4,201; 6,285; 4,012 *[4,012; 4,201; 6,285]*

10. 52,612; 51,710; 56,102 *[51,710; 52,612; 56,102]*

11. 152,736; 125,736; 137,528 *[125,736; 137,528; 152,736]*

12. 701; 7,001; 71 *[71; 701; 7,001]*

PURPOSE Provide another opportunity for review and practice.

Materials have available: calculators

Using the Extra Practice

The Extra Practice can be used to provide further practice during a lesson or as a review later in the chapter.

Using the Additional Practice

The sections below provide additional practice that you can assign. You may wish to write these exercises on the chalkboard or put them on a reproducible master.

Problem-Solving Strategy: Make a Table page 15
Solve.

1 Akoni has 11 marbles. He has 6 more red marbles than blue marbles. He has twice as many blue marbles as yellow marbles. How many of each color does he have? **8 red marbles, 2 blue marbles, and 1 yellow marble**

2 Ashley paid $8.95 for a book. Keira paid $7 more than Ashley her book. Ken paid $2 less than Keira for his book. How much di Keira and Ken each pay for their books? **$15.95; $13.95**

3 **Logical reasoning** A stuffed animal, a toy guitar, and a doll were prizes at a carnival. Brandon did not choose the doll. Keisha did not choose the stuffed animal. Cassie chose the guitar. What did Keisha choose?
Keisha chose the doll.

4 Antonio works at a local grocery store. He earns $6 for each hou he works. Last week, he worked 2 hours on Tuesday, 4 hours on Friday, and 2 hours on Saturday. How much did he earn that wee **$48**

Round Numbers page 23
Round to the nearest ten.

1 47	**2** 314	**3** 4,098	**4** 6,152	**5** 79,99
50	310	4,100	6,150	80,00

Round to the nearest hundred.

6 448	**7** 9,105	**8** 45,051	**9** 38,649	**10** 508,9
400	9,100	45,100	38,600	509,0

Round to the nearest thousand.

11 4,099	**12** 9,601	**13** 25,741	**14** 98,389	**15** 399,5
4,000	10,000	26,000	98,000	400,0

Solve.

16 When rounding to the nearest ten, what is the greatest number that rounds to 620? **624**

17 When rounding to the nearest t what is the least number that rounds to 620? **615**

18 A special code is on facing pages in Joanne's secret code book. The total of the page numbers is 49. What are the numbers of the pages on which you will find the secret code? **24 and 25**

19 When Onida walks 3 blocks to the park and another 4 blocks to the grocery, she is halfway to school. How many blocks will she walk from home to school and back? **28 blocks**

Additional Practice

p. 15 Solve. Explain your methods. [Explanations may vary.]

1. **Logical Reasoning** Teri, Tom, and Tim play sports. They are hockey, soccer, and golf. Tim and Teri do not play golf. Tim plays hockey. Which sport does each person play? [Teri—soccer; Tom—golf; Tim—hockey]

2. José has 21 books. He has twice as many history books as mysteries. He has one more sport book than mystery. How many books of each kind does he have? [10 history books, 5 mysteries, 6 sport books]

3. Lee surveyed his class on their favorite beverages. His survey showed 6 preferred orange juice, 9 liked milk, 8 chose cider, and 5 selected ice tea. How many chose a drink made from fruit? [14 students]

4. Alex placed red, blue, and green markers in a row. The two markers on the left are green and blue. The green is in the middle. How are the markers placed? [blue, green, red]

p. 23 Round to the nearest ten.

1. 268–page book [270]
2. 42 minutes [40]
3. 217,296 species of insects [217,300]

Round to the nearest hundred.

4. 13,796 students [13,800]
5. 5,468 acres [5,500]
6. 13,643 residents [13,600]

Round to the nearest thousand.

7. 4,382 miles of trails [4,000]
8. 12,419 gallons of water [12,000]
9. 161,682 visitors [162,000]

Millions page 27

Write the number in standard form and in expanded form.

1. five million, six hundred three thousand, two hundred twenty-five **5,603,225; 5,000,000 + 600,000 + 3,000 + 200 + 20 + 5**

2. four million, nine hundred fifty-six thousand, one **4,956,001; 4,000,000 + 900,000 + 50,000 + 6,000 + 1**

3. six million, three hundred ninety-two thousand, nine hundred **6,392,900; 6,000,000 + 300,000 + 90,000 + 2,000 + 900**

4. three million, five hundred seven thousand, ninety **3,507,090; 3,000,000 + 500,000 + 7,000 + 90**

5. two million, one hundred nine thousand, sixty-seven **2,109,067; 2,000,000 + 100,000 + 9,000 + 60 + 7**

6. nine million, two hundred thousand, six hundred thirty-seven **9,200,637; 9,000,000 + 200,000 + 600 + 30 + 7**

Solve.

7. Suppose you save 100 pennies every day. If you continue at that rate, how many days will it take you to save 1,000,000 pennies? Explain your answer. **10,000 d; there are 10,000 hundreds in a million.**

8. The highest volcano on Mars is recorded at 78,000 feet above the surface. Is this an actual or a rounded number? Explain your answer. **Rounded; no one has been to Mars to measure.**

Problem Solvers at Work page 31

Solve.

1. May surveyed 26 students to find out their favorite color. She recorded the data in a tally table. Which color was favored by the most students? **blue**

Favorite Colors of Students

Color	Number of Students
Red	JHT //
Blue	JHT ///
Yellow	////
Green	JHT //

2. Suppose the choices—both green—of two new students are added to the table. Will this change the answer to problem 1? Explain. **Yes; more students now prefer green.**

3. Describe what happens if two students change their choices— one from blue to yellow and one from green to yellow. **Possible answer: Red and blue tie as the most-favored colors.**

4. There are about 900 species of endangered birds. In 1978, there were about 300 species of endangered birds. By how many has the number of endangered species increased? **about 600 species**

5. A hummingbird visits about 2,000 flowers each day to gather nectar. Use this information to write and answer a question. **Students may write questions involving addition or subtraction.**

Extra Practice **487**

DEVELOPING NUMBER SENSE

This section provides another opportunity for students to reinforce number sense.

Find the claims that you think are reasonable. *[c, d]*

a. The tallest building in the world is 5,816 mm tall.

b. The largest fish in the world weighs 985g.

c. An airplane can fly about 800 miles per hour.

d. Kevin can do 23 sit-ups per minute.

e. On average, there are 800,000,000 people who use the Grand Central Terminal in New York City daily.

f. The fastest speed attained by a railed vehicle is 6,121 meters per hour.

p. 27 Write the number in standard form and in expanded form.

1. five million, twenty-nine thousand, sixteen *[5,029,016; 5,000,000 + 20,000 + 9,000 + 10 + 6]*

2. nine million, one hundred seven thousand, two hundred forty *[9,107,240; 9,000,000 + 100,000 + 7,000 + 200 + 40]*

3. two million, thirty-four thousand, ninety-one *[2,034,091; 2,000,000 + 30,000 + 4,000 + 90 + 1]*

4. one million, one hundred one thousand, eleven *[1,101,011; 1,000,000 + 100,000 + 1,000 + 10 + 1]*

5. seven million, two hundred sixteen thousand *[7,216,000; 7,000,000 + 200,000 + 10,000 + 6,000]*

6. seven million, three hundred sixty-five thousand, twenty-one *[7,365,021; 7,000,000 + 300,000 + 60,000 + 5,000 + 20 + 1]*

p. 31 Solve. Use the line plot to solve problems 1–2. Explain your methods. *[Explanations may vary.]*

ON WHICH DAY DO PEOPLE DO THEIR GROCERY SHOPPING?

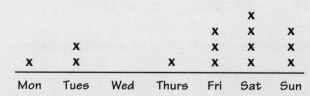

| Mon | Tues | Wed | Thurs | Fri | Sat | Sun |

1. On which day do most people do their grocery shopping? *[Saturday]*

2. How many people were surveyed? *[14 people]*

3. I am a number with the digits 2, 5, 7, 1, 8. If you round me to the nearest thousand, I am 51,000. I have 7 in the one's place. What number am I? *[51,287]*

487

PURPOSE Provide another opportunity for review and practice.

Materials have available: calculators, play money.

Using the Extra Practice

The Extra Practice can be used to provide further practice during a lesson or as a review later in the chapter.

Using the Additional Practice

The sections below provide additional practice that you can assign. You may wish to write these exercises on the chalkboard or put them on a reproducible master.

Count Money and Make Change page 41 Answers may vary. Possible answers a
Use play money to show the amount of money given.
in two ways.

1 26¢
1q, 1p; 5n, 1p

2 $1.02
1 one-dollar bill,
2p; 4q, 2p

3 $6.36
See below.

4 $11.45
See below.

Solve.

5 Sari bought a toy for $6.25. How much change did she get from $10? **$3.75**

6 List at least ten ways to show 7
using nickels, dimes, and quarte
See below.

3. 6 one-dollar bills, 3d, 6p; 1 five-dollar bill, 1 one-dollar bill, 1q, 1d, 1p
4. 1 ten-dollar bill, 1 one-dollar bill, 4d, 1n; 11 one-dollar bills, 1q, 2d

Compare, Order, and Round Money page 43
Write the amounts in order from least to greatest.

1 $1.15, $1.51, $5.51, $5.11
$1.15, $1.51, $5.11, $5.51

2 $25.83, $25.28, $5.75, $15.57
$5.75, $15.57, $25.28, $25.83

Solve.

3 An amount rounded to the nearest 10¢ is $11.50, to the nearest dollar is $12, and to the nearest $10 is $10. What could the amount be? Possible answers: $11.50, $11.51, $11.52, $11.53, $11.54

4 Karly paid with a ten-dollar bill. Her change was 4 one-dollar bills, 2 quarter 1 nickel, and 3 pennies. How much was her purchase? $5.42

Addition Strategies page 45
Add mentally.

1 200 + 568
768

2 $746 + $222
$968

3 462 + 321
783

4 $123 + $3
$444

5 816 + 183 999

6 195 + 308 + 105
608

7 520 + 113 + 280
913

Solve.

8 Banana Hut sold 215 shirts one week and 174 shirts the next week. How many shirts were sold in all? 389 shirts

9 Which would you rather have—1 ten-dollar bill, 11 quarters, and 10 pennies or 12 one-dollar bills, 3 quarters, and 1 dime? Explain. Answers may vary. Both represent the same amount of money: $12.85.

6. Possible answers: 3 quarters; 2 quarters, dimes, 1 nickel; 2 quarters, 1 dime, 3 nickels; 2 dimes, 11 nickels; 1 dime, 13 nickels; 15 nickels

488 Extra Practice

Additional Practice

p. 41 Use play money to show the amount of money in two ways.
[Answers may vary. Check student's work.]

1. 48¢

2. $1.73

3. 92¢

4. $14.45

5. $8.68

6. $3.14

p. 43 Write the amounts in order from least to greatest.

1. $4.25, $4.18, $4.52 [$4.18, $4.25, $4.52]

2. $21.85, $2.58, $15.73, $12.58 [$2.58, $12.58, $15.73, $21.85]

3. $17.51, $11.71, $171.51, $175.71 [$11.71, $17.51, $171.51, $175.71]

4. $3,876.68, $3,768.39, $3,867.51 [$3,768.39, $3,867.51, $3,876.68]

p. 45 Add mentally.

1. 43 + 26
[69]

2. 61 + 17
[78]

3. 38 + 41
[79]

4. 55 + 31
[86]

5. 24 + 64
[88]

6. 36 + 23
[59]

7. 432 + 265
[697]

8. 503 + 115
[618]

9. $216 + $372
[$588]

10. 724 + 253
[977]

11. $389 + $510
[$899]

12. $824 + $123
[$947]

13. 642 + 253
[895]

14. $773 + $214
[$987]

15. 627 + 222
[849]

Estimate Sums page 47

Estimate. Round to the nearest ten or ten cents.

1 $0.55 + $0.97
$1.60

2 $0.92 + $0.21
$1.10

3 58 + 99
160

4 48 + 22
70

Estimate. Round to the nearest hundred or dollar.

5 153 + 246
400

6 637 + 152
800

7 $6.39 + $9.67
$16.00

8 8,469 + 743
9,200

Solve.

9 A model costs $15.96 and a puzzle costs $4.24. Can you purchase both items with $20.00? Explain. No; the estimate is $20, but the actual cost is $20.20.

10 Bly paid with a five-dollar bill and 3 quarters. His change was 21¢. How much was his purchase? $5.54

Add Whole Numbers page 51

Add. Remember to estimate.

1
43
+ 36
79

2
72
+ 89
161

3
385
+ 828
1,213

4
3,764
+ 144
3,908

5
$3.26
+ 8.75
$12.01

Solve.

6 Last year, attendance was about 95,000 people. This year, 9,500 more people are expected. What is the expected attendance this year? about 104,500 people

7 Po, Rae, and Dee sell pads, rings, and dolls. The first letter of the item and name are not the same. Po sells dolls. What do Rae and Dee sell? Rae—pads, Dee—rings

Three or More Addends page 53

Add. Remember to estimate.

1
32
65
+ 19
116

2
$4.28
6.53
+ 8.12
$18.93

3
6,203
475
+ 634
7,312

4
356
482
27
+ 72
937

5
1,111
3,333
88
+ 77
4,609

Solve.

6 You have a twenty-dollar bill. Can you buy three craft items costing $6.46, $11.31, and $3.55? Explain. No; the total cost is $21.32, $21.32 > $20.

7 ALGEBRA: PATTERNS Show the next step.

DEVELOPING ALGEBRA SENSE

This section provides another opportunity for students to reinforce algebraic ideas.

Find the one that does not name the number. Use mental math to solve.

1. 12 [c]   **a.** 6 + 6   **b.** 6 × 2   **c.** 20 ÷ 5   **d.** 18 − 6

2. 32 [a]   **a.** 3 + 2   **b.** 30 + 2   **c.** 40 − 8   **d.** 21 + 11

3. 250 [b]   **a.** 150 + 100   **b.** 500 × 2   **c.** 205 + 45   **d.** 300 − 50

4. 186 [d]   **a.** 23 + 163   **b.** 190 − 4   **c.** 115 + 71   **d.** 1 + 8 + 6

5. 986 [c]   **a.** 900 + 86   **b.** 542 + 444   **c.** 579 + 210   **d.** 345 + 641

---

p. 47 Estimate. Round to the nearest ten or ten cents.

1. $0.23 + $0.55
[$0.80]

2. $1.99 + $0.28
[$2.30]

4. 65 + 48
[120]

5. 92 + 19
[110]

p. 51 Add. Remember to estimate.

1.
37
+ 24
[61]

2.
$4.56
+ 3.72
[$8.28]

3.
23,417
+ 66,247
[89,664]

4. $37,724 + $752
[$38,476]

5. 5,109 + 7,424
[12,533]

6. 527,814 + 639,148
[1,166,962]

p. 53 Add. Remember to estimate.

1.
28
53
+ 71
[152]

2.
416
23
853
+ 15
[1,307]

3.
468
921
3,574
+ 821
[5,784]

4. 271 + 5,566 + 4,728 + 634 [11,199]

5. $13.58 + $4.18 + $6.94 [$24.70]

6. 40 + 6,200 + 700 [6,940]

7. 10,589 + 4,692 + 3,175 [18,456]

> **PURPOSE** Provide another opportunity for review and practice.
>
> **Materials** have available: calculators, play money

Using the Extra Practice

The Extra Practice can be used to provide further practice during a lesson or as a review later in the chapter.

Using the Additional Practice

The sections below provide additional practice that you can assign. You may wish to write these exercises on the chalkboard or put them on a reproducible master.

---

5. Possible answer: They could buy 2 hamburgers and 2 bags of chips, but they would
Subtraction Strategies page 59   have nothing to drink.
Subtract mentally.

1. 42 − 9 **33** 2. 53¢ − 12¢ **41¢** 3. 56 − 15 **41** 4. $805 − $79 **$10**

Use the menu to solve.

5. Liza and Evan have $8.00 together. What can they have for lunch if they spend as much money as possible? **See above.**

Menu			
Hot dog	$1.75	Hamburger	$3.25
Milk	.85	Lemonade	.95
Pretzel	.95	Chips	.75

Estimate Differences page 61
Estimate. Round to the nearest ten or ten cents.

1. 84 − 39 **40** 2. $4.44 − $2.52 **$1.90** 3. $42.28 − $16.15 **$26.10** 4. 567 − 296 **270**

Estimate. Round to the nearest hundred or dollar.

5. 851 − 363 **500** 6. 847 − 385 **400** 7. 8,096 − 304 **7,800** 8. $28.03 − $ **$21.00**

Estimate. Round to the nearest thousand or ten dollars.

9. 3,053 − 1,843 **1,000** 10. $63.95 − $8.72 **$50.00** 11. 8,763 − 2,933 **6,000** 12. 9,393 − 27 **9,000**

Solve.

13. Last year the Skating Program earned $596. This year the goal of the organizers is to earn $725. About how much more do they hope to earn this year? **about $100**

14. **ALGEBRA** Find the value for each symbol. Every symbol has the same value when it appears.

♣ + ♣ = 8
♦ + ♣ = 10
♦ + ♣ + ♣ = Δ
Δ = 14, ♣ = 4, ♦ = 6

Subtract Whole Numbers page 65
Subtract. Remember to estimate.

1.
```
  48
− 25
  23
```
2.
```
  84
− 37
  47
```
3.
```
  419
−  62
  357
```
4.
```
  $35.86
− 17.88
  $17.98
```
5.
```
  $7.24
−  2.55
  $4.69
```

Solve.

6. A sign is 18 inches wide. How much space will be on the left side if it is centered on a wall that is 36 inches wide? **9 in.**

7. A sketch pad costs $3.98, a brush costs $2.19, and a set of paints costs $5.68. What is the total cost? **$11.85**

Additional Practice

p. 59 Subtract mentally.

1. 31 − 7 *[24]*   2. 75 − 15 *[60]*   3. 82¢ − 8¢ *[74¢]*

4. 528 − 307 *[221]*   5. $7.89 − $1.15 *[$6.74]* 6. 201 − 80 *[121]*

p. 61 Estimate. Round to the nearest hundred or dollar.

1. 563 − 460 *[100]*   2. 652 − 217 *[500]*

3. 7,982 − 563 *[7,400]*   4. $21.55 − $8.95 *[$13]*

Estimate. Round to the nearest thousand or ten dollars.

5. 5,824 − 2,611 *[3,000]* 6. 6,185 − 592 *[5,000]*

7. 9,015 − 7,815 *[1,000]* 8. $38.47 − $12.64 *[$30]*

p. 65 Subtract. Remember to estimate.

1.
```
  84
− 31
 [53]
```
2.
```
  426
−  52
 [374]
```
3.
```
  $8.24
−  3.07
 [$5.17]
```

4.
```
  7,250
− 5,327
 [1,923]
```
5.
```
  $45.26
−  23.74
 [$21.52]
```
6.
```
  52,814
−  8,365
 [44,449]
```

7. 73,582 − 62,947 *[10,635]*   8. $638 − $475 *[$163]*   9. 205,721 − 136,482 *[69,239]*

oblem-Solving Strategy: Choose the Operation page 67

lve.

Lily's family drove 1,045 miles to a family reunion. Then, they drove 485 miles to a friend's home. How far did they travel in all?
1,530 mi

Caleb counts 18 wheels on bicycles and cars. There are more cars than bicycles. How many cars and bicycles are there? **4 cars, 1 bicycle**

2 Park tickets cost $1.50 for each car and $2.00 for each person. How much change will 2 people in a car get from a ten-dollar bill?
$4.50

4 A ranger's shift is from 10:30 A.M. until 5:00 P.M. with $\frac{1}{2}$ hour off for lunch and a $\frac{1}{2}$ hour break. How long does the ranger work?
$5\frac{1}{2}$ h

btract Across Zero page 69

btract. Remember to estimate.

603	**2** 500	**3** $50.30	**4** 8,060	**5** 9,001
− 72	− 387	− 26.15	− 926	− 6,504
531	**113**	**$24.15**	**7,134**	**2,497**

lve.

Write a problem that uses the numbers 3,050 and 5,008 and can be solved using subtraction.
Problems may vary.

7 Hal has $40. A new coat costs $28.73. How much change will he receive? **$11.27**

oblem Solvers at Work page 73

lve.

Mitchell has two friends on the Internet. Akoni lives 3,045 miles away, and Juan lives 1,268 miles away. How much closer does Mitchell live to Juan than to Akoni?
1,777 mi

One amusement park charges $37.75 for each adult ticket. Children under 12 can get in for $24.25. Mr. and Mrs. Hill are going to the park. How much will their tickets cost? **$75.50**

Jewel receives 35¢ in change. One coin is a quarter. List all the other coins she might receive to make up the total amount. **Possible answers: 1 dime, 2 nickels, 1 nickel and 5 pennies, 10 pennies**

Spatial reasoning Use graph paper to arrange and shade six squares in as many different shapes as you can. Each square must share at least one side with another square.
Answers may vary. Check that the squares share at least one adjacent side.

DEVELOPING NUMBER SENSE

This section provides another opportunity for students to reinforce number sense.

Use front-end estimation to find the sum or difference.

1. 44 + 23 *[60]*
2. 237 + 45 *[240]*
3. 108 + 429 *[500]*
4. $12.98 + $8.57 *[18]*
5. $30.98 + $21.99 *[$50]*
6. 1,247 + 6,583 *[7,000]*
7. 812 − 533 *[300]*
8. $71.99 − $23.65 *[$50]*
9. 110 − 42 *[60]*
10. 8,075 − 1,314 *[7,000]*

---

p. 67 Solve. Explain your methods. *[Explanantions may vary.]*

1. Beth bought a gallon of paint at $14.95 and a brush for $3.50. How much did she pay? *[$18.45]*

2. Kyle has $12.53 in his pocket. He bought a hammer and nails for $9.18. How much does he have left? *[$3.35]*

p. 69 Subtract. Remember to estimate.

1.	2.	3.
190	$60.50	8,005
− 87	− 33.15	− 927
[103]	*[$27.35]*	*[7,078]*

4. 5,004 − 2,182 *[2,822]*
5. 7,000 − 3,486 *[3,514]*

p. 73 Solve. Explain your method. *[Explanations may vary.]*

1. Rosa bought school supplies. She bought a box of pencils for $1.19 and a note book for $3.99. She has $10. How much did her supplies cost? *[$5.18]*

2. A sticker book has 8 pages. Each page has 6 rows. Each row has 4 stickers. How many stickers are in the book? *[192 stickers]*

3. Doris bought a new shirt on sale for $29.49. It usually sells for $38.95. How much did she save? *[$9.46]*

4. Barry bought lunch at school. His sandwich was $0.75, milk was $0.50, and an apple was $0.30. How much did he pay for lunch? *[$1.55]*

PURPOSE Provide another opportunity for review and practice.

Materials have available: calculators

Using the Extra Practice

The Extra Practice can be used to provide further practice during a lesson or as a review later in the chapter.

Using the Additional Practice

The sections below provide additional practice that you can assign. You may wish to write these exercises on the chalkboard or put them on a reproducible master.

4. She is late; quarter to nine is before 9 o'clock and 9:01 is after 9 o'clock.

Time page 83

Write the time in two different ways.

1 Possible answers: 2:15; two fifteen; fifteen minutes after two; quarter after two

2 `5:55` Possible answers: 5:55; five fifty-five; fifty-five minutes after five; five minutes to six

3 Possible answers: 9:10; ten; t minut after

Solve.

4 School starts at quarter to nine. Jocelyn arrives at 9:01. Is she late or on time? How do you know? See above.

5 Benjamin saved $22.89. Then he found $1.72 in the park. How much money does he have now? **$24.61**

Elapsed Time page 87

Tell what time it will be:

1 1 h 30 min after 6:15 P.M.
7:45 P.M.

2 40 min after 2:10 A.M.
2:50 A.M.

Solve.

3 Use the digits 2, 4, 7, and 9 to write numbers that are greater than seven thousand, five hundred. **7,924; 7,942; 9,247; 9,274; 9,427; 9,472; 9,724; 9,742**

4 Frank's soccer practice always end at 4:00 P.M. It lasts 90 minutes. What time does practice start? **2:30 P.M.**

Problem-Solving Strategy: Work Backward page 89

Solve. Explain your methods. Explanations may vary.

1 School starts at 8:45 A.M. It takes Ray 15 minutes to walk to school. What is the latest time he can leave for school and not be late? **8:30 A.M.**

2 Kathy had $1.58 left after buying a book for $9.95. How much money did she have before her purchase? **$11.53**

3 January has 44,640 minutes. During leap years, February has 41,760 minutes. April has 43,200 minutes. Write the numbers in order from least to greatest. **41,760; 43,200; 44,640**

4 Write the extra information in this problem. Then solve it. Oscar pays 25¢ for a 5-mile bus trip to Len's house. How far does he ride in all to visit Len and return home? **25¢ for a bus trip; 10 mi**

Additional Practice

p. 83 Write the time in two different ways. *[Possible responses shown.]*

1.

[2:17; two seventeen; seventeen minutes after two]

2. `4:30`

[4:30; half past four; thirty minutes after four]

3. `8:47`

[8:47; forty-seven minutes after eight; thirteen minutes before nine]

4.

[3:25; three twenty-five; twenty five minutes after three]

5.

[6:55; fifty-five minutes after six; five minutes before seven]

6. `9:08`

[9:08; eight minutes after nine]

p. 87 Tell what time it was.

1. 30 min before 4:25
[3:55]

2. 3 h 25 min before 4:45 P.M.
[1:20 P.M.]

3. 3 h 15 min before 10:50 P.M.
[7:35 P.M.]

4. 4 h 50 min before 2:35 P.M.
[9:45 A.M.]

p. 89 Solve.

1. Using his calculator, Daren starts with a number, adds 6, subtracts 7, adds 5, subtracts 9. The final number is 38. What is his starting number? [43]

2. Lara must leave for a party at 7:30 P.M. She needs 1 hr 10 min to get ready. What is the latest time that she can start getting ready? [6:20 P.M.]

Range, Median, and Mode page 93
Find the median, range, and mode for the set of data.

1 Weights of Dogs (in pounds):
68 13 25 88 49 68 52
52; 75; 68

2 Amounts Saved by 7 Students:
$95 $60 $3 $36 $86 $36 $57
$57; $92; $36

Use the data in ex. 1–2 to tell whether the sentence is *true* or *false*. Then, explain your answer.

3 The heaviest dog weighs 52 pounds more than the lightest dog. **False; the range is 75 pounds.**

4 More students saved $36 than any other amount. **True; the mode is $36.**

Solve.

5 Yolanda buys stickers costing 35¢, 50¢, 85¢, 35¢, and 75¢. She says the mode price is 50¢. Tell why you agree or disagree with her.
Disagree, because the mode is 35¢—the median is 50¢.

6 **Spatial reasoning** List as many ways as you can to sort these shapes. **Possible answers: by size, by shape, by shading, by corners/no corners**

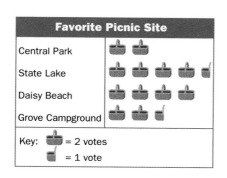

Pictographs page 95
Use the pictograph for problems 1–6.

1 Which site has the most votes? How many votes did it receive? **State Lake; 9 votes**

2 How many students chose Grove Campground as the picnic site? **5 students**

3 How many more students chose State Lake than chose Daisy Beach as the picnic site? **1 student**

4 How many students were surveyed? **26 students**

5 How would the pictograph change if each stands for 1 vote? **The number of symbols would increase.**

6 Which site has votes that can be added to the votes for Central Park to equal the sum of the votes for the other two sites? **Daisy Beach**

Favorite Picnic Site	
Central Park	
State Lake	
Daisy Beach	
Grove Campground	

Key: = 2 votes = 1 vote

a DEVELOPING ALGEBRA SENSE

This section provides another opportunity for students to reinforce algebraic ideas.

Rule: Add 7		Rule: ◆ [Subtract 4]		Rule: ◆ [Subtract 6]	
Input	Output	Input	Output	Input	Output
6	◆ [13]	13	9	14	8
9	◆ [16]	15	11	11	5
14	◆ [21]	11	7	9	3
16	◆ [23]	9	5	17	11

---

p. 93 Find the median, range, and mode for each set of data.

1. Spelling grades: 80 85 85 95 100 85 90
[range: 20, median: 85, mode: 85]

2. Bowling scores: 103 92 112 86 109
[range: 26, median: 103, mode: none]

3. Prices of shirts: $34 $24 $16 $22 $24
[range: $18, median: $24, mode: $24]

4. Ages of children: 2 2 4 7 5 11 15 10 9
[range: 13, median: 7, mode: 2]

5. Temperatures during one week in January:
35 37 40 31 38 26 31
[range: 14, median: 35, mode: 31]

6. Minutes spent on homework last week:
45 35 50 75 40
[range: 40, median: 45, mode: none]

p. 95 Use the pictograph for problems 1–4.

Favorite Types of Books of Fourth Graders	
Adventure	📖 📖 📖
Mystery	📖
General Fiction	📖 📖 📖 📖 📖
Non-Fiction	📖 📖 📖 📖

Each 📖 = 6 votes

1. Which type of book was the most popular? *[general fiction]* least popular? *[mystery]*

2. How many students were surveyed? *[72 students]*

3. How many more students prefer general fiction to adventure? *[9 students]*

Chapter 3 — EXTRA PRACTICE

PURPOSE Provide another opportunity for review and practice.

Materials have available: calculators

Using the Extra Practice

The Extra Practice can be used to provide further practice during a lesson or as a review later in the chapter.

Using the Additional Practice

The sections below provide additional practice that you can assign. You may wish to write these exercises on the chalkboard or put them on a reproducible master.

Bar Graphs page 103
Use the bar graph for problems 1–5.

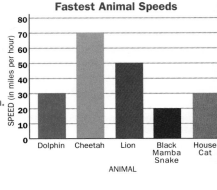

Fastest Animal Speeds

1 Which animal is the slowest? What is its speed? black mamba snake; 20 mi per hour

2 Which two animals have the same speed? How do you know? Dolphin, and house cat; the bars are the same length.

3 How much faster is a cheetah than a lion? 20 mi per hour

4 A human's fastest speed is about 28 miles per hour. Which animals are faster than a human? cheetah, lion, dolphin, and house cat

5 Can you list the animals in order from fastest to slowest by looking at the bars and not reading the scale numbers? Explain your answer. Answers may vary. Possible answer: Yes; list the animals according to the length of the bars from tallest to shortest.

Ordered Pairs page 105
Use the map to find the ordered pair for the location.

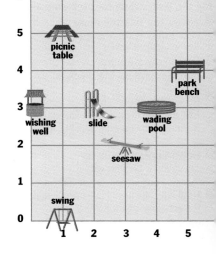

1 Picnic table (1, 5)

2 Slide (2, 3)

3 Wading pool (4, 3)

Tell what is found at the location on the map.

4 (1, 0) swing

5 (3, 2) seesaw

Solve.

6 The entrance to the park is above the wishing well and to the left of the park bench. What is the ordered pair that describes its location? (0, 4)

Additional Practice

p. 103 Use the bar graph for problems 1–3.

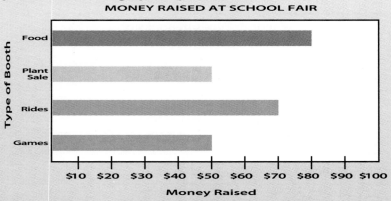

MONEY RAISED AT SCHOOL FAIR

1. Which type of booth made the most money? [food]

2. Which two types of booths made the same amount of money? [plant sale and games]

3. How much money was raised at the School Fair? [$250]

p. 105 Use the map to find the ordered pair for the location.

1. Library [8,4]
2. Fire Station [3,8]
3. School [7,2]
4. Movie Theater [2,4]
5. Train Station [6,5]
6. Supermarket [3,0]

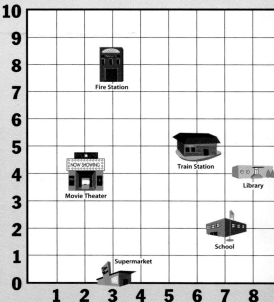

Line Graphs page 109

Use the line graph for problems 1–5.

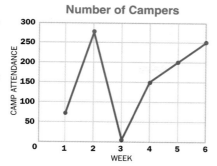

Number of Campers

1 How many campers attended week 4?
150 campers

2 During which week were there the fewest campers? Why do you think this happened? **Week 3; answers may vary.**

3 Which weeks had the highest attendance? **weeks 2 and 6**

4 Between which two weeks did the attendance increase the most? **between weeks 1 and 2**

5 What is the range in the number of campers? **275 campers**

6 Art class is held from 2:15 P.M. to 3:45 P.M. How long is the class? **90 min, or 1 h 30 min**

Problem Solvers at Work page 113

Solve. Explain your methods. Explanations may vary.

1 The Backyard Club paid $15.62 for a pizza and juices. They gave a tip of $2.50. How much did they spend in all? **$18.12**

2 Keiko gave the clerk 2 five-dollar bills and 3 quarters. She received 2 dimes and 4 pennies in return. How much was her purchase? **$10.51**

3 **Logical reasoning** Jan is in front of Bob but behind Flo on the trail. Gary is in front of Flo. Who is in the lead on the trail? **Gary**

4 Add a sentence so that you can solve the problem, then solve it. Cal has a flute lesson at 3:15 P.M. It takes him 20 minutes to walk home. What time will he get home? **Answers may vary. Possible answer: The lesson ends at 3:45 P.M., and he walks home; 4:05 P.M.**

5 In 1995, Mother's Day was on May 14 and Father's Day was on June 18. In 1996, Mother's Day was on May 12 and Father's Day was on June 16. How many days were between these special days in each of the years? **35 d**

6 Use the line graph at the top of the page. When the attendance for week 7 is graphed, the line will go up. How many students could be attending that session? Explain your answer. **Answers may vary. Answers could include any number greater than 250, although given the data, the attendance probably will not exceed 300 campers.**

Extra Practice **495**

DEVELOPING NUMBER SENSE

This section provides another opportunity for students to reinforce number sense.

Copy and complete the graph to solve. Explain your reasoning.

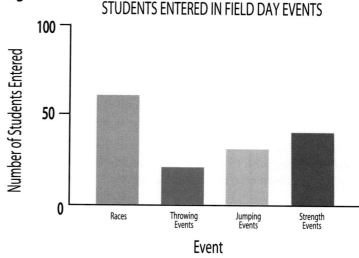

STUDENTS ENTERED IN FIELD DAY EVENTS

1. About how many students signed up to race? *[60 students]*

2. About how many students entered throwing events? *[20 students]*

3. About how many students participated in strength events? *[40 students]*

4. About how many students entered in field day events? *[b]*
   a. between 50 and 100
   b. between 100 and 150
   c. between 200 and 300
   d. more than 300

---

p. 109 Use the line graph for problems 1–4.

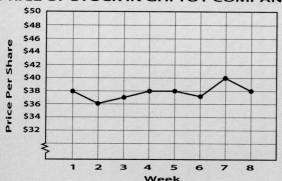

PRICE OF STOCK IN GHI TOY COMPANY

1. What was the value of the stock at the end of the first week? *[$38]*

2. What was the highest price the stock reached? *[$40]*

3. Between which two weeks did the stock gain the most value? *[sixth and seventh]*

4. How much did the value of the stock change between weeks 4 and 5? *[It did not change.]*

p. 113 Solve. Explain your methods. *[Explanations may vary.]*

1. Henry went for a bike ride. He left his home at 3:50 P.M. and returned 1 hr 40 min later. When did he get home? *[5:30 P.M.]*

2. Rita had 24 stickers. Don had 6 stickers. Rita gave some of her stickers to Don. Now they have the same number of stickers. How many stickers do Rita and Don each have now? *[15 stickers]*

3. Playing a computer game, John scored 830, 1125, 920, 1200, and 975. What is the range of his scores? What are the median and the mode? *[Range: 370, median: 975, mode: none]*

4. Joni went to the market with $10. She wants to buy bread for $1.89, sandwich meat for $3.69, and juices for $3.99. Does she have enough money? *[Yes: the items add up to $9.57].*

5. **Write a problem** about elapsed time. Solve it and have others solve it. *[Check students' problems.]*

Chapter 4 — EXTRA PRACTICE

PURPOSE Provide another opportunity for review and practice.

Materials have available: calculators

Using the Extra Practice

The Extra Practice can be used to provide further practice during a lesson or as a review later in the chapter.

Using the Additional Practice

The sections below provide additional practice that you can assign. You may wish to write these exercises on the chalkboard or put them on a reproducible master.

Meaning of Multiplication page 127

12. $1 \times 12 = 12$, $2 \times 6 = 12$, $3 \times 4 = 12$, $4 \times 3 = 12$, $6 \times 2 = 12$, $12 \times 1 = 12$

Multiply using any method.

1 3×8 24 2 8×2 16 3 4×5 20 4 7×4 28 5 9×3 27

6 1×5 5 7 2×6 12 8 3×4 12 9 6×6 36 10 3×5 15

Solve.

11 The baseball league has 6 teams. Each team has 9 positions. What is the least number of players in the league? **54 players**

12 Use tiles to find two numbers that have a product of 12. Write a multiplication sentence for each way you can find. **See above.**

---

2 Through 5 as Factors page 131

Multiply using any method.

1 3×2 6 2 3×6 18 3 4×4 16 4 6×5 30

5 9×2 18 6 3×7 21 7 4×7 28 8 7×5 35

9 2×4 8 10 3×3 9 11 4×8 32 12 5×3 15

Solve.

13 Leonard made four 2-point baskets and two 3-point baskets. How many points did he score altogether? **14 points**

14 Latisha practices tennis for 1 hour every other day. How many hours does she practice tennis in 2 weeks? **7 h**

---

6 and 8 as Factors page 133

Multiply using any method.

1 6×3 18 2 8×0 0 3 6×8 48 4 8×9 72 5 6×2 12

6 6×1 6 7 8×8 64 8 6×7 42 9 8×7 56 10 6×9 54

11 8×3 24 12 6×4 24 13 8×5 40 14 6×6 36 15 8×4 32

Solve.

16 Arthur's high school plays 8 football games each year. How many games can he attend during his 4 years of high school? **32 games**

17 Kenicka bought a drink for $0.75 and a hot dog for $1.50. She received $3.00 in change. How much money did she give the clerk? **$5.25**

Additional Practice

p. 127 Multiply using any method.

1. 3×4 [12] 2. 4×6 [24] 3. 0×9 [0]

4. $\begin{array}{r} 5 \\ \times 1 \\ \hline [5] \end{array}$ 5. $\begin{array}{r} 2 \\ \times 8 \\ \hline [16] \end{array}$ 6. $\begin{array}{r} 7 \\ \times 9 \\ \hline [63] \end{array}$

p. 131 Multiply using any method.

1. 3×6 [18] 2. 4×4 [16] 3. 5×6 [30]

4. $\begin{array}{r} 9 \\ \times 4 \\ \hline [36] \end{array}$ 5. $\begin{array}{r} 3 \\ \times 5 \\ \hline [15] \end{array}$ 6. $\begin{array}{r} 5 \\ \times 5 \\ \hline [25] \end{array}$

p. 133 Multiply using any method.

1. 4×8 [32] 2. 6×3 [18] 3. 6×1 [6]

4. 3×6 [18] 5. 7×8 [56] 6. 0×6 [0]

7. 6×9 [54] 8. 8×8 [64] 9. 6×8 [48]

10. 1×8 [8] 11. 6×7 [42] 12. 7×6 [42]

13. 5×6 [30] 14. 8×7 [56] 15. 6×6 [36]

16. 2×6 [12] 17. 8×2 [16] 18. 6×4 [24]

7 and 9 as Factors page 137

Multiply mentally.

1 7 × 2 14   **2** 9 × 1 9   **3** 7 × 7 49   **4** 9 × 4 36   **5** 7 × 9 63

6 9 × 5 45   **7** 7 × 1 7   **8** 9 × 7 63   **9** 7 × 0 0   **10** 9 × 9 81

11 7 × 3 21   **12** 7 × 6 42   **13** 9 × 6 54   **14** 7 × 8 56   **15** 9 × 8 72

Solve.

16 Marik competed in a kite-making contest. The judges gave him these scores: 9, 9, 8, 8, 9, 9. How many points did he score in all? **52 points**

17 Each of 7 teams has 4 players. Write a multiplication and an addition sentence to show the total number of players. **7 × 4 = 28, 4 + 4 + 4 + 4 + 4 + 4 + 4 = 28**

Problem-Solving Strategy: Find a Pattern page 139

Solve. Explain your methods. Explanations may vary.

1 Chris alternates sprinting and jogging. She sprints for 30 seconds and then jogs for 3 minutes. She has trained 9 minutes. Will she sprint or jog for the next 30 seconds? **jog**

2 Spatial reasoning Copy and complete the diagram.

3 Jason treated himself and 2 friends to a baseball game and a juice. Tickets were $6 each and juice was $1 each. How much did he spend? **$21**

4 Write the information needed to solve the problem. Then solve it. The school has 6 jump ropes and 5 balls for each class. How many balls does the school have in all?

4. Need: number of classes in school; possible solution: 7 classes, 35 balls.

Three Factors page 141

Multiply.

1 (6 × 2) × 4   48   **2** 4 × (8 × 2)   64   **3** 5 × (2 × 4)   40   **4** 3 × (9 × 2)   54   **5** 2 × (5 × 3)   30

6 (3 × 7) × 3   63   **7** (6 × 2) × 2   24   **8** 4 × (2 × 7)   56   **9** 2 × (2 × 3)   12   **10** (9 × 2) × 2   36

Solve.

11 Casey lives 2 miles from school. He rides his bike to and from school 3 days each week. How many miles does he ride during his commute in 1 week? **12 mi**

12 Nathan does 15 minutes of warm-up stretches, 45 minutes of exercise, and 15 minutes of cool-off stretches. To finish at 6:45 P.M., what time should he start? **5:30 P.M.**

Extra Practice   **497**

✴ *a* DEVELOPING ALGEBRA SENSE

This section provides another opportunity for students to reinforce algebraic ideas.

Find the missing number.

1. 8 × ◆ = 4 × 8   **2.** ◆ × 7 = 7 × 5   **3.** 7 × 9 = ◆ × 7
[4]   *[5]*   *[9]*

4. 3 × 4 × ◆ = 0   **5.** 3 × 9 × ◆ = 27   **6.** 8 × ◆ = 8
[0]   *[1]*   *[1]*

7. 4 × 7 × 2 = 4 × ◆ × 7 *[2]*   **8.** 8 × 3 × 2 = 3 × ◆ × 8 *[2]*

Find the value of each symbol.

9. ♠ × 8 = 32   **10.** ■ × ■ = 16

    ♠ × ♣ = 24   ■ × 5 = Δ × 20

    ♠ × ◆ = ♣ × ♣   ■ × 8 × ∇ = ∇ × 9 × Δ

    [♠ = 4, ♣ = 6, ◆ = 9]   *[■ = 4, Δ = 1, ∇ = 0]*

---

p. 137 Multiply mentally.

1. 7 × 5   **2.** 9 × 4   **3.** 6 × 7
[35]   *[36]*   *[42]*

4. 9 × 9   **5.** 9 × 8   **6.** 2 × 7
[81]   *[72]*   *[14]*

p. 139 Solve. Explain your methods. *[Explanations may vary.]*

1. The box office is giving away free hot dogs for every 5 tickets sold. Mina buys 27 tickets. How many free hot dogs will she get? *[5]*

2. At the Super Bowl in 1991, 39 points were scored. The New York Giants beat the Buffalo Bills by one point. What was the final score? *[Giants 20; Bills 19]*

p. 141 Multiply.

1. 3 × 2 × 8 *[48]*   **2.** 5 × 1 × 7 *[35]*   **3.** 3 × 9 × 3 *[81]*

4. 2 × 7 × 2 *[28]*   **5.** 3 × 7 × 2 *[42]*   **6.** 4 × 5 × 2 *[40]*

7. 8 × 3 × 3 *[72]*   **8.** 2 × 2 × 9 *[36]*   **9.** 8 × 1 × 4 *[32]*

10. 6 × 2 × 3 *[36]*   **11.** 4 × 2 × 9 *[72]*   **12.** 2 × 6 × 2 *[24]*

13. 2 × 8 × 2 *[32]*   **14.** 7 × 4 × 2 *[56]*   **15.** 9 × 3 × 1 *[27]*

PURPOSE Provide another opportunity for review and practice.

Materials have available: calculators

Using the Extra Practice

The Extra Practice can be used to provide further practice during a lesson or as a review later in the chapter.

Using the Additional Practice

The sections below provide additional practice that you can assign. You may wish to write these exercises on the chalkboard or put them on a reproducible master.

Meaning of Division page 149
Draw an array. Find the quotient. Check students' drawings.

1 $14 \div 2$ 7   **2** $48 \div 8$ 6   **3** $16 \div 4$ 4   **4** $18 \div 9$ 2   **5** $27 \div 3$ 9

6 $21 \div 7$ 3   **7** $36 \div 4$ 9   **8** $12 \div 3$ 4   **9** $24 \div 6$ 4   **10** $3 \div 3$ 1

Solve. Use the bar graph to answer.

11 Which game had the most points scored? Which had the least? **Game 4; Game 2**

12 The league record is 40 points scored in 5 games. Did this team break the record? Explain. **No; they scored 27 points in all; 27 < 40.**

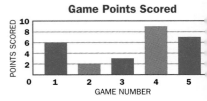

Game Points Scored

(bar graph: POINTS SCORED vs GAME NUMBER)

2 Through 5 as Divisors page 151
Divide.

1 $6 \div 2$ 3   **2** $18 \div 3$ 6   **3** $24 \div 3$ 8   **4** $32 \div 4$ 8   **5** $30 \div 5$ 6

6 $2\overline{)18}$ 9   **7** $3\overline{)15}$ 5   **8** $4\overline{)20}$ 5   **9** $5\overline{)25}$ 5   **10** $5\overline{)30}$ 6

Solve.

11 A 2-digit number can be divided evenly by 3 and 4. The sum of its digits is 6. What is the number? **24 or 60**

12 Find the value for each symbol. The value is the same in all equations.
♣ × ♣ = 25
♦ ÷ ♣ = 3
♦ + ♣ + ♣ = ♥
♦ = 15, ♣ = 5, ♥ = 25

6 Through 9 as Divisors page 153
Divide.

1 $18 \div 6$ 3   **2** $49 \div 7$ 7   **3** $72 \div 8$ 9   **4** $63 \div 9$ 7   **5** $54 \div 9$ 6

6 $6\overline{)42}$ 7   **7** $7\overline{)56}$ 8   **8** $7\overline{)35}$ 5   **9** $8\overline{)64}$ 8   **10** $9\overline{)27}$ 3

Solve.

11 The food for a picnic costs $45. The cost is to be split evenly between 9 people. How much will each person pay? **$5**

12 Each tour group consists of 5 people. A class of 30 students decides to take the tour. How many tour groups will they need for everyone? **6 tour groups**

Additional Practice

p. 149 Divide using any method.

1. $30 \div 5$ [6]   **2.** $28 \div 7$ [4]   **3.** $18 \div 3$ [6]

4. $9\overline{)45}$ [5]   **5.** $8\overline{)48}$ [6]

p. 151 Divide.

1. $20 \div 4$ [5]   **2.** $32 \div 4$ [8]   **3.** $15 \div 5$ [3]

4. $2\overline{)18}$ [9]   **5.** $3\overline{)21}$ [7]   **6.** $2\overline{)0}$ [0]

p. 153 Divide.

1. $40 \div 8$ [5]   **2.** $42 \div 6$ [7]   **3.** $27 \div 9$ [3]

4. $16 \div 8$ [2]   **5.** $56 \div 7$ [8]   **6.** $24 \div 6$ [4]

7. $63 \div 9$ [7]   **8.** $24 \div 8$ [3]   **9.** $14 \div 7$ [2]

10. $8\overline{)72}$ [9]   **11.** $6\overline{)36}$ [6]   **12.** $7\overline{)35}$ [5]

13. $6\overline{)12}$ [2]   **14.** $9\overline{)54}$ [6]   **15.** $8\overline{)64}$ [8]

2 × 5 = 10, 5 × 2 = 10,   2. 4 × 9 = 36, 9 × 4 = 36,   3. 6 × 9 = 54, 9 × 6 = 54,
10 ÷ 2 = 5, 10 ÷ 5 = 2   36 ÷ 4 = 9, 36 ÷ 9 = 4   54 ÷ 6 = 9, 54 ÷ 9 = 6

Fact Families page 155   4. 9 × 9 = 81, 81 ÷ 9 = 9
Find the fact family for the set of numbers.

1 2, 5, 10   **2** 4, 9, 36   **3** 6, 9, 54   **4** 9, 9, 81
See above.   See above.   See above.   See above.

Multiply or divide.

5 6 × 5 30   **6** 63 ÷ 7 9   **7** 8 × 6 48   **8** 24 ÷ 4 6   **9** 3 × 7 21

10 72 ÷ 8 9   **11** 2 × 7 14   **12** 40 ÷ 8 5   **13** 6 × 7 42   **14** 56 ÷ 7 8

Solve.

15 One rose costs $2. How much would it cost to buy each member of your family one rose? Use your data to write a fact family.
Answers may vary. Possible answer: $8 for family members—2 × 4 = 8, 4 × 2 = 8, 8 ÷ 2 = 4, 8 ÷ 4 = 2

16 **ALGEBRA: PATTERNS** Find the rule. Then show the next set of dots.
• • • • • • • • •   • • • • • • •

Remainders page 157
Divide.

1 20 ÷ 4   **2** 38 ÷ 5   **3** 32 ÷ 7   **4** 65 ÷ 9   **5** 55 ÷ 6
5   7 R3   4 R4   7 R2   9 R1

6 28 ÷ 3   **7** 45 ÷ 7   **8** 38 ÷ 6   **9** 77 ÷ 8   **10** 50 ÷ 8
9 R1   6 R3   6 R2   9 R5   6 R2

Solve.

11 A pictograph shows that 18 students like hockey and 24 students like tennis. What could each symbol stand for if only whole symbols are used in the graph?
1, 2, 3, or 6

12 Kelly is making banners to take to the basketball game. Each banner will be 3 feet long. She has a roll of paper 25 feet long. How many banners can she make? **8 banners**

Problem Solvers at Work page 161
Solve. Explain your methods. Explanations may vary.

1 Kiley works 2 hours each day at the golf-pro shop. He earns $24 for 2 days work. How much does he earn per hour? **$6**

2 Chane bowled two games and scored 85 and 113. Emilio scored 98 and 99. Who scored more points in all? How do you know?
See below.

3 **Spatial reasoning** How many small cubes make up the large block?

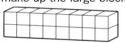

16 small cubes

4 Felix, Marla, Hillary, and Liam are on a relay team. Marla runs before Liam. Felix follows Hillary. Hillary follows Liam. In what order do they run? **Marla, Liam, Hillary, Felix**

2. Chane; he scored 198 points, Emilio scored 197 points, 198 > 197.

DEVELOPING NUMBER SENSE

This section provides another opportunity for students to reinforce number sense.

Compare. Use <, >, or =.

1. 8 × 4 ■ 2 × 2 × 8 [=]   **2.** 3 × 3 × 7 ■ 6 × 7 [>]

3. 9 × 4 × 2 ■ 3 × 3 × 8 [=]   **4.** 4 × 2 × 9 ■ 3 × 3 × 9 [<]

5. 2 × 9 × 2 ■ 5 × 0 × 9 [>]   **6.** 3 × 2 × 2 ■ 3 × 5 × 1 [<]

7. 24 ÷ 6 ■ 24 ÷ 4 [<]   **8.** 9 ÷ 1 ■ 7 ÷ 1 [>]

9. 36 ÷ 6 ■ 36 ÷ 9 [>]   **10.** 64 ÷ 8 ■ 2 × 4 [=]

11. 0 ÷ 8 ■ 8 × 0 [=]   **12.** 81 ÷ 9 ■ 1 × 2 × 3 × 4 [<]

---

p. 155 Find the fact family for the set of numbers.

1. 5, 7, 35
[5 × 7 = 35;
7 × 5 = 35;
35 ÷ 5 = 7;
35 ÷ 7 = 5]

2. 6, 8, 48
[6 × 8 = 48;
8 × 6 = 48;
48 ÷ 8 = 6;
48 ÷ 6 = 8]

3. 81, 9
[9 × 9 = 81;
81 ÷ 9 = 9]

4. 5, 30, 6
[5 × 6 = 30;
6 × 5 = 30;
30 ÷ 5 = 6;
30 ÷ 6 = 5]

5. 7, 42, 6
[6 × 7 = 42;
7 × 6 = 42;
42 ÷ 6 = 7;
42 ÷ 7 = 6]

6. 36, 4, 9
[4 × 9 = 36;
9 × 4 = 36;
36 ÷ 4 = 9;
36 ÷ 9 = 4]

Multiply or divide.

7. 4 × 7 [28]   **8.** 48 ÷ 8 [6]   **9.** 9 × 3 [27]

10. 21 ÷ 3 [7]   **11.** 4 × 5 [20]   **12.** 28 ÷ 7 [4]

13. 5)45 [9]   **14.** 8 × 8 [64]   **15.** 6)54 [9]

p. 157 Divide.

1. 17 ÷ 3 [5 R 2]   **2.** 31 ÷ 4 [7 R 3]   **3.** 27 ÷ 9 [3]

4. 9)68 [7 R 5]   **5.** 6)15 [2 R 3]   **6.** 5)31 [6 R 1]

p. 161 Solve. Explain your method. [Explanations may vary.]

1. Practice for the track team begins daily at 3:30 P.M. and ends at 5:15 P.M. How long is the daily practice? [1 h 45 min]

2. Members of the tennis team practice in groups of 4. If 24 girls are on the team, how many groups can practice? [6 groups]

PURPOSE Provide another opportunity for review and practice.

Materials have available: calculators

Using the Extra Practice

The Extra Practice can be used to provide further practice during a lesson or as a review later in the chapter.

Using the Additional Practice

The sections below provide additional practice that you can assign. You may wish to write these exercises on the chalkboard or put them on a reproducible master.

Multiplication Patterns page 171
Multiply mentally.

1 4×20
80

2 3×30
90

3 8×60
480

4 5×80
400

5 2×50
100

6 3×700
2,100

7 6×500
3,000

8 7×300
2,100

9 4×400
1,600

10 6×200
1,200

11 $8 \times 3,000$
24,000

12 $4 \times 6,000$
24,000

13 $3 \times 4,000$
12,000

14 $6 \times 5,000$
30,000

15 $7 \times 8,000$
56,000

Solve.

16 It takes Karen 7 minutes to print a report from her computer. How long will it take to print 60 reports?
420 min, or 7 h

17 **ALGEBRA: PATTERNS** Explain how you found your answer.
5, 12, 19, 26, 33, ■, ■ 40, 47; added 7 to the previous number.

18 Carlos gets paid $2 for every word in his article. If his article has 7,000 words, how much will he be paid? $14,000

19 Lee gave 6 and 800 as factors with a product of 4,800. Give another pair of factors with the same product. **Possible answers: 8 and 600; 4 and 1,200; 2 and 2,400**

Estimate Products page 173
Estimate the product.

1 6×39
240

2 6×96
600

3 7×43
280

4 8×60
480

5 5×86
450

6 7×568
4,200

7 6×701
4,200

8 4×652
2,800

9 5×979
5,000

10 6×337
1,800

11 $4 \times 6,593$
28,000

12 $5 \times 7,593$
40,000

13 $4 \times 9,103$
36,000

14 $6 \times 5,045$
30,000

15 $3 \times 8,453$
24,000

16 39 × 5
200

17 56 × 6
360

18 19 × 7
140

19 14 × 8
80

20 84 × 6
480

Solve.

21 Bicycle helmets cost $9 each. Kneepads cost $3 each. About how much will 187 helmets and 308 kneepads cost? **$2,700**

22 **Logical reasoning** Which two numbers do *not* belong? Explain your reasoning.
20, 27, 62, 70, 328, 429
See below.

23 The bicycle race started at 9:30 A.M., and the last person finished the race at 4:45 P.M. How long did the race last? **7 h 15 min**

24 Identify any extra information. There are 387 bicycles in each of four stores. Each bicycle has 5 reflectors. About how many bicycles are there? **Each bicycle has 5 reflectors.**

22. Possible answer: 62 and 70 do not have 2 in the tens place.

500 Extra Practice

Additional Practice

p. 171 Multiply mentally.

1. 6×300
[1,800]

2. 7×40
[280]

3. 6×600
[3,600]

4. 3×70
[210]

5. 2×900
[1,800]

6. 4×700
[2,800]

7. $5 \times 1,000$
[5,000]

8. 8×800
[6,400]

9. $4 \times 5,000$
[20,000]

10. $2 \times 7,000$
[14,000]

11. $3 \times 3,000$
[9,000]

12. $7 \times 8,000$
[56,000]

p. 173 Estimate the product.

1. 39 × 4
[160]

2. 71 × 6
[420]

3. 788 × 5
[4,000]

4. 67 × 6
[420]

5. 995 × 5
[5,000]

6. 1,034 × 3
[3,000]

7. 7×453
[3,500]

8. 8×845
[6,400]

9. $9 \times 4,376$
[36,000]

10. $2 \times 6,067$
[12,000]

11. $5 \times 7,897$
[40,000]

12. $3 \times 5,934$
[18,000]

Use Models to Multiply page 177
Find the total number of squares in the rectangle without counting all the squares.

1

65 squares

2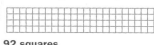

92 squares

3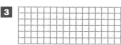

102 squares

4

39 squares

5

132 squares

6

120 squares

Multiply using any method.

7 39	**8** 93	**9** 19	**10** 91	**11** 72
× 5	× 6	× 4	× 3	× 5
195	156	76	328	216

Multiply 2-Digit Numbers page 181
Multiply.

1 83	**2** 93	**3** 82	**4** 91	**5** 72
× 3	× 6	× 4	× 3	× 5
249	558	328	273	360

6 75	**7** 97	**8** 43	**9** 78	**10** 27
× 8	× 4	× 5	× 2	× 6
600	388	215	156	162

11 6 × 55	**12** 8 × 99	**13** 7 × 30	**14** 4 × 76	**15** 5 × 36
330	792	210	304	180

16 4 × 61	**17** 2 × 58	**18** 3 × 42	**19** 9 × 22	**20** 7 × 44
244	116	126	198	308

21 3 × 48	**22** 5 × 47	**23** 4 × 83	**24** 3 × 98	**25** 5 × 26
144	235	332	294	130

Solve.

26 Peter gives $3 to charity from every piñata he sells. If he sold 68 piñatas this week, how much money will he give? **$204**

27 The large piñata holds 768 candies. The small piñata holds 75 candies. How many more candies does a large piñata hold? **693 more candies**

Extra Practice **501**

a DEVELOPING ALGEBRA SENSE

This section provides another opportunity for students to reinforce algebraic ideas.

Find the missing number.

1. 3,056 = ◆ + 50 + 6 *[3,000]*   **2.** 3 × 87 = ◆ × 3 = *[87]*

3. 6 × 17 × 10 = 6 × ◆ × 17 *[10]*   **4.** 2,903 × ◆ = 2,903 *[1]*

5. 4 × 789 = (4 × ◆) + (4 × 80) + (4 × 9) *[700]*

---

p. 177 Find the total number of squares in the rectangle without counting all the squares.

1.

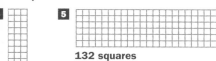

[96 squares]

2.

 *[45 squares]*

Find the product using any method.

3. 18	**4.** 32	**5.** 65
× 4	× 3	× 5
[72]	*[96]*	*[325]*

6. 6 × 19 *[114]*   **7.** 8 × 16 *[128]*   **8.** 7 × 27 *[189]*

p. 181 Multiply.

1. 82	**2.** 67	**3.** 74
× 4	× 6	× 5
[328]	*[402]*	*[370]*

4. 66	**5.** 90	**6.** 56
× 7	× 8	× 3
[462]	*[720]*	*[168]*

7. 5 × 72 *[360]*   **8.** 6 × 76 *[456]*   **9.** 5 × 34 *[170]*

10. 9 × 88 *[792]*   **11.** 6 × 77 *[462]*   **12.** 4 × 83 *[332]*

13. 4 × 68 *[272]*   **14.** 9 × 43 *[387]*   **15.** 2 × 89 *[178]*

PURPOSE Provide another opportunity for review and practice.

Materials have available: calculators

Using the Extra Practice

The Extra Practice can be used to provide further practice during a lesson or as a review later in the chapter.

Using the Additional Practice

The sections below provide additional practice that you can assign. You may wish to write these exercises on the chalkboard or put them on a reproducible master.

Problem-Solving Strategy:
Solve Multistep Problems page 183
Solve.

1 Carole is designing outfits for five action figures. Each action figure has outfits that sell for $2.39, $2.99, $2.99, and $3.99. What is the cost of buying all the outfits for the action figures? **$61.80**

2 Lee bakes 55 batches of cookie Each batch has 9 pounds of cookies. If he needs to meet a target of 550 pounds of cookies how many more pounds of cooki does Lee need to bake? **55 lbs**

3 Karen rounds the median price to estimate the cost of rolls of paper. Her prices are $45.59, $37.50, $46.75, $39.00, and $51.99. What is Karen's estimate for 9 rolls of paper? **Possible answer: $450**

4 James walks 4 miles every morning and 6 miles every evening. Steve walks 7 miles every morning and 2 miles every evening. Who walks more in a week? How much more? **James; 7 mi**

5 Robert leaves work at 5:00 P.M. He shops for 45 minutes and then takes 30 minutes to get home. What time does he get home? **6:15 P.M.**

6 A bag of fruit costs $4, and a bo of fruit costs seven times as mu as a bag. How much will Mei spe if she buys 7 bags and 4 boxes? **$140**

Multiply Greater Numbers page 191
Multiply.

1 984 × 2 = **1,968**	**2** 802 × 9 = **7,218**	**3** 455 × 8 = **3,640**	**4** 274 × 6 = **1,644**	**5** 772 × 7 = **5,404**
6 607 × 5 = **3,035**	**7** 910 × 9 = **8,190**	**8** 1,023 × 5 = **5,115**	**9** 5,605 × 7 = **39,235**	**10** 2,345 × 3 = **7,035**

11 6 × 555 **3,330**   **12** 8 × 909 **7,272**   **13** 6 × 354 **2,124**   **14** 4 × 747 **2,988**   **15** 5 × 398 **1,990**

16 5 × 8,033 **40,165**   **17** 9 × 6,765 **60,885**   **18** 5 × 9,003 **45,015**   **19** 4 × 4,888 **19,552**   **20** 9 × 8,439 **75,951**

Solve.

21 **Make a decision** Machine 1 fills 3,905 pies in an hour. Machine 2 fills 800 in 2 hours. Which machine would you buy? Why? **Machine 1; possible answer: it fills 7,810 pies in 2 h.**

22 Fruity Juices packs 907 boxes o a train for delivery. Every day, 8 trains leave the station. How ma boxes can Fruity Juices deliver i 6 days? **43,536 boxes**

Additional Practice

p. 183 Solve. Explain your methods. [Explanations may vary.]

1. Aja unloads 4 boxes of games and 3 boxes of paint sets. There are 24 games or 15 paint sets in each box. How many things does Aja unload? [141 things]

2. It takes Joel 35 minutes to walk to school. He plays in the yard for 15 minutes until the bell rings. If he leaves for school at 7:10 A.M., when does the bell ring? [8:00 A.M.]

3. Carl spends $84.76 at the grocery store and $6.78 at the bakery. He started with $120. How much money does he have now? [$28.46]

4. School t-shirts come in 3 designs. Each design is available in 2 colors. Nina orders 32 of each type of shirt. How many shirts does she order? [192 shirts]

p. 191 Multiply.

1. 723 × 3 = [2,169]   **2.** 608 × 6 = [3,648]   **3.** 519 × 4 = [2,076]

4. 1,723 × 3 = [5,169]   **5.** 8,043 × 5 = [40,215]   **6.** 6,762 × 7 = [47,334]

7. 8 × 309 [2,472]   **8.** 9 × 265 [2,385]   **9.** 4 × 896 [3,58

10. 5 × 4,678 [23,390]   **11.** 8 × 4,009 [32,072]   **12.** 7 × 7,097 [49,

6. Students should write problems that can be solved using mental math, paper and pencil, or a calculator.

Multiply with Money page 193

Multiply.

1	**2**	**3**	**4**	**5**
$0.47	$0.16	$0.22	$0.38	$0.73
× 5	× 8	× 7	× 5	× 4
$2.35	$1.28	$1.54	$1.90	$2.92

6	**7**	**8**	**9**	**10**
$1.53	$1.80	$2.77	$4.82	$3.33
× 6	× 9	× 8	× 3	× 4
$9.18	$16.20	$22.16	$14.46	$13.32

11 4 × $0.85
$3.40

12 7 × $9.09
$63.63

13 6 × $6.35
$38.10

14 5 × $0.03
$0.15

15 4 × $3.98
$15.92

16 7 × $0.06
$0.42

17 5 × $5.48
$27.40

18 4 × $3.42
$13.68

19 9 × $9.22
$82.98

20 8 × $9.49
$75.92

21 3 × $59.64
$178.92

22 8 × $49.54
$396.32

23 4 × $68.37
$273.48

24 7 × $11.38
$79.66

25 7 × $66.24
$463.68

Solve.

26 Tía buys 4 flower patches for her new denim jacket. Each patch costs $3.75. How much does Tía spend on patches? **$15**

27 Tía buys 3 yards of red ribbon and 2 yards of gold ribbon. Each yard of red ribbon costs $0.45. Each yard of gold ribbon costs $0.85. What is the total cost? **$3.05**

Problem Solvers at Work page 197

Solve. Explain your method.

1 Rashid wants to hike for at least 20 miles. The hiking paths he wants to use are 3 miles, 4 miles, 7 miles, 8 miles, and 9 miles long. Give three ways that Rashid can meet his goal. **See below.**

2 Heather and her family are allowed 400 pounds of luggage. She and her two brothers each have luggage that weighs 70 pounds. Her parents' luggage weighs 160 pounds. If Heather carries an extra bag, what is the most it can weigh? **30 lb**

3 Karl bought 4 books. Three of the books cost $6.85, $24.99, and $29.50. He got $3.28 in change from $80. How much did the fourth book cost? **$15.38**

4 Rosa starts to list factors that give the product 192. She gives 8 and 24 as an answer. Give two more pairs of factors. **Possible answers: 2 and 96, 3 and 64, 4 and 48, 6 and 32, 12 and 16**

5 Marsha says she can solve 4 × 725 by finding 4 × 700 and 4 × 25 and adding both products. Is she correct? Why or why not? Yes; 725 can be renamed as 700 + 25.

6 **Write a problem** that can be solved by finding 7 × 44. Solve it. Did you use mental math, paper and pencil, or a calculator? Why? **See above.**

1. Possible answer: twice along both the 3-mi and 7-mi paths, five times along the 4-mi path, twice along the 7-mi path and once along the 8-mi path

Extra Practice **503**

DEVELOPING NUMBER SENSE

This section provides another opportunity for students to reinforce number sense.

Estimate. Write >, <, or =.

1. 345 + 452 ■ 700 *[>]*

2. 912 − 592 ■ 400 *[<]*

3. 3 × 47 ■ 150 *[<]*

4. 4 × 82 ■ 320 *[>]*

p. 193 Multiply.

1.	**2.**	**3.**
$0.37	$0.44	$0.65
× 4	× 8	× 7
[$1.48]	[$3.52]	[$4.55]

4.	**5.**	**6.**
$0.09	$4.78	$9.09
× 7	× 3	× 3
[$0.63]	[$14.34]	[$27.27]

7. 6 × $0.05 *[$0.30]* **8.** 5 × $0.80 *[$4.00]* **9.** 9 × $4.21 *[37.89]*

10. 8 × $3.28 *[$26.24]* **11.** 7 × $17.89 *[$125.23]* **12.** 4 × $89.67 *[$358.68]*

p. 197 Solve. Explain your methods. *[Explanations may vary.]*

1. Falco bought 2 CDs for $12.99. He also bought a battery for $4.76. He paid with a $20 bill and received $2.00 as change. How much was the tax on his purchase? *[$0.25]*

2. Write a problem about shopping. Use items and prices from local stores. Trade problems. Solve at least three problems written by classmates. *[Check students' problems.]*

PURPOSE Provide another opportunity for review and practice.

Materials have available: calculators

Using the Extra Practice

The Extra Practice can be used to provide further practice during a lesson or as a review later in the chapter.

Using the Additional Practice

The sections below provide additional practice that you can assign. You may wish to write these exercises on the chalkboard or put them on a reproducible master.

Multiplication Patterns page 207
Multiply mentally.

1. 50×100
5,000

2. 30×40
1,200

3. 80×60
4,800

4. 60×90
5,400

5. 20×300
6,000

6. 400×90
36,000

7. 300×30
9,000

8. 80×400
32,000

9. 70×900
63,000

10. 40×500
20,000

11. $20 \times 2,000$
40,000

12. $60 \times 7,000$
420,000

ALGEBRA Find the missing number.

13. $30 \times \blacksquare = 27,000$
900

14. $\blacksquare \times 90 = 54,000$
600

15. $\blacksquare \times 4,000 = 280,000$
70

Solve.

16. A recycling bin holds about 100 cans. About how many cans have been recycled when the bin has been filled 20 times? **about 2,000 cans**

17. Lenora receives 8¢ for each bottle she returns. She returns 10 bottles. Then she spends 35¢. How much money does she have left? **45¢**

Estimate Products page 209   Estimates may vary. Estimates shown are by
Estimate the product by rounding. rounding each factor to its greatest place.

1. 38×42
1,600

2. 57×52
3,000

3. 405×24
8,000

4. 77×827
64,000

5. 29×541
15,000

6. 651×84
56,000

7. $11 \times 5,602$
60,000

8. $49 \times 2,204$
100,000

9. $\begin{array}{r} 18 \\ \times\, 74 \\ \hline 1,400 \end{array}$

10. $\begin{array}{r} 23 \\ \times\, 45 \\ \hline 1,000 \end{array}$

11. $\begin{array}{r} 304 \\ \times\, 26 \\ \hline 9,000 \end{array}$

12. $\begin{array}{r} 491 \\ \times\, 63 \\ \hline 30,000 \end{array}$

13. $\begin{array}{r} 3,217 \\ \times\, 53 \\ \hline 150,000 \end{array}$

Solve.

14. Zena's class spends 15 minutes picking up trash each week. Estimate how many minutes they pick up trash in 13 weeks. **about 200 min**

15. Jay bikes 2 miles to work. Alex bikes twice as far as Jay. Frank bikes twice as far as Alex. How far is Frank from his place of work? **8 mi**

Additional Practice

p. 207 Multiply mentally.

1. 70×100 [7,000]   2. 30×50 [1,500]   3. $2,000 \times 80$ [160,000]

4. 90×400 [36,000]   5. 80×80 [6,400]   6. $50 \times 9,000$ [450,000]

Algebra Find the missing number.

7. $30 \times \blacklozenge = 9,000$ [300]

8. $70 \times \blacklozenge = 1,400$ [20]

9. $\blacklozenge \times 1,000 = 9,000$ [9]

10. $40 \times \blacklozenge = 1,600$ [40]

11. $\blacklozenge \times 30 = 3,000$ [100]

12. $80 \times \blacklozenge = 7,200$ [90]

p. 209 Estimate the product by rounding. *[Estimates may vary. Estim~* *shown are by rounding each factor to its greatest place.]*

1. 23×768 [16,000]   2. $53 \times \$92$ [\$4,500]   3. $89 \times 4,621$ [450,0~

4. $\$624 \times 37$ [\$24,000]   5. $5,736 \times 82$ [480,000]   6. 92×321 [27,000~

7. $\$81 \times 48$ [\$4,000]   8. $5,293 \times 33$ [150,000]   9. $2,846 \times 79$ [240,0~

10. $\begin{array}{r} 478 \\ \times\, 36 \\ \hline [20,000] \end{array}$

11. $\begin{array}{r} \$6,159 \\ \times\, 83 \\ \hline [\$480,000] \end{array}$

12. $\begin{array}{r} 2,149 \\ \times\, 67 \\ \hline [140,000] \end{array}$

Multiply 2-Digit Numbers page 213

Find the product. Use any method.

1 19 × 40 760	2 20 × 14 280	3 11 × 46 506	4 34 × 27 918	5 23 × 12 276
6 26 × 21 546	7 34 × 16 544	8 41 × 32 1,312	9 29 × 19 551	10 44 × 14 616
11 14 × 19 266	12 21 × 30 630	13 32 × 32 1,024	14 26 × 15 390	15 19 × 44 836

Solve.

16 **Logical reasoning** The product of two numbers is 1,800. One number is twice the value of the other. What are the two numbers? **30 and 60**

17 There are 12 inches in 1 foot. How many inches deep is a pond with a depth of 15 feet? **180 in.**

Multiply 2-Digit Numbers page 217

Multiply using any method. Remember to estimate.

1 21 × 50 1,050	2 35 × 13 455	3 24 × 15 360	4 13 × 37 481	5 41 × 23 943
6 72 × 31 2,232	7 18 × 44 792	8 29 × 53 1,537	9 66 × 33 2,178	10 $0.12 × 17 $2.04
11 38 × 20 760	12 19 × 52 988	13 $0.24 × 61 $14.64	14 12 × 32 384	15 74 × 11 814

Solve.

16 A farmer's stand sells 3 melons for $5.50. A market sells melons for $2 each. How much less do 6 melons cost at the stand than at the market? **$1**

17 Callan started picking strawberries at 8:30 A.M. She worked for 3 hours 20 minutes. When did she stop? **11:50 A.M.**

Extra Practice **505**

DEVELOPING ALGEBRA SENSE

This section provides another opportunity for students to reinforce algebraic ideas.

Study these examples.

2 ● 4 = 9
3 ● 8 = 25
0 ● 6 = 1
3 ● 7 = 22

The operator ● means to multiply the two numbers and then add 1 to the product.

2 × 4 = 8
8 + 1 = 9

Study the examples to find the meaning of the operator. Then use the operator to find the answers.

1. 3 ▲ 5 = 10
6 ▲ 4 = 122
10 ▲ 10 = 22
8 ▲ 3 = 133
5 ▲ 2 = ◆ *[9]*

[1. The operator ▲ means to find the sum of the two numbers and then add 2.]

2. 9 ◆ 3 = 5
12 ◆ 2 = 9
6 ◆ 0 = 5
7 ◆ 5 = 1
8 ◆ 3 = ◆ *[4]*

[2. The operator ◆ means to find the difference of the two numbers and then to subtract 1.]

3. 9 ★ 9 = 83
5 ★ 5 = 27
6 ★ 3 = 20
7 ★ 5 = 37
6 ★ 2 = ◆ *[14]*

[3. The operator ★ means to find the product of the two numbers and then add 2.]

4. 10 ▮ 3 = 23
9 ▮ 2 = 20
5 ▮ 4 = 14
8 ▮ 1 = 17
4 ▮ 3 = ◆ *[11]*

[4. The operator ▮ means to multiply the first number by 2 and then add the second number.]

p.213 Multiply using any method.

1. 54 × 30 *[1,620]*	**2.** 35 × 50 *[1,750]*	**3.** 42 × 37 *[1,554]*
4. 57 × 21 *[1,197]*	**5.** 36 × 40 *[1,440]*	**6.** 14 × 29 *[406]*
7. 47 × 47 *[2,209]*	**8.** 82 × 20 *[1,640]*	**9.** 14 × 67 *[938]*

p.217 Multiply using any method. Remember to estimate.

1. 23 × 14 *[322]*	**2.** 81 × 25 *[2,025]*	**3.** $36 × 40 *[$1,440]*
4. 83 × 22 *[1,826]*	**5.** $91 × 18 *[1,638]*	**6.** 58 × 60 *[3,480]*

7. 77 × 14 *[1,078]* **8.** 63 × 72 *[4,536]* **9.** 54 × 35 *[1,890]*

Chapter 6 — EXTRA PRACTICE

PURPOSE Provide another opportunity for review and practice.

Materials have available: calculators

Using the Extra Practice

The Extra Practice can be used to provide further practice during a lesson or as a review later in the chapter.

Using the Additional Practice

The sections below provide additional practice that you can assign. You may wish to write these exercises on the chalkboard or put them on a reproducible master.

---

1. Simon—deserts, Greta—panthers, Malik—whales, Yoko—wetlands

Problem-Solving Strategy: Use Alternate Methods page 223
Solve. Use the bar graph to answer problems 3–5. Explain your methods. Explanations may vary.

1 Simon, Greta, Malik, and Yoko work to save deserts, panthers, whales, or wetlands. Greta saves animals. Malik saves animals from boats. Yoko saves wetlands. Who works with which resource? See above.

2 Copy the rectangle and show as many ways as you can to color one half. Answers may vary. 6 ways if each quarter is entirely colored

3 How many hours did students work during Week 1? 16 h

4 How many more hours were worked during the first two weeks than during the last two weeks? 8 h

5 During which weeks were the same number of hours worked? Weeks 2 and 5, and Weeks 3 and 4

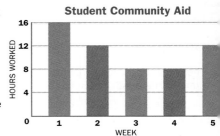

Student Community Aid

Multiply 3-Digit Numbers and Money page 225
Multiply. Remember to estimate.

1 107	**2** 394	**3** 583	**4** 460	**5** 809
× 73	× 21	× 22	× 34	× 45
7,811	8,274	12,826	15,640	36,405

6 $6.41	**7** $0.29	**8** $1.98	**9** $5.03	**10** $2.40
× 17	× 31	× 64	× 37	× 28
$108.97	$8.99	$126.72	$186.11	$67.20

11 42 × 118 = 4,956   **12** 22 × 372 = 8,184   **13** 36 × 511 = 18,396   **14** 13 × 309 = 4,017

Solve.

15 The Cho family conserves water and uses about 178 gallons less per month than they used to use. Estimate how much less water they will use over 2 years. Answers may vary depending on method used.

16 A regular light bulb lasts about 750 hours. An energy-saving bulb lasts about 10,000 hours. How many more hours does the energy saving bulb last? 9,250 h

---

Additional Practice

p. 223 Solve.

1. A class of 23 students collected newspaper for recycling. Each student collected 15 pounds of newspaper. How many pounds of newspapers did they collect? *[345 pounds]*

2. I am a number less than 40. The sum of my digits is 9. If you add 4 to me, you get a multiple of 5. If you subtract 6 from me, you get a multiple of 6. What number am I? *[36]*

3. One class sold 31 flats of plants for $12 each. They needed $300 for a field trip. Did they earn enough money? *[Yes, underestimate: 30 × $10 = $300]*

4. The cost of a weekend campout is $37 each. How much money must the class raise for 27 students to participate? *[$999]*

p. 225 Multiply. Remember to estimate.

1. 281	**2.** 620	**3.** 805
× 25	× 38	× 53
[7,025]	*[23,560]*	*[42,665]*

4. $0.72	**5.** $5.08	**6.** $5.17
× 18	× 42	× 12
[$12.96]	*[$213.36]*	*[$62.04]*

7. 12 × 521 *[6,252]*   **8.** 24 × $0.56 *[$13.44]*

9. 41 × 804 *[32,964]*   **10.** 57 × $0.03 *[$1.71]*

11. 11 × 741 *[8,151]*   **12.** 38 × $5.06 *[$192.28]*

Multiply Greater Numbers page 227

Multiply mentally.

1	**2**	**3**	**4**	**5**
3,000	9,000	11,000	48,000	31,000
× 40	× 70	× 30	× 20	× 30
120,000	630,000	330,000	960,000	930,000

Multiply using any method. Remember to estimate.

6	**7**	**8**	**9**	**10**
879	$5.38	5,309	$12.15	4,006
× 72	× 21	× 18	× 83	× 69
63,288	$112.98	95,562	$1,008.45	276,414

11	**12**	**13**	**14**	**15**
$46.03	5,131	$32.05	8,060	$24.26
× 24	× 17	× 36	× 23	× 21
$1,104.72	87,227	$1,153.80	185,380	$509.46

16 27 × 1,365
36,855

17 3,815 × 34
129,710

18 $28.16 × 31
$872.96

19 16 × $31.08
$497.28

Solve.

20 One club sold T-shirts to celebrate Earth Day. An adult's shirt sold for $15, and a child's shirt sold for $9. The club sold 1,230 adults' shirts and 462 children's shirts. How much money did the club make in sales? **$22,608**

21 At one time, it was estimated that 2 million, 100 thousand tons of used motor oil seeped into our waterways. Write this number in both standard and expanded forms. **2,100,000 and 2,000,000 + 100,000**

Problem Solvers at Work page 231

Solve. Tell whether you can estimate to solve problems 1–2. Explain your methods. Explanations may vary.

1 The Morales family lowered the temperature in their house and saved from $30 to $50 each month from November through April. How much did they save over the 6 months? **Possible answer: $180 to $300; yes; only estimates are given.**

2 The animal shelter had a race to raise money. Howie had pledges of $14.25 for each of the 15 miles he ran in the race. How much money did he earn for the shelter? **Possible answer: $213.75; no; an exact answer is necessary.**

3 A grocery store gives customers a 3¢ discount each time they bring their own bag. How much will you save by using your own bag once a week for one year? **156¢, or $1.56**

4 **Spatial reasoning** Copy the three shapes. Then try to fit them together to form a square.

DEVELOPING SPATIAL SENSE

This section provides another opportunity for students to reinforce spatial sense.

Show as many different ways as you can to color half of the shape. [Check students' work.]

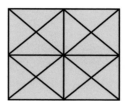

---

p. 227 Multiply using any method. Remember to estimate.

1. 692	**2.** $12.78	**3.** 4,020
× 82	× 35	× 18
[56,744]	[$447.30]	[72,360]

4. $57.35	**5.** 62,100	**6.** 37,500
× 42	× 61	× 18
[$2,408.70]	[3,788,100]	[675,000]

7. 31 × 4,720 [146,320]   **8.** $21.48 × 18 [$386.64]

9. 591 × 38 [22,458]   **10.** 33 × 6,210 [204,930]

11. $32.51 × 21 [$682.71] **12.** 473 × 52 [24,596]

p. 233 Solve. Explain your methods. [Explanations may vary.]

1. The Reed family recycles an average of 24 aluminum cans each week. About how many aluminum cans will they recycle in a year? [About 1,000 aluminum cans]

2. Bessie kept a water usage chart. She found that she uses an average of 75 gallons of water each day. At that rate, about how much water will she use in a year? [About 32,000 gallons]

3. A scout troup saves aluminum cans. They sold 418 pounds of cans to a recycling center for $0.42 a pound. Did they raise $200? [No, 418 × $0.42 = $175.56]

4. The sum of two numbers is 68. The product of these two numbers is 480. What are the numbers? [60 and 8]

5. **Make a decision** Would you buy one 6-pack soda for $2.25 or 6 cans of soda for $.40 each. Explain. [one 6-pack, 6 × $0.40 = $2.40, $2.25 < $2.40]

Depth of Oceans

Ocean	Average Depth in Feet	Area Covered in Square Miles
Arctic	3,407	5,105,700
Atlantic	11,730	33,420,000
Indian	12,598	28,350,500
Pacific	12,925	64,186,300

Endangered Animal Populations

Animal Species	Location	Estimated Population in 1970s	Estimated Population in 1990s
Arabian oryx	Asia	35	1,000
African elephant	Africa	1,300,000	600,000
Black rhinoceros	Africa	15,000	4,500
Florida cougar	North America	20	50
Hawaiian monk seal	Hawaiian Islands	2,000	1,000
Indian tiger	Asia	2,500	4,000
Japanese crane	Hokkaido, Japan	220	450
Mauritius parakeet	Africa	50	10
Nene *(similar to a goose)*	Oceania	750	500
Orangutan	Asia	150,000	100,000
Polar bear	Arctic region	5,000	40,000
Red wolf	Texas and Louisiana	100	300
Siberian tiger	Asia	130	400
Woolly spider monkey	South America	3,000	500

Heights of Mountains

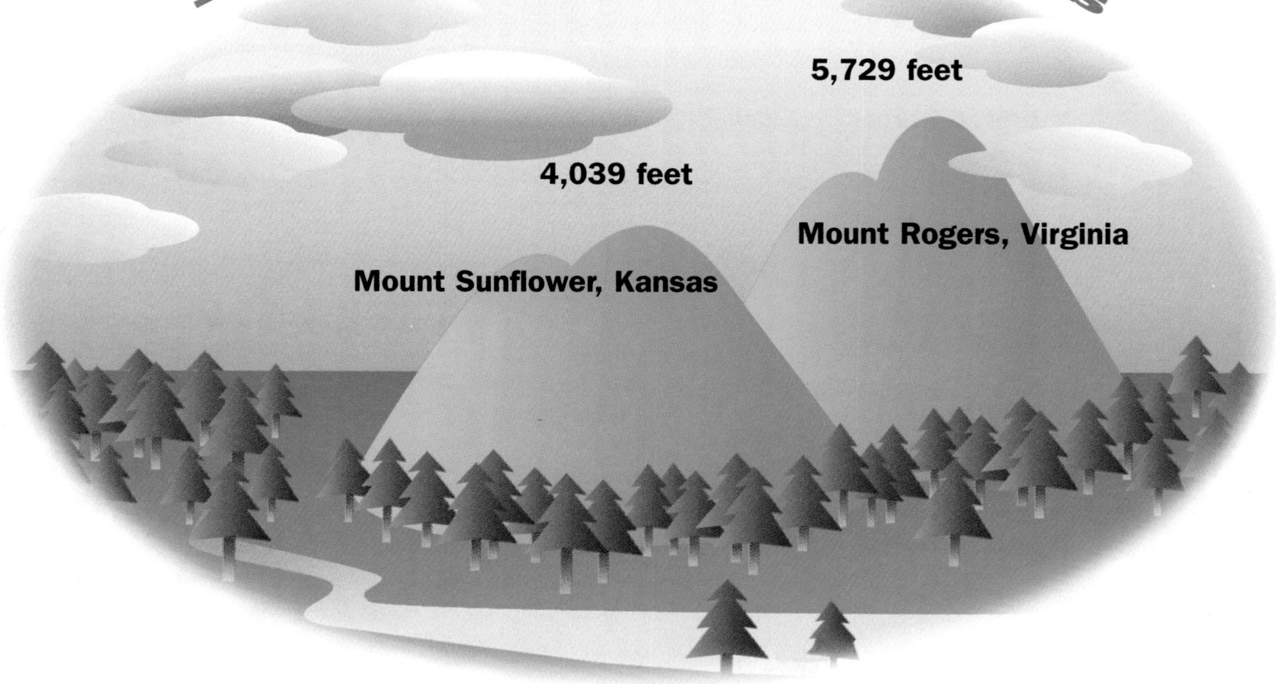

5,729 feet

4,039 feet

Mount Rogers, Virginia

Mount Sunflower, Kansas

Notes and Coins from Different Countries

Country	Note	Coins	Relationship
Botswana	1 pula	50 thebes 25 thebes 10 thebes 5 thebes 2 thebes 1 thebe	100 thebes = 1 pula
China	1 yuan	5 fen 2 fen 1 fen	100 fen = 1 yuan
India	1 rupee	50 paise 25 paise 20 paise	100 paise = 1 rupee
Peru	1 inti	50 centimos 10 centimos 5 centimos	100 centimos = 1 inti
Russia	1 ruble	50 kopeks 20 kopeks 15 kopeks 10 kopeks 5 kopeks 3 kopeks 2 kopeks 1 kopek	100 kopeks = 1 ruble
United States	1 dollar	50 cents 25 cents 10 cents 5 cents 1 cent	100 cents = 1 dollar

KIM'S WEIGHT

AGE	1	2	3	4	5
WEIGHT IN POUNDS	15	23	30	34	41

AGE	6	7	8	9	10
WEIGHT IN POUNDS	47	55	62	70	75

Giant Trees of the United States

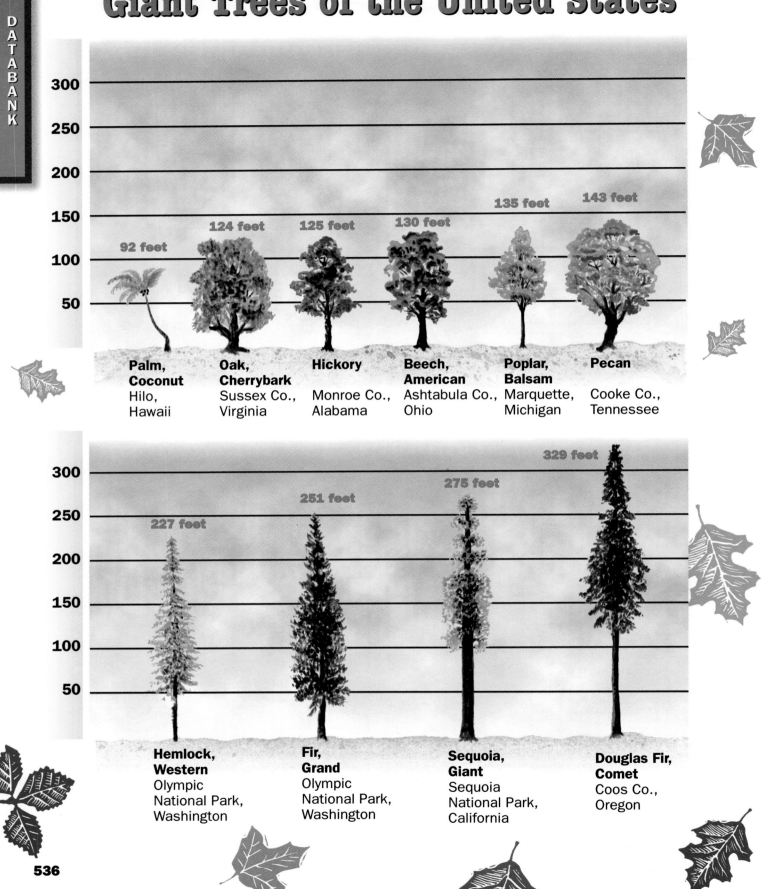

300
250
200
150
100
50

92 feet
124 feet
125 feet
130 feet
135 feet
143 feet

Palm, Coconut
Hilo, Hawaii

Oak, Cherrybark
Sussex Co., Virginia

Hickory
Monroe Co., Alabama

Beech, American
Ashtabula Co., Ohio

Poplar, Balsam
Marquette, Michigan

Pecan
Cooke Co., Tennessee

300
250
200
150
100
50

227 feet
251 feet
275 feet
329 feet

Hemlock, Western
Olympic National Park, Washington

Fir, Grand
Olympic National Park, Washington

Sequoia, Giant
Sequoia National Park, California

Douglas Fir, Comet
Coos Co., Oregon

Orange Computer Company

Item	Price
X610 laptop computer	$3,899.00
Z14 external modem	$109.00
3.8Y CD-ROM drive	$299.00
76B laser printer	$549.00

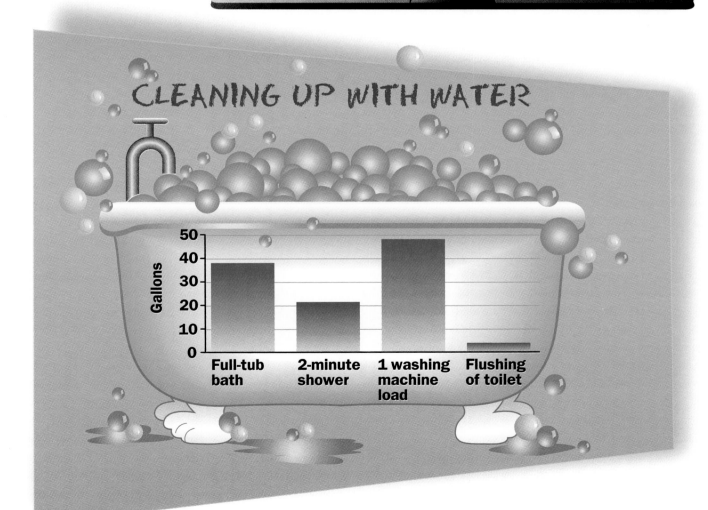

CLEANING UP WITH WATER

Mediterranean Sea

Gulf of Mexico

Pacific Ocean

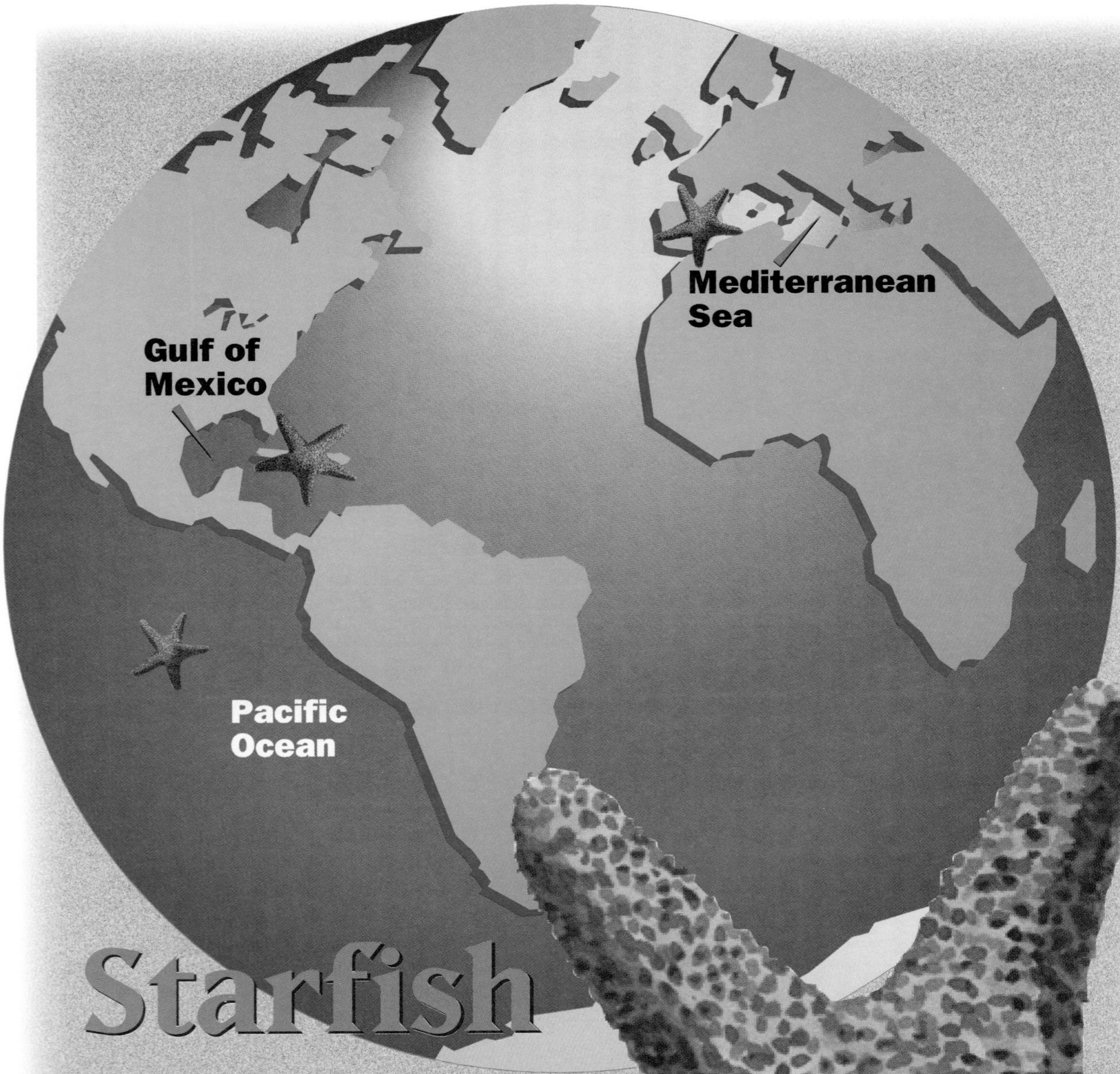

Starfish

There are 1,600 known species of starfish. The largest starfish, found in the Gulf of Mexico in 1968, had an arm span measuring 54 in. but weighed only $2\frac{1}{2}$ oz. The heaviest, found in the Pacific Ocean, weighed 13 lb and had an arm span of 25 in. The smallest known starfish, which has an arm span of $\frac{1}{2}$ in., is found in the Mediterranean Sea.

POPULATION OF CAPITAL CITIES

State	Capital of State	Population of Capital
Arizona	Phoenix	983,392
Iowa	Des Moines	193,187
Hawaii	Honolulu	365,272
Idaho	Boise	125,738
Louisiana	Baton Rouge	219,513

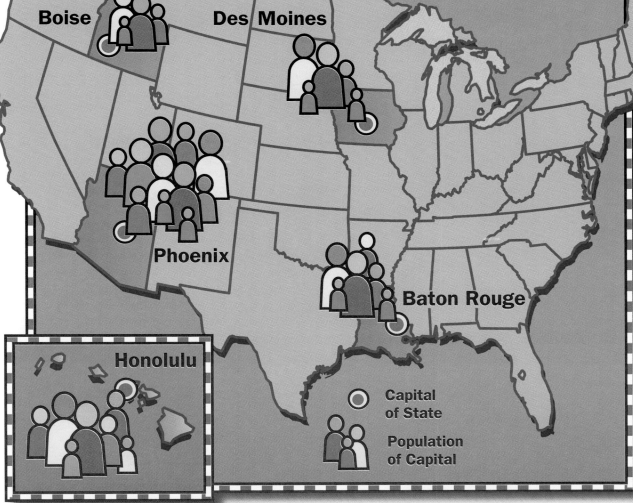

SHAPES IN REAL LIFE

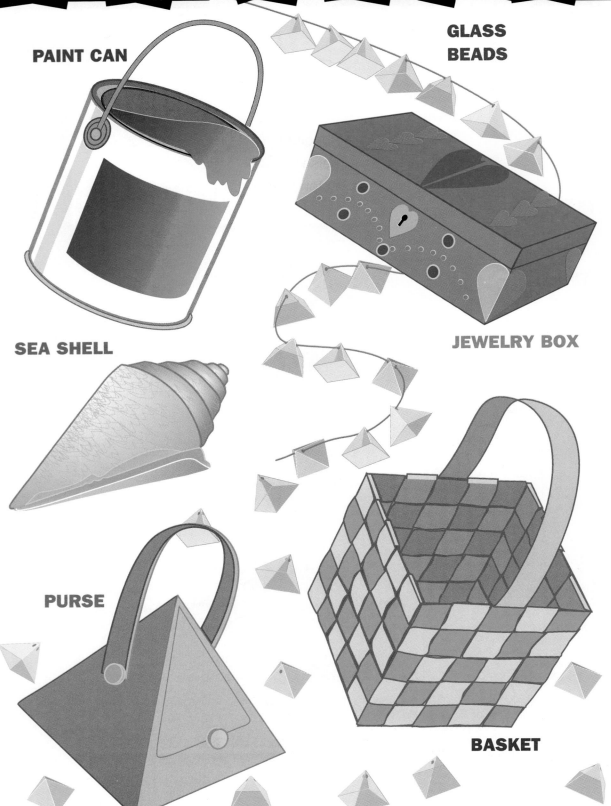

PAINT CAN

GLASS BEADS

SEA SHELL

JEWELRY BOX

PURSE

BASKET

540

THINGS SOME FOURTH GRADERS IN COLORADO LIKE TO DO

Activity		Number of Students
Color pictures	卌 卌 I	11
Take photographs	卌 卌 卌	15
Watch it rain	卌 III	8
Collect foreign coins	IIII	4
Collect old jewelry	III	3
Collect sports posters	卌 III	8
Swim	卌 卌 卌 III	18
Play roller hockey	卌 卌 IIII	14
Go fishing	卌 卌 I	11
Garden	卌 II	7
Make electrical things	卌 卌 卌 IIII	19

Apples Picked by Families

Family	Number of Pounds Picked
The Smiths	38
The Garcias	$25\frac{1}{2}$
The Lohs	$40\frac{3}{4}$
The Crowleys	51

The Story of the Ballpoint Pen

In early times, people wrote with pens made of long reeds. Pens made of goose or swan quills were introduced in Europe around A.D. 600. Workable fountain pens were not invented until 1884. Fountain pens were different from quills in that they had metal points and they could hold their own supply of ink. The first fountain pen was developed by an American named Lewis Waterman.

The idea for a ballpoint pen was patented as early as 1888, but it took a long time to get the pen to work properly. Early ballpoints would only write on rough surfaces. They also tended to leak. The ink in a ballpoint pen is quite thick, but it still must be able to flow smoothly onto the ball so that it can be applied to the paper without skipping and dry almost immediately. It was not until 1944 that two Hungarian inventors named Laszlo and George Biro found the right consistency for the ink and produced a successful ballpoint pen.

Glossary

(*Italicized terms* are defined elsewhere in this glossary.)

A

abacus A counting board used to solve number problems by sliding beads along rods or wires.

acute angle An angle with a measure less than a *right angle.*

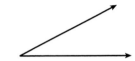

addend A number to be added.
Example: 5 + 4 = 9
The addends are 5 and 4.

addition An operation on two or more numbers that tells *how many in all.*

Example: 9 + 3 = 12 ← sum
      ↑ ↑
     addends

A.M. A name for time between 12:00 midnight and 12:00 noon.

angle A figure formed by two *rays* with the same *endpoint.*

area The number of *square units* needed to cover a surface.

array Objects or symbols displayed in rows and columns.

o   o   o   o

o   o   o   o

o   o   o   o

o   o   o   o

Associative Property When adding or multiplying, the grouping of the numbers does not affect the result.

Examples: 3 + (4 + 5) = (3 + 4) + 5
           2 × (3 × 9) = (2 × 3) × 9

average A *statistic* found by adding two or more numbers and dividing their *sum* by the total number of *addends.* (*See* mean.)

Example: 92 + 84 + 73 = 249
        249 ÷ 3 = 83 ← average

B

bar graph A graph that displays *data* using bars of different heights.

C

capacity The amount a container can hold.

centimeter (cm) A *metric unit* of *length.* (*See* Table of Measures.)

circle A closed, curved *2-dimensional figure.* All the points on the circle are the same distance from the center.

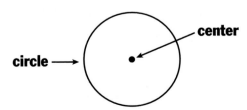

closed figure A figure that starts and ends at the same point.

clustering *Estimating* a *sum* by changing the *addends* that are close in value to one common number and then multiplying that number by the number of *addends*.

Example: 47 + 55 + 59
Estimate: 3 × 50 = 150

common denominator A *denominator* that is a *multiple* of the denominators of two or more fractions.

Example: 48 is a common denominator of $\frac{1}{12}$ and $\frac{1}{8}$.

Commutative Property When adding or multiplying, the order of the numbers does not affect the result.

Examples: 5 + 8 = 8 + 5 = 13
9 × 3 = 3 × 9 = 27

compatible numbers Changing numbers to other numbers that form a basic fact to *estimate* an answer.

Example:
133 ÷ 4 becomes 120 ÷ 4 = 30

composite number A whole number that has *factors* other than itself and 1.

Example: 8 is a composite number. Its factors are 1, 2, 4, and 8.

cone A *3-dimensional figure* whose base is a *circle*.

congruent figures Figures that have the same shape and size.

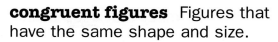

cube A *3-dimensional figure* with six square sides of equal *length*.

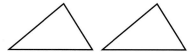

cubic unit A unit for measuring *volume*.

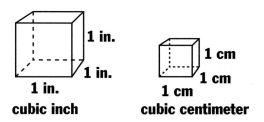

cubic inch   cubic centimeter

cup (c) A *customary unit* of *capacity*. (*See* Table of Measures.)

customary system A system of measurement whose basic units include *inch, ounce,* and *pound*. (*See* Table of Measures.)

customary unit A unit of measurement in the *customary system*.

cylinder A *3-dimensional figure* with two *faces* that are *circles*.

data Information.

decagon A *polygon* with ten sides and ten *angles*.

decimal A number that uses *place value* and a *decimal point* to show tenths, hundredths, and thousandths.

decimal point A period separating the ones and the tenths in a decimal number.
Examples: 0.3, 4.9, 24.752
↑   ↑   ↑
decimal points

decimeter (dm) A *metric unit* of *length.* (*See* Table of Measures.)

degree Celsius (°C) A *metric unit* for measuring *temperature.*

degree Fahrenheit (°F) A *customary unit* for measuring *temperature.*

denominator The number below the bar in a *fraction.*
Example: $\frac{3}{4}$ ← denominator

diagonal A *line segment* that connects two *vertices* but is not a side.

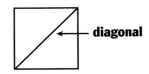
← diagonal

difference The number obtained by subtracting one number from another.
Example: $10 - 6 = 4$ ← difference

dividend A number to be divided.

divisible by One number is divisible by another if the *remainder* is 0 after dividing.

division An operation on two numbers that tells *how many groups* or *how many in each group.* Division can also tell *how many are left over.*
Example : quotient
↓
9 R1 ← remainder
divisor → 5$\overline{)46}$ ← dividend

divisor The number by which the *dividend* is divided.

edge A *line segment* where two *faces* of a *3-dimensional figure* meet.

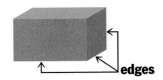
edges

elapsed time The amount of time taken to go from start to finish.

endpoint A point at either end of a *line segment.* The beginning point of a *ray.*

equivalent fractions Two or more fractions that name the same number.
Examples: $\frac{1}{3}$, $\frac{2}{6}$, and $\frac{3}{9}$

estimate To find an answer that is close to the exact answer.

even number A number that ends in 0, 2, 4, 6, or 8.

expanded form A way of writing a number as the *sum* of the values of its digits.
Example: 1,489 can be written as $1,000 + 400 + 80 + 9$.

exponent A number that tells how many times a given number is used as a *factor*.

Example: $10^3 = 10 \times 10 \times 10 = 1,000$

↑
exponent

face A side of a *3-dimensional figure*.

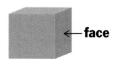
← face

fact family A group of related facts using the same numbers.

Examples: $3 + 2 = 5$ $2 + 3 = 5$
$5 - 2 = 3$ $5 - 3 = 2$

$2 \times 4 = 8$ $4 \times 2 = 8$
$8 \div 2 = 4$ $8 \div 4 = 2$

factors Numbers that are multiplied to give a *product*.

Example: $7 \times 8 = 56$
The factors are 7 and 8.

favorable outcomes Winning results in a *probability* experiment.

flip To move a figure over a *line*; reflection.

fluid ounce (fl oz) A *customary unit* of *capacity*. (*See* Table of Measures.)

foot (ft) A *customary unit* of *length*. (*See* Table of Measures.)

fraction A number that names part of a whole or part of a group.

Examples: $\frac{2}{3}$, $\frac{7}{10}$, $\frac{1}{100}$

gallon (gal) A *customary unit* of *capacity*. (*See* Table of Measures.)

gram (g) A *metric unit* of *mass*. (*See* Table of Measures.)

Grouping Property When adding or multiplying, the grouping of the numbers does not affect the result.

Examples:
$(3 + 5) + 7 = 15$ $(2 \times 4) \times 5 = 40$
$3 + (5 + 7) = 15$ $2 \times (4 \times 5) = 40$

height The distance from the base to the top of a figure.

heptagon A *polygon* with seven sides and seven *angles*.

hexagon A *polygon* with six sides and six *angles*.

improper fraction A fraction with a *numerator* that is greater than or equal to the *denominator*.

inch (in.) A *customary unit* of *length*. (*See* Table of Measures.)

intersecting lines Lines that meet or cross at a common point.

is greater than (>) Symbol to show that the first number is greater than the second.

Example: 439 > 436

is less than (<) Symbol to show that the first number is less than the second.

Example: 852 < 872

key The part of a graph that tells how many items each picture symbol stands for. (*See* pictograph.)

kilogram (kg) A *metric unit* of *mass.* (*See* Table of Measures.)

kilometer (km) A *metric unit* of *length.* (*See* Table of Measures.)

kite A *quadrilateral* with two pairs of touching *congruent* sides.

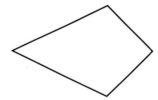

length The measurement of distance between two *endpoints.* (*See also* 2-dimensional figure, 3-dimensional figure.)

line A straight path that goes in two directions without end.

line graph A graph that uses lines to show changes in *data.*

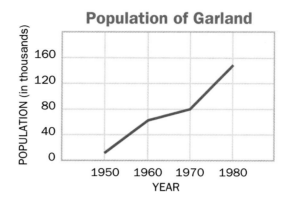

line of symmetry A line on which a figure can be folded so that its two halves match exactly.

line plot A vertical *graph* that uses Xs above a line to show *data.*

Example:

What is Your Favorite Pet?

	x		
	x		
x	x		
x	x	x	
x	x	x	x
Dog	**Cat**	**Fish**	**Snake**

line segment A straight path that has two *endpoints.*

liter (L) A *metric unit* of *capacity.* (*See* Table of Measures.)

mass A measurement that indicates how much of something there is. It is measured by *kilograms* and *grams.*

median The middle number in a group of numbers ordered from the least to the greatest.
Example: The median of 4, 5, and 7 is 5.

meter (m) A *metric unit* of *length.* (*See* Table of Measures.)

metric system A decimal system of measurement whose basic units include *meter, liter,* and *gram.* (*See* Table of Measures.)

metric unit A unit of measurement in the *metric system.*

mile (mi) A *customary unit* of *length.* (*See* Table of Measures.)

milliliter (mL) A *metric unit* of *capacity.* (*See* Table of Measures.)

millimeter (mm) A *metric unit* of *length.* (*See* Table of Measures.)

mixed number A number that has a whole number and a *fraction.*
Example: $8\frac{5}{6}$

mode The number or numbers that occur most often in a collection of *data.*
Example: 2, 6, 1, 6, 4, 8, 6
    The mode is 6.

multiple The *product* of a number and any whole number.
Example: 8 is a multiple of 4 because $2 \times 4 = 8$.

multiplication An operation that tells *how many in all* when equal groups are combined.
Example: $5 \times 8 = 40$
    ↑ ↑ ↑
    factors product

numerator The number above the bar in a *fraction.*
Example: $\frac{3}{5}$ ← numerator

obtuse angle An angle with a measure that is greater than a *right angle.*

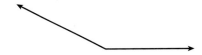

octagon A *polygon* with eight sides and eight *angles.*

odd number A number that ends in 1, 3, 5, 7, or 9.

open figure A figure that does not start and end at the same point.

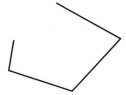

ordered pair A pair of numbers that gives the location of a point on a graph, map, or grid.

GLOSSARY

Order Property When adding or multiplying, the order of the numbers does not affect the result.

Examples: $8 + 9 = 17$ $4 \times 5 = 20$
$9 + 8 = 17$ $5 \times 4 = 20$

ordinal number A number used to tell order or position.

Example: second

ounce (oz) A *customary unit* of *weight*. (*See* Table of Measures.)

parallel lines Lines that never intersect.

parallelogram A *quadrilateral* with both pairs of opposite sides parallel.

pattern A series of numbers or figures that follows a rule.

Examples: 1, 3, 5, 7, 9, 11, . . .

pentagon A *polygon* with five sides and five *angles*.

perimeter The distance around a *closed figure.*

period Each group of three digits in a *place-value* chart.

Example: 527,000

Thousands Period			Ones Period		
Hundred Thousands	Ten Thousands	Thousands	Hundreds	Tens	Ones
5	2	7	0	0	0

perpendicular lines Lines that intersect to form square corners.

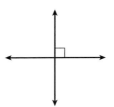

pictograph A graph that shows *data* by using picture symbols. A *key* tells how many items each picture symbol stands for.

pint (pt) A *customary unit* of *capacity.* (*See* Table of Measures.)

place value The value of a digit based on its position in a number.

P.M. A name for time between 12 noon and 12 midnight.

polygon A closed *2-dimensional figure* formed by *line segments.* The sides do not cross each other.

possible outcome Any of the results that could occur in a *probability* experiment.

pound (lb) A *customary unit* of *weight.* (*See* Table of Measures.)

prime number A *whole number* greater than 1 with only itself and 1 as *factors.*

Examples: 7 is a prime number. 2 is the only even number that is prime.

prism A *3-dimensional figure* with two parallel *congruent* bases and *rectangles* or *parallelograms* for faces.

probability A number from 0 to 1 that measures the likelihood of an event happening.

product The result of *multiplication.*

Example: $6 \times 8 = 48$ ← product

pyramid A *3-dimensional figure* that is shaped by *triangles* on a base.

quadrilateral A *polygon* with four sides.

quart (qt) A *customary unit* of *capacity.* (*See* Table of Measures.)

quotient The result of *division.*

Example: $35 \div 7 = 5$ ← quotient

range The *difference* between the greatest and the least numbers in a group of numbers.

ray A *2-dimensional figure* that has one *endpoint* and goes on forever in one direction.

rectangle A polygon with four sides and four square corners.

rectangular prism A *3-dimensional figure* with six rectangular *faces.*

regroup To name a number in a different way.

Example: 23 can be regrouped as 2 tens 3 ones or as 1 ten 13 ones.

remainder The number left over after dividing.

Example: $43 \div 7 = 6$ R1← remainder

rhombus A *parallelogram* with all four sides the same *length.*

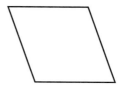

right angle An *angle,* or square corner, formed by *perpendicular lines.*

rounding (round) Finding the nearest ten, hundred, thousand, and so on.

Example: 868 rounded to the nearest hundred is 900.

scale Marks that are equally spaced along a line and are used to measure.

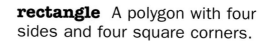

similar shapes Figures that are the same shape but are different sizes.

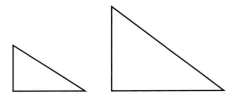

simplest form A *fraction* in which the *numerator* and *denominator* have no common *factor* greater than 1.

skip-count To count by twos, threes, fours, and so on.

Examples:
2, 4, 6, 8, 10, . . . 3, 6, 9, 12, . . .

slide To move a figure along a *line*; translation.

sphere A *3-dimensional figure* that has the shape of a round ball.

spreadsheet A computer program that arranges *data* and formulas in table form.

square A *2-dimensional figure* that has four equal sides and four square corners.

square pyramid A *pyramid* whose base is a *square.*

square unit A unit for measuring *area.*

Examples: square inch (in.^{2}), square foot (ft^2), square centimeter (cm^2), and square meter (m^2)

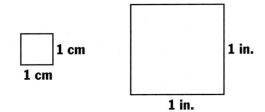

standard form The usual or common way to write a number.

statistics The collecting and arranging of *data* on a particular subject.

subtraction An operation on two numbers that tells *how many are left* when some are taken away. Subtraction is also used to compare two numbers.

Example: $14 - 8 = 6$ ← difference

sum The result of *addition.*

Example: $9 + 6 = 15$ ← sum

temperature A measurement that tells how hot or cold something is.

tessellation Related shapes that cover a flat surface without leaving any gaps; for example, the design on a checkerboard.

3-dimensional figure A figure that has *length, width,* and *height.*

time line A *line* that shows times or dates as points along a *line segment.*

trapezoid A *quadrilateral* with exactly one pair of *parallel* sides.

triangle A *polygon* with three sides and three *angles*.

triangular prism A *prism* whose opposite *faces* are *triangles*.

triangular pyramid A *pyramid* whose base is a *triangle*.

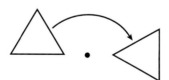

turn To rotate a figure around a point; rotation.

2-dimensional figure A figure that has only *length* and *width*.

variable A symbol used to represent a number or group of numbers.

vertex The common point of the two *rays* of an *angle*, two sides of a *polygon*, or three or more *edges of a 3-dimensional figure*.

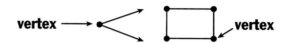

vertex

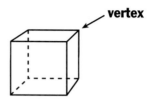

volume The number of *cubic units* that fit inside a *3-dimensional figure*.

weight A measure of how heavy something is.

width The measurement of the shorter of the sides of a *rectangle* that is not a *square*. (*See also* 2-dimensional figure, 3-dimensional figure.)

yard (yd) A *customary unit* of length. (*See* Table of Measures.)

Table of Measures

Time

60 seconds (s) = 1 minute (min)
60 minutes (min) = 1 hour (h)
24 hours = 1 day (d)
7 days = 1 week (wk)
12 months (mo) = 1 year (y)
about 52 weeks = 1 year
365 days = 1 year
366 days = 1 leap year

Metric Units

LENGTH
1 centimeter (cm) = 10 millimeters (mm)
10 centimeters = 1 decimeter (dm)
10 decimeters = 1 meter (m)
1,000 meters = 1 kilometer (km)

MASS
1 kilogram (kg) = 1,000 grams (g)

CAPACITY
1 liter (L) = 1,000 milliliters (mL)

TEMPERATURE
0° Celsius (°C) . . . Water freezes
100° Celsius . . . Water boils

Customary Units

LENGTH
1 foot (ft) = 12 inches (in.)
1 yard (yd) = 36 inches
1 yard = 3 feet
1 mile (mi) = 5,280 feet
1 mile = 1,760 yards

WEIGHT
1 pound (lb) = 16 ounces (oz)

CAPACITY
1 cup (c) = 8 fluid ounces
1 pint (pt) = 2 cups
1 quart (qt) = 2 pints
1 gallon (gal) = 4 quarts

TEMPERATURE
32° Fahrenheit (°F) . . . Water freezes
212° Fahrenheit . . . Water boils

Symbols

<	is less than	°	degree	$\overrightarrow{AB}$	ray AB
>	is greater than	$\overleftrightarrow{AB}$	line AB	$\angle ABC$	angle ABC
=	is equal to	$\overline{AB}$	line segment AB	(5, 3)	ordered pair 5, 3